Co

# Cognitive Linguistics: Basic Readings

*Edited by*
Dirk Geeraerts



Mouton de Gruyter
Berlin · New York

Mouton de Gruyter (formerly Mouton, The Hague)
is a Division of Walter de Gruyter GmbH & Co. KG, Berlin

♾ Printed on acid-free paper
which falls within
the guidelines of the ANSI
to ensure permanence and durability.

*Library of Congress Cataloging-in-Publication Data*

Cognitive linguistics : basic readings / edited by Dirk Geeraerts.
p. cm. – (Cognitive linguistics research ; 34)
Includes bibliographical references.
ISBN-13: 978-3-11-019084-7 (hardcover : alk. paper)
ISBN-10: 3-11-019084-2 (hardcover : alk. paper)
ISBN-13: 978-3-11-019085-4 (pbk. : alk. paper)
ISBN-10: 3-11-019085-0 (pbk. : alk. paper)
1. Cognitive grammar. I. Geeraerts, Dirk, 1955–
P165.C6424 2006
415–dc22
2006023786

*Bibliographic information published by the Deutsche Nationalbibliothek*

The Deutsche Nationalbibliothek lists this publication in the Deutsche Nationalbibliografie; detailed bibliographic data are available in the Internet at http://dnb.d-nb.de.

ISBN-13: 978-3-11-019085-4
ISBN-10: 3-11-019085-0



Cover design: Martin Zech, Bremen.
Typesetting: Selignow Verlagsservice, Berlin
Printed in Germany

# Contents

# Publication sources

## Chapter 1. Cognitive Grammar

Ronald W. Langacker

1990 Chapter 1. Introduction in *Concept, Image, and Symbol: The Cognitive Basis of Grammar*, Ronald W. Langacker, 1–32. Berlin/New York: Mouton de Gruyter. (Reprint of An introduction to cognitive grammar. *Cognitive Science* 10(1): 1–40. 1986.)

## Chapter 2. Grammatical construal

Leonard Talmy

1988 The relation of grammar to cognition. In *Topics in Cognitive Linguistics*, Brygida Rudzka-Ostyn (ed.), 165–205. Amsterdam/Philadelphia: John Benjamins.

## Chapter 3. Radial network

Claudia Brugman and George Lakoff

1988 Cognitive topology and lexical networks. In *Lexical Ambiguity Resolution: Perspectives from Psycholinguistics, Neuropsychology, and Artificial Intelligence*, Steven L. Small, Garrison W. Cottrell, and Michael K. Tanenhaus (eds.), 477–508. San Mateo, CA: Morgan Kaufmann.

## Chapter 4. Prototype theory

Dirk Geeraerts

1989 Prospects and problems of prototype theory. *Linguistics* 27(4): 587–612.

## Chapter 5. Schematic network

David Tuggy

1993 Ambiguity, polysemy, and vagueness. *Cognitive Linguistics* 4(3): 273–290.

## Chapter 6. Conceptual metaphor

George Lakoff

1993 The contemporary theory of metaphor. In *Metaphor and Thought*, Andrew Ortony (ed.), 202–251. Cambridge: Cambridge University Press.

## Chapter 7. Image schema

Raymond W. Gibbs, Jr. and Herbert L. Colston

1995 The cognitive psychological reality of image schemas and their transformations. *Cognitive Linguistics* 6(4): 347–378.

## Chapter 8. Metonymy

William Croft

1993 The role of domains in the interpretation of metaphors and metonymies. *Cognitive Linguistics* 4(4): 335–370.

## Chapter 9. Mental spaces

Gilles Fauconnier and Mark Turner

1998 Conceptual integration networks. *Cognitive Science* 22(2): 133–187.

## Chapter 10. Frame semantics

Charles J. Fillmore

1982 Frame semantics. In *Linguistics in the Morning Calm*, Linguistic Society of Korea (ed.), 111–137. Seoul: Hanshin Publishing Company.

## Chapter 11. Construction Grammar

Adele E. Goldberg

1992 The inherent semantics of argument structure: The case of the English ditransitive construction. *Cognitive Linguistics* 3(1): 37–74.

## Chapter 12. Usage-based linguistics

Michael Tomasello

2000 First steps toward a usage-based theory of language acquisition. *Cognitive Linguistics* 11(1/2): 61–82.

# Introduction
# A rough guide to Cognitive Linguistics

*Dirk Geeraerts*

So this is the first time you visit the field of Cognitive Linguistics, no? You may need a guide then. Sure, when you move through the following chapters of this volume, you get to see a top twelve of sights that you should not miss: a delightful dozen of articles written by authorities in the field that each introduce one of the conceptual cornerstones of the theoretical framework of Cognitive Linguistics. Still, to give you a firm reference point for your tour, you may need some initiation to what Cognitive Linguistics is about. That's what the present chapter is for: it provides you with a roadmap and a travel book to Cognitive Linguistics. It's only a rough guide, to be sure: it gives you the minimal amount of background that you need to figure out the steps to be taken and to make sure that you are not recognized as a total foreigner or a naïve apprentice, but it does not pretend to supply more than that.

To understand what you may expect to find in this brief travel guide, we need to introduce one of the characteristic ideas of Cognitive Linguistics first – the idea, that is, that we should not just describe concepts and categories by means of an abstract definition, but that we should also take into account the things that the definition is about, if we are to achieve an adequate level of knowledge. Take birds: you can define birds as a certain type of animal with certain characteristics (like having wings, being able to fly, and being born from eggs), but if you want to get a good cognitive grip on what birds are, you will want to have a look at some typical birds like robins and sparrows and doves, and then maybe also at some less typical ones, like chickens and ostriches.

It's no different when you are dealing with linguistic theories. You have to know about the scientific content of the theory, that is to say, the abstract definition of the approach: the topics it deals with, the specific perspective it takes, and the observations it makes. But you also have to know about the sociology of the theory: the people it involves, the conferences where they meet, the channels in which they publish. Introductions to linguistics tend to focus on the first perspective only, but the present guide will take the second into account just as much as the first.

## 1. What is so special about this place?

Theories in linguistics tend to be fairly insular affairs: each theoretical framework tends to constitute a conceptual and sociological entity in its own right, with only a limited number of bridges, market places or even battlegrounds shared with other approaches. Cognitive Linguistics, when considered in the light of this metaphor, takes the form of an archipelago rather than an island. It is not one clearly delimited large territory, but rather a conglomerate of more or less extensive, more or less active centers of linguistic research that are closely knit together by a shared perspective, but that are not (yet) brought together under the common rule of a well-defined theory. The present volume contains an introduction to twelve fundamental parts of that theoretical conglomerate – a tour of twelve central islands, if you wish: Cognitive Grammar, grammatical construal, radial network, prototype theory, schematic network, conceptual metaphor, image schema, metonymy, mental spaces, frame semantics, construction grammar, and usage-based linguistics.

We will define in a moment what links hold these concepts together and why each of them separately is important, but at this point, the chief thing is to realize that there is no single, uniform theoretical doctrine according to which these research topics belong together: Cognitive Linguistics is a flexible framework rather than a single theory of language. From the point of view of category structure (one of the standard topics for analysis in Cognitive Linguistics), this recognition is again one way in which Cognitive Linguistics illustrates its own concepts. As we mentioned a moment ago, Cognitive Linguistics emphasizes the fact that defining a category may involve describing some of its principal members rather than just giving an abstract definition. But it also stresses that the abstract definition need not consist of a single set of defining characteristics that belong uniquely and distinctively to that category. Think of birds again: when we describe the features of birds, we soon notice that the features we would like to think of as definitional for birds are not shared by all members of the species: we may even find birds like the penguin or the kiwi, that have no wings to speak of, cannot fly, and don't have feathers but that are rather covered with some kind of fluff. In such cases, we say that a category has a family resemblance structure: different types of birds resemble each other like the members of a family would, but there is no single set of attributes that necessarily shows up in all the members of the family. Again, it is no different with a linguistic framework like Cognitive Linguistics: it constitutes a cluster of many partially overlapping approaches rather than a single well-defined theory that identifies in an all-or-none fashion whether something belongs to Cognitive Linguistics or not.

Then again, the recognition that Cognitive Linguistics has not yet stabilized into a single uniform theory should not prevent us from looking for fundamental common features and shared perspectives among the many forms of research that come together under the label of Cognitive Linguistics. An obvious question to start from relates to the 'cognitive' aspect of Cognitive Linguistics: in what sense exactly is Cognitive Linguistics a cognitive approach to the study of language?

Terminologically speaking, we now need to make a distinction between Cognitive Linguistics (the approach represented in this reader), and uncapitalized cognitive linguistics – referring to all approaches in which natural language is studied as a mental phenomenon. Cognitive Linguistics is but one form of cognitive linguistics, to be distinguished from, for instance, generative grammar and many other forms of linguistic research within the field of cognitive science. What, then, determines the specificity of Cognitive Linguistics within cognitive linguistics?

There are a number of characteristics that need to be mentioned: one basic principle that is really, really foundational, and four tenets that spell out this fundamental notion. The foundational point is simply that language is all about meaning. As it says in the Editorial Statement of the very first issue of the journal Cognitive Linguistics, published in 1990, this approach sees language 'as an instrument for organizing, processing, and conveying information' – as something primarily semantic, in other words. Now, it may seem self-evident to you that a 'cognitive' approach to language focuses on meaning, but if you are familiar with generative grammar (i.e. Chomskyan linguistics), you will know that this is a theory that thinks of language primarily in formal terms: as a collection of formal, syntactic structures and rules (or constraints on such structures and rules). And generative grammar is definitely also a 'cognitive' conception of language, one that attributes a mental status to the language. So we have to be careful with the term *cognitive* in *Cognitive Linguistics*. It does not only signal that language is a psychologically real phenomenon (and that linguistics is part of the cognitive sciences), but also that the processing and storage of information is a crucial design feature of language. Linguistics is not just about knowledge of the language (that's the focus of generative grammar), but language itself is a form of knowledge – and has to be analyzed accordingly, with a focus on meaning.

Conversely, Cognitive Linguistics is not the only linguistic approach focusing on meaning: there are diverse forms of functional approaches to language that go in the same direction. And further, formal semantics is clearly a semantically oriented approach as well. It lies beyond the scope of this introduction to provide a systematic comparison with these other semantic approaches, but you will certainly be interested in what is particular about the way in which Cognitive Linguistics deals with meaning. So that brings us to the four specific characteristics that we announced earlier: each of them says something specific about the way Cognitive Linguistics thinks about meaning. (By the way, the captions we use to introduce the features may sound formidable, but don't worry: an explanation follows.)

### LINGUISTIC MEANING IS PERSPECTIVAL

Meaning is not just an objective reflection of the outside world, it is a way of shaping that world. You might say that it construes the world in a particular way, that it embodies a perspective onto the world. The easiest way to understand the point is to think of spatial perspectives showing up in linguistic expressions, and the way in which the same objective situation can be construed linguistically in different ways. Think of a situation in which you are standing in your back garden and you want to express where you left your bicycle. You could then both say *It's behind the house* and *It's in front of the house*. These would seem to be contradictory statements, except that they embody different perspectives.

In the first expression, the perspective is determined by the way you look: the object that is situated in the direction of your gaze is in front of you, but if there is an obstacle along that direction, the thing is behind that obstacle. In this case, you're looking in the direction of your bicycle from the back garden, but the house blocks the view, and so the bike is behind the house.

In the second expression, however, the point of view is that of the house: a house has a canonical direction, with a front that is similar to the face of a person. The way a house is facing, then, is determined by its front, and the second expression takes the point of view of the house rather than the speaker, as if the house were a person looking in a certain direction. Such multiple perspectivizations (and not just spatial ones!) are everywhere in the language, and Cognitive Linguistics attempts to analyze them.

### LINGUISTIC MEANING IS DYNAMIC AND FLEXIBLE

Meanings change, and there is a good reason for that: meaning has to do with shaping our world, but we have to deal with a changing world. New experiences and changes in our environment require that we adapt our semantic categories to transformations of the circumstances, and that we leave room for nuances and slightly deviant cases. For a theory of language, this means that we cannot just think of language as a more or less rigid and stable structure – a tendency that is quite outspoken in twentieth century linguistics. If meaning is the hallmark of linguistic structure, then we should think of those structures as flexible. Again, we don't have to look far for an example. Think back to what we said about birds: there is no single, rigid set of defining features that applies to all and only birds, but we have a flexible family resemblance structure that is able to deal with marginal cases.

### LINGUISTIC MEANING IS ENCYCLOPEDIC AND NON-AUTONOMOUS

If meaning has to do with the way in which we interact with the world, it is natural to assume that our whole person is involved. The meaning we construct in and through the language is not a separate and independent module of the mind, but it reflects our overall experience as human beings. Linguistic meaning is not separate from other forms of knowledge of the world that we have, and in that sense it is encyclopedic and non-autonomous: it involves knowledge of the world that is integrated with our other cognitive capacities. There are at least two main aspects to this broader experiential grounding of linguistic meaning.

First, we are embodied beings, not pure minds. Our organic nature influences our experience of the world, and this experience is reflected in the language we use. The *behind/in front of* example again provides a clear and simple illustration: the perspectives we use to conceptualize the scene derive from the fact that our bodies and our gaze have a natural orientation, an orientation that defines what is in front of us and that we can project onto other entities, like houses.

Second, however, we are not just biological entities: we also have a cultural and social identity, and our language may reveal that identity, i.e. languages may embody the historical and cultural experience of groups of speakers (and individuals). Again, think of birds. The encyclopedic nature of language implies that we have to take into account the actual familiarity that people have with birds: it is not just the general definition of *bird* that counts, but also what we know about sparrows and penguins and ostriches etc. But these experiences will differ from culture to culture: the typical, most familiar birds in one culture will be different from those in another, and that will affect the knowledge people associate with a category like 'bird'.

### LINGUISTIC MEANING IS BASED ON USAGE AND EXPERIENCE

The idea that linguistic meaning is non-autonomously integrated with the rest of experience is sometimes formulated by saying that meaning is experientially grounded – rooted in experience. The experiential nature of linguistic knowledge can be specified in yet another way, by pointing to the importance of language use for our knowledge of a language.

Note that there is a lot of abstract structure in a language: think for instance of the pattern Subject – Verb – Direct Object – Indirect Object that you find in a sentence like *Mary sent Peter a message.* In many languages, such structures are not directly observable: what we do observe, i.e. what constitutes the experiential basis for our knowledge of the language, is merely a succession of words (and even that is not entirely without problems, but let's pass over those). So the question arises: how does this more concrete level of words relate to the abstract level where you find functional categories like Subject and Direct Object? In more traditional terms, the question reads: how does the lexicon relate to the syntax?

But if we think of grammatical patterns as having an experiential basis in concrete, observable strings of words, there is yet another step we have to take: the 'observable strings of words' do not exist in the abstract; they are always part of actual utterances and actual conversations. The experience of language is an experience of actual language use, not of words like you would find them in a dictionary or sentence patterns like you would find them in a grammar. That is why we say that Cognitive Linguistics is a usage-based model of grammar: if we take the experiential nature of grammar seriously, we will have to take the actual experience of language seriously, and that is experience of actual language use. Again, from the point of view of mainstream twentieth century linguistics, that is a fairly revolutionary approach. An existing tradition tended to impose a distinction between the level of language structure and the level of language use – in the terms of Ferdinand de Saussure (generally known as the founder of modern linguistics), between *langue* and *parole*. Generally (and specifically in the tradition of generative grammar), *parole* would be relatively unimportant: the structural level would be essential, the usage level epiphenomenal. In a usage-based model that considers the knowledge of language to be experientially based in actual speech, that hierarchy of values is obviously rejected.

## 2. What does the tour include?

You are right, of course: the first exploration of Cognitive Linguistics in the previous section remains somewhat superficial and abstract. You now have a general idea of what type of scenery to expect in the Cognitive Linguistics archipelago, but you would like to get acquainted with the specific islands, i.e. you now know what the overall perspective of Cognitive Linguistics entails, but you hardly know how it is put into practice. In this section, we will have a look at the twelve basic concepts that are introduced by the dozen articles in this collection, and we will show how these concepts relate to the overall picture that was drawn in the previous pages.

As a preliminary step, let us observe that each of the characteristics that we discussed earlier defines a number of specific questions for Cognitive Linguistics. The *perspectival* nature of meaning raises questions about the specific mechanisms of construal present in a language: what kinds of semantic construal, imagery, conceptual perspectivization do languages implement? The *dynamic* nature of meaning raises questions about the process of meaning extension: what are the mechanisms of semantic flexibility, and how do the various readings of a linguistic expression relate to each other? The *encyclopedic* nature of meaning raises questions about the interdisciplinary links of language to the other cognitive capacities: to what extent are the cognitive mechanisms at work in natural language shared by other cognitive systems? And the *usage-based* nature of meaning raises questions about the relationship between syntax and lexicon, and the acquisition of language: what kind of experience do children need to learn a language?

These questions are illustrated in various ways by the articles in the collection, but before we can make that explicit, we need to introduce the articles separately, and say something about the way in which they are grouped together. Roughly, there are four groups of concepts and articles, corresponding to the four features that we identified before. The following pages pay specific attention to the logic behind the basic concepts that we introduce: why is it that these concepts are so important to Cognitive Linguistics? What you should see, in particular, is how they turn the fundamental features that we discussed in the previous section, into a concrete practice of linguistic description. Reading through the following pages will give you an initial idea of what you can expect in the volume, but of course, until you get there yourself, you will never really know what it is about.

## 2.1. The perspectival nature of grammar

The first two concepts, COGNITIVE GRAMMAR and GRAMMATICAL CONSTRUAL, illustrate the overall organization of a grammar that focuses on meaning. If conceptual perspectivization is the central function of a grammar, the typical formal categories of grammatical description (like word classes or inflection) will have to be reinterpreted from a semantic point of view. In the context of Cognitive Linguistics, two authorities in particular are systematically exploring these phenomena: Ronald W. Langacker, and Len Talmy. The two initial papers in the volume will introduce you to the thought of these two major thinkers – towering figures in the context of Cognitive Linguistics, who have both provided the approach with some of its basic vocabulary.

### COGNITIVE GRAMMAR

Cognitive Grammar is the specific name that Langacker uses for his theory of language. The paper included in the present volume originates from 1986, but is here reprinted in the form in which it was published in 1990. It specifies a number of basic features of Cognitive Grammar that are still valid, and that form an interesting backdrop for the rest of the articles in the present collection. Langacker starts off with the very idea of a perspectival grammar – although he uses a slightly different terminology: he talks about grammar as conceptualization and imagery. He introduces a number of high level general features of grammatical 'imagery' (profiling, specificity, scope, salience) and then tackles the key question how to build a descriptive framework for a grammar that starts from the assumption, simplistically, that language is meaning and that meaning is conceptualization.

Central to his answer is the idea that a grammar is not built up out of grammatical rules on the one hand and a lexicon on the other (the idea that you traditionally find in generative grammar). Rather, a grammar consists of 'symbolic units', where a symbolical unit is a conventional pairing of a form and a meaning. You can obviously think of lexical items here, but symbolic units can be more abstract than that, like when nouns are claimed to instantiate the abstract notion 'thing', and verbs the abstract notion 'process'. Given that you take the notion of symbolic unit as the basis for a grammar, there are two questions that immediately crop up, and Langacker does not fail to address them.

First, what could be the notional, conceptual characterization of abstract entities like word classes? What do we mean when we say that the meaning of nouns is 'thing' and that of verb is 'process'? On conceptual grounds, Langacker distinguishes between a number of basic classes of predications: entities and things versus relations, and within the relational predicates, stative relations, complex atemporal relations, and processes. The formal word classes of a language will typically express a basic type of predication. For instance, while nouns express the notion of 'thing' (a bounded entity in some domain), adjectives will typically be stative relational predicates.

Second, if you have a grammar with no rules but only symbolic units, how do you achieve compositionality, i.e. how do you ensure that different symbolic units may be combined to build larger units, like phrases or sentences? Here, the trick is to recognize that many predicates have open slots. If, for instance, the meaning of *above* is defined in terms of a stative relationship between what Langacker calls a 'trajector' and a 'landmark', the trajector and the landmark are only included schematically, as an open slot, in the meaning of *above.* Filling out the slots with other predicates then compositionally yields phrases like *the lamp above the table.*

In the course of Langacker's paper, you will come across a number of concepts that will play a central role in some of the other chapters included in the present collection: the schematic network idea (which will come to the fore in Chapter 5), the notion of domain matrix (which will play an essential role in Chapter 8), and the concept of a construction and a continuum between lexicon and grammar (which will constitute the focus of Chapter 11 and Chapter 12).

## GRAMMATICAL CONSTRUAL

Talmy never suggested a specific label for his approach to grammatical description, but the label *grammatical construal* captures very well what he is doing: what are the forms and patterns of construal (in the sense of conceptual perspectivization through language) that are realized by the grammatical structure of a language? This adjective *grammatical* is quite important here: Talmy focuses on the specific types of conceptual construal that are expressed by those aspects of natural language that have to do with syntax and morphology, rather than the lexicon. In Langacker's article, we noticed a specific interest in the relationship between the lexical dimension of the language, and the structural dimension – the syntax and the morphology. Talmy notes that there are some forms of conceptual construal that are hardly ever expressed by the grammatical structure (like color), whereas others (like the distinction between singular and plural) are typically expressed by syntax and morphology. The bulk of Talmy's paper, then, provides an overview of different types of conceptual construal systems that are typical for the structural, grammatical rather than the lexical subsystem of natural languages.

## 2.2. The dynamic nature of grammar

If natural language signs are flexible, we will need a model to describe how the different readings of the expressions relate to each other. Several such models for the polysemic architecture of expressions have been proposed by Cognitive Linguistics, and the three concepts in this group describe the most important of them.

### RADIAL NETWORK

The radial network model describes a category structure in which a central case of the category radiates towards novel instances: less central category uses are extended from the center. The paper featured in this collection, 'Cognitive topology and lexical networks' by Claudia Brugman and George Lakoff is based on Brugman's seminal analysis of the preposition *over*. The study was seminal not just in the sense that it popularized the radial network model, but also because it spawned a whole literature on the analysis of prepositions (more on this in the *Further reading* chapter). Brugman suggests the 'above and across' reading of *over* (as in *the plane flew over*) as central, and then shows how less central readings extend from the central case. These can be concrete extensions, as in a 'coverage' reading (*the board is over the hole*), but also metaphorical ones, as in temporal uses (*over a period of time*).

### PROTOTYPE THEORY

Radial categories constitute but one type of a broader set of models that fall under the heading of *prototype theory*. For instance, the importance of specific birds in the category structure of *bird* (this is a point we drew the attention to before) belongs in the same set of phenomena as the radial set idea. The paper 'Prospects and problems of prototype theory' by Dirk Geeraerts presents a systematic overview of the different prototype-theoretical phenomena that are mentioned in the literature. Specific attention is paid to the mutual relations that exist among these phenomena: it is argued that *prototype* is itself a prototypically structured concept, i.e. that there is no single definition that captures all and only the diverse forms of 'prototypicality' that linguists have been talking about.

### SCHEMATIC NETWORK

Prototype theory as described in the previous article is a generalization over the radial network model. But there is another generalization to introduce: the schematic network model. What this adds to the radial network and prototype models is the idea that the dynamism of meaning may also involve a shift along a taxonomical dimension. This may need some explanation. Note that we can think of birds at different levels of conceptual abstraction (or schematicity, as it is also called). At one level, we have a prototypical idea of birds as living beings that have feathers and wings and that can fly. If we stay on this level, we can move from the central prototype cases (the ones that correspond to the central concept) to peripheral cases, like birds without feathers and wings (we mentioned penguins and kiwis before). But there are other levels at which you can think of birds: more specific ones (as when you think about individual birds, like your great-uncle's parrot) and more general ones (like when you group bird species into categories like 'fowl', 'birds of prey', 'water birds' etc.).

Moving from a more specific to a more general level is called 'schematization', and the resulting model of readings for an expression is called a schematic network. The idea of schematic networks is implicit in prototype theory, but it has been made most explicit by Ronald W. Langacker. The concept plays an important role in construction grammar (see below), but here, in David Tuggy's paper 'Ambiguity, polysemy and vagueness', it is applied to a crucial question about meaning: the relationship between vagueness and polysemy: in a schematic network, you accept that what is polysemy (different meanings) at one level is vagueness (a less specified meaning potential) at an other, more schematic level. In a very clear and graphical way, Tuggy shows how this shift between levels is a contextual effect: in one situation we may use an expression rather more vaguely, in another we use it at a more specific, polysemous level.

The consequences for our conception of semantic dynamism are tremendous. The dynamism of meaning does not just imply that it is easy to add new meanings to the semantic inventory of an expression, but also that we should not think of this overall structure of meanings as stable. The semantics of lexical and constructional units is not a bag of meanings, but is a (prototypically and schematically) structured meaning potential that is sensitive to contextual effects.

## 2.3. The non-autonomy of grammar

If meaning is non-autonomous and encyclopedic, it is important to investigate the way in which different types of experience interact with each other. How for instance does our bodily experience of a sensory or motor kind relate to our more abstract thought, and are there any conceptual mechanisms that cut across the sensorimotor and the abstract mode of human knowledge? The four papers brought together in this group show how Cognitive Linguistics deals with the encyclopedic entrenchment of linguistic meaning, from both perspectives: what is the role of general cognitive mechanisms, and how do specific domains of experience interact?

Two of the four concepts that will be introduced are not specific for Cognitive Linguistics: metaphor and metonymy are traditional concepts in natural language semantics. Cognitive Linguistics has however brought new perspectives to the study of both metaphor and metonymy, and we will see in what sense. The other two concepts were newly introduced by Cognitive Linguistics. Incidentally, the fact that metaphor and metonymy are traditionally known as mechanisms of semantic change, makes clear that there is a certain degree of overlap between the present group of concepts and the previous one: some of the concepts mentioned here may also be seen as illustrations of the dynamic nature of meaning.

### CONCEPTUAL METAPHOR

Conceptual metaphor is probably the best known aspect of Cognitive Linguistics: if you've heard only vaguely about Cognitive Linguistics, conceptual metaphor is likely to be the notion that you've come across. You will have learnt by now that there is much more to Cognitive Linguistics, but still, Conceptual Metaphor Theory occupies a major place in the cognitive linguistic research program. Conceptual Metaphor Theory rests on the recognition that a given metaphor need not be restricted to a single lexical item, but may generalize over different expressions. Such general patterns may then be summarized in an overall statement like LOVE IS WAR, a pattern that ranges over expressions like the following:

> He is known for his many rapid *conquests*. She *fought for* him, but his mistress *won out*. He *fled from* her advances. She *pursued* him *relentlessly*. He is slowly *gaining ground* with her. He *won* her hand in marriage. He *overpowered* her. She is *besieged* by suitors. He has to *fend* them *off*. He *enlisted the aid* of her friends. He *made an ally* of her mother. Theirs is a *misalliance* if I've ever seen one.

This way of thinking about metaphor was introduced in George Lakoff's and Mark Johnson's book *Metaphors we live by* of 1980, a book that has achieved something of a bestseller status. The article included here, Lakoff's 'The contemporary theory of metaphors' gives a systematic overview of the theoretical and practical features of Conceptual Metaphor Theory.

You will notice how the two aspects of non-autonomy that were mentioned earlier show up in conceptual metaphor theory. First, metaphor is treated as a general cognitive mechanism, not as a specifically linguistic one that works on the level of individual expressions. Second, metaphor involves the interaction between different domains of experience: a source domain (in the example, war) and a target domain (love). This notion of domain will turn out to be crucially important for the other concepts in this group as well.

### IMAGE SCHEMA

An image schema is a regular pattern that recurs as a source domain (or a structuring part of a source domain) for different target domains. Typical image schema's include containment, path, scales, verticality, and center-periphery. The recurrence of image schemas may be illustrated by a closer look at the containment schema. It occurs in conceptual metaphors in which containment is the source domain for widely diverse target domains like the visual field (*in* sight, *out of* sight, go *out of* view, *inside* someone's field of vision), time (*in* two hours, he's *into* the first year of his retirement, do something *in* a short period), difficulties (get yourself *into* difficulties, we're *in* this together, how do we get *out of* this, to be *in* a mess), obligations (what are you getting *into*, no way *out*, can he get *out* of it), and the self as contained in the body (withdraw *into* oneself, a young man *in* an old man's body, there's an insecure person *inside*).

Characteristically, image schemas involve some form of sensory or motor experience, like a spatial configuration in the case of containment. In that sense, the appearance of image schemas in metaphors is typical for the encyclopedic, non-autonomous nature of meaning: prelinguistic domains, like the sensorimotor or spatial ones are mapped onto more abstract domains, providing them with structure. The notion of image schema, like the notion of conceptual metaphor, was introduced into Cognitive Linguistics by George Lakoff in his collaboration with the philosopher Mark Johnson. The paper included here, 'The cognitive psychological reality of image schemas and their transformations' by Ray Gibbs and Herb Colston, examines the psychological reality of image schemas: how can you prove, by means of experimental methods, that image schemas do indeed have a psychological reality?

In this sense, the paper is not just important as an illustration of the notion of image schema, but also for methodological reasons. The particular theoretical perspective of Cognitive Linguistics has a number of far-reaching methodological consequences. For one thing, treating meaning as a mental phenomenon and focusing on language as a cognitive tool implies that a rapprochement with the methodology of psychological research is obvious: experimental methods should bear fruit in Cognitive Linguistics just like they do in psychology. For another, the idea that grammar is usage-based implies that the analysis of actual usage data (as in corpora, specifically) should play an important role in Cognitive Linguistics. The paper by Gibbs and Colston is an example of such an experimental approach. An example of a corpus-based methodology is presented in Tomasello's paper in this volume.

However, neither the use of an experimental method nor the use of corpus data is as yet a dominant methodology in Cognitive Linguistics. They constitute emerging tendencies that are likely to gain in importance in the course of the following years, but a lot of the work done in Cognitive Linguistics is still based on a more traditional analytic methodology.

### METONYMY

There is yet another way in which thinking in terms of domains plays a role in Cognitive Linguistics, viz. in the analysis of metonymy. In the tradition of lexical semantics, metaphor and metonymy are distinguished on the basis of the type of semantic association they involve. Metaphor is supposed to be based on similarity (if love is war, it is *like* war in a number of respects), whereas metonymy is said to be based on contiguity – a somewhat vague notion that could be clarified in terms of 'actual proximity or association'. For instance, when you fill up your car, you don't fill the entire vehicle with fuel, but only the gas tank. The name of the whole comes to stand for the part, and part and whole are associated in reality.

Now, metonymy research in Cognitive Linguistics received an important impetus from the recognition that metonymy could receive a definition that is nicely complementary to that of metaphor. If metaphor is seen as a mapping from one domain to the other, metonymy can be seen as a mapping *within* a single domain. The shift from whole to part in *car* is a shift within the physical, spatial domain. This view on the relationship between metaphor and metonymy was already made in Lakoff and Johnson's *Metaphors we live by*, but the article 'The role of domains in the interpretation of metaphors and metonymies' by William Croft adds an innovative perspective. The relevant shift, Croft argues, is not necessarily one within a single domain, but it may be a shift within a domain matrix.

The domain matrix is a notion introduced by Ronald W. Langacker: it captures the idea that a concept may be simultaneously defined in various domains. For instance, Shakespeare is not only defined as a physical person, but also in the literary domain, as an author. So, when you say that you have read the whole of Shakespeare, you metonymically mean the entirety of his literary production, rather than the person. What Croft suggests, then, is to define metonymy overall in terms of such a domain matrix.

MENTAL SPACES

If metaphor is analyzed as a mapping from one domain to another, the question arises how such mappings take place: how does the structure of the source domain get mapped onto the target domain? The notion of conceptual integration developed by Gilles Fauconnier, and represented here by the paper 'Conceptual integration networks' by Gilles Fauconnier and Mark Turner, provides a descriptive framework to answer that question. It distinguishes between four spaces: a source input space, a target input space, a blend between both, and a so-called generic space. For instance (to use an example first described by Seana Coulson), you can think of 'trashcan basketball' as a game in which you throw crumpled pieces of paper into a trashcan, as you might do in an office environment or in a student dorm. The game of basketball is one input space, and the office or the dorm situation the other. The mapping between the two spaces associates the ball with the piece of paper, the basket with the trashcan, the players with the students or the office people, and further elaborations are possible. This mapping creates a blended space, and the relevant features of the blend are not just directly derived from the original input spaces. On the contrary, you may find emergent structure that is specific to the blended space: the fact that the trashcan would normally be placed on the ground, in contrast with a basketball ring, would certainly influence the way the game is played. The fourth type of space, the generic space, contains the common structure of the input spaces; in this case, it would be the space of someone throwing an object into a container.

The description of the four spaces may also explain some of the alternative names that the conceptual integration approach is known by: the *blending* or the *mental spaces* approach. As mentioned, the conceptual integration approach clearly links up with the analysis of metaphor as mapping across domains: one might say that the trashcan example elaborates the metaphor 'a trashcan is a basketball ring'. However, the blending analysis is more general than the study of metaphor. Conceptual integration has proved to be useful in a wide variety of phenomena, many of which are not even remotely associated with metaphorical processes. Counterfactuals are a case in point. *If Beethoven were alive, he would use a synthesizer* creates a blended space between the present-day musical situation and the historical space of Beethoven as an innovative composer, but you cannot really say that the conceptual process is a metaphorical one.

## 2.4. The experiential grounding of grammar

You will remember that the experiential nature of language raised the question of the relationship between lexicon and syntax. Cognitive Linguistics provides a specific answer to that question that links up with what we said about prototype theory and schematic networks: we can think of a grammar as a schematic network with abstract patterns at the schematic level, and the lexicalized instantiations of those patterns (the words and strings of words that fill the patterns) at a more specific level. From the point of view of mainstream twentieth century linguistics, this is a bit of a strange idea. If you assume (as generative grammar so vehemently stressed) that grammar is a set of rules, the lexical items instantiating those roles are not all that important: you basically need an inventory of items, but the real work is done by the rules.

However, Ronald W. Langacker has pointed out that there is a fallacy here: the so-called rule/list fallacy, i.e. the idea that what can be handled by rules should not be listed. If you start from that assumption, you get a strict separation between lexicon and syntax. But if you think in terms of schematic networks, such a separation is not necessary at all: you can both describe abstract patterns and their concrete lexicalizations. In fact, you *have* to, because there are prototypicality effects that you may need to describe. An indirect object construction of the type Subject – Verb – Direct Object – Indirect Object is typically filled by verbs like *give* or *tell*, and less typically so by verbs like *envy*. It is part of our grammatical knowledge that we recognize those typicalities (just like we recognize blackbirds as more typical birds than ostriches).

The specific form in which this idea is realized in Cognitive Linguistics, is in the form of construction grammars. The plural is deliberate here: since there are various forms of construction grammar, Construction Grammar is a family of theories rather than a single well-defined approach. The three papers in this group all involve Construction Grammar, but it is the paper by Goldberg (Chapter 11, the second one in the group) that introduces the approach most directly. The first paper in the group presents frame semantics, which is one of the important sources for Construction Grammar. The final paper show how the principles of Construction Grammar can be applied in language acquisition research.

### FRAME SEMANTICS

Frame semantics is the specific approach to natural language semantics developed by Charles Fillmore. The article included here, 'Frame semantics', sets out the basics of the theory. One essential starting-point is the idea that one cannot understand the meaning of a word (or a linguistic expression in general) without access to all the encyclopedic knowledge that relates to that word. This obviously ties in with the non-autonomous nature of natural language semantics: that meaning in natural language is not separated from other forms of knowledge implies that it is not very useful to maintain a strict separation between world knowledge and knowledge of linguistic meaning. While this recognition would be shared by all forms of semantics in Cognitive Linguistics, the individual identity of frame semantics involves the specific structures of encyclopedic knowledge that it invokes. Basically, these 'frames' are things happening and occurring together in reality. For example, in order to understand the word *sell,* you need to have world knowledge about the situation of commercial transfer. This comprises, apart from the act of selling, a person who sells, a person who buys, goods to be sold, money or another form of payment, and so on.

A semantic frame of this type is a coherent structure of related concepts where the relations have to do with the way the concepts co-occur in real world situations. Knowledge of the frame is necessary for an adequate knowledge of the words referring to the concepts in the frame: a word activates the frame, highlights individual concepts within the frame, and often determines a certain perspective in which the frame is viewed. In the standard commercial transaction example, for instance, *sell* construes the situation from the perspective of the seller and *buy* from the perspective of the buyer.

Although frame semantics was originally applied predominantly to the semantic description of words, there is a close relationship with Construction Grammar. Words like *sell* come with their own set of constructions (like *sell something to someone* or *sell something for a certain price*), and the different constructions reflect different ways in which the frame can be highlighted. In this way, frame semantics can be integrated with Construction Grammar as one way of specifying the semantics of constructions. Overall, we can now see that frame semantics occupies a transitional position in our grouping of concepts. On the one hand, if we focus on the way in which it uses structured encyclopedic knowledge as the background for the description of meanings in natural language, it belongs with the previous group of papers: it describes one of the ways in which conceptual knowledge of an encyclopedic (i.e. not specifically linguistic) nature is structured. On the other hand, if we concentrate on the input that frame semantics provides for the description of construction types, it links up with the present group of articles.

## CONSTRUCTION GRAMMAR

Simplistically, a grammatical construction is any string of words or morphemes exhibiting a coherent pattern, whether it be an entire sentence or a clause or a phrase (like a noun phrase or a verb phrase) or a complex lexeme (like a phrasal verb). And of course, the abstract pattern itself may also be called a 'construction'. In classical contemporary grammars, an indirect object pattern of the type Subject – Predicate – Indirect Object – Direct Object would be considered a derived structure, built up from the functional classes Subject, Predicate etc. That is to say, the rules of the grammar would be defined in such a way that a grammatical pattern of the form Subject – Predicate – Indirect Object – Direct Object could be assembled on the basis of the relevant functional building blocks. In Cognitive Linguistics, a pattern of this type is considered to be non-derived, i.e. is taken to be a sign of the language, or, if you wish, an (abstract) expression in its own right.

As you can read in Adele Goldberg's paper 'The inherent semantics of argument structure: The case of the English ditransitive construction', there are a number of advantages to such an approach, two of which may be mentioned here, to give you a first idea of why thinking in terms of constructions may be interesting. First, if a construction is treated as an entity in its own right, it is possible that the whole has characteristics that cannot be straightforwardly derived from the constituent components. This is a property known as non-compositionality: the meaning of the whole is not necessarily a compositional function of the meaning of the parts. Second, if any construction is a distinct element of the inventory of linguistic signs for a given language, you can treat constructions like any other category – according to the usual practice of Cognitive Linguistics. That is to say, it will then be quite normal to describe not just the meaning and the form of the category, but also its salient members. In the case of constructions, we may then think primarily of the lexical elements that can fill the slots of the construction (like the verbs that occupy the predicate role in the indirect object construction). Or in other words: describing grammar as a schematic network with lexical elements at the bottom and more abstract patterns higher up in the network is completely congenial to a construction grammar approach.

### USAGE-BASED LINGUISTICS

Defining Cognitive Linguistics as a usage-based model of language has a number of consequences, like the straightforward methodological conclusion that cognitive linguists will have to invest in the analysis of real language use if they are to live up to their self-declared status. You would expect a lot of corpus research in Cognitive Linguistics, then, but to be honest, this is a trend that is clearly emerging, but that has not yet gained as prominent a status as one would expect.

Using corpora of observed speech is natural in language acquisition research, though: if you wish to study how children acquire their language, you will obviously want to observe and analyze their developing language. Also, language acquisition is a domain par excellence to test a usage-based model of language that believes that our experience of actual speech determines how we come by more abstract patterns. In fact, if our more schematic knowledge is based on our more concrete knowledge of lexical instantiations of such patterns, you should be able to observe 'lexical bootstrapping' effects: the specific words in which we begin to learn certain constructions, determine how we learn the construction. That is exactly what Michael Tomasello investigates in his paper 'First Steps toward a Usage-based Theory of Language Acquisition', which is part of a long-term research effort to develop a theory of language acquisition that ties in with Cognitive Linguistics and Construction Grammar.

If you are familiar with the history of contemporary linguistics, you will appreciate how important such an attempt is. The generative grammar idea that language is a separate module of the mind is very much based on an argument from language acquisition: if we do not assume that language is genetically wired in, the argument goes, we couldn't explain at all how the acquisition of language proceeds so quickly as it actually does. This is particularly the case, the argument continues, because the input children get (the language they are exposed to) is not sufficient to explain how they could learn all the intricacies of natural language syntax. This is the 'poverty of stimulus' argument. Obviously, if Tomasello succeeds in his attempt to explain how children can learn language through abstraction from the actual input they get, a central tenet of generative grammar will be overturned.

## 2.5. A conceptual map

Let us summarize. What we have shown in this (somewhat detailed) introduction to the tour of twelve papers is how they introduce, discuss, illustrate concepts that follow logically from the central characteristics of Cognitive Linguistics that we learned about in the previous section. It will not come as a surprise to you that these twelve concepts are far from being the only relevant or interesting ones that have been developed in the context of Cognitive Linguistics – but they are certainly among the most basic ones. When you read the individual papers, it may be wise to refer back once in a while to the characterizations that you find in the foregoing pages: they will help you not to lose track and to interpret the conspicuous features of the papers.

In Figure 1, the relations between the various papers are graphically represented. The fundamental features of Cognitive Linguistics (the perspectival, dynamic, non-autonomous, experiential nature of natural language) are mentioned in the corners of the figure. Intermediate between these cornerstones and the twelve central concepts, you will find six fields of research that emerged in the foregoing discussion as the logical link between the fundamental features and the central concepts: the conceptual characterization of the grammar, the search for models of polysemy, the analysis of mechanisms of polysemy, the importance of thinking in terms of domains of experience, the relationship between grammar and lexicon, and the relationship between structure and usage. The arrows in the figure indicate how each more specific concept is motivated by a more general one for instance: looking at mechanisms of categorial polysemy is one way of getting a grip on the dynamic nature of linguistic meaning, and in a next step, conceptual metaphor is one of the specific mechanisms of categorial polysemy.

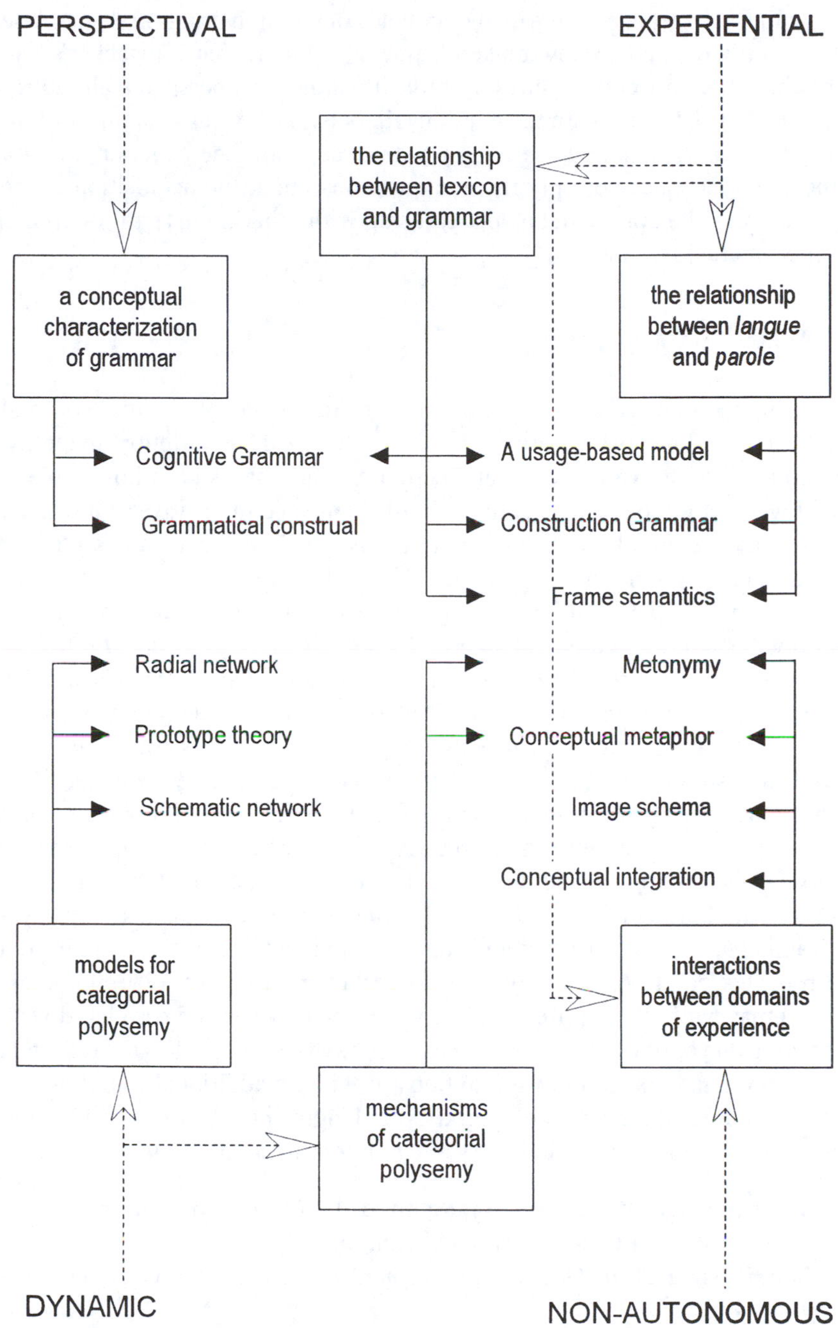


*Figure 1.* A conceptual map of Cognitive Linguistics

Adding the intermediate level with the six fields of research brings in extra subtlety in the overview. We can now make clear, for instance, that Langacker's paper with which the collection opens, not only illustrates the perspectival nature of grammar, but also deals with the relationship between lexical structure and morpho-syntax. In the same way, the figure illustrates how the experiential nature of the grammar does not only involve questions about the acquisition and the architecture of the grammar, but also links up with thinking in terms of domains and their mutual relations.

## 3. Where do you go next?

Let us assume that, after roaming the present introductory volume, you really like the look and feel of Cognitive Linguistics. It's a safe assumption, in fact: you are bound to be drawn in by an intellectual climate that is both hospitable and inspiring, open-minded and exciting, wide-ranging and innovative. But where do you go after the initial tour d'horizon that has won your heart? Let's go over a few trajectories that might cater to your personal interests.

A first thing to do would be to complete your initiation by reading the companion volume to the present collection. In several ways, *Cognitive Linguistics: Current Applications and Future Perspectives* (edited by Gitte Kristiansen, Michel Achard, René Dirven and Francisco J. Ruiz de Mendoza) is deliberately complementary to the book that you are holding in your hands: it does not focus on Cognitive Linguistics basics, but rather describes the contemporary state of affairs in the main fields of application of Cognitive Linguistics. Also, it does not consist of existing papers, but only contains newly written articles that have the explicit purpose of presenting current discussions and domains. Taken together, the two volumes will thoroughly familiarize you with Cognitive Linguistics, way beyond the fragmented and uncertain knowledge that an incidental visit would impart.

From that point on, you may want to go beyond the level of introductions, and you may, with the acquired confidence of the experienced traveler, do some journeying on your own. However, in case your self-assurance has not reached an optimal level and you would want to boost it with an additional round of introductory reading, there are some good book-length introductions to Cognitive Linguistics that may help you. Here's a list of commendable texts.

- Friedrich Ungerer and Hans-Jörg Schmid. 1996. *An Introduction to Cognitive Linguistics*. London/New York: Longman.
- Violi, Patrizia. 2001. *Meaning and Experience*. Bloomington: Indiana University Press.
- John R. Taylor. 2003. *Linguistic Categorization*. Third Edition. Oxford: Oxford University Press.

- René Dirven and Marjolijn Verspoor. 2004. *Cognitive Exploration of Language and Linguistics.* Second Revised Edition. Amsterdam, Philadelphia: John Benjamins.
- William Croft and D. Alan Cruse. 2004. *Cognitive Linguistics.* Cambridge: Cambridge University Press.
- Vyvian Evans and Melanie Green. 2006. *Cognitive Linguistics. An Introduction*. Edinburgh: Edinburgh University Press.

Once you are ready to leave the introductory level, there are basically two things to do: deepen your understanding of the existing body of work in Cognitive Linguistics, and keep aware of current developments. With regard to the former, a first set of routes to explore is provided by the present volume itself: accompanying each of the chapters included in the collection, you find a broadly conceived set of suggestions for further reading in the *Epilogue.* They will direct you to elaborations and discussions of the basic concepts that are presented here – and to some of the less basic (but no less important) concepts developed in the field of Cognitive Linguistics. Alternatively (or in parallel), you could have a look at the forthcoming *Handbook of Cognitive Linguistics*, edited by Dirk Geeraerts and Hubert Cuyckens and published by Oxford University Press. It's a collection of some fifty commissioned articles that each offer an in-depth treatment of one of the manifold aspects of Cognitive Linguistics.

To keep in touch with new work, you would certainly want to be aware of new publications. So, what are the journals and the book series that you need to keep an eye on? Note that a lot of studies in Cognitive Linguistics are now being published in general publication channels and by a wide variety of international publishers. Here, only journals and book series that are specifically dedicated to Cognitive Linguistics are mentioned.

Two journals need to be cited: *Cognitive Linguistics*, and the *Annual Review of Cognitive Linguistics.* The former, published by Mouton De Gruyter, is the official journal of the International Cognitive Linguistics Association (more about which in the next section). The journal was founded by Dirk Geeraerts in 1990. Consecutive editors-in-chief so far were Arie Verhagen and Adele Goldberg. The latter journal, published by the John Benjamins Publishing Company under the auspices of the Spanish Cognitive Linguistics Association, first appeared in 2003. It is led by Francisco Ruiz de Mendoza. The journal *Cognitive Linguistics* is not only the most reputable journal in the field, it also comes with a considerable bonus. A subscription to *Cognitive Linguistics* includes a copy of the digital *Bibliography of Cognitive Linguistics* – and indispensable bibliographical tool compiled through the relentless efforts René Dirven (undoubtedly the major organizational force behind the entire Cognitive Linguistics enterprise). The bibliography now covers 7000 publications (no, you won't have to read them all to be recognized as an accomplished cognitive linguist), and it will be regularly updated in the following years.

Five book series specifically dedicated to work in Cognitive Linguistics need to be mentioned. *Cognitive Linguistic Research* or CLR is the oldest and most complete series. Published by Mouton de Gruyter of Berlin, it was launched at the same time as the journal *Cognitive Linguistics*, and now numbers over thirty volumes. Recently, *Cognitive Linguistic Research* (with Dirk Geeraerts as managing editor) has received a companion series in the form of *Applications of Cognitive Linguistics* or ACL (managed by Gitte Kristiansen) – a series that will focus on the descriptive applications of Cognitive Linguistics, while *Cognitive Linguistic Research* harbors the more theoretically relevant studies. The other main publisher for Cognitive Linguistics, the John Benjamins Publishing Company of Amsterdam, features three specifically relevant (but as yet less extensive) series. While *Human Cognitive Processing* (edited by Marcelo Dascal, Raymond W. Gibbs and Jan Nuyts) has a broad cognitive orientation, the two other series are more specific: *Cognitive Linguistics in Practice* (edited by Günter Radden) covers the field from a textbook oriented perspective, and *Constructional Approaches to Language* (edited by Mirjam Fried and Jan-Ola Östman) specifically deals with Construction Grammar.

If you are interested in following what is going on in Cognitive Linguistics, note that the book series are not just monograph series. A lot of what is being published in the series consists of collective volumes with thematically interconnected articles. In many cases, these constitute selections of papers presented at Cognitive Linguistics conferences. Because quite a lot of relevant work is being published in such collective volumes, you will profit from keeping an eye on them once you've become a Cognitive Linguistics aficionado.

When you've reached this stage, you will be ready to take a step into the world and take part in some real life Cognitive Linguistics activities. Where would you go? All self-respecting cities and countries have their own festivals and fiesta, and becoming part of the crowd involves participating in the celebrations. In Cognitive Linguistics, the main community event is without any doubt the biannual ICLC or Cognitive Linguistics Conference. The first ICLC took place in 1989 in Duisburg, Germany. It was one of the so-called LAUD symposia (where LAUD stands for Linguistic Agency of the University of Duisburg) that had been organized by René Dirven since 1977 and where some of the world's most distinguished linguists were invited to present their work. The Duisburg conference was of crucial importance for the institutionalization and the international expansion of Cognitive Linguistics: it was there and then that the International Cognitive Linguistics Association or ICLA was founded (the conference was accordingly rebaptized as the First International Cognitive Linguistics Conference), that plans were made to launch the journal *Cognitive Linguistics*, and that the monograph series *Cognitive Linguistics Research* was announced. Cognitive Linguistics as an intellectual movement is too self-critical to recognize any historical sites or places of pilgrimage, but if ever a commemorative plate were to be considered, Duisburg would be a likely candidate.

The following ICLC conferences were consecutively held in Santa Cruz, US (1991, organized by Gene Casad), Leuven, Belgium (1993, organized by Dirk Geeraerts), Albuquerque, US (1995, organized by Sherman Wilcox), Amsterdam, The Netherlands (1997, organized by Theo Jansen and Gisela Redeker), Stockholm, Sweden (1999, organized by Erling Wande), Santa Barbara, US (2001, organized by Ronald W. Langacker), Logroño, Spain (2003, organized by Francisco J. Ruiz De Mendoza), and Seoul, South Korea (2005, organized by Hyon-Sook Shin). The tenth ICLC in 2007, organized by Elzbieta Tabakowska, has its venue at the Jagiellonian University of Krakow in Poland.

Next to the ICLC's, there are a number of local events that you may consider attending. The LAUD conferences are now being organized bi-annually in Landau, Germany, in the year between the ICLC conferences. That holds for a number of other regular meetings, like the US-based Cognitive Structure, Discourse and Language conference, which reached its eighth edition in 2006; or the International Conference on Construction Grammar, which had its fourth edition in 2006.

An important part in the organization of workshops and symposia in Cognitive Linguistics is currently played by the ICLA affiliates. These are ICLA branches defined by region or country (and occasionally by language). The first one to be founded was the Spanish Cognitive Linguistics Association, whose affiliation was formally approved at the 1999 ICLC. The year 2001 saw the affiliation of the Finnish, the Polish, and the Slavic Cognitive Linguistics Associations. Further affiliates include the Russian Association of Cognitive Linguists (2004), the German Cognitive Linguistics Association (2005), the Discourse and Cognitive Linguistics Association of Korea (2005), the Association Française de Linguistique Cognitive (2005), the Japanese Cognitive Linguistics Association (2005), the Conceptual Structure, Discourse and Language Association (2005), and the UK Cognitive Linguistics Association (2006). Further local branches are likely to emerge, and all of them are likely to organize regular meetings. If you are interested in following what is on the agenda, you may want to consult the ICLA website: it contains a calendar of Cognitive Linguistics events, and supplies links to the individual websites of the ICLA affiliates. This is the ICLA address: http://www.cognitivelinguistics.org/

Meetings, lectures, workshops, symposia, and conferences are also announced on Cogling, a mailing list for disseminating ICLA news, queries, and discussions of interest to cognitive linguists. Again, details about subscribing may be found on the ICLA website. Incidentally, the website also offers an overview of the courses or programs in Cognitive Linguistics that are offered at many places around the globe.

Once you get to one of the conferences, who would you be likely and/or eager to meet? Thinking in terms of people, the key figures of Cognitive Linguistics are George Lakoff, Ronald W. Langacker, and Leonard Talmy. Round this core of founding fathers, who originated Cognitive Linguistics in the late 1970s and the early 1980s, two chronologically widening circles of cognitive linguists may be discerned. (The lists that follow are obviously indicative only: they are not meant to exclude anyone, but only to give you an idea of the different 'generations' of cognitive linguists.)

A first wave, coming to the fore in the second half of the 1980s and the beginning of the 1990s, consists of the early collaborators and colleagues of the key figures, together with a first generation of students. Names that come to mind include those of Gilles Fauconnier, Eve Sweetser, Mark Johnson, Mark Turner, Raymond W. Gibbs, William Croft, Adele Goldberg, Dave Tuggy, Gene Casad, Laura Janda, Suzanne Kemmer, Sally Rice, Ricardo Maldonado, Karen Van Hoek, Geoff Nathan, Margaret Winters, Sherman and Phyllis Wilcox, Margaret Freeman.

Simultaneously, a number of people in mostly Western and Central Europe took up the ideas of Cognitive Linguistics and contributed to their international dissemination. Names include those of René Dirven (to repeat: his instrumental role in the expansion of Cognitive Linguistics can hardly be overestimated), Brygida Rudzka-Ostyn, John Taylor, Zoltan Kövecses, Chris Sinha, Brigitte Nerlich, Arie Verhagen, Barbara Lewandowska-Tomaszczyk, Elzbieta Tabakowska, Peter Harder, Günter Radden, Susanne Niemeier, Martin Pütz, Hans-Jörg Schmid, Hubert Cuyckens and the author of the present introduction.

The mid 1990s and later witnessed a second wave of expansion, with second generation students and a further geographical spread directed largely towards Asia and the rest of Europe. Names include those of Alan Cienki, Michel Achard, Joe Grady, Tim Rohrer, Seana Coulson, Todd Oakley, Gary Palmer, Jose M. Garcia-Miguel, Antonio Barcelona, Francisco Ruiz de Mendoza, Carlos Inchaurralde, Andrej Kibrik, Ekaterina Rakhilina, Michael Tomasello, Ted Sanders, Wilbert Spooren, Gerard Steen, Stefan Grondelaers, Stefan Gries, Anatol Stefanowitsch, Yo Matsumoto.

In addition, you might profit from the occasion to rub elbows with people who would perhaps not describe themselves unreservedly as cognitive linguists (coming as they do from other theoretical families or other disciplines, or simply because they like their independence), but who would show up at the Cognitive Linguistics conferences because they have relevant things to say: linguists like Charles Fillmore, Joan Bybee, Elizabeth Traugott, Östen Dahl, Jan Nuyts, or psychologists like Melissa Bowerman, Dedre Gentner, and Dan Slobin.

## 4. Why would you want to come back?

So now you know your way around in Cognitive Linguistics. You can walk the walk and talk the talk, and there's no way that you'd be exposed as a novice. But why would you be coming back? What would be a good reason to become a permanent resident? An obvious but relatively superficial motivation would be the diversity of the panorama: there's a lot to be found in the Cognitive Linguistics archipelago, and the framework is not so strict as to stifle creativity. It's a lively, colorful, varied environment, and you're likely to find some corner of special significance to you, where you can do your thing and meet people with similar interests. But beyond that? What would be the long-term importance of Cognitive Linguistics?

Let us try to take a bird's eye view of the history of linguistics, and see exactly where Cognitive Linguistics fits in, and why it could be important for the future of linguistics. Agreed, you can only achieve this sort of extreme synthesis if you allow for massive simplification: let us try to keep that in mind as a proviso when we do the exercise.

The development of linguistics in the twentieth century, then, is characterized by a succession of two dominant approaches: the structuralist one, and the generativist one. Currently, in the first decade of the 21st century, the generativist paradigm is no longer the principal framework, but there clearly is no new central approach yet. If one looks at Cognitive Linguistics from this perspective, there are indications that Cognitive Linguistics combines a number of tendencies that may also be found in other contemporary developments in theoretical linguistics – viz. in the broad range of functionalist approaches to linguistics. By combining these tendencies, Cognitive Linguistics taps directly into the undercurrent of contemporary developments. Specifically, if we recognize that *decontextualization* is a fundamental underlying characteristic of the development of grammatical theory in twentieth century linguistics, Cognitive Linguistics strongly embodies the *recontextualizing* tendency that is shared by most functionalist approaches.

The logic behind the decontextualization of twentieth century grammar may be grasped if we take our starting-point in De Saussure, the founding father of the structuralist approach. The Saussurean distinction between *langue* (the language system) and *parole* (the use of the language system in actual usage) creates an internally divided grammar, a conception of language with, so to speak, a hole in the middle. On the one hand, *langue* is defined by De Saussure as a social system, a set of collective conventions, a common code shared by a community. On the other hand, *parole* is an individual, psychological activity that consists of producing specific combinations from the elements that are present in the code. When *langue* and *parole* are defined in this way, there is a gap between both: what is the factor that bridges the distance between the social and the psychological, between the community and the individual, between the system and the application of the system, between the code and the actual use of the code?

The father of generative grammar, Noam Chomsky, provided an answer by introducing a distinction between competence and performance: the missing link between social code and individual usage is the individual's knowledge of the code. Performance, in the Chomskyan sense, is basically equivalent with Saussurean *parole*, but competence interiorizes the notion of the linguistic system. Competence is the internal grammar of the language user, the knowledge that the language user has of the linguistic system and that he or she puts to use in actual performance.

Remarkably, however, Chomsky introduces a new gap into the system. Rather than the threefold classification that one might expect, he restricts his conception of language to a new dichotomy: the social aspects of language are largely ignored. In comparison with a ternary distinction distinguishing between *langue*, competence, and *parole*/performance (between social system, individual knowledge of the system, and individual use of the system), the binary distinction between competence and performance creates a new empty slot, leaving the social aspects of language largely out of sight.

This apparent lack of interest for language as a social sign system links up logically with the Chomskyan emphasis on the genetic nature of natural language. Where, in fact, does the individual knowledge of the language come from? If the source of linguistic knowledge is not social, what else can it be than an innate and universal endowment? If the language is not learned through acculturation in a linguistic community, what other source could there be for linguistic knowledge except genetics?

Further restrictions follow. Meanings constitute the variable, contextual, cultural aspects of language par excellence. Because social interaction, the exchange of ideas, changing conceptions of the world are primarily reflected in the meaning of linguistic expressions, meanings are less interesting from a genetic point of view. Also, if the lexicon is the main repository of linguistically encoded meaning, studying the lexicon is of secondary importance: the focus will fall on the abstract syntactic patterns. And finally, if linguistics focuses on formal rule systems, the application of the rule systems in actual usage is relatively uninteresting. If the rules define the grammar, it is hard to see what added value could be derived from studying the way in which the rules are actually put to use. The study of performance, in other words, is just as secondary as research into the lexicon.

In short, generative grammar led to a severe decontextualization of the grammar, separating the autonomous grammatical module from different forms of context: through the basic Chomskyan shift from *langue* to competence, linguistics is separated from the social context of language as a social code; through the focus on the genetic aspects of the language, linguistics is separated from the cognitive context of lived individual experience; through the focus on formal rule systems, linguistics is separated from the situational context of actual language use.

Compared to this, Cognitive Linguistics is very much a recontextualizing approach. First, it is an outspoken attempt to give meaning a central position in the architecture of the grammar. Second, in contrast with formal semantics, the conception of meaning that lies at the basis of this approach is not restricted to a referential, truth-functional type of meaning – the type of meaning that you could express in logical terms. Linguistic structures are thought to express conceptualizations, and conceptualization goes further than mere reference. As we have seen, it involves imagery in the broadest sense of the word: ways of making sense, of imposing meaning. Also, the conceptualizations that are expressed in natural language have an experiential basis, i.e., they link up with the way in which human beings experience reality, both culturally and physiologically. In this sense, Cognitive Linguistics embodies a fully contextualized conception of meaning. Third, the link between linguistic performance and grammar is re-established by the view that language is usage-based, i.e. that there is a dialectic relationship between *langue* and *parole*.

We can observe, then, that the various characteristics of Cognitive Linguistics that you learned about in the first section of this introductory chapter and that were further spelled out in twelve crucial concepts, can be summarized under one general denominator: the *recontextualization* of grammar. If we assume, next, that this recontextualizing tendency is an underlying trend in contemporary cognitive-functionalist linguistics, Cognitive Linguistics is probably one of the most outspoken representatives of this tendency. Surely, it is not the only one, and there are whole disciplines in linguistics that are devoted to the exploration of specific forms of context, like sociolinguistics dealing with the social context, or pragmatics and text linguistics dealing with the level of *parole*. But Cognitive Linguistics is specific in the extent to which it tries to integrate these different tendencies into an overall model of language.

All of this does not mean, however, that Cognitive Linguistics has reached its goal yet. To begin with, because it is far from being alone in pursuing a recontextualized line of linguistic research, one of the major tasks for its future development will be to systematically confront similar approaches within the broad cognitive-functionalist domain and see to what extent theoretical and empirical convergences are possible. That is not going to be self-evident, given that Cognitive Linguistics is not even a theoretically uniform framework on its own account.

Further, we cannot say that Cognitive Linguistics has already realized all the consequences of the decontextualizing stance. For one thing, seeing language in the context of the mind at large would seem to imply a lively interdisciplinary interaction with the other sciences of the mind, but that is a trend that is only gradually emerging in mainstream cognitive linguistic circles. For an other, recontextualizing language in its social context implies an awareness of the variation that is inherent in the social life of language. Here again, sociolinguistically oriented studies inspired by Cognitive Linguistics are only beginning to come into view.

In short, there is still a quite a lot to be done. Ultimately, that may well be the best reason for coming back: not what has already been achieved, but what still has to be done – all the exciting, inviting paths for further exploration. So we will meet there, right?

# Chapter 1
# Cognitive Grammar

## Introduction to *Concept, Image, and Symbol*
*Ronald W. Langacker*

Despite the diversity of contemporary linguistic theory, certain fundamental views are widely accepted without serious question. Points of widespread agreement include the following: (i) language is a self-contained system amenable to algorithmic characterization, with sufficient autonomy to be studied in essential isolation from broader cognitive concerns; (ii) grammar (syntax in particular) is an independent aspect of linguistic structure distinct from both lexicon and semantics; and (iii) if meaning falls within the purview of linguistic analysis, it is properly described by some type of formal logic based on truth conditions. Individual theorists would doubtlessly qualify their assent in various ways, but (i)–(iii) certainly come closer than their denials to representing majority opinion.

Since 1976, I have been developing a linguistic theory that departs quite radically from these assumptions. Called "cognitive grammar" (alias "space grammar"), this model assumes that language is neither self-contained nor describable without essential reference to cognitive processing (regardless of whether one posits a special *faculté de langage*). Grammatical structures do not constitute an autonomous formal system or level of representation: they are claimed instead to be inherently symbolic, providing for the structuring and conventional symbolization of conceptual content. Lexicon, morphology, and syntax form a continuum of symbolic units, divided only arbitrarily into separate components; it is ultimately as pointless to analyze grammatical units without reference to their semantic value as to write a dictionary which omits the meanings of its lexical items. Moreover, a formal semantics based on truth conditions is deemed inadequate for describing the meaning of linguistic expressions. One reason is that semantic structures are characterized relative to knowledge systems whose scope is essentially open-ended. A second is that their value reflects not only the content of a conceived situation, but also how this content is structured and construed.

Cognitive grammar is therefore quite distinct from any version of generative theory. Moreover, it departs from most varieties of traditional and formal semantics, as well as the newer "situation semantics" of Barwise and Perry (1983), by

Originally published in 1990 as Chapter 1. Introduction in *Concept, Image, Symbol: The Cognitive Basis of Grammar*, Ronald W. Langacker, 1–32. Berlin/New York: Mouton de Gruyter. (Reprinted with permission from An introduction to cognitive grammar. *Cognitive Science* 10(1): 1–40. 1986).

equating meaning with conceptualization (or cognitive processing). It agrees in this regard with the "procedural semantics" of Miller and Johnson-Laird (1976) and Johnson-Laird (1983), and with the linguistic theories of Chafe (1970) and Jackendoff (1983); however, it is very different from all of these in its conception of grammatical organization and its specific proposals concerning semantic structure. Although cognitive grammar is not a direct outgrowth or a variant of any other linguistic theory, I do consider it compatible with a variety of ongoing research programs. Among these are Lakoff's work on categorization (1982, 1987); Fauconnier's study of mental spaces (1985); Haiman's ideas on iconicity and encyclopedic semantics (1980, 1983, 1985); Talmy's research on spatial terms, force dynamics, and the meanings of grammatical elements (1975, 1977, 1978, 1983, 1985a, 1985b, 1988a, 1988b); the proposals of Moore and Carling concerning the nonautonomy of linguistic structure (1982); Fillmore's conception of frame semantics (1982); Wierzbicka's insightful investigation into the semantics of grammar (1988); the growing body of research on metaphor and image schemas (Johnson 1987; Lakoff and Johnson 1980; Lakoff and Turner 1989; Sweetser 1984, 1987); recent studies of grammaticization (Bybee 1988; Kemmer 1988; Sweetser 1988; Traugott 1982, 1986, 1988); and the rich, multifaceted work in a "functional" vein by scholars too numerous to cite individually (though Givón 1979, 1984, 1989 must certainly be mentioned).

This chapter affords an overview of cognitive grammar as I myself conceive it. The topics it briefly covers will all be taken up again in later chapters of Langacker (1991a) and examined in greater detail. Readers interested in still further discussion and illustration of the theory will find it in the following works: Casad 1982, 1988; Cook 1988, 1989; Hawkins 1984, 1988; Janda 1984, 1988, 1993; Langacker 1981, 1982, 1985, 1987, 1988a, 1988b, 1991b; Lindner 1981, 1982; Poteet 1987; Rice 1987a, 1987b, 1988; Smith 1985a, 1985b, 1987, 1989; Tuggy 1980, 1981, 1986, 1988, 1989; Vandeloise 1984.

## 1. Linguistic semantics

Meaning is equated with conceptualization. Linguistic semantics must therefore attempt the structural analysis and explicit description of abstract entities like thoughts and concepts. The term conceptualization is interpreted quite broadly: it encompasses novel conceptions as well as fixed concepts; sensory, kinesthetic, and emotive experience; recognition of the immediate context (social, physical, and linguistic); and so on. Because conceptualization resides in cognitive processing, our ultimate objective must be to characterize the types of cognitive events whose occurrence constitutes a given mental experience. The remoteness of this goal is not a valid argument for denying the conceptual basis of meaning.

Most lexical items have a considerable array of interrelated senses, which define the range of their conventionally sanctioned usage. These alternate senses are conveniently represented in network form; Figure 1 depicts a fragment of the network associated with the noun *ring*. Certain senses are "schematic" relative to others, as indicated by the solid arrows. Some represent "extensions" from others (i.e. there is some conflict in specifications), as indicated by the dashed-line arrows. The nodes and categorizing relationships in such a network differ in their degree of entrenchment and cognitive salience – for instance, the heavy-line box in Figure 1 corresponds to the category prototype. The precise configuration of such a network is less important than recognizing the inadequacy of any reductionist description of lexical meaning. A speaker's knowledge of the conventional value of a lexical item cannot in general be reduced to a single structure, such as the prototype or the highest-level schema. For one thing, not every lexical category has a single, clearly determined prototype, nor can we invariably assume a high-level schema fully compatible with the specifications of every node in the network (none is shown in Figure 1). Even if such a structure is posited, moreover, there is no way to predict precisely which array of extensions and elaborations – out of all those that are conceivable and linguistically plausible – have in fact achieved conventional status. The conventional meaning of a lexical item must be equaled with the entire network, not with any single node.

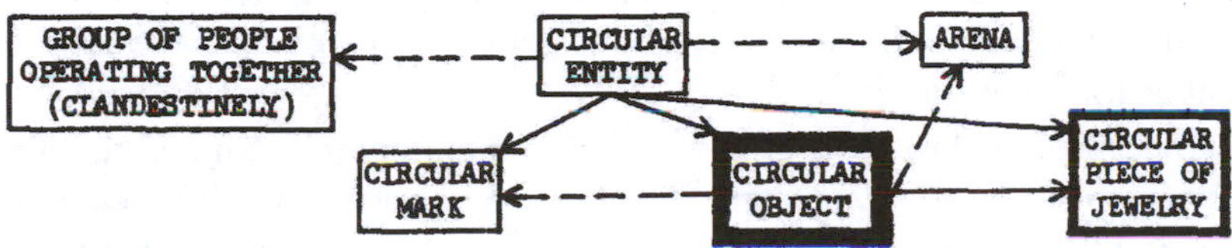


*Figure 1.*

Because polysemy is not our central concern, we will nevertheless focus on individual nodes. What is required to adequately characterize any particular sense of a linguistic expression? Specifically rejected is the idea that a semantic structure reduces to a bundle of features or semantic markers (cf. Katz and Fodor 1963). Rejected as well is the notion that all meanings are described directly in terms of semantic primitives. It is claimed instead that semantic structures (which I call "predications") are characterized relative to "cognitive domains", where a domain can be any sort of conceptualization: a perceptual experience, a concept, a conceptual complex, an elaborate knowledge system, etc. The semantic description of an expression therefore takes for its starting point an integrated conception of arbitrary complexity and possibly encyclopedic scope. The basic observation supporting this position is that certain conceptions presuppose others for their characterization. We can thus posit hierarchies of conceptual complexity, where structures at a given level arise through cognitive operations (including simple coordination) performed on the structures at lower levels. Crucially, the cognitive domains required by linguistic predications can occur at any level in such hierarchies.

Consider some examples. The notion *hypotenuse* is readily characterized given the prior conception of a right triangle, but incoherent without it; *right triangle* therefore functions as the cognitive domain for *hypotenuse*. Central to the value of *elbow* is the position of the designated entity relative to the overall configuration of the human arm (try explaining what an elbow is without referring in any way to an arm!), so *arm* is a domain for *elbow*. Similarly, *tip* presupposes the conception of an elongated object, and *April*, of the calendrical cycle devised to plot the passage of a year. A meaningful description of *shortstop* or *sacrifice fly* is possible only granted substantial knowledge of the rules and objectives of baseball. The implications of this position are apparent: the full and definitive characterization of a semantic structure must incorporate a comparable description of its domain, and ultimately of the entire hierarchy of more fundamental conceptions on which it depends. Pushing things to their logical conclusion, we must recognize that linguistic semantics is not an autonomous enterprise, and that a complete analysis of meaning is tantamount to a complete account of developmental cognition. This consequence is terribly inconvenient for linguistic theorists imprinted on autonomous formal systems, but that is not a legitimate argument against its validity.

What occupies the lowest level in conceptual hierarchies? I am neutral as to the possible existence of innately specified conceptual primitives. It is however necessary to posit a number of "basic domains", i.e. cognitively irreducible representational spaces or fields of conceptual potential. Among these basic domains are the experience of time and our capacity for dealing with two- and three-dimensional spatial configurations. There are basic domains associated with the various senses: color space (an array of possible color sensations), coordinated with the extension of the visual field; the pitch scale; a range of possible temperature sensations (coordinated with positions on the body); and so on. Emotive domains must also be assumed. It is possible that certain linguistic predications are characterized solely in relation to one or more basic domains, e.g. time for *before,* color space for *red,* or time and the pitch scale for *beep.* However most expressions pertain to higher levels of conceptual organization and presuppose nonbasic domains for their semantic characterization.

Most predications also require more than one domain for their full description, in which case I refer to the set as a "complex matrix", as illustrated for *knife* in Figure 2. One dimension of its characterization is a shape specification (or a family of such specifications). Another is the canonical role of a knife in the process of cutting. Additional properties are its inclusion in a typical place setting with other pieces of silverware; specifications of size, weight, and material; information about the manufacture of knives; the existence of knife-throwing acts in circuses; and so on indefinitely. Obviously these specifications are not all on a par. They differ greatly in their degree of "centrality", i.e. the likelihood of their activation on a given occasion of the expression's use. Moreover, some are probably incorporated as components of others – for instance, Figure 2 plausibly suggests that a shape specification is typically included in the conceptions constituting other domains of the complex matrix. I do however adopt an "encyclopedic" view of semantics (Haiman 1980). There is no sharp dividing line such that all specifications on one side are linguistically relevant and all those on the other side clearly irrelevant. Any facet of our knowledge of an entity is capable in principle of playing a role in determining the linguistic behavior of an expression that designates it (e.g. in semantic extension, or in its combination with other expressions).

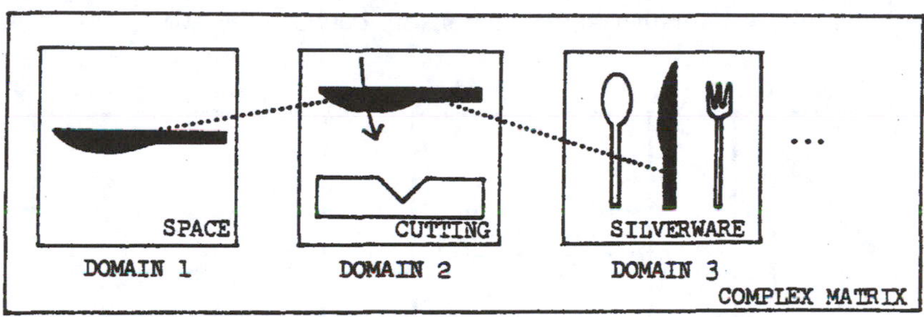


*Figure 2.*

If we succeed in identifying and describing the domain or complex matrix invoked by a linguistic predication, we have not yet finished its characterization. Equally significant for semantic structure is the "conventional imagery" inherent in the meaning of an expression. By imagery, I do not mean sensory images *à la* Shepard (1978) or Kosslyn (1980), though sensory images – as one type of conceptualization – are quite important for semantic analysis. I refer instead to our manifest capacity to structure or construe the content of a domain in alternate ways. This multifaceted ability is far too often neglected in semantic studies. Let us explore its dimensions and briefly note their grammatical significance.

## 2. Dimensions of imagery

The first dimension of imagery, observed in every linguistic predication, is the imposition of a "profile" on a "base". The base of a predication is its domain (or each domain in a complex matrix). Its profile is a substructure elevated to a special level of prominence within the base, namely that substructure which the expression "designates".[1] Some examples are sketched in Figure 3, with the profile given in heavy lines. The base (or domain) for the characterization of *hypotenuse* is the conception of a right triangle; for *tip*, the base is the conception of an elongated object; and for *uncle*, a set of individuals linked by kinship relations. The base is obviously essential to the semantic value of each predication, but it does not per se constitute that value: a hypotenuse is not a right triangle, a tip is not an elongated object, and an uncle is not a kinship network. The meaning of *hypotenuse*, *tip*, and *uncle* is in each case given only by the selection of a particular substructure within the base for the distinctive prominence characteristic of a profile. An expression's semantic value does not reside in either the base or the profile individually, but rather in the relationship between the two.

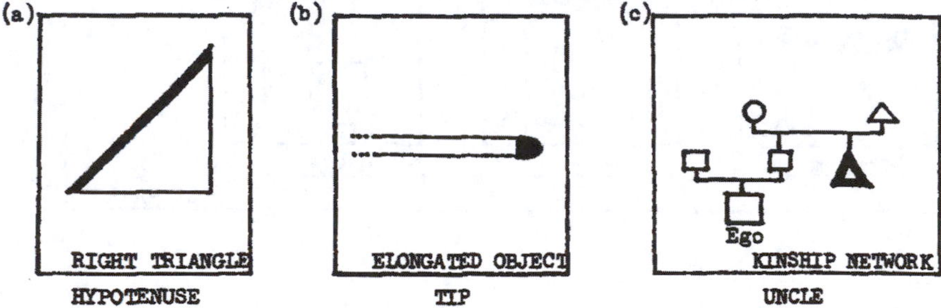


*Figure 3.*

Some further examples will demonstrate both the descriptive utility and the grammatical import of these constructs. The predications in question represent specific senses of *go*, *away*, and *gone*, namely those illustrated in (1):

(1) a. *I think you should go now.*
    b. *China is very far away.*
    c. *When I arrived, he was already gone.*

Consider first the particular sense of *go* that is diagramed in Figure 4(a). This is a relational rather than a nominal predication, i.e. it profiles the "interconnections" among conceived entities; these interconnections are indicated in Figure 4 by the heavy dashed lines. The relevant domains are space and time. With the passage of time, one individual, referred to here as the "trajector" (tr), moves from a position within the neighborhood of another individual, the "landmark" (lm), to a final position outside that neighborhood. Only four states of the process are shown explicitly, but they represent a continuous series. The dotted lines indicate that the trajectors "correspond" from one state to the next (i.e. they are construed as identical), as do the landmarks. *Away* profiles a relationship that is identical to the final state of *go:* the trajector is situated outside the vicinity of the landmark. Observe now that the participle *gone* profiles this same relationship, but it does so with respect to a different base. The base for *away* is simply the spatial domain, but the base for *gone* is the process profiled by *go* – something cannot be *gone* except by virtue of the process of going. The semantic contribution of the past participial inflection is to restrict the profile of the stem, in this case *go*, to its final state. *Gone* thus differs from *go* by virtue of its profile, and from *away* by virtue of its base.

A second dimension of imagery is the "level of specificity" at which a situation is construed. For example, the same situation might be described by any of the sentences in (2):

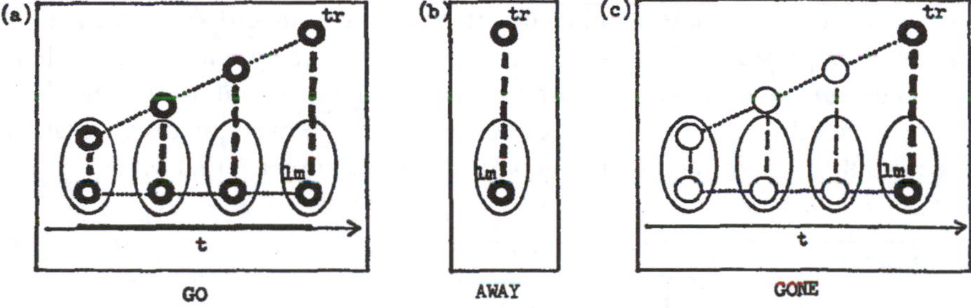


*Figure 4.*

(2) a. *That player is tall.*
b. *That defensive player is over 6' tall.*
c. *That linebacker is about 6' 5" tall.*
d. *That middle linebacker is precisely 6' 5" tall.*

Each of these sentences can be regarded as schematic for the one that follows, which elaborates its specifications and confines their possible values to a narrower range. It is well known that lexical items form hierarchies with respect to level of specificity, e.g. *animal* → *reptile* → *snake* → *rattlesnake* → *sidewinder.* Relationships of schematicity are also important for grammatical structure. Consider the combination of *break* and *the cup* to form the composite expression *break the cup.* As part of its internal structure, the predicate *break* makes schematic reference to two central participants. The combination of *break* and *the cup* is effected through a correspondence established between one of these participants (its landmark) and the entity profiled by *the cup,* which is characterized with far greater specificity. One of the component expressions thus elaborates a schematic substructure within the other, as is typically the case in a grammatical construction.

A third dimension of imagery pertains to the "scale" and "scope of predication". The scope of a predication is the extent of its coverage in relevant domains. A predication's scope is not always sharply delimited or explicitly indicated, but the construct is nonetheless of considerable structural significance (cf. Langacker 1991a: Chapter 2). Consider the notion *island* with respect to the various scopes indicated in Figure 5. The outer box, scope (a), is presumably sufficient to establish the land mass as an island, but scope (b) is at best problematic. There is no precise requirement on how extensive the body of water surrounding an island must be, but the narrow strip of water included in (b) does not have the necessary expanse (e.g. it could simply be a moat, and the land inside a moat is not thought of as an island). Similarly, the finger of land projecting out into the water qualifies as a *peninsula* given scope (c), but not (d); only from the former can we determine that the overall land mass is quite large relative to the finger-like projection. We can see that predications often imply a particular scale by noting the infelicity of using *island* to designate a handful of mud lying in the middle of a puddle. In my own speech, *bay* and *cove* are quite comparable in meaning except that *bay* specifies the requisite configuration of land and water on a larger scale.

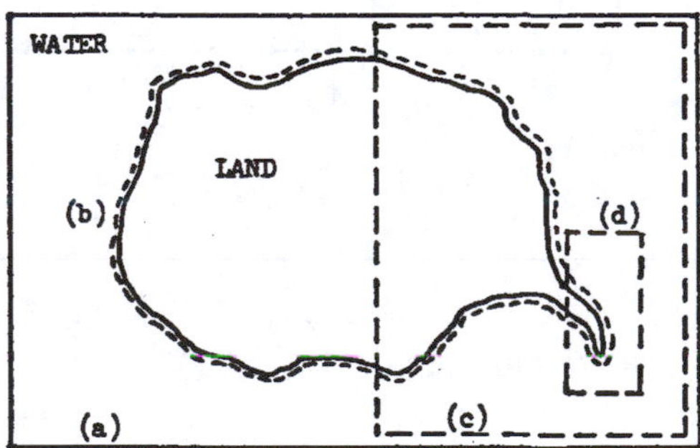


*Figure 5.*

Body-part terms illustrate the semantic and structural significance of these constructs. Essential to the characterization of terms like *head, arm,* and *leg* is the position of the profiled entity relative to the body as a whole, whose conception thus functions as their domain and immediate scope of predication. Each of these designated entities functions in turn as immediate scope of predication for other body-part terms defined on a smaller scale, e.g. *hand*, *elbow*, and *forearm* in the case of *arm*. *Hand* then furnishes the immediate scope of predication for *palm*, *thumb*, and *finger*, on a still smaller scale, and *finger* for *knuckle*, *fingertip*, and *fingernail*. This hierarchical organization has structural consequences. For example, sentences like those in (3), where *have* pertains to part-whole relationships, are most felicitous (other things being equal) when the subject designates the immediate scope of predication for the object (cf. Bever and Rosenbaum 1970; Cruse 1979).

(3) a. *A finger has 3 knuckles and 1 nail.*
    b. *??An arm has 14 knuckles and 5 nails.*
    c. *???A body has 56 knuckles and 20 nails.*

A similar restriction can be observed with noun compounds. We find numerous terms like *fingertip*, *fingernail*, *toenail*, *eyelash*, and *eyelid*, where the first element of the compound constitutes the immediate scope of predication for the second.[2] Compare this to the nonexistence and oddity of expressions like **bodytip*, **arm-nail*, **footnail*, **facelash*, and **headlid* to designate the same entities.

In certain grammatical constructions the scope of predication plays a specific structural role. A case in point is the "nested locative" construction exemplified in (4).

(4) a. *The quilt is upstairs in the bedroom in the closet on the top shelf behind the boxes.*
    b. *The rake is in the yard by the back fence near the gate.*

Each locative expression confines the subject to a specific "search domain", which then constitutes the scope of predication for the locative that follows. Thus in (4a) the locative *upstairs* confines the quilt to an upper story, and *in the bedroom* is construed relative to this restricted region – only an upstairs bedroom need be considered. The search domain imposed by this second locative functions in turn as the scope of predication for *in the closet,* and so on. Formally, these relationships are handled by positing a correspondence between the search domain of each locative and the scope of predication of its successor. Apart from the abstractness of the entities concerned, this correspondence is just like that found in any instance of grammatical combination (e.g. between the landmark of *break* and the profile of *the cup* in *break the cup*).

The relative salience of a predication's substructures constitutes a fourth dimension of imagery. Salience is of course a very general notion, so its descriptive significance depends on our ability to sort out the various contributing factors. One factor is the special prominence associated with profiling (considered previously). A number of others can be discerned, but only two will be discussed: the relative prominence of relational participants, and the enhanced salience of elements that are explicitly mentioned.

Relational predications normally manifest an asymmetry in the portrayal of the relational participants. This asymmetry is not strictly dependent on the content of the predication, and is consequently observable even for expressions designating symmetrical relationships, e.g. *resemble*. I maintain that *X resembles Y* and *Y resembles X* are semantically distinct (even granting their truth-conditional equivalence): the former characterizes X with reference to Y, and the latter describes Y with reference to X. We can similarly employ either *X is above Y* or *Y is below X* to describe precisely the same conceived situation, but they differ in how they construe this situation; in the former, Y functions as a point of reference – a kind of landmark – for locating X, whereas the latter reverses these roles. The subtlety of the contrast with predications like these hardly diminishes its significance for linguistic semantics and grammatical structure. The asymmetry is more apparent in cases like *go*, *hit*, *enter*, and *approach*, where one participant moves in relation to another (which is stationary so far as the verb itself is concerned), but its characterization must be abstract enough to accommodate the full range of relational expressions.

I attribute this inherent asymmetry to figure/ground organization (for discussion, see Langacker 1987: Chapter 6). A relational predication elevates one of its participants to the status of figure. I refer to this participant as its "trajector"; other salient participants are referred to as "landmarks". This terminology is inspired by prototypical action verbs, where the trajector is usually the initial or primary mover, but the definitions make no specific reference to motion and are therefore applicable to any relational expression. The trajector/landmark asymmetry underlies the subject/object distinction, but the former notions have considerably broader application. In particular, a schematic trajector and landmark are imputed to a relational predication's internal structure, regardless of whether these entities receive (or are capable of receiving) separate expression. The verb *read* consequently has a trajector and a landmark in all the sentences of (5), despite the fact that both are made explicit (by elaborative noun phrases) only in (5a):

(5) a. *David read a new book.*
  b. *David is reading.*
  c. *The best way to learn is to read.*

The terms subject and object are generally reserved for overt noun phrases that elaborate a relational trajector and primary landmark at the clausal level. By contrast, trajector/landmark asymmetry is characteristic of relational predications at any level of organization, even if left implicit.

The enhanced salience of explicitly mentioned elements can be illustrated by the semantic contrast between pairs of expressions like the following: *father* vs. *male parent*; *pork* vs. *pig meat*; *oak* vs. *oak tree*; *triangle* vs. *three-sided polygon*; and *sink* vs. *passively descend through a medium under the force of gravity.* I am not concerned here with differences in connotation or information content – for sake of discussion, let us accept the members of each pair as equivalent in these respects. My claim is that the paired expressions nevertheless contrast semantically because the second expression in each case explicitly mentions certain semantic components and thereby renders them more prominent than they would otherwise be. Even for a speaker who knows perfectly well that pork comes from pigs, the expression *pig meat* renders this provenience more salient than does *pork*, simply because the former incorporates a symbolic unit that specifically designates this source. In similar fashion, the inclusion of the designated entity in a broader class of geometrical figures is highlighted by *three-sided polygon*, but remains latent in the case of *triangle.*

A linguistically appropriate characterization of meaning should accommodate such differences. Cognitive grammar defines the meaning of a complex expression as including not only the semantic structure that represents its composite sense, but also its "compositional path": the hierarchy of semantic structures reflecting its progressive assembly from the meanings of component expressions. Let us assume, for example, that the composite semantic values of *pork* and *pig meat* are identical. As an unanalyzable morpheme, *pork* symbolizes this notion directly, so its compositional path consists of the single semantic structure [PORK]. However *pig meat* is "analyzable", i.e. speakers recognize the semantic contribution of its component morphemes. The meaning of *pig meat* therefore incorporates not only the composite structure [PORK], but also the individually symbolized components [PIG] and [MEAT], together with the relationship that each of them bears to the composite value. The two expressions arrive at the same composite value through different compositional paths (a degenerate path in the case of *pork*), with the consequence that they differ in meaning.

Besides accounting for the semantic contrast between simple and composite expressions, this conception of meaning has the advantage of resolving a classic problem of truth-conditional semantics. The problem is posed by semantically anomalous expressions, e.g. * *perspicacious neutrino* and **truculent spoon,* which lack truth conditions and thus ought to be meaningless and semantically equivalent. Not only is this counterintuitive, but it also predicts – quite incorrectly – the semantic anomaly of sentences like those in (6), which contain anomalous constituents.

(6) a. *There is no such thing as a perspicacious neutrino.*
b. *It is meaningless to speak of a truculent spoon.*

In the present framework, anomalous expressions are indeed both meaningful and nonsynonymous. Though a coherent composite conceptualization fails to emerge for **perspicacious neutrino*, it has a semantic value, consisting of the meanings of its components together with their specified mode of combination (as determined by the grammatical construction). The same is true for **truculent spoon*, and because its components are different from those of **perspicacious neutrino*, so is its semantic value. Lacking a coherent composite sense, these meanings are defective, but they are meanings nonetheless. Sentences like (6) are semantically well-formed precisely because they comment on the anomaly of a constituent.

I will mention two more dimensions of imagery only in passing, though each is multifaceted and merits extended discussion. One is the construal of a situation relative to different background assumptions and expectations. To take just one example, either (7a) or (7b) might be used to describe the same state of affairs:

(7) a. *He has a few friends in high places.*
b. *He has few friends in high places.*
c. *Few people have any friends in high places.*
d. **A few people have any friends in high places.*

Intuitively, the difference between *few* and *a few* is that the former is somehow negative, and the latter more positive. This is corroborated by (7c) and (7d): *any*, which requires a negative context (cf. Klima 1964), is compatible with *few*, but not with *a few*. Analytically, I suggest that *few* construes the specified quantity as being less than some implicit norm, whereas *a few* construes the quantity relative to a baseline of zero. These respective predications therefore indicate departure from an implicit reference point in a negative vs. a positive direction.

The final dimension of imagery is perspective, which subsumes a number of more specific factors: orientation, assumed vantage point, directionality, and how objectively an entity is construed. Orientation and vantage point are well known from the ambiguity of sentences like (8a). The contrast between (8b) and (8c) shows the importance of directionality, even for situations that appear to involve no motion.

(8) a. *Brian is sitting to the left of Sally.*
b. *The fall falls gently to the bank of the river.*
c. *The hill rises gently from the bank of the river.*
d. *The balloon rose swiftly.*

I suggest, though, that (8b)–(8d) all involve motion in an abstract sense of the term (see Langacker 1991a: Chapter 5). Described in (8d) is physical motion on the part of a mover construed "objectively", by which I mean that it is solely an object of conceptualization, maximally differentiated from the conceptualizer (i.e. the speaker and/or hearer). Motion along a similar trajectory is implied in (8c), but in this case the movement is abstract and the mover is construed "subjectively": the mover is none other than the conceptualizer, in his role as the agent (rather than the object) of conceptualization. Gradations between physical and abstract motion on the one hand, and between objective and subjective construal of conceived entities on the other, are important to the analysis of numerous linguistic phenomena.[3]

## 3. Grammar as image

Lexicon and grammar form a continuum of symbolic elements. Like lexicon, grammar provides for the structuring and symbolization of conceptual content, and is thus imagic in character. When we use a particular construction or grammatical morpheme, we thereby select a particular image to structure the conceived situation for communicative purposes. Because languages differ in their grammatical structure, they differ in the imagery that speakers employ when conforming to linguistic convention. This relativistic view does not per se imply that lexicogrammatical structure imposes any significant constraints on our thought processes – in fact I suspect its impact to be rather superficial (cf. Langacker 1976). The symbolic resources of a language generally provide an array of alternative images for describing a given scene, and we shift from one to another with great facility, often within the confines of a single sentence. The conventional imagery invoked for linguistic expression is a fleeting thing that neither defines nor constrains the contents of our thoughts.

The most obvious contribution of grammar to the construal of a scene pertains to designation. Grammatical constructions have the effect of imposing a particular profile on their composite semantic value. When a head combines with a modifier, for example, it is the profile of the head that prevails at the composite structure level. Consider a simple situation in which a lamp is suspended over a table. Starting from such simple expressions as *the lamp*, *the table*, *above*, and *below*, we can combine them in alternate ways to form composite expressions that profile different facets of the scene. *The lamp above the table* naturally designates the lamp. By choosing *the table* for the head, and appropriately adjusting the prepositional phrase modifier, we obtain instead *the table below the lamp*, which profiles the table. Another option is to add the proper form of *be* to the prepositional phrase, converting it into a process predication designating the extension of the locative relationship through a span of conceived time, e.g. *is above the table*. When a subject is then supplied, the resulting sentence *The lamp is above the table* also profiles the temporally extended locative relationship.

Let us further explore the sense in which grammar embodies conventional imagery by considering the semantic contrast between (9a) and (9b).

(9) a. *Bill sent a walrus to Joyce.*
    b. *Bill sent Joyce a walrus.*

The standard transformational analysis of these sentences treats them as synonymous and derives them from a common deep structure; depending on the particular choice of deep structure, *to* is either deleted or inserted transformationally, and the nonsubject nominals are permuted in the course of deriving the surface form of either (9a) or (9b). Cognitive grammar does not posit abstract deep structures, and neither sentence type is derived from the other – they are claimed instead to represent alternate construals of the profiled event. Examples (9a) and (9b) differ in meaning because they employ subtly different images to structure the same conceived situation.

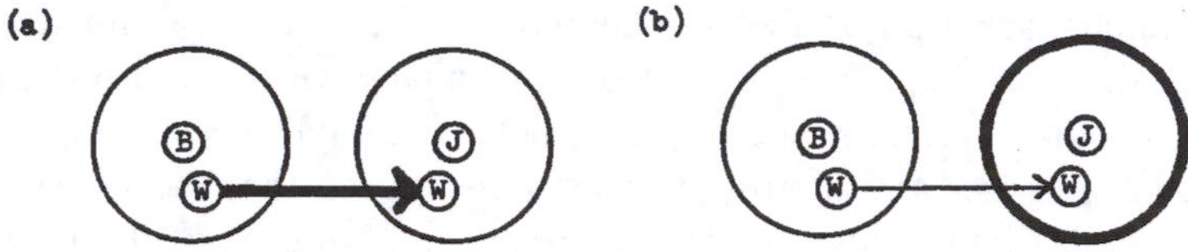


*Figure 6.*

The essentials of the analysis are sketched in Figure 6, where the small circles represent Bill, Joyce, and the walrus; the large circles stand for the regions over which Bill and Joyce exercise dominion; and heavy lines indicate a certain degree of relative prominence. Up to a point the sentences are semantically equivalent. Each symbolizes a conception in which a walrus originates in the domain under Bill's control and – at Bill's instigation – follows a path that results in its eventual location within the region under Joyce's control. The semantic contrast resides in the relative salience of certain facets of this complex scene. In (9a), the morpheme *to* specifically designates the path followed by the walrus, thereby rendering this aspect of the conceptualization more prominent than it would otherwise be, as indicated in Figure 6(a). In (9b), on the other hand, *to* is absent, but the juxtaposition of two unmarked nominals (*Joyce* and *a walrus*) after the verb symbolizes a possessive relationship between the first nominal and the second. Consequently

(9b) lends added prominence to the configuration that results when the walrus completes its trajectory, namely that which finds it in Joyce's possession, as indicated in Figure 6(b).

All of the content present in one conception may be presumed to figure in the other as well – what differs is the relative salience of substructures. This subtle difference in imagery has an impact on the felicity of using *to* or the double-object construction for certain types of situations.[4] Consider the data in (10):

(10) a. *I sent a walrus to Antarctica.*
  b. *?I sent Antarctica a walrus.*
  c. *I sent the zoo a walrus.*

Example (10a) is fully acceptable because *to* emphasizes the path traversed by the walrus, and a continent can perfectly well be construed as the endpoint of a path. However, it is harder to construe a continent as a possessor exercising control over other entities, so (10b), which specifically places Antarctica in a possessor role, is felt to be marginal. The status of (10c) depends on the construal of *zoo.* If the zoo is simply construed as a place, it is difficult to view it as a possessor, and (10c) is questionable for the same reason as (10b). But a zoo is also an institution, and it is conventional in English to treat institutions as being analogous to people, which allows them to function linguistically as agents, possessors, and so forth. Example (10c) is consequently well formed to the extent that this second construal prevails. As viewed in the present framework, then, judgments of well-formedness often hinge on the interplay and compatibility of images, and are influenced by subtle shifts in context, intended meaning, or how a speaker chooses to structure and interpret a situation.

The examples in (11)–(13) provide further illustration.

(11) a. *I gave the fence a new coat of paint.*
  b. *?I gave a new coat of paint to the fence.*

(12) a. *I cleared the floor for Bill.*
  b. *?I cleared Bill the floor.*
  c. *I cleared Bill a place to sleep on the floor.*

(13) a. *I baked her a cake.*
  b. *?I mowed her the lawn.*

It is conventional in English to employ possessive locutions for part-whole relations, so construing a fence as the possessor of a new coat of paint, in the manner of (11a), is quite natural. It is more difficult to envisage a coat of paint moving along a path to the fence; (11b) is thus a bit less natural, because *to* renders the path more prominent than the eventual possessive relationship.[5] The sentences in (12)–(13) bring out another consequence of the analysis. Because the two constructions are claimed to be parallel (i.e. neither is derived from the other) and semantically distinct, it is to be expected that the double-object construction – having no intrinsic connection with *to* – might serve as an alternative to other prepositions also. It is well known from transformational studies (where the fact has long been problematic) that the double-object construction alternates with *for* as well as *to*. With *for* also the double-object construction is restricted to instances where the first object is plausibly construed as winding up in possession of the second. In (12), for example, Bill does not come to possess the floor just because I clear it for him, so (12b) is peculiar; (12c) is perfectly acceptable, however, since the additional context provided by the second nominal (a *place to sleep on the floor*) makes it apparent that the spot in question effectively comes under Bill's control and lies at his disposal by virtue of the act of clearing it. The data in (13) is similarly explained. Baking someone a cake puts the cake at that person's disposal, but mowing a lawn can hardly have a comparable effect under normal circumstances.

## 4. Grammatical organization

The ultimate goal of linguistic description is to characterize, in a cognitively realistic fashion, those structures and abilities that constitute a speaker's grasp of linguistic convention. A speaker's linguistic knowledge is procedural rather than declarative, and the internalized grammar representing this knowledge is simply a "structured inventory of conventional linguistic units". The term "unit" is employed in a technical sense to indicate a thoroughly mastered structure, i.e. one that a speaker can activate as a preassembled whole without attending to the specifics of its internal composition. A unit can therefore be regarded as a cognitive routine. The inventory of conventional units is "structured" in the sense that some units function as components of others (i.e. they constitute subroutines).

I speak of an "inventory" of conventional units to indicate that a grammar is nongenerative and nonconstructive. That is, I reject the standard notion that a grammar is properly conceived as an algorithmic device giving a well-defined class of expressions ("all and only the grammatical sentences of a language") as output. This conception is viable only if one imposes arbitrary restrictions on the scope of linguistic structure and makes gratuitous assumptions about its character. It is commonly assumed, for example, that judgments of grammaticality are categorical rather than matters of degree; that figurative language is properly excluded from the domain of linguistic description; and that a motivated distinction can be made between semantics and pragmatics. Although such assumptions support the notion that language is self-contained and cognitively autonomous, there is little factual basis for their adoption.

Instead, I conceive the grammar of a language as merely providing the speaker with an inventory of symbolic resources, among them schematic templates representing established patterns in the assembly of complex symbolic structures. Speakers employ these symbolic units as standards of comparison in assessing the conventionality of novel expressions and usages, whether of their own creation or supplied by other speakers. The novel symbolic structures evaluated in this fashion are not a well-defined set and cannot be algorithmically derived by the limited mechanisms of an autonomous grammar. Rather their construction is attributed to problem-solving activity on the part of the language user, who brings to bear in this task not only his grasp of linguistic convention, but also his appreciation of the context, his communicative objectives, his esthetic sensibilities, and any aspect of his general knowledge that might prove relevant. The resulting symbolic structures are generally more specific than anything computable from linguistic units alone, and often conflict with conventional expectations (e.g. in metaphor and semantic extension). Assessing their conventionality (or "well-formedness") is a matter of categorization: categorizing judgments either sanction them as elaborations of schematic units or recognize them as departing from linguistic convention as currently established.

Only three basic types of units are posited: semantic, phonological, and symbolic. A symbolic unit is said to be "bipolar", consisting of a semantic unit defining one pole and a phonological unit defining the other: [[SEM]/[PHON]]. That lexical units have this bipolar character is uncontroversial; *pencil*, for example, has the form [[PENCIL]/[pencil]], where capital letters abbreviate a semantic structure (of indefinite internal complexity), and a phonological structure is represented orthographically. A pivotal claim of cognitive grammar is that grammatical units are also intrinsically symbolic. I maintain, in other words, that grammatical morphemes, categories, and constructions all take the form of symbolic units, and that nothing else is required for the description of grammatical structure.

Symbolic units vary along the parameters of complexity and specificity. With respect to the former, a unit is minimal (a "morpheme") if it contains no other symbolic units as components. For instance, despite its internal complexity at both the semantic and the phonological poles, the morpheme *sharp* is minimal from the symbolic standpoint, whereas *sharpen*, *sharpener*, and *pencil sharpener* are progressively more complex. With respect to the second parameter, symbolic units run the gamut from the highly specific to the maximally schematic. Each sense of *ring* depicted in Figure 1, for example, combines with the phonological unit [ring] to constitute a symbolic unit. Some of these senses are schematic relative to others, so the symbolic units in question vary in their level of specificity at the semantic pole. Basic grammatical categories (e.g. noun, verb, adjective, adverb) are represented in the grammar by symbolic units that are maximally schematic at both the semantic and the phonological poles. A noun, for instance, is claimed to instantiate the schema [[THING]/[X]], and a verb the schema [[PROCESS]/[Y]], where [THING] and [PROCESS] are abstract notions to be described later, and [X] and [Y] are highly schematic phonological structures (i.e. they specify little more than the presence of "some phonological content").

A grammatical rule or construction is represented in the grammar by a symbolic unit that is both complex and schematic. For example, the morphological rule illustrated by the deverbal nominalizations *teacher, helper, hiker, thinker, diver,* etc. consists in a complex unit that incorporates as components the verb schema [[PROCESS]/[Y]] and the grammatical morpheme [[ER]/[er]] (i.e. the suffix *-er,* which is attributed substantial though schematic semantic content). This unit further specifies how the component structures are integrated, conceptually and phonologically, to form a composite symbolic structure. Using "-" to indicate this integration (examined later), we can write the constructional schema as follows: [[[PROCESS]/[Y]]-[[ER]/[er]]]. Its internal structure is exactly parallel to that of an instantiating expression, e.g. [[[TEACH]/[teach]]-[[ER]/[er]]], except that in lieu of a specific verb stem it contains the schema for the verb-stem category.

One constructional schema can be incorporated as a component of another. In the top portion of Figure 7(a), the schema just described combines with the noun schema [[THING]/[X]] to form a higher-order constructional schema, which speakers presumably extract to represent the commonality of *pencil sharpener, lawn mower, mountain climber, back scratcher, taxi driver,* and so on. The lower portion of 7(a) represents the lexical unit *pencil sharpener,* which conforms to the specifications of this schema but elaborates it greatly. The arrow labeled (a) indicates that the upper structure as a whole is judged schematic for the overall expression; this categorizing relationship is what specifies the membership of the expression in the class that the schema characterizes. This global categorizing relationship is based on local categorizations between component structures: relationship (b) identifies *pencil* as a member of the noun class; (c) categorizes *sharpener* as a deverbal nominalization derived by *-er*; and (d) classes *sharpen* as a verb.[6] The full set of categorizing relationships of this sort constitutes the expression's "structural description". Observe that *pencil sharpener* has a conventional meaning which is considerably more specific than anything derivable compositionally from the meanings of its parts – a pencil sharpener is not simply 'something that sharpens pencils'. Given the nonconstructive nature of the present model, we can nevertheless accept the expression as a valid instantiation of the construction in question, without relegating the unpredictable semantic specifications to the realm of extralinguistic knowledge. The constructional schema is not responsible for assembling the expression, but only for its categorization.

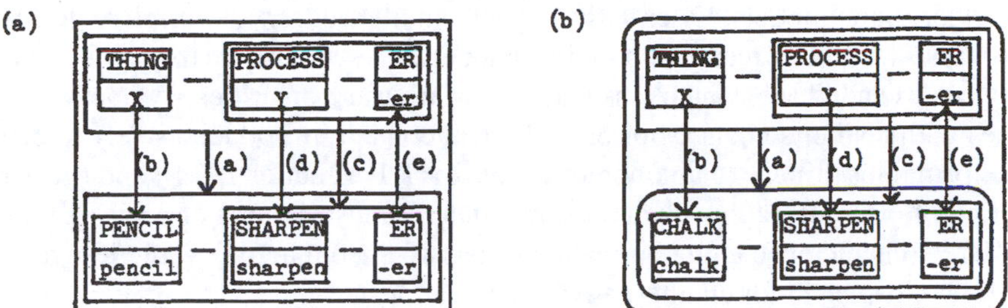


*Figure 7.*

All of the structures and categorizing relationships in Figure 7(a) have the status of units, which I indicate by enclosing them in boxes or square brackets. What about a novel expression on the same model, for example *chalk sharpener*? Its organization is sketched in Figure 7(b), where a closed curve (as opposed to a box) indicates a structure that does not yet constitute a unit. The assembly of this novel symbolic structure is largely prefigured by existing units, including the constructional schema, the components *chalk* and *sharpener,* and the categorization of *chalk* as a noun. Taken as a whole, however, neither the full expression *chalk sharpener* nor its categorization by the constructional schema (relationship (a)) has unit status. It does not matter for our purposes whether a speaker employs the existing units to construct or simply to understand the novel expression – in either case, all of the structures and relationships in 7(b) figure in its composition and structural description, and in either case its contextual meaning may incorporate specifications that are obvious from the situation being described (which functions as the domain for the composite expression) but are not supplied by the conventional meanings of its components. Despite this lack of full compositionality, the expression may well recur with sufficient frequency to become established as a conventional unit parallel to *pencil sharpener, lawn mower,* etc. If so, its contextual meaning (in an appropriately schematized form) becomes the conventional meaning of the new lexical unit. Full semantic compositionality is therefore not a hallmark of either novel expressions as they are actually understood or the fixed expressions which result from their conventionalization.

This conception of grammar makes it possible to impose the following restriction on linguistic analyses: the only units permitted in the grammar of a language are (i) semantic, phonological, and symbolic structures that occur overtly in linguistic expressions; (ii) structures that are schematic for those in (i); and (iii) categorizing relationships involving the structures in (i) and (ii). I call this the "content requirement", and consider it to be intrinsically more restrictive (at least in a certain, possibly nontechnical sense) than the constraints generally imposed on algorithmic models. Essentially, it rules out all arbitrary descriptive devices, i.e. those with no direct grounding in phonetic or semantic reality. Among the devices excluded are contentless features or arbitrary diacritics; syntactic dummies with neither semantic nor phonological content, introduced solely to drive the formal machinery of autonomous syntax (cf. Perlmutter 1978); and the derivation of overt structures from abstract, underlying structures of a substantially different character (e.g. the derivation of passives from actives – see Langacker (1991a: Chapter 4) for an alternative account).

## 5. Grammatical classes

The content requirement proscribes the use of diacritic features. How, then, does a grammar indicate the behavior and class membership of conventional units? Some classes are characterized on the basis of intrinsic semantic and/or phonological content. In this event, a schematic unit is extracted to represent the shared content, and class membership is indicated by categorizing units reflecting the judgment that individual members instantiate the schema. The vowel [i], for example, is classed as a high vowel by virtue of the categorizing unit [[HIGH VOWEL]→[i]], where [HIGH VOWEL] is a schematic phonological structure which neutralizes the properties that distinguish one high vowel from another. Similarly, among the categorizing units depicted in Figure 7(a), relationships (b) and (d) identify *pencil* and *sharpen* as a noun and a verb respectively, whereas relationship (a) identifies *pencil sharpener* as an instance of the grammatical construction characterized by the overall schema. Only symbolic structures with actual semantic and phonological content figure in these relationships.

Obviously, though, the membership of many grammatical classes is not fully predictable on the basis of semantic or phonological properties, e.g. the class of nouns that voice *f* to *v* in the plural (*leaf/leaves*, but *reef/reefs*), or the class of verbs that conventionally occur in the double-object construction described earlier (cf. Green 1974; Oehrle 1977). The fact that morphological and syntactic behavior is often not fully predictable is generally taken as establishing the independence of grammar as a distinct aspect of linguistic structure. However, this conclusion does not actually follow from the observation – the tacit reasoning behind it confounds two issues that are in principle distinct: (i) what KINDS of structures there are; and (ii) the PREDICTABILITY of their behavior. The present framework accommodates unpredictable behavior without positing arbitrary diacritics or rule features. To say that *leaf* (but not *reef*) voices *f* to *v* in the plural is simply to say that the composite symbolic structure *leaves* (but not *reeves*) is included among the conventional units of the grammar. Similarly, to say that *send* participates in the double-object construction amounts to positing the constructional schema [send NP NP], where the verb is specific but the two noun phrases are characterized only schematically. The nonoccurrence of *transfer* in this construction is reflected in the grammar by the nonexistence of the parallel symbolic unit [transfer NP NP].[7]

Crucial to the claim that grammatical structure resides in symbolic units alone is the possibility of providing a notional characterization of basic grammatical categories, nouns and verbs in particular. The impossibility of such a characterization is a fundamental dogma of modern linguistics, but the standard arguments that appear to support it are not immune to criticism. For one thing, they presuppose an objectivist view of meaning, and thus fail to acknowledge sufficiently our capacity to construe a conceived situation in alternate ways. Consider the argument based on verb/noun pairs which refer to the same process, e.g. *extract* and *extraction*. Such pairs demonstrate the impossibility of a notional definition only if one assumes that they are semantically identical, yet this is not a necessary assumption when meaning is treated as a subjective phenomenon. It is perfectly coherent to suggest that the nominalization of *extract* involves a conceptual reification of the designated process, i.e. the verb and noun construe it by means of contrasting images. Another type of argument against a notional characterization pivots on the confusion of prototypes with abstract schemas. In the case of nouns, for instance, discussions of notional definitions generally focus on physical objects (or perhaps "persons, places, and things"), which are clearly prototypical; the existence of nouns like *extraction*, which do not conform to this prototype, is then taken as demonstrating that nouns are not a semantic class. Obviously, a schematic characterization of the class – one compatible with the specifications of all class members – cannot be identified with the category prototype representing typical instances. If a schematic characterization is possible at all, it must be quite abstract, accommodating both physical objects and many other sorts of entities as special cases.

Cognitive grammar posits a number of basic classes that differ in the nature of their profile (see Langacker 1991a: Chapter 3 for extensive discussion). As previously indicated, a noun is a symbolic structure that designates a thing, where "thing" is a technical term defined as a "region in some domain"; in the case of count nouns, the profiled region is further specified as being "bounded". Because physical objects occupy bounded regions in three-dimensional space, expressions which designate such objects qualify as count nouns, but the definition does not specifically refer to them or to the spatial domain in particular. Examples of count nouns characterized with respect to other domains include *moment* (a bounded region in time), *paragraph* (a delimited portion of a written work), and *B-flat* (a minimal, point-like region on the musical scale). Observe that the bounding implied by a count noun need not be sharp or precise, and it may be imposed as a matter of construal when objective factors do not suggest any demarcation. Where, for instance, does one's *midriff* begin or end?

Contrasting with nouns are "relational" expressions, which profile the "interconnections" among conceived entities. The term "entity" is employed in a maximally general way, and subsumes anything we might have occasion to refer to for analytic purposes: things, relations, boundaries, points on a scale, and so on. Interconnections can be regarded as cognitive operations that assess the relative position of entities within the scope of predication. It is speculated that only four basic types of assessment are necessary, provided that cognitive domains have been properly described: inclusion (INCL), coincidence (COINC), separation (SEP), and proximity (PROX). Significantly, the interconnecting operations defining a relational conception commonly associate entities other than the major relational participants (trajector and primary landmark), or associate selected facets of these participants rather than treating them as undifferentiated wholes.

By way of illustration, consider the predicate [ABOVE], sketched in Figure 8. Its domain is space organized in terms of vertical and horizontal dimensions, including an implicit reference point $O_V$ (the vertical origin). The major relational participants are both things, characterized only schematically; one is further identified as the trajector (relational figure).[8] Among the entities invoked by specifications of this predicate are the horizontal and vertical projections of the trajector ($h_t$, $v_t$) and of the landmark ($h_l$, $v_l$). The expression *above* is optimally employed when the horizontal projections of the trajector and landmark coincide, i.e. [$h_t$ COINC $h_l$], but is tolerated so long as they remain in proximity to one another: [$h_t$ PROX $h_l$]. With respect to the vertical dimension, on the other hand, their projections must not coincide – the specification [$v_t$ SEP $v_l$] is obligatory. The pivotal specification of [ABOVE] is provided by an operation interconnecting two entities that are still more abstract. Let [$O_V > v_t$] be the operation which registers the displacement of the trajector from the vertical origin, and [$O_V > v_l$] that of the landmark. The specification in question resides in a higher-order operation assessing the relative magnitudes of the component operations: [($O_V > v_t$) INCL ($O_V > v_l$)].

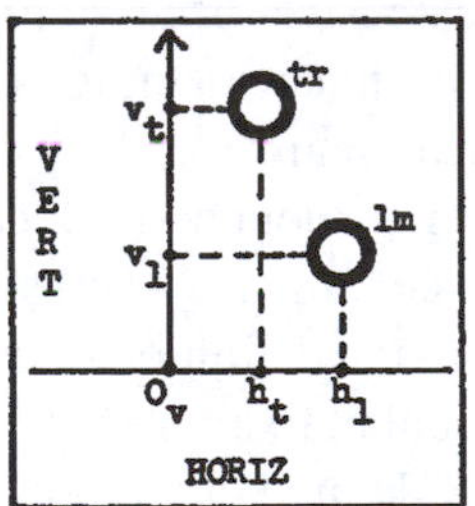


*Figure 8.*

Interconnecting operations of roughly this sort must somehow figure in the cognitive representation of a relational notion (though I take no position on the specifics of their implementation). [ABOVE] is a "simple atemporal relation" (or "stative" relation), in the sense that its specifications portray a single, internally consistent configuration. We must also recognize "complex" atemporal relations, where such is not the case. Consider the contrast between (14a) and (14b).

(14) a. *There is a bridge across the river.*
b. *A hiker waded across the river.*

Distinct senses of *across* are involved, diagramed in Figures 9(a) and (b). In 9(a), the trajector (in this case the bridge) simultaneously occupies all the points on a path leading from one side of the primary landmark (the river) to the other. In 9(b), on the other hand, the trajector still occupies all the points on the path leading from one side of the landmark to the other, but does so only successively through time. The profiled relationship involves indefinitely many distinct configurations (or states), of which only a few are represented diagramatically. This sense of *across* is consequently a complex atemporal relation.[9]

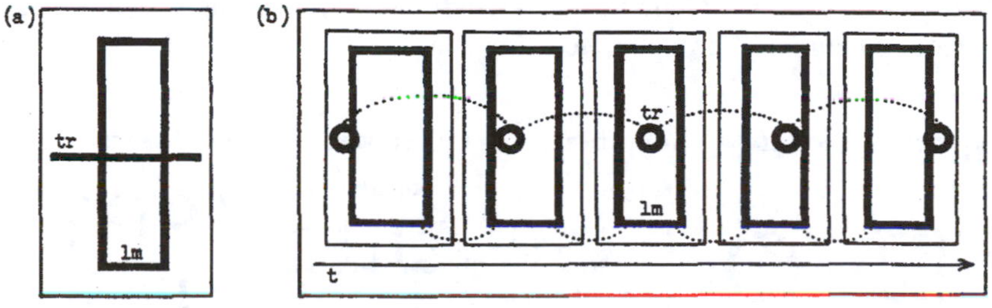


*Figure 9.*

Atemporal relations contrast with "processes", which define the class of verbs. The distinction between a process and a complex atemporal relation involves the contrast between "sequential" and "summary scanning" (see Langacker 1991a: Chapter 3). Sequential scanning is the mode of processing we employ when watching a motion picture or observing a ball as it flies through the air. The successive states of the conceived event are activated serially and more or less instantaneously, so that the activation of one state begins to decline as that of its successor is initiated; essentially, we follow along from one state to the next as the event unfolds.[10] On the other hand, summary scanning is what we employ in mentally reconstructing the trajectory a ball has followed (e.g. in identifying a pitch as a curve, fastball, or slider and diagraming its degree of curvature). The component states are activated successively but cumulatively (i.e. once activated they remain active throughout), so that eventually they are all coactivated as a simultaneously accessible whole. The difference between a complex atemporal relation (like *across*) and the corresponding verb (*cross*) is therefore attributed not to their intrinsic content, but rather to the mode of scanning employed in their activation – a matter of conventional imagery.

Abbreviatory notations for the basic classes of predications are presented in Figure 10. A circle is the natural choice to represent a thing. A simple atemporal (or stative) relation profiles the interconnections between two or more conceived entities, where an entity can be either a thing or another relation. (Dashed lines represent these interconnections, and by convention the uppermost of the interconnected entities will be taken as the trajector unless otherwise indicated.) A complex atemporal relation consists of a sequence of stative relations scanned in summary fashion. A process is comparable to a complex atemporal relation in profiling a sequence of relational configurations, but has certain other properties as well: (i) the component states are conceived as being distributed through time; (ii) these states are scanned in sequential fashion; and (iii) the trajector is always a thing (never a relation). The arrow in Figure 10(e) stands for conceived time, and the heavy-line bar along this arrow indicates that the component states are scanned sequentially through processing time.

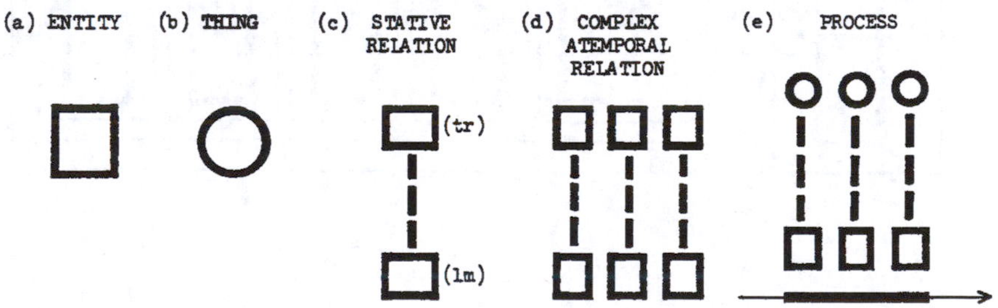


*Figure 10.*

## 6. Grammatical constructions

Grammar resides in patterns for the successive combination of symbolic structures to form more and more elaborate symbolic expressions. It is described by a structured inventory of "grammatical constructions", each of which specifies the relation between two or more "component" structures and the "composite" structure resulting from their integration. The essential structures and relationships in a grammatical construction are spelled out in Figure 11, where [SEM$_3$/PHON$_3$] is the composite structure formed by integrating the component expressions [SEM $_1$/ PHON $_1$] and [SEM $_2$/ PHON $_2$]. The two diagrams are notational variants: 11(b) is an "exploded" version of 11(a); it shows the component and composite structures separately at each pole.

Four symbolic relationships are indicated in Figure 11. The ones labeled $s_1$ and $s_2$ hold between the semantic and the phonological poles of each component expression, whereas $s_3$ indicates that the composite phonological structure symbolizes the composite semantic structure. The fourth relationship, $s_i$, reveals an important sense in which grammar is said to be inherently symbolic: the integration of component structures at the phonological pole serves to symbolize the integration of the corresponding component structures at the semantic pole. Consider the plural noun *walls.* At the phonological pole, the component structures are integrated by the suffixation of *-s* to *wall,* which involves the appropriate temporal sequencing, syllabic organization, and minor phonetic adjustments. It is precisely the fact that *-s* suffixes to *wall* (and not to some other noun stem) which symbolizes the fact that the plurality it expresses is predicated of the notion *wall* in particular (rather than the thing designated by some other noun in the sentence). Or to put it in other terms, the symbolic association $s_i$, does not hold between a semantic and a phonological structure per se – instead it associates the RELATIONSHIPS between two semantic and two phonological structures.

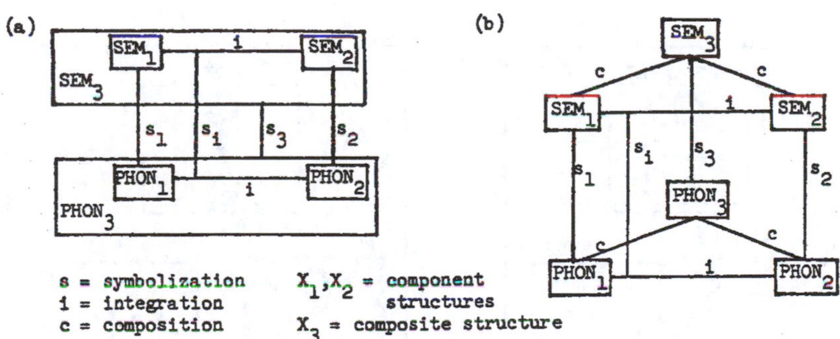


*Figure 11.*

Integration and composition work in essentially the same way at the phonological pole and the semantic pole, but we will confine our attention to the latter. I suggest that the integration of two component structures always involves "correspondences" being established between certain of their substructures. The corresponding substructures provide points of overlap between the component predications, which are necessary if a coherent composite conception is to emerge. The composite structure is obtained by superimposing the specifications of corresponding substructures. In those instances where there is some conflict in their specifications, a fully consistent composite notion cannot be formed, and the result is what we perceive as semantic anomaly (or the violation of "selectional restrictions").

The semantic pole of a typical construction is sketched in Figure 12(a), which diagrams the integration of *above* and *the table* to form the prepositional phrase *above the table* (I will ignore the semantic contribution of the definite article). [ABOVE] profiles a stative relation in oriented space between two things, each characterized only schematically. [TABLE] profiles a thing characterized in far greater detail with respect to numerous domains; purely for sake of diagramatic convenience, it is represented by a mnemonic shape specification. The integration of these component predications is effected by a correspondence established between the landmark of [ABOVE] and the profile of [TABLE] (correspondences are represented by dotted lines). By superimposing the specifications of these corresponding substructures, and adopting the relational profile of [ABOVE], we obtain the composite predication (ABOVE - TABLE), which designates a stative relation involving a schematic trajector and a specific landmark. Note that the compositional process results in "vertical" correspondences between elements of the component and composite structures, in addition to the "horizontal" correspondence(s) linking the components.[11]

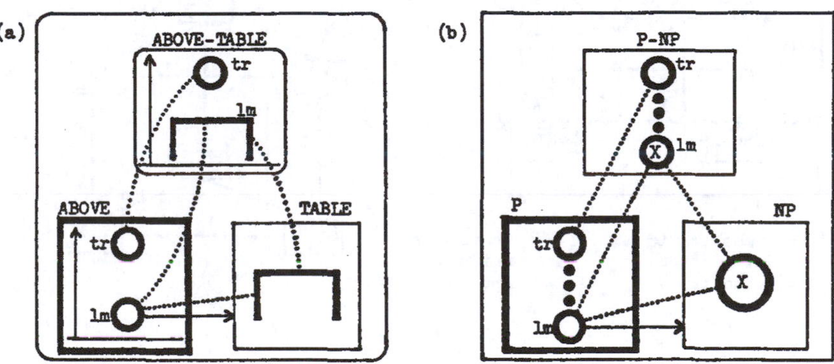


*Figure 12.*

Semantics is not fully compositional. When first assembled, an expression's composite structure may invoke a domain or incorporate specifications (e.g. the orientation of the table) that are not predictable from the component structures or other conventional units. Because such specifications are part of how the expression is actually understood in context, and may well be included in its conventional semantic value should the expression be established as a unit, it is arbitrary to exclude them from the purview of semantic analysis. There are nevertheless conventional patterns of composition that determine central aspects of a composite structure's organization. These are represented in the grammar by constructional schemas, whose internal structure is parallel to that of the specific expressions which instantiate them. For example, the grammar of English includes a schema for the prepositional-phrase construction. Its phonological pole specifies the contiguity and linear ordering of the preposition and its noun-phrase object; its semantic pole, given in Figure 12(b), is precisely analogous to 12(a) except that the component and composite structures are schematic rather than specific. The first component is schematic for the class of prepositions. Basically, it is identified only as a stative relation whose trajector and primary landmark are both things. The other component is the noun-phrase schema: it profiles a thing, and implies additional content (labeled X), but does not itself specify the nature of this content. As in the specific structure 12(a), a correspondence holds between the landmark of P and the profile of NP, and the composite structure is formed by superimposing the specifications of these correspondents (and adopting the relational profile of P). Speakers can employ this constructional schema in the computation and evaluation of novel expressions. It serves as the structural description of any expression which it categorizes when so employed.

This construction has various properties that can be regarded as prototypical. There are just two component structures, one of them relational and the other nominal. A correspondence holds between two highly prominent substructures: the profile of the nominal predication, and the primary landmark (one facet of the profile) of the relational predication. Moreover, there is a substantial asymmetry in the degree of specificity at which the predications characterize the corresponding elements – the landmark of [ABOVE] is quite schematic, whereas by comparison the profile of [TABLE] is specified in considerable detail. I have indicated this diagramatically by an arrow (standing for a relationship of schematicity) between [ABOVE]'s landmark and the other predication as a whole. Finally, it is the relational predication which lends its profile to the composite structure (i.e. *above the table* designates a stative relation, not a thing). I thus refer to [ABOVE] in 12(a) as the construction's "profile determinant", and make this role explicit by putting the box enclosing this predication in heavy lines.

None of the properties just cited is invariant except the existence of at least one correspondence between substructures of the components. By recognizing these properties as prototypical rather than imposing them as absolute requirements, we obtain the flexibility needed to accommodate the full range of attested construction types. It is probably necessary, for example, to allow more than just two component structures at a particular level of constituency (e.g. for coordinate expressions such as *X, Y, and Z*). It need not be the case that one component structure is relational and the other nominal – in fact, there need be no relational component at all. Appositional constructions involving two nominal predications, e.g. *my good friend Ollie North*, are straightforwardly accommodated in this framework by means of a correspondence established between the nominal profiles. In all the examples cited so far, the corresponding elements have been things that either constitute or are included within the profile of the component structure. Often, however, the correspondents are relational substructures, and they need not be in profile. Consider once more the sense of *gone* diagramed in Figure 4(c). The component structures are [GO], which designates a process, and one particular semantic variant of the past-participial morpheme. This particular predication profiles the final state of an otherwise unprofiled process that constitutes its base. The participial morpheme itself characterizes this process quite schematically; only in combination with a verb stem is the nature of the process made specific. Their integration is effected by a correspondence between the specific process profiled by [GO] and the schematic process functioning as the base within the participial predication. By superimposing their specifications, and adopting the profile contributed by the grammatical morpheme, we obtain a composite structure that profiles just the final state of the process [GO].

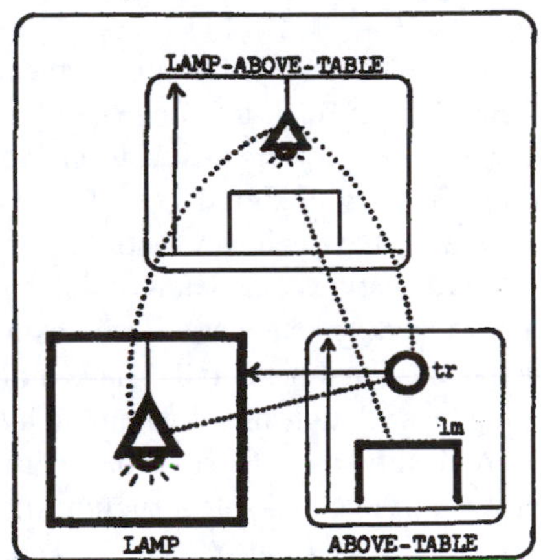


*Figure 13.*

A factor we have not yet considered is "constituency", which pertains to the order in which symbolic structures are progressively assembled into larger and larger composite expressions. Clearly, the composite structure resulting from the integration of component structures at one level of organization can itself be employed as a component structure at the next higher level, and so on indefinitely. In Figure 13, for example, the composite structure (ABOVE-TABLE) from Figure 12(a) functions as a component structure, combining with [LAMP] to derive the composite semantic value of the noun phrase *the lamp above the table*. At this second level of organization, it is the schematic trajector of the relational predication that is put in correspondence with the profile of the nominal predication; moreover, it is this latter which functions as the construction's profile determinant. The composite structure (LAMP-ABOVE-TABLE) consequently designates the lamp, not its locative relationship vis-à-vis the table, though this relationship is included as a prominent facet of its base.

Some grammatically significant observations can be made on the basis of these examples. For one thing, we see that either a relational or a nominal predication is capable of serving as the profile determinant in a construction. In Figure 12, it is the relation [ABOVE] which contributes the profile of the composite expression, whereas in Figure 13 it is the nominal [LAMP]. Moreover, the constructs now at our disposal permit workable and revealing characterizations of certain fundamental grammatical notions that have long been problematic, namely "head", "modifier", and "complement". At a given level of organization, a construction's head can be identified with its profile determinant. *Above* is thus the head within the prepositional phrase *above the table,* whereas *lamp* is the head within the noun phrase *the lamp above the table*. In appositional expressions like *my good friend Ollie North* there is no real basis for singling out either component noun phrase as the head. But that is precisely what we expect: because their profiles correspond, and each corresponds to the profile of the composite structure, it is arbitrary to say that the latter inherits its profile from either one of the component structures (as opposed to the other).

To the extent that one component structure, taken as a whole, serves to elaborate a salient substructure within the other, I will speak of the elaborating component as being "conceptually autonomous", and the elaborated component as "conceptually dependent". In Figure 12(a), then, [TABLE] is conceptually autonomous with respect to [ABOVE] because it elaborates the latter's schematic landmark. In Figure 13, similarly, [LAMP] is autonomous by virtue of elaborating the schematic trajector of the dependent predication (ABOVE-TABLE). The notions modifier and complement can now be characterized explicitly in a way that reconstructs the normal usage of these traditional terms: a "modifier" is a conceptually dependent predication that combines with a head, whereas a "complement" is a conceptually autonomous predication that combines with a head. *The table* is consequently a complement (or "argument") of *above* in *above the table,* and this entire prepositional phrase functions as a modifier of *lamp* in *the lamp above the table*. What about appositional constructions? Because there is no basis for recognizing either component structure as the head (and often no autonomous/dependent asymmetry), the definitions are correctly found to be inapplicable. In *my good friend Ollie North,* neither *my good friend* nor *Ollie North* is considered a modifier or a complement of the other.

This conception of grammatical structure has numerous descriptive advantages, only a few of which will be noted at this juncture. One advantage is that it readily accommodates variability of constituency, which is in fact quite common. The present framework does not posit phrase trees of the sort familiar from generative studies, nor does it rely on phrase structure configurations for the definition of grammatical relations. Constituency is simply the sequence in which component symbolic structures are progressively assembled into more and more elaborate composite expressions. Though a specific order of assembly commonly becomes conventionalized as the sole or default-case sequence, the choice is not inherently critical in this model, because alternate constituencies often permit the same composite structure to be derived. Moreover, because grammatical relations are not defined in configurational terms, a unique constituency is not essential. What identifies *the table* as the object of *above* in *above the table,* for example, is the fact that the noun phrase elaborates the preposition's landmark. Though constituency happens to be invariant in this case, the critical factor in defining the prepositional-object relation is the correspondence established between the landmark of the preposition and the profile of the noun phrase.

We can better appreciate these points with regard to sentences like the ones in (15).

(15) a. *Alice likes liver.*
b. *Liver Alice likes.*
c. *Alice likes, but most people really hate, braised liver.*

Sentence (15a) exhibits the normal, default-case NP + VP constituency of English clauses: *liver* elaborates the schematic landmark of *likes* at the first level of constituency, yielding a processual predication with a specified landmark and schematic trajector; *Alice* then elaborates the trajector of *likes liver* at the second level to derive a process predication whose trajector and landmark are both specific. It should be apparent, however, that the same composite structure will result if the constituents combine in the opposite order, with *Alice* elaborating the schematic trajector of *likes,* and then *liver* the schematic landmark of *Alice likes.* This alternative constituency is available for exploitation, with no effect on grammatical relations, whenever special factors motivate departure from the default-case arrangement. Two such factors are illustrated here. In (15b) we observe the topicalization of the direct-object noun phrase, normally described as a movement transformation. There is no need in this framework to derive this sentence type by transformation – it can be assembled directly through the alternate compositional path. The second type of situation arises in conjoined structures when two verbs have different subjects but share the same object, as in (15c). In lieu of the transformational process of "Right Node Raising", which supposedly derives this type of sentence from conjoined clauses of normal NP + VP constituency, we can once again assemble the overt structure directly. The two subject-verb constituents are put together first and then combined in a coordinate structure. A direct object NP is subsequently added, being integrated simultaneously with each conjunct through a correspondence between its profile and the conjunct's relational landmark.

Also eliminable in this framework is the raising rule needed in certain transformational accounts (e.g. Keyser and Postal 1976) to handle agreement between a subject and an auxiliary verb, as in (16).

(16) *The lamp is above the table.*

The rationale for a raising rule goes something like this: (i) a verb is assumed to agree with its own subject; (ii) *the lamp* is not the logical subject of *be*, which – if anything – has a clause for its underlying subject; (iii) hence, to account for agreement, some rule must raise *the lamp* from its position as subject of *above* and make it the subject of *be*. However the need for such a rule is obviated given a proper analysis of *be* and a suitably flexible conception of grammatical constructions.

The semantic pole of (16) is outlined in Figure 14.[12] Pivotal to the analysis is the semantic value attributed to *be*, of which three main features are relevant. First, *be* is a true verb, i.e. a symbolic expression that profiles a process. Second, all the component states of the designated process are construed as being identical; this is indicated by the dotted correspondence lines internal to [BE] that link the three states which are explicitly represented (additional correspondence lines specify that the trajector is the same from one state to the next, as is the landmark). Third, apart from this specification of identity, the profiled process is maximally schematic. *Be* is one of numerous verbs in English which designate a process consisting of the extension through time of a stable situation (see Langacker 1991a: Chapter 3) – others include *have*, *resemble*, *like*, *know*, *contain*, *slope*, *exist*, and so on – but it abstracts away from the specific content that distinguishes these predications from one another. In summary, [BE] follows through time, by means of sequential scanning, the evolution of a situation that is construed as being stable but not further specified (except for its relational character).

Any single component state of [BE] constitutes a schematic stative relation. At the first level of constituency in Figure 14, the more specific stative relation (ABOVE-TABLE) is put in correspondence with a representative state of [BE], the latter serving as profile determinant. The result is the composite predication (BE-ABOVE-TABLE), which is like [BE] except that all the specifications inherited from (ABOVE-TABLE) are attributed to the situation followed sequentially through time. Observe that the landmark of (BE-ABOVE-TABLE) is now specific, whereas its trajector remains schematic. At the second level of constituency, this schematic trajector is elaborated by [LAMP] to derive the composite structure (LAMP-BE-ABOVE-TABLE), which represents the composite meaning of the full sentence. It profiles the extension through time of a stable situation in which the lamp and the table participate in a particular locative relationship.

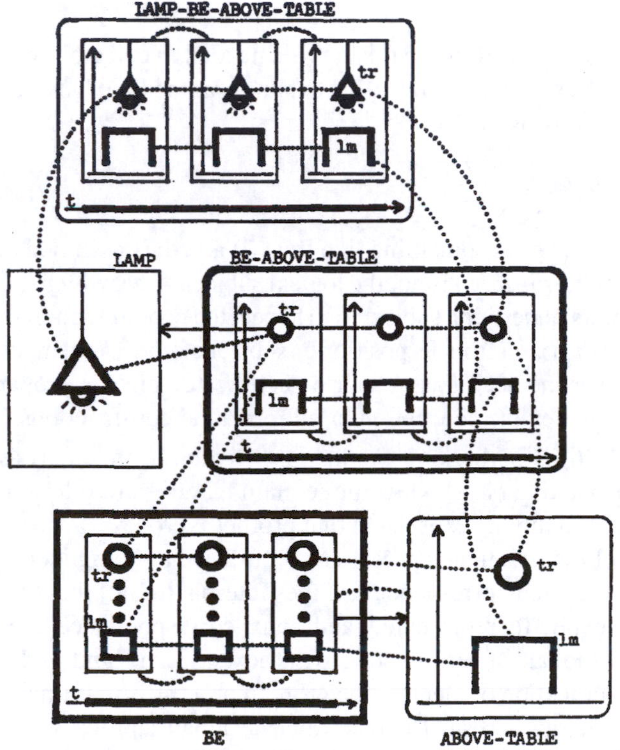


*Figure 14.*

Observe that the sentence is assembled directly, in accordance with its surface constituency. In particular, there is no "raising" rule which derives it from a hypothetical underlying structure by changing the grammatical relation of the subject NP. But does *the lamp* function as the subject of *be,* as their agreement presumably requires? It certainly does, given the way grammatical relations are defined in this framework. A subject NP is one which elaborates the schematic trajector of a relational predication by virtue of a correspondence established between that trajector and its own profile. With respect to Figure 14, note first that [BE] does in fact have a schematic trajector, characterized as both a thing (not a clause) and a relational participant. Moreover, [BE]'s trajector does correspond to the profile of *the lamp,* when both horizontal and vertical correspondences are taken into account: the profile of [LAMP] corresponds to the trajector of (BE-ABOVE-TABLE), which in turn corresponds vertically to the trajector of [BE]. It is simply incorrect, in this analysis, to claim that *be* has no nonclausal subject, or that *the lamp* is not its "logical" subject in (16). With no special apparatus, the analysis establishes a relationship between *the lamp* and *be* which is perfectly adequate as a basis for agreement.

Finally, the analysis permits a simple and natural account of sentences like (17b), in which an auxiliary verb functions as a pro form:

(17) a. Q: *What is above the table?*
b. A: *The lamp is.*

As highly schematic process predications, auxiliary verbs are perfectly suited to this role, and sentences of this type are derivable without any deletion operation. Because constituency is potentially variable in this framework, we can derive (17b) just by combining *the lamp* and *be* directly. A correspondence is established between the profile of the former and the schematic trajector of the latter. *Be* is the profile determinant, so the composite structure designates a process involving the evolution of a stable situation through time. Apart from its trajector, identified as the lamp, this situation is characterized only schematically.

## 7. Conclusion

This initial presentation of cognitive grammar has itself been quite schematic. I do however hope to have shown that currently predominant linguistic theories do not represent the only possible way of conceiving the nature of language structure and linguistic investigation. By taking a radically different perspective on questions of meaning and grammar, it is possible to formulate a coherent descriptive framework which promises to be both cognitively realistic and linguistically well-motivated.

## Notes

1. Observe that designation, in my technical sense of the term, does not pertain to the relation between a linguistic expression and the world – rather it is a relationship holding between a cognitive domain as a whole and certain of its subparts. I do not know whether profiling reduces to any independently established cognitive phenomenon. Possibly it constitutes one level of figure/ground organization, but not every figure is a designatum.
2. In these expressions *eye* is evidently construed as the eye region, not the eyeball itself.
3. The constructs needed to make this notion of subjectivity/objectivity precise are introduced in Langacker 1985 and 1987, Chapters 3 and 7. For vantage point and orientation, see Langacker (1991a: Chapter 2) and Vandeloise 1984.
4. Goldsmith 1980 presents a very similar analysis.
5. The importance of conventionality should be emphasized. Often a speaker is led to employ a particular image simply because an alternative construction, which might seem more appropriate, happens not to be conventionally established. For instance, many verbs of transfer (e.g. *transfer* itself) are not employed in the double-object construction; the *to*-construction represents the speaker's only option with such verbs.
6. At this level of organization, we can ignore the fact that *sharpen* is morphematically complex. The double-headed arrow labeled (e) in Figure 7 indicates identity of the associated structures.
7. Fuller discussion is provided in Langacker (1991a: Chapter 10). (See also Langacker 1987: Chapter 11.)
8. By reversing the trajectory/landmark assignation, we obtain the predicate [BELOW].
9. I omit the dashed line standing for the profiled interconnections, because the nature of these interconnections is implicit in the position of the major participants within the diagrams. Note that I regard these diagrams as heuristic in character, not as formal objects. They are analogous to the sketch a biologist might draw to illustrate the major components of a cell and their relative position within it.
10. Only for convenience do I speak of discrete states – a process is more accurately viewed as continuous.
11. The component structures are enclosed in boxes, to indicate that *above* and *the table* have the status of units. Closed curves surround the composite structure and the construction as a whole on the presumption that *above the table* is a novel expression (in the text, parentheses serve this purpose).
12. Omitted are the semantic contributions of the definite article and the verb inflection on *be*. Note that our concern is not the nature of agreement (cf. Langacker 1991a: Chapter 11), but rather the issue of whether *the lamp* can be considered the subject of *be* in accordance with assumption (i).

## References

Barwise, Jon and John Perry
1983 *Situations and Attitudes*. Cambridge, MA, and London: MIT Press/Bradford.

Bever, Thomas G. and Peter S. Rosenbaum
1970 Some lexical structures and their empirical validity. In *Readings in English Transformational Grammar*, Roderick A. Jacobs and Peter S. Rosenbaum (eds.), 3–19. Waltham, MA: Ginn.

Bybee, Joan L.
1988 Semantic substance vs. contrast in the development of grammatical meaning. In *Proceedings of the Annual Meeting of the Berkeley Linguistics Society* 14: 247–264.

Casad, Eugene H.
1982 Cora locationals and structured imagery. Unpublished Ph.D. dissertation, University of California, San Diego.
1988 Conventionalization of Cora locationals. In *Topics in Cognitive Linguistics*, Brygida Rudzka-Ostyn (ed.), 345–378. Amsterdam/Philadelphia: Benjamins.

Chafe, Wallace L.
1970 *Meaning and the Structure of Language*. Chicago: University of Chicago Press.

Cook, Kenneth W.
1988 A cognitive analysis of grammatical relations, case, and transitivity in Samoan. Unpublished Ph.D. dissertation, University of California, San Diego.
1989 A cognitive account of the Samoan *lavea* and *galo* verbs. Linguistic Agency University of Duisburg.

Cruse, D.Allan
1979 On the transitivity of the part-whole relation. *Journal of Linguistics* 15: 29–38.

Fauconnier, Gilles
1985 *Mental Spaces: Aspects of Meaning Construction in Natural Language*. Cambridge, MA and London: MIT Press/Bradford.

Fillmore, Charles J.
1982 Frame Semantics. In *Linguistics in the Morning Calm*, Linguistic Society of Korea (ed.), 111–137. Seoul: Hanshin.

Givón, Talmy
1979 The time-axis phenomenon. *Language* 49: 890–925.
1984 *Syntax: A Functional-Typological Introduction*. Volume 1. Amsterdam/Philadelphia: Benjamins.
1989 *Mind, Code, and Context: Essays in Pragmatics*. Hillsdale, NJ: Erlbaum.

Green, Georgia M.
1974 *Semantics and Syntactic Regularity*. Bloomington: Indiana University Press.

Haiman, John
1980 Dictionaries and encyclopedias. *Lingua* 50: 329–357.
1983 Iconic and economic motivation. *Language* 59: 781–819.

1985 *Natural Syntax: Iconicity and Erosion.* Cambridge: Cambridge University Press.

Hawkins, Bruce W.

1984 The semantics of English spatial prepositions. Unpublished Ph.D. dissertation, University of California, San Diego.

1988 The natural category MEDIUM: An alternative to selection restrictions and similar constructs. In *Topics in Cognitive Linguistics*, Brygida Rudzka-Ostyn (ed.), 231–270. Amsterdam/Philadelphia: Benjamins.

Jackendoff, Ray

1983 *Semantics and Cognition.* (Current Studies in Linguistics 8.) Cambridge, MA: MIT Press.

Janda, Laura A.

1984 A semantic analysis of the Russian verbal prefixes *za-, pere-, do-*, and *ot-*. Unpublished Ph.D. dissertation, University of California, Los Angeles.

1988 The mapping of elements of cognitive space onto grammatical relations: An example from Russian verbal prefixation. In *Topics in Cognitive Linguistics*, Brygida Rudzka-Ostyn (ed.), 327–343. Amsterdam/Philadelphia: Benjamins.

1993 *A Geography of Case Semantics: The Czech Dative and the Russian Instrumental.* Berlin/New York: Mouton de Gruyter.

Johnson, Mark

1987 *The Body in the Mind: The Bodily Basis of Meaning, Imagination, and Reason.* Chicago/London: University of Chicago Press.

Johnson-Laird, Philip N.

1983 *Mental Models.* Cambridge, MA: Harvard University Press.

Katz, Jerrold J. and Jerry A. Fodor

1963 The structure of a semantic theory. *Language* 39: 170–210.

Kemmer, Suzanne E.

1988 The middle voice: A typological and diachronic study. Unpublished Ph.D. dissertation, Stanford University.

Keyser, Samuel Jay and Paul M. Postal

1976 *Beginning English Grammar.* New York: Harper & Row.

Klima, Edward S.

1964 Negation in English. In *The Structure of Language: Readings in the Philosophy of Language*, Jerry A. Fodor and Jerrold J. Katz (eds.), 246–323. Englewood Cliffs, NJ: Prentice-Hall.

Kosslyn, Stephen Michael

1980 *Image and Mind.* Cambridge, MA: Harvard University Press.

Lakoff, George

1982 Categories: An essay in cognitive linguistics. In *Linguistics in the Morning Calm*, Linguistic Society of Korea (ed.), 139–193. Seoul: Hanshin.

1987 *Women, Fire, and Dangerous Things: What Categories Reveal about the Mind.* Chicago/London: University of Chicago Press.

Lakoff, George and Mark Johnson

1980 *Metaphors We Live By.* Chicago/London: University of Chicago Press.

Lakoff, George and Mark Turner
1989 *More than Cool Reason: A Field Guide to Poetic Metaphor.* Chicago/London: University of Chicago Press.

Langacker, Ronald W.
1976 Semantic representations and the linguistic relativity hypothesis. *Foundations of Language* 14: 307–357.
1981 The integration of grammar and grammatical change. *Indian Linguistics* 42: 82–135.
1982 Remarks on English aspect. In *Tense-Aspect: Between Semantics and Pragmatics*, Paul J. Hopper (ed.), 265–304. (Typological Studies in Language 1.) Amsterdam/Philadelphia: Benjamins.
1985 Observations and speculations on subjectivity. In *Iconicity in Syntax*, John Haiman (ed.), 109–150. (Typological Studies in Language 6.) Amsterdam/Philadelphia: Benjamins.
1987 *Foundations of Cognitive Grammar.* Volume 1: *Theoretical Prerequisites.* Stanford: Stanford University Press.
1988a An overview of cognitive grammar. In *Topics in Cognitive Linguistics*, Brygida Rudzka-Ostyn (ed.), 3–48. Amsterdam/Philadelphia: Benjamins.
1988b A view of linguistic semantics. In *Topics in Cognitive Linguistics*, Brygida Rudzka-Ostyn (ed.), 49–90. Amsterdam/Philadelphia: Benjamins.
1991a *Concept, Image, and Symbol. The Cognitive Basis of Grammar.* Berlin/New York: Mouton de Gruyter.
1991b *Foundations of Cognitive Grammar.* Volume 2: *Descriptive Application.* Stanford: Stanford University Press.

Lindner, Susan
1981 A lexico-semantic analysis of English verb-particle constructions with UP and OUT. Unpublished Ph.D. dissertation, University of California, San Diego.
1982 What goes up doesn't necessarily come down: The ins and outs of opposites. In *Papers from the Regional Meeting of the Chicago Linguistic Society* 18: 305–323.

Miller, George A. and Philip N. Johnson-Laird
1976 *Language and Perception.* Cambridge, MA: Harvard/Belknap.

Moore, Terence and Christine Carling
1982 *Language Understanding: Towards a Post-Chomskyan Linguistics.* New York: St. Martin's Press.

Oehrle, Richard T.
1977 Review of Green 1974. *Language* 53: 198–208.

Perlmutter, David M.
1978 Impersonal passives and the unaccusative hypothesis. In *Proceedings of the Annual Meeting of the Berkeley Linguistics Society* 4: 157–189.

Poteet, Stephen
1987 Paths through different domains: A cognitive grammar analysis of Mandarin *dào.* In *Proceedings of the Annual Meeting of the Berkeley Linguistics Society* 13: 408–421.

Rice, Sally
1987a Towards a transitive prototype: Evidence from some atypical English passives.

In *Proceedings of the Annual Meeting of the Berkeley Linguistics Society* 13: 422–434.

1987b Towards a cognitive model of transitivity. Unpublished Ph.D. dissertation, University of California, San Diego.

1988 Unlikely lexical entries. In *Proceedings of the Annual Meeting of the Berkeley Linguistics Society* 14: 202–212.

Shepard, Roger N.

1978 The mental image. *American Psychologist* 33: 125–137.

Smith, Michael B.

1985a An analysis of German dummy subject constructions. In *Proceedings of the Annual Meeting of the Pacific Linguistics Conference* 1: 412–425.

1985b Event chains, grammatical relations, and the semantics of case in German. In *Papers from the Regional Meeting of the Chicago Linguistic Society* 21: 388–407.

1987 The semantics of dative and accusative in German: An investigation in cognitive grammar. Unpublished Ph.D. dissertation, University of California, San Diego.

1989 Cases from conceptual categories: Evidence from German. Linguistic Agency University of Duisburg.

Sweetser, Eve E.

1984 Semantic structure and semantic change: A cognitive linguistic study of modality, perception, speech acts, and logical relations. Unpublished Ph.D. dissertation, University of California, Berkeley.

1987 Metaphorical models of thought and speech: A comparison of historical directions and metaphorical mappings in two domains. In *Proceedings of the Annual Meeting of the Berkeley Linguistics Society* 13: 446–459.

1988 Grammaticalization and semantic bleaching. In *Proceedings of the Annual Meeting of the Berkeley Linguistics Society* 14: 389–405.

Talmy, Leonard

1975 Sematic and syntax in motion. In *Syntax and Semantics 4*, John Kimball (ed.), 181–238. New York: Academic Press.

1977 Rubber-sheet cognition in language. In *Papers from the Regional Meeting of the Chicago Linguistic Society* 13: 612–628.

1978 Figure and ground in complex sentences. In *Universals of Human Language*, volume 4: *Syntax*, Joseph H. Greenberg (ed.), 625–649. Stanford: Stanford University Press.

1983 How language structures space. In *Spatial Orientation: Theory, Research, and Application*, Herbert Pick and Linda Acredolo (eds.), 225–282. New York: Plenum Press.

1985a Force dynamics in language and thought. In *Papers from the Parasession on Causatives and Agentivity*, William H. Eilfort et al. (eds.), 293–337. Chicago: Chicago Linguistic Society.

1985b Lexicalization patterns: Semantic structure in lexical forms. In *Language Typology and Syntactic Description*. Volume 3: *Grammatical Categories and the Lexicon*, Timothy Shopen (ed.), 57–149. Cambridge: Cambridge University Press.

1988a Force dynamics in language and cognition. *Cognitive Science* 12: 49–100.
1988b The relation of grammar to cognition. In *Topics in Cognitive Linguistics*, Brygida Rudzka-Ostyn (ed.), 165–205. Amsterdam/Philadelphia: Benjamins.

Traugott, Elizabeth C.
1982 From propositional to textual and expressive meanings: Some semantic-pragmatic aspects of grammaticalization. In *Perspectives on Historical Linguistics*, Winfred P. Lehmann and Yakov Malkiel (eds.), 245–271. Amsterdam/Philadelphia: Benjamins.
1986 From polysemy to internal semantic reconstruction. In *Proceedings of the Annual Meeting of the Berkeley Linguistics Society* 12: 539–550.
1988 Pragmatic strengthening and grammaticalization. In *Proceedings of the Annual Meeting of the Berkeley Linguistics Society* 14: 406–416.

Tuggy, David
1980 ¡Ethical dative and possessor omission sí, possessor ascension no! In *Work Papers of the Summer Institute of Linguistics, University of North Dakota* 24: 97–141.
1981 The transitivity-related morphology of Tetelcingo Nahuatl: An exploration in space grammar. Unpublished Ph.D. dissertation, University of California, San Diego.
1986 Noun incorporations in Nahuatl. In *Proceedings of the Annual Meeting of the Pacific Linguistics Conference* 2: 455–469.
1988 Náhuatl causative/applicatives in cognitive grammar. In *Topics in Cognitive Linguistics*, Brygida Rudzka-Ostyn (ed.), 587–618. Amsterdam/Philadelphia: Benjamins.
1989 The affix-stem distinction in Orizaba Náhuatl. Linguistic Agency University of Duisburg.

Vandeloise, Claude
1984 Description of space in French. Unpublished Ph.D. dissertation, University of California, San Diego.

Wierzbicka, Anna
1988 *The Semantics of Grammar.* (Studies in Language Companion Series 18.) Amsterdam/Philadelphia: Benjamins.

# Chapter 2
# Grammatical construal

## The relation of grammar to cognition[1]
*Leonard Talmy*

### 0. Introduction

A fundamental design feature of language is that it has two subsystems which can be designated as the grammatical and the lexical (as these are characterized below). Why is there this universal bifurcation when, in principle, a language could be conceived having only a single system, the lexical? The explanation in this paper is that the two subsystems have distinct semantic functions, ones that are indispensable and complementary. To develop this account further, we must first note that we take a sentence (or other portion of discourse) to evoke in the listener a particular kind of experiential complex, here to be termed a "cognitive representation" or "CR".[2] Now, the grammatical and lexical subsystems in a sentence seem generally to specify different portions of a CR. Together, the grammatical elements of a sentence determine the majority of the *structure* of the CR, while the lexical elements together contribute the majority of its *content*. Lexical elements do incorporate some of the same structural indications that grammatical elements express, but when the two are in association or in conflict within a sentence, it is generally always the grammatical elements' specifications of structure that are determinative.[3] The grammatical specifications in a sentence, thus, provide a conceptual framework or, imagistically, a skeletal structure or scaffolding, for the conceptual material that is lexically specified.

More generally, across the spectrum of languages, the grammatical elements that are encountered, taken together, specify a crucial set of concepts. This set is highly restricted: only certain concepts appear in it, and not others, as seen below. The purport of the present paper is that this set of grammatically specified notions collectively constitutes the fundamental conceptual structuring system of language. That is, this cross-linguistically select set of grammatically specified concepts provides the basic schematic framework for conceptual organization within the cognitive domain of language.

Thus, grammar, broadly conceived, is the determinant of conceptual structure within one cognitive domain, language, and as such is the main object of

Originally published in 1988 in *Topics in Cognitive Linguistics*, Brygida Rudzka-Ostyn (ed.), 165–205. Amsterdam/Philadelphia: John Benjamins. Reprinted with permission.

this paper's study. But such a study directly opens out into a broader investigation across other cognitive domains, such as visual perception and reasoning, as discussed at the end of the paper. That is, the greater issue, toward which the present study ultimately aims, is the general character of conceptual structure in human cognition.

The present investigation into the semantics of grammar is of a scope that follows in a progression from previous types of study. These have mostly been either an in-depth semantic analysis of a selected grammatical element (or class of elements) of particular interest within a language, e.g., the Turkish evidential suffix *-mis* (Slobin and Aksu 1982); or an exposition of the meanings and functions of all the grammatical elements of a single language, say, as in a grammar of Dyirbal (Dixon 1972); or a cross-linguistic typology of the different kinds of grammatical devices used for a single semantic function, say, to indicate the interrogative (Ultan 1978). Some previous work has also treated broader issues of grammatical meaning (Sapir 1921; Boas 1938; Whorf 1956, Jakobson 1971). But the present study is perhaps the first to address grammatical expression in language at the superordinate level, with the aim of determining the semantic and cognitive properties and functions of this structural component of language as a whole.[4]

The terms "grammatical" and "lexical" as employed here require some immediate elaboration. The distinction between the two is made formally – i.e., without reference to meaning – on the basis of the traditional linguistic distinction between "open-class" and "closed-class". A class of morphemes is considered open if it is quite large and readily augmentable relative to other classes. A class is considered closed if it is relatively small and fixed in membership. We can identify the particular classes belonging to these two types. The open classes of elements – i.e., the lexical classes – are the roots of nouns, verbs, and adjectives.[5] Everything else is closed-class – and is here considered to be, quite generally, "grammatical". Among the overt elements of this type are such bound forms as inflections and derivations, such free forms as determiners, prepositions, conjunctions, and particles, and perhaps also such suprasegmental forms as intonation patterns. Included among abstract, or implicit, closed-class forms are grammatical categories and grammatical relations, word order, and perhaps also paradigms and "zero" forms. Additionally here are regular combinations of simpler closed-class forms, tending to have a unified or integrated semantic function – what are below called "grammatical complexes", including grammatical constructions and syntactic structures.[6]

The issues presented in this introduction are treated below in three sections. Section 1 examines the notions specified by a heuristic sampling of grammatical elements, outlines the kinds of constraints on such notions, proposes a property held in common by such notions but largely absent from excluded notions, and contrasts such grammatically specified notions with ones that are lexically specified. Section 2 presents a number of categories in which grammatically specified notions are seen to pattern, as well as broader conceptual systems in which these categories in turn participate, ending with the identification of four comprehensive "imaging systems". This section, further, examines the interactions of grammatical specifications with lexical specifications within categories and the nesting of such interactions across categories, as well as the cognitive processes that accompany these interactions. And Section 3 presents an explanation of the function of grammatical specification, as well as possibilities of its relations to other cognitive systems.

## 1. The nature of grammatically specified notions

In this section we examine a small sampling of grammatical forms for the particular component notions that they specify. The sample will give a heuristic indication of the kinds of notions that get grammatically specified as well as of the kinds of notions that possibly never do. By contrast, it will be seen that the excluded kinds can be readily specified by lexical elements. A particular property will be seen to run through most of the grammatical notions. To indicate this property at the outset, it is preponderantly the case that grammatical specifications of structure are relativistic or topology-like, and exclude the absolute or the metrically Euclidean. Finally, a systematic difference is shown between the characteristics of grammatically specified notions and of lexically specified ones.

We begin with a simple demonstration that the concepts specified by grammatical forms are constrained in two ways: as to their categories and as to the membership of these categories. Many languages have inflections on the noun that specify the *"number"* of the object referred to by the noun, for example its *'singularity'* or *'plurality'*, like the English -∅ and -*s*. By contrast, no languages appear to have inflections that specify the *"color"* of the object referred to by a noun, e.g., its *'redness'* or *'blueness'*. Here, single quotes enclose "notions", while double quotes enclose categories of notions. The "number" category can be specified grammatically and in that form is readily seen to play a structuring role in a CR.[7] The "color" category is perhaps never found specified by grammatical elements, though it is readily found specified by lexical elements, e.g., English *red* and *blue*. Further, though, even within a conceptual category acceptable for grammatical expression, there are great constraints on the particular notions that can be specified. Thus, "number" notions that are expressed grammatically include little more than 'singular', 'dual', 'trial', 'plural', and 'paucal'. They apparently never include, say, 'even', 'odd', 'dozen', or 'numerable', whereas such notions, again, *can* be specified lexically, as shown by the words just used.

Given such constraints on grammatically specifiable notions, we can seek properties that hold in common for included notions but need not apply to excluded notions. In this regard, consider a deictic like the English *this* or *that* as in *This/That chair is broken.* A closed-class element of this type specifies the location of an indicated object as being, in effect, on the speaker-side or the non-speaker-side of a conceptual partition drawn through space (or time or other qualitative dimension). This integral specification can be analyzed as containing the component notions enclosed by quotes in (I):

(1) (a, b) a 'partition' that divides a space into 'regions'/'sides'
(c–e) the 'locatedness' (a particular relation) of a 'point' (or object idealizable as a point) 'within' a region
(f, g) (a side that is the) 'same as' or 'different from'
(h, i) a 'currently indicated' object and a 'currently communicating' entity

Notions that might at first be ascribed to such deictics, such as of distance or perhaps size, prove not to apply, on the evidence of sentence-pairs like (2):

(2) a. This speck is smaller than that speck.
b. This planet is smaller than that planet.

The scenes referred to by (2a) and (b) differ greatly, involving tiny objects millimeters apart or huge objects parsecs apart. But the sentences differ only lexically, not grammatically. Hence, the scenes' differences as to the magnitude of size or distance must arise from the lexical elements, they cannot be traced to the deictics (or other grammatical elements) in the sentences. Thus, the notions specified by a *this* or a *that* are abstracted away from any particularities of magnitude and so, to this extent, are genuinely *topological.* Their specification of a conceptual partition remains constant, but this partition's distance can – by the characterization of topology as "rubber-sheet geometry" – be "stretched" indefinitely without challenge to any semantic constraints of the deictics. This finding about deictics alerts us to noticing whether any grammatical elements make specifications about magnitude. A spot check through English and various other languages suggests that – while there are grammatical specifications for *relative* magnitude[8] – there are possibly never any for absolute or quantified magnitude, whether of size, distance, or other parameters. We can provisionally conclude that the referents of grammatical elements have the topological property of being "magnitude-neutral".

For another case, consider the type of adposition that specifies, for a moving object, certain characteristics of path and of reference-point or -frame. An example of this type is English *through* as used, for instance, in *I walked through the woods.* In this usage, *through* specifies, broadly, 'motion along a line that is within a medium'. The component notions contained here include those in (3):

(3) (a) 'motion'
(b–e) which can be understood as 'one-to-one correspondences' between 'adjacent' points of 'space' and adjacent points of 'time'
(f) motion that describes a 'line' (i.e., a 'linear extent')
(g) the locatedness of a line within a 'medium'
(h, i) a medium, i.e., a region of three-dimensional space set apart by the locatedness within it of 'material' that is in a 'pattern of distribution' with properties and a range of variation still to be determined

It can be first observed, from a sentence-pair like (4), that the concept specified by *through* is indifferent to particulars of shape or contour in the linear path described by the moving object. This is evident here because, as before, the two sentences differ only lexically, not grammatically – they both use *through* while referring to different path contours. Another cross-linguistic spot check of closed-class elements suggests that they largely have this further topological property of being "shape-neutral".

(4) a. I zig-zagged through the woods.
b. I circled through the woods.

With a sentence pair like (5), it can be further determined that the 'rate' of motion is not specified by *through, a* finding that also appears quite general among grammatical elements. And (6) shows that *through,* again like grammatical elements generally, excludes specification of the 'kind of material' involved – here, comprising the "medium" – and of the 'sensorimotor characteristics' attendant on executing the action involved – as, here, those attendant on wading in liquid vs. weaving amidst obstacles. Thus, it can be further held that grammatical elements are generally rate-neutral, material-neutral, and sense/motor-neutral.

(5) (a/b) I crept / dashed through the woods.
(6) (a/b) I walked through the water / woods.

In the aim of ascertaining any properties common to grammatically specified notions, the notions examined above are gathered together in (7). For heuristic purposes, the notions are provisionally divided into two groups on the basis of their relation to topology. In group (a) are combined the notions that properly belong to the specific mathematical system of topology and, with them, the intuitively comparable notions that might belong to a language-based system of topology – one that perhaps could serve as the model for the construction of a new topology-like mathematical system.[9] In group (b) are the notions that fall outside any usual conception of topological properties. The number of notions in the first group is fourteen, while the second has six – an indication of a preponderant propensity for grammatical elements to specify quasi-topological notions. The ratio in this direction is in fact improved if we consider that even several notions in group (b) – the bottom three – resemble topological ones in the sense of involving relativistic relationships between quantities rather than absolutely fixed quantities.

(7) *some notions found to be specified by grammatical elements*

| a. *topological or topology-like* | | b. *non-topological* |
|---|---|---|
| point | singularity | material |
| linear extent | plurality | space |
| locatedness | same | time |
| within | different | motion |
| region | „adjacency" of points | medium |
| side | one-to-one correspondence | entity currently indicated/communicating |
| partition | pattern of distribution | |

In the complementary aim of ascertaining any properties excluded from grammatical specification, the categories of notions found above *not* to be specified by the elements investigated are listed in (8). Rather than topological, topology-like, or relativistic, these notions involve Euclidean-geometric concepts – e.g., fixed distance, size, contour, and angle – as well as quantified measure, and various particularities of a quantity: in sum, characteristics that are absolute or fixed.

(8) *some categories of notions seemingly rarely or never specified by grammatical elements*

| | |
|---|---|
| absolute/quantified magnitude (of distance, size, etc.) | kind of material |
| shape/contour of line | sensorimotor characteristics |
| rate | color |

The provisional conclusion to be drawn from these findings is that, if grammatical specifications generally correspond to (linguistic-) cognitive structuring, then the nature of that structure is largely relativistic or topological rather than absolute or Euclidean.

This preponderant requirement for conceptual neutralities among closed-class elements is in sharp contrast with the referential freedom of lexical items, which can express not only structural abstractions but also wide-ranging specificities. For example, specificity as to magnitude is seen in nouns like *inch* and *mile;* as to shape, in nouns like *circle,* adjectives like *square,* and verbs like *ricochet;* as to rate, in verbs like *dawdle* and *hurry;* in material, in a noun and verb like *iron* and *bleed;* as to sensorimotor characteristics in *watch* and *wade;* and, of course, as to color by such adjectives as *red* and *blue.*

To elaborate further the contrast between the grammatical and the lexical type of specification, consider the full complement of both element-types in a single whole sentence, viz., that selected in (9):

(9) A rustler lassoed the steers.

We first list the grammatical elements present in the sentence and the notions that they specify in (10):

(10)

| | | |
|---|---|---|
| a. | -ed | 'occurring at a time before that of the present communication' |
| b. | the | 'has ready identifiability for the addressee' |
| c. | *a* | 'not before in discussion or otherwise readily identifiable for the addressee' |
| d. | -s | 'multiple instantiation of object' |
| e. | a...-Ø | 'unitary instantiation of object' |
| f. | the grammatical category of "verb" for *lasso* | 'event character' |
| g/h. | the grammatical category of "noun" for *rustlerlsteer* | 'entity character' |
| i/j- | the grammatical relations of "subject'V'object" for *rustlerlsteer* | 'agent'/'patient' (among the possibilities) |
| k. | active voice | 'point-of-view at the agent' |
| 1. | intonation, word order, pattern of auxiliaries | 'the Speaker "knows" the Situation to be true and asserts it' |

The lexical items in the sentence have specifications that can be characterized as in (11):

(11) *a complex of concepts involving:*

a. *rustler:* a person, property ownership, illegality, mode of activity
b. *steer:* object of particular appearance, physical makeup, etc.
relation to animal kingdom
castration
institution of breeding for human consumption
c. *lasso:* certain objects (a body and a lasso) in particular configurations
certain movement sequences
accompanying cognitive intending, directing, monitoring, etc.

In surveying the two lists, we can see these differences emerge: The grammatical elements are more numerous, and their specifications seem more spare and simpler, and more structural in function. Together, their specifications seem to establish the main delineations of the scene organization and communicative setting of the CR evoked by the sentence. The lexical elements are fewer in number, but their specifications are greater in quantity and complexity, and function more to contribute content than structure. The lexical specifications are greater in three ways: compared to a grammatical specification, each has a) more total information, b) greater intricacy of information, and c) more different types of information together. Taken together, their specifications comprise most of the conceptual content of the *CR* scene that is evoked by the sentence.

These grammatical-lexical differences can be set into further relief by in turn varying each element-type while keeping the other constant. Thus, varying only the grammatical elements of (9), as is done in (12), seems to alter the scene organization and discourse properties of the referent event but to leave its basic contents intact:

(12) Will the rustlers lasso a steer?

By contrast, varying only (9)'s lexical elements, as in (13), shifts us to a new scene altogether, and yet the basic breakup of the scene and of its communicative setting seems to remain the same:

(13) A machine stamped the envelopes.

## 2. Categories of grammatically specified notions

The preceding sampling of grammatical elements has yielded a set of notions helpful toward discovering common semantic properties. But the set has been small and unstructured. With a broader and more systematic investigation, patterns of organization among the notions become evident. Grammatically specified notions can be seen to pattern in categories, and the categories, in turn, in integrated systems, as presented below. And within these notional patterns can be seen certain regularities of function and process. These patterns and regularities constitute principal features of conceptual organization in language.

Several such features are brought forward below. One feature is an extensive homology between the representation of space and that of time. The first category, "dimension", includes this space-time homology, and largely crosscuts the remaining categories. These categories will, in the majority, apply to both space and time, and parallel examples from each dimension will be presented side by side.

Another feature is that, of the member notions of any category represented in a language, often each notion will be incorporated in at least some lexical items. Correlatively, the language will often contain grammatical forms that interact with each lexicalization type in a way that yields the expression of another notion of the category. Each such type of interaction can be regarded as a type of cognitive operation that converts the indication of one notion to that of another within the same category. A corollary feature is that a language with grammatical forms for converting from notion A to notion B frequently has forms as well for conversion in the reverse direction – that is, it can also trigger the reverse cognitive operation.[10]

Some of the grammatical forms in a language function specifically to perform a particular conversion operation. Others simply make structural specifications that can come into conflict with the specification of a neighboring lexical item. In such cases, the basic pattern is that the grammatical form's specification always takes precedence, and triggers a kind of operation, a "shift", in the lexical item's referent that brings it into accord."

As a note on methodology in what follows, efforts were made to determine categories on the basis of particular grammatical meanings encountered, rather than to posit the categories as part of an a priori schema which then sought corroborative examples. In the research leading to this paper, grammatical forms were sampled from a range of languages, but an effort has been made to take most of the exemplification from English.

## 2.1. Dimension

The category of "dimension" has two principal member notions, 'space' and 'time'. The kind of entity that exists in space is – in respectively continuous or discrete form – 'matter' or 'objects'. The kind of entity existing in time is, correspondingly, 'action' or 'events' – terms here used neutrally as to whether the entity is static or changing. These notions thus relate as in (14):[12]

| (14) | *dimension* | *continuous* | *discrete* |
|---|---|---|---|
| | space: | matter | objects |
| | time: | action | events |

Homologies between the linguistic structuring of space and of time will be indicated in the categories that follow. But here we can indicate operations of conversion between these two main members of the dimension category. Thus, a verb root that lexicalizes expression of an event or of action as a temporal quantity can be associated with grammatical forms, including nominalizations, that signal a cognitive operation of "reification". By the semantic effect of this operation, the referent becomes conceptualized as an object or a mass, one that can participate in many of the same activities (such as being given or gotten) as a physical quantity, as well as in many of the corresponding syntactic constructions (including pluralization and modification: ...*gave me two quick calls*), as exemplified in (15). (A way of representing the grammatical complexes involved here and in the next operation is presented in connection with the following category.)

| (15) | *an event:* | *reified as an object:* |
|---|---|---|
| | John called me. | John gave me a call. |
| | I was called by John. | I got a call from John. |
| | *action:* | *reified as mass:* |
| | John helped me. | John gave me some help. |
| | I was helped by John. | I got some help from John. |

The reverse conversion also occurs. A noun referring to an object or mass can be associated with grammatical forms, including verb-forming derivations, that signal a cognitive operation of "actionalizing". By this operation, the physical referent is melded together with some of the activity in which it participates, with the semantic effect that much of the referent's tangible concrete character is backgrounded, subordinated to a conceptualization in terms of a process of occurrence, as illustrated in (16):

(16)

| *object(s)/mass:* | *actionalized as:* |
|---|---|
| Hail(stones) came in through the window | It hailed in through the window. |
| Ice is forming over the windshield. | It is icing up over the windshield. |
| I removed the pit from the cherry. | I pitted the cherry. |

## 2.2. Plexity

The category here to be termed "plexity" is a quantity's state of articulation into equivalent elements. Where the quantity consists of only one such element, it is "uniplex", and where it consists of more than one, it is "multiplex". When the quantity involved is matter, plexity is, of course, equivalent to the traditional linguistic category of "number" with its component notions "singular" and "plural". But the present notions are intended to capture the generalization from matter over to action, which the traditional notions do not do.[13]

Specifications as to plexity are made by both lexical items and grammatical elements, and there is interplay between the two when they are both in association. Example English lexical items that basically specify a uniplex referent are – for matter and action, respectively – *bird* and *(to) sigh*. They can occur with grammatical elements that themselves specify a uniplexity, like those italicized in (17a) (many languages have here a more regular, overt system of markers than English). But they can also occur with grammatical elements that specify a multiplexity, as in (17b). In this association, such elements can be thought to trigger a particular cognitive operation, one of "multiplexing". By this operation, an original solo referent is, in effect, copied onto various points of space or time.

(17)

| | *matter* | *action* |
|---|---|---|
| a. uniplex | *A* bird flew in. | He sighed (once). |
| b. multiplex | Birds flew in. | He *kept sighing*. |

The reverse of the preceding pattern is also found in language. First, there are lexical items that intrinsically specify a multiplexity. English examples are *furniture* or *timber* (i.e., 'standing trees') for matter and *breathe* for action, as used in (18a). And, too, there are grammatical forms able to appear in association with these, as in (18b), that signal an operation the reverse of multiplexing – one that can be called "unit-excerpting". By this operation, a single instance of the specified equivalent units is taken and set in the foreground of attention.

(18) *matter*

*action*

a. *multiplex* Furniture overturned in the earthquake.
She breathed without pain.

b. *uniplex* A *piece of* furniture overturned in the earthquake.
She *took a* breath / breathed *in* without pain.

The English grammatical forms seen above that signaled multiplexing – *-s* and *keep -ing* – consisted solely of explicit morphemes. The forms that signal unit-excerpting differ in that they also include abstract elements: particular grammatical categories that require the insertion of one out of a certain set of lexical items, as represented in (19c,d). The forms can, moreover, contain two or more independent elements. These forms are here considered to be "grammatical complexes", comparable to other grammatical constructions or indeed to lexical complexes (collocations): they combine distinct elements within a structural whole serving a single overall semantic function. Actually, by one analysis, all grammatical forms are complexes, merely ranked along a dine of elaborateness. Under this analysis, a grammatical form includes not only any explicit and generic elements, but also the semantic and syntactic category memberships of its input and output forms, as represented throughout (19). Thus, the English multiplexing forms, in (19a,b), are merely at the simpler end of a continuum:

(19)

(a)

$$\Big[ [\_\_\_]_{N_{upx}} + \textit{-s} \Big]_{N_{mpx}}$$

e.g., *bird: birds*

(b)

$$\Big[ \textit{keep} + [\_\_\_]_{V_{upx}} + \textit{-ing} \Big]_{V_{mpx}}$$

e.g., *sigh: keep sighing*

(c)

$$\left[ N_{unit}\ \textit{of} \ + \ [\_\_]_{N_{mpx}} \right]_{N_{upx}}$$

e.g., *furniture: a piece of furniture*

(d)

$$\left[ V_{dummy} \ + \ [\,[\_\_]_{V_{mpx}} + \text{DERIV}\,]_{N_{upx}} \right]_{V_{upx}}$$

e.g., ***breathe: take a breath***

(d′)

$$\left[ [\_\_]_{V_{mpx}} + \text{PTC} \right]_{V_{upx}}$$

e.g., ***breathe: breathe in***

Support is lent to the thesis that a more elaborate grammatical complex can have a semantic unity by the existence, within the same or another language, of a simpler form with the same semantic function. As an example of just this circumstance, the English unit-excerpting complex for nouns, which is rather elaborate, is paralleled in function by a simple suffix in Yiddish, either *-l* or *-ele* (otherwise indicating diminutives), as illustrated in (20):

(20) *zamd* 'sand': *zemdl* 'grain of sand'
*groz* 'grass': *grezl* 'blade of grass'
*shney* 'snow': *shneyele* 'snowflake'

### 2.3. State of boundedness

When a quantity is specified as "unbounded", it is conceived as continuing on indefinitely with no necessary characteristic of finiteness intrinsic to it. When a quantity is specified as "bounded", it is conceived to be demarcated as an individuated unit entity. In application to nouns, these notions largely correspond to the traditional linguistic distinction between "mass" and "count", and in application to verbs they can correspond to "imperfective" and "perfective", among other terms (the closeness of these correspondences varies with different usages of the traditional terms). However, as with plexity, the concepts designated by the new terms are intended to capture the commonality between the space and time dimensions and to generalize over their usually separate analyses.

Among English examples of lexical items, *water* and *(to) sleep* basically specify unbounded quantities, whereas *sea* and *(to) dress* basically specify bounded ones. These specifications are demonstrated by the fact that these words are, respectively, unacceptable and acceptable in construction with the grammatical complex "*in* $\text{NP}_{\text{extent-of-time}}$", which itself specifies boundedness, as seen in (21):

| (21) | | *matter* | *action* |
|---|---|---|---|
| a. | *unbounded* | *We flew over water in 1 hr. | *She slept in 8hrs. |
| b. | *bounded* | We flew over a sea in 1 hr. | She dressed in 8mins. |

As with plexity, there exist grammatical elements that can, in construction with a lexical item, shift its basic specification for state of boundedness to the opposite value. Those acting in this way on an unbounded-type lexical item, in effect, trigger a cognitive operation of "bounding", or "portion-excerpting". By this operation, a portion of the specified unbounded quantity is demarcated and placed in the foreground of attention. Examples of such grammatical elements in English are shown in (22).

The reverse of the preceding pattern also exists. The English nouns *shrub* and *panel* each refer intrinsically to a bounded entity. But the grammatical elements *-ery* and *-ing* can be added to them, yielding *shrubbery* and *paneling,* forms which now refer to unbounded quantities. In effect, the grammatical elements have triggered a cognitive operation of "debounding" whereby the quantity formerly within bounds is now conceptualized in a form with indefinite extension. In English, however, such elements are not productive; they cannot, for example, be used with *sea* to yield the meaning 'pelagic water', nor with *(a) tear* to yield 'lachrymal fluid'.[14]

(22)

*matter:*

$$\left[ N_{\text{bounded-quantity}}\ \textit{of} + [\underline{\quad\quad}]_{N_{\text{unbd}}} \right]_{N_{\text{bd}}}$$

*e.g., water: body of water*

*action:*

$$\left[ [\underline{\quad\quad}]_{V_{\text{unbd}}} + \textit{for}\ N_{\text{extent-of-time}} \right]_{V_{\text{bd}}}$$

e.g., *sleep: sleep for an hour*

## 2.4. State of dividedness

The category of "state of dividedness" refers to a quantity's internal segmentation. A quantity is "discrete" (or "particulate") if it is conceptualized as having breaks, or interruptions, through its composition. Otherwise, the quantity is conceptualized as "continuous".[15]

Both lexical and grammatical elements are sensitive, in their specifications, to the distinctions of this category. But there appear to be no grammatical elements that solely specify discreteness or continuity for a quantity, nor any that signal an operation for reversing a quantity's lexically specified state of dividedness. If forms of the latter type existed, we can describe how they would behave. A grammatical form for a continuous-type lexical item would signal an operation of "discretizing", whereby the originally continuous referent would become conceptualized as a particulate aggregation. Conversely, a grammatical form for a discrete-type lexical item would trigger an operation of "melding", whereby the separate elements of the original referent would be conceptualized as having fused together into a continuum.

Although such grammatical forms seem lacking, there do exist certain indirect or inexplicit mechanisms for these operations. Thus, the continuity specified by the noun *water* can be reconceptualized as discrete with the locution *particles of*, as in: *Water / Particles of water filled the vessel.* However, the grammatical complex used here does not directly specify this shift but, like the complexes in Sections 2.5. and 2.13., comprises a several-stage sequence of other cognitive operations. In the reverse direction, there appears to be a general conceptual tendency for a basically discrete-type referent of a lexical root to undergo at least some degree of spontaneous melding, without the addition of any explicit grammatical forms.

Thus, *foliage*, *timber*, and *furniture*, as contrasted with *leaves*, *trees*, and *pieces of furniture*, tend to evoke referents with a degree of blurring and fusion across their component elements.

Because the category of dividedness has limited realization by itself, further treatment of it will be deferred until the next section, where it can be seen in interaction with the other categories.

## 2.5. The disposition of a quantity: A system of categories

The preceding four categories of attributes – dimension, plexity, boundedness, and dividedness – all pertain to a quantity simultaneously and, taken together, can be considered to constitute a *system* of attributes that may be termed a quantity's "disposition". The intersections of these categories form an array that can be schematized as in (23).

(23)

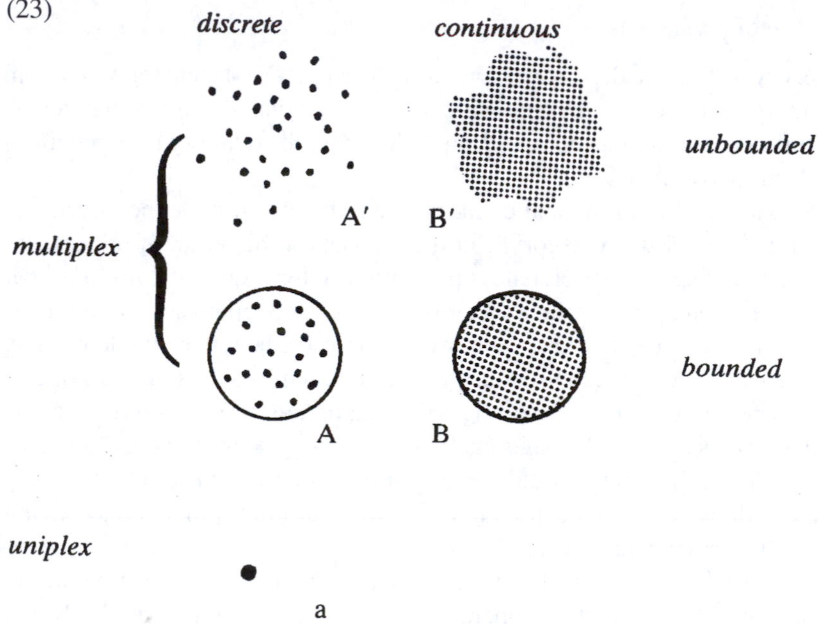


+ the distinction between *matter* and *action,* which crosscuts all of the above[16]

Each intersection of attributes indicated here is specified by various lexical items (although one, a bounded multiplexity for action, is quite minimally represented in English). An example or two (most seen earlier) is given for each intersection in (24) :[17]

| (24) | | | | |
|---|---|---|---|---|
| | A': | timber/furniture | B': | water |
| | | (to) breathe | | (to) sleep |
| | A: | (a) family | B: | (a) sea/panel |
| | | (to) molt | | (to) empty |
| | | (The bird molted.) | | (The tank emptied.) |
| | a: | (a) bird | | |
| | | (to) sigh | | |

Now if the particular contentful referent for which one chooses a lexical item happens to be wedded, by that lexical item, to an unwanted set of structural specifications, there generally are grammatical means available for converting this to a desired set. Such means range in directness from specifying the single relevant operation to involving a circuitous sequence of operations (cf. Section 2.13. on "nesting"). A number of starting- and ending-points for such conversions, and the means for accomplishing them, are indicated in (25):

| (25) | | | | |
|---|---|---|---|---|
| | A' → A | a stand of timber | B' → B | a body of water |
| | | breathe for an hour | | sleep for an hour |
| | A' → a | a piece of furniture | ---- | |
| | | take a breath / breathe in | | |
| | A → a | a member of a family | ---- | |
| | | ?molt a single feather | | |
| | A → A' | members of a family | B → B' | paneling |
| | | (A → a → A') | | |
| | | molt and molt | | empty and empty |
| | a → A' | trees | ---- | |
| | | keep sighing | | |
| | a → A | a stand of trees | ---- | |
| | | (a → A' → A) | | |
| | | sigh for a while | | |

## 2.6. Degree of extension

Implicit in the vertical dimension of the schematic arrangement in (23) is a further category that can be called "degree of extension". This category has three principal member notions, terms for which are given in (26) together with schematic representations of the notions for the linear case. Lexical items referring to either matter or action may be taken to incorporate specifications as to their referent's basic degree of extension, and three examples of these for the linear spatial case are also shown in (26) :[18]

(26)

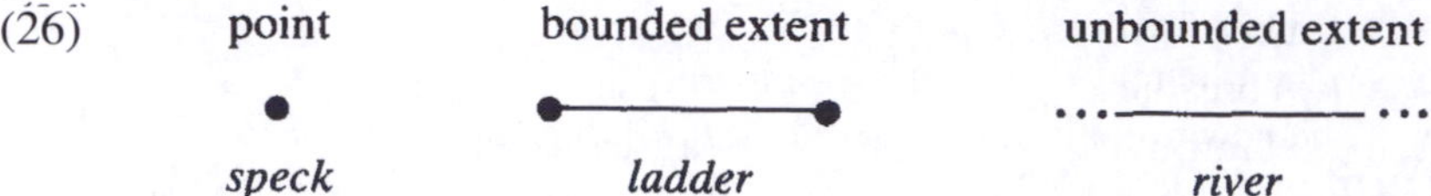


Now a lexical referent that is perhaps most basically conceived as of one particular degree of extension can, by various grammatical specifications that induce a shift, be reconceptualized as of some other degree of extension. For a first example, consider the event referent of *climb a ladder,* which seems basically of bounded linear extent in the temporal dimension, as is in fact manifested in (27) in conjunction with the grammatical element "*in* + $\mathrm{NP}_{\text{extent-of-time}}$":

(27) She climbed up the fire-ladder in 5 minutes.

With a different accompanying grammatical form, like the "*at* + $\mathrm{NP}_{\text{point-of-time}}$" in (28), (as well as different contextual specifications), the event referent of the preceding can be shifted toward a conceptual schematization as a point of time – i.e., as being point-durational:

(28) Moving along on the training course,
she climbed the fire-ladder at exactly midday.

This shift in the cognized extension of the event can be thought to involve a cognitive operation of "reduction" or, alternatively, "adoption of a long-range perspective". This shift can also go in the other direction. The event referent can be conceptually schematized as an unbounded extent by the effect of grammatical forms like *"keep -ing", "-er and -er",* and *"as* + S", as in (29):

(29) She kept climbing higher and higher up the fire-ladder as we watched.

Here there would seem to have taken place a cognitive operation of "magnification", or "adoption of a close-up perspective". By this operation, a perspective point is established from which the existence of any exterior bounds falls outside of view and attention – or, at most, is asymptotically approachable.

The preceding event referent was continuous, but a discrete case can exhibit the same shifts in extension. One such case, perhaps to be considered as most basically of bounded extent, is shown with that degree of extension in (30a). But the referent can also be idealized as a point, as in (30b) (clearly, the cows would not all have died at the same moment, and yet the spread of their death times is conceptually collapsed into such a single moment). Or, the referent can be schematized as an unbounded extent, as in (30c):

(30) a. The cows all died in a month.
b. When the cows all died, we sold our farm.
c. The cows kept dying (and dying) until they were all gone.

The alternative schematizations of extension just seen as specifiable for an event referent are generally also available for an object referent. Thus, e.g., the referent of *(a) box* can be specified for idealization as a point or as a bounded extent (of area or volume). Some grammatical elements making such specifications are illustrated in (31). Also set forth here are the homologies between these and the event-specific elements:

| (31) | | |
|---|---|---|
| | *point* | The box is 20 feet away from the wall. |
| | | I read the book 20 years ago. |
| | *bounded extent* | The box is 2 feet across. |
| | | I read the book in 2 hours. |
| | *(point within) bounded extent* | The ball is in the box. |
| | | She left while I read the letter. |

## 2.7. Pattern of distribution

The pattern of distribution of matter through space or of action through time is a further category of notions that can be both grammatically and lexically specified.[19] For action through time – the only dimension we will be looking at here – this category together with the preceding one largely constitute the traditional category of "aspect".

Several of the main patterns of distribution for action through time are shown schematically in (32) (the dots here, which represent situatedness in complementary states, should really be adjacent, but they are sketched apart with a connecting line to show the crossing of state-interfaces). Also shown are illustrative English verbs, both non-agentive and agentive, that incorporate these patterns.

(32)

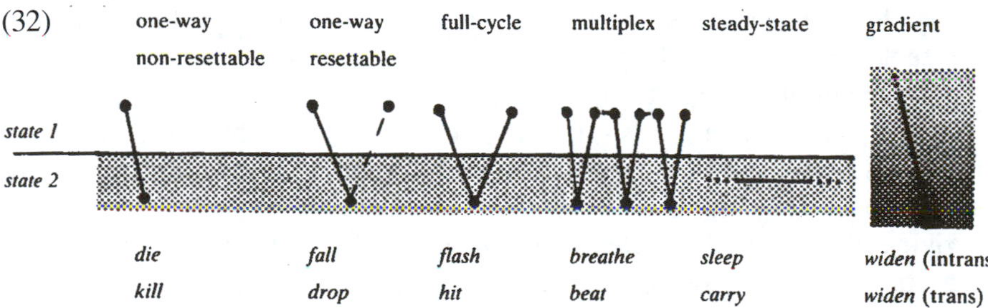

One can determine that these verbs incorporate the specifications indicated by noting the grammatical forms with which they can and cannot occur (or, to put the latter case in our terms: ...grammatical forms toward whose specifications they will not [readily] shift). A full demonstration is not in order here, but a few examples show the principle: The resettable type of a one-way event is distinguished from the non-resettable type by its compatibility with iterative expressions, as in: *He fell 3 times;* the non-resettable type cannot occur here: **He died 3 times.* This same one-way form is distinguished from a full-cycle form by its ability to appear in sentences like: *He fell and then got up,* which the latter cannot do: **The beacon flashed and then went off.* A gradient type can appear with adverbs of augmentation, as in *The river progressively widened,* unlike a steady-state type: * *She progressively slept.* And so on.

Grammatical elements can, of course, also specify differing patterns of temporal distribution, and the present form of diagramming can readily reveal some of their distinctions. Thus, the closed-class elements *back* and *again,* singly and in combination, can indicate versions of full-cycle, sesqui-cycle, and double-cycle patterns, as shown in (33):

(33)

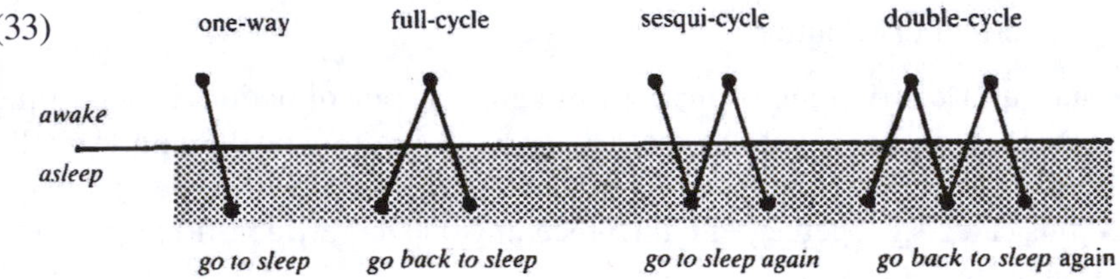


Now consider the circumstance where a verb of one distribution type appears with grammatical forms of another type. The resultant seems invariably to be that the verb shifts its specifications into conformity with those of the grammatical forms. For an example we again take *die,* whose basic specifications can be adjudged as point-durational one-way non-resettable – schematizable, now more precisely, as: ●. This verb is used with its basic specifications in a sentence like (34a). But in a sentence like (34b), the grammatical form *"be + -ing"* induces a shift. In effect, the infinitesimal interval between the two states involved for *die* – viz., 'aliveness' and 'deadness' – is spread out, with the creation thereby of an extent-durational gradient. This is the shift in the distribution pattern's structural type. But concomitantly, a shift in the basic contentful referent is engendered. Instead of 'dying', the new gradient refers to 'moribundity'. The distinction becomes clear in noting that, as the conception is structured linguistically, one can have been dying without having died, and, correlatively, one can have died without having been dying.[20]

(34) a. He died as she looked on.
b. He was (slowly) dying as she looked on.

## 2.8. Axiality

The adjectives in a pair like *well/sick* behave contrarily when in association with grammatical forms specifying degree like *slightly* and *almost,* as seen in (35a), and they select for different readings of temporal forms like *"in* + $NP_{extent\text{-}of\text{-}time}$", as seen in (35b). In this, perhaps surprisingly, they parallel the behavior of certain kinds of expressions that specify spatial relations, e.g., *at the border I past the border:*

(35)

a. He's slightly { sick / past the border. | *well / *at the border. }

He's almost { well / at the border. | ?sick / ?past the border. }

b. He got well / to the border in 5 days. – i.e., progressively in the course of
He got sick / past the border in 5 days. – i.e., first after the elapse of

This behavior can be accounted for by positing that such adjectives, in referring to a more generic notional parameter, such as that of 'health', are not simply "opposites" but, rather, presuppose a schematic axis that is structured and directed in a particular way. Each adjective, then, labels a different portion of that axis. The adjectives here seem in particular to presuppose a directed line bounded at one end; *well* refers to the end-point while *sick* refers to the remainder of the line, correlating greater magnitude with greater distance along the line. These are the "axial properties", or "axiality", of the lexical items, i.e., the specific relations each has to a particular conceptual axis and to other lexical items with referents along the same axis. It is the lexicalization of such axiality that can align adjectives with expressions of spatial relation. Grammatical forms like the ones just above also have axial properties, and these can function in consonance with those of a lexical item, as in the acceptable cases of (35), now schematized as to axiality in (36):

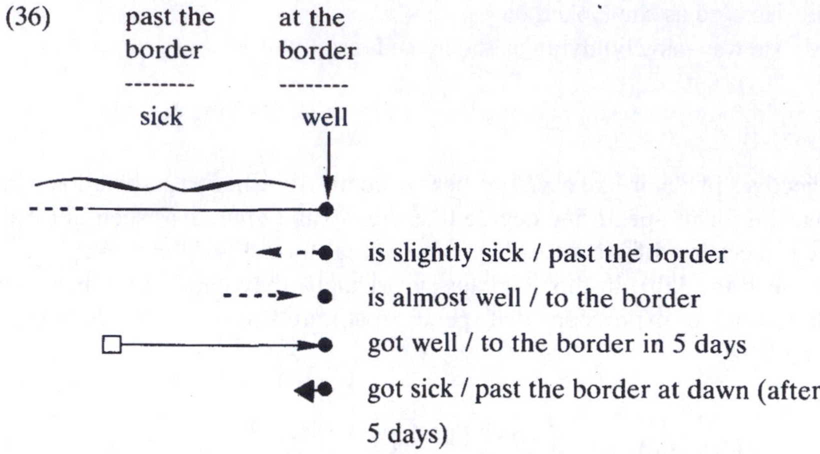


In other cases, though, the axiality of a grammatical form can conflict with that of a lexical item and, accordingly, can cause the latter to shift. Thus, *sick* in (37) – now associated with grammatical forms that refer to an end-point – shifts from its basic "directed shaft" type of axiality, and indeed from its reference to an axis of 'health'; it now specifies the end-point of an axis pertaining to 'feeling physically bad'.

(37) (After exposure to the virus, he felt worse and worse and)
he was almost sick at one point. / he finally got sick in 3 days.[21]

## 2.9. Perspectival mode

As seen earlier, a particular event, whether static or changing, can have a pattern of distribution through time that is perhaps most basically associated with or intrinsic to it in its own right. But, in addition, language has the means for specifying an independent schema as to how one is to attend to the event. This schema includes the location and deployment of the perspective point one adopts from which to regard the event and the distribution of one's attention over the event. This category of specifications, here called the "perspectival mode", can either conform with or diverge from the event's own basic pattern of distribution. Two principal members of the category are characterized in (38):

(38) the assuming of:
  a. a steady-state long-range perspective point with global scope of attention
  b. a moving close-up perspective point with local scope of attention

For illustration, consider first an example with a basically steady-state referent, viz., objects in location. The (38a) type of perspectival mode – the one more congruent with such a referent – is invoked in (39a), multiply specified there by the set of grammatical forms shown underlined, namely, plural forms, an adverbial expression of spatial dispersion, and the locative preposition *in*. But these can be replaced by grammatical forms coding for the (38b) perspectival mode – as in (39b) with singular forms, an adverbial expression of temporal dispersion, and the motion preposition *through*. Thereby, the evoked CR is converted to one where one's perspective and attention or one's own projected location shifts in turn from object to object. In effect, a steady-state multiplexity of objects has been converted to a sequential multiplexity of events consisting of conceptualized encounters with the objects.

(39) a. There *are* houses *at various points* in the valley.
  b. There *is a* house *every now and then through* the valley.

For representing certain static spatial configurations, the moving-perspective mode, though non-congruent in character, is greatly favored over the steady-state mode. Thus, the ready colloquial formulation of (40b) for moving-perspective is matched in the global steady-state mode of (40a) only by a stilted scientific style:

(40) a. The wells' depths form a gradient that correlates with their locations on the road.
  b. The wells get deeper the further down the road they are.

The reverse of the preceding circumstances also exists. That is, a sequential multiplexity of events, an example of which is represented in (41 a) with the more congruent moving-perspective mode, can also become the object of a fixed global viewing, as represented in (41b). Metaphorically, the effect here is as if the vertical time line is tilted up into present-moment horizontality for integrated or summational assessment.

(41) a. I took *an* aspirin *time after time during / in the course of* the last hour.
  b. I *have* taken *a number of* aspirin*s in the* last hour.[22]

## 2.10. Level of synthesis

The category to be considered now pertains to bounded quantities, like those schematized in the A/B row in (23). One form of locution already seen to specify such quantities is the particular type of "NP *of* NP" construction illustrated in (42a). Here the second NP specifies the *identity* of the quantity involved, itself conceptualized as without intrinsic bounds, while the first NP specifies the *bounding,* or *"portion-excerpting",* per se of the quantity. Moreover, in addition to such a pure operation of bounding, the first NP can further specify the particular *form* or *configuration* that the excerpted portion has, as in (42b):[23]

(42) a. a set of trees a body of water
b. a cluster of trees a puddle/drop of water

The two NPs here can be seen as coding for two different "levels of synthesis". Describing this for the internally discrete case, e.g., *a cluster of trees,* we can say that the second NP specifies an unsynthesized multiplexity of independent elements, while the first NP specifies a particular Gestalt synthesized out of that multiplexity.

Furthermore, language can mark an additional cognitive distinction here. Either level of synthesis can be placed in the foreground of attention while the other level is placed in the background. One grammatical device for marking this is the placement of the foregrounded NP at the head of the larger nominal construction (in English, placing it first), as shown in (43a). With the use of this device, moreover, predications can be made that pertain solely to one level of synthesis or the other, as seen in (43b):

(43) a. the cluster of trees / the trees in the cluster
b. That cluster of trees is small.
The trees in that cluster are small.

There are certain forms, furthermore, whose referents are keyed to applying to only one or the other level of synthesis. Thus, *together (toward each other)* tends to correlate with multiple objects at large, while *in upon -self* tends to correlate with a composite formed therefrom, as seen in (44):

(44) The bricks in the pyramid came crashing together / *in upon themselves.
The pyramid of bricks came crashing in upon itself / * together.

The preceding phenomena have involved the shift of attention from a multiplexity to a Gestalt that it can constitute, a process that can be called "Gestalt formation". Also encountered in language are means for specifying the reverse: shifting attention from a Gestalt to components seen as constituting it, in a process of "componentializing". This procedure can take place when the starting lexical item specifies an entity taken to be already at the more synthetic level, as is the case with *iceberg* in (45a). By grammatical devices like those in (45b), such an entity can be analytically converted from conception as a coherent whole to one of component parts and their interrelations. Again we encounter a surface form – *in two* – that correlates with only one level of synthesis and not the other:

(45) a. The iceberg broke in two.
b. The two halves of the iceberg broke apart (*in two).

The two levels of synthesis with the two directions of conceptual shift applicable to them define four notional types, as indicated in (46). The term *Figure* is used here as described in Talmy (1978b, 1983).

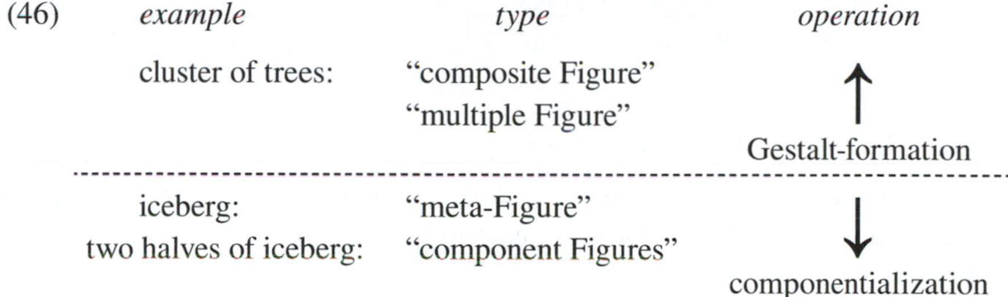

(46)
example
type
operation
cluster of trees:
"composite Figure"
"multiple Figure"
Gestalt-formation
iceberg:
"meta-Figure"
two halves of iceberg:
"component Figures"
componentialization


## 2.11. Level of exemplarity

A further cognitive distinction can be specified for a multiplexity of objects. This distinction does not affect the basic reference to all the members of the multiplexity, but addresses how attention is directed and distributed within that multiplexity. Either the *full complement* of the multiplexity is in the foreground of attention, with perhaps individual items here and there singled out in the background of attention. Or a single *exemplar* out of the multiplexity is placed in the foreground of attention, with the remaining items more dimly conceived in the background of attention. This distinction as to "level of exemplarity" is specified by grammatical devices in perhaps most languages. But English stands out in the extensiveness of its specifications: there are different pairs of grammatical forms that mark the distinction for a number of different types of multiplexity. A rather full list of these pairs is indicated in (47), with examples showing first the full-complement form and then the counterpart exemplar form:

(47) a. Oysters have siphons / a siphon.
An oyster has siphons / a siphon.[24]

b. All oysters have siphons / a siphon.
   Every oyster has siphons / a siphon
c. All the members raised their hand(s).
   Each member raised his hand(s).[25]
d. Many members raised their hand(s).
   Many a member raised his hand(s).
e. Some members here and there raised their hand(s).
   A member here and there raised his hand(s).
f. Members one after another raised their hand(s).
   One member after another raised his hand(s).
g. Hardly any members raised their hand(s).
   Hardly a member raised his hand(s).
h. No members raised their hand(s).
   No member (Not a member) raised his hand(s).
i. She held a gun in both hands.
   She held a gun in either hand.[26]

## 2.12. Other categories and processes

A number of further notional categories and cognitive processes can be discerned in language, but there is opportunity here to present briefly only two additional examples:

*Scene-division properties.* A lexical item can have particular "scene-division properties", that is, a principal breakup of its referent into parts and participants. For example, the referent of the English verb *serve* breaks up into an activity, an item served, and a social dyad involving the two roles of 'host' and 'guest' – this last being its particular "personation" type (Talmy 1985a) – as illustrated in (48a). But grammatical forms can also have scene-division properties. Thus, a subject-plus-reflexive-object complex has a single-role specification. When such a grammatical form occurs with a dyadic verb like *serve,* it triggers an operation of "monad-formation": the verb's referent shifts to one with monadic personation, as in (48b). In this shifted state, its referent is equivalent to that of an intrinsically monadic expression, like that in (48c):[27]

(48) a. The host served me some dessert from the kitchen.
     b. I served myself some dessert from the kitchen.
     c. I went and got some dessert from the kitchen.

*Associated attributes.* Lexical expressions like *apartment* and *hotel room,* in addition to their basic denotations, may be taken to have "associated attributes" – here, respectively, those of 'permanent residence' and 'temporary lodging.' Such attributes may mesh or conflict with the specifications of another element in the same sentence. The attributes of the above two nominals mesh and conflict respectively, e.g., with the closed-class directional adverb *home,* which specifies a permanent residence. In the case of conflict, as in (49b), a cognitive process operates on the lexical item to leave its essential characteristics intact but replace its associated attributes with the closed-class element's specifications:

(49) a. He drove home to his apartment.
 b. He drove home to his hotel room.

## 2.13. Nesting: An interaction of categories

A number of what can be considered "meta-properties" govern the behavior of categories of grammatical notions, in general and with respect to one another. One of these, the capacity for nesting, already illustrated in Section 2.5., can be readily presented here: The operations and shifts described throughout Section 2 need not take place singly. The output of one can serve as the input to another, thereby building up hierarchical levels of embedding. While there are a number of interesting examples of this for different types of matter and action, we will go directly to illustrating one of the longer cases in (50):

(50) a. The beacon flashed (as I glanced over).
 b. The beacon kept flashing.
 c. The beacon flashed 5 times in a row.
 d. The beacon kept flashing 5 times at a stretch.
 e. The beacon flashed 5 times at a stretch for 3 hours.

In (50a), the lexical verb *flash* appears with its basic structural specification as a point-durational full-cycle uniplex event. This undergoes the operation of multiplexing, to yield the unbounded multiplexity in (50b). This then undergoes bounding in (50c). This bounded multiplexity then first goes through the operation of reduction to become schematized as a new point-like uniplex quantity, and this is in turn multiplexed, yielding (50d). This new unbounded multiplexity is finally then bounded in (50e). The nesting of structural specifications in this last stage can be represented schematically as in (51):

(51) [('''') - ('''')......('''') - ('''')]

Quite analogous to this temporal nesting, except for the lack of specific numerals, is the spatial example in (52):

(52) a. A duck landed on the pond.
b. Ducks landed on the pond
c. A flock of ducks landed on the pond.
d. Flocks of ducks landed on the pond.
e. A group of flocks of ducks landed on the pond.

## 2.14. Four imaging systems

Most of the preceding categories of grammatically specified notions, together with categories not discussed here, group together under four much broader conceptual systems, ones that can be understood as principal "imaging systems" of language. These are great complexes in language that organize the structuring and the "viewing" of conceptual material. The four systems outlined here (there are additional ones) are relatively independent of each other in content, with each adding a distinct conceptual parameter to those of the others, but their contributions can be coordinated and linked, at times by individual grammatical forms.

The first imaging system is "structural schematization". This system comprises all the forms of conceptual delineation that can be ascribed to a quantity, or to the pattern in which two or more quantities are interrelated, whether in space or time or some other conceptual dimension. A number of the categories of notions presented above are part of this system. After "dimension", all the categories pertaining to the disposition of a quantity and its generalizations belong here, in particular, the categories of plexity, state of boundedness, state of dividedness, degree of extension, pattern of distribution, and axiality. Belonging here, too, are the category of scene-division properties and that of the "partitioning" of space or time that is specified by such deictics as *this* and *that,* described in Section 1. A further major component of this imaging system is the spatial or temporal "geometric" schematization, including the topology-like kind, that is specified especially by the adpositional systems of languages. This was only touched on here in Section 1's discussion of the English preposition *through,* but it is an extensive domain, one treated at length in such works as Bennett (1975), Gruber (1965), Jackendorf (1977), Langacker (1986), Talmy (1975, 1982, 1983), Herskovits (1986).

The second imaging system is the "deployment of perspective". Given a structurally schematized scene, this system pertains to how one places one's "mental eyes" to look out upon that scene, including the location, the distance away, and the movement pattern of this conceptual perspective point. Belonging to this system from the discussion above is the category of perspectival mode, with its options of a steady-state or a moving perspective point. Also here is the category of degree of extension, when its alternatives are interpreted as "adopting a long-range vs. a close-up perspective".

The third imaging system is “distribution of attention”. Given a schematized scene and a vantage from which to regard it, this system pertains to the allocation of attention that one can direct differentially over the aspects of the scene. Belonging here from the discussion above are the categories of level of synthesis and level of exemplarity, as well as the component of the perspectival mode category that involves global vs. local scope of attention. In addition, a major category, not treated here, comprises the obligatory “Figure/Ground” distinctions that language imposes on a referent scene. Here, within a scene, there is ascribed to one element the status of “Figure”, with its attentional primacy, and to another element the status of “Ground”, with its function in the background of attention as a reference object for the localizing of the Figure (Talmy 1978b, 1978c, 1983). Additionally in this imaging system are such grammatically marked discourse concepts as focus, topic, comment, given and new.

The fourth imaging system, not treated here at all, is “force dynamics”, which, given a structured scene, involves the forces that the elements of the scene exert on each other. Comprehended here are the notions of force exerted by one quantity on another, as well as notions of resistance to such force, the overcoming of such resistance, blockage to the exertion of force, and the removal of such blockage. The system of force dynamics includes the traditional linguistic concepts of the “causative”, but is a generalization over those concepts (Talmy 1976, 1985b).

## 3. Further cognitive connections

Grammatically specified structuring appears to correspond, in certain of its functions and characteristics, to the structuring in other cognitive domains, such as that of visual perception, compared below, or those of inference and memory. In particular, perhaps the principal overarching function of the structuring common across cognitive domains is that of providing conceptual *coherence,* that is, acting as a means for integrating and unifying a body of otherwise disparate conceptual material. In language and, as suggested below, in vision, this fundamental function has three main global forms of realization: coherence across a conceptual inventory, coherence within a scene, and coherence through time.

Across the inventory of notions available for expression within any one language, grammatical specifications bring coherence principally by constituting a *classification* of the vast variety of conceived and perceived material. They gather different portions of the material together into subdivisions distinct from each other. By this, any particular currently cognized element is associated with its implicit “subdivision-mates”. An illustrative case here are the twenty-plus motion-related prepositions in English, such as *through* and *into,* which together subdivide the conceptual domain of ‘paths considered with respect to reference-objects’.

This domain covers a great and varied range, but any particular "path" generally falls within the purview of one or another preposition, associated there with other "paths". To a certain extent, such associations can be regarded as arbitrary or idiosyncratic. Thus, as seen earlier, classed together by *through* are such dissimilar cases as a straightforward liquid-parting course (walking through water) and a zig-zag obstacle-avoiding course (walking through woods). The question arises why such distinctions should be effaced by the grammatical system, while they are observed by the lexical and other cognitive systems. Why are grammatical elements – say, such prepositions – not a large and open class marking indefinitely many distinctions? One may speculate that the cognitive function of such classification lies in unifying contentful material within a single conceptual system and in rendering it manipulable – i.e., amenable to transmission, storage, and processing – and that its absence would render content an intractable agglomeration.

Providing coherence within a cognized scene was the function of grammatical structuring that was originally indicated in the Introduction. There it was put forward that the grammatical elements of any particular sentence together specify the structure of the cognitive representation evoked by that sentence. Their specifications act as a scaffolding or framework across which contentful material can, in effect, be splayed or draped. It can be posited that such structuring is necessary for a disparate quantity of contentful material to be able to cohere in any sensible way and hence to be amenable to simultaneous cognizing as a Gestalt. That is, without such structuring, not only does the inventory of concepts available for expression in a language become less coherent, but also any selection of such concepts concurrently juxtaposed by a sentence would tend to be only a collection of elements, rather than elements assembled so as to convey an integrated idea or thought complex.

In the course of discourse, a great welter of notions are expressed in rapid succession, posing the potential problem of an unconnected sequence of ideational elements. But grammatically specified structuring is a principal contributor to the conceptual coherence through time that is requisite here. Through such structuring, a cognitive continuity is maintained through this flux and a coherent Gestalt is summated over time. A language can have a great stock of closed-class elements participating in this function, for example, such English forms as *"yes, but", moreover, nevertheless, besides, instead, also.* Such forms direct the illocutionary flow, specify the "logical tissue" of the discourse, and limn out its rhetorical framework. That is, these grammatical forms establish a structure that extends over a span of time, and thus provides a conceptual level with temporal constancy amidst more fleeting aspects of content.

The preceding three global forms of grammatically specified structuring apply over the scope of any single language but, as indicated in the Introduction, a fourth form must also be recognized that holds for language in general. While each language has to some extent a different set of grammatical specifications, there is great commonality across languages, so one can posit that each set is drawn from an innate inventory of concepts available for serving a structuring function in language.

Further, though, a qualifying property of this inventory can be adduced. It can be observed that grammatically specified concepts range cross-linguistically from ones that are of extremely widespread (perhaps universal) occurrence and of broad application within a language, down to ones appearing in a scant few languages with minimal application. Thus, the innate inventory of available structuring notions that is posited here seems to be *graduated* as to significance for the language faculty (cf. the tabular listing of grammatical notions in Talmy (1985a:126ff)). For example, the notions 'entity' and 'occurrence' as expressed by the grammatical categories "noun" and "verb" are of great application and probably universal distribution, the notional category "number" seems of roughly middle standing in the ranking, while notions like 'in the morning' and 'in the evening' are expressed inflectionally on the verb in just a few languages.

Notably, compared to spatio-temporal structuring, the notional category of "affect" is rather low in the graduated inventory of concepts that language draws on for structuring purposes, a fact that is significant considering its importance in other cognitive domains (cf. the other cross-domain differences noted below). The affect category does have scattered representation, for example 'affection' expressed by diminutive affixes, 'scorn' by pejoratives, 'concern' by a conjunction like *lest,* and 'hurt' by the "adversive" construction (as in the English: *My flowers all died* on me.). But seemingly no language has a system of closed-class forms marking major affect distinctions in the way that, say, the modal system in English specifies distinctions of force opposition (Talmy 1985b). Such an affect system can easily be imagined, however. Consider a parent addressing a child in danger near an open window. Grammatical systems readily allow the parent to refer to the spatial structure in this situational complex – *Get away from the window!* – leaving the affectual component to be inferred. But there is no closed-class form comparable to a modal, one that we could represent as "FEAR", as in *FEAR the window!,* that would allow the parent to refer to the affectual component of the complex and leave the spatial component to be inferred. Comparably, to a child near a freshly painted wall and about to harm it, a parent would likely again express the spatial structure – *Get away from the wall!* – leaving the affect to be inferred. There is no closed-class affect form for 'like, be nice to', which we could represent as "FAVOR", that the parent could use instead – *FAVOR the wall!* – thereby leaving the spatial component for inference.

Parallels can now be drawn between the structuring system operating in language and that in visual perception (cf. Jackendoff 1987).[28] The principal function of structure to provide coherence appears common across the two cognitive domains, and the three global forms of such coherence just outlined for language correspond to comparable forms in the operation of vision.

First, as proposed in cognitive psychology, the perception of any particular object is mediated by its association with related objects in a schema for that object type, and the set of such Schemas constitutes a classificatory system (Neisser 1967). This posited functioning of visual perception thus parallels the classificatory function of linguistic structure across a language's conceptual inventory.

Second, there is a parallel between the linguistic coherence within a *referent* scene and the visual coherence within a *perceptual* scene. The welter of optical sensations registered at any one moment from some whole visual scene is rendered coherent by the perception of structural delineations running through it. For example, one looking at, say, the interior of a restaurant from one corner of the room does not see simply a pastiche of color daubs and curves but, rather, perceives a structured whole that includes the framework of the room, the spatial pattern of tables and people, and the individuated tables and people themselves. And seeing a person in some posture involves perceiving a structural framework in the human figure, as Marr (1982) describes this in his treatment of the "3-D model" in visual perception. Children's line drawings of scenes and stick-figure sketches of people, animals, and objects (Kellogg 1970) demonstrate our early capacity to abstract structure from visual scenes and scene parts.

Third, one can observe a parallel between the coherence through time in linguistic discourse and that in visual perception. If the viewer in the illustrative restaurant now walks through the room, the patterns in which visual stimuli and the perception of structure change give rise in turn to the perception of a coherent continuity of path and view occurring within an overall "scene-structure constancy".

It is reasonable to assume that, in addition to these language-vision parallels in global structuring, a number of particular structuring devices match across the two domains. Perhaps most of the grammatically specified conceptual categories treated in this paper – including, for example, state of boundedness and level of exemplarity – correspond to structuring factors in visual perception. Further, the first three of the broader linguistic systems for conceptual organization, the "imaging systems" outlined in Section 2.14., seem also to correspond to broader systems of visual organization.

One can adduce still further parallels between language and vision as to the properties of their structuring. The topology-like character of grammatical specifications may have some parallel in the character of the perceived delineations of a scene, or internal structure of a figure, or plan of a path to be followed through obstacles. Such perceptions of structure seem in certain respects to abstract away from Euclidean particularities of exact magnitude, shape, or angle, and more to involve qualitative or approximate spatial relationships. As a further parallel, the capacity of grammatical specifications to nest, one within another, and form embedded structuring seems to correspond to embedded structuring within a visual scene. The restaurant scene above was described in terms of an overall framework that embedded a spatial pattern, itself consisting of individuated objects. Marr's (1982) analysis of an object like the human figure then continues the embedding, with perceived structurings of the body ranked from its overall linearity, to its stick-figure-like limb structure, and further to its articulations of these components.

Whereas the preceding has outlined a set of parallels between language and vision, significantly, each of these two cognitive domains has prominent structuring devices that play little or no role in the other domain. Thus, in visual perception, three major parameters that structure (parts of) a scene are bilateral symmetry (moving or static), rotation, and dilation (expansion or contraction) (Gibson 1966; Palmer 1983) and, if color can be treated as structural, it is a fourth. In language, by contrast, grammatical specification of symmetry is minimal, perhaps limited entirely to the notion 'reciprocal'. Closed-class indication of rotation is limited in English to the prepositions and verb particles *around* and *over,* and is barely augmented in other languages. Dilation is grammatically expressed in English by the verb particles *in* and *out* when referring to radial motion (*spread out / I shrink in*) and, again, such notions are not greatly more elaborated in other languages. And color, of course, was this paper's original example of a conceptual category *not* grammatically specified.

In the other direction, there are several prominent linguistic categories of seemingly little structural function in visual perception. Examples are "status of reality", as expressed, e.g., by inflections for mood, "status of knowledge", as expressed by evidentials, and "comparison of alternatives", as expressed by a category of particles that includes *instead, only,* and *also.* Further possible examples are "relative temporal location", as expressed by tense markings, "degree", as expressed by adjective inflections and modifiers (e.g., English *-er, -est, almost, too*), and "force dynamics", as expressed by modals (Talmy 1985b).

While language may not share these conceptual structuring categories with visual perception, it may well do so with other cognitive domains. Thus, its closed-class category "status of knowledge", which distinguishes such notions as 'known as fact', 'inferred', 'deduced', and 'considered probable' is very likely related to a set of basic parameters in our reasoning faculty. And, significantly, certain conceptual categories in language have a structuring apparently similar to that of conceptual models that form part of our broader faculty for conceptualization, in particular, our naive or folk models ("mental models" – cf. Gentner and Stevens 1982; Lakoff 1987) as well as models in early science. For example, Talmy (1985b) demonstrates that the way in which language structures its concepts of causation and force interactions greatly parallels the conceptual structuring of naive physics and medieval physics (cf. diSessa 1988), while all three of these forms differ conceptually in a similar way from modern physics.

Generalizing from all these findings, the possibility is that there is a fundamental core to conceptual structure that is common across cognitive domains – a core that thus epitomizes the nature of conceptual structure for human cognition – but that each domain has features of structuring, and perhaps also functions for structuring, that are not shared by others. Determining the overall and particular character of conceptual structure is the aim of the research advanced in the present study, one requiring a cooperative venture among the cognitive disciplines.

## Notes

1. This paper is a moderately revised and fully rewritten version of Talmy (1978a). Since 1978, the amount of additional material on the present subject, both descriptive and theoretical, has grown to be quite extensive. The present version incorporates a certain amount of this new material, as well as bibliographic updating, but the remainder will be reserved for an entirely new paper at a later date.
2. The word "evoke" is used because the relationship is not direct. The CR is an emergent, compounded by various cognitive processes out of the referential meanings of the sentence elements, understanding of the present situation, general knowledge, etc.
   Our term "cognitive representation" is similar in purport to Fillmore's (1975) "scene" but is chosen over that more specifically visual term. The linguistically evoked complex can include much from other sense modalities (notably somesthetic/kinesthetic and auditory) as well as abstract conceptual aspects. More recently, Lakoff's (1987) notion of an "idealized cognitive model", or ICM, points toward a comparable mental entity.
3. For their part, grammatical elements are generally more unalloyed in their indication of structure. They *can* express more contentful concepts, but this is largely limited. An example of it is in English *upon* as used in *We marched/rode/sailed/rushed upon them (e.g., the enemy)*, where *upon* incorporates the notion of 'attack', seemingly equivalent to the paraphrase 'into attack upon'.
4. More recently, research on different aspects of this broader scope has included work by Jackendoff (1983), Bybee (1985), Slobin (1985), Morrow (1986), and Langacker (1987).
5. Not included are regular adverbs, which seem in all languages to be derived from the three open classes just mentioned, rather than to comprise in their own right an open class of specifically adverbial roots. Of possible inclusion as a type of open class are the systems of ideophones, or "expressive forms" found, for example, in a number of Asian and African languages. Also includable, at a level above that of basic elements, are "lexical complexes" (collocations) like English *kick the bucket* or *have it in for.*

6. More accurately, rather than a dichotomy between an open and a closed type of class, there appears to be a cline. A class can range from having quite few members, like that of number inflection in English, to having very many, like that of noun roots in English, and the class's properties may correspondingly range from relatively more grammatical to more lexical. There exist some mid-sized classes – e.g., the several score individual classifiers of Chinese, or the three dozen or so instrumental prefixes in the polysynthetic verb of Atsugewi (Talmy 1972, 1985a) – that appear to have properties part grammatical and part lexical in character.
7. One can note, for example, the effect on one's cognitive representation in considering first the sentence *I looked at the dog* and then *I looked at the dogs*. The addition of the grammatical element *-s* has a major effect on the delineational breakup of – to put it visually – the scene before the mind's eye.
8. For example, augmentative and diminutive elements, insofar as they refer to actual size, seem to specify size relatively greater or lesser than the norm for the particular object indicated. And closed-class elements specifying distance – like English *just* or *way,* as in *just/way up there* – specify notions of 'near' and 'far' that are relative to the referent situation.
9. The properties of the specifically linguistic form of topology require determination. In this regard, consider the English preposition *in*, which in one main usage specifies a plane so curved as to define a volume of space. The referent of this morpheme, as in mathematical topology, is magnitude-neutral: *in the thimble / volcano;* and it is shape-neutral: *in the well / trench*. But in addition, its referent is *closure-neutral,* i.e., indifferent to whether the curved plane leaves an opening or is wholly closed: *in the bowl / ball*. And it is *discontinuity-neutral,* i.e., indifferent to whether the curved plane is solid or gapped: *in the bell jar / birdcage*. These last two properties would form a proper part of language's topological system, whereas they are strictly excluded from mathematical topology.
10. In many cases, a language favors only one such direction, having much lexicalization with notion A and simple grammatical means for reaching notion B, but in the reverse direction having only little lexicalization and complex grammatical forms. Languages differ typologically in the directions they favor. This issue will not be taken up here, but is treated at length in Talmy (1985a).
11. Shifts are actually one member of a *set* of "reconciliation processes" – including blends, juxtapositions, schema-juggling, and blockage – that can be triggered by the association of a grammatical and a lexical form with incompatible structural specifications. In the non-shift processes, the grammatical specification does not take precedence over the lexical one, but plays an equal role with it. Of all these processes, this paper treats mostly shifts, but an additional number are discussed in Talmy (1977).
12. In addition to space and time, language represents other conceptual dimensions that also belong to the present category. For an example, recall from Section 1 that *this* and *that* specify a partition drawn through space – and can do so through time as well – and indicate that a referent entity is on the same or the other side of the partition as the speaker. Now consider the English pronouns *you* and *they* in their indefinite usage (akin to German *man* or French *on).* These also specify a partition, but one drawn through "identificational space", understood as a new conceptual dimension.

They indicate, respectively, that 'the average person' is or is not identified with the speaker in some relevant respect, i.e., is on the same or the other side of the identificational partition as the speaker. Thus, a person who smokes that is visiting a new neighborhood can ask a passer-by about the purchase of cigarettes with *you,* but about the sale of cigarettes with *they:*

(i) Where can you buy cigarettes around here?
Where do they sell cigarettes around here?

But a person looking for a location to open a tobacco shop would ask a business consultant in the neighborhood about purchases and sales with the reverse assignment of *you* and *they:*

(ii) Where can you sell cigarettes around here?
Where do they buy cigarettes around here?

13. It is true that there are the traditional terms "semelfactive" and "iterative" referring, respectively, to one and more than one instantiation of an event. But there is no real equivalent to number: "aspect" includes too much else about the temporal structure of action. And in any case, none of the traditional terms refers generically to both the dimensions.
14. The mechanism actually resorted to in many such cases, including that of *tear,* is the use of the plural, as in:
(i) Tears flowed through that channel in Hades.
There seems to be a sequence of cognitive operations here in getting from a bounded to an unbounded quantity. Speculatively, the bounded quantity is first treated as a uniplex entity, it is then multiplexed, the resultant entities are conceived as spatially juxtaposed, and their boundaries are lastly effaced, thereby creating an unbounded continuum.
15. The present category may be prone to confusion with the preceding one. Contributory here is the normal meaning range of *continuous,* which as easily covers 'boundlessness' as it does 'internal seamlessness'. However, the two categories can vary independently. Thus, in the preceding section, the lexical examples given for unboundedness, *water* and *sleep,* happened also to be internally continuous; but the same demonstration of unboundedness could have been made with internally discrete examples like *timber* and *breathe.*
In general, unbounded forms share many properties, whether continuous or discrete. Thus, mass nouns and plural count nouns, both unbounded, share many syntactic characteristics not shared by singular count nouns, e.g.:
(i) a / every – book / *ink / *books;
(ii) all / a lot of / more / some [unstressed] / 0 [generic] – ink / books / *book; 0 ['progressively more'] (e.g., *The machine consumed ink / books / *book for an hour.*)
16. For schematizing action along the one-dimensional time axis, an adaptation of the two-dimensional A', B', A, and B diagrams would be necessary – and can be readily visualized.
17. The lexical types for several of these intersections, it should be noted, do have traditional terms. Thus, nominal forms of the a, A or A', and B' types, respectively, have been called count nouns, collective nouns, and mass nouns. And verbal forms of the a

and B' types, respectively, have been called punctual and durative verbs. The matrix presented here augments, systematizes, and generalizes the traditional notions.

18. This category can be considered a generalization over the earlier category of "state of boundedness" by the inclusion of the "uniplexity" notion. It can in turn itself be generalized – becoming the category *"pattern* of extension" – by the further inclusion of such notions as a quantity bounded at one end but unbounded at the other (see Talmy 1983).
19. This category clearly patterns with the preceding five within a single system of notions, one that would be an expansion or generalization over "disposition of a quantity".
20. Our main purpose here is to note the shift in structural distribution type. The shift in content will doubtless prove part of a larger pattern as well, but this is not yet worked out.
21. The category of axiality can be seen as an extension of the preceding category, pattern of distribution. The two categories address temporal stasis or change, involving both spatial relations (e.g., *fall* there, *past the border* here) and qualitative states (e.g., *die/flash, awake/asleep* there, *sick/well* here). But where the preceding category focused on discrete states, the present category elaborates the notion of a scalar quantity functioning in conjunction with a discrete state. Due to their structural character, these two categories pattern together with all the categories after "dimension" as part of a single broad conceptual system of "structural schematization", described below in Section 2.14., and are thereby distinguished from the categories described next, which belong to different conceptual systems.
22. The use of the perfect here points to a principal function of perfect forms in general: They can indicate the temporal counterpart of matter located within a bounded extent of space, of the type seen in (i). That is, a sentence containing the perfect, as in (ii), suggests a paraphrase like that in (iii), which is homologous with (i):
    (i) There were 5 aspirins on the table.
    (ii) I have taken 5 aspirins in the last hour.
    (iii) There were 5 aspirin-takings in the last hour.
    (In support of this interpretation, as pointed out to me by Peyton Todd, the perfect seems always to involve a temporal span bounded at both ends.)
23. All three notions here – (a) identity of a quantity, (b) portion-excerpting from that quantity, (c) configuration of that portion – can be respectively represented by three distinct NPs together in a construction, as in:
    (i) a clustering (c) of a set (b) of trees (a).
    Many lexical items conflate the specification of two or all of these notions at once. Thus, conflating (c) and (b) is a *cluster* 'a clustering configuration of a set' and a *drop* 'a small globular form of an amount (of a liquid)'. A lexical item conflating all three notions is a *tear* 'drop of lachrymal fluid'. (See Talmy 1985a for a general treatment of "conflation".)
24. For the plural form *oysters*, the plural form *siphons* is ambiguous as to whether there are one or more siphons per oyster. All the other combinations unambiguously indicate the number of siphons per oyster. Thus, the exemplar form is always unambiguous in this regard – one of its advantages over the full-complement form. This same arrangement holds through the list.
25. The difference between *each* and *every* arising in this analysis can now be added to

those observed elsewhere (e.g., Vendler 1968). *Each* is the exemplar counterpart of the full-complement expression *all the,* but not of *all* without *the.* Thus, **Each oyster has a siphon* cannot function as a generic assertion. *Every* is not as unilaterally aligned in this way, but does serve more naturally as the counterpart of *all* without *the.*

26. One more pair can be added to this list by adjoining two complementary unpaired forms from two different languages. The English form *some,* as in *some friends of mine*, is a full-complement form requiring the plural and has no exemplar counterpart in the singular. The corresponding Italian form *qualche*, as in *qualche amico mio*, requires the singular and lacks a plural counterpart.
27. Though the grammatical complex in (48b) is determinative in setting the role-number as monadic, a trace of the verb's original scene-division type does remain. In the CR, the metaphoric suggestion of a dyad is blended in, as if both 'host' and 'guest' are together present in the "I", perhaps as separate subparts of the single person. For this reason, (48b) is not the complete semantic equal of (48c). Such blending is, beside shifting, another major process of reconciliation between incompatible specifications, referred to in note 11.
28. Clearly, the language-related faculty of the brain evolved to its present character in the presence of other already existing cognitive domains, including that of vision, and no doubt developed in interaction with their mechanisms of functioning, perhaps incorporating some of these.

## References

Bennett, David C.
1975 *Spatial and Temporal Uses of English Prepositions. An Essay in Stratificational Semantics.* London: Longman.

Boas, Franz
1938 Language. In *General Anthropology*, Franz Boas (ed.), 124–145. Boston: Heath & Co.

Bybee, Joan L.
1985 *Morphology: A Study of the Relation between Meaning and Form.* Amsterdam/Philadelphia: John Benjamins.

diSessa, Andrea
1988 Knowledge in pieces. In *Constructivism in the Computer Age*, George Forman and Peter Pufall (eds.), 49–70. Hillsdale, N.J.: Erlbaum.

Dixon, Robert M. W.
1972 *The Dyirbal Language of North Queensland.* London: Cambridge University Press.

Fillmore, Charles J.
1975 An Alternative to Checklist Theories of Meaning. *Proceedings of the First Annual Meeting of the Berkeley Linguistics Society* 123–131.

Gentner, Dedre, and Albert L. Stevens (eds.)
1982 *Mental Models*. Hillsdale, N.J.: Erlbaum.

Gibson, James J.
1966 *The Senses Considered as Perceptual Systems*. Boston: Houghton Mifflin.

Gruber, Jeffrey S.
1965 Studies in Lexical Relations. Doctoral dissertation, MIT. Reprinted as part of *Lexical Structures in Syntax and Semantics*. Amsterdam: North-Holland, 1976.

Herskovits, Annette
1986 *Language and Spatial Cognition: An Interdisciplinary Study of the Prepositions in English*. Cambridge: Cambridge University Press.

Jackendoff, Ray
1977 Toward a cognitively viable semantics. In *Georgetown University Round Table on Languages and Linguistics*, Clea Rameh (ed.), 59–80. Washington, D.C.: Georgetown Unversity Press.
1983 *Semantics and Cognition*. Cambridge, MA: MIT Press.
1987 *Consciousness and the Computational Mind*. Cambridge, MA: MIT Press.

Jakobson, Roman
1971 Boas' view of grammatical meaning. *Selected Writings of Roman Jakobson*, vol. 2: *Word and Language*, 489–496. The Hague: Mouton.

Kellogg, Rhoda
1970 *Analyzing Children's Art*. Palo Alto: Mayfield.

Lakoff, George
1987 *Women, Fire, and Dangerous Things: What Categories Reveal about the Mind*. Chicago/London: University of Chicago Press.

Langacker, Ronald W.
1986 An introduction to Cognitive Grammar. *Cognitive Science* 10: 1–40.
1987 *Foundations of Cognitive Grammar*. Vol. 1: *Theoretical Prerequisites*. Stanford, CA: Stanford University Press.

Marr, David
1982 *Vision*. San Francisco: Freeman & Co.

Morrow, Daniel
1986 Grammatical morphemes and conceptual structure in discourse processing. *Cognitive Science* 10: 423–455.

Neisser, Ulrich
1967 *Cognitive Psychology*. New York: Meredith.

Palmer, Stephen
1983 The psychology of perceptual organization: A transformational approach. In *Human and Machine Vision*, Jacob Beck, Barbara Hope, and Azriel Rosenfeld (eds.), 269–339. New York: Academic Press.

Sapir, Edward
1921 *Language*. New York: Harcourt, Brace & Company.

Slobin, Dan I. and Ayhan A. Aksu
1982 Tense, aspect and modality in the use of the Turkish evidential. In *Tense – Aspect: Between Semantics and Pragmatics*, Paul Hopper (ed.), 185–200. Amsterdam/Philadelphia: John Benjamins.

Slobin, Dan I.

1985 Crosslinguistic evidence for the language-making capacity. In *The Crosslinguistic Study of Language Acquisition*, vol. 2, Dan I. Slobin (ed.), 1157–1256. Hillsdale, N.J.: Erlbaum.

Talmy, Leonard

1972 Semantic Structures in English and Atsugewi. Doctoral dissertation, University of California, Berkeley.

1975 Semantics and syntax of motion. In *Syntax and Semantics,* vol. 4, John P. Kimball (ed.), 181–238. New York: Academic Press.

1976 Semantic causative types. In *The Grammar of Causative Constructions* (Syntax and Semantics 6.), Masayoshi Shibatani (ed.), 43–116. New York: Academic Press.

1977 Rubber-sheet cognition in language. *Papers from the Thirteenth Regional Meeting of the Chicago Linguistic Society* 612–628.

1978a The relation of grammar to cognition – a synopsis. *Proceedings of TINLAP* 2 (*Theoretical Issues in Natural Language Processing*), David Waltz (ed.), 14–24. New York: Association for Computing Machinery.

1978b Figure and ground in complex sentences. In *Universals of Human Language,* vol. 4: *Syntax,* Joseph H. Greenberg (ed.), 625–649. Stanford, CA: Stanford University Press.

1978c Relations between subordination and coordination. In *Universals of Human Language*, vol. 4: *Syntax*, Joseph H. Greenberg (ed.), 487–513. Stanford, CA: Stanford University Press.

1982 Borrowing semantic space: Yiddish verb prefixes between Germanic and Slavic. *Proceedings of the Eighth Annual Meeting of the Berkeley Linguistics Society* 231–250.

1983 How language structures space. In *Spatial Orientation: Theory, Research, and Application,* Herbert Pick and Linda Acredolo (eds.), 225–282. New York: Plenum Press.

1985a Lexicalization patterns: semantic structure in lexical forms. In *Language Typology and Syntactic Description,* vol. 3: *Grammatical Categories and the Lexicon*, Timothy Shopen (ed.), 57–149. Cambridge: Cambridge University Press.

1985b Force dynamics in language and thought. *Papers from the Parasession on Causatives and Agentivity at the Twenty-First Regional Meeting of the Chicago Linguistic Society* 293–337.

Ultan, Russell

1978 Some general characteristics of interrogative systems. In *Universals of Human Language*, vol. 4: *Syntax*, Joseph H. Greenberg (ed.), 211–248. Stanford, CA: Stanford University Press.

Vendler, Zeno

1968 Each and Every, Any and All. In *Linguistics and Philosophy*, 70–96. Ithaca: Cornell University Press.

Whorf, Benjamin L.

1956 *Language, Thought, and Reality.* John B. Carroll (ed.). Cambridge, MA: MIT Press.

# Chapter 3
# Radial network

## Cognitive topology and lexical networks*

*Claudia Brugman and George Lakoff*

This article is a rather long and detailed study of a polysemous lexical item – the English word *over* – paying specific attention to the character of the relations among its senses. Polysemy is a subtype of lexical ambiguity, contrasting with homonymy, wherein a single lexical form is associated with more than one meaning, and those meanings are unrelated. In the case of polysemy, one word is taken as having senses which are related. The distinction is an important one for the resolution of lexical ambiguity, for, as we will show in the bulk of this article, the way semantic information is stored in a lexical entry may differ depending on whether that lexical entry is taken as reflecting homonymy or polysemy. We will show that the common practice of giving a list of meanings of ambiguous items is neither the only way, nor, for polysemous words, the most efficient way, of storing such semantic information. We will argue instead that a network-style mode of storage is cognitively real, and that this allows for a maximum of shared, and otherwise related, information between senses.

Network-style representation is common in many areas of AI. But we use it here not by notational fiat but as part of a much more general conception of categorization, explored at length in Lakoff (1987). That work provides detailed empirical evidence and theoretical argument against the classical view of categories as collections of objects characterized by lists of necessary-and-sufficient conditions, and in favor of an enriched view of categories. On that view, categories may contain a great deal of internal structure – for instance, that one member of a category should be more exemplary of that category than some other member; that the boundaries of the category are not always clear-cut; that categories may be characterized in part with respect to their contrast with other categories. The category structure utilized here is called a "radial" structure, with a central member and a network of links to other members. Each noncentral member of the category is either a variant of the central member or is a variant on a variant The theoretical claim being made is that a polysemous lexical item is a radial category of senses.

Originally published in *Lexical Ambiguity Resolution: Perspectives from Psycholinguistics, Neuropsychology, and Artificial Intelligence,* Steven L. Small, Garrison W. Cottrell, and Michael K. Tanenhaus (eds.), 477–508. San Mateo, CA: Morgan Kaufmann. Reprinted with permission from Elsevier.

What is important for our purposes is that the kind of network structure found here is not made up ad hoc to characterize this set of facts. Instead, this is a common category structure that occurs in domains other than the lexicon.

There is an important consequence of using the general theory of radial categories to characterize polysemy. In the general theory, the links between members of the network are not arbitrary. The theory of radial categories comes with a characterization of possible link types. In the case of polysemy, the link types are the types of relations linking the senses of the word. In general, some of the links may involve shared information, some may involve the relation between a general and a specific case, and some may be metaphoric. In the case under discussion, most of the links are what we have called "image-schema transformations." But overall there is only a small number of types of relations between senses of words, and this study is one of many that is being carried out in an attempt to figure out what they are.

Such studies are significant in a number of respects. They show that the relations between senses are not arbitrary, but are rather *principled, systematic,* and *recurrent* throughout the lexicon. Moreover, the relationships are natural, in the sense that they are either relationships that arise naturally within the cognitive system, or they are characterized by metaphors that have an independent existence in the conceptual system. From an explanatory point of view, the natural and independently motivated character of the links allows us to explain why polysemy should exist as a general phenomenon. From the point of view of language processing studies, it suggests that the lexicon has a structure that is made use of in processing.

## 1. Cognitive topology versus semantic features

The traditional mode of representing lexical information, whether in linguistics or in cognitive science, has been the use of semantic features. Semantic features arise in general within the symbol manipulation paradigm in cognitive science: they are finitary symbols with no inherent meaning, but are to be made meaningful by being connected to things in the world. The features have no inherent structure, and any relationships among them are to be specified by a calculus characterizing permissible operations on the symbols.

One reason that we have chosen the example of *over* is that it demonstrates the inadequacy of feature analyses and shows the need for an oriented cognitive topology, which characterizes structures oriented relative to the human body that apply generally to spatial situations, structures like paths, bounded regions, tops, etc. Structures in a cognitive topology differ from semantic features in a number of ways: they are inherently meaningful (arising from sensory-motor operations), they have an inherent structure, they are analog rather than finitary, and the relationships among them arise naturally via the operation of the human sensory-motor system.

The evidence in this paper suggests that there are two respects in which cognitive topology is superior to feature analysis for *over.*

> The topological properties of the concepts are necessary to characterize "image-schema transformations" in terms that are cognitively natural, rather than in terms of an arbitrary calculus.

We will discuss this issue at the end of the paper. To facilitate the comparison between topological and feature analyses, we will use both types of representation in this paper. The drawings indicate the topological representation, while the names (such as 1.VX.C.E) indicate feature representations. We will demonstrate that, while feature representations might be useful in computer simulations, only topological representations characterize the cognitive reality of the meanings of words like *over*:

> Topological concepts are needed in order to account for how prepositions can be used to characterize an infinity of visual scenes.

The semantics of even the most basic spatial senses of *over* is such that a feature analysis simply will not do. Take, for example, the sense of *over* in *The ball went over the net.* Given a scene with a ball moving with respect to a net, there is an infinity of trajectories of the ball relative to the net that *over* will fit and another infinity that it will not fit. To characterize those two infinities, one needs concepts that generalize over possible trajectories and properties of the landscape: this sense of *over* requires two bounded regions, and a path from one to the other that is oriented vertically relative to the net. In short, what is needed is an oriented cognitive topology with elementary structures (paths, bounded regions), orientations (vertical), and means of fitting them together into an overall gestalt.

Our reason for going into this issue in such detail is as follows: It is sometimes claimed that the Symbol Manipulation Paradigm is necessary to account adequately for natural language. In fact, the reverse is true. The Symbol Manipulation Paradigm cannot account for natural language semantics. For a lengthy discussion, see Langacker (1987).

## 2. Two levels of prototype structure

The lexical representation of *over* actually contains two levels of topological structure. First, each sense of *over* is a complex topological structure. Second, all the senses together form a radial category, which is itself a complex topological structure. It is crucial to distinguish these two levels: The first is the level of semantic content and the second is the level at which that content is structured in the lexicon.

Correspondingly, there are two levels of prototype structure – one at each level. At the second level, the level of lexical structure, the central sense in the radial category is the prototypical sense of *over.* But at the first level, the level of semantic content for each particular sense of *over,* the nature of prototypicality is quite different. At this level, prototypicality concerns the degree of fit of some real-world relation to an individual sense of the word. For example, consider *The plane flew over the mountain.* The best fit is where the path goes right above the center of the mountain. As the path of flight moves away from the center of the mountain, the degree of fit lessens.

This introduction does not provide the whole story: we will not fully motivate the independent existence of all principles that relate senses, and we cannot do justice to the question of how contrasting lexical categories and the conventionalization of boundaries figure in a full semantic description of this item. The chief concern here is to provide a detailed example of how a lexical ambiguity of a specific kind can be given a reasonably complete description and to show the kinds of theoretical apparatus required for that description. To sum up: the critical features of this description are that feature-based descriptions are inadequate, that a topological representation appears to be needed, and that the senses of a polysemous item form a radially-structured lexical network.

## 3. The problem

To get some sense of the problem, let us consider a handful of the senses of *over:*

The painting is *over* the mantel.
The plane is flying *over* the hill.
Sam is walking *over* the hill.
Sam lives *over* the hill.
The wall fell *over.*
Sam turned the page *over.*
Sam turned *over.*
She spread the tablecloth *over* the table.
The guards were posted all *over* the hill.
The play is *over.*
Do it *over,* but don't *overdo* it.

Look *over* my corrections, and don't overlook any of them.
You made *over* a hundred errors.

Even this small number of examples shows enormous complexity. The problem Brugman undertook was how to describe all these senses and the relations among them. The analysis we will be presenting is a minor refinement of the semantic aspect of the earlier analysis. Let us begin with what was found to be the central sense.

## 4. The above-across sense

The central sense of *over* combines elements of both *above* and *across* (see Figure 18.1). In this example, the plane is understood as a trajector (TR) oriented relative to a landmark (LM). TR and LM are generalizations of the concepts figure and ground (Langacker 1983, 1987). In this case the landmark is unspecified. The arrow in the figure represents the PATH that the TR is moving along. The LM is what the plane is flying over. The PATH is *above* the LM. The dotted lines indicate the extreme boundaries of the landmark. The PATH goes all the way *across* the landmark from the boundary on one side to the boundary on the other. Although the figure indicates noncontact between the TR and LM, the central sense is neutral on the issue of contact. As we will see shortly, there are instances with contact and instances without contact. In this respect the schema cannot be drawn with complete accuracy. Any drawing would have to indicate contact or the lack of it. The image-schema is neutral, and that is part of what makes it schematic. What we have here is an abstract schema that cannot itself be imaged concretely, but which structures images. We will return below to the question of what it means for an image-schema to structure an image.

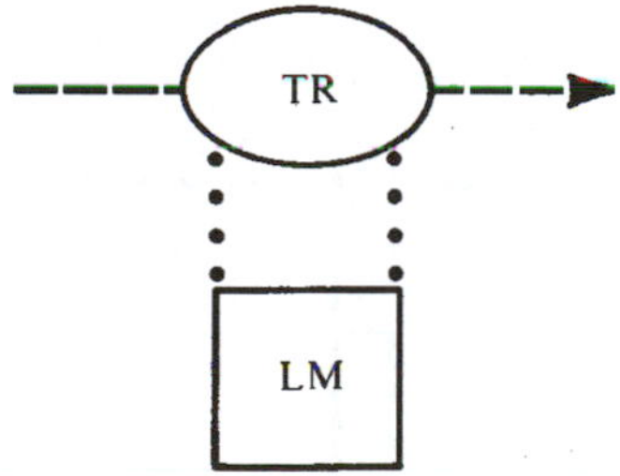


*Figure 1.* The plane flew over. Name: Schema 1

Let us now turn to some special cases of the schema in Figure 1. These are instances of the schema that are arrived at by adding information, in particular, by further specifying the nature of the landmark and by specifying whether or not there is contact. We will consider four kinds of landmark specifications: (1) LM is a point, that is, the landmark is viewed as a point with no internal structure. (2) LM is extended, that is, the landmark extends over a distance or area. (3) LM is vertical. (4) LM is both extended and vertical. For each such case, we will consider two further specifications: contact between TR and LM, and noncontact. Each schema will be named using the following abbreviations: X: extended, V: vertical, C: contact, NC: no contact. Thus, the schema name '1.VX.C' stands for the special case of schema 1 in which the landmark is both vertical and extended (VX) and there is contact (C) between the LM and TR.

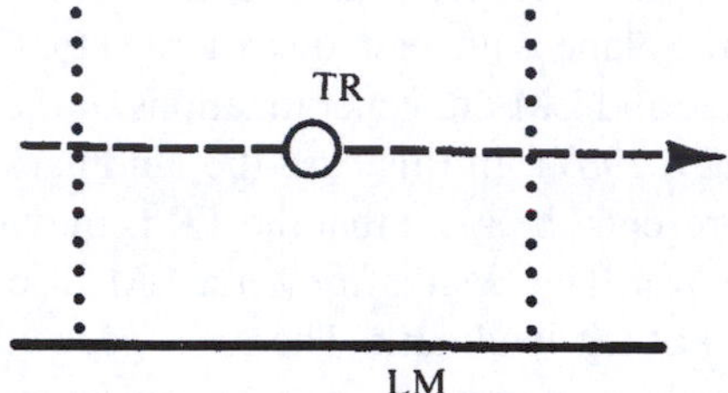


*Figure 2.* The bird flew over the yard. Name: Schema 1.X.NC

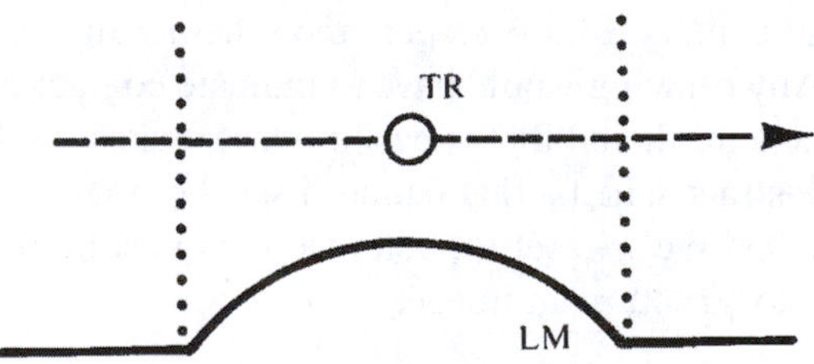


*Figure 3.* The plane flew over the hill. Name: Schema 1.VX.NC

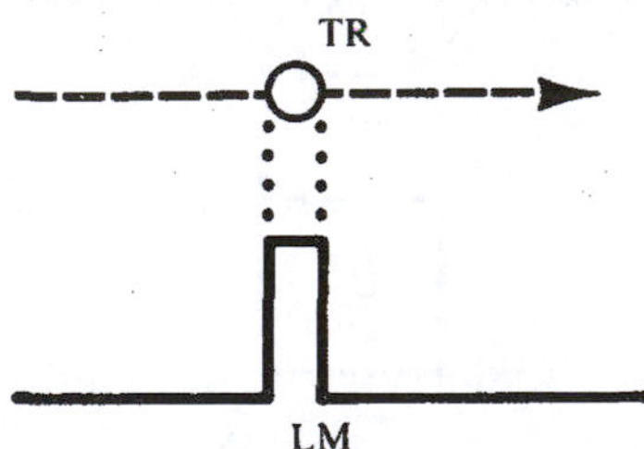


*Figure 4.* The bird flew over the wall. Name: Schema 1.V.NC

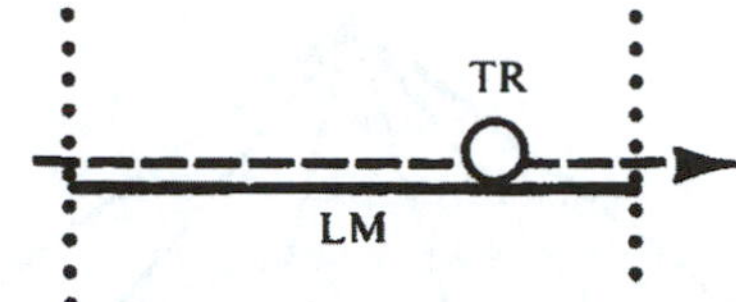


*Figure 5.* Sam drove over the bridge. Name: Schema 1.X.C

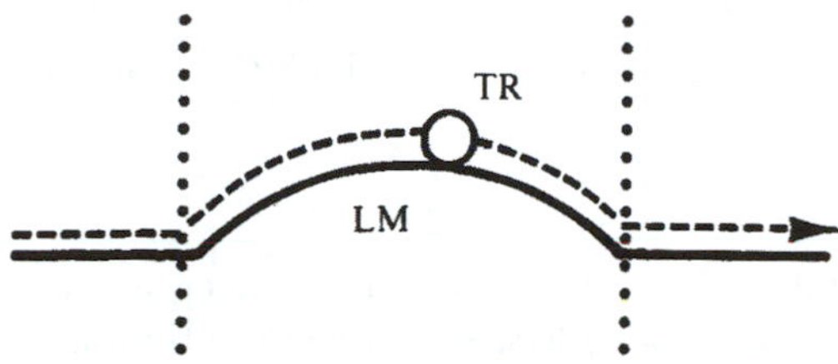


*Figure 6.* Sam walked over the hill. Name: Schema 1.VX.C

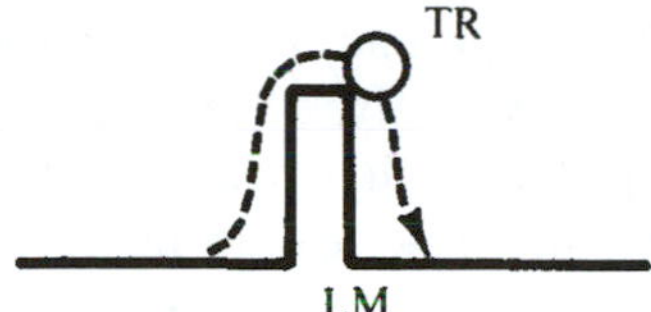


*Figure 7.* Sam climbed over the wall. Name: Schema 1.V.C

The schemas in Figures 2–7 can be related by a diagram in Figure 8.

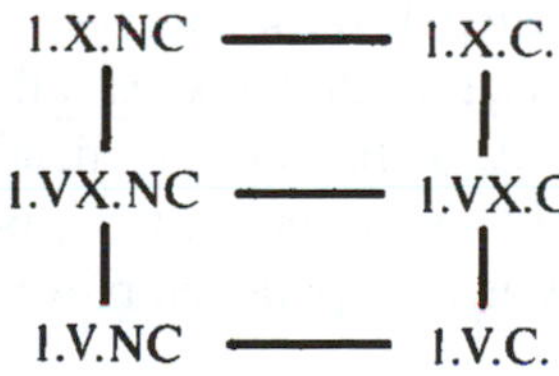


*Figure 8.* Links among schemas

These links indicate similarity. Thus, all the schemas are linked, as are all the schemas that share noncontact. Moreover, each pair of schemas that share everything except for the contact parameter are linked. In addition, they are all linked to schema 1 (see Figure 1), since they are all instances of that schema.

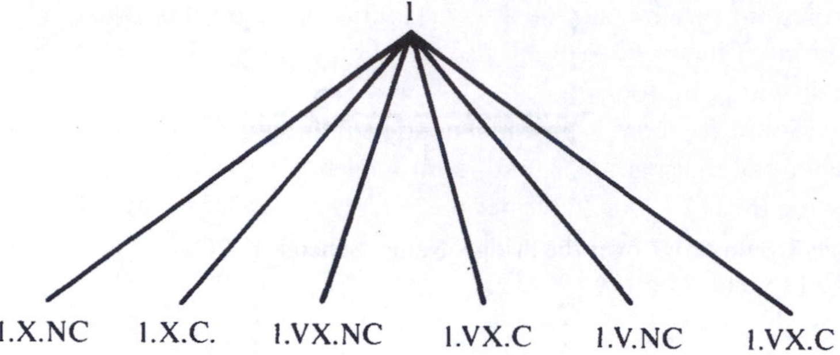


*Figure 9.*

The schemas in Figures 2–7 can be viewed in two equivalent ways. Take, for example, a sentence like *Sam walked over the hill* in Figure 6. We can think of *over* in this sentence as being represented by the minimally-specified schema 1 of Figure 1, and we can think of the additional information as being added by the object and the verb. Thus, a hill is vertical and extended (VX) and walking requires contact (C) with the ground. Let us refer to this as the *minimal specification interpretation*. Equivalently, we can view the minimally-specified *over* of Figure 1 as generating all the fully-specified schemas of Figure 2–7. On this *full specification interpretation,* we can think of the *over* in *Sam walked over the hill* as having the full specification of schema 1.VX.C in Figure 7. The verb *walk* would then match the contact (C) specification, and the direct object *hill* would match the vertical extended (VX) specification. The difference is whether the verb and direct object *add* the VX and C information or whether they *match* it.

These two interpretations make slightly different claims about the lexical representation of *over* in these sentences. On the minimal specification interpretation, only schema 1 exists in the lexicon; the other schemas all result from information added by the verb and direct object. On the full specification interpretation, there is a lexical representation for all these schemas; the more specific schemas are generated by schema 1 plus the general parameters we have discussed: C–NC and X–VX–V.

On the basis of what we have said so far, these two interpretations are completely equivalent; there is no empirical difference between them, and no a priori reason to choose between them. There is, however, additional evidence that favors the full specification interpretation, and we will be citing it throughout the remainder of this case study. We will be arguing that the senses of *over* form a chain with schema 1 at the center. On the full specification interpretation, the schemas in Figures 2–7 are part of that chain. Some of those schemas form links to other senses. The existence of such links suggests that the full specification interpretation is correct. Consider the following case, where there is a focus on the end-point of the path. We will use the abbreviation E in naming schemas where there is end-point focus.

In Figure 10, there is an understood path that goes over the hill, and Sam lives at the end of that path. The end-point focus is not added by anything in the sentence, neither *hill,* nor *lives,* nor *Sam. Over* here has an additional sense which is one step away from schema 1.VX.C – a sense in which end-point focus (E) is added to yield schema 1.VX.C.E.

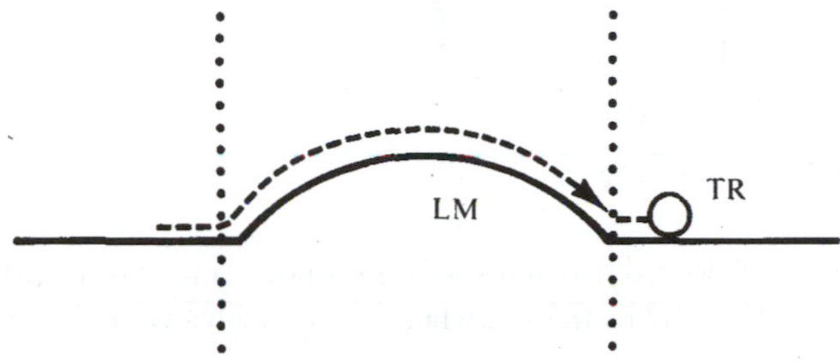


*Figure 10.* Sam lives over the hill. Name: Schema 1.VX.C.E

But end-point focus cannot be freely added to just any of the schemas in Figures 18.2–18.7. It can only be added to those with an extended landmark, as in Figure 18.11.

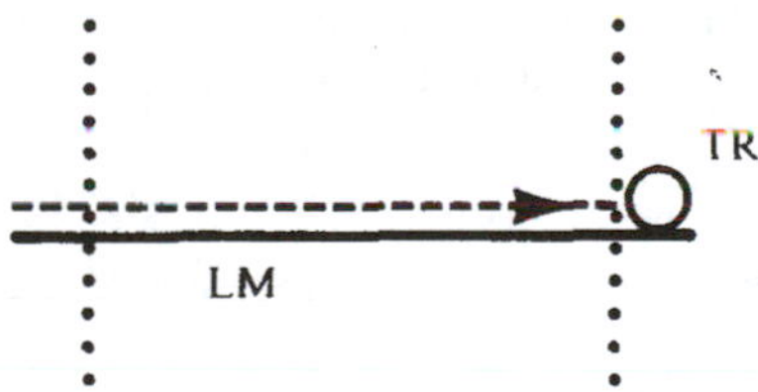


*Figure 11.* Sausalito is over the bridge. Name: Schema 1.X.C.E

In these cases, *over* has the sense of 'on the other side of' as a result of end-point focus. However, *over* does not in general mean 'on the other side of'. For example, sentences like *Sam lives over the wall* and *Sam is standing over the door,* if they occur at all, cannot mean that he lives, or is standing, on the other side of the door and the wall. And a sentence like *Sam is sitting over the spot,* can only mean that he is sitting *on* it, not that he is sitting on the other side of it. Thus there is no end-point focus schema corresponding to schema 1.V.C of Figure 6.

Assuming the full specification interpretation, we can extend the chain in Figure 8 to include the schemas in Figures 10 and 11, which is illustrated in Figure 12.

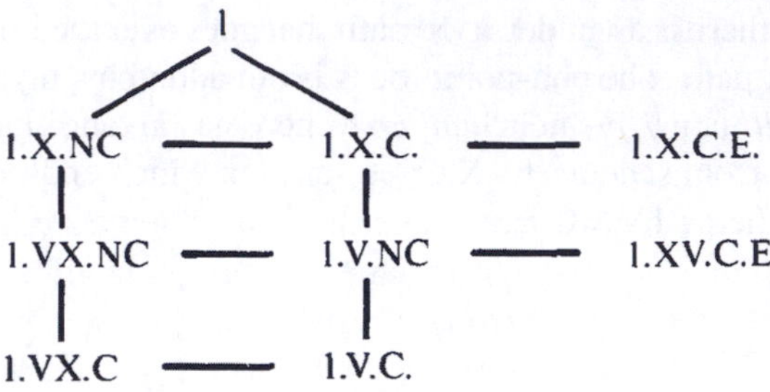


*Figure 12.* Links among schemas

So far, we have considered two types of links among schemas: *instance links* and *similarity links*. Here are examples, where '←' indicates an instance link and '↔' indicates a similarity link:

Instance link: 1 1 1.V.C
Similarity links: 1.VX.NC ↔ 1.VX.C

Thus, the link between schema 1 and schema 1.V.C is an instance link, with 1.V.C being an instance of 1. And the link between schema 1.VX.NC and schema 1.VX. C is a similarity link, where 1.VX and C are shared.

So far, we have looked only at instances of the *above-across* sense. And we have only looked at the least interesting links between schemas. Let us now turn to other senses and more interesting kinds of links.

## 5. The above sense

*Over* has a stative sense, with no PATH. It is roughly equivalent in meaning to *above* (see Figure 13).

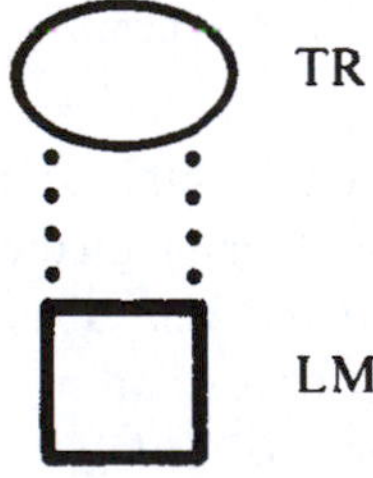


*Figure 13.* Hang the painting over the fireplace. Name: Schema 2

Schema 2 has no particular constraints on either the TR or LM. It is linked to schema 1 in that it has the TR above the LM. However, it differs from schema 1 in two respects: First, it has no PATH and no boundaries; in other words, the *across-sense* is missing. Second, it does not permit contact between the TR and LM. The no-contact requirement can be seen in examples like *The helicopter is hovering over the hill.* If the helicopter lands, it is no longer *over* the hill, it is *on* the hill.

From time to time, linguists have suggested that schema 2 is *the core meaning* of the preposition *over,* that is, that schema 2 is present in all the uses of *over* as a preposition. It should be clear from what we have seen so far that this is false. Since schema 2 requires no contact, it cannot be present in those cases where contact occurs, for example, in schema 1.X.C exemplified by *Sam drove over the bridge.* Schema 2 also does not occur in the cases of end-point focus, such as schema 1.VX.C.E, which is exemplified by *Sam lives over the hill.* In this case, the TR is not above the LM.

One of the instances of schema 2 is the case where the TR is one-dimensional (which we will abbreviate as 1DTR – see Figure 14).

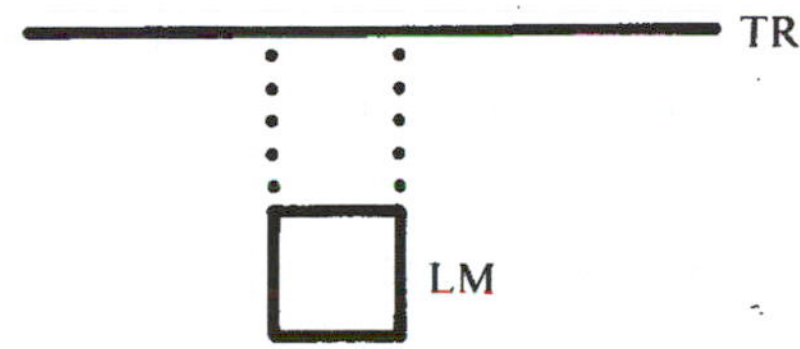


*Figure 14.* The power line streches over the yard. Name: Schema 2.1DTR

This schema is a minimal variant of schema 1.X.NC, exemplified by *The bird flew over the yard,* as shown in Figure 2. The extended path in Figure 2 corresponds to the one-dimensional solid trajector in Figure 14. We will call this kind of link between schemas a *transformational link.* This particular link between an extended path (X.P) and a one-dimensional trajector (1DTR) will be represented as:

X.P ↔ 1DTR

This relationship is not directly reflected in the naming system for schemas that we have adopted. However, we can state the relationship more systematically if we do a little renaming of a sort that reflects image-schema decompositions. Let us use ABV for the 'above' subschema. And let us use PATH (P) for the 'across' subschema. Schema 1 would be renamed ABV.P, and schema 1.X.NC of Figure

2 would be renamed ABV.NC.X.P. This name would reflect the fact that in this schema the TR is moving above (ABV) the LM, along a path (P), where the landmark is extended (X) and there is no contact between TR and LM (NC). Correspondingly, schema 2 would be renamed ABV.NC, and schema 2.1DTR in Figure 15 would be renamed ABV.NC.1DTR.

Schema 1.X.NC = ABV.NC.X.P
Schema 2.1DTR = ABV.NC.1DTR

This decomposition displays the relationship between the schemas directly. The schemas are transforms of one another, given the transformational link X.P ↔ 1DTR.

It is important to bear in mind the difference between similarity links and transformational links. In the case of similarity links, the link is defined by shared subschemas. In the relationship described above, there are, indeed, shared subschemas: both schemas contain ABV.NC. But the transformational link is not a matter of *shared* subschemas, but of *related* subschemas.

The links among the schemas that we have described so far can be represented by the following diagram in Figure 15.

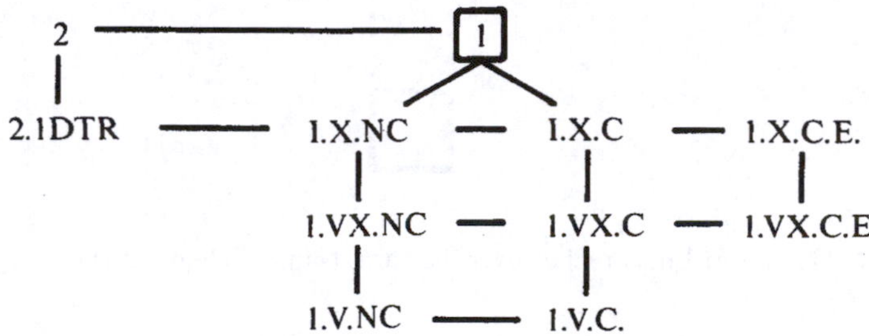


*Figure 15.* Links among schemas

## 6. The covering senses

There is a group of schemas for *over* that have to do with covering. This group is linked to the grid of Figure 15 in two ways. The basic covering schema is a variant of schema 2, where the TR is at least 2-dimensional and extends across the boundaries of the LM.

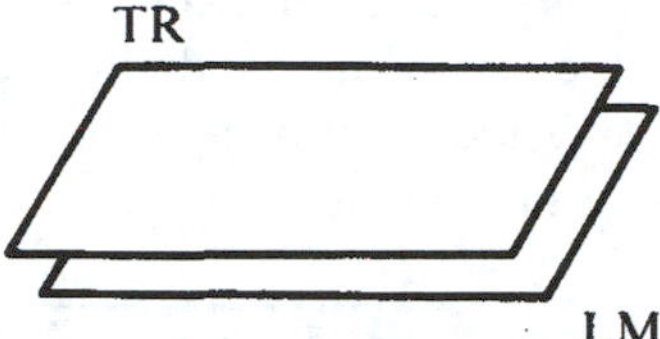


*Figure 16.* The board is over the hole. Name: Schema 3

There are two differences between schema 2 and schema 3. The first is that schema 2 is unspecified for the dimension of the trajector, while schema 3 must be at least 2-dimensional. But while schema 2 requires noncontact, schema 3 is neutral with respect to contact, allowing either contact or lack of it.

There is a minimal variant of schema 3 in which the TR moves to the position in schema 3. This schema is composed of schema 3 plus a path (P) indicating motion to the final position.

Schema 3.P.E (see Figure 17) is linked to schema 1. It shares motion of the TR above and across the LM. It also shares a lack of specification for contact. Schema 3.P.E differs from schema 1 in two ways. It is specified for the dimension of the trajector and it has end-point focus, which indicates that the final state is that of schema 3.

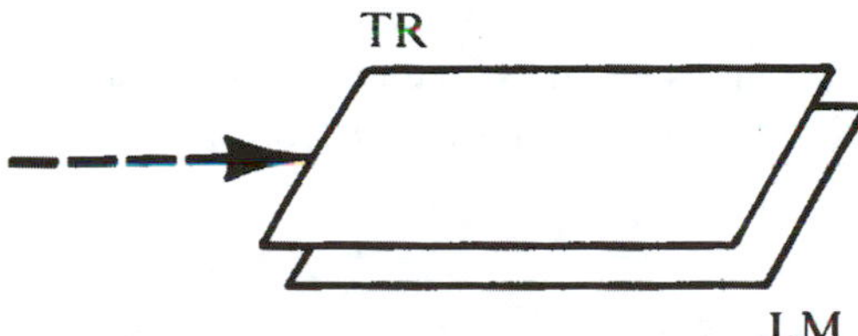


*Figure 17.* The city clouded over. Name: Schema 3.P.E.

There are two covering schemas in which *over* is paired with a mass quantifier that quantifies regions of the landmark, e.g., *all, most, a lot of, entire,* etc. The quantifier *all* may combine with *over* in this sense to form the unit *all over.* The first of these two schemas has a *multiplex* (MX) trajector, that is, a trajector made up of many individuals.

> He has freckles over most of his body.
> There are specks of paint all over the rug.
> There is sagebrush over the entire valley floor.

In these cases, the individuals – the individual hairs, specks of paint, and bushes – don't completely cover the part of the landmark quantified over. Rather, the landmark has small regions which jointly cover its surface (or most of it), and there is at least one trajector in each region.

*Figure 18.* The guards are posted all over the hill. Name: Schema 3.MX

The relationship between schema 3 and schema 3.MX (see Figure 18) is the relationship between a continuous region (or mass) and a multiplex entity. Such relationships are very common in language. Compare *cows* (multiplex) and *cattle* (mass). Quantifiers like *all* and *most* can occur with either masses (*all gold, most wine*) or multiplex entities (*all ducks, most trees*). The relationship between multiplex entities and masses is a natural visual relationship. Imagine a large herd of cows up close – close enough to pick out the individual cows. Now imagine yourself moving back until you can no longer pick out the individual cows. What you perceive is a mass. There is a point at which you cease making out the individuals and start perceiving a mass. It is this perceptual experience upon which the relationship between multiplex entities and masses rests. The image transformation that relates multiplex entities and masses characterizes the link between schema 3 and schema 3.MX. We can characterize that transformational link as follows:

MX ↔ MS

There is a second covering schema for *over* in which *over* is associated with a mass quantifier. It is a minimal variant on schema 3.MX in which the points representing the multiplex entity of 3.MX are joined to form a path (P) which 'covers' the landmark. Examples are:

I walked all over the hill.
We've hiked over most of the Sierras.
I've hitchhiked over the entire country.

We can represent this schema in Figure 19. This schema is linked to schema 3.MX by an image transformation that forms a path through a collection of points. We will represent this transformational linkage as:

MX ↔ MX.P

Schema 3.MX.P is also minimally linked to schema 3.P. In schema 3.P, the landmark is gradually covered as the trajector moves along the path. This is also true in schema 3.MX.P.

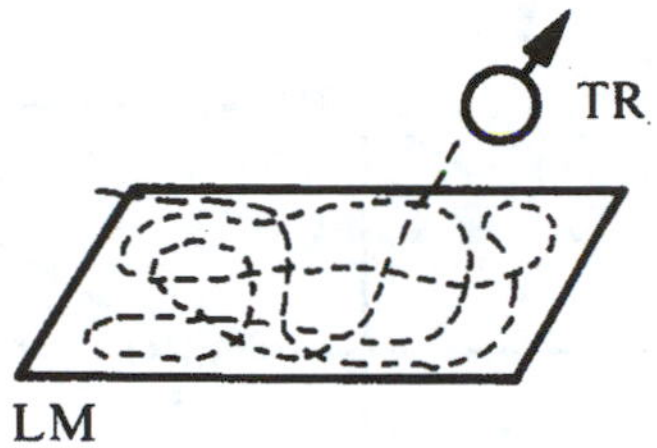


*Figure 19.* I walked all over the hill. Name: Schema 3.MX.P

The covering schemas all have variants in which the TR need not be above (that is, higher than) the LM. In all cases, however, there must be an understood viewpoint from which the TR is blocking accessibility of vision to at least some part of the landmark.

> There was a veil over her face.
> As the rain came down, it froze and ice spread all over the windshield.
> There were flies all over the ceiling.
> The spider had crawled all over the ceiling.

We will refer to these as *rotated* (RO) schemas, though with no suggestion that there is actual mental rotation degree-by-degree involved. One might suggest that instead of rotation from the vertical, there is simply a lack of specification of orientation. If there were, we would expect that the contact restrictions would be the same in all orientations. However, they are not. The rotated versions of the MX schemas – 3.MX and 3.MX.P – require contact, while the unrotated versions do not. Here are some typical examples that illustrate the distinction:

> Superman flew all over downtown Metropolis. (TR above LM, noncontact)
> *Superman flew all over the canyon walls. (TR not above LM, noncontact)
> Harry climbed all over the canyon walls. (TR not above LM, contact)

Thus, Superman's flying *alongside* the canyon walls does not constitute flying *over* them.

We will add 'RO' to the names of the unrotated covering schemas to yield names for the corresponding covering schemas. The rotated covering schemas have the following names: 3.RO, 3.P.RO, 3.MX.RO, and 3.MX.P.RO. Figure 20 is a diagram indicating the links among the covering schemas and the links to the other *over* schemas. And Figure 21 indicates the overall linkage among the schemas discussed so far.

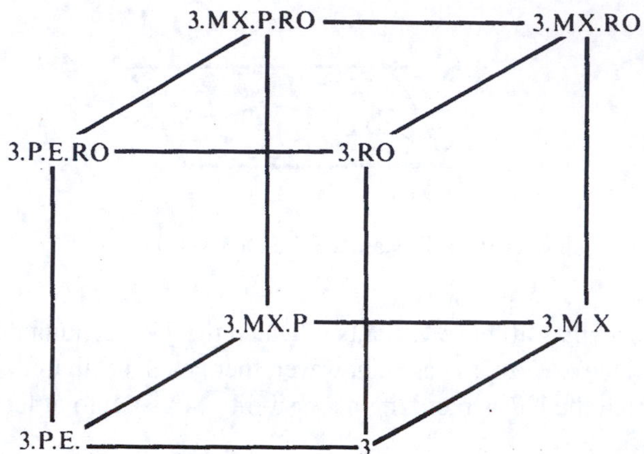


*Figure 20.* Links among covering schemas

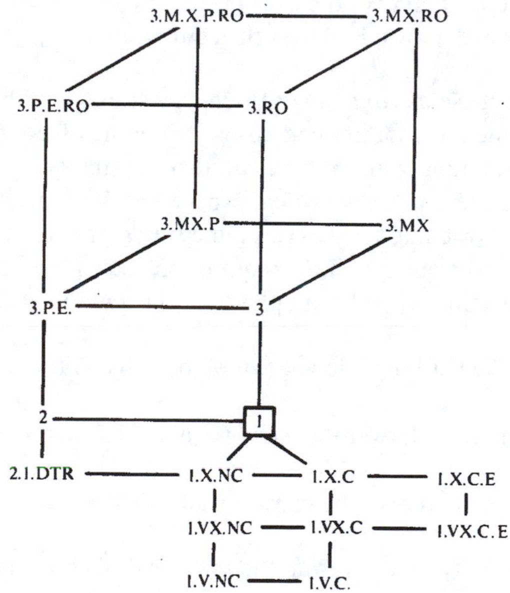


*Figure 21.* Links among schemas discussed so far

## 7. The reflexive schemas

Perhaps the most remarkable of the discoveries made by Lindner (1981, 1982) was the discovery of *reflexive trajectors.* The concept can be illustrated most simply using the example of *out.* The simplest use of *out* occurs in cases like *Harry ran out of the room.* We can represent this by the schema in Figure 22.

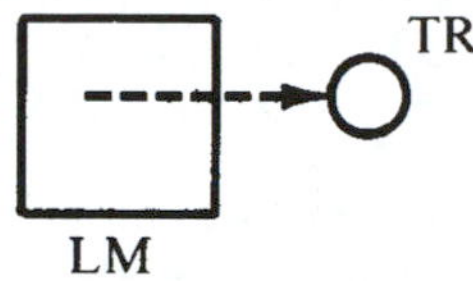


*Figure 22.* Harry ran out of the room.

In this diagram the container (the room) is the landmark, and the trajector (Harry) moves from the interior to the exterior of the room. But this schema won't do for cases of *out* like:

The syrup spread out.
The posse spread out.
They stretched out the taffy.
We rolled out the carpet.

Here the relevant trajectors are the syrup, the posse, the taffy, and the carpet. But they are not moving *out* with respect to any other landmark. Take the case of the syrup. Pour some syrup on a table. It will have a certain outer boundary at first; but the boundary moves. Some of the syrup that was inside the initial boundary is now outside that initial boundary. The syrup, or at least part of it, is moving 'out' relative to its own prior boundary. We can schematize this in Figure 23.

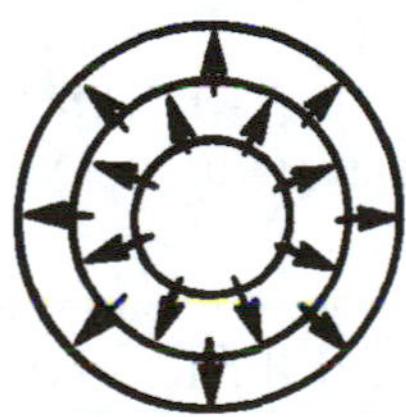

*Figure 23.* The syrup spread out.

In short, the syrup is its own landmark: TR = LM. Such a relation between a landmark and a trajector is called *reflexive*. Since there is only one entity under consideration, it is referred to as a *reflexive trajector.*

The '=' in 'TR = LM' is not strict identity; it is 'identity' of *part of* a bounded mass relative to itself as it *used to be* bounded. As we will see below, there are several ways in which 'TR = LM' can be realized. An important one is when parts of a single entity act as TR and other parts of the same entity act as LM. This kind of reflexive trajector occurs in the case of *over.* Consider examples like:

Roll the log over.

Here a major part (roughly half) of the log is moving above and across the rest. That is, half the log is acting as landmark and the rest as trajector. The same is true in a case like

Turn the paper over.

Both of these are variations on schema 1; they differ only in that LM = TR in the sense just described.

*Figure 24.* Roll the log over. Name: Schema 4

We can represent the schema for these cases in Figure 24. Schema 4 can be viewed as a transform of schema 1, with schema 4 adding the condition TR = LM. We will represent such a transformational link as

NRF $\leftrightarrow$ RF

where 'NRF' means "nonreflexive" and 'RF' means "reflexive". If we had chosen to name schema 4 according to its status as a variant of schema 1, we would have called it 1.RF.

The path of *over* in schema 4 traces a semi-circle above and across other parts of the thing being moved. We will refer to this as a *reflexive path.* There is a variant on schema 4 in which no part of the thing moving moves above or across any other part; instead, the entity as a whole traces the reflexive path. This occurs in cases like

The fence fell over.
Sam knocked over the lamp.

These are cases where the TR is initially vertical and moves so as to follow the last half of a reflexive path (RFP). The schema represented is as in Figure 25. The relationship between schemas 4 and 4.RFP can be stated as follows: In schema 4, half of the TR follows the whole reflexive path; in schema 4.RPF, all of the TR follows the last half of the reflexive path.

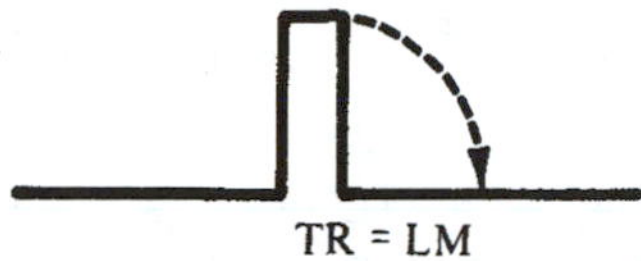


*Figure 25.* The fence fell over. Name: Schema 4.RFP

This schema is not only a variant of schema 4. It is also a minimal variant of one of the most common instances of schema 1, the instance that characterizes *over* in *The dog jumped over the fence.* In this case, there is a vertical landmark and the path of the trajector both begins and ends on the ground (G). This results in a semi-circular path (see Figure 26). If we take the reflexive transform of this schema, letting TR = LM, we get the schema of Figure 25 – schema 4.RFP. Thus, schema 4.RFP has close links to two other schemas.

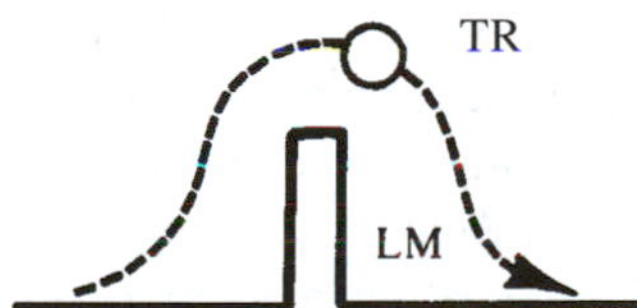


*Figure 26.* The dog jumped over the fence. Name: 1.V.NC.G

## 8. The excess schema

When *over* is used as a prefix, it can indicate excess, as in:

The bathtub overflowed.
I overate.
Don't overextend yourself.

The excess schema for *over* is a variation on one of the instances of schema 1, in particular, schema 1.X.C.E of Figure 11. In schema 1.X.C.E, there is an extended landmark; the trajector has moved across the boundaries of the landmark, and there is focus on the end-point, which is past the boundary. The excess schema has all these characteristics. It differs from schema 1.X.C.E in three respects. First, it is oriented vertically, with the end-point at the top. Second, it is understood as indicating amount via the MORE IS UP metaphor (see Lakoff and Johnson 1980). Third, the path is taken as indicating the course of an activity, via the ACTIVITY IS A JOURNEY metaphor. Fourth, the boundary point is taken as the upper limit of what is normal for that activity. Thus, being beyond that boundary point indicates excess.

The excess schema is thus not merely an image-schema, but a complex image-schema that makes use of an image-schema (schema 1.X.C.E), an orientation transformation from horizontal to vertical, two metaphors (MORE IS UP and AN ACTIVITY IS A JOURNEY), and propositional information about what is normal. In link diagrams, we will refer to the excess schema as schema 5.

## 9. The repetition schema

One of the most common uses of *over* is to indicate repetition, as in

Do it over.

*Over* here is used an adverb. As in the case of the *over* of excess, the *over* of repetition makes use of a complex schema built on an instance of schema 1, namely, schema 1.X.C. This schema has an extended landmark, and indicates motion above and across it (see Figure 5). The repetition schema uses schema 1.X.C, and adds two metaphors to it. Again, the path is metaphorically understood as the course of the activity. This is via the very general ACTIVITY IS A JOURNEY metaphor. The landmark is understood metaphorically as an earlier completed performance of the activity. This is a special-purpose metaphor, which is, to my knowledge, used only in this complex schema. This is the part of the repetition schema for *over* that is *not motivated by an occurrence elsewhere in the conceptual system.* It is what makes this sense of *over* somewhat idiosyncratic.

At this point, we are in a position to give a link diagram that shows a good deal of the complexity of *over.* In that diagram, we will refer to the repetition schema as schema 6. Figure 27 displays all the links we have discussed so far. A number of additional metaphorical links will be discussed below.

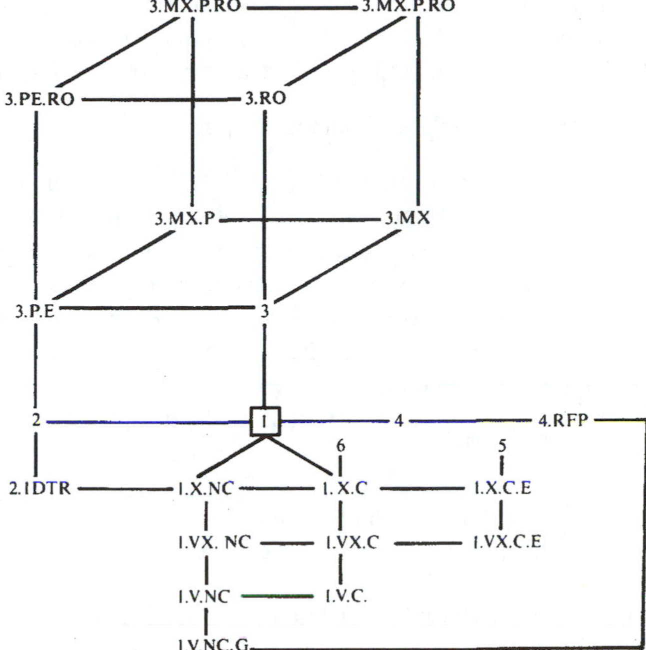


*Figure 27.*

Figure 27 shows what is meant by a *radial* structure. schema 1 occupies a central position; it and its instances are of primary importance in the system of links. The links correspond to what Wittgenstein called 'family resemblances.' The links are sometimes defined by shared properties. But frequently they are defined not by shared properties, but by transforms or by metaphors.

## 10. Some metaphorical senses

It is extremely common for metaphors to apply to image-schemas. A great many metaphorical models use a spatial domain as their source domain. Among the most common source domains for metaphorical models are containers, orientations, journeys (with paths and goals), vertical impediments, etc. In this section, we will give a number of cases where *over* has a metaphorical sense based on an image-schema discussed above.

She has a strange power *over* me.

This is an instance of a very common metaphor: CONTROL IS UP, LACK OF CONTROL IS DOWN (see Lakoff and Johnson 1980). *Over* in this sentence is an extension of schema 2 (Figure 14), where the trajector is simply above the landmark.

Sam was passed *over* for promotion.

Here we have an instance of schema 1 (Figure 1). Two metaphorical mappings apply to it. The first is CONTROL IS UP, LACK OF CONTROL IS DOWN. This entails that the person who passed over Sam was in control of Sam's status. The second metaphor the applies to this schema is another common one: CHOOSING IS TOUCHING. This occurs in such sentences as *He was tapped for service* and *The boss handpicked his successor.* Since the schema indicates that there is no contact, it is entailed that Sam was not chosen.

We are now in a position to make sense of the difference between *overlook* and *oversee.*

You've overlooked his accomplishments.
We need to find someone who can oversee this operation.

The *over* in *overlook* is based on schema 2.1 DTR (Figure 5). There are two metaphors involved. The first is a metaphor for understanding vision: SEEING IS TOUCHING. This occurs in examples like *I couldn't take my eyes off of her, Her eyes picked out every detail of the pattern, He undressed her with his eyes,* and *He fixed his gaze on the entrance.* According to this metaphor, one's gaze goes from one's eyes to what one sees. You see whatever your gaze touches. Under the metaphorical mapping, the path in schema 2.1DTR is the gaze. Since there is no contact in schema 2.1DTR, the metaphorical gaze doesn't touch the landmark; thus the subject of *overlook* is *not* looking at, and therefore does *not* see, the landmark. The second metaphor is the general MIND-AS-BODY metaphor (see Sweetser 1984). The relevant aspect of that metaphor is the part in which LOOKING AT SOMETHING IS TAKING IT INTO CONSIDERATION. Accordingly, *I'll take a look at it* normally entails *I'll consider it.* Therefore, to overlook someone's accomplishments is *not* to take them into consideration.

The *over* in *oversee* is based on schema 2 (Figure 15), in which the TR is above the LM. There are a metaphor and a metonymy that are relevant to this example. The metaphor is CONTROL IS UP. Thus, the one who does the overseeing has control over the persons overseen. The metonymy is SEEING SOMETHING DONE STANDS FOR MAKING SURE THAT IT IS DONE. This metonymy is based on an idealized model in which making sure of something typically involves seeing it. Because of this metonymic relation. *See that he gets his money* means *Make sure that he gets his money.* Thus, to *oversee* means to be in control and make sure that something is done.

We can now compare *overlook* to *look over.*

Look *over* my corrections, but don't overlook any of them.

The *over* in *look over* is based on schema 3.MX.P (Figure 18), and the SEEING IS TOUCHING metaphor. The resulting complex schema is one in which the subject's gaze traces a path that 'covers' the direct object, *corrections.* In the resulting schema, the gaze does make contact with the landmark. The MIND-AS-BODY metaphor again yields a sense of *look* in which looking at something involves taking it into consideration. Thus, when one looks over X, one directs one's attention to a representative sampling that 'covers' X, and one takes into consideration each subpart that one directs attention to.

## 11. Motivation

Before we go on, it is worth commenting on what is and what is not being explained in these analyses. We are not explaining why *oversee, overlook,* and *look over* mean what they mean. Their meanings cannot be predicted from the meanings of *over, look,* and *see.* But their meanings are not completely arbitrary. Given the range of spatial meanings of *over,* and given the metaphors present in the conceptual system that English is based on, it *makes sense* for these words to have these meanings. We are explaining just why it makes sense and what kind of sense it makes.

In each of these cases, the metaphorical and metonymic models exist in the conceptual system independently of the given expression. For example, we understand seeing metaphorically in terms of a gaze that goes out of one's eyes and touches the object seen. This metaphorical understanding is present regardless of whether any of the expressions just discussed have those meanings. Similarly, the schemas for *over* exist for expressions in the spatial domain independently of the existence of *oversee, overlook,* and *look over.* What one learns when one learns these words is which of the independently existing components of their meaning are actually utilized. Each of these expressions is a specialized 'assembly' of independently existing parts. The only arbitrariness involved is the knowledge that such an assembly exists.

The psychological claim being made here is that it is easier to learn, remember, and use such assemblies which use existing patterns than it is to learn, remember, and use words whose meaning is inconsistent with existing patterns. What is being explained is not why those expressions mean what they mean, but why those are natural meanings for them to have. Thus, if one is going to have a word that means 'to fail to take into consideration,' it is more natural to use *overlook* than to use an existing unrelated word like *sew,* or a complex word whose components are in conflict with the meaning, such as *underplan,* or *taste at,* or *rekick.* It is common sense that such expressions would not be used with such a meaning, and we are characterizing the nature of that 'common sense.'

As we have mentioned before, such an explanation requires going beyond the predictable/arbitrary dichotomy. It requires introducing the concept of *motivation.* Thus, the meaning of *overlook,* though not predictable, is motivated – motivated by one of the spatial schemas for *over* and by two metaphors in the conceptual system. Similarly, all of the noncentral schemas for *over* in the chain given in Figure 27 are motivated – motivated by other senses and by principles of linking.

## 12. More metaphorical senses

There are some additional common metaphorical senses of *over* that are worth discussing. Take *get over* in

Harry still hasn't gotten *over* his divorce.

This use of *over* is based on schema 1.VX.C (Figure 6), and two metaphors. In the first metaphor, obstacles are understood in terms of vertical landmarks – which may be extended or not. This metaphorical model is the basis for expressions such as *There is nothing standing in your way.* The second metaphorical model is one that understands LIFE as a JOURNEY. This occurs in sentences like *It's time to get on with your life.* In the above use, the divorce in an obstacle (metaphorically, a vertical extended landmark) on the path defined by life's journey.

Pete Rose is over the hill.

Over the hill makes use of schema 1.VX.C.E (Figure 10) and a metaphor for understanding a career in terms of a journey over a vertical extended landmark like a hill. In this metaphorical model of a career, one *starts at the bottom,* may *go all the way to the top,* and then *goes downhill.* Thus, *over the hill* means that one has already reached and passed the peak, or "high point," of one's career and will never have that high a stature again.

The rebels overthrew the government.

This is an instance of schema 4.RFP (Figure 25) and the CONTROL IS UP metaphor. Before the event takes place, the government is in control (metaphorically upright), and afterwards it is not in control (metaphorically down).
He turned the question over in his mind.

This is an instance of schema 4 (Figure 24), plus an instance of the MIND-AS-

BODY metaphor in which THINKING ABOUT SOMETHING IS EXAMINING IT. This metaphorical model occurs in such sentences as *Let us now examine the question of factory chickens.* In examining a physical object, one turns it over in order to get a look at all sides of it. Questions are metaphorically understood as having sides, and when one turns a question over in one's mind, one is examining all sides of it.

The play is over.

Here we have an instance of schema 1.X.C.E (Figure 11). In general, activities with a prescribed structure are understood as extended landmarks, and performing such an activity is understood metaphorically as traveling along a prescribed path over that landmark. When one gets to the end, the activity is *over.* Thus, games, plays, and political campaigns can be characterized at their end as being *over.*

## 13. Image-schemas as links between perception and reason

Two of our major sources of information are vision and language. We can gain information through either perceiving something directly or being told it. And we can reason about that information, no matter what its source. We can even reason using information from both sources simultaneously, which suggests that it is possible for us to encode information from both sources in a single format. We would like to suggest that image-schemas provide such a format.

It is our guess that image-schemas play a central role in both perception and reason. We believe that they structure our perceptions and that their structure is made use of in reason. The analysis of *over* that we have just given is rich enough for us to discuss such questions in some detail. Let us begin with the following question. Are the image-schema transformations we have discussed natural, and if so, what is the source of their 'naturalness'?

## 14. The nature of image-schema transformations

There are certain very natural relationships among image-schemas, and these motivate polysemy, not just in one or two cases, but in case after case throughout the lexicon. Natural image-schema transformations play a central role in forming radial categories of senses. Take, for example, the end-point-focus transformation. It is common for words that have an image-schema with a path to also have the corresponding image-schema with a focus on the end-point of the path. We saw this in *over* in cases like

Sam walked *over* the hill. (path)
Sam lives *over* the hill. (end-of-path)

Pairs such as this are common.

Harry walked *through* that doorway. (path)
The passport office is *through* that doorway. (end-of-path)

Sam walked *around* the comer. (path)
Sam lives *around* the comer. (end-of-path)

Harriet walked *across* the street. (path)
Harriet lives *across* the street. (end-of-path)

Mary walked *down* the road. (path)
Mary lives *down* the road. (end-of-path)

Sam walked *past* the post office. (path)
Sam lives *past* the post office. (end-of-path)

It should be noted that although such pairs are common, they are not fully productive.

Sam walked *by* the post office. (path)
Sam lives *by* the post office. (= *near,* ≠ end-of-path)

Here, *by* has a path schema, but no corresponding end-point schema.

Sam *ran from* the house. (path)
Sam stood three *feet from* the house. (end-of-path)

Sam ran *to* the house. (path)
*Sam stood (three feet) *to* the house. (≠ end-of-path)

*From* allows both path and end-of-path schemas, but *to* only allows a path schema.

Path schemas are so naturally related to end-point schemas that people sometimes have to think twice to notice the difference. The same is true of the schema transformation that links multiplex and mass schemas. It is natural for words that have a mass schema to also have a multiplex schema.

*All* men are mortal. (MX)
*All* gold is yellow. (MS)

She bought *a lot of* earrings. (MX)
*She bought *a lot of* jewelry. (MS)

This schema transformation, of course, doesn't hold for all quantifiers:

She bought *two* earrings. (MX)
*She bought *two* jewelry. (MS)

There are also verbs which have both schemas:

He *poured* the juice through the sieve. (MS)
The fans *poured* through the gates. (MX)

This will also work for other verbs of liquid movement, such as *spill, flow,* etc.

The wine *spilled* out over the table. (MS)
The fans *spilled* out over the field. (MX)

There is a special case of the multiplex-mass transformation in which the multiplex entity is a sequence of points and the mass is a one-dimensional trajector. A variety of prepositions permit both schemas.

There are guards posted *along* the road. (MX)
There is a fence *along* the road. (1DTR)

He coughed *throughout* the concert. (MX)
He slept *throughout* the concert. (1DTR)

There were stains *down* his tie. (MX)
There were stripes *down* his tie. (1DTR)

There is a natural relationship not only between a one-dimensional trajector and a sequence of points. There is also a natural relationship between a one-dimensional trajector and a zero-dimensional moving trajector that traces a path.

Sam *went* to the top of the mountain. (0DMTR)
The road *went* to the top of the mountain. (1DTR)

Sam ran *through* the forest. (0DMTR)
There is a road *through* the forest. (1DTR)

Sam walked *across* the street. (0DMTR)
There was a rope stretched *across* the street. (1DTR)

Finally, there is a natural relationship between nonreflexive and reflexive trajectors. Here are some examples:

He stood *apart* from the crowd. (NRF)
The book fell *apart.* (RF)

She walked *up* to me. (NRF)
Let's cuddle *up.* (RF)

She poured the syrup *out* of the jar. (NRF)
The syrup spread *out* over the pancakes. (RF)

Let us consider for a moment what is natural about these image-schema transformations.

*Path-focus/end-point-focus:* It is a common experience to follow the path of a moving object until it comes to rest, and then to focus on where it is. This corresponds to the path-focus / end-point-focus transformation.

*Multiplex/mass:* As one moves further away, a group of individuals: at a certain point begins to be seen as a mass. Similarly, a sequence of points is seen as a continuous line when viewed from a distance.

*0DMTR/1DTR:* When we perceive a continuously-moving object, we can mentally trace the path it is following. This capacity is reflected in the transformation linking zero-dimensional moving trajectors and a one-dimensional trajector.

*NRF/RF:* Given a perceived relationship between a TR and a LM which are two separate entities, it is possible to perceive the same relationship between (a) different parts of the same entity or (2) earlier and later locations of the same entity, where one part or location is considered LM and the other TR.

In short, these schema transformations are anything but arbitrary. They are direct reflections of our visual experiences.

The fact that image-schemas are a reflection of our sensory and general spatial experience is hardly surprising, yet it plays a very important role in the theory of image-schemas. Perhaps we can see that significance most easily by contrasting the image-schema transformations we have described with the names we have given to them. Take the transformation name 'MX ↔ MS.' The names 'MX' and 'MS' are arbitrary relative to the character of what they name: a group of individual entities and a mass. The transformation is a natural relationship, but the name of the transformation is just a collection of arbitrary symbols.

This distinction is important because of certain versions of the Symbol Manipulation Paradigm. On one theory of image-representation – the 'prepositional theory' – visual scenes are represented by arbitrary symbols which are linked together in network structures. Arbitrary symbols such as X and Y are taken as standing for some aspect of a scene, such as a point or an edge or a surface or an entire object. Other symbols are used to express relations among these symbols, for example, 'ABV(X,Y)' and 'C(X,Y)' might represent relations which are supposed to correspond to 'X is above Y' and 'X is in contact with Y,' but which, so far as the computer is concerned, are just symbols. Such a symbolization describes how various parts – points, edges, surfaces, etc. – are related to one another. Objects in a scene are described using such symbolizations.

According to the Symbol Manipulation Paradigm as applied to visual information and mental imagery (Pylyshyn 1981), only such propositional representations are mentally real, while images are not real. This view stems from taking the Symbol Manipulation Paradigm *very* seriously. Since digital computers work by the manipulation of such arbitrary symbols, the strong version of the Symbol Manipulation Paradigm *requires* not only that visual perception and mental imagery be characterizable in such a 'propositional' form, but also that such symbolic representations, and only those, are mentally real.

The names that we have given to the image schemas, as well as to the image-schema transformations, are in keeping with feature representations. They have the properties that (1) they are arbitrary, in the sense that the internal structure of symbols plays no role in how the symbols interact or what they mean; (2) they are inherently meaningless, and have to be assigned meanings; and (3) they are finitary in nature. Such feature-style names are in these respects opposite from the corresponding image-schemas, which (1) are nonarbitrary, in the sense that they have an internal structure that plays a crucial role in what they mean and how they interact; (2) they are inherently meaningful; and (3) they are analog in nature.

Suppose that, instead of merely using such symbols as convenient names, we chose to take such a use of symbols seriously, as one would have to if one were to adopt the Symbol Manipulation Paradigm for Cognitive Science. According to that paradigm, topological representations such as image-schemas are not available as cognitive representations; all that is available are symbolic representations, which would look like the symbolic names we have given and would have their properties. The Symbol Manipulation Paradigm would thus make the implicit claim that the cognitively natural image-schema transformations of the sort we described did not exist. In their place would be arbitrary transformations relating the names we have given. Instead of a natural explanation of types of polysemy, we would have no explanation at all, but only an arbitrary description. We consider the lack of such explanatory force intolerable.

For instance, consider the relationship between the *over* of *The bird flew over the yard* and that of *The power line stretches over the yard.* These are adjacent senses in the network, linked by the natural relationship between a zero-dimensional moving trajector and a corresponding one-dimensional stationary trajector. If there were no such natural relation between the senses, they would not be adjacent in the network. Thus, the configuration of *the* network is anything but arbitrary; it is determined by an account of what constitutes a "natural" link type. Since it is the topological character of the representations that makes such relationships natural, it is that topological nature that makes the configurations of the networks nonarbitrary. If symbolic feature representations are substituted for the topological representations, then the naturalness of the relationships disappears and, with it, the explanation for what is linked to what. In short, there are natural reasons for the extensions of certain senses to other senses, and those reasons must be given in a cognitively adequate account of polysemy.

## 16. Conclusion

Systematic polysemy of the sort we have just seen is a pervasive phenomenon in language. It is so common and automatic that we often do not even notice it. Yet, as we have seen, simple basic processes like image-schema transformations and metaphors can interact to form rather large networks that characterize the natural relationships among the senses of polysemous words.

Our primary conclusion is that lists will not do; networks of the kind we have described are needed to characterize the relationships among the senses of polysemous words.

Our secondary conclusion is that features will not do. Oriented topological representations using image-schemas are necessary for two reasons: (1) to account for the range of scenes that concepts like *over* can fit, and (2) to account for the naturalness of image-schema transformations. This suggests that the Symbol Manipulation Paradigm, which cannot tolerate the existence of such representations using a cognitive topology, is inadequate for natural language semantics.

## Note

* This paper is a shortened version of a discussion of polysemy and image-schemas that appears as case study 2 in Lakoff 1987. It is published here with permission of the University of Chicago Press. That study, in turn, was based on Brugman's University of California M.A. thesis (Brugman 1981). Portions of this work were supported by grant no. BNS-8310445 of the National Science Foundation and a grant by the Sloan Foundation to the Institute of Cognitive Studies at the University of California, Berkeley.

## References

Brugman, Claudia
1981 Story of *over.* M.A. thesis, University of California, Berkeley.
Lakoff, George
1987 *Women, Fire, and Dangerous Things: What Categories Reveal about the Mind.* Chicago: University of Chicago Press.
Lakoff, George, and Mark Johnson
1980 *Metaphors We Live By.* Chicago: University of Chicago Press.
Langacker, Ronald W.
1983 Remarks on English aspect. In *Tense and Aspect: Between Semantics and Pragmatics*, P. Hopper (ed.), 265–304. Amsterdam: Benjamins.
1987 *Foundations of Cognitive Grammar,* Vol. 1. Stanford: Stanford University Press.
Lindner, Susan
1981 A lexico-semantic analysis of verb-particle constructions with *up* and *out.* Ph.D. dissertation, University of California, San Diego.
1982 What goes up doesn't necessarily come down: The ins and outs of opposites. In *Papers from the Eighteenth Regional Meeting of the Chicago Linguistic Society*, 305–323.
Pylyshyn, Zenon
1981 The imagery debate: Analogue media versus tacit knowledge. *Psychological Review* 87: 16–45.
Sweetser, Eve E.
1984 Semantic structure and semantic change. Ph.D. dissertation, University of California, Berkeley.

# Chapter 4
# Prototype theory

## Prospects and problems of prototype theory*
*Dirk Geeraerts*

### 1. Prototype theory within linguistics

The starting-point of the prototypical conception of categorial structure is summarized in the statement that

> when describing categories analytically, most traditions of thought have treated category membership as a digital, all-or-none phenomenon. That is, much work in philosophy, psychology, linguistics, and anthropology assumes that categories are logical bounded entities, membership in which is defined by an item's possession of a simple set of criterial features, in which all instances possessing the criterial attributes have a full and equal degree of membership. In contrast, it has recently been argued ... that some natural categories are analog and must be represented logically in a manner which reflects their analog structure (Rosch and Mervis 1975: 573–574).

As we shall see in section 2, the exact definition of the concept of prototypicality as used in linguistics is not without problems. The major part of this introduction to the prototypicality-based studies collected here will, in fact, consist of an attempt at clarification of some of the problematic aspects of the way in which the notion of prototype has been used in linguistics. To begin with, however, we shall be concerned with a brief overview of the state of the art in linguistic prototype theory.[1]

The theory originated in the mid 1970s with Eleanor Rosch's research into the internal structure of categories. (Overviews may be found in Rosch 1978, 1988, and Mervis and Rosch 1981; the basic research is reported on mainly in Heider 1972; Rosch 1973, 1975, 1977; Rosch and Mervis 1975; Rosch, Simpson and Miller 1976; Rosch et al. 1976.) From its psycholinguistic origins, prototype theory has moved mainly[2] in two directions. On the one hand, Rosch's findings and proposals were taken up by formal psycholexicology (and more generally, information-processing psychology), which tries to devise formal models for human conceptual memory and its operation, and which so, obviously, borders on Artificial Intel-

Originally published in 1989 in *Linguistics* 27(4): 587–612. A section of the original paper describing the various contributions to the thematic issue has been omitted from the present reprint.

ligence. Excellent overviews of the representational and experimental issues at stake here are Smith and Medin (1981), and Medin and Smith (1984); an interesting sample of current research may be found in Neisser (1987). On the other hand, prototype theory has had a steadily growing success in linguistics since the early 1980s, as witnessed by a number of recent monographs and collective volumes in which prototype theory and its cognitive extensions play a major role (Wierzbicka 1985; Lakoff 1987; Langacker 1987; Craig 1986; Holland and Quinn 1987; Rudzka-Ostyn 1988; Lehmann 1988a; Hüllen and Schulze 1988; Tsohatzidis 1989; Taylor 1989). It is with the latter development that we shall be concerned with here.

Against the background of the development of linguistic semantics, prototype theory may be defined primarily in contrast with the componential model of semantic analysis that was current in transformational grammar and that is stereotypically associated with Katz and Fodor's analysis of *bachelor* (Katz and Fodor 1963); in an early defense of a prototypical approach, Fillmore (1975) called this the 'checklist theory' of meaning. The prototypists' reaction against this featural approach had, however, the negative side-effect of creating the impression that prototypical theories rejected any kind of componential analysis. This is a misconception for the simple reason that there can be no semantic description without some sort of decompositional analysis. As a heuristic tool for the description and comparison of lexical meanings, a componential analysis retains its value (a value that, incidentally, it did not acquire with the advent of componential analysis as an explicit semantic theory, but which had been obvious to lexicographers from time immemorial). Rather, the difficulties with the neostructuralist kind of feature analysis that grew out of structuralist field theory lie elsewhere; it is not the use of decomposition as a descriptive instrument that causes concern, but the status attributed to the featural analysis. Two important points have to be mentioned.

In the first place, as suggested by the quotation at the beginning of this introduction, featural definitions are classically thought of as criterial, i.e. as listing attributes that are each indispensable for the definition of the concept in question, and that taken together suffice to delimit that concept from all others. In contrast, prototype theory claims that there need not be a single set of defining attributes that conform to the necessity-cum-sufficiency requirement.[3]

In the second place, prototype theory is reluctant to accept the idea that there is an autonomous semantic structure in natural languages which can be studied in its own right, in isolation from the other cognitive capacities of man. In particular, meaning phenomena in natural languages cannot be studied in isolation from the encyclopedic knowledge individuals possess; it is precisely the presupposition that there exists a purely linguistic structure of semantic oppositions that enables structuralist and neostructuralist semantics to posit the existence of a distinction between semantic and encyclopedic knowledge. Prototype theory tends to minimize the distinction primarily for methodological reasons: because linguistic categorization is a cognitive phenomenon just like the other cognitive capacities of man, it is important to study it in its relationship to these other capacities. More specific arguments have also been formulated to show that the distinction between an encyclopedic and a semantic level of categorial structure is untenable.[4] For instance, given that the flexible extendibility of prototypical concepts is a synchronic characteristic of linguistic structure, and given the fact that these extensions may be based indiscriminately on allegedly encyclopedic or on allegedly semantic features, the distinction between both kinds of information loses its synchronic relevance. Take the case of metaphor: before *lion* acquires the meaning 'brave man', the feature 'brave' is not structurally distinctive within the semasiological structure of *lion*, and hence, it has to be considered encyclopedic according to structuralist theories. But if it can be accepted (and this is of course the crucial point) that the metaphorical extension of *lion* towards the concept 'brave man' is not just a question of diachronic change, but is merely an effect of the synchronic flexibility of lexical items, the feature clearly acquires semantic status. If, furthermore, the argument can be repeated in the sense that such synchronic metaphorical extensions may be based on any allegedly encyclopedic attribute, the distinction between semantic and encyclopedic concepts as a whole falls.[5]

The matter need not, to be sure, be settled here. What is important for our introductory purposes is rather to see what exactly prototype theory objects to in componential theories of the Katzian type. First, the suggestion that lexical concepts are criterial in the classical sense, and second, the suggestion that there exists a purely linguistic level of conceptual structuring that is neatly separated from other, 'encyclopedic' forms of conceptual information, and that may thus be studied autonomously, in methodological isolation from other kinds of cognitive research. As against these points of view, prototype theory defends a non-criterial conception of categorial structure, and an interdisciplinary methodological perspective that takes into account relevant research from the other cognitive sciences. (The very transposition of the prototypical approach from experimental psychology to linguistics derives from this attitude.)

But this historical positioning of prototype theory with regard to its immediate predecessors within the field of lexical semantics clearly does not explain why it has turned out to be such a successful alternative. Why did (and does) the prototypical approach appeal to a sizeable part of the linguistic community? On the one hand, the historical development of generative grammar had raised a considerable amount of interest in semantic matters. It should not be forgotten, in fact, that it was only after the incorporation of a semantic component into the transformational framework that Chomskyanism became internationally popular; the universal appeal of the generative Standard Theory was at least partly due to the promises held by its Katzian semantic component. On the other hand, the promises were not fulfilled. Within the generative paradigm, Generative Semantics (which most strongly embodied the semantic approach) withered in favor of Autonomous Syntax, in which semantics hardly played a role worthy of note. Outside the generative approach, formal semantics of the Montagovian kind was too narrowly restricted to sentential meaning to be able to hold the attention of those who were interested primarily in the internal structure of natural language categories (and not primarily in the way these categories combine into larger unities).[6] In short, as far as semantics was concerned, there was a gap in the linguistic market of the early 1980s that was not filled by the major approaches of the day.[7]

But again, recognizing that there was an interest in the semantics of natural language categories to which prototype theory could appeal does not tell the whole story. Why didn't people simply stick to the componential theory popularized by Katz, or to the rival axiomatic method of representation – even if these gradually moved out of the centre of the linguistic attention as Autonomous Syntax and Formal Semantics took over? In general, there are a number of methodological requirements people nowadays expect of linguistic theories: descriptive adequacy (mainly in the form of a broad empirical scope), explanatory depth, productivity, and formalization. Although prototype theory rates much lower on the formalization scale than either the axiomatic or the featural approach, its assets with regard to the other three points are considerable.

In the first place, it tackles a number of semantic phenomena that had been swept under the rug by the more structurally minded approaches. The fuzzy boundaries of lexical categories, the existence of typicality scales for the members of a category, the flexible and dynamic nature of word meanings, the importance of metaphor and metonymy as the basis of that flexibility – these are all intuitively obvious elements of the subject matter of semantics that were largely neglected by structural semantics. It is true that they were occasionally pointed at as an indispensable aspect of any full-fledged semantic theory: think, for instance, of Weinreich's remark (1966: 471) that a semantic theory should be able to deal with 'interpretable deviance', or Uhlenbeck's plea (1967) for a dynamic conception of word meaning.[8] These remarks did not, however, have much effect as far as theory formation was concerned. In particular, it is only with the advent of prototype theory that contemporary linguistics developed a valid model for the polysemy of lexical items. This is perhaps the single most appealing characteristic of prototype theory: here at last is a descriptive approach to lexical meaning in which our pretheoretical intuitions about gradedness, fuzziness, flexibility, clustering of senses etc. receive due attention.

In the second place, prototype theory appears to be a productive theory not just in the sense that its insights into the structure of lexical categories can be easily applied in various fields of the lexicon, but also in the sense that it may be extended towards other aspects of linguistics. Whereas prototype theory started with being descriptively fruitful in lexical semantics, it soon became theoretically fruitful in the sense that other areas of linguistics were taken into consideration. A few recent examples of such extensions may suffice: phonology (Nathan 1986), morphology (Bybee and Moder 1983; Post 1986), syntax (Van Oosten 1986; Ross 1987), historical linguistics (Winters 1987; Aijmer 1985), markedness theory (Van Langendonck 1986), theoretical lexicography (Geeraerts 1985c). Through these and similar extensions,[9] prototype theory has become one of the cornerstones of Cognitive Linguistics, which tries to account for the interaction between language and cognition on all levels of linguistic structure: one need only have a look at the prominent place attributed to a prototypical conception of categorial structure in Langacker (1987) (one of the basic works of the Cognitive Linguistic approach) to appreciate its importance.[10] In this sense, the development of prototype theory into Cognitive Linguistics contains exciting promises of a unified cognitive theory of linguistic categorization.

In the third place, the explanatory depth of prototype theory resides partly in its generalizable character, but also in its interdisciplinary nature. The importance of its genetic link with psycholinguistics can only be fully appreciated against the background of the Chomskyan requirements with regard to theories of grammar. Chomsky's methodology is, in fact, in the awkward position of declaring linguistics a cognitive science, but refusing to deal directly with the findings of the other sciences of the mind. Roughly stated, Chomskyan linguistics claims to reveal something about the mind, but imperviously prefers a strictly autonomist methodology over the open dialogue with psychology that would seem to be implied by such a claim. Prototype theory's linguistic application of psycholinguistic findings, on the other hand, takes the Chomskyan ideal of cognitive explanatory depth to its natural consequences, viz. of giving up the methodological autonomy of linguistics in favor of an interdisciplinary dialogue with the other cognitive sciences.[11] Prototype theory takes the cognitive claims of Chomskyanism methodologically seriously by its interdisciplinary openness. This is all the more important at a moment when Cognitive Science is emerging as an interdisciplinary cluster of psychology, neuroscience, Artificial Intelligence, and philosophy. It is probably one of the reasons for the appeal of prototype theory that its interdisciplinary connections hold the promise of linking linguistics to the most important development that the human sciences are currently witnessing.

## 2. Definitional problems, first series: 'Prototype' as a prototypical notion

The appeal of prototype theory should not, however, obscure the fact that the exact definition of prototypicality is not without problems. The purpose of this section (and the following) is to analyze the sources of the confusion by making clear that prototypicality is itself, in the words of Posner (1986), a prototypical concept. As a first step, we shall have a look at four characteristics that are frequently mentioned (in various combinations) as typical of prototypicality. In each case, a quotation from early prototype studies is added to illustrate the point.

(i) Prototypical categories cannot be defined by means of a single set of criterial (necessary and sufficient) attributes:

> We have argued that many words ... have as their meanings not a list of necessary and sufficient conditions that a thing or event must satisfy to count as a member of the category denoted by the word, but rather a psychological object or process which we have called a prototype (Coleman and Kay 1981: 43).

(ii) Prototypical categories exhibit a family resemblance structure, or more generally, their semantic structure takes the form of a radial set of clustered and overlapping meanings:[12]

> The purpose of the present research was to explore one of the major structural principles which, we believe, may govern the formation of the prototype structure of semantic categories. This principle was first suggested in philosophy; Wittgenstein (1953) argued that the referents of a word need not have common elements to be understood and used in the normal functioning of language. He suggested that, rather, a family resemblance might be what linked the various referents of a word. A family resemblance relationship takes the form AB, BC, CD, DE. That is, each item has at least one, and probably several, elements in common with one or more items, but no, or few, elements are common to all items (Rosch and Mervis 1975: 574–575).

(iii) Prototypical categories exhibit degrees of category membership; not every member is equally representative for a category:

> By prototypes of categories we have generally meant the clearest cases of category membership defined operationally by people's judgments of goodness of membership in the category ... we can judge how clear a case something is and deal with categories on the basis of clear cases in the total absence of information about boundaries (Rosch 1978: 36).

(iv) Prototypical categories are blurred at the edges:

> New trends in categorization research have brought into investigation and debate some of the major issues in conception and learning whose solution had been unquestioned in earlier approaches. Empirical findings have established that ... category boundaries are not necessarily definite (Mervis and Rosch 1981: 109).

As a first remark with regard to these characteristics, it should be noted that they are not the only ones that may be used in attempts to define the prototypical conception of categorization. Two classes of such additional features should be mentioned.

On the one hand, there are characteristics that do not pertain (as the four mentioned above) to the structure of categories, but that rather pertain to the epistemological features of so-called non-Aristotelian categories.[13] For instance, the view that prototypical categories are not 'objectivist' but 'experiential' in nature (Lakoff 1987) envisages the epistemological relationship between concepts and the world rather than the structural characteristics of those concepts. In particular, it contrasts the allegedly classical view that 'categories of mind ... are simply reflections of categories that supposedly exist objectively in the world, independent of all beings', with the view that 'both categories of mind and human reason depend upon experiential aspects of human psychology' (Lakoff 1982: 99). Such an epistemological rather than structural characterization of natural concepts also has a methodological aspect to it; it entails that prototypical categories should not be studied in isolation from their experiential context. While such an epistemological or methodological conception of prototypical categorization is extremely valuable, we shall take a structural point of view in the following pages; we shall try to determine whether it is possible to give a coherent, structurally intrinsic characterization of prototypical categories.

On the other hand, there are structural characteristics of prototypical concepts that can be reduced to the four basic structural features mentioned above. For instance, in my own work on prototypical categorization, I have repeatedly stressed the flexibility of prototypical concepts (1983, 1985a), together with the fact that a distinction between semantic and encyclopedic components of lexical concepts cannot be maintained in the case of prototypical concepts (1985b). But the flexibility of prototypical categories is linked in a straightforward manner with the fourth characteristic: uncertainties with regard to the denotational boundaries of a category imply that it need not be used in a rigidly fixed manner. Similarly, the absence of a clear dividing line between encyclopedic and purely semantic information follows from this very flexibility together with the first and second characteristic. As illustrated in the previous section, the possibility of incorporating members into the category that do not correspond in every definitional respect with the existing members entails that features that are encyclopedic (non-definitional) with regard to a given set of category members may turn into definitional features with regard to a flexibly incorporated peripheral category member. The resemblance between central and peripheral cases may be based on allegedly encyclopedic just as well as on allegedly 'semantic' features. In short, features of prototypicality that are not included among the ones mentioned in (i)–(iv) may often be reduced to those four, and this in turn justifies a preliminary restriction of the discussion to the latter.

A second remark with regard to the four characteristics is concerned with the fact that they are systematically related along two dimensions. On the one hand, the third and the fourth characteristic take into account the referential, extensional structure of a category. In particular, they have a look at the members of a category; they observe, respectively, that not all referents of a category are equal in representativeness for that category, and that the denotational boundaries of a category are not always determinate. On the other hand, these two aspects (centrality and non-rigidity) recur on the intensional level, where the definitional rather than the referential structure of a category is envisaged. For one thing, non-rigidity shows up in the fact that there is no single necessary and sufficient definition for a prototypical concept. For another, family resemblances imply overlapping of the subsets of a category. To take up the formulation used in the quotation under (ii) above, if there is no definition adequately describing A, B, C, D, and E, each of the subsets AB, BC, CD, and DE can be defined separately, but obviously, the 'meanings' that are so distinguished overlap. Consequently, meanings exhibiting a greater degree of overlapping (in the example: the senses corresponding with BC and CD) will have more structural weight than meanings that cover peripheral members of the category only. In short, the clustering of meanings that is typical of family resemblances implies that not every meaning is structurally equally important (and a similar observation can be made with regard to the components into which those meanings may be analyzed). The systematic links between the characteristics mentioned at the beginning are schematically summarized in Table 1.

As a third remark, it should be noted that the four characteristics are often thought to be co-extensive, in spite of incidental but clear warnings such as Rosch and Mervis's remark that a family resemblance structure need not be the only source of prototypicality (1975: 599). Admittedly, it is easy to consider them to be equivalent; already in the quotations given above, partial reasons for their mutual interdependence can be found. More systematically, the following links between the four characteristics might be responsible for the idea that prototypicality necessarily entails the joint presence of all four.

*Table 1.* Characteristics of prototypicality

| | NON-EQUALITY<br>differences in structural weight | NON-RIGIDITY<br>flexibility and vagueness |
|---|---|---|
| EXTENSIONALLY | degrees of representativity | absence of clear boundaries |
| INTENSIONALLY | clusters of overlapping senses | absence of classical definition |

First, linking the first to the second characteristic is the argument mentioned above: if there is no single definition adequately describing the extension of an item as a whole, different subsets may be defined, but since the members of a category can usually be grouped together along different dimensions, these subsets are likely to overlap, i.e., to form clusters of related meanings.

Second, linking the second to the third characteristic is the idea that members of a category that are found in an area of overlapping between two senses carry more structural weight than instances that are covered by only one meaning. Representative members of a category (i.e., instances with a high degree of representativity) are to be found in maximally overlapping areas of the extension of a category. (In the example, A and E are less typical members that B, C, and D, which each belong to two different subsets.)

Third, linking the third to the fourth characteristic is the idea that differences in degree of membership may diminish to a point where it becomes unclear whether something still belongs to the category or not. Categories have referentially blurred edges because of the dubious categorial status of items with extremely low membership degrees.

And fourth, linking the fourth to the first characteristic is the idea that the flexibility that is inherent in the absence of clear boundaries prevents the formulation of an essence that is common to all the members of the category. Because peripheral members may not be identical with central cases but may only share some characteristics with them, it is difficult to define a set of attributes that is common to all members of a category and that is sufficient to distinguish that category from all others.

These circular links between the four characteristics are, however, misleading. A closer look at some (familiar and less familiar) examples of prototypicality reveals that they need not co-occur.

### BIRD

The concept *bird* (one of Rosch's original examples of prototypicality) shows that natural categories may have clear-cut boundaries. At least with regard to our own, real world, the denotation of *bird* is determinate; educated speakers of

English know very well where birds end and non-birds begin. They know, for instance, that a bat is not a bird but that a penguin is. Of course, the principled indeterminacy described by Waismann (1952) as 'open texture' remains: when confronted with an SF creature (a post-World War III mutant) that looks like a bird but talks like a man, we would not be sure whether it should be called a bird or not. A boundary problem that is typical for a prototypical organization of the lexicon would then arise. As it functions now, however, in present-day English, *bird* is denotationally clearly bounded, the archaeopteryx notwithstanding.[14] As has been remarked elsewhere (Lakoff 1987), the existence of prototypicality effects in clearly bounded concepts such as *bird* implies that a strict distinction has to be made between degree of membership and degree of representativity. Membership in the category *bird* is discrete; something is or is not a bird. But some birds may be birdier than others: the swallow does remain a more typical bird than the ostrich.

### RED

Color terms such as *red* constituted the starting-point for prototypical research; drawing on the views developed in Berlin and Kay (1969), Rosch's earliest work is an experimental demonstration of the fact that the borderline between different colors is fuzzy (there is no single line in the spectrum where red stops and orange begins), and of the fact that each color term is psychologically represented by focal colors (some hues are experienced as better reds than others) (Heider 1972; Heider and Olivier 1972). These prototypical characteristics on the extensional level are not matched on the definitional level. If *red* can be analytically defined at all (i.e., if it does not simply receive an ostensive definition consisting of an enumeration of hues with their degree of focality), its definition might be 'having a color that is more like that of blood than like that of an unclouded sky, that of grass, that of the sun, that of ... (etc., listing a typical exemplar for each of the other main colors)'. Such a definition (cp. Wierzbicka 1985: 342) does not correspond with either the first or the second characteristic mentioned above.

### ODD NUMBER

Armstrong, Gleitman and Gleitman (1983) have shown experimentally that even a mathematical concept such as *odd number* exhibits psychological representativity effects. This might seem remarkable, since *odd number* is a classical concept in all other respects: it receives a clear definition, does not exhibit a family resemblance structure or a radial set of clustered meanings, does not have blurred edges. However, Lakoff (1982) has made clear that degrees of representativity among odd numbers are not surprising if the experiential nature of concepts is taken into account. For instance, because the even or uneven character of a large number can be determined easily by looking at the final number, it is no wonder that uneven numbers below 10 carry more psychological weight: they are procedurally of primary importance.

VERS

As I have tried to show elsewhere (1988a), the first characteristic mentioned above is not sufficient to distinguish prototypical from classical categories, since, within the classical approach, the absence of a single definition characterized by necessity-cum-sufficiency might simply be an indication of polysemy. This means that it has to be shown on independent grounds that the allegedly prototypical concepts are not polysemous, or rather, it means that prototypical lexical concepts will be polysemous according to a definitional analysis in terms of necessary and sufficient conditions (the classical definition of polysemy), but univocal according to certain other criteria. These criteria may be found, for instance, in native speakers' intuitions about the lexical items involved, intuitions that may be revealed by tests such as Quine's (1960) or Zwicky and Sadock's (1975). In this sense, the first characteristic has to be restated: prototypical categories will exhibit intuitive univocality coupled with analytical (definitional) polysemy, and not just the absence of a necessary-and-sufficient definition.

Once this revision of the first characteristic is accepted, it can be demonstrated that the first and the second criterion need not co-occur. Lexical items that show clustered overlapping of senses may either conform or not conform to the revised first characteristic. An example of the first situation is the literal meaning of *bird*, an example of the second situation the Dutch adjective *vers*, which corresponds roughly with English *fresh* (except for the fact that the Dutch word does not carry the meaning 'cool'). Details of the comparison between both categories may be found in the paper mentioned above; by way of summary, Figures 1 and 2 represent the definitional analysis of both items. The distinction in intuitive status between *vers* and *bird* can be demonstrated by means of the Quinean test (roughly, a lexical item is ambiguous if it can be simultaneously predicated and negated of something in a particular context). Thus, taking an example based on the corresponding ambiguity in the English counterpart of *vers*, it would be quite normal to state that the news meant in the sentence *there was no fresh news from the fighting*[15] is fresh in one sense ('recent, new') but not in another ('in optimal condition'): it makes sense to say that the news is at the same time fresh and not fresh. By contrast, it would be intuitively paradoxical to state that a penguin is at the same time a bird and not a bird (disregarding figurative extensions of the semantic range of *bird*). Nevertheless, the definitional analyses in Figures 1 and 2 make clear that both concepts exhibit prototypical clustering. In both cases, too, the structural position of the instances just discussed (news, penguin) is not in the central area with maximal overlapping. In short, then, the revised version of the first characteristic need not coincide with the second characteristic.

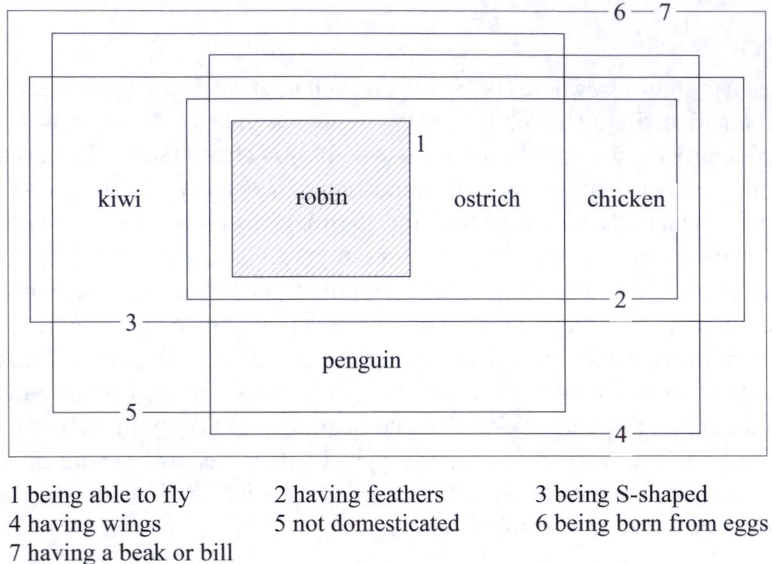


*Figure 1.* A definitional analysis of *bird*

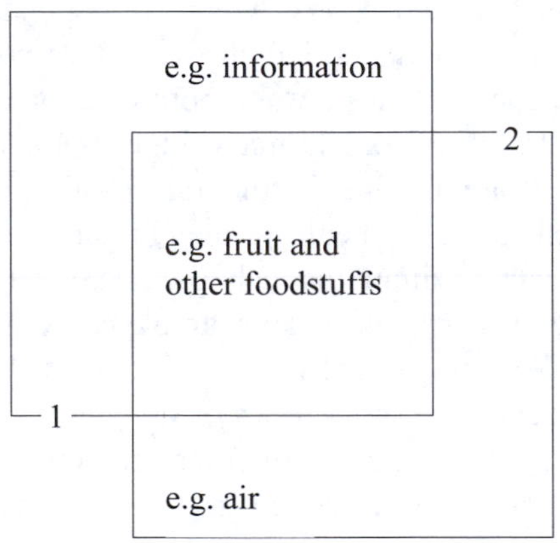


*Figure 2.* A definitional analysis of *vers*

The insight derived from a closer look at the four examples just described may be summarized as in Table 2. It is now easy to see to what extent 'prototypicality' is itself a prototypical notion. There is no single set of attributes that is common to all of the examples discussed here. Rather, they exhibit a family resemblance structure based on partial similarities. In this sense, the set of prototypical concepts characterized by clustering of senses overlaps with the subset characterized by fuzzy boundaries (because of *vers*), and so on. At the same time, some concepts are more typically prototypical than others. (*Bird* and *vers* are more prototypical than *red*.) Notice, in particular, that the category *fruit* makes a good candidate for prototypical prototypicality, in the sense that it seems to combine all four characteristics. It shares the prototypical characteristics of *bird*, but in addition, things such as coconuts and, perhaps, tomatoes, seem to point out that the denotational boundary of *fruit* is less clear-cut than that of *bird*.

However, although the examples considered above do not have a set of attributes in common, they do share a single feature, viz. degrees of membership representativity. It is highly dubious, though, whether this feature alone suffices to distinguish prototypical concepts from classical concepts. If the possibility of a single necessary-and-sufficient definition is one of the features par excellence with which the classical conception has been identified, it might justifiably be claimed that degrees of representativity are entirely compatible with the classical conception of categorization. It is, in fact, in that sense that Armstrong, Gleitman and Gleitman (1983) deal with a category such as *odd number*. The experiments used by Rosch to measure degrees of representativity are not, they claim, indicative of prototypicality since they occur with classical, rigidly definable concepts such as *odd number*. To say the least, representativity effects are only a peripheral prototypical attribute according to Table 2 (cp. Lakoff 1986). But at the same time, the debate over the status of *odd number* shows that the concept 'prototypical concept' has no clear boundaries: it is not immediately clear whether a concept such as *odd number* should be included in the set of prototypical concepts or not.

*Table 2.* The prototypicality of 'prototypicality'

| | BIRD | VERS | RED | ODD NUMBER |
|---|---|---|---|---|
| absence of classical definition | + | – | – | – |
| clusters of overlapping senses | + | + | – | – |
| degrees of representativity | + | + | + | + |
| absence of clear boundaries | – | + | + | – |

Of course, contrary to the situation in everyday speech, such a boundary conflict should not be maintained in scientific speech. A discipline such as linguistics should try to define its concepts as clearly as possible, and the purpose of this section is precisely to show that what has intuitively been classified together as instances of prototypical categories consists of distinct phenomena that have to be kept theoretically apart. In line with prototype theory itself, however, such an attempt at clear definition should not imply an attempt to define the 'true nature' or the 'very essence' of prototypicality. Determining an 'only true kind' of prototypicality is infinitely less important than seeing what the phenomena are and how they are related to each other by contrast or similarity.

Still, there might seem to be one way in which decent sense could be made of the question what the true meaning of prototypicality would be. To begin with, let us note that the prototypical character attributed to the concept of prototypicality also shows up in the fact that the notion 'prototype' is an extremely flexible one. This can be illustrated in two ways. First, the lexical item *prototypical* is spontaneously used to name a number of phenomena that are linked by metonymy, next to the phenomena linked by similarity that are brought together in Table 2. The lexical item does not only characterize structural features of concepts, and the concepts exhibiting those features themselves, but sometimes even particular (viz., highly representative) instances of the categories in question (the robin as a prototypical bird). Second, context may stress one feature of prototypical organization rather than another (cp. the priming effects in Rosch 1975). The general purpose of one's investigations may lead one to devote more attention to one aspect of the prototypical cluster than to another. To name a few examples: degrees of representativity are important for language development studies (if it is taken into account that most concepts in early language development are acquired via their exemplars), while clustered overlapping of senses will come to the fore in linguistic or lexicographical studies into the structure of polysemy. And a cognitive interest into the epistemological principles underlying natural language will attach more weight to the decoupling of intuitive univocality and analytical, definitional polysemy.[16]

In this respect, the question with regard to the true nature of prototypicality might be transformed into the question what might be the most interesting (or perhaps even the most important) perspective for studying and defining prototypicality. But here again, the 'ultimate essence fallacy' exposed by prototype theory itself lurks round the corner: there will be different preferences for one perspective rather than another, but there will be no single ultimately and eternally most important conception of prototypicality.

In short, the foregoing analysis corroborates Wierzbicka's remark that there are 'many senses' to the notion *prototype*, and that 'the notion prototype has been used in recent literature as a catch-all notion' (1985: 343). However, a more systematic analysis than Wierzbicka's reveals that this very multiplicity of usage also supports Cognitive Semantics, in the sense that it shows that the same categorization principles may guide common sense and scientific thinking. This is, then, a further indication of the metatheoretical relevance of a cognitive conception of linguistic categorization, which I have explored at length elsewhere (1985b). At the same time, it has become clear that one of the major tasks for the further development of prototype theory is the closer investigation of the prototypically clustered characteristics of prototypicality. A major reference in this respect is Lakoff's attempt (1987: chapter 4–8) to determine which different kinds of conceptual models may lie at the basis of prototypicality effects.

## 3. Definitional problems, second series: 'Prototype theory' as a prototypical notion

Whereas the previous section made clear that prototypicality as used in linguistic semantics is a prototypically structured concept, it should now be noted that the prototype-theoretical movement as well is a prototypically structured approach to semantics. There are, in other words, central as well as more peripheral examples of prototypical theories. In particular, there exist a number of theories that combine aspects of the classical approach to semantic structure with aspects of the prototypical conception. In this section, two approaches will be considered that are to some extent semi-classical as well as semi-prototypical; each of both embodies a strategy for reinstating particular aspects of the classical view against the background of an overall cognitive point of view.

To begin with, some of the clarity and neatness of the classical approach may be recovered by concentrating on the prototypical centre of a category. If the non-classical indeterminacy of lexical concepts stems primarily from the flexible extendibility of concepts, discreteness may be reinstalled by avoiding the problems of clustered polysemy, i.e., by restricting the definitional analysis to the prototypical centre of the category. This approach is vigorously carried through by Wierzbicka (1985), who explicitly defends the discreteness of semantics by introspectively considering only the clear, salient centre of lexical categories. In a discussion of Labov's experimental investigation into the non-classical characteristics of everyday concepts (1973), she notes:[17]

> To state the meaning of a word, it is not sufficient to study its applicability to things; what one must do above all is to study the structure of the concept which underlies and explains that applicability. In the case of words describing natural kinds or kinds of human artefacts, to understand the structure of the concept means to describe fully and accurately the *idea* (not just the visual image) of a typical representative of the kind: the prototype. And to describe it fully and accurately

> we have to discover the internal logic of the concept. This is best done not through interviews, not through laboratory experiments, and not through reports of casual, superficial impressions or intuitions ... but through methodical introspection and thinking (1985: 19).

It should be noted immediately that Wierzbicka's reinstatement of discreteness does not imply that her definitions do in fact always consist of necessary-and-sufficient conditions, and she acknowledges as much (1985: 60). In this respect, Wierzbicka's approach is only partly a departure from the hard core of prototype-theoretical studies: the absence of necessary-and-sufficient conditions for the definition of certain core concepts is accepted, but the avoidance of the clustered polysemy problem 'tidies up' the semantic description and reinstates some of the classical neatness. Neither does Wierzbicka's approach imply that lexical items are always univocal; in her dictionary of English speech act verbs (1987), several items receive multiple definitions. Each of the definitions does, however, constitute a highly salient meaning, and again, by disregarding peripheral kinds of usage, the clustered or radial structure of the polysemy of lexical items does not enter the picture. The question to be asked, then, is whether Wierzbicka's restriction of the description to the salient meanings of a category is useful and adequate from a cognitive point of view.

From a methodological point of view, the periphery of natural, non-uniquely definable categories is as interesting as their salient centre(s), because it is precisely the relationship between both that typically characterizes natural categories. Cognitive Linguistics is not only interested in what constitutes the centre of a category, but also in how this centre can be extended towards peripheral cases, and how far this extension can go. The mechanisms for incorporating marginal cases into a category at the same time restrict the flexibility of that concept; it is only by studying peripheral cases, for instance, that an answer may be found with regard to the question how dissimilar things can be before they are no longer recognized as basically the same. If, in other words, flexible polysemization is indeed one of the major characteristics of natural language categories, a deliberate restriction of the description to the salient meanings of a category is methodologically less propitious, as it may lead to a neglect of this basic feature.[18]

A second strategy for salvaging aspects of the classical approach is to invoke sociolinguistic mechanisms such as Putnam's 'division of linguistic labor' (1975). According to Putnam, ordinary language users possess no more than 'stereotypical' knowledge about natural kinds, that is to say, they are aware of a number of salient characteristics, such as the fact that water is a transparent, thirst-quenching, tasteless liquid. The technical definition of *water* as $H_2O$, on the other hand, is to be located primarily with scientific experts. It is the experts' knowledge that ultimately determines how natural kind terms are to be used. On the one hand, a 'division of linguistic labor' ensures that there are societal experts who know that water is $H_2O$, that there is a distinction between elms and beech, how to recognize gold from pyrites, and so on. On the other hand, laymen attune their own linguistic usage to that of the expert scientists, technicians, etc.. The members of the non-specialized group are not required to have expert knowledge, but if they wish to be considered full-fledged members of the linguistic community, they are supposed to know the 'stereotype' connected with a category. A stereotype is, thus, a socially determined minimum set of data with regard to the extension of a category. Given the similarity between Putnam's stereotypes and the prototypes of Cognitive Linguistics (both consist roughly of the most salient information connected with a category), the division of linguistic labor might be used to rescue the classical view of concepts.[19] Expert definitions being classical (they specify an essentialist 'hidden structure' for natural kinds), the stereotypical concepts of everyday language users might now be seen as hardly more than a sloppy derivative of those classically defined expert categories. 'True' (expert) definitions would be classical, and stereotypical/prototypical concepts might be dismissed as sociolinguistically secondary phenomena.

It should be remarked immediately that such a reinstatement of the classical view is not as obvious for other words than the natural kind terms for which Putnam's theory is in fact intended (what is the expert definition of the preposition *for*?). Moreover, as a sociolinguistic theory about the social factors that determine how lexical items may be used, the 'division of linguistic labor' theory is incomplete to say the least. The primacy of expert definitions would seem to imply that natural language follows the developments and discoveries of science in a strict fashion. In actual fact, however, natural language categorization is not only determined by the state of affairs in the sciences, but also by the communicative and cognitive requirements of the linguistic community in its own right. One of Putnam's own examples may serve as an illustration. Although science has discovered that *jade* refers to two kinds of materials (one with the 'hidden structure' of a silicate of calcium and magnesium, the other being a silicate of sodium and aluminium), ordinary usage continues to refer to both substances indiscriminately as *jade*. That is to say, categorization in everyday language is not entirely dependent upon scientific research, but seems to be determined at least in part by independent criteria: if the classificatory exigencies of everyday communicative interaction do not call for a distinction between the two kinds of jade, the scientific splitting of the category is largely ignored. This implies that an investigation into everyday language categorization as an independent cognitive system is justified. More generally, if Putnam's view is seen as a theory about the sociolinguistic structure of semantic norms, his hierarchical model (with experts at one end and laymen at the other) is only one among a number of alternatives, some of which (such as the one described by Bartsch 1985) link up closely with a prototypical conception of categorial structure. At the same time, however, it should be admitted that the relationship between classical scientific categorization and prototypical common-sense categorization may be explored in more depth than is yet the case.[20]

To summarize: the confusion associated with the notion of prototypicality is further increased by the fact that more straightforwardly prototypical approaches are surrounded by hybrid theories that contain particular strategies for combining classical discreteness with typically prototypical phenomena. We have discussed two such approaches (one in which the strategy in question is methodological, and another one in which it is sociolinguistic), but this does not mean that these are the only ones that might be mentioned.[21] The two approaches mentioned here are, however, particularly revealing, as they link up with two important currents in the history of Western thought. The first one simplifyingly boils down to the view that the mind is neat (if you look hard enough into it), but that the world is fuzzy: the non-discreteness that Cognitive Linguistics is concerned with arises from the fact that we have to apply clear-cut mental categories to an external reality that is so to say less well organized. The conception that the world of mental entities is somehow better organized than the outside world is obviously an idealistic one (though it does not constitute the only possible kind of idealism); Wierzbicka herself stresses the Platonist character of her approach. On the other hand, Putnam's view that science is neat whereas everyday language is fuzzy, links up with the empiricist objectivism of the Ideal Language branch of analytical philosophy: the objective structure of reality is best described by the language of science, and everyday language is at best a weak derivative of scientific categorization, at worst a conceptual muddle teeming with philosophical pseudo-problems. As the previous discussion suggests that hard-core Cognitive Linguistics steers clear of both the idealist and the objectivist option, we have here one more indication[22] for the necessity of a further investigation into the epistemological, philosophical background of the prototypical conception of categorial structure.

## Notes

1. The discussion in section 2 will make clear that the term *prototype theory* should be used with care, since the theoretical uniformity that it suggests tends to obliterate the actual distinctions between the diverse forms of prototypicality discussed in the literature. The term is used here as a convenient reference mark only, to indicate a number of related theoretical conceptions of categorial structure that share an insistence on any or more of the various kinds of prototypicality effects discussed in section 2.
2. Though not exclusively: see Rosch (1988: 386).
3. Notice that this claim applies just as well to the axiomatic, postulate-based form of

description that developed as the major representational alternative for Katzian componential analysis. The notion of criteriality is just as much part and parcel of the classical versions of the axiomatic alternative as it is of Katzian feature analysis.

4. See, among others, Haiman (1980) and Geeraerts (1985b).
5. The distinction between semantic and encyclopedic concepts against which Cognitive Semantics reacts is often misconstrued. In particular, in the statement that there is no principled distinction between semantic and encyclopedic information, the words *semantic* and *encyclopedic* are not used (as implied by Lehmann 1988b) in the senses 'as may be found in dictionaries' and 'as may be found in encyclopedias', respectively. Rather, the rejected distinction refers to an alleged distinction within an individual language user's conceptual memory; it involves the presupposition that there is an independent level of semantic information that belongs to the language and that is distinct from the individual's world knowledge. The kind of information that is typically found in encyclopedias involves scientific information of the kind 'ovulation triggered by copulation' for the item *cat* (the example is Lehmann's); but while the distinction between scientific and laymen's knowledge is primarily a social one, this kind of 'encyclopedic' information is only relevant for the psychological perspective of Cognitive Semantics if the individual lexicon to be described is that of someone with a certain amount of scientific knowledge of cats (or if, through sociolinguistic idealization, the average language user's lexicon may be supposed to contain that piece of scientific information).
6. There are, of course, exceptions such as Dowty (1979) to confirm the rule. The historical sketch of the advent of prototype theory given here is treated more thoroughly in Geeraerts (1988b).
7. As the semantic interests of the former audience of Generative Semantics were so to say no longer envisaged by the leading theories of the day, it does not come as a total surprise, from this point of view, to find George Lakoff, one of the leading Generative Semanticists, again as one of the leading cognitivists.
8. These antecedents are not the only ones that might be mentioned. I have elsewhere (1988c) drawn the attention to the similarities between the prestructuralist, historical tradition of semantic research and present-day Cognitive Semantics, but there are other (admittedly non-mainstream) traditions of semantic research with which Cognitive Semantics is methodologically related: think, e.g., of the anthropological research of Malinowski, Firth, and the London School in general. Even a structuralist such as Reichling has held views about the structure of polysemy that come close to the point of view of prototype theory: his influential work on the word as the fundamental unit of linguistics (1935) contains an analysis of the Dutch word spel that is awkwardly similar to Wittgenstein's remarks about the German equivalent Spiel. The point to be stressed is this: as a theory about the (radial, clustered, dynamically flexible) structure of polysemy, prototype theory is to a considerable extent a rediscovery of views that were paramount during the prestructuralist era of the development of lexical semantics, and that lingered on below the surface in the structuralist and transformationalist periods.
9. Because of their large scope, the functionalist approach of Seiler (1986) and the naturalist approach of Dressler (1985) are particularly interesting for the use of prototypicality with regard to various aspects of the formal organization of language.

10. A bibliography of work in Cognitive Linguistics is to be found in Dirven (1988). It is worth mentioning that Cognitive Linguistics is currently in a stage of organization: a first international conference of Cognitive Linguistics was held in Duisburg in March 1989, and a new journal entitled Cognitive Linguistics, published by Mouton, is scheduled to start appearing in the beginning of 1990.
11. Next to the link with psycholinguistics, there is a connection with Artificial Intelligence research, through the correspondences between the notion of prototypicality and that of frame; see Fillmore (1977). It needs to be stressed, though, that the link is relatively weak; specifically, the correspondence just mentioned is to a certain extent counterbalanced by Lakoff's criticism (1987) of the objectivist assumptions of mainstream Artificial Intelligence research (but then again, one of Lakoff's current research projects involves a connectionist approach to the formal modeling of Cognitive Semantic notions such as metaphorical image schemata). In general, sorting out the relationship between Cognitive Semantics and Artificial Intelligence-oriented Cognitive Science will be one of the major tasks for the further development of Cognitive Semantics.
12. See Lakoff (1987: chapter 6) for the notion of a radial set, and compare Givon (1986) for a comparison between the views of Wittgenstein and those of prototype theory. The stress Givon places on the distinctions between both is slightly exaggerated, as it tends to obscure their mutual rejection of the so-called classical theory. See also the next footnote.
13. The 'so-called' is added to stress, first, that the views of Aristotle also contain features that correspond rather with a cognitive than with a 'classical' approach, and second (more generally), that the philosophical position of prototype theory is in need of further elucidation. The present situation is rather muddled: while the classical Roschian position is to characterize prototype theory as non-Aristotelian and Wittgensteinian, Givon (1986) has argued that prototype theory is non-Wittgensteinian (see the previous note), but whereas Givon also describes prototype theory as non-Platonic, Wierzbicka (to whom we shall come back in section 3) precisely presents an explicitly Platonic version of prototype theory. More generally, the philosophical position of prototype theory has so far been discussed mainly against the background of classical philosophy (Aristotle and Plato), and against the background of contemporary analytical philosophy (see Lakoff 1987). This means that a large part of the history of Western philosophy passes unmentioned; this is to be regretted, as the post-Cartesian period in the history of philosophy is concerned with epistemological questions that are of immediate interest to Cognitive Semantics. In particular, if it can be accepted that one of the major epistemological aspects of a prototypical conception of categorial structure resides in the fact that categories are interpretive schemata that are used flexibly and dynamically in our encounters with reality, a major philosophical reference point for prototype theory will lie with those philosophical theories that recognize the constitutive role of existing knowledge with regard to new experiences. As I have argued elsewhere (1985b), the Husserlian phenomenological movement (as represented, specifically, by Maurice Merleau-Ponty) provides a good starting-point for a further confrontation with philosophy.
14. The archaeopteryx is probably regarded as a species separate from either bird or reptile.

15. The example is taken from the *Longman Dictionary of Contemporary English*.
16. Considered from this point of view, Lakoff's radial sets as such are not particularly unclassical: structured polysemy as such is entirely compatible with the classical view. Kleiber (1988) offers an insightful discussion of the theoretical consequences of the growing importance of the structure of polysemy in prototype-theoretical research.
17. For a more extended discussion of Wierzbicka's views, see Geeraerts (1988d).
18. Notice that the restriction to the prototypical centre of categories correlates with Wierzbicka's Platonic, introspective methodology: it seems probable that the applications of a category that can be accessed introspectively are only the more salient ones; peripheral cases probably do not always pass the threshold of conscious attention. What is interesting from a cognitive point of view, however, is the way people spontaneously categorize and classify things, not the way in which they introspectively reflect upon their own conceptualizations. Any attempt to describe the peripheral instances of a category together with its prototypical centre can therefore not be restricted to an introspective methodology.
19. This is not say that Putnam actually intended his stereotypical theory as such an attempted rescue: his problems lay with the notion of reference rather than with those of polysemy and categorial structure. My remarks about Putnam are an investigation into some of the possible consequences of the notion of division of linguistic labor, not an attempt to give an account of Putnam's view in its original setting. Further, it has to be mentioned that some of Putnam's later philosophical views open up entirely different perspectives for a confrontation with Cognitive Semantics; in particular, see Lakoff (1987) on Putnam and anti-objectivism.
20. An interesting contribution to such an exploration is found in Lakoff (1987: chapter 12), where it is claimed that scientific categories are far from being as classical as is usually assumed.
21. Again, see Lakoff (1987: chapter 9) for some more examples; they are situated within formal psycholexicology rather than within linguistics.
22. Next, that is, to the remarks made in footnote 13.

## References

Aijmer, Karen
1985 The semantic development of *will*. In *Historical Semantics – Historical Word-Formation*, Jacek Fisiak (ed.), 11–21. Berlin/New York: Mouton de Gruyter.

Armstrong, Sharon L., Lila R. Gleitman, and Henry Gleitman
1983 What some concepts might not be. *Cognition* 13: 263–308.

Bartsch, Renate
1985 *Sprachnormen: Theorie und Praxis.* Tübingen: Niemeyer Verlag.

Berlin, Brent and Paul Kay
1969 *Basic Color Terms.* Berkeley: University of California Press.

Bybee, Joan and Carol L. Moder
1983 Morphological classes as natural categories. *Language* 59: 251–270.

Craig, Colette (ed.)
1986 *Noun Classes and Categorization.* Amsterdam/Philadelphia: John Benjamins.

Dirven, René
1988 Bibliography of Cognitive Linguistics. Duisburg: Linguistic Agency of the University of Duisburg.

Dowty, David
1979 *Word Meaning and Montague Grammar.* Dordrecht: Reidel.

Dressler, Wolfgang
1985 *Morphophonology.* Ann Arbor: Karoma.

Fillmore, Charles J.
1975 An alternative to checklist theories of meaning. In *Proceedings of the First Annual Meeting of the Berkeley Linguistics Society*, Cathy Cogen, Henry Thompson, and James Wright (eds.), 123–131. Berkeley: Berkeley Linguistics Society.
1977 Scenes–and–frames semantics. In *Linguistic Structures Processing*, Antonio Zampolli (ed.), 55–81. Amsterdam: North Holland Publishing Company.

Geeraerts, Dirk
1983 Prototype theory and diachronic semantics: A case study. *Indogermanische Forschungen* 88: 1–32.
1985a *Paradigm and Paradox. Explorations into a Paradigmatic Theory of Meaning and its Epistemological Background.* Leuven: Universitaire Pers.
1985b Les données stéréotypiques, prototypiques et encyclopédiques dans le dictionnaire. *Cahiers de Lexicologie* 46: 27–43.
1985c Cognitive restrictions on the structure of semantic change. In *Historical Semantics - Historical Word Formation*, Jacek Fisiak (ed.), 127–153. Berlin/New York: Mouton de Gruyter.
1988a On necessary and sufficient conditions. *Journal of Semantics* 5: 275–291.
1988b Katz revisited: aspects of the history of lexical semantics. In *Understanding the Lexicon*, Werner Hüllen and Rainer Schulze (eds.), 23–35. Tübingen: Max Niemeyer Verlag.
1988c Cognitive Grammar and the history of lexical semantics. In *Topics in Cognitive Linguistics*, Brygida Rudzka–Ostyn (ed.), 647–677. Amsterdam/Philadelphia: John Benjamins.
1988d Review of Anna Wierzbicka, Lexicography and Conceptual Analysis. *Language in Society* 17: 449–455.

Givon, Talmy
1986 Prototypes: between Plato and Wittgenstein. In *Noun Classes and Categorization*, Colette Craig (ed.), 78–102. Amsterdam/Philadelphia: John Benjamins.

John Haiman
1980 Dictionaries and encylopedias. *Lingua* 50: 329–357.

Heider, Eleanor R.
1972 Universals in color naming and memory. *Journal of Experimental Psychology* 93: 10–20.

Heider, Eleanor R. and Olivier, D.C.
1972 The structure of color space in naming and memory for two languages. *Cognitive Psychology* 3: 337–354.
Holland, Dorothy and Naomi Quinn (eds.)
1987 *Cultural Models in Language and Thought*. Cambridge: Cambridge University Press.
Hüllen, Werner and Rainer Schulze (eds.)
1988 *Understanding the Lexicon. Meaning, Sense, and World Knowledge in Lexical Semantics*. Tübingen: Niemeyer.
Katz, Jerrold J. and Jerry A. Fodor
1963 The structure of a semantic theory. *Language* 39, 170–210.
Kleiber, Georges
1988 Prototype, stéréotype: un air de famille? *DRLAV. Revue de Linguistique* 38: 1–61.
Labov, William
1973 The boundaries of words and their meanings. In *New Ways of Analysing Variation in English*, Charles J. Bailey and Roger Shuy (eds.), 340–373. Washington: Georgetown University Press.
Lakoff, George
1982 Categories and cognitive models. Trier: Linguistic Agency of the University of Trier. Also as: *Berkeley Cognitive Science Report* no. 2. Berkeley: Institute for Human Learning.
1986 Classifiers as a reflection of mind. In *Noun Classes and Categorization,* Colette Craig (ed.), 13–51. Amsterdam/Philadelphia: John Benjamins.
1987 *Women, Fire, and Dangerous Things. What Categories Reveal about the Mind*. Chicago: The University of Chicago Press.
Langacker Ronald W.
1987 *Foundations of Cognitive Grammar I*. Stanford: Stanford University Press.
Lehmann, Winfred P. (ed.)
1988a *Prototypes in Language and Cognition*. Ann Arbor: Karoma.
Lehmann Winfred P.
1988b Review of R. Langacker, Foundations of Cognitive Grammar. *General Linguistics* 28: 122–30.
Medin, Doug L. and Edward E. Smith
1984 Concepts and concept formation. *Annual Review of Psychology* 35: 113–138.
Mervis, Carolyn B. and Eleanor Rosch
1981 Categorization of natural objects. *Annual Review of Psychology* 32: 89–115.
Nathan, Geoffrey S.
1986 Phonemes as mental categories. In *Proceedings of the Twelfth Annual Meeting of the Berkeley Linguistics Society*, Vassiliki Nikiforidou, Mary VanClay, Mary Niepokuj, Deborah Feder (eds.), 212–224. Berkeley: Berkeley Linguistics Society.
Neisser, Ulrich
1987 *Concepts and Conceptual Development. Ecological and Intellectual Factors in Categorization*. Cambridge: Cambridge University Press.

Posner, Michael
1986 Empirical studies of prototypes. *Noun classes and categorization*, Colette Craig (ed.), 53–61. Amsterdam/Philadelphia: John Benjamins.

Post, Michael
1986 A prototype approach to denominal adjectives. In *Linguistics across Historical and Geographical Boundaries*, Dieter Kastovsky and Aleksander Szwedek (eds.), II: 1003–1013. Berlin/New York: Mouton De Gruyter.

Putnam, Hilary
1975 The meaning of Meaning. In *Mind, Language, and Reality. Philosophical Papers II*, Hilary Putnam, 215–271. Cambridge: Cambridge University Press.

Quine, Willard V.O.
1960 *Word and Object*. Cambridge, Mass.: MIT Press.

Reichling, Anton
1935 *Het Woord*. Zwolle: Tjeenk Willink.

Rosch, Eleanor
1973 On the internal structure of perceptual and semantic categories. In *Cognitive Development and the Acquisition of Language*, Timothy E. Moore (ed.), 111–144. New York: Academic Press.
1975 Cognitive representations of semantic categories. *Journal of Experimental Psychology: General* 104: 192–233.
1977 Human categorization. In *Studies in Cross–cultural Psychology I,* Warren, Neil (ed.), 1–49. New York: Academic Press.
1978 Principles of categorization. In *Cognition and Categorization*, Eleanor Rosch and Barbara B. Lloyd (eds.), 27–48. Hillsdale, NJ: Lawrence Erlbaum.
1988 Coherences and categorization: A historical view. In *The Development of Language and Language Researchers. Essays in Honor of Roger Brown*, Frank Kessel (ed.), 373–392. Hillsdale, NJ: Lawrence Erlbaum.

Rosch, Eleanor and Carolyn B. Mervis
1975 Family resemblances: Studies in the internal structure of categories. *Cognitive Psychology* 7: 573–605.

Rosch, Eleanor, Carolyn B. Mervis, Wayne D. Gray, David Johnson, and Penny Boyes–Braem
1976 Basic objects in natural categories. *Cognitive Psychology* 8: 382–439.

Rosch, Eleanor, Carol Simpson, and Scott R. Miller
1976 Structural bases of typicality effects. *Journal of Experimental Psychology: Human Perception and Peformance* 2: 491–502.

Ross, John R.
1987 Islands and syntactic prototypes. In *Papers from the 23rd Annual Meeting of the Chicago Linguistic Society*, Barbara Need, Eric Schiller, and Anna Bosch (eds.), 309–320. Chicago: Chicago Linguistic Society.

Rudzka–Ostyn, Brygida
1988 Semantic extensions into the domain of verbal communication. In *Topics in Cognitive Linguistics*, Brygida Rudzka–Ostyn (ed.), 507–553. Amsterdam/ Philadelphia: John Benjamins.

Smith, Edward E. and Doug Medin

1981 *Categories and Concepts*. Cambridge, MA: Harvard University Press.

Taylor, John

1989 *Linguistic Categorization. Prototypes in Linguistic Theory*. Oxford: Clarendon Press.

Tsohatzidis, Savas L. (ed.)

1989 *Meanings and Prototypes. Studies on Linguistic Categorization*. London: Routledge and Kegan Paul.

Uhlenbeck, Eugenius M.

1967 The dynamic nature of word meaning. *Actes du Xe Congrès International des Linguistes* II, 679–685. Bucarest: Editions de l'Academie.

Van Langendonck, Willy

1986 Markedness, prototypes, and language acquisition. *Cahiers de l'Institut de Linguistique de Louvain* 12: 39–76.

Van Oosten, Jeanne

1986 The nature of subjects, topics, and agents: a cognitive explanation. Bloomington: Indiana University Linguistics Club.

Waismann, Friedrich

1952 Verifiability. In *Logic and Language (First Series)*, Anthony Flew (ed.), 117–144. Oxford: Basil Blackwell.

Weinreich, Uriel

1966 Explorations in semantic theory. *Current Trends in Linguistics* III: 395–479.

Wierzbicka, Anna

1985 *Lexicography and Conceptual Analysis*. Ann Arbor: Karoma.

1987 *English Speech Act Verbs: A Semantic Dictionary*. Sydney: Academic Press.

Winters, Margaret

1987 Syntactic and semantic space: the development of the French subjunctive. In *Papers from the Seventh International Conference on Historical Linguistics*, Anna G. Ramat, Onofrio Carruba, and Giulano Bernini (eds.), 607–618. Amsterdam/Philadelphia: John Benjamins.

Wittgenstein, Ludwig

1953 *Philosophische Untersuchungen. Philosophical Investigations*. Oxford: Basil Blackwell.

Zwicky, Arnold and Jerry Sadock

1975. Ambiguity tests and how to fail them. In *Syntax and Semantics 4*, John Kimball (ed.), 1–36. New York: Academic Press.

# Chapter 5
# Schematic network

## Ambiguity, polysemy, and vagueness

*David Tuggy*

### 1. Introduction: Tests for ambiguity vs. vagueness

The difference between ambiguity and vagueness is a matter of whether two or more meanings associated with a given phonological form are distinct (ambiguous), or united as non-distinguished subcases of a single, more general meaning (vague). A standard example of ambiguity is *bank* "financial institution" vs. *bank* "land at river edge", where the meanings are intuitively quite separate; in *aunt* "father's sister" vs. *aunt* "mother's sister", however, the meanings are intuitively united into one, "parent's sister". Thus ambiguity corresponds to separation, and vagueness to unity, of different meanings.

Several kinds of tests have been proposed to render this difference measurable. The "logical" test of Quine (1960) will not centrally concern us here; it involves seeing if a sentence "X and not X" can be true; the (supposed) acceptability of *This is the bank* [river edge] *but it is not the bank* [financial institution] indicates that *bank* is ambiguous; the unacceptability of *I have an aunt* [father's sister] *but I do not have an aunt* [mother's sister] indicates vagueness for *aunt.* There is a "definitional" test (since Aristotle) which involves seeking a meaning common to the two; if such is found, then it is taken as the correct definition, and it is vague as to the differences between the original two meanings. Thus since there is (supposedly) no meaning common to the two meanings of *bank* it is ambiguous; since for *aunt* there is a common meaning (parent's sister), it takes precedence over the two more specific meanings and the word is ambiguous. The "linguistic" tests (Lakoff 1970 and others) will concern us more; they involve grammatical constructions which are taken as requiring semantic identity, such as "X does/did Z and so does/did Y". If Z as done by X and Z as done by Y can be given "crossed" readings without the semantic oddness known as zeugma, the meaning of Z is taken to be vague; if zeugma results, Z is ambiguous. Thus the ordinariness of *I have an aunt* [father's sister] *and so does Bill* [have an aunt (mother's sister)] indicates that the meanings are taken to be the same, and thus *aunt* is vague; the unacceptability of the zeugmatic *I went to the bank* [financial

Originally published in 1993 in *Cognitive Linguistics* 4(3): 273–290.

institution] *and so did Bill* [go to the bank (river edge)], which could only be said facetiously, indicates that *bank* is ambiguous. A fourth distinction which is sometimes mentioned (e.g. Kempson 1977: 182) is that puns can be constructed with ambiguous but not vague structures; thus a pirate burying his gold at the edge of the river could be said to be *putting his money in the bank,* which is an (admittedly bad) pun; such a pun could not be readily made, if at all, on the two meanings of *aunt.*

Geeraerts (1993) argues that (a) the three tests do not always agree with each other, and (b) by changing the context, all three tests can be made to yield indeterminate results. He is particularly concerned to demonstrate that even for the standard paradigm examples of ambiguity, if you try hard enough you can get the tests to yield equivocal results. He concludes that the conception of ambiguity and vagueness as classical categories with fixed boundaries and no gradations of membership is, at the least, strongly called into question. The possibility that they are categories formed on a prototype pattern thus merits investigation.

## 2. The fuzzy borderline between ambiguity and vagueness

### 2.1. Polysemy

Geeraerts' conclusions are supported solidly by a different sort of data, not the paradigm cases but rather borderline cases where there is clearly a meaning common to the sub-meanings in question (and thus by the definitional test there is only one meaning), but nevertheless there are strong enough differences in meaning to produce equivocal results or judgments of ambiguity from the linguistic tests.[1] These cases are traditionally considered under the rubric of polysemy:[2] traditional definitions (e.g. Lyons 1977: 550; Zwicky and Sadock 1975: 2) have lexical ambiguity (or homonymy) as involving two lexemes, polysemy a single lexeme with different distinct senses, and vagueness a lexeme with a single but nonspecific meaning, i.e., the lexeme may subsume other meanings but those meanings are not distinguished from each other or from the more inclusive "true" meaning. Thus polysemy is a sort of halfway point between ambiguity and vagueness. As Deane (1988: 327, 345) puts it, "In effect, the three types form a gradient between total semantic identity and total semantic distinctness", and "Polysemy seems somehow to straddle the border between identity and distinctness."

Any conscientious lexicographer will admit to at least occasional difficulty in deciding whether two clearly related meanings associated with the same phonological form are to be listed as a single entry in the dictionary or not (e.g. Hartmann's (1983: 6–7) discussion of senses of *bank*); most make frequent use of sub-entries and sub-sub-entries to ease the difficulty. These cases constitute massive evidence, from any and every language, that the categories of ambiguity and vagueness are not absolute.

### *2.1.1. The verb* paint

For an English example, consider the meaning(s) of the verb *paint.* A structure such as *she is painting (it)* can conventionally be used to refer to an indefinitely large number of situations, including the following (and many others): (i) painting a portrait in oils on canvas, (ii) painting a landscape with watercolors on paper, (iii) painting *trompe l'oeil* on the interior wall and floor of a house, (iv) painting a mural on the exterior wall of a public building, (v) painting a decorative border on an interior wall, (vi) painting the walls of a room with a single color of paint for decorative purposes but also to preserve them, (vii) painting the exterior of a house primarily to preserve it, (viii) painting furniture, (ix) painting a car with an air gun, (x) painting stripes on a parking lot or roadway by driving a paint-spraying machine, (xi) applying makeup to the face, or (xii) applying iodine or some other colored disinfectant to the body after or prior to an incision, with a swabbing motion. The concepts coded by *paint* in these different situations clearly have something important in common: they all involve applying some colored substance to a surface. This, by the Aristotelian definitional test, is the meaning of the word, which is therefore presumably vague. However, the different situations vary along a number of parameters such as the nature of the substance applied (usually it is a liquid, properly called *paint* [N], which dries into a thin tough layer on the surface, but not in the cases of (xi–xii)), the nature of the surface and the extent to which it is covered as a whole, whether one color or a combination of colors is applied, the instrument used for application (usually a brush or less typically a roller, but not in (ix–xii)), the kind of physical activity involved in the application, the purpose of the application (with protection and visual esthetic enhancement being the two major types), the kinds of abilities and training needed to do the application properly, etc. Many cases are obviously closer to each other than others along these parameters; e.g. (i) and (ii) are much closer than (i) and (x) or (i) and (xii).

### *2.1.2. Ambivalent results on the linguistic tests*

The linguistic tests yield equivocal results in cases of this sort. If I have been painting a watercolor landscape (ii) and Jane a portrait in oils (i), a sentence like (1) *I have been painting and so has Jane* is perfectly normal, indicating vagueness rather than ambiguity for *paint.* If I have been painting stripes on the road (x), however, while Jane painted a portrait, (1) feels zeugmatic: I do not believe I could utter it except facetiously. This indicates that *paint* is ambiguous. Combinations of (i) and (xi) or (i) and (xii) would be even more anomalous and clearly zeugmatic. If I was painting the exterior of a house (vii) and Jane a portrait, the sentence would still strike me as odd, but not nearly as odd as clear cases of zeugma do. I would not judge that this oddness amounts to a clear indication of either ambiguity or vagueness, rather it might be taken to indicate something in between.[3] If I were painting a mural on a wall (iv), it would be better; if she were painting a mural and I doing the more normal wall painting of (vi) or (vii) I think it would be almost, but still not entirely, normal; if she were painting a decorative border on a wall (v) and I a flat coat of paint (vi), the sentence would be quite normal. The acceptability of sentence (1) in the different cases is not a discrete, binary property, and it seems to correlate at least roughly to the closeness of the kinds of painting along the parameters mentioned above.

### *2.1.3. The influence of context*

Equally importantly, the linguistic context can affect the acceptability of such test sentences. For instance, when the stem *paint* is used with the nominalizing suffix *-er,* the distinctions of purpose of painting and skills and training needed to paint well become more important. Thus, although sentence (1) is almost normal in a case of (iv) and (vi) or (vii) (mural vs. normal wall painting), it sounds facetious to say, if Jane and I do those activities professionally, (2) *I am a painter and so is Jane*. If I paint stripes on a road for a living and she paints oil portraits (i and x), it sounds downright ludicrous. On the other hand, I could say, non-facetiously, (3) *When I'm painting I try to get the color on evenly, and so does Jane,* with virtually any combination of the kinds of painting involved.

If *paint* is used transitively further differences emerge. In cases (i–ii) and usually (iii–v) the direct object designates not the surface to which paint is applied, but either the artistic figure created in paint on that surface, or something of which that artistic figure is a representation. A similar construal is also normal for (x), though roadway stripes are not precisely "artistic figures", and the direct object designates only the stripes themselves, not anything which they might represent. Marginally in (iii–iv) and (x), more easily in (v) and (xii), and normally in (vi–ix) and (xi) the object is the surface. Example (xii), however, would normally take the disinfectant as object. This means that for some combinations (e.g. (v) and (xii) a sentence like (4) *I have been painting it and so has Jane* is not possible since there is no referent of *it* that can normally do service in both cases. In other cases the same object can be construed, but its relationship to the process of painting is different in the two cases, and thus the sentence still does not work: e.g., if Jane is painting my house in sense (ii) (i.e., creating an artistic representation of it in watercolors on paper) and I am painting it in sense (vi) or (vii) (as a housepainter), to say (5) *I am painting the house and so is Jane* can only be facetious. Similarly

(6) *Jane is painting her grandfather's portrait – bright green* sounds like a pun on senses (i) and (vi) or (vii).

### 2.1.4. Summary

So, is *paint* ambiguous, or is it vague? Both, or perhaps neither. A full answer would require elucidating more carefully than we have done here the relationships among all these meanings and many others, including figurative meanings (*paint a gloomy picture of the prospects for peace*), nominal meanings, and so forth. These meanings are separable, yet they can also be correctly united. *Webster's New Collegiate Dictionary* makes separate entries for nominal and verbal meanings, treating them exactly as it does clearly ambiguous forms,[4] with multiple subdivisions of both entries (the verb entry lists 4 transitive and 2 intransitive meanings, plus submeanings for a total of 12 definitions; the noun entry has 3 main meanings and a total of 7 definitions). *The American Heritage Dictionary* lists only one main entry, with nominal and verbal subsections (6 nominal and 10 verbal definitions); other dictionaries do it still differently. I do not think anyone would want to say that one dictionary is right and the others wrong: rather we are dealing with very complex groupings of meanings which can be rightly united (treated as vague) for some purposes and distinguished (treated as ambiguous) for others. The dictionary makers have made intelligent, even praiseworthy choices for the purposes they have in mind, but the meanings they are representing do not fall into classical categories, internally homogeneous and with absolute boundaries between them; thus no one way of splitting them up, or of uniting them, is absolutely right.[5]

Thousands of other examples, from every language I know, could be given to illustrate the same point: the same set of meanings can be both separable (ambiguous-like) and unitable (vague-like). Any time a dictionary entry has sub-entries, and especially sub-sub-entries, the dictionary makers have in effect said "these meanings are united, but they are also usefully distinguished." And surely our native speaker intuitions confirm the same point. A chess *set*, a *set* in tennis, a *set* of dishes, and a *set* in logic; or *breaking* a stick, a law, a horse, water, ranks, a code, and a record; in each case the meanings are clearly rather different from each other, but do they not have something in common as well? Our seeing the differences between them does not cancel out our ability to see them as the same thing (and thus call them by the same name). We see what is common between getting food ready to eat and counselling a person about to be traumatized, and that accounts for us calling both activities *preparing,* yet it feels like a pun when you hear on the radio advice on how to prepare your turkey for Thanksgiving dinner – by breaking it to him gently ("Tom, are you religious?"). Wrenches, keys, and faucets have a lot in common, and that doubtless is why they are all called *llave* in Spanish, but must we therefore suppose that Spanish speakers don't distinguish them? Rather the evidence, from the linguistic tests, would show that they can and often do do so. A Náhuatl speaker can certainly distinguish the rising of the sun from leaving a house from a chicken hatching or a seed sprouting, but he calls all these processes (and others) *kisa* 'emerge', and they clearly do have important elements in common, some more than others.

### 2.2. Diachronic change

Another issue that is problematic for a model which posits classical categories for ambiguity and vagueness, with no gradation between them, is diachronic change. It is common for meanings that at one stage are united (vague) to become separate over time (occasionally the opposite occurs as well), and the change seems to be gradual rather than abrupt. For instance, Lewis (1967: 139), after a careful delineation of cumulative small changes in the meanings of *sense*, says of the juridical vs. grammatical meanings of *sentence*: "This is an excellent example of the merely homophonic status to which the different uses of a word are finally reduced. If you said 'Jeremy Taylor can boast the longest sentence of any English writer' and someone replied 'Poor Wilde had a longer one', this would be a pure pun."

### 2.3. Summary

In sum, then, the synchronic existence of cases where the borderline between ambiguity and vagueness is blurred, together with instances of gradual diachronic change across that border, casts doubt on whether there is an absolute, hard and fast line of demarcation between the two categories.

## 3. A cognitive model

If a model of ambiguity and vagueness (or ambiguity, polysemy, and vagueness) as well-defined categories, internally homogenous and with clear boundaries, does not work, what does? Categories based on prototypes have proved useful for analyzing many other linguistic distinctions (e.g., Lakoff 1987; Langacker 1987); perhaps they are appropriate for this one as well. I would suggest the following model within Langacker's Cognitive Grammar framework.[6]

### 3.1. Categorization in Cognitive Grammar

Following Langacker (1987, etc.), we call what two cognitive structures have in common a "schema", and represent its relationship to its elaborations (or subcases) by arrows from the schema to each elaboration (Figure 1a); such relationships form the basis for categorization.[7] Both schemas and their elaborations can coexist in a language; they exist to the degree that they are established (entrenched) in speakers' minds through repeated usage. Well-entrenched structures, *ceteris paribus*, are more salient than less-entrenched structures, i.e., they occur more energetically. Entrenchment can be viewed as a kind of enduring salience, i.e., salience apart from relatively transitory effects such as directed attention or heightened activation due to contextual factors. Degree of salience is represented by the thickness and continuity of a box enclosing the structure in question (and secondarily by grayscaling the representation of the structure itself): thus Figure 1b shows a salient structure A and a less salient structure B, both subsumed by marginally salient schema C; if transitory salience effects are not factored in, the degree of salience will be equivalent to the degree of entrenchment. Another parameter which we should distinguish is elaborative distance, which we represent by the length of the arrows from schema to elaboration:[8] a schema is distant from its elaborations when relatively many specifications of the elaborations must be despecified to form the schema, and close when relatively few must be despecified. Thus in Figure 1c, C is at a greater elaborative distance from A and B than in 1b. (One might, for example, take A, B, and C in 1b to be CAT, WEASEL, and MAMMAL THAT EATS MICE, respectively, while in 1c they might be DOG, STOOL, and THING WITH LEGS FOUND IN HUMAN DWELLINGS.)

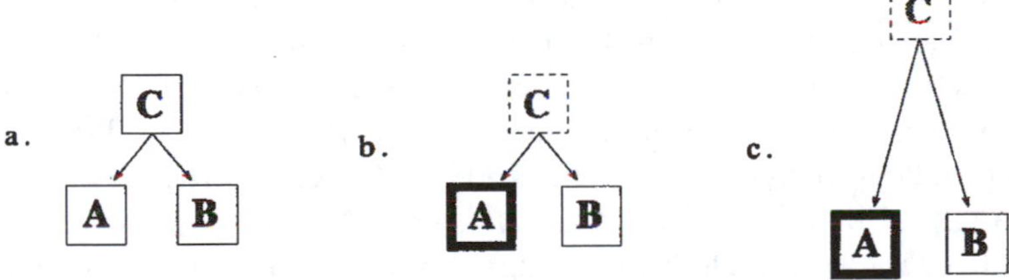


*Figure 1.* Schemas and elaborations

It will be readily seen that the Aristotelian definitional test amounts to looking to see if there is a schema subsuming two meanings and making that the definition. Many linguists seem to operate on the assumption that once such a schema is found, the subcases it subsumes may be safely ignored, regardless of their degree of entrenchment or salience. I am suggesting, however, that to the degree that they are salient they must not be ignored.

## 3.2. The characterization of ambiguity and vagueness

The prototypical case of ambiguity is where two semantic structures, associated with the same phonological structure (which is called their *phonological pole*), are both well-entrenched (and therefore salient), while there is no well-entrenched and elaboratively close schema, also linked to the phonological pole, subsuming them.[9] This is represented in Figure 2a.[10] Prototypical vagueness, on the other hand, involves meanings which are not well-entrenched but which have a relatively well-entrenched, elaboratively close schema subsuming them, as represented in Figure 2e.[11]

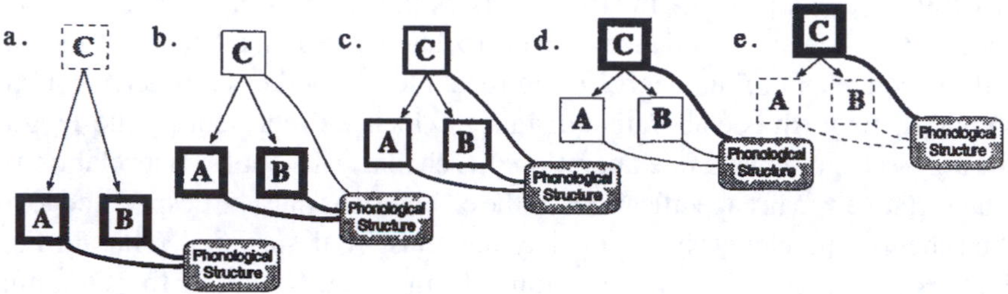


*Figure 2.* The ambiguity–vagueness cline

Elaborateness (non-schematicity) of a semantic structure correlates with a smaller extensionality; the extension of a schema includes those of its elaborations. Thus Figure 2 corresponds to Figure 3, where Venn diagrams represent the extension of the structures involved.[12] Again thickness and continuity of the lines (with gray-scaling) represents salience, and relative size represents schematic distance. 3a, like 2a, represents prototypical ambiguity, and 3e, like 2e, prototypical vagueness. It is perhaps more intuitively obvious from this sort of diagram that in the ambiguous case it is easy to separate the meanings and hard to unite them, whereas in the vague case it is relatively hard to separate them and easy to unite them.

It is important to realize that Figure 3 is a representation of the *extension* of the concepts (i.e., of the range of cases characterized by each concept's cognitive specifications), not a representation of the extent of the cognitive specifications themselves (such as is implied by diagrams utilizing the "container" metaphor, e.g., Langacker 1987: 75, Figure 2.4a, and many other places). More extensive specifications (greater "elaboration") corresponds to a lesser extension: thus a diagram like Figure 4, representing the extent of semantic specifications, would represent the same semantic structures as Figure 3 in quite opposite fashion (4a = 3a, 4c= 3c, 4e= 3e). The diagrams in Figure 4 make it clear that the schema is completely *immanent* to its elaborations (Langacker 1987: 180, 438–439): i.e., they contain all its specifications and more; the schema comprises those specifications which are common to the two subcases. Again relative size of a schema vs. its subcase represents cognitive distance: when the schema is much smaller than the subcase that means the subcase adds many specifications to those of the schema and is thus quite distant from it.

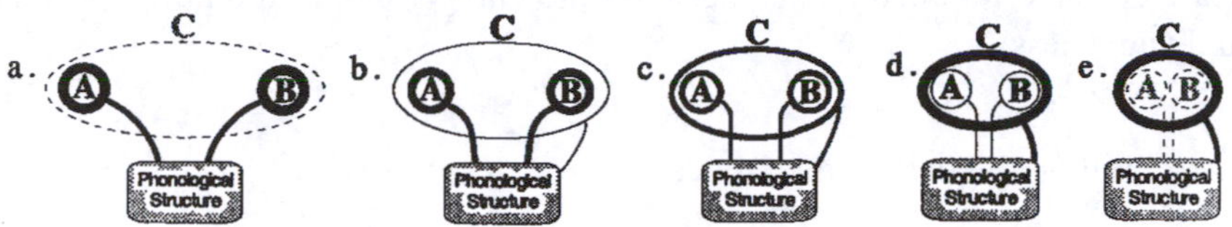


*Figure 3.* The ambiguity–vagueness cline showing extensionality of semantic structures

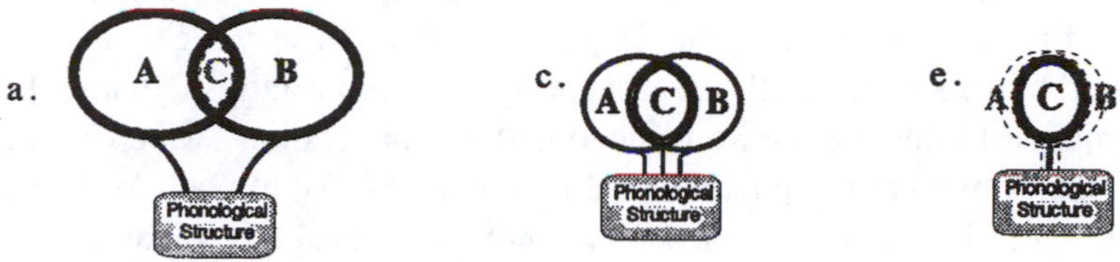


*Figure 4.* The ambiguity–vagueness cline showing extent of semantic structures

For many purposes, speakers will "filter out" specifications below a certain level of salience. If the threshold of salience is set higher than the level of salience of any uniting schema in 2a/3a or of the elaborate structures (the subcases) in 2e/3e, 2a/3a will have two completely separate meanings attached to the same phonological pole, while 2e/3e has only one meaning. (A rough visual analog to imposing such a threshold can be achieved by squinting more or less tightly at Figures 2–6.[13]) This corresponds exactly to the traditional characterizations of the ambiguity/vagueness distinction.

### 3.3. The in-between cases: Polysemy

Since the differences between Figure 2a and 2e (3a and 3e) are gradual, we can expect to find cases in the middle, where a schema exists but is not salient and/or is distant (2b/3b), or where the subcases are somewhat salient but not so much so as the schema (2d/3d), or even where both the schema and the subcases are salient (2c/3c). These of course are the polysemous cases discussed in section 2.1, the border straddling cases, with meanings both clearly separable and clearly united. But the important thing is that the differences among the categories are gradual, not absolute.

Note that if a high enough threshold of salience is imposed (if a speaker "squints" tightly enough), the schema in 2b (3b) is filtered out, leaving a configuration which is effectively the same as 2a (3a). Similarly, if the threshold of salience is set above the level of salience of the sub-cases in 2d (3d), 2d (or 3d) becomes effectively equivalent to 2e (3e). This, together with the influence of contextual salience mentioned below (3.4.3), makes it even more impossible to draw absolute boundary lines between the categories of ambiguity, polysemy, and vagueness.

## 3.4. Fitting the data to the model

### *3.4.1. Straightforward cases*

This model fits with the sorts of phenomena we find in languages. The case of *bank* "financial institution" and "edge of a river" fits very nicely at the ambiguous end of the spectrum: the two meanings are well established, and the nearest schema subsuming the two would be something like "Thing", which is quite distant and is not linked to the phonological pole /baenk/ (5a, cf. 2a). At the vague end (5e, cf. 2e) we can place *aunt*, with the non-salient subcases "father's sister" vs. "mother's sister" subsumed at a minimal elaborative distance under the concept "parent's sister", which is clearly better established and thus more salient than they as a meaning of *aunt*. An example of 2c (5c) would be the notions of artistic painting (including painting in oils and watercolors as in (i–ii) above) and of typical utilitarian painting (subsuming (vi–viii) and others): both well-established concepts, but clearly united under an also well-established schema not greatly distant from the subcases.

### *3.4.2. Flexibility*

Figure 2 of course oversimplifies things. Although elaborative distance between a schema and its elaborations tends to correlate inversely to entrenchment of the schema, the parameters are not absolutely parallel; Figure 2 does not represent this. Also one typically is dealing not with two or three meanings but with many more, arranged in multiply overlapping hierarchies – cf. Figure 6, of which 5c is an abbreviation, with 5c=6a–c. (Figure 6 itself is of course far from exhaustive of the meaning of *paint*.) Furthermore it is relatively rare for the subcases in question to have the same degree of salience; they are more likely to differ along this parameter, as in 1b–c (and, again, 6). These would all be valid criticisms if the presentation in Figure 2 were intended as absolute, but they are in fact predicted by the model, which has built into it the flexibility to accommodate them. Granted that Figure 2 is incomplete in this way, the main point nevertheless remains valid: To the degree that a group of meanings and any schema subsuming them approaches the configuration given in 2a, we can call it a case of ambiguity, and to the degree that it approaches 2e, it is vagueness.

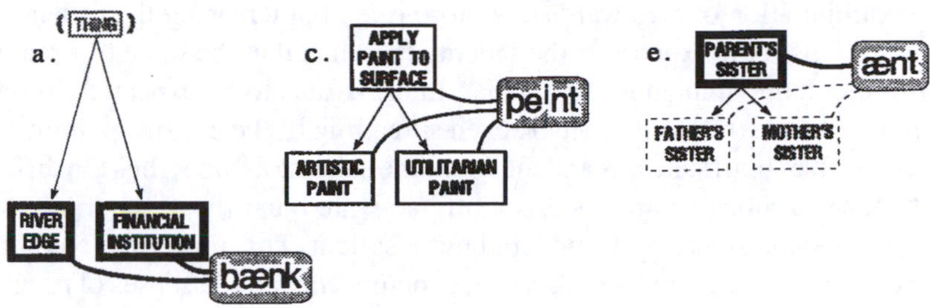


*Figure 5.* Typical examples along the ambiguity–vagueness cline

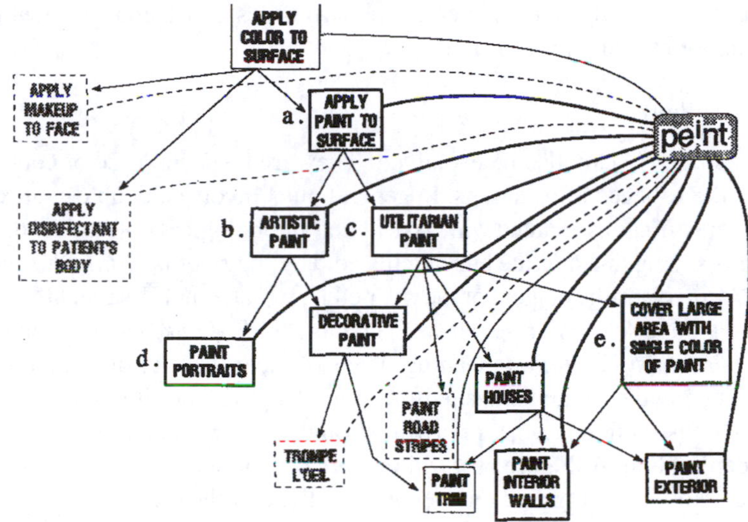


*Figure 6.* Paint

### *3.4.3. The influence of context*

Given this model, the influence of context comes for free. For salience is not a static characteristic, but a dynamic one. Among the factors enhancing it is entrenchment, as previously noted, but also degree of activation produced by context.[14] When a cognitive structure has itself been recently activated, whether in the linguistic or in some other cognitive context, or when structures closely linked to it have been activated, it retains a residual activation, and it will reactivate at a higher level of energy.[15] Thus when the word *painter* or even more especially the phrase *be a painter* is used as in sentence (2) above, the specifications attached to *-er* "one who does the verb professionally", and to the phrase *be a* V-*er,* enhance the salience of those portions of the meaning(s) of *paint* which have to do with innate abilities and skills employed, purpose for which done, and so on. This moves the configuration of 5c towards one more like 2b, increasing the salience of the elaborations at the expense of the schema. The fact that the same two readings of *paint* feel more ambiguous in (2) than in (1) is thus to be expected. In sentence (3), in contrast, the focus is on the even spreading of the color in painting, which characterizes both subcases and therefore the schema as well; thus the differences between the subcases are not especially activated and the schema (i.e., what is common to the subcases) is rendered more salient. This moves the configuration of 5c towards one more like 2d, which explains why all the senses of *paint* test as vague by sentence (3).[16] When *paint* is used intransitively, as in (1), the nature of the object is less salient: When it is used transitively, as in (4) or (5), it is rendered more salient, and must match in the two cases construed for identity-of-sense anaphora to function normally.

### 3.4.4. *Puns*

Puns like (6) can also be explained: They are a special case of context enhancing the salience of meanings. In general puns involve a double context, in which two meanings associated with a particular phonological pole are rendered salient. Thus saying that a pirate burying his gold by the river is *putting his money in the bank* involves the context of the river edge, which renders salient that meaning of *bank,* but also the phrase *put (your) money in the bank,* which strongly activates the *financial institution* meaning. The two meanings are overlaid on each other, producing the semantic discomfort we call a pun. The situation in (6) is similar: The construction *paint X's portrait* strongly activates, and thus renders salient, a meaning like (i) (Figure 6d), while *paint Y color* activates something like (vi–ix) (6e). Both meanings are thus rendered salient by the context, yielding a configuration like 2b, and overlaid on each other. In exactly the same way, the phrase *prepare your turkey for Thanksgiving dinner* renders salient one meaning of *prepare,* while the continuation *by breaking it to him gently* renders another meaning salient, and the superimposition of the two salient meanings constitutes a pun.

### 3.4.5. *Diachronic change*

And, finally, the model clearly shows the distinction between ambiguity and vagueness to be a gradual one, with synchronic variation of meanings along the parameters of differentiation. This brings ease to the problem of diachronic change from one category to the other. There is no hard and fast boundary that a form needs to jump all at once: it can straddle the fence indefinitely, shifting its weight back and forth, before gradually moving more to one side than the other.

## 4. Summary

I commend this model to you on the following grounds:

(1) The theoretical constructs involved are well motivated on independent grounds (see extensive argumentation in Langacker 1987 and elsewhere).

(2) The traditional view of the ambiguity/vagueness distinction is seen as essentially correct; its intuitive characterizations fit the model nicely. It was only wrong if the categories were made absolute.

(3) The value of the traditional linguistic and definitional tests is affirmed: they clearly and correctly distinguish prototypically vague from prototypically ambiguous structures. The different behavior of ambiguous and vague structures in puns also fits into the model.

(4) The model correctly allows for a range of in-between (polysemous) cases, neither ambiguous nor vague in the prototypical sense (although in the cases we examined they are predictably vague by the definitional test).

(5) The influence of context (including the possibility of puns between related senses of a polysemous form) is accounted for automatically.

(6) The gradual nature of the ambiguity/vagueness distinction allows for gradual rather than abrupt diachronic shifting from one category to the other.

# Notes

1. Quine's logical test is difficult for me to apply in these cases (as in most others). Applying it, for instance, to examples mentioned below, I could say, of a case of painting stripes in a parking lot (x) or even more of swabbing iodine (xii), "She's painting, but she's not (really) *painting"*. By that I would mean that what she is doing may be properly called painting, but it is not painting proper, i.e. it is not the prototypical kind of painting. This might be taken as indicating ambiguity, but it is not very satisfactory; it does not precisely yield the "painting in one sense but not the other" reading that Quine was after. Also it does not work for more prototypical cases – e.g. (i), or (vi) or (vii). In general, however, to say of a person in any of these situations "She's painting, but she's not painting", with no special intonation, seems infelicitous if not anomalous. This rather indicates vagueness. On the other hand, "This is the bank but it's not the bank" is far from felicitous for me as well. Kempson (1977: 129), for rather different reasons, also concludes that "the characterization of ambiguity as the simultaneous assignment to a sentence of the values true and false has not provided a criterion for deciding unclear cases; it merely accentuates the point of disagreement."
2. Traditional treatments of polysemy, however, tend to concentrate on cases in which the senses involved are not as closely related as those I am interested in: e.g., they would be more likely to discuss whether the nominal and verbal senses of *paint* can

be considered the same lexeme than to consider the distinctions among verbal senses I list in (i–xii).

3. Lyons (1977: 554) considers such in-between cases with the verb *play:* "Could we delete the second occurrence of the form *plays* in [*She plays chess better than she plays the flute*]? And what about [*?He played scrum-half in the afternoon and Hamlet in the evening*]?" Lyons concludes that "It may well be that the whole notion of discrete lexical senses is ill-founded."
4. "1paint *vb"* vs. "2paint *n".* The treatment is thus exactly parallel to that of "1painter *n* ... one that paints" (with subcases for artists and for housepainters and such) vs. "2painter *n* [... prob. fr. MF pendoir ...]: a line used for securing or towing a boat" vs. "3painter *n* ... [alter. of *panther*]... COUGAR"; three meanings with little or nothing in common beyond designating a thing of some sort. Cf. Lyons' (1977: 21–22) comment, "The fact that there are two separate entries means that the compilers or editors of the dictionary have decided that two distinct lexemes are involved (and not one lexeme with two meanings").
5. Langacker's discussion of the notion "lexical item" (1987: 388) is apropos: "A category is *coherent* to the extent that its members are densely linked by well-entrenched categorizing relationships of minimal distance. ... The coherence of a category is naturally a matter of degree ... To the extent that a semantic network with common symbolization [i.e. linked to a common phonological pole] approximates a coherent category, we can reasonably speak of a *lexical item.* Despite its convenience, however, this construct is more a descriptive fiction than a natural unit of linguistic organization. Not only is coherence inherently a matter of degree, but also the definition allows a single network to be divided into lexical items in multiple and mutually inconsistent ways. I regard this as a realistic characterization of the phenomena in question."
6. Most of this discussion is prefigured to some extent in Tuggy (1981: 56–59, 72), and I have been using the essence of the diagram in Figure 2 at least since 1984. Nevertheless, and although Langacker (1988: 137–139) credits my work, the ideas involved rest crucially on constructs of his theory, and in any case they came to me at least in part through discussions with him, Sue Lindner, Mary Ellen Ryder, Jeff Burnham, Barbara Levergood, and others. Thus I can claim no absolute credit for them.
7. For the discussion of this paper an essentially Aristotelian definition of *schema* is adequate, in which the schema contains only (and all) material common to the subcases, and any concept which includes that material is a subcase. This, while not the only possible conceptualization, is doubtless the prototypical one, and is that described repeatedly by Langacker (e.g. 1987: 68, 132–138). The main point of this paper with respect to it is that (i) the existence of such a schema as part of the meaning of a lexical item does not preclude the existence of its subcases: in fact the subcases may well be more salient than the schema; and (ii) such variations in salience among a schema and its subcases account for the non-absoluteness of the distinctions between ambiguity, (polysemy), and vagueness.

   A separate question is whether this conception of a schema is sufficient. (This is one of the important issues addressed by Geeraerts 1993.) Specifically, can a schema contain "either/or" specifications, or lists of alternative characteristics which do not have anything in common, or can it consist of specifications which are not characteristic (e.g. can one speak of a "schema" uniting *checkmate* and *pawn,* consisting of the game of chess, which figures saliently in the meaning of both but characterizes neither)? Although I do not argue it here, I believe such "schemas" (if the term is appropriate to use for them) do indeed serve to unite concepts into categories and thus are relevant to the concerns of this paper. Langacker (e.g. 1987: 69, 92–93) speaks at length of a relationship of "partial schematicity" or "extension" in which there is conflict between the specifications of the "schema" and the "elaboration", using it to describe the relationship between a prototype and non-prototypical members of the same category, or between the literal and figurative senses of a metaphor, or a grammatical pattern and an ill-formed instance of that pattern; the prototypical kind of schematicity is the limiting case along a parameter of compatibility, in which there is no conflict of specifications. I would expect that there are other parameters involved in the other cases of non-prototypical "schemas" (those involving alternatives or lists, non-characteristic specifications, etc.), and that the prototypical schematicity will again prove to be the limiting and most salient case. In any case, I believe that the conclusions outlined above still hold: Both the uniting concept (of whatever type) and the concepts which it unites may exist simultaneously, and differences in salience among them will make the configurations we recognize as ambiguity and vagueness non-absolute.

8. The limitations of 2-dimensional representation make this convention impracticable for most purposes; it should not be taken too seriously in Figure 6, for instance. It has not to my knowledge been used in other publications on Cognitive Grammar.

9. Ultimately there will always be some schema uniting any two cognitive structures, even if it be only the superschema ENTITY (Langacker 1987: 198), which corresponds to the notions "concept" or "cognitive structure". Frequently there is even some slightly more fully specified schema; e.g. THING, which unites the two meanings of *bank* (5a), or LARGE PHYSICAL THING, which would unite the river edge sense of *bank* with the physical building sub-sense of the financial institution sense. The important things to notice, however, are that such a schema will be quite distant in cases of clear ambiguity, and, more importantly, that it will not be linked directly to the phonological pole of the lexical item in question. Thus THING is not a meaning of /baenk/.

   Another consideration, closely related to elaborative distance, is the possible existence of schemas intermediate between the uniting schema and the elaborations, but not linked to the same phonological pole. The uniting schema will not usually still be linked to the phonological pole in such a case. One example, however, might be the schema MOST IMPORTANT PART, which is arguably a meaning of *head* (it is used productively, especially with adjectival *head*). Although the cutting piece of a machine designed for cutting is its most important part and in some cases it is called a *head* (e.g., in a milling machine), in many other cases it is not (e.g., in a carpenter's plane or a pair of scissors).

10. In Figures 2–6 the connecting links from phonological structures are represented as varying in salience directly with the salience of the semantic structures to which they connect. Actually it is in some sense the salience of the link which is primary. For assessing position along the ambiguity/vagueness continuum, what counts is not salience of meanings as they might be measured objectively, from some outside viewpoint, but rather their salience as measured from the phonological pole as point

of access. E.g., the concept THING is, in and of itself, presumably quite a salient one in English speakers' minds, probably more so than RIVER EDGE or FINANCIAL INSTITUTION, but it is not directly accessed from the phonological structure /baenk/, so from the perspective of that phonological structure it is relatively non-salient, as represented in Figure 5a.

11. Figures 2a and e are essentially the same configurations as Langacker's (1988: 138) Figures 3b and 3a.
12. This diagram may be instructively compared with Geeraerts' (1991: 202) representation of the meaning of *vers*; if Figure 6 were converted into this type of diagram the result would be similarly complex. Note however that Geeraerts' diagram does not represent salience, except in the cross-hatching that marks the area which includes the "most central meaning".
13. This is somewhat misleading in that squinting requires effort; the default case of looking is to have the eyes wide open. In cognition presumably the default case is rather to have a fairly high threshold of salience (i.e., to attend only to structures which are quite highly activated), and it will require effort to lower that threshold and "see" more detail (cf. Kosslyn 1980: 53, 165–166; Langacker 1987: 381).
14. We are here dealing with what happens from the perspective of a hearer decoding speech. Things are doubtless more complex from the perspective of a thinker, for whom volition and other factors are more active in establishing what cognitive structures are salient. It is here that Geeraerts' "searchlight" metaphor (see Geeraerts 1993: 258–260, 263) is especially appropriate; the thinker can turn the searchlight of salience (heightened cognitive activity) where he wants to (and has the mental energy to), not just where the lights are already on most strongly. He then, if he wishes to communicate as a speaker, can construct a context which will evoke parallel saliences for the hearer; it is the hearer's decoding of such a communication that we are dealing with. Even here, of course, volition and other factors can enter the picture; hearers are also active thinkers. But when these other factors are allowed to counteract the effect of context, they generally foul up the communication process. In ideal communication between a skilled speaker and a cooperative hearer, the pre-established saliences of entrenchment and the influence of context are the most important factors determining what is salient in the hearer's mind.
15. This same mechanism is what accounts for hearers' choosing of one possible meaning instead of others because it fits the context. Thus if one says *The current slammed the boat against the bank* or *the current carried the boat into the reeds,* the specifications of *current* and *boat,* involving as they do the notions of water moving in a stream, produce a secondary activation in concepts closely linked with them, such as *bed* (of the stream) or the river edge sense of *bank* or the aquatic plant sense of *reed.* This makes it quite improbable that hearers of the sentences will think of the financial institution sense of *bank* or the musical instrument sense of *reed* at all, much less to the exclusion of the river edge or aquatic plant sense. Of course a larger context (e.g., of a flood overflowing a town, with perhaps an orchestra bravely carrying on despite the water rising around them) might render those meanings salient instead or as well. If both meanings are simultaneously salient, the sentences will feel like puns (3.4.4).
16. In a context of overt comparison, any feature whatsoever which two homophonous

semantic structures have in common can function as a salient schema, rendering the configuration vague and allowing identity-of-sense anaphora to function. This is the significance of Deane's sentence (1988: 345): *Financial banks resemble those you find by rivers: they control, respectively, the flow of money and of water.* As Deane says, "in effect, the context temporarily creates a single category".

In the extreme case, where the only relevant feature two semantic structures have in common is linkage to the same phonological pole, a context of naming or definition can set up just that as the most salient feature. This is the point of Geeraerts' sentence: *Daddy, what exactly do you call a bank: the place where we moor the boat or the place where I bring my savings? – Well, son, the place where we moor the boat is a bank, but so is the place where you bring your savings* (Geeraerts 1993: 245).

## References

*The American Heritage Dictionary of the English Language*
1978 New College Edition. Boston: Houghton Mimin.

Aristotle
1984 Post. Anal. II.xiii. In *The Complete Works of Aristotle: The Revised Oxford Translation*, Jonathan Barnes (ed.). Princeton: Princeton University Press.

Deane, Paul
1988 Polysemy and cognition. *Lingua* 75: 325–361.

Geeraerts, Dirk
1991 The lexicographical treatment of prototypical polysemy. In Tsohatzidis (ed.), 195–210.
1993 Vagueness's puzzles, polysemy's vagaries. *Cognitive Linguistics* 4(3): 223–272.

Hartmann, R. R. K.
1983 On theory and practice. In *Lexicography: Principles and Practice*, R. R. K. Hartmann (ed.), 3–11. London: Academic Press.

Kempson, Ruth M.
1977 *Semantic Theory.* Cambridge: Cambridge University Press.

Kimball, John P. (ed.)
1975 *Syntax and Semantics*, vol. 4. New York: Academic Press.

Kosslyn, Stephen Michael
1980 *Image and Mind*. Cambridge, MA: Harvard University Press.

Lakoff, George
1970 A note on vagueness and ambiguity. *Linguistic Inquiry* 1: 357–359.
1987 *Women, Fire and Dangerous Things. What Categories Reveal about the Mind.* Chicago: University of Chicago Press.

Langacker, Ronald W.
1987 *Foundations of Cognitive Grammar.* vol. 1: *Theoretical Prerequisites.* Stanford, CA: Stanford University Press.
1988 A usage-based model. In Rudzka-Ostyn (ed.), 127–161.

1991 *Concept, Image, and Symbol: The Cognitive Basis of Grammar.* Berlin/New York: Mouton de Gruyter.

Lewis, Clive S.
1967 *Studies in Words.* 2nd edition. New York: Cambridge University Press.

Lyons, John
1977 *Semantics.* 2 vols. Cambridge: Cambridge University Press.

Quine, Willard V. 0.
1960 *Word and Object.* Cambridge, MA: MIT Press.

Rudzka-Ostyn, Brygida (ed.)
1988 *Topics in Cognitive Linguistics.* Amsterdam/Philadelphia: John Benjamins.

Tuggy, David
1981 The transitivity-related morphology of Tetelcingo Nahuatl: An exploration in Space grammar. Doctoral dissertation, University of California, San Diego.

Tsohatzidis, Savas L. (ed.)
1991 *Meanings and Prototypes: Studies in Linguistic Categorization.* London/New York: Routledge.

*Webster's New Collegiate Dictionary*
1977 Springfield, MA: Merriam.

Zwicky, Arnold M. and Jerrold M. Sadock
1975 Identity tests and how to fail them. In Kimball (ed.), 1–36.

# Chapter 6
# Conceptual metaphor

## The contemporary theory of metaphor*
## *George Lakoff*

*Do not go gentle into that good night.*
Dylan Thomas
*Death is the mother of beauty.*
Wallace Stevens, "Sunday Morning"

### 1. Introduction

These famous lines by Thomas and Stevens are examples of what classical theorists, at least since Aristotle, have referred to as metaphor: instances of novel poetic language in which words like "mother," "go," and "night" are not used in their normal everyday sense. In classical theories of language, metaphor was seen as a matter of language, not thought. Metaphorical expressions were assumed to be mutually exclusive with the realm of ordinary everyday language: everyday language had no metaphor, and metaphor used mechanisms outside the realm of everyday conventional language.

The classical theory was taken so much for granted over the centuries that many people didn't realize that it was just a theory. The theory was not merely taken to be true, but came to be taken as definitional. The word "metaphor" was defined as a novel or poetic linguistic expression where one or more words for a concept are used outside of their normal conventional meaning to express a "similar" concept.

But such issues are not matters for definitions; they are empirical questions. As a cognitive scientist and a linguist, one asks: what are the generalizations governing the linguistic expressions referred to classically as "poetic metaphors"? When this question is answered rigorously, the classical theory turns out to be false. The generalizations governing poetic metaphorical expressions are not in language, but in thought: they are general mappings across conceptual domains. Moreover, these general principles which take the form of conceptual mappings, apply not just to novel poetic expressions, but to much of ordinary everyday language.

In short, the locus of metaphor is not in language at all, but in the way we conceptualize one mental domain in terms of another. The general theory of meta-

Originally published in 1993 in *Metaphor and Thought*, Andrew Ortony (ed.), 202–251. Cambridge: Cambridge University Press. Reprinted with permission.

phor is given by characterizing such cross-domain mappings. And in the process, everyday abstract concepts like time, states, change, causation, and purpose also turn out to be metaphorical.

The result is that metaphor (that is, cross-domain mapping) is absolutely central to ordinary natural language semantics, and that the study of literary metaphor is an extension of the study of everyday metaphor. Everyday metaphor is characterized by a huge system of thousands of cross-domain mappings, and this system is made use of in novel metaphor.

Because of these empirical results, the word "metaphor" has come to be used differently in contemporary metaphor research. It has come to mean "a cross-domain mapping in the conceptual system." The term "metaphorical expression" refers to a linguistic expression (a word, phrase, or sentence) that is the surface realization of such a cross-domain mapping (this is what the word "metaphor" referred to in the old theory). I will adopt the contemporary usage throughout this chapter.

Experimental results demonstrating the cognitive reality of the extensive system of metaphorical mappings are discussed by Gibbs (1993). Mark Turner's 1987 book *Death Is the Mother of Beauty*, whose title comes from Stevens' great line, demonstrates in detail how that line uses the ordinary system of everyday mappings. For further examples of how literary metaphor makes use of the ordinary metaphor system, see *More Than Cool Reason: A Field Guide to Poetic Metaphor* by Lakoff and Turner (1989) and *Reading Minds: The Study of English in the Age of Cognitive Science* by Turner (1991).

Since the everyday metaphor system is central to the understanding of poetic metaphor, we will begin with the everyday system and then turn to poetic examples.

## 1.1. Homage to Ready

The contemporary theory that metaphor is primarily conceptual, conventional, and part of the ordinary system of thought and language can be traced to Michael Reddy's (1993) now classic essay, "The Conduit Metaphor," which first appeared in the first edition of Ortony (1993[1979]). Reddy did far more in that essay than he modestly suggested. With a single, thoroughly analyzed example, he allowed us to see, albeit in a restricted domain, that ordinary everyday English is largely metaphorical, dispelling once and for all the traditional view that metaphor is primarily in the realm of poetic or "figurative" language. Reddy showed, for a single, very significant case, that the locus of metaphor is thought, not language, that metaphor is a major and indispensable part of our ordinary, conventional way of conceptualizing the world, and that our everyday behavior reflects our metaphorical understanding of experience. Though other theorists had noticed some of these characteristics of metaphor, Reddy was the first to demonstrate them by rigorous linguistic analysis, stating generalizations over voluminous examples.

Reddy's chapter on how we conceptualize the concept of communication by metaphor gave us a tiny glimpse of an enormous system of conceptual metaphor. Since its appearance, an entire branch of linguistics and cognitive science has developed to study systems of metaphorical thought that we use to reason and base our actions on, and that underlie a great deal of the structure of language.

The bulk of the chapters in Ortony (1993[1979]), in which the present article appeared originally, were written before the development of the contemporary field of metaphor research. My chapter therefore contradicts much that appears in the other chapters of Ortony (1993[1979]), many of which make certain assumptions that were widely taken for granted in 1977. A major assumption that is challenged by contemporary research is the traditional division between literal and figurative language, with metaphor as a kind of figurative language. This entails, by definition, that: what is literal is not metaphorical. In fact, the word "literal" has traditionally been used with one or more of a set of assumptions that have since proved to be false:

### 1.2. Traditional false assumptions

- All everyday conventional language is literal, and none is metaphorical.
- All subject matter can be comprehended literally, without metaphor.
- Only literal language can be contingently true or false.
- All definitions given in the lexicon of a language are literal, not metaphorical.
- The concepts used in the grammar of a language are all literal; none are metaphorical.

The big difference between the contemporary theory and views of metaphor prior to Reddy's work lies in this set of assumptions. The reason for the difference is that, in the intervening years, a huge system of everyday, conventional, conceptual metaphors has been discovered. It is a system of metaphor that structures our everyday conceptual system, including most abstract concepts, and that lies behind much of everyday language. The discovery of this enormous metaphor system has destroyed the traditional literal-figurative distinction, since the term "literal," as used in defining the traditional distinction, carries with it all those false assumptions.

A major difference between the contemporary theory and the classical one is based on the old literal-figurative distinction. Given that distinction, one might think that one "arrives at" a metaphorical interpretation of a sentence by "starting" with the literal meaning and applying some algorithmic process to it (see

Searle 1993). Though there do exist cases where something like this happens, this is not in general how metaphor works, as we shall see shortly.

### 1.3. What is not metaphorical

Although the old literal-metaphorical distinction was based on assumptions that have proved to be false, one can make a different sort of literal-metaphorical distinction: those concepts that are not comprehended via conceptual metaphor might be called "literal." Thus, although I will argue that a great many common concepts like causation and purpose are metaphorical, there is nonetheless an extensive range of non-metaphorical concepts. A sentence like *the balloon went up* is not metaphorical, nor is the old philosopher's favorite *the cat is on the mat.* But as soon as one gets away from concrete physical experience and starts talking about abstractions or emotions, metaphorical understanding is the norm.

## 2. The contemporary theory: Some examples

Let us now turn to some examples that are illustrative of contemporary metaphor research. They will mostly come from the domain of everyday conventional metaphor, since that has been the main focus of the research. I will turn to the discussion of poetic metaphor only after I have discussed the conventional system, since knowledge of the conventional system is needed to make sense of most of the poetic cases.

The evidence for the existence of a system of conventional conceptual metaphors is of five types:

- Generalizations governing polysemy, that is, the use of words with a number of related meanings
- Generalizations governing inference patterns, that is, cases where a pattern of inferences from one conceptual domain is used in another domain
- Generalizations governing novel metaphorical language (see Lakoff and Turner 1989)
- Generalizations governing patterns of semantic change (see Sweetser 1990)
- Psycholinguistic experiments (see Gibbs 1990)

We will be discussing primarily the first three of these sources of evidence, since they are the most robust.

## 2.1. Conceptual metaphor

Imagine a love relationship described as follows:

> Our relationship has hit a *dead-end street.*

Here love is being conceptualized as a journey, with the implication that the relationship is *stalled*, that the lovers cannot *keep going the way they've been going*, that they must *turn back*, or abandon the relationship altogether. This is not an isolated case. English has many everyday expressions that are based on a conceptualization of love as a journey, and they are used not just for talking about love, but for reasoning about it as well. Some are necessarily about love; others can be understood that way:

> Look *how far we've come.*
> It's been *a long, bumpy road.*
> We can't *turn back* now.
> We're at a *crossroads.*
> We may have to *go our separate ways.*
> The relationship isn't *going anywhere.*
> We're *spinning our wheels.*
> Our relationship is *off the track.*
> The marriage is *on the rocks.*
> We may have to *bail out* of this relationship.

These are ordinary, everyday English expressions. They are not poetic, nor are they necessarily used for special rhetorical effect. Those like *look how far we've come*, which aren't necessarily about love, can readily be understood as being about love.

As a linguist and a cognitive scientist, I ask two commonplace questions:

- Is there a general principle governing how these linguistic expressions about journeys are used to characterize love?
- Is there a general principle governing how our patterns of inference about journeys are used to reason about love when expressions such as these are used?

The answer to both is yes. Indeed, there is a single general principle that answers both questions, but it is a general principle that is neither part of the grammar of English, nor the English lexicon. Rather, it is part of the conceptual system underlying English. It is a principle for understanding the domain of love in terms of the domain of journeys.

The principle can be stated informally as a metaphorical scenario:

> The lovers are travelers on a journey together, with their common life goals seen as destinations to be reached. The relationship is their vehicle, and it allows them to pursue those common goals together. The relationship is seen as fulfilling its purpose as long as it allows them to make progress toward their common goals. The journey isn't easy. There are impediments, and there are places (crossroads) where a decision has to be made about which direction to go in and whether to keep traveling together.

The metaphor involves understanding one domain of experience, love, in terms of a very different domain of experience, journeys. More technically, the metaphor can be understood as a mapping (in the mathematical sense) from a source domain (in this case, journeys) to a target domain (in this case, love). The mapping is tightly structured. There are ontological correspondences, according to which entities in the domain of love (e.g., the lovers, their common goals, their difficulties, the love relationship, etc.) correspond systematically to entities in the domain of a journey (the travelers, the vehicle, destinations, etc.).

To make it easier to remember what mappings there are in the conceptual system, Johnson and I (Lakoff and Johnson 1980) adopted a strategy for naming such mappings, using mnemonics which suggest the mapping. Mnemonic names typically (though not always) have the form: TARGET-DOMAIN IS SOURCE-DOMAIN, or alternatively, TARGET-DOMAIN AS SOURCE-DOMAIN. In this case, the name of the mapping is LOVE IS A JOURNEY. When I speak of the LOVE IS A JOURNEY metaphor, I am using a mnemonic for a set of ontological correspondences that characterize a mapping, namely:

THE LOVE-AS-JOURNEY MAPPING
- The lovers correspond to travelers.
- The love relationship corresponds to the vehicle.
- The lovers' common goals correspond to their common destinations on the journey.

Difficulties in the relationship correspond to impediments to travel. It is a common mistake to confuse the name of the mapping, LOVE IS A JOURNEY, for the mapping itself. The mapping is the set of correspondences, Thus, whenever I refer to a metaphor by a mnemonic like LOVE IS A JOURNEY, I will be referring to such a set of correspondences.

If mappings are confused with names of mappings, another misunderstanding can arise. Names of mappings commonly have a propositional form, for example, LOVE IS A JOURNEY. But the mappings themselves are not propositions. If mappings are confused with names for mappings, one might mistakenly think that, in this theory, metaphors are propositional. They are anything but that: metaphors are mappings, that is, sets of conceptual correspondences.

The LOVE-AS-JOURNEY mapping is a set of ontological correspondences that characterize epistemic correspondences by mapping knowledge about journeys onto knowledge about love. Such correspondences permit us to reason about love using the knowledge we use to reason about journeys. Let us take an example. Consider the expression, *we're stuck,* said by one lover to another about their relationship. How is this expression about travel to be understood as being about their relationship?

*We're stuck* can be used of travel, and when it is, it evokes knowledge about travel. The exact knowledge may vary from person to person, but here is a typical example of the kind of knowledge evoked. The capitalized expressions represent entities in the ontology of travel, that is, in the source domain of the LOVE-IS-A-JOURNEY mapping given above.

> Two TRAVELERS are in a VEHICLE, TRAVELING WITH COMMON DESTINATIONS. The VEHICLE encounters some IMPEDIMENT and gets stuck, that is, becomes nonfunctional. If the travelers do nothing, they will not REACH THEIR DESTINATIONS. There are a limited number of alternatives for action:
> They can try to get the vehicle moving again, either by fixing it or getting it past the IMPEDIMENT that stopped it.
> They can remain in the nonfunctional VEHICLE and give up on REACHING THEIR DESTINATIONS.
> They can abandon the VEHICLE.
> The alternative of remaining in the nonfunctional VEHICLE takes the least effort, but does not satisfy the desire to REACH THEIR DESTINATIONS.

The ontological correspondences that constitute the LOVE IS A JOURNEY metaphor map the ontology of travel onto the ontology of love. In doing so, they map this scenario about travel onto a corresponding love scenario in which the corresponding alternatives for action are seen. Here is the corresponding love scenario that results from applying the correspondences to this knowledge structure. The target domain entities that are mapped by the correspondences are capitalized:

> Two LOVERS are in a LOVE RELATIONSHIP, PURSUING COMMON LIFE GOALS. The RELATIONSHIP encounters some DIFFICULTY, which makes it nonfunctional. If they do nothing, they will not be able to ACHIEVE THEIR LIFE GOALS. There are a limited number of alternatives for action:
> They can try to get it moving again, either by fixing it or getting it past the DIFFICULTY.

They can remain in the nonfunctional RELATIONSHIP, and give up on ACHIEVING THEIR LIFE GOALS.
They can abandon the RELATIONSHIP.
The alternative of remaining in the nonfunctional RELATIONSHIP takes the least effort, but does not satisfy the desire to ACHIEVE LIFE GOALS.

This is an example of an inference pattern that is mapped from one domain to another. It is via such mappings that we apply knowledge about travel to love relationships.

## 2.2. Metaphors are not mere words

What constitutes the LOVE AS JOURNEY metaphor is not any particular word or expression. It is the ontological mapping across conceptual domains, from the source domain of journeys to the target domain of love. The metaphor is not just a matter of language, but of thought and reason. The language is secondary. The mapping is primary, in that it sanctions the use of source domain language and inference patterns for target domain concepts. The mapping is conventional, that is, it is a fixed part of our conceptual system, one of our conventional ways of conceptualizing love relationships.

This view of metaphor is thoroughly at odds with the view that metaphors are just linguistic expressions. If metaphors were merely linguistic expressions, we would expect different linguistic expressions to be different metaphors. Thus, *We've hit a dead-end street* would constitute one metaphor. *We can't turn back now* would constitute another, entirely different metaphor. *Their marriage is on the rocks* would involve still a different metaphor. And so on for dozens of examples. Yet we don't seem to have dozens of different metaphors here. We have one metaphor, in which love is conceptualized as a journey. The mapping tells us precisely how love is being conceptualized as a journey. And this unified way of *conceptualizing* love metaphorically is realized in many different *linguistic* expressions.

It should be noted that contemporary metaphor theorists commonly use the term "metaphor" to refer to the conceptual mapping, and the term "metaphorical expression" to refer to an individual linguistic expression (like *dead-end street*) that is sanctioned by a mapping. We have adopted this terminology for the following reason: Metaphor, as a phenomenon, involves both conceptual mappings and individual linguistic expressions. It is important to keep them distinct. Since it is the mappings that are primary and that state the generalizations that are our principal concern, we have reserved the term "metaphor" for the mappings, rather than for the linguistic expressions.

In the literature of the field, small capitals like LOVE IS A JOURNEY are used as mnemonics to name mappings. Thus, when we refer to the LOVE IS A JOURNEY metaphor, we are referring to the set of correspondences discussed above. The English sentence *love is a journey,* on the other hand, is a metaphorical expression that is understood via that set of correspondences.

### 2.3. Generalizations

The LOVE IS A JOURNEY metaphor is a conceptual mapping that characterizes a generalization of two kinds:

- Polysemy generalization: a generalization over related senses of linguistic expressions, for example, *dead-end street*, *crossroads*, *stuck*, *spinning one's wheels*, *not going anywhere*, and so on.
- Inferential generalization: a generalization over inferences across different conceptual domains.

That is, the existence of the mapping provides a general answer to two questions:

- Why are words for travel used to describe love relationships?
- Why are inference patterns used to reason about travel also used to reason about love relationships?

Correspondingly, from the perspective of the linguistic analyst, the existence of such cross-domain pairings of words and of inference patterns provides evidence for the existence of such mappings.

### 2.4. Novel extensions of conventional metaphors

The fact that the LOVE-IS-A-JOURNEY mapping is a fixed part of our conceptual system explains why new and imaginative uses of the mapping can be understood instantly, given the ontological correspondences and other knowledge about journeys. Take the song lyric, *We're driving in the fast lane on the freeway of love.* The traveling knowledge called upon is this: when you drive in the fast lane, you go a long way in a short time and it can be exciting and dangerous. The general metaphorical mapping maps this knowledge about driving into knowledge about love relationships. The danger may be to the vehicle (the relationship may not last) or the passengers (the lovers may be hurt emotionally). The excitement of the love journey is sexual. Our understanding of the song lyric is a consequence of the preexisting metaphorical correspondences of the LOVE IS A JOURNEY metaphor.

The song lyric is instantly comprehensible to speakers of English because those metaphorical correspondences are already part of our conceptual system.

The LOVE IS A JOURNEY metaphor and Reddy's Conduit Metaphor were the two examples that first convinced me that metaphor was not a figure of speech, but a mode of thought, defined by a systematic mapping from a source to a target domain. What convinced me were the three characteristics of metaphor that I have just discussed:

1. The systematicity in the linguistic correspondences.
2. The use of metaphor to govern reasoning and behavior based on that reasoning.
3. The possibility for understanding novel extensions in terms of the conventional correspondences.

## 2.5. Motivation

Each conventional metaphor, that is, each mapping, is a fixed pattern of conceptual correspondence across conceptual domains. As such, each mapping defines an open-ended class of potential correspondences across inference patterns. When activated, a mapping may apply to a novel source domain knowledge structure and characterize a corresponding target domain knowledge structure.

Mappings should not be thought of as processes, or as algorithms that mechanically take source domain inputs and produce target domain outputs. Each mapping should be seen instead as a fixed pattern of ontological correspondences across domains that may, or may not, be applied to a source domain knowledge structure or a source domain lexical item. Thus, lexical items that are conventional in the source domain are not always conventional in the target domain. Instead, each source domain lexical item may or may not make use of the static mapping pattern. If it does, it has an extended lexicalized sense in the target domain, where that sense is characterized by the mapping. If not, the source domain lexical item will not have a conventional sense in the target domain, but may still be actively mapped in the case of novel metaphor. Thus, the words *freeway* and *fast lane* are not conventionally used of love, but the knowledge structures associated with them are mapped by the LOVE IS A JOURNEY metaphor in the case of *We're driving in the fast lane on the freeway of love.*

## 2.6. Imageable idioms

Many of the metaphorical expressions discussed in the literature on conventional metaphor are idioms. On classical views, idioms have arbitrary meanings, but within cognitive linguistics, the possibility exists that they are not arbitrary, but rather motivated. That is, they do not arise automatically by productive rules, but they fit one or more patterns present in the conceptual system. Let us look a little more closely at idioms.

An idiom like *spinning one's wheels* comes with a conventional mental image, that of the wheels of a car stuck in some substance – mud, sand, snow, or on ice – so that the car cannot move when the motor is engaged and the wheels turn. Part of our knowledge about that image is that a lot of energy is being used up (in spinning the wheels) without any progress being made, that the situation will not readily change of its own accord, that it will take a lot of effort on the part of the occupants to get the vehicle moving again – and that may not even be possible.

The LOVE IS A JOURNEY metaphor applies to this knowledge about the image. It maps this knowledge onto knowledge about love relationships: a lot of energy is being spent without any progress toward fulfilling common goals, the situation will not change of its own accord, it will take a lot of effort on the part of the lovers to make more progress, and so on. In short, when idioms have associated conventional images, it is common for an independently motivated conceptual metaphor to map that knowledge from the source to the target domain. For a survey of experiments verifying the existence of such images and such mappings, see Gibbs (1990).

### 2.7. Mappings are at the superordinate level

In the LOVE-IS-A-JOURNEY mapping, a love relationship corresponds to a vehicle. A vehicle is a superordinate category that includes such basic level categories as car, train, boat, and plane. The examples of vehicles are typically drawn from this range of basic level categories: car (*long bumpy road*, *spinning our wheels*), train (*off the track*), boat (*on the rocks*, *foundering*), plane (*just taking off*, *bailing out*). This is not an accident: in general, we have found that mappings are at the superordinate rather than the basic level. Thus, we do not find fully general submappings like A LOVE RELATIONSHIP IS A CAR; when we find a love relationship conceptualized as a car, we also tend to find it conceptualized as a boat, a train, a plane, and so forth. It is the superordinate category VEHICLE not the basic level category CAR that is in the general mapping.

It should be no surprise that the generalization is at the superordinate level, while the special cases are at the basic level. After all, the basic level is the level of rich mental images and rich knowledge structure. (For a discussion of the properties of basic level categories, see Lakoff 1987: 31–50.) A mapping at the superordinate level maximizes the possibilities for mapping rich conceptual structures in the source domain onto the target domain, since it permits many basic level instances, each of which is information rich.

Thus, a prediction is made about conventional mappings: the categories mapped will tend to be at the superordinate rather than the basic level. One tends not to find mappings like A LOVE RELATIONSHIP IS A CAR or A LOVE RELATIONSHIP IS A BOAT. Instead, one tends to find both basic level cases (e.g., both cars and boats), which indicates that the generalization is one level higher, at the superordinate level of the vehicle. In the hundreds of cases of conventional mappings studied so far, this prediction has been borne out: it is superordinate categories that are used in mappings.

## 3. Basic semantic concepts that are metaphorical

Most people are not too surprised to discover that emotional concepts like love and anger are understood metaphorically. What is more interesting, and I think more exciting, is the realization that many of the most basic concepts in our conceptual systems are also normally comprehended via metaphor – concepts like time, quantity, state, change, action, cause, purpose, means, modality, and even the concept of a category. These are concepts that enter normally into the grammars of languages, and if they are indeed metaphorical in nature, then metaphor becomes central to grammar.

I would like to suggest that the same kinds of considerations that lead to our acceptance of the LOVE IS A JOURNEY metaphor lead inevitably to the conclusion that such basic concepts are often, and perhaps always, understood via metaphor.

### 3.1. Categories

Classical categories are understood metaphorically in terms of bounded regions, or "containers." Thus, something can be *in* or *out* of a category, it can be *put into* a category or *removed from* a category. The logic of classical categories is the logic of containers (see Figure 1).

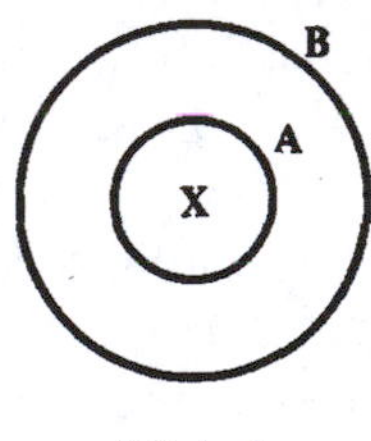


*Figure 1.*

If X is in container A and container A is in container B, then X is in container B.

This is true not by virtue of any logical deduction, but by virtue of the topological properties of containers. Under the CLASSICAL CATEGORIES ARE CONTAINERS metaphor, the logical properties of categories are inherited from the logical properties of containers. One of the principal logical properties of classical categories is that the classical syllogism holds for them. The classical syllogism,

> Socrates is a man.
> All men are mortal.
> Therefore, Socrates is mortal.

is of the form:

> If X is in category A and category A is in category B, then X is in category B.

Thus, the logical properties of classical categories can be seen as following from the topological properties of containers plus the metaphorical mapping from containers to categories. As long as the topological properties of containers are preserved by the mapping, this result will be true.

In other words, there is a generalization to be stated here. The language of containers applies to classical categories and the logic of containers is true of classical categories. A single metaphorical mapping ought to characterize both the linguistic and logical generalizations at once. This can be done provided that the topological properties of containers are preserved in the mapping.

The joint linguistic-and-inferential relation between containers and classical categories is not an isolated case. Let us take another example.

### 3.2. Quantity and linear scales

The concept of quantities involves at least two metaphors. The first is the well-known MORE IS UP, LESS IS DOWN metaphor as shown by a myriad of expressions like *prices rose*, *stocks skyrocketed*, *the market plummeted*, and so on. A second is that LINEAR SCALES ARE PATHS. We can see this in expressions like:

> John is *far* more intelligent than Bill.
> John's intelligence *goes way beyond* Bill's.
> John is *way ahead of* Bill in intelligence.

The metaphor maps the starting point of the path onto the bottom of the scale and maps distance traveled onto quantity in general.

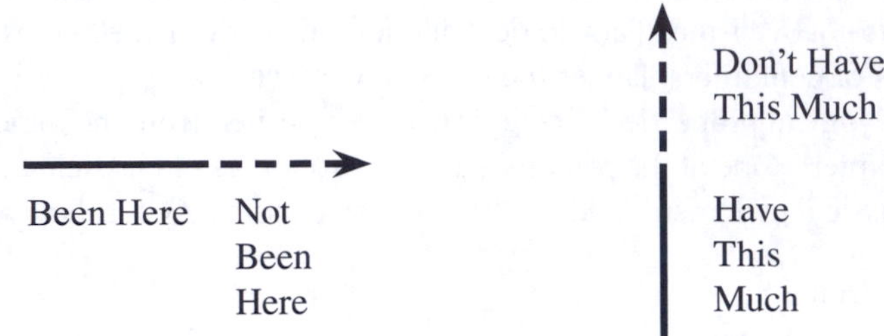


*Figure 2.*

What is particularly interesting is that the logic of paths maps onto the logic of linear scale (see Figure 2).

> Path inference: if you are going from A to C, and you are now at an intermediate point B, then you have been at all points between A and B and not at any points between B and C.

Example: If you are going from San Francisco to New York along Route 80, and you are now at Chicago, then you have been to Denver but not to Pittsburgh.

> Linear scale inference: if you have exactly $50 in your bank account, then you have $40, $30, and so on, but not $60, $70, or any larger amount.

The form of these inferences is the same. The path inference is a consequence of the cognitive topology of paths. It will be true of any path image-schema. Again, there is a linguistic-and-inferential generalization to be stated. It would be stated by the metaphor LINEAR SCALES ARE PATHS, provided that metaphors in general preserve the cognitive topology (that is, the image-schematic structure) of the source domain.

Looking at the inferential structure alone, one might suggest a non-metaphorical alternative in which both linear scales and paths are instances of a more general abstract schema. But when *both* the inferential and lexical data are considered, it becomes clear that a metaphorical solution is required. An expression like *ahead of* is from the spatial domain, not the linear scale domain: *ahead* in its core sense is defined with respect to one's head – it refers to the direction in which one is facing. To say that there is no metaphorical mapping from paths to scales is to say that *ahead of* is not fundamentally spatial and characterized with respect to heads; it is to claim rather that *ahead* is very abstract, neutral between space and linear scales, and has nothing to do with heads. This would be a bizarre analysis.

Similarly, for sentences like *John's intelligence goes beyond Bill's*, the nonmetaphorical analysis would claim that *go* is not fundamentally a verb of motion at all, but is somehow neutral between motion and a linear relation. This would also be bizarre. In short, if one grants that *ahead of* and *go* are fundamentally spatial, then the fact that they can also be used of linear scales suggests a metaphor solution. There could be no such neutral sense of *go* for these cases, since *go beyond* in the spatial sense involves motion, while in the linear scale sense, there is no motion or change, but just a point on a scale. Here the neutral case solution is not even available.

### 3.3. The Invariance Principle

In the examples we have just considered, the image-schemas characterizing the source domains (containers, paths) are mapped onto the target domains (categories, linear scales). This observation leads to the following hypothesis, called "The Invariance Principle":

> Metaphorical mappings preserve the cognitive topology (that is, the image-schema structure) of the source domain, in a way consistent with the inherent structure of the target domain.

What the Invariance Principle does is guarantee that, for container schemas, interiors will be mapped onto interiors, exteriors onto exteriors, and boundaries onto boundaries; for path-schemas, sources will be mapped onto sources, goals onto goals, trajectories onto trajectories, and so on.

To understand the Invariance Principle properly, it is important not to think of mappings as algorithmic processes that "start" with source domain structure and wind up with target domain structure. Such a mistaken understanding of mappings would lead to a mistaken understanding of the Invariance Principle, namely, that one first picks all the image-schematic structure of the source domain, then one copies it onto the target domain unless the target domain interferes.

One should instead think of the Invariance Principle in terms of constraints on fixed correspondences: if one looks at the existing correspondences, one will see that the Invariance Principle holds: source domain interiors correspond to target domain interiors; source domain exteriors correspond to target domain exteriors, and so forth. As a consequence it will turn out that the image-schematic structure of the target domain cannot be violated: One cannot find cases where a source domain interior is mapped onto a target domain exterior, or where a source domain exterior is mapped onto a target domain path. This simply does not happen.

### 3.4. Target domain overrides

A corollary of the Invariance Principle is that image-schema structure inherent in the target domain cannot be violated, and that inherent target domain structure limits the possibilities for mappings automatically. This general principle explains a large number of previously mysterious limitations on metaphorical mappings. For example, it explains why you can give someone a kick, even if that person doesn't have it afterward, and why you can give someone information, even if you don't lose it. This is a consequence of the fact that inherent target domain structure automatically limits what can be mapped. For example, consider that part of your inherent knowledge of actions that says that actions do not continue to exist after they occur. Now consider the ACTIONS ARE TRANSFERS metaphor, in which actions are conceptualized as objects transferred from an agent to a patient, as when one gives someone a kick or a punch. We know (as part of target domain knowledge) that an action does not exist after it occurs. In the source domain, where there is a giving, the recipient possesses the object given after the giving. But this cannot be mapped onto the target domain since the inherent structure of the target domain says that no such object exists after the action is over. The target domain override in the Invariance Principle explains why you can give someone a kick without his having it afterward.

### 3.5. Abstract inferences as metaphorical spatial inferences

Spatial inferences are characterized by the topological structure of image schemas. We have seen cases such as CATEGORIES ARE CONTAINERS and LINEAR SCALES ARE PATHS where image-schema structure is preserved by metaphor and where abstract inferences about categories and linear scales are metaphorical versions of spatial inferences about containers and paths. The Invariance Principle hypothesizes that image-schema structure is always preserved by metaphor.

The Invariance Principle raises the possibility that a great many, if not all, abstract inferences are actually metaphorical versions of spatial inferences that are inherent in the topological structure of image-schemas. I will now turn to other cases of basic, but abstract, concepts to see what evidence there is for the claim that such concepts are fundamentally characterized by metaphor.

### 3.6. Time

It has often been noted that time in English is conceptualized in terms of space. The details are rather interesting.

Ontology: Time is understood in terms of things (that is, entities and locations) and motion.
Background condition: The present time is at the same location as a canonical observer.
Mapping:
Times are things.
The passing of time is motion.
Future times are in front of the observer; past times are behind the observer.
One thing is moving, the other is stationary; the stationary entity is the deictic center.
Entailment:
Since motion is continuous and one-dimensional, the passage of time is continuous and one-dimensional.
Special case 1:
The observer is fixed; times are entities moving with respect to the observer.
Times are oriented with their fronts in their direction of motion.

Entailments:
If time 2 follows time 1, then time 2 is in the future relative to time 1.
The time passing the observer is the present time.
Time has a velocity relative to the observer.
Special case 2:
Times are fixed locations; the observer is moving with respect to time.
Entailment:
Time has extension, and can be measured.
An extended time, like a spatial area, may be conceived of as a bounded region.

This metaphor, TIME PASSING IS MOTION, with its two special cases, embodies a generalization that accounts for a wide range of cases where a spatial expression can also be used for time. Special case 1, TIME PASSING IS MOTION OF AN OBJECT, accounts for both the linguistic form and the semantic entailments of expressions like:

The time will come when . . . The time has long since gone when . . . The time for action has arrived. That time is here. In the weeks following next Tuesday . . . On the preceding day . . . I'm looking ahead to Christmas.

> Thanksgiving is coming up on us. Let's put all that behind us. I can't face the future. Time is flying by. The time has passed when . . .

Thus, special case 1 characterizes the general principle behind the temporal use of words like *come*, *go*, *here*, *follow*, *precede*, *ahead*, *behind*, *fly*, *pass*, accounting not only for why they are used for both space and time, but why they mean what they mean.

Special case 2, TIME PASSING IS MOTION OVER A LANDSCAPE, accounts for a different range of cases, expressions like:

> There's going to be trouble down the road. He stayed there for ten years. He stayed there a long time. His stay in Russia extended over many years. He passed the time happily. He arrived on time. We're coming up on Christmas. We're getting close to Christmas. He'll have his degree within two years. I'll be there in a minute.

Special case 2 maps location expressions like *down the road*, *for* + location, *long*, *over*, *come*, *close to*, *within*, *in*, *pass*, onto corresponding temporal expressions with their corresponding meanings. Again, special case 2 states a general principle relating spatial terms and inference patterns to temporal terms and inference patterns.

The details of the two special cases are rather different; indeed, they are inconsistent with one another. The existence of such special cases has an especially interesting theoretical consequence: words mapped by both special cases will have inconsistent readings. Take, for example, the *come* of *Christmas is coming* (special case 1) and *We're coming up on Christmas* (special case 2). Both instances of *come* are temporal, but one takes a moving time as first argument and the other takes a moving observer as first argument. The same is true of *pass* in *The time has passed* (special case 1) and in *He passed the time* (special case 2).

These differences in the details of the mappings show that one cannot just say blithely that spatial expressions can be used to speak of time, without specifying details, as though there were only one correspondence between time and space. When we are explicit about stating the mappings, we discover that there are two different – and inconsistent – subcases.

The fact that time is understood metaphorically in terms of motion, entities, and locations accords with our biological knowledge. In our visual systems, we have detectors for motion and detectors for objects/locations. We do not have detectors for time (whatever that could mean). Thus, it makes good biological sense that time should be understood in terms of things and motion.

## 3.7. Duality

The two special cases (location and object) of the TIME PASSING IS MOTION metaphor are not merely an accidental feature of our understanding of time. As we shall see below, there are other metaphors that come in such location/ object pairs. Such pairs are called "duals," and the general phenomenon in which metaphors come in location/object pairs is referred to as "duality."

## 3.8. Simultaneous mappings

It is important to recall that metaphorical mappings are fixed correspondences that can be activated, rather than algorithmic processes that take inputs and give outputs. Thus, it is *not* the case that sentences containing conventional metaphors are the products of a real-time process of conversion from literal to metaphorical readings. A sentence like *The time for action has arrived* is not understood by first trying to give a literal reading to *arrive,* and then, on failing, trying to give it a temporal reading. Instead, the metaphor TIME PASSING IS MOTION is a fixed structure of existing correspondences between the space and time domains, and *arrive* has a conventional extended meaning that makes use of that fixed structure of correspondences.

Thus, it is possible for two different parts of a sentence to make use of two distinct metaphorical mappings at once. Consider a phrase like, *within the coming weeks.* Here, *within* makes use of the metaphor of time as a stationary landscape which has extension and bounded regions, whereas *coming* makes use of the metaphor of times as moving objects. This is possible because the two metaphors for time pick out different aspects of the target domain. *The coming weeks* conceptualizes those weeks as a whole, in motion relative to the observer. *Within* looks inside that whole, conceptualizing it as a bounded region with an interior. Each mapping is used partially. Thus, although the mappings – as wholes – are inconsistent, there are cases where parts of the mappings may be consistently superimposed. The Invariance Principle allows such parts of the mappings to be picked out and used to characterize reasoning about different aspects of the target domain.

Simultaneous mappings are very common in poetry. Take, for example, the Dylan Thomas line "Do not go gentle into that good night." Here *go* reflects DEATH IS DEPARTURE, *gentle* reflects LIFE IS A STRUGGLE, with death as defeat. *Night* reflects A LIFETIME IS A DAY, with death as night. This one line has three different metaphors for death, each mapped onto different parts of the sentence. This is possible since mappings are fixed correspondences.

There is an important lesson to be learned from this example. In mathematics, mappings are static correspondences. In computer science, it is common to represent mathematical mappings by algorithmic processes that take place in real time. Researchers in information processing psychology and cognitive science also commonly represent mappings as real-time algorithmic procedures. Some researchers from these fields have mistakenly supposed that the metaphorical mappings we are discussing should also be represented as real-time, sequential algorithmic procedures, where the input to each metaphor is a literal meaning. Any attempt to do this will fail for the simultaneous mapping cases just discussed.

## 4. Event structure

I now want to turn to some research by myself and some of my students (especially Sharon Fischler, Karin Myhre, and Jane Espenson) on the metaphorical understanding of event structure in English. What we have found is that various aspects of event structure, including notions like states, changes, processes, actions, causes, purposes, and means, are characterized cognitively via metaphor in terms of space, motion, and force.

The general mapping we have found goes as follows:

*The event structure metaphor*
- States are locations (bounded regions in space).
- Changes are movements (into or out of bounded regions).
- Causes are forces.
- Actions are self-propelled movements.
- Purposes are destinations.
- Means are paths (to destinations).
- Difficulties are impediments to motion.
- Expected progress is a travel schedule; a schedule is a virtual traveler, who reaches prearranged destinations at prearranged times.
- External events are large, moving objects.
- Long term, purposeful activities are journeys.

This mapping generalizes over an extremely wide range of expressions for one or more aspects of event structure. For example, take states and changes. We speak of being *in* or *out* of a state, *of going into* or *out of* it, of *entering* or *leaving* it, of getting *to* a state or emerging *from* it.

This is a rich and complex metaphor whose parts interact in complex ways. To get an idea of how it works, consider the submapping "Difficulties are impediments to motion." In the metaphor, purposive action is self-propelled motion toward a destination. A difficulty is something that impedes motion to such a destination. Metaphorical difficulties of this sort come in five types: blockages;

features of the terrain; burdens; counter-forces; lack of an energy source. Here are examples of each:

> Blockages:
>> He got over his divorce. He's trying to get around the regulations. He went through the trial. We ran into a brick wall. We've got him boxed into a corner.
>
> Features of the terrain:
>> He's between a rock and a hard place. It's been uphill all the way. We've been bogged down. We've been hacking our way through a jungle of regulations.
>
> Burdens:
>> He's carrying quite a load. He's weighed down by a lot of assignments. He's been trying to shoulder all the responsibility. Get off my back!
>
> Counterforces:
>> Quit pushing me around. She's leading him around by the nose. She's holding him back.
>
> Lack of an energy source:
>> I'm out of gas. We're running out of steam.

To see just how rich the event structure metaphor is, consider some of its basic entailments:

- Manner of action is manner of motion.
- A different means for achieving a purpose is a different path.
- Forces affecting action are forces affecting motion.
- The inability to act is the inability to move.
- Progress made is distance traveled or distance from goal.

We will consider examples of each of these one by one, including a number of special cases.

> Aids to action are aids to motion:
>> It is smooth sailing from here on in. It's all downhill from here. There's nothing in our way.
>
> A different means of achieving a result is a different path:
>> Do it this way. She did it the other way. Do it any way you can. However you want to go about it is fine with me.
>
> Manner of action is manner of motion:
>> We are moving/running/skipping right along. We slogged through it. He is flailing around. He is falling all over himself. We are leaping over hurdles. He is out of step. He is in step.

Careful action is careful motion:

I'm walking on eggshells. He is treading on thin ice. He is walking a fine line.

Speed of action is speed of movement:

He flew through his work. He is running around. It is going swimmingly. Keep things moving at a good clip. Things have slowed to a crawl. She is going by leaps and bounds. I am moving at a snail's pace.

Purposeful action is self-propelled motion to a destination; this has the following special cases:

Making progress is forward movement:

We are moving ahead. Let's forge ahead. Let's keep moving forward. We made lots of forward movement.

Amount of progress is distance moved:

We've come a long way. We've covered lots of ground. We've made it this far.

Undoing progress is backward movement:

We are sliding backward. We are backsliding. We need to backtrack. It is time to turn around and retrace our steps.

Expected progress is a travel schedule; a schedule is a virtual traveler, who reaches prearranged destinations at prearranged times:

We're behind schedule on the project. We got a head start on the project. I'm trying to catch up. I finally got a little ahead.

Starting an action is starting out on a path:

We are just starting out. We have taken the first step.

Success is reaching the end of the path:

We've reached the end. We are seeing the light at the end of the tunnel. We only have a short way to go. The end is in sight. The end is a long way off.

Lack of purpose is lack of direction:

He is just floating around. He is drifting aimlessly. He needs some direction.

Lack of progress is lack of movement:

We are at a standstill. We aren't getting any place. We aren't going anywhere. We are going nowhere with this.

External events are large moving objects:

Special case 1: Things

How're things going? Things are going fine with me. Things are going against me these days. Things took a turn for the worse. Things are going my way.

Special case 2: Fluids

> You gotta go with the flow. I'm just trying to keep my head above water. The tide of events . . . The winds of change. . . . The flow of history . . . I'm trying to get my bearings. He's up a creek without a paddle. We're all in the same boat.

Special case 3: Horses

> Try to keep a tight rein on the situation. Keep a grip on the situation. Don't let things get out of hand. Wild horses couldn't make me go. "Whoa!" (said when things start to get out of hand).

Such examples provide overwhelming empirical support for the existence of the event structure metaphor. And the existence of that metaphor shows that the most common abstract concepts – TIME, STATE, CHANGE, CAUSATION, ACTION, PURPOSE and MEANS – are conceptualized via metaphor. Since such concepts are at the very center of our conceptual systems, the fact that they are conceptualized metaphorically shows that metaphor is central to ordinary abstract thought.

### 4.1. Inheritance hierarchies

Metaphorical mappings do not occur isolated from one another. They are sometimes organized in hierarchical structures, in which "lower" mappings in the hierarchy inherit the structures of the "higher" mappings. Let us consider an example of a hierarchy with three levels:

Level 1: *The event structure metaphor*
Level 2: A PURPOSEFUL LIFE IS A JOURNEY
Level 3: LOVE IS A JOURNEY; A CAREER IS A JOURNEY

To refresh your memory, recall:

*The event structure metaphor*
- Target domain: Events   Source domain: Space
- States are locations (bounded regions in space).
- Changes are movements (into or out of bounded regions).
- Causes are forces.
- Actions are self-propelled movements.
- Purposes are destinations.
- Means are paths to destinations.
- Difficulties are impediments to motion.
- Expected progress is a travel schedule; a schedule is a virtual traveler, who reaches prearranged destinations at prearranged times.
- External events are large, moving objects.

– Long-term, purposeful activities are journeys.

In our culture, life is assumed to be purposeful, that is, we are expected to have goals in life. In the event structure metaphor, purposes are destinations and purposeful action is self-propelled motion toward a destination. A purposeful life is a long-term, purposeful activity, and hence a journey. Goals in life are destinations on the journey. The actions one takes in life are self-propelled movements, and the totality of one's actions form a path one moves along. Choosing a means to achieve a goal is choosing a path to a destination. Difficulties in life are impediments to motion. External events are large moving objects that can impede motion toward one's life goals. One's expected progress through life is charted in terms of a life schedule, which is conceptualized as a virtual traveler that one is expected to keep up with.

In short, the metaphor A PURPOSEFUL LIFE IS A JOURNEY makes use of all the structure of the event structure metaphor, since events in a life conceptualized as purposeful are subcases of events in general.

A PURPOSEFUL LIFE IS A JOURNEY
– Target domain: Life Source domain: Space
– The person leading a life is a traveler.
– Inherits event structure metaphor, with:
Events = significant life events
Purposes = life goals

Thus we have expressions like:

> He got a head start in life. He's without direction in his life. I'm where I want to be in life. I'm at a crossroads in my life. He'll go places in life. He's never let anyone get in his way. He's gone through a lot in life.

Just as significant life events are special cases of events, so events in a love relationship are special cases of life events. Thus, the LOVE IS A JOURNEY metaphor inherits the structure of the LIFE IS A JOURNEY metaphor. What is special about the LOVE IS A JOURNEY metaphor is that there are two lovers who are travelers and that the love relationship is a vehicle. The rest of the mapping is a consequence of inheriting the LIFE IS A JOURNEY metaphor. Because the lovers are in the same vehicle, they have common destinations, that is, common life goals. Relationship difficulties are impediments to travel.

LOVE IS A JOURNEY
– Target domain: Love Source domain: Space
– The lovers are travelers.

- The love relationship is a vehicle.
- Inherits the LIFE IS A JOURNEY metaphor.

A career is another aspect of life that can be conceptualized as a journey. Here, because STATUS IS UP, a career is actually a journey upward. Career goals are special cases of life goals.

A CAREER IS A JOURNEY
- Target domain: Career   Source domain: Space
- A careerist is a traveler.
- Status is up.
- Inherits LIFE IS A JOURNEY, with life goals = career goals. Ideal: to go as high, far, and fast as possible.

Examples include:

> He clawed his way to the top. He's over the hill. She's on the fast track. He's climbing the corporate ladder. She's moving up in the ranks quickly.

This inheritance hierarchy accounts for a range of generalizations. First, there are generalizations about lexical items. Take the word *crossroads*. Its central meaning is in the domain of space, but it can be used in a metaphorical sense to speak of any extended activity, of one's life, of a love relationship, or of a career.

> I'm at a crossroads on this project. I'm at a crossroads in life. We're at a crossroads in our relationship. I'm at a crossroads in my career.

The hierarchy allows one to state a general principle: *crossroads* is extended lexically via the submetaphor of the event structure metaphor that LONG-TERM PURPOSEFUL ACTIVITIES ARE JOURNEYS. All its other uses are automatically generated via the inheritance hierarchy. Thus, separate senses for each level of the hierarchy are not needed.

The second generalization is inferential in character. Thus the understanding of difficulties as impediments to travel occurs not only in events in general, but also in a purposeful life, in a love relationship, and in a career. The inheritance hierarchy guarantees that this understanding of difficulties in life, love, and careers is a consequence of such an understanding of difficulties in events in general.

The hierarchy also allows us to characterize lexical items whose meanings are more restricted: Thus, *climbing the ladder* refers only to careers, not to love relationships or to life in general.

Such hierarchical organization is a very prominent feature of the metaphor system of English and other languages. So far we have found that the metaphors higher up in the hierarchy tend to be more widespread than those mappings at lower levels. Thus, the event structure metaphor is very widespread (and may even be universal), while the metaphors for life, love, and careers are much more restricted culturally.

### 4.2. Duality in the event structure system

In our discussion of time metaphors, we noted the existence of an object/location duality. There were two related time metaphors. In both, the passage of time was understood in terms of relative motion between an observer and a time. In the object-dual, the observer is fixed and times are moving objects. In the location-dual, the opposite is true. The observer moves and times are fixed locations in a landscape.

The event structure system that we have seen so far is based wholly on location. But there is another event structure system that is the dual of the one we have just discussed – a system based on objects rather than locations. In both systems, CHANGE IS MOTION and CAUSES ARE FORCES that control motion. The difference is this:

- In the location system, change is the motion of the thing-changing to a new location or from an old one.
- In the object system, the thing-changing doesn't necessarily move. Change is instead the motion of an object to, or away from, the thing-changing.

In addition, the object in motion is conceptualized as a possession and the thing-changing as a possessor. Change is thus seen as the acquisition or loss of an object. Causation is seen as giving or taking. Here are some examples:

> I have a headache. (The headache is a possession)
> I got a headache. (Change is acquisition – motion to)
> My headache went away. (Change is loss – motion from)
> The noise gave me a headache. (Causation is giving – motion to)
> The aspirin took away my headache. (Causation is taking – motion from)

We can see the duality somewhat more clearly with a word like "trouble":

> I'm in trouble. (Trouble is a location)
> I have trouble. (Trouble is an object that is possessed)

In both cases, trouble is being attributed to me, and in both cases, trouble is metaphorically conceptualized as being in the same place as me (co-location) – in one case, because I possess the trouble-object and in the other case, because I am in the trouble-location. That is, attribution in both cases is conceptualized metaphorically as co-location. In *I'm in trouble*, trouble is a state. A state is an attribute conceptualized as a location. Attributes (or properties) are like states, except that they are conceptualized as possessible objects.

Thus, STATES ARE LOCATIONS and ATTRIBUTES ARE POSSESSIONS are duals, since possession and location are special cases of the same thing – co-location – and since states and attributes are also special cases of the same thing – what can be attributed to someone.

Given this, we can see that there is an object-version of the event structure metaphor:

– Attributes are possessions.
– Changes are movements (of possessions, namely, acquisitions or losses).
– Causes are forces (controlling the movement of possessions, namely, giving or taking away).

These are the duals of:

– States are locations.
– Changes are movements (to or from locations).
– Causes are forces (controlling movement to or from locations).

Similarly, ACTIONS ARE SELF-PROPELLED MOVEMENTS (to or from locations) has as its object-dual ACTIONS ARE SELF-CONTROLLED ACQUISITIONS OR LOSSES. Thus, there is a reason why one can "take" certain actions – one can take a shower, or take a shot at someone, or take a chance.

The submapping PURPOSES ARE DESTINATIONS also has a dual. Destinations are desired locations and so the submapping can be rephrased as PURPOSES ARE DESIRED LOCATIONS, and ACHIEVING A PURPOSE IS REACHING A DESIRED LOCATION. Replacing "location" by "object," we get the dual PURPOSES ARE DESIRED OBJECTS, and ACHIEVING A PURPOSE IS ACQUIRING A DESIRED OBJECT (or ridding oneself of an undesirable one).

Here are some examples:

> ACHIEVING A PURPOSE IS ACQUIRING A DESIRED OBJECT
> They just handed him the job. It's within my grasp. It eluded me. Go for it. It escaped me. It slipped through my hands. He is pursuing a goal. Reach for/grab all the gusto you can get. Latch onto a good job. Seize the opportunity. He found success.

There is also a hierarchical structure in the object-version of the event structure metaphor. A special case of getting an object is getting an object to eat. Hence:

ACHIEVING A PURPOSE IS GETTING SOMETHING TO EAT
He savored the victory. All the good jobs have been gobbled up. He's hungry for success. The opportunity has me drooling. This is a mouth-watering opportunity.

Traditional methods of getting things to eat are hunting, fishing, and agriculture. Each of these special cases can be used metaphorically to conceptualize achieving (or attempting to achieve) a purpose.

TRYING TO ACHIEVE A PURPOSE IS HUNTING
I'm hunting for a job. I bagged a promotion. The pennant is in the bag.

The typical way to hunt is to use projectiles (bullets, arrows, etc.)

I'm shooting for a promotion. I'm aiming for a career in the movies. I'm afraid I missed my chance.

TRYING TO ACHIEVE A PURPOSE IS FISHING
He's fishing for compliments. I landed a promotion. She netted a good job. I've got a line out on a good used car. It's time to fish or cut bait.

TRYING TO ACHIEVE A PURPOSE IS AGRICULTURE
It's time I reaped some rewards. That job is a plum. Those are the fruits of his labor. The contract is ripe for the picking.

I will not try to survey all the dualities in the English metaphor system, but it is worth mentioning a few to see how subtle and persuasive dualities are. Take, for example, the LIFE IS A JOURNEY metaphor, in which goals in life are destinations, that is, desired locations to be reached. Since the dual of PURPOSES ARE DESTINATIONS is PURPOSES ARE DESIRED OBJECTS, the dual of LIFE IS A JOURNEY is a metaphor in which life is an activity through which one acquires desired objects. In this culture, the principal activity of this sort is business, and hence, LIFE IS A BUSINESS is the dual of LIFE IS A JOURNEY.

A PURPOSEFUL LIFE IS A BUSINESS
He has a rich life. It's an enriching experience. I want to get a lot out of life. He's going about the business of everyday life. It's time to take stock of my life.

Recall that LOVE IS A JOURNEY is an extension of A PURPOSEFUL LIFE IS A JOURNEY. It happens that LOVE IS A JOURNEY has a dual that is an extension of the dual of A PURPOSEFUL LIFE IS A JOURNEY, which is A PURPOSEFUL LIFE IS A BUSINESS. The dual of LOVE IS A JOURNEY is LOVE IS A PARTNERSHIP, that is, a two-person business. Thus, we speak of lovers as "partners," there are marriage contracts, and in a long-term love relationship the partners are expected to do their jobs and to share in both responsibilities (what they contribute to the relationship) and benefits (what they get out of it). Long-term love relationships fail under the same conditions as businesses fail – when what the partners get out of the relationship is not worth what they put into it.

Duality is a newly discovered phenomenon. The person who first discovered it in the event structure system was Jane Espenson, a graduate student at Berkeley who stumbled upon it in the course of her research on causation metaphors. Since Espenson's discovery, other extensive dualities have been found in the English metaphor system. It is not known at present, however, just how extensive dualities are in English, or even whether they are all of the location/object type.

At this point, I will leave off discussing the metaphor system of English, although hundreds of other mappings have been described to date. The major point to take away from this discussion is that metaphor resides for the most part in this huge, highly structured, fixed system, a system anything but "dead." Because it is conventional, it is used constantly and automatically, with neither effort nor awareness. Novel metaphor uses this system, and builds on it, but only rarely occurs independently of it. It is most interesting that this system of metaphor seems to give rise to abstract reasoning, which appears to be based on spatial reasoning.

### 4.3. Invariance again

The metaphors I have discussed primarily map three kinds of image schemas: containers, paths, and force-images. Because of the complexity of the subcases and interactions, the details are intricate, to say the least. However, the Invariance Principle does make claims in each case as to what image-schemas get mapped onto target domains. I will not go through most of the details here, but so far as I can see, the claims made about inferential structure are reasonable ones.

For example, the logic of force-dynamics does seem to map, via the submapping CAUSES ARE FORCES, onto the logic of causation. The following are inferences from the logic of forces inherent in force dynamics:

- A stationary object will move only when force is applied to it; without force, it will not move.
- The application of force requires contact; thus, the applier of the force must be in spatial contiguity with the thing it moves.
- The application of force temporarily precedes motion, since inertia must be overcome before motion can take place.

These are among the classic inferential conditions on causation: spatial contiguity, temporal precedence, and that A caused B only if B wouldn't have happened without A.

At this point, I would like to take up the question of what else the Invariance Principle would buy us. I will consider two cases that arose while Mark Turner and I were writing *More Than Cool Reason* (Lakoff and Turner 1989). The first concerns image-metaphors and the second, generic-level metaphors. But before I move on to those topics, I should mention an important consequence of invariance.

Johnson and I argued in *Metaphors We Live By* (Lakoff and Johnson 1980) that a complex propositional structure could be mapped by metaphor onto another domain. The main example we gave was ARGUMENT IS WAR. Kövecses and I, in our analysis of anger metaphors (Lakoff 1987: case study 1; Kövecses 1990), also argued that metaphors could map complex propositional structures. The Invariance Principle does not deny this, but it puts those claims in a very different light. Complex propositional structures involve concepts like time, states, changes, causes, purposes, quantity scales, and categories. If all these abstract concepts are characterized metaphorically, then the Invariance Principle claims that what we had called propositional structure is really image-schematic structure. In other words:

– So-called propositional inferences arise from the inherent topological structure of the image-schemas mapped by metaphor onto concepts like time, states, changes, actions, causes, purposes, means, quantity, and categories.

I have taken the trouble to discuss these abstract concepts to demonstrate this consequence of the Invariance Principle: what have been seen in the past as propositional inferences are really image-based inferences. If the Invariance Principle is correct, it has a remarkable consequence:

– Abstract reasoning is a special case of image-based reasoning.

Image-based reasoning is fundamental and abstract reasoning is image-based reasoning under metaphorical projections to abstract domains.

To look for independent confirmation of the Invariance Principle, let us turn to image metaphors.

## 5. Novel metaphors

### 5.1. Image metaphors

There are kinds of metaphors that function to map one conventional mental image onto another. These contrast with the metaphors I have discussed so far, each of which maps one conceptual domain onto another, often with many concepts in the source domain mapped onto many corresponding concepts in the target domain. Image metaphors, by contrast, are "one-shot" metaphors: they map only one image onto one other image.

Consider, for example, this poem from the Indian tradition:

> Now women-rivers
> belted with silver fish
> move unhurried as women in love
> at dawn after a night with their lovers
> (Merwin and Masson 1981: 71)

Here the image of the slow, sinuous walk of an Indian woman is mapped onto the image of the slow, sinuous, shimmering flow of a river. The shimmering of a school of fish is imagined as the shimmering of the belt.

Metaphoric image mappings work in the same way as all other metaphoric mappings: by mapping the structure of one domain onto the structure of another. But here, the domains are conventional mental images. Take, for example, this line from Andre Breton:

> My wife . . . whose waist is an hourglass.

This is a superimposition of the image of an hourglass onto the image of a woman's waist by virtue of their common shape. As before, the metaphor is conceptual; it is not in the words themselves, but in the mental images. Here, we have a mental image of an hourglass and of a woman, and we map the middle of the hourglass onto the waist of the woman. Note that the words do not tell us which part of the hourglass to map onto the waist, or even that only part of the hourglass shape corresponds to the waist. The words are prompts for us to map from one conventional image to another. Similarly, consider:

> His toes were like the keyboard of a spinet.
> (Rabelais *The Descriptions of King Lent*, trans. J. M. Cohen)

Here, too, the words do not tell us that an individual toe corresponds to an individual key on the keyboard. The words are prompts for us to perform a conceptual mapping between conventional mental images. In particular, we map aspects of the part-whole structure of one image onto aspects of the part-whole structure of another. Just as individual keys are parts of the whole keyboard, so individual toes are parts of the whole foot.

Image mapping can involve more than mapping physical part-whole relationships. For example, the water line of a river may drop slowly and that slowness is part of a dynamic image, which may be mapped onto the slow removal of clothing:

> Slowly slowly rivers in autumn show
> sand banks
> bashful in first love woman
> showing thighs
> (Merwin and Masson 1981: 69)

Other attributes are also mapped: the color of the sand bank onto the color of flesh, the quality of light on a wet sand bank onto the reflectiveness of skin, the light grazing of the water's touch receding down the bank onto the light grazing of the clothing along the skin. Notice that the words do not tell us that any clothing is involved. We get that from a conventional mental image. Part-whole structure is also mapped in this example. The water covers the hidden part of the bank just as the clothing covers the hidden part of the body. The proliferation of detail in the images limits image mappings to highly specific cases. That is what makes them one-shot mappings.

Such mappings of one image onto another can lead us to map knowledge about the first image onto knowledge about the second. Consider the following example from the Navaho:

> My horse with a mane made of short rainbows.
> (*War God's Horse Song I*, words by Tall Kia ahni, interpreted by Louis Watchman)

The structure of a rainbow, its band of curved lines for example, is mapped onto an arc of curved hair, and many rainbows onto many such arcs on the horse's mane. Such image mapping allows us to map our evaluation of the source domain onto the target. We know that rainbows are beautiful, special, inspiring, larger than life, almost mystic, and that seeing them makes us happy and inspires us with awe. This knowledge is mapped onto what we know of the horse: it too is awe-inspiring, beautiful, larger than life, almost mystic. This line comes from a poem containing a series of such image mappings:

My horse with a hoof like a striped agate,
with his fetlock like a fine eagle plume:
my horse whose legs are like quick lightning
whose body is an eagle-plumed arrow:
my horse whose tail is like a trailing black cloud.

Image metaphors raise two major issues for the general theory of metaphor:

- How do they work? What constrains the mappings? What kinds of internal structures do mental images have that permit some mappings to work readily, others only with effort, and others not at all?
- What is the general theory of metaphor that unifies image metaphors with all the conventional metaphors that map the propositional structure of one domain onto the propositional structure of another domain?

Turner and I (Lakoff and Turner 1989) have suggested that the Invariance Principle could be an answer to both questions. We suggest that conventional mental images are structured by image-schemas and that image metaphors preserve image-schematic structure, mapping parts onto parts and wholes onto wholes, containers onto containers, paths onto paths, and so on. The generalization would be that all metaphors are invariant with respect to their cognitive topology, that is, each metaphorical mapping preserves image-schema structure.

## 5.2. Generic-level metaphors

When Turner and I were writing *More Than Cool Reason*, we hypothesized the existence of what we called "generic-level metaphors" to deal with two problems we faced – first, the problem of personification and second, the problem of proverbs, which requires an understanding of analogy. I shall discuss each in turn.

### *5.2.1. Personification*

In studying a wide variety of poems about death in English, we found that, in poem after poem, death was personified in a relatively small number of ways: drivers, coachmen, footmen; reapers, devourers and destroyers, or opponents in a struggle or game (say, a knight or a chess opponent). The question we asked was: why these? Why isn't death personified as a teacher or a carpenter or an ice cream salesman? Somehow, the ones that occur repeatedly seem appropriate. Why?

In studying personifications in general, we found that the overwhelming number seem to fit a single pattern: events (like death) are understood in terms of actions by some agent (like reaping). It is that agent that is personified. We thus hypothesized a very general metaphor, EVENTS ARE ACTIONS, which combines with other, independently existing metaphors for life and death. Consider, for example, the DEATH IS DEPARTURE metaphor. Departure is an event. If we understand this event as an action on the part of some causal agent – someone who brings about, or helps to bring about, departure – then we can account for figures like drivers, coachmen, footmen, and so forth. Take the PEOPLE ARE PLANTS metaphor. In the natural course of things, plants wither and die. If we see that event as a causal action on the part of some agent, that agent is a reaper. So far, so good. But why destroyers and devourers? And what about the impossible cases?

Destroying and devouring are actions in which an entity ceases to exist. The same is true of death. The overall shape of the event of death is similar in this respect to the overall shapes of the events of destroying and devouring. Moreover, there is a causal aspect to death: the passage of time will eventually result in death. Thus, the overall shape of the event of death has an entity that over time ceases to exist as the result of some cause. Devouring and destroying have the same overall event shape. That is, it is the same with respect to causal structure and the persistence of entities over time.

Turner (1987) had noticed a similar case in *Death Is the Mother of Beauty,* his classic work on kinship metaphor. In expressions like *necessity is the mother of invention*, or *Edward Teller was the father of the H-bomb*, causation is understood in terms of giving birth or fathering, what Turner called the CAUSATION IS PROGENERATION metaphor. But, as he observed (Turner 1987: 145–148), this metaphor could not be used for just any instance of causation. It could only be used for cases that had the overall event shape of progeneration: something must be created out of nothing, and the thing created must persist for a long time (as if it had a life).

Thus, for example, we can speak of Saussure as the father of modern synchronic linguistics, or of New Orleans as giving birth to jazz. But we cannot use this metaphor for a single causal action with a short-lived effect. We could not speak of Jose Canseco as the father of the home run he just hit, or of that home run as giving birth to the Oakland As' victory in the game. We could, however, speak of Babe Ruth as the father of modern home-run hitting, and of home runs giving birth to the era of baseball players as superstars. The overall event shape of the target domain limits the applicability of the metaphor.

Recalling Turner's observation about CAUSATION IS PROGENERATION, we therefore hypothesized that EVENTS ARE ACTIONS is constrained in the following way: the action must have the same overall event shape as the event. What is preserved across the mapping is the causal structure, the aspectual structure, and the persistence of entities. We referred to this as "generic-level structure."

The preservation of generic-level structure explained why death is not metaphorized in terms of teaching, or filling the bathtub, or sitting on the sofa. These actions do not have the same causal and overall event structure, they do not share "generic-level structure."

### *5.2.2. Proverbs*

In Asian figures – proverbs in the form of short poems – the question arises as to what the limitations are on the interpretation of a proverb. Some interpretations are natural; others seem impossible. Why?

Consider the following example from *Asian Figures*, translated by William Merwin.

> Blind
> blames the ditch

To get some sense of the possible range of interpretations, consider the following application of the proverb:

> Suppose a presidential candidate knowingly commits some personal impropriety (though not illegal and not related to political issues) and his candidacy is destroyed by the press's reporting of the impropriety. He blames the press for reporting it, rather than himself for committing it. We think he should have recognized the realities of political press coverage when he chose to commit the impropriety. We express our judgment by saying, "Blind / blames the ditch."

Turner and I (1989) observed that the knowledge structure used in comprehending the case of the candidate's impropriety shared certain things with knowledge structure used in comprehending the literal interpretation of "Blind / blames the ditch." That knowledge structure is the following:

- There is a person with an incapacity, namely, blindness.
- He encounters a situation, namely a ditch, in which his incapacity, namely his inability to see the ditch, results in a negative consequence, namely, his falling into the ditch.
- He blames the situation, rather than his own incapacity.
- He should have held himself responsible, not the situation.

This specific knowledge schema about the blind man and the ditch is an instance of a general knowledge schema, in which specific information about the blindness and ditch are absent. Let us refer to it as the "generic-level schema" that structures our knowledge of the proverb. That generic level knowledge schema is:

- There is a person with an incapacity.
- He encounters a situation in which his incapacity results in a negative consequence.
- He blames the situation rather than his own incapacity.
- He should have held himself responsible, not the situation.

This is a very general schema characterizing an open-ended category of situations. We can think of it as a variable template that can be filled in many ways. As it happened, Turner and I were studying this at the time of the Gary Hart scandal. Hart, a presidential candidate, committed certain sexual improprieties during a campaign, had his candidacy dashed, and then blamed the press for his downfall. "Blind / blames the ditch" fits this situation. Here's how:

- The person is the presidential candidate.
- His incapacity is his inability to understand the consequences of his personal improprieties.
- The context he encounters is his knowingly committing an impropriety and the press's reporting it.
- The consequence is having his candidacy dashed.
- He blames the press.
- We judge him as being foolish for blaming the press instead of himself.

If we view the generic-level schema as mediating between the proverb "Blind / blames the ditch" and the story of the candidate's impropriety, we get the following correspondence:

- The blind person corresponds to the presidential candidate.
- His blindness corresponds to his inability to understand the consequences of his personal improprieties.
- Falling into the ditch corresponds to his committing the impropriety and having it reported.
- Being in the ditch corresponds to being out of the running as a candidate.
- Blaming the ditch corresponds to blaming the press coverage.
- Judging the blind man as foolish for blaming the ditch corresponds to judging the candidate as foolish for blaming the press coverage.

This correspondence defines the metaphorical interpretation of the proverb as applied to the candidate's impropriety. Moreover, the class of possible ways of filling in the generic-level schema of the proverb corresponds to the class of possible interpretations of the proverb. Thus, we can explain why "Blind / blames the ditch" does not mean *I took a bath* or *My aunt is sitting on the sofa* or any of the myriad things the proverb cannot mean.

All the proverbs that Turner and I studied turned out to involve this sort of generic-level schema, and the kinds of things that turned up in such schemata seemed to be pretty much the same in case after case. They include:

- Causal structure
- Temporal structure
- Event shape; that is, instantaneous or repeated, completed or open-ended, single or repeating, having fixed stages or not, preserving the existence of entities or not, and so on
- Purpose structure
- Modal structure
- Linear scales

This is not an exhaustive list, but it includes most of the major elements of generic-level structure we discovered. What is striking to us about this list is that everything on it is, under the Invariance Principle, an aspect of image-schematic structure. In short, if the Invariance Principle is correct, the way to arrive at a generic-level schema for some knowledge structure is to extract its image-schematic structure.

The metaphoric interpretation of such discourse forms as proverbs, fables, allegories, and so on seems to depend on our ability to extract generic-level structure. Turner and I have called the relation between a specific knowledge structure and its generic-level structure the GENERIC IS SPECIFIC metaphor. It is an extremely common mechanism for comprehending the general in terms of the specific.

If the Invariance Principle is correct, then the GENERIC IS SPECIFIC metaphor is a minimal metaphor that maps what the Invariance Principle requires it to and nothing more. Should it turn out that generic-level structure is exactly image-schematic structure, then the Invariance Principle would have enormous explanatory value. It would obviate the need for a separate characterization of generic-level structure. Instead, it would itself characterize generic-level structure, explaining possible personifications and the possible interpretations for proverbs.

### 5.3. Analogy

The GENERIC IS SPECIFIC metaphor is used for more than just the interpretation of proverbs. Turner (1991) has suggested that it is also the general mechanism at work in analogic reasoning and that the Invariance Principle characterizes the class of possible analogies. We can see how this works with the Gary Hart example cited above. We can convert that example into an analogy with the following sentence: *Gary Hart was like a blind man who fell into a ditch and blamed the ditch.* The mechanism for understanding this analogy makes use of:

- A knowledge schema for the blind man and the ditch
- A knowledge schema concerning Gary Hart
- The GENERIC IS SPECIFIC metaphor

The GENERIC IS SPECIFIC metaphor maps the knowledge schema for the blind man and the ditch into its generic-level schema. The generic-level schema defines an open-ended category of knowledge schemata. The Gary Hart schema is a member of that category, since it fits the generic-level schema given the correspondences stated above.

It appears at present that such analogies use this metaphorical mechanism. But it is common for analogies to use other metaphorical mechanisms as well, for instance, the Great Chain Metaphor and the full range of conventional mappings in the conceptual system. Sentences like *John is a wolf* or *Harry is a pig* use the Great Chain metaphor (see Lakoff and Turner 1989: Chapter 4).

A good example of how the rest of the metaphor system interacts with GENERIC IS SPECIFIC is the well-known example of Glucksberg and Keysar (1993), *my job is a jail*. First, the knowledge schema for a jail includes the knowledge that a jail imposes extreme physical constraints on a prisoner's movements. The GENERIC IS SPECIFIC metaphor preserves the image-schematic structure of the knowledge schema, factoring out the specific details of the prisoner and the jail: X imposes extreme physical constraints on Y's movements. But now two additional conventional metaphors apply to this generic-level schema: The event structure metaphor, with the submetaphor ACTIONS ARE SELF-PROPELLED MOVEMENTS, and PSYCHOLOGICAL FORCE IS PHYSICAL FORCE. These metaphors map "X imposes extreme physical constraints on Y's movements" into "X imposes extreme psychological constraints on Y's actions." The statement *my job is a jail* imposes an interpretation in which X = my job and Y = me, and hence yields the knowledge that "my job imposes extreme psychological constraints on my actions." Thus, the mechanism for understanding *my job is a jail* uses very common, independently existing metaphors: GENERIC IS SPECIFIC, PSYCHOLOGICAL FORCE IS PHYSICAL FORCE, and the Event Structure Metaphor.

### 5.4. The Glucksberg-Keysar Claim

I mention this example because of the claim by Glucksberg and Keysar (1993) that metaphor is simply a matter of categorization. In personal correspondence, however, Glucksberg has written, "We assume that people can judge and can also infer that certain basic level entities, such as 'jails,' typify or are emblematic of a metaphoric attributive category such as 'situations that are confining, unpleasant, etc.' " Glucksberg and Keysar give no theory of how it is possible to have such a "metaphoric attributive category" – that is, how it is possible for one kind of thing (a general situation) to be metaphorically categorized in terms of a fundamentally spatial notion like "confining." Since Glucksberg is not in the business of describing the nature of conceptual systems, he does not see it as his job to give such an account. I have argued in this essay that the general principle governing such cases is the Event Structure Metaphor. If such a metaphor exists in our conceptual system, then the Glucksberg-Keysar "jail" example is accounted for automatically and their categorization theory is not needed. Indeed, the category he needs – "situations that are confining, unpleasant, etc." – is a "metaphoric attributive category." That is, to get the appropriate categories in their categorization theory of metaphor he needs an account of metaphor. But given such an account of metaphor, the metaphor-as-categorization theory becomes unnecessary.

Even worse for the Glucksberg-Keysar theory, it cannot account for either everyday conceptual metaphor of the sort we have been discussing or for really rich poetic metaphor, such as one finds in the works of, say, Dylan Thomas, or for image metaphor of the sort common in the examples cited above from the Sanskrit, Navaho, and surrealist traditions. Since it does not even attempt to deal with most of the data covered by the contemporary theory of metaphor, it cannot account for "how metaphor works."

## 5.5. More on novel metaphor

At the time most of the chapters in Ortony (1993[1979]) were written (the late 1970s), "metaphor" was taken to mean "novel metaphor," since the huge system of conventional metaphor had barely been noticed. The authors therefore never took up the question of how the system of conventional metaphor functions in the interpretation of novel metaphor. We have just seen one such example. Let us consider some others.

As common as novel metaphor is, its occurrence is rare by comparison with conventional metaphor, which occurs in most of the sentences we utter. Our everyday metaphor system, which we use to understand concepts as commonplace as TIME, STATE, CHANGE, CAUSATION, PURPOSE, and so forth is constantly active, and is used maximally in interpreting novel metaphorical uses of language. The problem with all the older research on novel metaphor is that it completely missed the major contribution played by the conventional system.

As Turner and I discussed in detail (Lakoff and Turner 1989), there are three basic mechanisms for interpreting linguistic expressions as novel metaphors: extensions of conventional metaphors, generic-level metaphors, and image metaphors. Most interesting poetic metaphor uses all these superimposed on one another. Let us begin with examples of extensions of conventional metaphors. Dante begins the *Divine Comedy:*

In the middle of life's road
I found myself in a dark wood.

"Life's road" evokes the domain of life and the domain of travel, and hence the conventional LIFE IS A JOURNEY metaphor that links them. "I found myself in a dark wood" evokes the knowledge that if it's dark you cannot see which way to go. This evokes the domain of seeing, and thus the conventional metaphor that KNOWING IS SEEING, as in *I see what you're getting at, his claims aren't clear, the passage is opaque*, and so forth. This entails that the speaker doesn't know which way to go. Since the LIFE IS A JOURNEY metaphor specifies destinations are life goals, the speaker must not know what life goals to pursue, that is, he is without direction in his life. All this uses nothing but the system of conventional metaphor, ordinary knowledge structure evoked by the conventional meaning of the sentence, and metaphorical inferences based on that knowledge structure.

Another equally simple case of the use of the conventional system is Robert Frost's

Two roads diverged in a wood, and I –
I took the one less traveled by,
And that has made all the difference.

Since Frost's language often does not overtly signal that the poem is to be taken metaphorically, incompetent English teachers occasionally teach Frost as if he were a nature poet, simply describing scenes. (I have actually had students whose high school teachers taught them that!) Thus, this passage could be read non-metaphorically as being just about a trip on which one encounters a crossroads. There is nothing in the sentence itself that forces one to a metaphorical interpretation. But, since it is about travel and encountering crossroads, it evokes a knowledge of journeys. This activates the system of conventional metaphor we have just discussed, in which long-term, purposeful activities are understood as journeys, and further, how life and careers can also be understood as one-person journeys (love relationships, involving two travelers, are ruled out here). The poem is typically taken as being about life and a choice of life goals, though it might also be interpreted as being about careers and career paths, or about some long-term, purposeful activity. All that is needed to get the requisite range of interpretations is the structure of conventional metaphors discussed above, and the knowledge structure evoked by the poem. The conventional mapping will apply to the knowledge structure yielding the appropriate inferences. No special mechanisms are needed.

### 5.6. Searle's theory

I will not pursue discussion of other more complex poetic examples, since they require lengthy treatment which can be found in Lakoff and Turner (1989), Turner (1987), and Turner (1991). Instead, I will confine myself to discussing three examples from John Searle (1993). Consider first Disraeli's remark, "I have climbed to the top of the greasy pole."

This could be taken nonmetaphorically, but its most likely metaphorical interpretation is via the CAREER IS A JOURNEY metaphor. This metaphor is evoked jointly by source domain knowledge about pole climbing, which is effortful, self-propelled, destination-oriented motion upward, and knowledge that the metaphor involves effortful, self-propelled, destination-oriented motion upward. Part of the knowledge evoked is that the speaker is as high as he can get on that particular pole, that the pole was difficult to climb, that the climb probably involved backward motion, that it is difficult for someone to stay at the top of a greasy pole, and that he will most likely slide down again. The CAREER IS A JOURNEY metaphor maps this knowledge onto corresponding knowledge about the speaker's career: he has as much status as he can get in that particular career, it was difficult to get to that point in the career, it probably involved some temporary loss of status along the way, it will be difficult to maintain this position, and he will probably lose status before long. All this follows with nothing more than the conventional CAREER-AS-JOURNEY mapping, which we all share as part of our metaphorical systems, plus knowledge about climbing greasy poles.

The second example of Searle's I will consider is *Sally is a block of ice*. Here there is a conventional metaphor that AFFECTION IS WARMTH, as in ordinary sentences like *she's a warm person*, *he was cool to me*, and so forth. *A block of ice* evokes the domain of temperature and, since it is predicated of a person, it also evokes knowledge of what a person can be. Jointly, both kinds of knowledge activate AFFECTION IS WARMTH. Since *a block of ice* is something very cold and not warmed quickly or easily, this knowledge is mapped onto Sally as being very unaffectionate and not able to become affectionate quickly or easily. Again, common knowledge and a conventional metaphor we all have is all that is needed.

Finally, Searle discusses *the hours crept by as we waited for the plane*. Here we have a verb of motion predicated of a time expression; the former activates the knowledge about motion through space and the latter activates the time domain. Jointly, they activate the TIME-AS-MOVING-OBJECT mapping. Again the meaning of the sentence follows only from everyday knowledge and the everyday system of metaphorical mappings.

Searle accounts for such cases by his Principle 4, which says that "we just do perceive a connection" which is the basis of the interpretation. This is vague and doesn't say what the perceived connection is or why we "just do" perceive it.

When we spell out the details of all such "perceived connections," they turn out to be the system of conceptual metaphors I have been describing. But given that system, Searle's theory and his principles become unnecessary.

In addition, Searle's account of literal meaning makes most of the usual false assumptions that accompany that term. Searle assumes that all everyday, conventional language is literal and not metaphorical. He would thus rule out every example of conventional metaphor described not only in this chapter, but in the whole literature of the field.

The study of the metaphorical subsystem of our conceptual system is a central part of synchronic linguistics because much of our semantic system, that is, our system of concepts, is metaphorical, as we saw above. Because this huge system went unnoticed prior to 1980, authors like Searle, Sadock, and Morgan could claim, incorrectly as it turns out, that metaphor was outside of synchronic linguistics and in the domain of principles of language use.

## 6. The experiential basis of metaphor

The conceptual system underlying a language contains thousands of conceptual metaphors – conventional mappings from one domain to another, such as the Event Structure Metaphor. The novel metaphors of a language are, except for image metaphors, extensions of this large conventional system.

Perhaps the deepest question that any theory of metaphor must answer is this: why do we have the conventional metaphors that we have? Or alternatively: is there any reason why conceptual systems contain one set of metaphorical mappings rather than another? There do appear to be answers to these questions for many of the mappings found so far, though they are in the realm of plausible accounts, rather than in the realm of scientific results.

Take a simple case: the MORE IS UP metaphor, as seen in expressions like prices rose; his income went down; unemployment is up; exports are down; the number of homeless people is very high.

There are other languages in which MORE IS UP and LESS IS DOWN, but none in which the reverse is true, where MORE IS DOWN and LESS IS UP. Why not? Contemporary theory postulates that the MORE IS UP metaphor is *grounded in experience* – in the common experiences of pouring more fluid into a container and seeing the level go up, or adding more things to a pile and seeing the pile get higher. These are thoroughly pervasive experiences; we encounter them every day of our lives. They have structure – a correspondence between the conceptual domain of quantity and the conceptual domain of verticality: MORE corresponds in such experiences to up and LESS corresponds to DOWN. These correspondences in real experience form the basis for the correspondences in the metaphorical cases, which go beyond real experience: *in prices rose* there is no correspondence in real experience between quantity and verticality, but understanding quantity in terms of verticality makes sense because of a regular correspondence in so many other cases.

Consider another case. What is the basis of the widespread KNOWING IS SEEING metaphor, as in expressions like I see what you're saying; his answer was clear; this paragraph is murky; he was so blinded by ambition that he never noticed his limitations? The experiential basis in this case is the fact that most of what we know comes through vision, and in the overwhelming majority of cases, if we see something, then we know it is true.

Consider still another case. Why, in the Event Structure Metaphor, is achieving a purpose understood as reaching a destination (in the location subsystem) and as acquiring a desired object (in the object subsystem)? The answer again seems to be correspondences in everyday experience. To achieve most of our everyday purposes, we either have to move to some destination or acquire some object. If you want a drink of water, you've got to go to the water fountain. If you want to be in the sunshine, you have to move to where the sunshine is. And if you want to write down a note, you have to get a pen or pencil. The correspondences between achieving purposes and either reaching destinations or acquiring objects is so utterly common in our everyday existence, that the resulting metaphor is completely natural.

But what about the experiential basis of A PURPOSEFUL LIFE IS A JOURNEY? Recall that the mapping is in an inheritance hierarchy, where life goals are special cases of purposes, which are destinations in the event structure metaphor. Thus, A PURPOSEFUL LIFE IS A JOURNEY inherits the experiential basis of PURPOSES ARE DESTINATIONS. Thus, inheritance hierarchies provide *indirect experiential bases,* in that a metaphorical mapping lower in a hierarchy can inherit its experiential basis indirectly from a mapping higher in the hierarchy.

Experiential bases motivate metaphors, they do not predict them. Thus, not every language has a MORE IS UP metaphor, though all human beings experience a correspondence between MORE and UP. What this experiential basis does predict is that no language will have the opposite metaphor LESS IS UP. It also predicts that a speaker of a language without that metaphor will be able to learn it much more easily than its reverse.

## 6.1. Realizations of metaphor

Consider objects like thermometers and stock market graphs, where increases in temperature and prices are represented as being up and decreases as being down. These are objects created by humans to accord with the MORE IS UP metaphor. They exhibit a correlation between MORE and UP and are much easier to read and understand than if they contradicted the metaphor, if, say, increases were represented as down and decreases as up.

Such objects are ways in which metaphors impose a structure on real life, through the creation of new correspondences in experience. And once created in one generation, they serve as an experiential basis for that metaphor in the next generation.

There are a great many ways in which conventional metaphors can be made real. They can be realized in obvious imaginative products such as cartoons, literary works, dreams, visions, and myths, but they can be made real in less obvious ways as well, in physical symptoms, social institutions, social practices, laws, and even foreign policy and forms of discourse and history.

Let us consider some examples.

### *6.1.1. Cartoons*

Conventional metaphors are made real in cartoons. A common example is the realization of the ANGER IS A HOT FLUID IN A CONTAINER metaphor, in which one can be *boiling mad* or *letting off steam*. In cartoons, anger is commonly depicted by steam coming out of the character's ears. Social clumsiness is indicated by having a cartoon character *fall on his face*.

### *6.1.2. Literary works*

It is common for the plot of a novel to be a realization of the PURPOSEFUL LIFE IS A JOURNEY metaphor, where the course of a life takes the form of an actual journey. *Pilgrim's Progress* is a classic example.

### *6.1.3. Rituals*

Consider the cultural ritual in which a newborn baby is carried upstairs to ensure his or her success. The metaphor realized in this ritual is STATUS IS UP, as in: he clawed his way to the top; *he climbed the ladder of success*; *you'll rise in the world.*

### *6.1.4. Dream interpretation*

Conceptual metaphors constitute the vocabulary of dream interpretation. The collection of our everyday conceptual metaphors makes dream interpretation possible. Consider one of the most celebrated of all examples, Joseph's interpretation of Pharaoh's dream from Genesis. In Pharaoh's dream, he is standing on the river bank when seven fat cows come out of the river, followed by seven lean cows that eat the seven fat ones and still remain lean. Pharaoh dreams again. This time he sees seven "full and good" ears of corn growing and then seven withered ears growing after them. The withered ears devour the good ears. Joseph interprets the two dreams as a single dream. The seven fat cows and full ears are good years and the seven lean cows and withered ears are famine years that follow the good years. The famine years devour what the good years produce. This interpretation makes sense to us because of a collection of conceptual metaphors in our conceptual system – metaphors that have been with us since biblical times. The first metaphor is TIMES ARE MOVING ENTITIES. A river is a common metaphor for the flow of time; the cows are individual entities (years) emerging from the flow of time and moving past the observer; the ears of corn are also entities that come into the scene. The second metaphor is ACHIEVING A PURPOSE IS EATING, where being fat indicates success, being lean indicates failure. This metaphor is combined with the most common of metonymies, A PART STANDS FOR THE WHOLE. Since cows and corn were typical of meat and grain eaten, each single cow stands for all the cows raised in a year and each ear of corn for all the corn grown in a year. The final metaphor is RESOURCES ARE FOOD, where using up resources is eating food. The devouring of the good years by the famine years is interpreted as indicating that all the surplus resources of the good years will be used up by the famine years. The interpretation of the whole dream is thus a composition of three conventional metaphors and one metonymy. The metaphoric and metonymic sources are combined to form the reality of the dream.

### *6.1.5. Myths*

In the event structure metaphor, there is a submapping EXTERNAL EVENTS ARE LARGE MOVING OBJECTS that can exert a force on you and thereby affect whether you achieve your goals. In English the special cases of such objects are "things," fluids, and horses. Pamela Morgan (in unpublished work) has observed that in Greek mythology, Poseidon is the god of the sea, earthquakes, horses, and bulls. The list might seem arbitrary, but Morgan observes that these are all large moving objects that can exert a force on you. Poseidon, she surmises, should really be seen as the god of external events.

### *6.1.6. Physical symptoms*

The unconscious mind makes use of our unconscious system of conventional metaphor, sometimes to express psychological states in terms of physical symptoms. For example, in the event structure metaphor, there is a submapping DIFFICULTIES ARE IMPEDIMENTS TO MOTION which has, as a special case, DIFFICULTIES ARE BURDENS. It is fairly common for someone encountering difficulties to walk with his shoulders stooped, as if *carrying a heavy weight* that is *burdening* him.

### 6.1.7. Social institutions

We have a TIME IS MONEY metaphor, shown by expressions like *he's wasting time*; *I have to budget my time*; *this will save you time*; *I've invested a lot of time in that*; *he doesn't use his time profitably*. This metaphor came into English use about the time of the industrial revolution, when people started to be paid for work by the amount of time they put in. Thus, the factory led to the institutional pairing of periods of time with amounts of money, which formed the experiential basis of this metaphor. Since then, the metaphor has been realized in many other ways. The budgeting of time has spread throughout American culture.

### 6.1.8. Social practices

There is a conceptual metaphor that SEEING IS TOUCHING, where the eyes are limbs and vision is achieved when the object seen is "touched." Examples are: *my eyes picked out every detail of the pattern*; *he ran his eyes over the walls*; *he couldn't take his eyes off of her*; *their eyes met*; *his eyes are glued to the TV*. The metaphor is made real in the social practice of avoiding eye "contact" on the street, and in the social prohibition against "undressing someone with your eyes."

### 6.1.9. Laws

Law is a major area where metaphor is made real. For example, CORPORATIONS ARE PERSONS is a tenet of American law, which not only enables corporations to be *harmed* or assigned *responsibility* so they can be sued when liable, but also gives them certain First Amendment rights.

### 6.1.10. Foreign policy

A STATE IS A PERSON is one of the major metaphors underlying foreign policy concepts. Thus, there are *friendly* states, *hostile* states, and so forth. Health for a state is economic health and strength is military strength. A threat to economic *health* can be seen as a death threat, as when Iraq was seen to have a *stranglehold* on the *economic lifeline* of the United States. Strong states are seen as male and weak states as female, so that an attack by a strong state on a weak one can be seen as a *rape*, as in the rape of Kuwait by Iraq. A *just war* is conceptualized as a fairy tale with villain, victim, and hero, where the villain attacks the victim and the hero rescues the victim. Thus, the United States and allies in the Gulf War were portrayed as having *rescued* Kuwait. As President Bush said in his address to Congress, "The issues couldn't have been clearer: Iraq was the villain and Kuwait, the victim."

### *6.1.11. Forms of discourse*

Common metaphors are often made real in discourse forms. Consider three common academic discourse forms: the guided tour, the heroic battle, and the heroic quest. The guided tour is based on the metaphor that THOUGHT IS MOTION, where ideas are locations and one reasons *step-by-step*, *reaches conclusions*, or fails to reach a conclusion if engaged in *circular reasoning*. Communication in this metaphor is giving someone a guided tour of some rational argument or of some *intellectual terrain*. This essay is an example of such a guided tour, where I, the author, am the tour guide who is assumed to be thoroughly familiar with the terrain and the terrain surveyed is taken as objectively real. The discourse form of the heroic battle is based on the metaphor that ARGUMENT IS WAR. The author's theory is the hero, the opposing theory is the villain, and words are weapons. The battle is in the form of an argument defending the hero's position and demolishing that of the villain. The heroic quest discourse form is based on the metaphor that knowledge is a valuable but elusive object that can be *discovered* if one perseveres. The scientist is the hero on a quest for knowledge, and the discourse form is an account of his difficult journey of discovery. What is *discovered* is a real entity.

What makes all these cases realizations of metaphors is that in each case something real is structured by conventional metaphor, and thereby made comprehensible, or even natural. What is real differs in each case: an object like a thermometer or graph, an experience like a dream, an action like a ritual, a form of discourse, and so forth. These examples reveal that much of what is real in a society or in the experience of an individual is structured and made sense of via conventional metaphor.

Experiential bases and realizations of metaphors are two sides of the same coin: they are both correlations in real experience that have the same structure as the correlations in metaphors. The difference is that experiential bases precede, ground, and make sense of conventional metaphorical mappings, whereas realizations follow, and are made sense of, via the conventional metaphors. And as we noted above, one generation's realizations of a metaphor can become part of the next generation's experiential basis for that metaphor.

## 7. Summary of results

As we have seen, the contemporary theory of metaphor is revolutionary in many respects. To give you some idea of how revolutionary, here is a list of the basic results that differ from most previous accounts.

### 7.1. The nature of metaphor

- Metaphor is the main mechanism through which we comprehend abstract concepts and perform abstract reasoning.
- Much subject matter, from the most mundane to the most abstruse scientific theories, can only be comprehended via metaphor. Metaphor is fundamentally conceptual, not linguistic, in nature.
- Metaphorical language is a surface manifestation of conceptual metaphor.
- Though much of our conceptual system is metaphorical, a significant part of it is nonmetaphorical. Metaphorical understanding is grounded in nonmetaphorical understanding.
- Metaphor allows us to understand a relatively abstract or inherently unstructured subject matter in terms of a more concrete, or at least more highly structured subject matter.

### 7.2. The structure of metaphor

- Metaphors are mappings across conceptual domains.
- Such mappings are asymmetric and partial.
- Each mapping is a fixed set of ontological correspondences between entities in a source domain and entities in a target domain.
- When those fixed correspondences are activated, mappings can project source domain inference patterns onto target domain inference patterns.
- Metaphorical mappings obey the Invariance Principle: The image-schema structure of the source domain is projected onto the target domain in a way that is consistent with inherent target domain structure.
- Mappings are not arbitrary, but grounded in the body and in everyday experience and knowledge.
- A conceptual system contains thousands of conventional metaphorical mappings which form a highly structured subsystem of the conceptual system.
- There are two types of mappings: conceptual mappings and image mappings; both obey the Invariance Principle.

### 7.3. Some aspects of metaphor

- The system of conventional conceptual metaphor is mostly unconscious, automatic, and used with no noticeable effort, just like our linguistic system and the rest of our conceptual system.
- Our system of conventional metaphor is “alive” in the same sense that our

system of grammatical and phonological rules is alive; namely, it is constantly in use, automatically, and below the level of consciousness.
- Our metaphor system is central to our understanding of experience and to the way we act on that understanding.
- Conventional mappings are static correspondences, and are not, in themselves, algorithmic in nature. However, this by no means rules out the possibility that such static correspondences might be used in language processing that involves sequential steps.
- Metaphor is mostly based on correspondences in our experiences, rather than on similarity.
- The metaphor system plays a major role in both the grammar and lexicon of a language.
- Metaphorical mappings vary in universality; some seem to be universal, others are widespread, and some seem to be culture specific.
- Poetic metaphor is, for the most part, an extension of our everyday, conventional system of metaphorical thought.

These are the conclusions that best fit the empirical studies of metaphor conducted over the past decade or so. Though many of them are inconsistent with traditional views, they are by no means all new, and some ideas – for example, that abstract concepts are comprehended in terms of concrete concepts – have a long history.

## 8. Concluding remarks

The evidence supporting the contemporary theory of metaphor is voluminous and grows larger each year as research in the field continues. The evidence, as we saw above, comes from five domains:

- Generalizations over polysemy
- Generalizations over inference patterns
- Generalizations over extensions to poetic cases
- Generalizations over semantic change
- Psycholinguistic experiments

I have discussed only a handful of examples of the first three of these, enough, I hope, to make the reader curious about the field.

Evidence is convincing, however, only if it can count as evidence. When does evidence fail to be evidence? Unfortunately, all too often. It is commonly the case that certain fields of inquiry are defined by assumptions that rule out the possibility of counterevidence. When a defining assumption of a field comes up against evidence, the evidence usually loses: the practitioners of the field must ignore the evidence if they want to keep the assumptions that define the field they are committed to.

Part of what makes the contemporary theory of metaphor so interesting is that the evidence for it contradicts the defining assumptions of so many academic disciplines. In my opinion, this should make one doubt the defining assumptions of all those disciplines. The reason is this: the defining assumptions of the contemporary theory of metaphor are minimal. There are only two.

1. The generalization commitment: To seek generalizations in all areas of language, including polysemy, patterns of inference, novel metaphor, and semantic change.
2. The cognitive commitment: To take experimental evidence seriously.

But these are nothing more than commitments to the scientific study of language and the mind. No initial commitment is made as to the form of an answer to the question of what is metaphor.

The defining assumptions of other fields do, however, often entail a commitment about the form of an answer to that question. It is useful, in an interdisciplinary volume of this sort, to spell out exactly what those defining assumptions are, since they will often explain why different authors reach such different conclusions about the nature of metaphor.

## 8.1. Literal meaning commitments

I started this chapter with a list of the false assumptions about literal meaning that are commonly made. These assumptions are "false" only relative to the kinds of evidence that support the contemporary theory of metaphor. If one ignores all such evidence, the assumptions can be maintained without contradiction.

Assumptions about literality are the locus of many of the contradictions between the contemporary theory of metaphor and various academic disciplines. Let us review those assumptions. In the discussion of literal meaning given above, I observed that it is taken as definitional that what is literal is not metaphorical. The "false assumptions and conclusions" that usually accompany the word "literal" are:

- All everyday conventional language is literal, and none is metaphorical.
- All subject matter can be comprehended literally, without metaphor.
- Only literal language can be contingently true or false.
- All definitions given in the lexicon of a language are literal, not metaphorical.
- The concepts used in the grammar of a language are all literal; none is metaphorical.

We will begin with the philosophy of language. The generalization commitment and the cognitive commitment are *not* definitional to the philosophy of language. Most philosophers of language would feel no need to abide by them, for a very good reason. The philosophy of language is typically not seen as an empirical discipline, constrained by empirical results, such as those that arise from the application of the generalization and cognitive commitments. Instead, the philosophy of language is usually seen as an a priori discipline, which can be pursued using the tools of philosophical analysis alone, rather than the tools of empirical research. Therefore, all the evidence that has been brought forth for the contemporary theory of metaphor simply will not matter for most philosophers of language.

In addition, the philosophy of language comes with its own set of defining assumptions, which entail many of the false assumptions usually associated with the word "literal." Most practitioners of the philosophy of language usually make one or more of the following assumptions.

- The correspondence theory of truth.
- Meaning is defined in terms of reference and truth.
- Natural language semantics is characterized by the mechanisms of mathematical logic, including model theory.

The very field of philosophy of language thus comes with defining assumptions that contradict the main conclusions of the contemporary theory of metaphor. Consequently, we can see why most philosophers of language have the range of views on metaphor that they have: they accept the traditional literal-figurative distinction. They may, like M. Johnson (1981), say that there is no metaphorical meaning, and that most metaphorical utterances are either trivially true or trivially false. Or, like Grice (1989: 34) and Searle (1993), they will assume that metaphor is in the realm of pragmatics, that is, that a metaphorical meaning is no more than the literal meaning of some other sentence which can be arrived at by some pragmatic principle. This is required, since the only real meaning for them is literal meaning, and pragmatic principles are those principles that allow one to say one thing (with a literal meaning) and mean something else (with a different, but nonetheless literal, meaning).

Much of generative linguistics accepts one or more of these assumptions from the philosophy of language. The field of formal semantics accepts them all, and thus formal semantics, by its defining assumptions, is at odds with the contemporary theory of metaphor. Formal semantics simply does not see it as its job to account for the generalizations discussed in this chapter. From the perspective of formal semantics, the phenomena that the contemporary theory of metaphor is concerned with are either nonexistent or uninteresting, since they lie outside the purview of the discipline. Thus Jerrold Sadock (1993) claims that metaphor lies outside of synchronic linguistics. Since he accepts mathematical logic as the correct approach to natural language semantics, Sadock must see metaphor as being outside of semantics proper. He must, therefore, also reject the enterprise of the contemporary theory of metaphor. And Morgan (1993), also accepting those defining assumptions of the philosophy of language, agrees with Grice and Searle that metaphor is a matter of pragmatics.

Chomsky's (1981) theory of government and binding also accepts crucial assumptions from the philosophy of language that are inconsistent with the contemporary theory of metaphor. Government and binding, following my early theory of generative semantics, assumes that semantics is to be represented in terms of logical form. Government and binding, like generative semantics, thus rules out the very possibility that metaphor might be part of natural language semantics as it enters into grammar. Because of this defining assumption, I would not expect government and binding theorists to become concerned with the phenomena covered by the contemporary theory of metaphor.

It is interesting that much of continental philosophy and deconstructionism is also characterized by defining assumptions at odds with the contemporary theory of metaphor. Nietzsche (see Johnson 1981) held that all language is metaphorical, a theory at odds with those results indicating that a significant amount of everyday language is not metaphorical (see subsection, "What is not metaphorical"). Much of continental philosophy, observing that conceptual systems change through time, assumes that conceptual systems are purely historically contingent, that there are no conceptual universals. Though conceptual systems do change through time, there do, however, appear to be universal, or at least very widespread, conceptual metaphors. The event structure metaphor is my present candidate for a metaphorical universal.

Continental philosophy also comes with a distinction between the study of the physical world, which can be scientific, and the study of human beings, which it says cannot be scientific. This is very much at odds with the conceptual theory of metaphor, which is very much a scientific enterprise.

Finally, the contemporary theory of metaphor is at odds with certain traditions in symbolic artificial intelligence and information processing psychology. Those fields assume that thought is a matter of algorithmic symbol manipulation, of the sort done by a traditional computer program. This defining assumption is inconsistent with the contemporary theory of metaphor in two respects.

First, the contemporary theory has an image-schematic basis. The Invariance Principle both applies to image metaphors and characterizes constraints on novel metaphor. Since symbol manipulation systems cannot handle image-schemas, they cannot deal with image metaphors or imageable idioms.

Second, those traditions must characterize metaphorical mapping as an algorithmic process, which typically takes literal meanings as input and gives a metaphorical reading as output. This runs counter to cases where there are multiple, overlapping metaphors in a single sentence, and which require the simultaneous activation of a number of metaphorical mappings.

The contemporary theory of metaphor is thus not only interesting for its own sake. It is especially interesting for the challenge it presents to other disciplines. If the results of the contemporary theory are accepted, the defining assumptions of whole disciplines are brought into question.

## Note

* This research was supported in part by grants from the Sloan Foundation and the National Science Foundation (IRI-8703202) to the University of California at Berkeley. The following colleagues and students helped with this essay in a variety of ways, from useful comments to allowing me to cite their research: Ken Baldwin, Claudia Brugman, Jane Espenson, Sharon Fischler, Ray Gibbs, Adele Goldberg, Mark Johnson, Karin Myhre, Eve Sweetser, and Mark Turner.

## References

Chomsky, Noam
1981 *Lectures on Government and Binding*. Dordrecht: Foris Publications.

Gibbs, Raymond W., Jr.
1990 Psycholinguistic studies on the conceptual basis of idiomaticity. *Cognitive Linguistics* 1: 417–462.
1993 Process and products in making sense of tropes. In *Metaphor and Thought*, Andrew Ortony (ed.), 252–276. Cambridge: Cambridge University Press.

Glucksberg, Sam and Boaz Keysar
1993 How metaphors work. In *Metaphor and Thought*, Andrew Ortony (ed.), 401–424. Cambridge: Cambridge University Press.

Grice, Paul
1989 *Studies in the Way of Words*. Cambridge, MA: Harvard University Press.

Johnson, M.
1981 *Philosophical Perspectives on Metaphor*. Minneapolis: University of Minnesota Press.

Kövecses, Zoltan
1990 *Emotion Concepts*. New York: Springer-Verlag.

Lakoff, George
1987 *Women, Fire, and Dangerous Things: What Categories Reveal about the Mind*. Chicago: University of Chicago Press.

Lakoff, George and Mark Johnson
1980 *Metaphors We Live By*. Chicago: University of Chicago Press.

Lakoff, George and Mark Turner
1989 *More Than Cool Reason: A Field Guide to Poetic Metaphor.* Chicago: University of Chicago Press.
Merwin, William S.
1973 *Asian Figures.* New York: Atheneum.
Merwin, William S. and Masson, J. Moussaieff (trans.)
1981 *The Peacock's Egg.* San Francisco: North Point Press.
Morgan, Pamela
1993 In *Metaphor and Thought*, Andrew Ortony (ed.). Cambridge: Cambridge University Press.
Ortony, Andrew (ed.)
1993 *Metaphor and Thought.* Cambridge: Cambridge University Press. (First edition published in 1979.)
Reddy, Michael
1993 The conduit metaphor. A case of frame conflict in our language about language. In *Metaphor and Thought*, Andrew Ortony (ed.), 164–201. Cambridge: Cambridge University Press.
Sadock, Jerrold
1993 Figurative speech and linguistics. In *Metaphor and Thought*, Andrew Ortony (ed.), 42–57. Cambridge: Cambridge University Press.
Searle, John R.
1993 Metaphor. In *Metaphor and Thought*, Andrew Ortony (ed.), 83–111. Cambridge: Cambridge University Press.
Sweetser, Eve
1990 *From Etymology to Pragmatics: The Mind-as-Body Metaphor in Semantic Structure and Semantic Change.* Cambridge: Cambridge University Press.
Turner, Mark
1987 *Death Is the Mother of Beauty: Mind, Metaphor, Criticism.* Chicago: University of Chicago Press.
1991 *Reading Minds: The Study of English in the Age of Cognitive Science.* Princeton: Princeton University Press.

# Chapter 7
# Image schema

## The cognitive psychological reality of image schemas and their transformations

*Raymond W. Gibbs, Jr. and Herbert L. Colston*

One of the important claims of cognitive semantics is that much of our knowledge is not static, propositional and sentential, but is grounded in and structured by various patterns of our perceptual interactions, bodily actions, and manipulations of objects (Johnson 1987, 1993; Lakoff 1987, 1990; Talmy 1988). These patterns are experiential gestalts, called *image schemas,* that emerge throughout sensorimotor activity as we manipulate objects, orient ourselves spatially and temporally, and direct our perceptual focus for various purposes (Johnson 1991).

Studies in cognitive linguistics suggest that over two dozen different image schemas and several image schema transformations appear regularly in people's everyday thinking, reasoning, and imagination (Johnson 1987; Lakoff 1987). Among these are the schematic structures of CONTAINER, BALANCE, SOURCE-PATH-GOAL, PATH, CYCLE, ATTRACTION, CENTER/PERIPHERY, and LINK. These image schemas cover a wide range of experiential structures that are pervasive in experience, have internal structure, and can be metaphorically elaborated to provide for our understanding of more abstract domains. For example, cognitive linguistic research has examined how image schemas are used to create grammatical forms (Langacker 1987, 1991), to represent the underlying meaning that relates the seemingly disparate senses of prepositions (Brugman and Lakoff 1988; Vandeloise 1993), to motivate verb-particle constructions, such as those focusing on *up* and *out* (Lindner 1983), adverbs, such as *very* (Brugman 1984), certain verbs, such as *take* (Norvig and Lakoff 1987), as well as to explain the many kinds of cognitive relationships that can form the basis of the extension of a category such as Japanese *hon* (Lakoff 1987). More recent investigations from linguistics and philosophy examined the role that image schemas have in motivating abstract metaphorical concepts, such as causation, death, and morality (Johnson 1993; Lakoff 1990; Lakoff and Turner 1989; Turner 1991).

Although these studies provide important evidence on image schemas in everyday thought and linguistic understanding, the question remains as to whether there exists independent empirical evidence on the psychological reality of image

Originally published in 1995 in *Cognitive Linguistics* 6(4): 347–378.

schemas. Our aim in this paper is to describe some of the findings from psycholinguistics, cognitive psychology, and developmental psychology that, in our view, support the claims of cognitive semantics about image schemas and their transformations.

There are two important reasons for considering this psychological evidence. First, cognitive linguists, following the cognitive commitment to construct theories that are consistent with what is known about the mind and brain (Lakoff 1990, 1993), should be aware of the experimental findings from neighboring disciplines, especially data that bear on the possible connections between perception, thought, and language. Second, psychologists are sometimes skeptical about theoretical notions from linguistics that are primarily based on an individual analyst's intuitions about linguistic structure and behavior. One of the main reasons for conducting experiments with large groups of people is to minimize the uncertainty in making inferences about thought and behavior in whole populations of people.

We do not entirely agree with the skepticism of psychologists about the theoretical claims of cognitive linguists (e.g., Kennedy and Vervaeke 1993). Yet we think there exist different kinds of empirical evidence from psychology that both psychologists and cognitive linguists should be aware of regarding the importance of image schemas in ordinary cognitive functioning. This paper describes some of this evidence. We begin by first elaborating the notion of image schemas and how they are transformed. We then review work from psycholinguistics that has explicitly examined how image schemas motivate people's understanding of word meaning. The next section of the paper describes work from cognitive psychology that seems quite consistent with claims for the importance of image schemas in everyday cognition. We then review work from developmental psychology that also supports the cognitive reality of image schemas. The final section discusses the significance of the different work from psychology for future studies in cognitive linguistics.

## 1. Image schemas and their transformations

Image schemas can generally be defined as dynamic analog representations of spatial relations and movements in space. Even though image schemas are derived from perceptual and motor processes, they are not themselves sensorimotor processes. Instead, image schemas are "primary means by which we construct or constitute order and are not mere passive receptacles into which experience is poured" (Johnson 1987: 30). In this way, image schemas are different from the notion of schemata traditionally used in cognitive science, which are abstract conceptual and propositional event structures (see Rumelhart 1980). By contrast, image schemas are imaginative and nonpropositional in nature and operate as organizing structures of experience at the level of bodily perception and movement. Image schemas exist across all perceptual modalities, something that must hold for there to be any sensorimotor coordination in our experience. As such, image schemas are at once visual, auditory, kinesthetic, and tactile.

We can illustrate what is meant by the notion of image schema, and how its internal structure is projected onto new domain via metaphor, by considering the BALANCE schema (Johnson 1987). The idea of balance is something that is learned "with our bodies and not by grasping a set of rules" (Johnson, 1987: 74). Balancing is such a pervasive part of our bodily experience that we are seldom aware of its presence in everyday life. We come to know the meaning of balance through the closely related experiences of bodily equilibrium or loss of equilibrium. For example, a baby stands, wobbles, and drops to the floor. It tries again and again, as it learns how to maintain a balanced erect posture. A young boy struggles to stay up on a two-wheeled bicycle as he learns to keep his balance while riding down the street. Each of us has experienced occasions when we have too much acid in our stomachs, when our hands get cold, our heads feel too hot, our bladders feel distended, our sinuses become swollen, and our mouths feel dry. In these and numerous other ways we learn the meanings of lack of balance or equilibrium. We respond to imbalance and disequilibrium by warming our hands, giving moisture to our mouths, draining our bladders, and so forth until we feel balanced once again. Our BALANCE image schema emerges, then, through our experiences of bodily equilibriums and disequilibriums and of maintaining our bodily systems and functions in states of equilibrium. We refer to these recurring bodily experiences as *image schemas* to emphasize means of structuring particular experiences schematically so that we can give order and connectedness to our perceptions and conceptions (Johnson 1987).

One of the most interesting things about image schemas is that they motivate important aspects of how we think, reason, and imagine. The same image schema can be instantiated in many different kinds of domains because the internal structure of a single schema can be metaphorically understood. Our BALANCE image schema, to continue with this example, is metaphorically elaborated in a large number of abstract domains of experience (e.g., psychological states, legal relationships, formal systems) (Johnson 1991). In the cases of bodily and visual balance, there seems to be one basic scheme consisting of a point or axis around which forces and weights must be distributed so that they counteract or balance off one another. Our experience of bodily balance and the perception of balance is connected to our understanding of balanced personalities, balanced views, balanced systems, balanced equilibrium, the balance of power, the balance of justice, and so on. In each of these examples, the mental or the abstract concept of balance is understood and experienced in terms of our physical understanding of balance. Image schemas have internal logic or structure that determine the roles these schemas can play in structuring various concepts and in patterns of reasoning. It is not the case that a large number of unrelated concepts (for the systematic, psychological, moral, legal, and mathematical domains) all just happen to make use of the same word *balance* and related terms (Johnson 1991). Rather, we use the same word for all these domains because they are structurally related by the same sort of underlying image schemas, and are metaphorically elaborated from them.

Image schemas do not simply exist as single entities, but are often linked together to form very natural relationships through different *image schema transformations*. Image schema transformations have been shown to play a special role in linking perception and reason. Among the most important image schema transformations are (Lakoff 1987: 443):

(a) *Path-focus to end-point focus*: Follow, in imagination, the path of a moving object, and then focus on the point where it comes to rest, or where it will come to rest.
(b) *Multiplex to mass*: Imagine a group of several objects. Move away (in your mind) from the group until the cluster of individuals start to become a single homogeneous mass. Now move back down to the point where the mass turns once again into a cluster.
(c) *Following a trajectory*: As we perceive a continuously moving object, we can mentally trace the path it has traversed or the trajectory it is about to traverse.
(d) *Superimposition*: Imagine a large sphere and a small cube. Increase the size of the cube until the sphere can fit inside it. Now reduce the size of the cube and put it within the sphere.

Each image schema transformation reflects important aspects of our visual, auditory, or kinesthetic bodily experience. To illustrate, consider how these transformations might apply to our earlier example of the image schema for balance or equilibrium. A situation where several of these transformations interact with the balance image schema is that of handling a group of animals. In order to successfully control and navigate a large number of animals, cattle or sheep perhaps, one needs to maintain the cohesiveness of the group. If a portion of the herd begins to drift apart from the whole, an instance of the Multiplex to mass transformation, equilibrium has been lost and action must be taken to restore it. Such a corrective action requires that the path of the drifters be ascertained, following a trajectory, and that their destination be determined and "headed off", path-focus to end-point focus. There are many examples like this that illustrate the role of image schemas and different transformations in structuring our understanding of real-world phenomena. We will consider other instances of image schema transformations as demonstrated in several studies from cognitive and developmental psychology. But we will first consider some of the experimental evidence on the role of image schemas in motivating people's understanding of word meaning.

## 2. Psycholinguistics and image schemas

Consider the word *stand* in the following sentences: *Please stand at attention. He wouldn't stand for such treatment. The clock stands on the mantle. The law still stands. He stands six-foot five. The part stands for the whole* and *She had a one-night stand with a stranger.* These sentences represent just a few of the many senses of *stand* that are common in everyday speech and writing. Some of these senses refer to the physical act of standing (e.g., *Please stand at attention, The clock stands on the mantle, He stands six-foot five),* while others have nonphysical, perhaps figurative, interpretations (e.g., *We stood accused of the crime, The part stands for the whole, He wouldn't stand for such treatment).* What are the principles that relate the meanings of polysemous words? For instance, what relates the different physical and nonphysical senses of *stand* in the examples noted above?

Some linguists in recent years have argued that many polysemous words resist being defined by a general, abstract, core sense (Brugman and Lakoff 1988; Fillmore 1982; Geeraerts 1993; Sweetser 1986). Cognitive linguists have suggested that the meanings of polysemous words can be characterized by metaphor, metonymy, and different kinds of image schemas (Lakoff 1987; Johnson 1987; Sweetser 1990). Under this view, the lexical organization of polysemous words is not a repository of random, idiosyncratic information, but is structured by general cognitive principles that are systematic and recurrent throughout the lexicon. Most important, perhaps, is the claim that these principles arise from our phenomenological, embodied experience. One possibility is that bodily experience partly motivates people's intuitions as to why different senses of *stand* have the meanings they do.

Gibbs et al. (1994) attempted to experimentally show that the different senses of the polysemous word *stand* are motivated by different image schemas that arise from our bodily experience of standing. Their general aim was to empirically demonstrate that the meanings of the polysemous word *stand* are not arbitrary for native speakers, but are motivated by people's recurring bodily experiences in the real world.

As a first step toward understanding how image schemas partly motivate the meanings of the polysemous word *stand,* a preliminary experiment sought to determine which image schemas best reflect people's recurring bodily experiences of standing. A group of participants were guided through a brief set of bodily exercises to get them to consciously think about their own physical experience of standing. For instance, participants were asked to stand up, to move around, bend over, to crunch, and to stretch out on their tip-toes. Having people actually engage in these bodily experiences facilitates participants' intuitive understandings of how their experience of standing related to many different possible image schemas. After this brief standing exercise, participants then read brief descriptions of 12 different image schemas that might possibly have some relationship to the experience of physical standing (e.g., VERTICALITY, BALANCE, RESISTANCE, ENABLEMENT, CENTER/PERIPHERY, LINKAGE). Finally, the participants rated the degree of relatedness of each image schema to their own embodied experience of standing. The results of this first study showed that five image schemas are primary to people's bodily experiences of standing (i.e., BALANCE, VERTICALITY, CENTER/PERIPHERY, RESISTANCE, and LINKAGE).

A second experiment investigated people's judgements of similarity for different senses of *stand*. The participants sorted 35 different senses of *stand* into five groups based on their similarity of meaning. An analysis of these groups revealed that participants did not sort physical senses of *stand* separately from the nonphysical or figurative senses. For example, the physical idea of standing in *to stand at attention* was often grouped with the metaphorical senses of *stand* in *let the issue stand* and *to stand the test of time*.

The third experiment in this series examined the relationship between the five image schemas for the physical experience of standing and the various senses of *stand* studied in Experiment 2. Once again, participants were first asked to stand up and focus on different aspects of their bodily experience of standing. As they did this, the participants were presented with verbal descriptions of the five image schemas BALANCE, VERTICALITY, CENTER/PERIPHERY, RESISTANCE, and LINKAGE. Afterwards, the participants were given a list of 32 senses of *stand* and asked to rate the degree of relatedness between each sense and the five image schemas.

The rating data from this third study allowed Gibbs et al. (1994) to construct an image schema profile for each of the 32 uses of *stand*. Several interesting similarities emerged in the image schema profiles for some of the 32 senses of *stand*. For example, *it stands to reason* and *as the matter now stands* both have the same image schema profile (in their rank-order of importance) of LINKAGE–BALANCE–CENTER/PERIPHERY–RESISTANCE–VERTICALITY. The expressions *don't stand for such treatment* and *to stand against great odds* are both characterized by the image schema profile RESISTANCE–CENTER/PERIPHERY–LINKAGE–BALANCE–VERTICALITY.

The primary goal of this study, though, was to assess whether the senses of *stand* seen as being similar in meaning in the second experiment were reliably predictable from the image schema profiles obtained in this study. Statistical analyses showed that knowing the image schema profiles for different senses of *stand* allowed us to predict 79% of all the groupings *of stand* in Experiment 2.

These data provide very strong support for the hypothesis that people's understandings of the meanings of *stand* are partly motivated by image schemas that arise from their bodily experiences of standing. A fourth study showed that participants' sortings of *stand* in different groups cannot be explained simply in terms of their understanding of the contexts in which these words appeared. Thus, people did not sort phrases, such as *don't stand for such treatment* and *to stand against great odds*, because these phrases refer to the same types of situations. Instead, it appears that people's similarity judgments are best attributed to their tacit understanding of how different patterns of image schemas motivate different uses of the polysemous word *stand*.

This psycholinguistic research has demonstrated that people make sense of different uses of *stand* because of their tacit understanding of several image schemas that arise partly from the ordinary bodily experience of standing. These image schemas, the most important of which are BALANCE, VERTICALITY, CENTER/PERIPHERY, RESISTANCE and LINKAGE, not only produce the grounding for many physical senses of *stand* (e.g., *he stands six-foot nine, stand in the way,* and *stand at attention*), but also underlie people's understanding of complex, metaphorical uses (e.g., *the part stands for the whole, as the matter now stands,* and *the engine can't stand the constant wear*). People perceive different senses of *stand* as similar in meaning partly on the basis of the underlying image schema profile for each use of the word in context.

This conclusion about the meanings of the word *stand* does not imply that people judge similarity of meaning between two senses of a word only on the basis of image schemas. Many aspects of word meaning that have little to do directly with image schemas certainly play some role in people's understanding of word meaning and their judgments of similarity of meaning for different senses of a polysemous word. At the same time, this experimental research does not imply that people automatically access some specific pattern of image schemas each time they encounter a particular use of a word. The main conclusion, though, from the experimental work is that people tacitly recognize some connection between these schematic bodily experiences and different aspects of linguistic meaning, including meanings that are highly abstract and/or metaphorical.

The psycholinguistic research on *stand* is, as far as we know, the only empirical work in psychology that has explicitly set out to investigate the possible role of image schemas in perception, thought, or language use. This work should be of interest to skeptics of cognitive linguistic ideas on image schemas because the methodology employed in these studies allowed for the independent assessment of bodily experience apart from any analysis of how the body might motivate linguistic expressions. Psychologists often contend that cognitive linguistic research suffers from circular reasoning in that it starts with an analysis of language to infer something about the mind and body which in turn motivates different aspects of linguistic structure and behavior. By independently assessing bodily experience of standing beforehand, Gibbs et al. (1994) were able to make specific predictions about people's understanding of different uses of *stand*. Making specific experimental predictions, which can be falsified, about people's linguistic behavior is an essential ingredient for psychologists if they are to accept the psychological reality of any hypothetical construct such as image schemas.

## 3. Cognitive psychology and image schemas

The possible relevance of cognitive psychology research to image schemas was first noted by Johnson (1987) and Lakoff (1987). They both described several studies on mental imagery that supported the idea that image schemas and their transformations play an important role in cognitive functioning. We will briefly consider these studies as well as describing several other lines of research on nonlinguistic information processing that are connected with the cognitive psychological reality of image schemas and their transformations.

One topic that might be especially relevant to image schemas and their transformations is the connection between imagery and perception. Research in imagery is of central importance to the long-standing debate in cognitive science concerning whether the human mind employs both propositional and analog representations. What does the study of mental imagery tell us about image schemas and their transformations?

The early research on mental imagery focused on the idea of selective interference. Consider first a classic study by Brooks (1968). Participants were presented with figures, such as the letter F, or sentences that were then taken away. Afterwards, the participants were asked to scan their mental images of the figures to answer specific questions. For the sentences, participants had to recall each word in the sentence sequentially and indicate if the word was a noun or not. For the line diagrams, which were in the form of block letters, participants had to imagine a particular comer of the diagram, and then proceed around the perimeter of the diagram and indicate if each corner of the letter that they imagined was an extreme outside corner or not. On both kinds of recall, participants were instructed to respond either verbally, by saying "yes" or "no", or visually, by pointing to a sheet with "yes" and "no" printed on it. Brooks found that the type of recall and the method of reporting conflicted if they were in the same modality. Participants were slower to respond visually than verbally when recalling the line diagram. Participants were also slower when responding verbally than visually when recalling the sentences. In general, imagery led to a drop in performance in tasks that used related processes. Other studies by Segal and Fusella (1970) showed that visual and auditory imagery can selectively interfere with the detection of signals from the same modality. Johnson (1987) suggested that the data from Brooks' study provided evidence for image schemas in that people seemed able to access certain modes of cognition, either recall of verbal information or visual imagery, through multiple channels, such as kinesthetic or verbal report.

Johnson (1987) and Lakoff (1987) also argued that several classic studies on mental rotation of images provide evidence in support of image schemas and their transformations. For example, participants in one study were presented with two-dimensional drawings of pairs of three-dimensional objects. The participants' task was to determine whether the two represented objects were identical except for orientation (Shepard and Metzler 1971). Some of the figures required rotation solely within the picture plane, while others required rotation in depth ("into" the page). The general result was that, whether for two- or three-dimensional rotations, participants seem to rotate the objects mentally at a fixed rate of approximately 60 degrees per second. Further experiments seemed to confirm this phenomenon (Cooper and Shepard 1982). Control studies demonstrate that mental imagery effects can not be easily explained in terms of verbal or other analytic strategies that might have been based on the initial description of a visual pattern (Bethell-Fox and Shepard 1988; Cooper and Podgorny 1976). These data show that we are constrained in our mental processes of manipulating things similarly to how we are constrained in our physical ability to manipulate things in the real world. Johnson (1987: 25) concluded from his discussion of the mental rotation data that "we can perform mental operations on image schemata that are analogs of spatial operations". In other words, the empirical data suggest that image schemas have a kinesthetic character as they are not tied to any single perceptual modality.

Does our ability to mentally rotate images truly reflect the operation of image schemata? To answer this question, we must be very clear about the differences between mental imagery as typically studied by cognitive psychologists and the idea of image schemas. Both Johnson and Lakoff note that image schemas are not the same as real images which they refer to as "rich" images. Image schemas are presumably more abstract than ordinary images and consist of dynamic spatial patterns that underlie the spatial relations and movement found in actual concrete images. Mental images are also temporary representations, while image schemas are permanent properties of embodied experience. Finally, image schemas are emergent properties of unreflective bodily experience, while mental images are the result of more effortful cognitive processes. For example, research shows that mental images are generated by assembling the parts of the image one part at a time (see Finke 1989).

Despite these differences, there are interesting similarities between mental images and image schemas that make the study of mental imagery especially relevant to our quest for the cognitive psychological reality of image schemas and their transformations. First, real images are typically not as rich and detailed as

Johnson and Lakoff originally implied. Various studies show that mental images are not mental pictures in the sense of providing a veridical copy of what has been perceived (Finke 1989). Visual images are typically constructed from the underlying concepts a person already knows (Chambers and Reisberg 1992; Intos-Peterson and Roskos-Ewoldsen 1989). Some aspects of mental images reflect the operation of visual and spatial representations. Even congenitally blind individuals perform quite successfully on various mental imagery tasks where they are first presented with the object studied tactically rather than visually (Kerr 1983; Zimler and Keenan 1983). These findings suggest that there is no reason to believe a visual representation is necessary for mental imagery. The representation of mental images is neither entirely visual nor entirely spatial. For example, Farah et al. (1988) note that there may be two anatomically distinct cortical systems for dealing with visual representations (one involved in representing the appearance of objects, the other to represent the location of objects in space). Other neuropsychological evidence shows that a patient with brain damage from an automobile accident suffered from several deficits in visual recognition but performed normally on most spatial mental imagery tasks. Most importantly, other aspects of mental imagery are constrained by people's kinesthetic knowledge which, for example, influences their ability to recognize permissible rotations of the body and different body parts (Parsons 1988, 1989).

In summary, although there are significant differences between mental imagery and image schemas, there is good evidence that both spatial and visual representation exist for mental imagery. This conclusion is quite consistent with the idea that different modes of perceptual/bodily experience give rise to cognitive schemes that have analoglike properties. To the extent, then, that people's mental images reflect the operation of various modalities and kinesthetic properties of the body, the experimental findings on mental imagery support the idea that image schemas play a significant role in certain aspects of perception and cognition.

One relatively new body of research that quite specifically points to the role of image schemas and their transformations in mental functioning comes from studies on representational momentum. Before considering these activities, consider first the bodily experience of momentum. This experience is pervasive in daily life. We experience visual momentum when we see heavy moving things continue to move even when encountering other objects. We experience kinesthetic momentum both when we are the object that the heavy moving thing encounters and when we are the heavy moving thing. We experience auditory momentum both as a correlate of visual and kinesthetic momentum and independently as when thunder builds up to a crescendo. We even experience internal momentum as when certain bodily functions build up such that they cannot be stopped. We abstract out of all of these similar experiences those aspects of form which they have in common or which are similar, which we refer to through language as momentum.

The term representational momentum was coined by Freyd and Finke (1984) to refer to an internalized representation of physical momentum. A variety of experiments have studied different aspects of representational momentum. The typical paradigm used to investigate representational momentum consists of the presentation of a sequence of three static images, referred to as the inducing stimuli, of an object (usually a simple geometric shape or a dot) which appears to be moving linearly or rotating in one direction. A final target position of the image is then presented and participants are asked to determine if this target image's position is the same as the third static image of the object. Figure 1 presents a schematic diagram of the experimental paradigm used to study representational momentum. People's participation in a representational momentum task involves their ability to follow in their imagination the path of a moving object and then focus on the point where it will come to rest (an example of the path-focus to end-point focus image schema transformation).

The classic finding from representational momentum studies is that participants' memory for the final position of an object undergoing implied motion is shifted toward the direction of the motion. The effect was first discovered for rotating objects (Freyd and Finke 1984) and was later extended to linearly moving objects (Finke and Freyd 1985;

Hubbard and Bharucha 1988). For example, if participants watch an image of an object which appears to be rotating, and then have to remember the final position of the object, they will typically report that the object's final position was further along in the rotation than it actually was. The same sort of effect holds for linearly moving objects. If participants watch an image of an object which appears to be moving along a linear path, and then have to remember this object's final position, they will report that the final position was further along the path than it actually was.

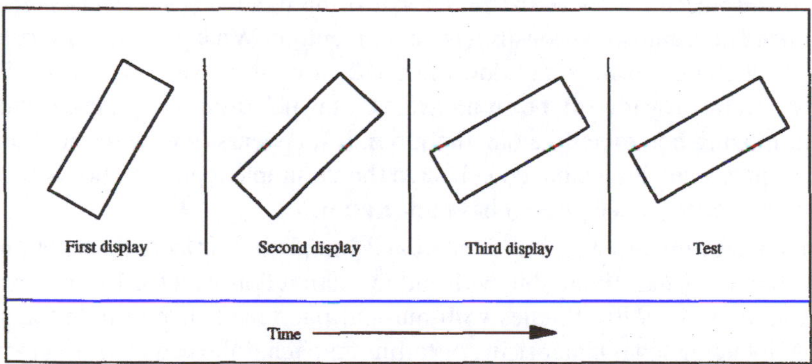


*Figure 1.* Schematic diagram of series of events in typical representational momentum experiment

What cognitive psychological principles best explain the phenomenon of representational momentum? The effect is not due to apparent motion because increasing the amount of time up to two seconds between the presentations of the static images still results in representational momentum (Finke and Freyd 1985). Representational momentum presumably "reflects the internalization in the visual system of the principles of physical momentum" (Kelly and Freyd 1987: 369). Indeed, many characteristics of real world physical momentum have been found in representational momentum. For instance, the apparent velocity of the inducing stimuli affects representational momentum (Freyd and Finke 1985; Finke et al. 1986). Participants' memory for the final position of a quickly moving object is displaced further along in its path than if the object is moving slowly. Apparent acceleration of the inducing stimuli also affects representational momentum in that objects which appear to be accelerating will produce a larger memory displacement (Finke et al. 1986). Also, displacements which go beyond what one would expect in real world momentum do not produce representational momentum, (Finke and Freyd 1985). If the target image of the object is in a position such that it corresponds to what would be the "next" position in the sequence of inducing images, or is even further along in the path or rotation than the "next" position, the representational momentum effect goes away.

Furthermore, memory displacement is greater for horizontal versus vertical motion (Hubbard and Bharucha 1988). This may be a result of the predominance of horizontal motion in our environment. Gravity also affects representational momentum (Hubbard and Bharucha 1988). Objects moving downward are displaced more along their direction of motion than objects moving upward. If an object is moving horizontally and then disappears, participants consistently mark its vanishing point to be lower than it actually was. The same result occurs with ascending oblique motion. Interestingly, descending oblique motion usually produces displacement above the actual vanishing point. These results suggest internalized environmental constraints on momentum. What goes up must come down, what comes down comes down faster than what goes up, things moving linearly usually drop toward the ground, and that which drops at an angle usually ends up moving horizontally along the ground. It appears that representational momentum is something more complicated than a simple representation of what an object's motion is like given it has momentum.

Finally, and importantly, representational momentum effects have not only been found for visual stimuli, but with auditory stimuli as well (Kelly and Freyd 1987; Freyd et al. 1990). Studies with musical pitch have demonstrated that a series of inducing tones either rising or falling in pitch, followed by a target tone either higher or lower in pitch than the third inducing tone produces the same representational momentum effects as with the studies using visual stimuli. This auditory representational momentum appears to not be simply due to a correlation with visual representational momentum, but rather seems only abstractly related to the latter (Kelly and Freyd 1987). Kelly and Freyd introduced the Gestalt property of "good continuation" as a possible explanation for the similarities between visual and auditory representational momentum, but discount the idea saying that it "cannot provide any explanation for the specific quantitative aspects of the phenomenon, such as the fact that the representational distortions increase with the implied velocity of the display. Such effects, however, are predicted by a model of the phenomenon based on physical momentum." (1987: 397).

Many aspects of the data on visual and auditory representational momentum can be explained in terms of image schemas and their transformations. First, the SOURCE–PATH–GOAL schema must underlie critical aspects of representational momentum as a person observes an object move from a starting position along some path toward an imagined goal. The SOURCE–PATH–GOAL schema must be one of the most basic image schemas that arise from our bodily experience and perceptual interactions with the world. Besides the schema of SOURCE–PATH–GOAL there may also be a specific schema for MOMENTUM. When we encounter the inducing stimuli in a representational momentum task, either visual or auditory, a stored representation for momentum is *not* activated. Instead, we use the image schema for MOMENTUM, derived jointly by our minds, bodies and our environment, to expect the next stimuli to be further along in the path, rotation or musical scale. Such an expectation would not occur using only the PATH image schema or FOLLOWING A TRAJECTORY transformation. These may provide the direction that a moving or rotating object is about to traverse, but they cannot account for an expectation concerning the distance that the object will travel given that it has momentum. Yet a MOMENTUM schema accounts for specific, quantitative aspects of visual representational momentum. Thus, our experience tells us that the faster something is moving, the more momentum it will have and thus the more distance it will travel when a stopping force is applied to it. Moreover, the notion of momentum as image schema also explains the cross modal aspects of representational momentum. We abstract away from our experiences of seeing momentum, hearing momentum and feeling momentum those aspects that are shared or which are similar to one another. Thus, we get the same kinds of effects in auditory as in visual representational momentum even though they are not always correlated in the environment (Kelly and Freyd 1987).

The research on visual and auditory representational momentum also illustrates different image schema transformations in that an image schema like momentum can be created by the transformation of other image schemas such as LANDMARK, PATH, BLOCKAGE, REMOVAL OF BLOCKAGE, and GOAL. Image schema transformations like these would function in representational momentum in the following way. First, we invoke the landmark image schema when we immediately attend to an object. As this object moves, we transform the landmark image schema into the path image schema in that our attention is now additionally focused upon the path of the landmark. This is known as the LANDMARK-PATH image schema transformation. We then invoke the BLOCKAGE image schema when the moving object disappears. This image schema is transformed into the REMOVAL OF BLOCKAGE image schema when the target stimuli appears. This transformation is known as the BLOCKAGE-REMOVAL image schema transformation. Finally, to determine the endpoint of the moving object given that it was a landmark moving along a path which encountered blockage which was subsequently removed, we transform the PATH image schema into a MOMENTUM image schema, and then that into an endpoint focus or goal image schema. This gives us information about the likely position of the object given that it had not encountered any blockage.

We use the position provided by image schema transformations to compare to the target stimuli in a representational momentum task. If there is a match between our expected position given by different image schema transformations and the target stimuli, we respond affirmatively. As the representational momentum literature has shown, however, we are frequently mistaken in saying that target positions which are further along the path correctly indicate the position the object would have. This mistake is produced by the PATH-END-POINT FOCUS image schema transformation. This transformation gives us information about where the object should be given that it was moving at a certain speed, in a certain direction, encountered blockage which was then removed. If we were instead relying only upon the information in memory on the actual position of the most recent image of the object, we would not make these errors.

In general, the research on representational momentum shows that different modes of experience, visual and auditory, are structured in very much the same way even though they are not always correlated in the environment. Internalized representations of real world physical momentum are not adequate because of the constraints imposed by our perceptual system. Externalized projections of our perceptions are not adequate because of the real world aspects like gravity. Gestalt principles are compelling in that they capture the flavor of abstracted repeating patterns of form of our bodily experience when interacting with our environment, but they are not adequate by themselves because they do not specify the quantitative details. On the other hand, image schemas and their transformations provide a useful way of explaining different aspects of representational momentum.

Our analysis of the image schemas and the transformations that might be involved in the empirical studies on representational momentum is meant to illustrate something about the importance of bodily experience in human perception and cognition. Many other studies in cognitive psychology show that dynamic events, not single, isolated occurrences, are the basic units of perception. In many cases, people find it easier to make sense of temporal events than they do of nontemporal ones, and of moving objects over those that are stationary (Gibson

1979; Michaels and Carello 1981). An elegant demonstration of these patterns is found in research conducted by Johansson (1973). In one experiment, lights were placed at the major joints of a person dressed in black and photographed in the dark. Viewing the lights as stationary, observers reported seeing only random arrangements of dots. However, if the person to whom the lights were attached moved by walking, hopping, doing situps, or any other familiar activity, observers will immediately and unmistakenly see a person engaged in that activity. If the lights stop moving, they return to what appears to be a random assemblage. Other evidence indicates that observers detect the sex and even the identity of a person walking to whom lights are attached (Koslowsky and Cutting 1977).

Johansson concluded that the perception of the gestalt pattern of an event progressing in time is basic in ordinary life. He proposed that the perception of a unique structure for continuously transforming point-lights was accomplished by the visual system according to some perceptual vector analysis. A similar conclusion has been offered for how people perceive the movements of the hands and arms through space in American Sign Language (Poizner et al. 1986). But the perception of dynamic events might also reflect the primacy of image schema transformations in human cognition. For example, the ability of observers to recognize that a set of moving lights form a person reflects the involvement of the MULTIPLEX-TO-MASS image schema transformation where an undifferentiated group of objects begins to take on a coherent, meaningful appearance once movement is detected. The perception of dynamic events over static ones also highlights the importance of the analog component of image schemas.

Beyond our image schematic ability to perceive meaningful configurations from the movement of random dots, people exhibit a capacity for noting meaningful resemblances between different sensory experiences. What enables people, for example, to recognize a resemblance between the faint twinkle of a dim star and a muted tone? When cross-modal similarities appear in language they typically take the form of similes and metaphors. The cross-sensory or synesthetic experience provides one of the simplest kinds of metaphoric language in which one mode of sensory or perceptual experience gets mapped onto another. Phrases such as *loud sunlight, bright thunder, murmur of sunlight,* and *sunlight roar* illustrate just some of the many thousands of examples of synesthesia. Although early studies suggested that synesthetic perception may be relatively rare in adults, studies in recent years suggest that synesthetic perception may rest on a universal understanding of cross-modal equivalence (Marks 1978). Synesthetic matches are not random. People do not arbitrarily combine colors, forms, and sounds. But people do make systematic connections between dimensions of specific modalities, for example, soft and low-pitched sounds are associated with dim or dark colors and as sounds get louder or higher in pitch, the colors gets brighter (Marks 1978, 1982).

Our ability to appreciate resemblances between relatively abstract properties of visual and auditory experiences may illustrate the emergence of various image schematic structures. We may, for instance, recognize that the image schematic structure for color might have a fixed correspondence with the image schematic structure for sounds. Marks et al. (1987) argue for the existence of abstract supra-dimensions of experience that make certain combinations of ideas more likely, more natural, than others (e.g., *loud* and *bright* go well together in a way that *loud* and *dark* do not). But we can better argue that constraints on permissible perceptual relations are provided by the invariance principle (Lakoff 1990), which holds that the mappings of source-to-target domain information in metaphors preserve the structural characteristics or cognitive topology of the source domains. Under this view, in synesthesia, people recognize invariant correspondences between the image schematic structure for auditory sounds and visual images and this constrains what combinations of synesthesia are most meaningful.

## 4. Image schemas and developmental research

Developmental psychologists have long debated the role of early sensorimotor behavior in cognitive development. Since Piaget's (1952, 1954) writings on how sensorimotor development underlies different aspects of cognitive growth, developmental psychologists have considered ways of linking patterns that emerge from young children's bodily and perceptual experience with later intellectual development. Although Piaget concluded that young infants understood little of the physical events that take place around them, more recent research conducted with sensitive methods suggests that young infants are capable of sophisticated physical reasoning (Baillargeon 1993; Spelke et al. 1992). In recent years, developmental psychologists have even argued that image schemas form the basis for certain concepts that appear to underlie physical reasoning in early childhood (Mandler 1992).

First consider the concept of animacy. People are able to judge motion to be animate on the basis of perceptual characteristics of which they are not aware. There are two broad types of onset of motion, self-instigated motion and caused motion. From early age, infants are sensitive to the difference between something starting to move on its own and something being pushed or otherwise made to move (Leslie 1988). Self-motion is the start of an independent trajectory where no other object or trajectory is involved. By itself an object starting to move without another visible trajector acting on it is not a guarantee of animacy (e.g., a wind-up toy).

Several kinds of simple perceptual analyses give conceptual meaning to a category of moving things. Mandler (1992) claimed that infants use image schemas as they generalize across the particulars of perception to a representation that encompasses some abstract characteristics the experiences have in common. For instance, adults think of biological motion as having certain rhythmic but unpredictable characteristics, whereas mechanical motion is thought of as undeviating unless it is deflected in some way. Given infants' concentrated attention on moving objects, some analysis of the animate trajectories must take place along with the analysis of the beginning of their paths. An example would be noticing that dogs bob up and down as well as follow irregular paths when they move. One study with 1- to 2-year-olds examined how children played with little models of a variety of animals and vehicles (Mandler et al. 1991). The children often responded to the animals by making them hop along the table, but they made the vehicles scoot in a straight line. Thus, very young children appear to understand differences in the movement of animate and inanimate objects.

Various image schemas may underlie young children's understanding of animacy. The contingency of animate movement not only involves such factors as one animate object following another, as described by the image schema LINKED PATHS, but also involves avoiding barriers and making sudden shifts in acceleration. Adults are sensitive to all of these aspects of animate movement (Stewart 1984), but it is not yet known whether infants are responsive to such movement, even though they appear to be perceptually salient. Nor has anyone considered how factors such as barrier avoidance might be represented in image schema form (Mandler 1992). Johnson (1987) described several FORCE schemas, such as BLOCKAGE and DIVERSION, that may be useful in describing barrier avoidance, but these schemas need to be further differentiated to account for animate and inanimate trajectories. One might represent animate and inanimate differences in response to blockage as a trajectory that shifts direction before contacting a barrier versus one that runs into a barrier and then either stops or bounces off from it (Mandler 1992).

Causality and inanimacy are two other concepts important to early conceptual development. The difference between self-motion and caused motion is that in the latter case the beginning of path involves another trajector. A hand picks up an object, whose trajectory then begins, or a ball rolls into another, starting the second one on its course. Leslie (1982, 1988) speculated that a concept of causality in infancy is derived from this kind of perception. His studies, which employed sophisticated dishabituation techniques, showed that infants as young as 4 months distinguished between the causal movement involved in one ball launching another and very similar events in which there is a small spatial or temporal gap between the two movements. In launching, the end-of-path of the first trajectory is the beginning-of-path trajector. In the noncausal case there is no connection between the end of one trajectory and the beginning of the next. Other research also shows that 10-month-old infants can differentiate between causal and non-causal events (Cohen and Oakes 1993), and that 10- to 12-month-olds can make sophisticated calibration judgments about collision events (Kotovesky and Baillargeon 1994).

These different findings on young children's spatial analyses suggest that physical causality might be represented before psychological causality, contrary to what is usually assumed in development (Piaget 1954). The specialization of causal understanding is usually said to begin only after infants experience many occasions of drawing objects to themselves or pushing them away. However, Leslie's (1982, 1988) data suggest that the ontogenetic ordering may be the other way around. The experience of intention or violation may not be required to form an initial conception of causality.

Consider now the child's acquisition of the concepts of containment and support. Containment is quite relevant to preverbal thinking and is an early part of conceptual development. Some concept of containment seems to be responsible for the better performance 9-month-old infants show on object-hiding tasks when the occluder consists of an upright container, rather than an inverted container or a screen (Freeman et al. 1980; Lloyd et al. 1981). These infants already appear to have a concept of containers as places where things disappear and reappear.

Image schemas may explain some of these data. For example, the CONTAINMENT schema has three structural elements (interior, boundary, and exterior) that primarily arise from two sources: (1) perceptual analysis of the differentiation of figure from ground, that is, seeing objects as bounded and having an inside that is separate from the outside (Spelke 1988); (2) perceptual analysis of objects going into and out containers. The list of containment relations that babies experience is long. Babies eat and drink, spit things out, watch their bodies being clothed and unclothed, are taken in and out of rooms, and so on.

Although Johnson (1987) emphasized bodily experience as the basis of the understanding of containment, it is not obvious that bodily experience per se is required for perceptual analysis to take place (Mandler 1992). Infants have many opportunities to analyze simple, easily visible containers such as bottles, cups, and dishes, and the acts of containment that make things disappear into and reappear out of them. Indeed, it might be easier to analyze the sight of milk going in and out of a cup than milk going into or out of one's mouth. Nevertheless, which ever way the analysis of containment gets started, one would expect the notion of food as something that is taken into the mouth to be an early conceptualization.

Another aspect that seems to be involved in an early concept of a container is that of support. True containers not only envelop things but support them as well. Infants as young as 3 months are surprised when support relations between objects are violated (Needham and Baillargeon 1991). Five-and-a-half-month-old infants are surprised when containers without bottoms appear to hold things (Kolstad 1991). Similarly, 9-month-old infants could judge whether a block could be supported by a box open at the top *only* when they were able to compare the widths of the block and the box in a single glance as the one was lowered into the other (Sitskoon and Smitsmon 1991). Finally, Baillargeon (1993) demonstrated that 12.5-month-old infants could determine whether a cloth cover with a small protuberance could hide a small tiger toy only when there were able to directly compare the size of the protuberance to that of the toy. These findings suggest that the notions of containments and support may be closely related from an early age. A primitive image schema of SUPPORT might require only a representation of contact between two objects in the vertical dimension (Mandler 1992).

An infant's understanding of opening and closing is also related to the development of containment. Piaget (1952) documented in detail the actions of 9- to 12-month-old infants performed while they were learning to imitate acts that they could not see themselves perform, such as blinking. Before infants accomplished the correct action, they sometimes opened and closed their mouths, opened and closed their hands, or covered and uncovered their eyes with a pillow. Piaget's observations testify to the perceptual analysis in which the infants were engaging and their analogical understanding of the structure of the behavior they were trying to reproduce. Such understanding seems a clear case of an image schema of the spatial movement involved when anything opens or closes, regardless of the particulars of the thing itself.

Finally, another source of evidence for the psychological reality of image schemas and their transformations comes from the developmental literature on object permanence. Object permanence refers to the belief that physical objects exist even when they are not in the presence of the sensory modalities. Piaget (1954) proposed that infants initially do not share adults' beliefs about occlusion events, but adopt the belief slowly over the first few years of life. One could argue that development of the notion of object permanence can be thought of as the development of several different image schemas, and the workings of transformations between them. Several studies have been conducted whose results are amenable to an image schema account. For example, Baillargeon (1987) has shown that 3.5- to 5.5-month old infants have no difficulty representing the existence of one, two, or even three hidden objects. Infants also appear to represent many of the properties of objects, such as their height, length, and trajectory (Baillargeon and DeVos 1991). Other studies show that infants know that hidden objects, like visible ones, cannot move through space occupied by other objects and an object cannot appear at two places in space without being transported from one point to the other (Baillargeon 1993). 3-month-old infants also appear to have developed knowledge of the physical aspects of people (Legerstee 1994).

These results on object permanence can be thought of as indicating the presence of various image schemas and transformations between them. We propose, following Mandler (1992), that the transformations LANDMARK, to BLOCKAGE, to REMOVAL OF BLOCKAGE, and finally back to LANDMARK underlie the demonstration of object permanence in the 4.5-month olds. The reason the 3.5-month olds do not exhibit object permanence is that they either have not developed one or more of these image schemas or are not yet capable of transforming them. The specific explanation requires more specific tests to determine which is true, but we suspect it has to do with blockage and removal of blockage. This follows from the fact that 3.5-month old infants can already focus on individual objects and thus appear to have developed the image schema for LANDMARK.

Our analysis of the role of image schemas in infants' reactions to physical events differs from many developmental psychologists' views on the origins of knowledge. Various scholars express doubt about the idea that infants' knowledge of physical events are derived as they learn about regularities in their perceptual environment (Spelke et al. 1993). Many psychologists argue that early development for perception, action, and reasoning is modular (Karmiloff-Smith 1992). But we wish to suggest that image schemas and their transformation have some functional role in infants' sensorimotor and cognitive systems.

We earlier discussed some of the research from cognitive psychology on cross-modal matching. There exists a similar line of studies in developmental psychology showing that young children find abstract similarities between different sensory experiences. Research in support of this conclusion has looked at how young children understand various multimodal movements. Detection of inter-modal relations is not just a case of association of two experiences that happen to occur simultaneously. For example, 3-month-old infants were familiarized with different visible and audible filmed events (Bahrick 1988). One film depicted a hand shaking a clear plastic bottle containing one very large marble. The other film depicted a hand shaking a similar bottle containing a number of very small marbles. Four conditions varied in their pairings of film and sound tracks as to whether the appropriate track (one or many marbles) was paired with a film or whether a track was synchronomous with the film or not. Only one group of infants was acquainted with films paired with the appropriate, synchronized sound tracks. After familiarization, an internal preference test was given to each group of infants with two films presented side-by-side while a single central track played. The data showed that learning did occur with greater familiarization, resulting in a preference for matching the film specified by its appropriate sound track. But, most importantly, learning was confined to just one group of infants, namely, those most familiar with the appropriate synchronized pairing of sight and sound. Equal opportunity to associate with an inappropriate sound track did not lead to a preference for that combination of the preference test. These findings show that very young children exhibit an ability to acquire abstract relations between events in different modalities.

A different line of research on how children find abstract similarities between different sensory experience comes from work on synesthesia. In one early study, infants were challenged to construct a similarity relationship between two events that shared no physical features or history of co-occurrence (e.g., a pulsing tone and paired slides of a dotted line and a solid line). Nine- to 12-month-old infants looked longer at the dotted line than the solid line in the presence of a pulsing tone suggesting that a metaphorical match was construed (Wagner et al. 1981). Similarly, they looked more at an arrow pointing upward when listening to an ascending tone and to a downward arrow when listening to a descending tone. The infants were thus able to recognize an abstract dimension that underlies two physically and temporally dissimilar events (e.g., discontinuity in the pulsing tone and discontinuity in the dotted line). Another study demonstrated that four-year-olds already perceive and conceive of similarities between pitch and brightness (e.g., low pitch equals dim; high pitch equals bright) and between loudness and brightness (e.g., soft equals dim; loud equals bright). These findings are especially important because they parallel the idea that adults project image schemas from one domain onto another, for example, conceptualizing quantity in terms of verticality (e.g., MORE IS UP and LESS IS DOWN.

Finally, more recent research examined whether infants can construe an abstract unity between a facial expression of emotion (e.g., joy) and an auditory event (e.g., an ascending tone), events that also share no physical features or history of co-occurrence (Phillips et al. 1990). The 7-month-old infants in this study did not categorize different facial expressions of joy and anger. But the infants did look significantly longer at joy, surprise, and sadness when these facial expressions were matched with ascending, pulsing, and descending and continuous tones, respectively. Because the auditory and visual events in this experimental task were substantially different, infants had to act upon the events within a short period of time to bring meaning (i.e., determine equivalences) to the disparity. Thus, infants had to determine the equivalence between both of a pair of facial expressions in concert with the auditory event. This is a striking demonstration of how infants metaphorically match disparate events to construe some meaning in facial expressions of emotion.

The various pieces of empirical evidence on young children's ability to find abstract relations between different sensory events fit in nicely with the claims about image schemas. For us to have meaningful, connected experiences, there must be regular patterns to our actions, perceptions, and conceptions. Image schemas reflect these recurring patterns and emerge through our bodily movements through space, our manipulation of objects, and our perception of the world in which we live.

## 5. General discussion

Our aim has been to explore different connections between ideas from cognitive linguistics on image schemas and their transformations and experimental data from psycholinguistics, cognitive psychology, and developmental psychology. The evidence we have reviewed provides only a small part of the experimental data that might be related to how image schemas and their transformations mediate and constitute different aspects of cognitive functioning. To be sure, many of the scholars whose studies we have cited would not immediately agree with our interpretation of their work in terms of image schemas and their transformations. Our discussion suggests that some empirical work, unbeknownst to the researchers who conducted these studies, might actually provide evidence for the cognitive psychological reality of image schemas and their transformations. Although image schemas do not underlie all aspects of meaning and cognition, they are a crucial, undervalued dimension of meaning that has not been sufficiently explored by psychologists.

The fact that one can talk about different kinds of image schemas and different ways in which these can be transformed certainly suggests that image schemas are definable mental representations. But how are image schemas represented given their cross-modal character? Where might image schemas be represented in the brain given that they arise from recurring bodily experiences that cut across vision, audition, kinesthetic movement and so on (i.e., are the SOURCE-PATH-GOAL or MOMENTUM schemas encoded in the visual cortex or some other part of the brain)? The abstract, yet still definable, character of image schemas does not provide easy answers to these questions. At this point, we can only suggest that linguists and psychologists be cautious in making concrete claims about how and where image schemas might be mentally represented. It is even possible that image schemas are not specific properties of the mind but reflect experiential gestalts that *never* get encoded as explicit mental representations. A different possibility is that image schemas might be characterized as emergent properties of our ordinary conceptual systems and therefore are not explicitly represented in any specific part of the mind. Connectionist or neural network systems provide the necessary architecture to model image schemas as emergent properties of human cognition. We raise these ideas to suggest just some of the possibilities of how image schemas might or might not be mentally represented.

There are several ways that looking at experimental work in different areas of psychology might enhance research in both psychology and cognitive linguistics on image schemas and their transformations. First, cognitive linguists should look closer at experimental evidence on nonlinguistic experience to see how different aspects of perception and cognition systematically relate to linguistic structure and behavior. For example, our discussion of representational momentum in mental imagery tasks suggests that certain image schematic properties might be related to various linguistic expressions. Consider the following utterances:

*I was bowled over by that idea.*
*We have too much momentum to withdraw from the election race.*
*I got carried away by what I was doing.*
*We better quit arguing before it picks up too much momentum and we can't stop.*
*Once he gets rolling, you'll never be able to stop him talking.*

These utterances reflect how the image schema for MOMENTUM allows discussion of very abstract domains of cognition, such as political support, control, arguments, and talking in terms of physical objects moving with momentum. We may be able to predict important aspects of the inferences people draw when understanding these sentences given what is known about representational momentum from cognitive psychological research.

One of the findings from representational momentum research is that people behave as if an apparently moving object continues to move even after encountering an obstacle. Essentially, the moving object appears to carry the obstacle along with it rather than deflecting off it or stopping. When understanding the sentence *I was bowled over by that idea,* people should infer that the idea was important and that the speaker was convinced by the idea. This follows from one of the characteristics of moving objects – the bigger objects are, the more momentum they have when moving. Accordingly, a big object encountering an obstacle should result in that obstacle being carried along with the big object. Applying the conceptual metaphor IDEAS ARE OBJECTS, one should infer when reading or hearing *I was bowled over by that idea* that the person encountering an important (big) idea would be convinced (carried along) by that idea.

Another result from the research on representational momentum is that objects moving with momentum are perceived as being unable to stop immediately. Even if a force is applied to stop the object, it will continue along for some distance before coming to rest. One might infer from this situation that if reaching a particular destination is desired, then the more momentum an object has the better are the chances for the object to reach the destination. We can apply this knowledge, along with the conceptual metaphor ACCOMPLISHMENTS ARE MOVEMENTS, to the sentence *We have too much momentum to withdraw from the election race* to infer that the candidates in the election race have a good chance (much momentum) to win the election, and therefore shouldn't attempt to withdraw (stop).

A related finding from representational momentum research is that an object with unchecked momentum will move a long distance, perhaps even overshooting some desired destination. This situation informs the inferences made on the sentence *I got carried away by what I was doing.* Specifically, a person doing something without monitoring the time involved or the resources devoted to doing it (an object moving with unchecked momentum) might result in devoting too much time or resources to the task (overshoot the desired destination).

A different aspect of the representational momentum research concerns the apparent speed and acceleration of the moving object. This factor affects the perceived amount of momentum that an object will have. Applying this finding to the sentence *Once he gets rolling, you'll never get him to stop talking* leads to the inference that interrupting (stopping) the person early in the conversation (when speed is low) will be easier than interrupting him later (when speed is high). This result also applies to the sentence *You had better stop the argument now before it picks up too much momentum and we can't stop it.* The inference here might be that arguments start off fairly innocuously (with low speed) but as they progress, things may be said which are unretractible (high speed). For both sentences, we understand that the talking or argument should be stopped as early as possible.

These analyses illustrate how findings from cognitive psychology can be applied to make predictions about people's understanding of linguistic expressions. Cognitive linguists would do well to consider in more detail, following the cognitive commitment, how experimental data relates to the analysis of linguistic structure and behavior. On the other hand, psychologists should consider how many of their experimental findings reflect human embodied experience. Many aspects of language, perception, and cognition may be, at least partly, motivated by image schemas that arise from recurring bodily experiences and our perceptual interactions with the world. Even though many psychologists hypothesize that much of our knowledge is innate and organized as incapsulated modules, significant aspects of how we learn, perceive, think, and use language are intimately intertwined with our ordinary bodily experience. One of our goals in writing this article is to urge psychologists to seek greater connections between their work in perception and cognition and people's ordinary bodily experience.

One significant challenge for both psychologists and cognitive linguists is to find better ways of empirically testing the role of image schemas in perception, cognition, and language. The main argument we have presented is that various empirical data are consistent with the cognitive reality of image schemas and their transformation. Yet we must find ways of *falsifying* the theory of image schemas. It is not enough to show that there are data consistent with image schemas, we must also make specific experimental predictions about human behavior based on our theoretical understanding of image schemas and their transformations. If we cannot make such experimental prediction, then the theory of image schemas will not be potentially falsifiable and will not be recognized by psychologists as having any significant cognitive reality. The psycho-linguistic research on *stand* demonstrates that it is possible to examine the psychological reality of image schemas in a falsification framework. We urge both psychologists and cognitive linguists to consider ways of doing similar kinds of experimental research.

Perhaps the greatest contribution of the work described in this article is that it provides additional information on what is especially cognitive about cognitive linguistics (Gibbs 1996). The embodied nature of thought and language can be illustrated not only from analyses of linguistic structure and behavior, but by experimentally examining many of the ways we perceive, learn, and imagine. Experimental studies are especially useful for understanding the important details of unconscious mental processing that cannot be obtained through introspective analysis of our phenomenological and linguistic experience.

## References

Bahrick, Lorraine

1988 Intermodal learning in infancy: Learning on the basis of two kinds of invariant relational in audible and visible events. *Child Development* 59: 197–209.

Baillargeon, Renée

1987 Object permanence in 3.5 and 4.5 month-old infants. *Developmental Psychology* 23: 655–664.

1993 The object concept revisited: New direction in the investigation of infant's physical knowledge. In *Visual Perception and Cognition in Infancy*, C. Granud (ed.), 265–313. Hillsdale, NJ: Erlbaum.

Baillargeon, Renée and Julie DeVos

1991 Object permanence in young infants: Further evidence. *Child Development* 114: 1227–1241.

Bethell-Fox, Charles and Roger Shepard

1988 Mental rotation: Effects of stimulus complexity and familiarity. *Journal of Experimental Psychology: Human Perception and Performance* 14: 12–23.

Brooks, Lee

1968 Spatial and verbal components of the act of recall. *Canadian Journal of Psychology* 22: 349–368.

Brugman, Claudia

1984 The very idea: A case-study in polysemy and cross-lexical generalization. In *Papers from the Twentieth Regional Meeting of the Chicago Linguistics Society*: 21–38.

Brugman, Claudia and George Lakoff

1988 Cognitive topology and lexical networks. In *Lexical Ambiguity Resolution*, S. Small, G. Cotrell, and M. Tannenhaus (eds.), 477–508. Palo Alto, CA: Morgan Kaufman.

Cohen, Leslie and Lisa Dukes

1993 How infants perceive a simple causal event. *Developmental Psychology* 29: 421–433.

Cooper, Lynn and Peter Podgorny

1976 Mental transformation and visual comparison processes: Effects of complexity and similarity. *Journal of Experimental Psychology: Human Perception and Performance* 2: 503–514.

Cooper, Lynn and Roger Shepard

1982 *Mental images and their transformations*. Cambridge: MIT Press.

Chambers, Deborah and Daniel Reisberg

1992 What an image depicts depends on what an image means. *Cognitive Psychology* 24: 145–174.

Farah, Martha, Katherine Hammond, David Levine, and Ronald Calvanio

1988 Visual and spatial mental imagery: Dissociable systems of representation. *Cognitive Psychology* 20: 439–462.

Fillmore, Charles J.

1982 Frame semantics. In *Linguistics in the Morning Calm*, The Linguistic Society of Korea (ed.), 111–137. Seoul: Hanshin.

Finke, Ronald

1989 *Principles of Mental Imagery*. Cambridge: MIT Press.

Finke, Ronald and Jennifer Freyd

1985 Transformations of visual memory induced by implied motions of pattern elements. *Journal of Experimental Psychology: Learning, Memory, and Cognition* 11: 780–794.

Finke, Ronald, Jennifer Freyd, and Gary Shyi

1986 Implied velocity and acceleration induce transformations of visual memory. *Journal of Experimental Psychology: General* 115: 175–188.

Freeman, Norman E., Sharon E. Lloyd, and Chris G. Sinha

1980 Infant search tasks reveal early concepts of containment and canonical usage of objects. *Cognition* 8: 243–262.

Freyd, Jennifer and Ronald Finke

1984 Representational momentum. *Journal of Experimental Psychology: Learning, Memory, and Cognition* 10: 126–132.

1985 A velocity effect for representational momentum. *Bulletin of the Psychonomic Society* 23: 443–446.

Freyd, Jennifer, J. Michael Kelly, and Michael DeKay

1990 Representational momentum in memory for pitch. *Journal of Experimental Psychology: Learning, Memory, and Cognition* 16: 1107–1117.

Geeraerts, Dirk

1993 Vagueness's puzzles, polysemy's vagaries. *Cognitive Linguistics* 4(3): 223–272.

Gibbs, Raymond W.

1994 *The Poetics of Mind: Figurative Thought, Language, and Understanding.* New York: Cambridge University Press.

1996 What's cognitive about cognitive linguistics? In *Cognitive Linguistics in the Redwoods: The Expansion of a New Paradigm in Linguistics,* Eugene H. Casad (ed.), 27–53. Berlin: Mouton de Gruyter.

Gibbs, Raymond W., Dinara Beitel, Michael Harrington, and Paul Sanders
1994 Taking a stand on the meanings of *stand:* Bodily experience as motivation for polysemy. *Journal of Semantics* 11: 231–251.

Gibson, James
1979 *The Ecological Approach to Visual Perception.* Boston: Houghton Mifflin.

Hubbard, Timothy and Jamshed Bharucha
1988 Judged displacement in apparent vertical and horizontal motion. *Perception and Psychophysics* 44: 211–221.

Intos-Peterson, Margaret and Barbara Roskos-Ewoldsen
1989 Sensory-perceptual qualities of images. *Journal of Experimental Psychology: Learning, Memory, and Cognition* 15: 188–199.

Johansson, Gunnar
1973 Visual perception of biological motion and a model for its analysis. *Perception and Psychophysics* 14: 201–211.

Johnson, Mark
1987 *The Body in the Mind.* Chicago: University of Chicago Press.
1991 Knowing through the body. *Philosophical Psychology* 4: 3–18.
1993 *Moral Imagination.* Chicago: University of Chicago Press.

Karmiloff-Smith, Annette
1992 *Beyond Modularity: A Developmental Perspective on Cognitive Science.* Cambridge: MIT Press.

Kelly, Michael and Jennifer Freyd
1987 Explorations of representational momentum. *Cognitive Psychology* 19: 369–401.

Kennedy, John and John Vervaeke
1993 Metaphor and knowledge attained via the body. *Philosophical Psychology* 6: 407–412.

Kerr, Nancy
1983 The role of vision in "visual imagery" experiments: Evidence from the congenitally blind. *Journal of Experimental Psychology: General* 112: 265–277.

Kolstad, Valerie
1991 Understanding of containment in 5.5 month-old infants. Poster presented at the meeting of the Society for Research in Child Development, Seattle: Washington.

Koslowski, Linda and James Cutting
1977 Recognizing the sex of a walker from a dynamic point-light display. *Perception and Psychophysics* 21: 575–580.

Kotovsky, Laura and Renée Baillargeon
1994 Calibration-based reasoning about collision events in 11-month old infants. *Cognition* 51: 107–129.

Lakoff, George
1987 *Women, Fire, and Dangerous Things: What Categories Reveal about the Mind.* Chicago: University of Chicago Press.
1990 The invariance hypothesis: Is abstract reason based on image-schemas? *Cognitive Linguistics* 1(1): 39–74.

1993 The contemporary theory of metaphor. In *Metaphor and Thought*. Volume 2, A. Ortony (ed.), 202–251. New York: Cambridge University Press.

Lakoff, George and Mark Turner
1989 *More than Cool Reason: A Field Guide to Poetic Metaphor.* Chicago: University of Chicago Press.

Langacker, Ronald
1987 *Foundations of Cognitive Grammar.* Vol. 1: *Theoretical Prerequisites.* Stanford: Stanford University Press.
1991 *Concept, Image, and Symbol: The Cognitive Basis of Grammar.* Berlin/New York: Mouton de Gruyter.

Legerstee, M.
1994 Patterns of 4-month old infant responses to hidden silent and sounding people and objects. *Early Development and Parenting* 2: 71–81.

Leslie, Alan
1982 The perception of causality in infants. *Perception* 11: 173–186.
1988 The necessity of illusion: Perception and thought in infancy. In *Thought without Language,* Lawrence Weiskrantz (ed.), 185–210. Oxford: Clarendon,

Lindner, Susan
1983 A lexico-semantic analysis of verb-particle constructions with *up* and *out.* Bloomington: Indiana University Linguistics Club.
1981 Spatial references systems and the canonicality effect in infant search. *Journal of Experimental Child Psychology* 32: 1–10.

Mandler, Jean
1992 How to build a baby; II, Conceptual primitives. *Psychological Review* 99: 587–604.

Mandler, Jean, Patricia Bauer, and Laraine McDonough
1991 Separating the sheep from the goats: Differentiating global categories. *Cognitive Psychology* 23: 263–298.

Marks, Lawrence
1978 *The Unity of the Senses: Interrelations among the Modalities.* New York: Academic Press.
1982 Synesthetic perception and poetic metaphor. *Journal of Experimental Psychology: Human Perception and Performance* 8: 15–23.

Marks, Lawrence, Robin Hammel, and Marc Bornstein
1987 Perceiving similarity and comprehending metaphor. *Monographs of the Society for Research in Child Development* 52: 1–102.

Michaels, Claire and Claudia Carello
1981 *Direct Perception.* Englewood Cliffs, NJ: Prentice-Hall.

Norvig, Peter and George Lakoff
1987 Taking: A study in lexical network theory. In *Proceedings of the 13th Annual Meeting of the Berkeley Linguistics Society,* Jon Aske, Natashia Beery, Laura Michaelis, and Hana Filip (eds.), 195–206. Berkeley: Berkeley Linguistics Society.

Parsons, Lawrence
1988 Imagined spatial transformations of one's body. *Journal of Experimental Psychology: General* 116: 172–191.

1989 Imagined spatial transformations of one's hands and feet. *Cognitive Psychology* 19: 178–241.

Phillips, Richard, Stephen Wagner, Christine Fell, and Mark Lynch
1990 Do infants recognize emotion in facial expressions? Categorical and metaphorical evidence. *Infant Behavior and Development* 13: 71–84.

Piaget, Jean
1952 *The Origins of Intelligence in Childhood.* New York: International Universities Press.
1954 *The Construction of Reality in the Child.* New York: Basic Books.

Poizner, Howard, Ed Klima, Ursula Bellugi, and Roger Livingston
1986 Motion analysis of grammatical processes in a visual-gestural language. In *Event Cognition: An Ecological Perspective*, V. McCabe and G. Balzano (eds.), 231–253. Hillsdale, NJ: Erlbaum.

Rumelhart, David
1980 Schemata: The building blocks of cognition. In *Theoretical Issues in Reading Comprehension*, Rand Spiro, Bertram Bruce, and William Brewer (eds.), 35–58. Hillsdale, NJ: Erlbaum.

Segal, Sydney and Vincent Fusella
1970 Influences of imaged pictures and sounds on detection of visual and auditory signals. *Journal of Experimental Psychology* 83: 458–464.

Shepard, Roger and Jacqueline Metzler
1971 Mental rotation of three-dimensional objects. *Science* 171: 701–703.

Sitskoorn, Margriet M., and Ad M. Smitsman
1991 Infants' visual perception of relative size in and containment and support events. Paper presented at the Biennial Meeting of the International Society for the Study of Behaviorial Development, Minneapolis.

Spelke, Elizabeth
1976 Infants' intermodal perception of events. *Cognitive Psychology* 8: 626–636.
1988 When perceiving ends and thinking begins: The apprehension of objects in infancy. In *Perceptual Development in Infancy*, Albert Yonas (ed.), 197–234. Hillsdale, NJ: Erlbaum.

Spelke, Elizabeth, Karen Breinlinger, Janet Macomber, and Kristen Jacobson
1993 Origins of knowledge. *Psychological Review* 99: 605–632.

Stewart, Judith
1984 Object motion and the perception of animacy. Paper presented at the meeting of the Psychonomics Society, San Antonio, Texas.

Sweetser, Eve
1986 Polysemy vs. abstraction: Mutually exclusive or complementary? In *Proceedings of the 12th Annual Meeting of the Berkeley Linguistics Society*, V. Nikiforidou, M. VarClay, M. Niepokuk, and D. Feder (eds.), 528–538. Berkeley: Berkeley Linguistic Society.
1990 *From Etymology to Pragmatics: The Mind-body Metaphor m Semantic Structure and Semantic Change.* New York: Cambridge University Press.

Talmy, Leonard
1988 Force dynamics in language and cognition. *Cognitive Science* 12: 49–100.

Turner, Mark
1991 *Reading Minds: English in the Age of Cognitive Science.* Princeton: Princeton University Press.
Vandeloise, Claude
1993 *Spatial Prepositions: A Case Study from French.* Chicago: University of Chicago Press.
Wagner, Susan, Ellen Winner, Diane Cicchetti, and Howard Gardner
1981 Metaphorical mappings in human infants. *Child Development* 52: 728–731.
Zimler, Jerome and Jan Keenan
1983 Imagery in the congenitally blind: How visual are visual images? *Journal of Experimental Psychology: Learning, Memory, and Cognition* 9: 269–282.

# Chapter 8
# Metonymy

## The role of domains in the interpretation of metaphors and metonymies*

*William Croft*

### 1. Introduction

Consider the following sentence:

(1) *Denmark shot down the Maastricht treaty,*

This sentence is generally taken to involve both metonymy and metaphor: the subject proper noun *Denmark is* a metonymy for 'the voters of Denmark', while the predicate *shot down is* a metaphor for 'cause to fail'. After the fact this is all quite straightforward. But how does the listener know that this sentence is not about a military act, or a particular piece of territory in Europe? The question this paper will address, though not fully answer, is: how are such "figurative" meanings constructed in a particular utterance? What leads speakers to not employ the basic or literal meanings of those words, or, if they do, to shift to the appropriate meaning?

This is a problem of semantic composition, that is, of the relation of the meaning of the whole to the meaning of the parts. Unlike the typical problems of semantic composition discussed in the formal semantic literature, where the meaning of the whole is at least in part determined by the meanings of the parts, the meaning of the parts here seems to be determined in part by the meaning of the whole. I will argue here that the "meaning of the whole" that affects the meanings of the parts is what I call the *conceptual unity of domain:* all of the elements in a syntactic unit must be interpreted in a single domain. In example 1, for instance, the domain is political activity.

Moreover, a large part (though not all) of what is going on in metaphorical and metonymic interpretation is adjustment of the domains of the component elements, and hence their meanings, to satisfy the conceptual unity of domain. I use the word "adjustment" here because the adjustment of domains is related to the conceptualization phenomena that Langacker calls *focal adjustments* (Langacker 1987: Chapter 3). In Section 2, I will describe a theory of word meaning

Originally published in 1993 in *Cognitive Linguistics* 4(4): 335–370.

and the role of domains in word meaning, taken largely from Langacker's model of cognitive grammar (Langacker 1987, 1991). In Section 3, I will describe the role of domains in metaphor and metonymy, and argue that metonymy as traditionally conceived usually involves a more general phenomenon of polysemy that critically involves domains. In Section 4, I discuss the relationship between metaphor and metonymy and semantic composition in cognitive grammar, arguing that metaphor applies to dependent predications and metonymy to autonomous predications (Langacker 1987: 8.3). Finally, in Section 5, I argue that the scope of the conceptual unity of domain is a dependent predication and the autonomous predications that it is dependent on, and that a listener's cognitive processing in "solving" the conceptual unity of domain requires reference to context.

## 2. Word meaning and domains in cognitive grammar

One of the central tenets of cognitive semantics is that the meaning of words is encyclopedic: everything you know about the concept is part of its meaning (Haiman 1980; Langacker 1987: 4.2.1). From this it follows that there is no essential difference between (linguistic) semantic representation and (general) knowledge representation; the study of linguistic semantics is the study of commonsense human experience. Thus, that aspect of "pragmatics" which involves the employment of "world knowledge" or "commonsense knowledge", and even contextual knowledge (since the speech act context is part of our world knowledge, albeit a very specific piece of knowledge), becomes part of semantics.

Not surprisingly, taking seriously the encyclopedic view of semantics rather drastically alters our view of most of the outstanding problems of semantics (without necessarily solving them, however; but at least they look much more natural). Although in theory all knowledge about an entity is accessible – that is, the whole knowledge network is accessible – some knowledge is more central (Langacker 1987: 4.2.2), and the pattern of centrality and peripherality is a major part of what distinguishes the meaning of one word from that of another. Langacker identifies four criteria for centrality: the extent to which knowledge of the concept applies to all entities categorized by the concept (*generic*), the extent to which knowledge of the concept applies to only those entities (*characteristic*; these two criteria together define cue validity, see Rosch 1978); the extent to which the knowledge is general knowledge in the speech community (*conventional*), and the degree to which the knowledge applies to the object itself as opposed to external entities (*intrinsic*).[1]

Understanding the meaning of a word in the encyclopedic view means entering the knowledge network at a certain point – more precisely, activating the network by activating it at a certain point or points:

> The entity designated by a symbolic unit can therefore be thought of as a *point of access* to a network. The semantic value of a symbolic unit is given by the open-ended set of relations ... in which this *access node* participates. Each of these relations is a cognitive routine, and because they share at least one component the activation of one routine facilitates (but does not always necessitate) the activation of another. (Langacker 1987: 163)

Thus, semantic space is the whole network of an individual's – and a community's – knowledge. This knowledge as a whole is not unstructured. Encyclopedic knowledge appears to be organized into experiential *domains* (Langacker 1987: 4.1; Lakoff 1987, among many others). The notion of a domain is central to the understanding of metaphor and metonymy. In particular, it is critical to identify when one is dealing with a single domain or different domains. Despite its centrality, the notion of domain has not been delineated in detail. It is related to the notion of a semantic field, as in the field theories of Trier and others. This work has come under considerable criticism, not least because the notion of semantic field is left undefined: "What is lacking so far, as most field-theorists would probably admit, is a more explicit formulation of the criteria which define a lexical field than has yet been provided" (Lyons 1977: 267).

The most carefully worked-out description of domains is found in Langacker (1987), some of which is based on Lakoff and Johnson (1980); the description that follows makes explicit some assumptions that are implicit in those works. But to understand the notion of a domain, we must begin by describing a central aspect of a concept symbolized by a word, its division into a profile and base. (What I am calling a "concept" is a semantic structure symbolized by a word; Langacker calls this a *predication,* and I will use these terms interchangeably. While there are concepts that do not – yet – have words that symbolize them, the notion of a concept is sufficiently difficult to identify independently of language that we will restrict ourselves to those that are already symbolized and therefore have a definite existence consecrated by the conventions of a language.)[2]

We will begin with Langacker's example of an arc of a circle (1987: 183–184). A concept, such as that of an arc, presupposes other concepts, in this case that of a circle. An arc is defined only relative to a circle; otherwise it would be merely a curved line segment. What we intuitively think of as the arc itself is the *profile;* the notion of a circle which it presupposes is its *base*. This idea is not totally new; one of its better-known manifestations is as a "frame" in artificial intelligence and linguistics. The concept of [ARC] is not just the profile but also the base; the concept is definable only relative to what it presupposes. (Searle 1979 also argues for the necessary inclusion of background assumptions in the definition of a word.) A circle itself is defined relative to two-dimensional space. The concept [CIRCLE] profiles that shape configuration, and has (two-dimensional) space as its base. (To be precise, it has shape as its base, and the concept of shape – not "a shape", but "shape" – is profiled in two-dimensional space. I return to this issue below.) In other words, a concept can function either as a profile or as a base for another concept profile.

The profile-base relation is not the same as the central-peripheral relation discussed above with respect to the encyclopedic definition of word meaning. The base is that aspect of knowledge which is necessarily presupposed in conceptualizing the profile. Peripheral knowledge is knowledge associated with a concept that is not as generic, characteristic, conventional, and intrinsic as more central knowledge. Peripheral knowledge is not presupposed knowledge, but additional, less central asserted knowledge. Of course, peripheral knowledge as well as central knowledge is organized in a profile-base fashion. This will be illustrated later.

Profile and base are conceptually interdependent. On the one hand, profiled concepts cannot be understood except against the background knowledge provided by the base. On the other hand, the base exists as a cognitively unified and delimited "chunk" of knowledge only by virtue of the concept or concepts defined with respect to it.

A particular base is almost always the base for several concept profiles. For example, a circle is the base not only for [ARC], but also [DIAMETER], [RADIUS], [CHORD], etc. This is what makes the base a domain, in the intuitive sense: several different concept profiles have it as a base. We can now define a domain as *a semantic structure that functions as the base for at least one concept profile* (typically, many profiles). As Taylor (1989: 84) notes, "In principle, any conceptualization or knowledge configuration, no matter how simple or complex, can serve as the cognitive domain for the characterization of meanings." We can say that the domain of a circle includes the concepts of an arc, a diameter, a radius, chord, etc. A circle itself is in the domain of two-dimensional space (actually, shape). This demonstrates that a particular semantic structure can be a concept in a domain (when it is profiled), or a domain itself (when it is functioning as the base to other concept profiles). We return to this point below.

Space itself does not appear to be profiled in a domain that serves as its base. Instead, it emerges directly from experience (cf. Lakoff and Johnson 1980: Chapter 12). Langacker calls space a *basic domain.* Basic domains are concepts that do not appear to be definable relative to other, more basic concepts, at least in the commonsense or folk model of experience. There are a substantial number of such basic domains; in fact, a good idea of the basic domains there are can be found by examining the higher divisions of a good thesaurus.

Langacker calls a nonbasic domain an *abstract domain.* The notion of a circle, functioning as a base, is an example of an abstract domain. An abstract domain itself is a concept that presupposes another domain. The other domain need not be a basic one. I noted above that shape is more precisely the base for [CIRCLE];

the concept of [SHAPE] is in turn profiled in two-dimensional space. (The other major concept profiled in space is [LOCATION].) One can have an arbitrarily deep nesting of abstract domains before reaching a basic domain. However, the base is usually taken to be just the domain immediately presupposed by the profiled concept. We will call this domain the *base domain* (or simply the base; this is also what Langacker calls the *scope of predication;* recall that a predication is a concept). Langacker (1987: 493) notes that the scope of predication/base "may sometimes constitute only a limited portion of relevant domains" (the involvement of multiple domains in the definition of a concept will be discussed below).

The relation between an abstract domain and the basic domain it presupposes is not a taxonomic relation (or, as Langacker calls such relations, a schematic one). It is a relationship of concept to background assumption or presupposition. This distinction is sometimes obscured by the English language. The word *shape* stands for the domain as a mass noun, but as a count noun (*a shape*) it is a more general or schematic concept subsuming [CIRCLE], [SQUARE], [TRIANGLE], etc. A more general or schematic concept is not the domain for the particular concept; in fact, it is itself profiled in the same domain as its particular concept. As will be seen below, it is not always easy to distinguish a taxonomic relation from an abstract-basic domain relation.

Langacker argues that some domains involve more than one *dimension* (1987: 150–151). An obvious case is space, which involves three dimensions (some concepts, such as [CIRCLE], need only two dimensions for their definition; others need only one). Many physical qualities that are grounded in the experience of sensory perception, such as temperature and pitch, are one-dimensional. Others, such as color, can be divided into hue, brightness and saturation. Generally, dimensions of a domain are all simultaneously presupposed by concepts profiled in that domain. This is the critical point: a concept may presuppose several different dimensions at once.

In fact, a concept may presuppose several different domains. For example, a human being must be defined relative to the domains of physical objects, living things, and volitional agents (and several other domains, e.g. emotion). The combination of domains simultaneously presupposed by a concept such as [HUMAN BEING] is called a *domain matrix*. Langacker (1987: 152) makes the important point that there is in principle only a difference of degree between dimensions of a domain and domains in a matrix. In practice, we are more likely to call a semantic structure a domain if there are a substantial number of concepts profiled relative to that structure. If there are few, if any, concepts profiled relative to that structure alone, but instead there are concepts profiled relative to that structure and another one, then those structures are likely to be called two dimensions of a single domain. The term "domain" implies a degree of cognitive independence not found in a dimension.

The domain structure presupposed by a concept can be extremely complex. We can begin by considering the domain of physical objects, commonly invoked as a basic domain. The physical object domain is in fact not a basic domain, but a domain matrix. It consists of the domains of matter (an object is made of matter), shape (since objects have a shape; even substances have a shape, although it is not fixed), and location (embodying the principle that two objects cannot occupy the same location). Matter is a basic domain but, as we noted above, shape and location are abstract domains based on space, which is a basic domain.

Physical objects are themselves very general. Let us now consider how one would define what seems to be a kind of physical object, the letter T. It is directly defined as a letter of the alphabet; its base (domain) is hence the alphabet. The alphabet is itself an abstract domain presupposing the notion of a writing system – it is not just an instance of a writing system, since the latter involves not just a set of symbols such as an alphabet but also the means of putting them together, including the order on a page, spaces for words, etc. The domain of writing systems in turn presupposes the activity of writing. The activity of writing must be defined in terms of human communication, which presupposes the notion of meaning – perhaps a basic domain, since the symbolic relation appears not to be reducible to some other relation – and of the visual sensations, since writing is communication via usually perceived inscriptions, rather than auditorily or through gestures. And since writing is an activity, the domains of time and force or causation (both basic domains; force is a generalization of causation, see Talmy 1988) are also involved in the domain matrix of writing, since the letter T is the product of an activity. Since it is a human activity, it presupposes the involvement of human beings. Human beings are living things with mental abilities, such as volition, intention and cognition (themselves dimensions of the mental domain or, better, domains in the matrix of the domain of the mind). Living things in turn are physical objects endowed with life. A diagram exhibiting all of the basic-abstract domain relations presupposed in defining the concept of the letter T is shown in Figure 1 (the basic domains are given in small capitals). From this, it can be seen that it is incorrect to describe the concept of the letter T simply as belonging to the domain of writing, as a typical informal theory of domains would most likely have it. The vast majority of concepts belong to abstract domains which are themselves profiled in complex domain matrices, often also abstract, and so ultimately presuppose a large array of basic domains, which I will call a *domain structure*.

It is not easy to distinguish profile-base relations from taxonomic ones (that is, type vs. instance). For example, is writing an instance of human communication, or is writing an instance of an activity that can only be understood in terms of the goals of human communication? I believe the latter is a more accurate description, and have described it as such. Likewise, since writing is an instance of human activity, human activity does not appear as a domain, but the various domains that it presupposes – time, change, force, volition – do appear, because anything presupposed by a human activity will be presupposed by any instance of it (cf. the discussion of the base of a circle and a shape above).

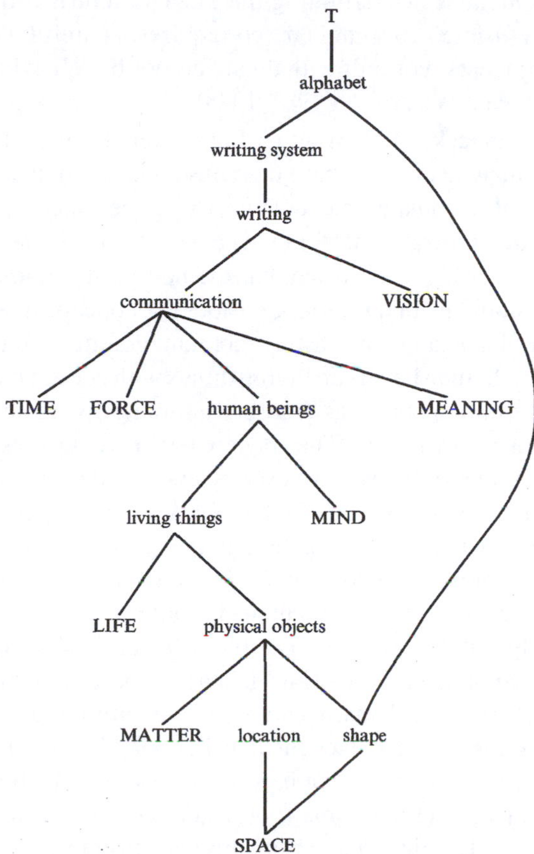


*Figure 1.* Domain structure underlying the concept of the letter T

It is also difficult to determine direct vs. indirect reference to a domain. Recall that Langacker argues that the definition of an arc does not directly presuppose two-dimensional space, but rather it presupposes a circle which in turn presupposes two-dimensional space. Thus, an arc is not directly a two-dimensional object per se, but only such by virtue of being a part of a circle. Likewise, the letter T is not directly a shape, but only such by virtue of being a letter of the alphabet. But in fact, is the letter T a shape by virtue of being a letter of the alphabet, or by virtue of being the physical product of the activity of writing? I believe it is best described as the former, since the set of symbols is a set of shapes.

Another similar problem in this example is the location of the domain of mental ability. The activity of writing is a volitional, intentional activity, so it presupposes the domain of mental ability. But mental ability is presupposed by writing because writing presupposes human involvement, and the human involvement involves volition and intention.[3] Determining the exact structure of the array of domains upon which a profiled concept is based requires a careful working out of the definitions of concepts, not unlike that carried out by Wierzbicka in her semantic analyses (see, e.g., Wierzbicka 1987, 1988).

It is not clear from Langacker 1987 whether Langacker considers the domain matrix of a concept to include only the base domains against which a concept is directly profiled or the entire domain structure underlying the concept profile. The example of the letter T demonstrates that for many concepts, the domain structure can be quite deep. There is some evidence that the notion of a domain matrix must include all of the domains in question. Consider the concepts [PERSON] and [BODY]. [PERSON] is profiled against the abstract domain of human beings. As the diagram above indicates, human beings are living things with certain mental abilities (recall the classic definition of man as a rational animal). Living things in turn are physical objects endowed with life. The concept [BODY] represents a person's physical reality (alive or dead). Its base is nevertheless still the abstract domain of human beings (or, more precisely, animals), but it profiles the physical object domain in the domain structure underlying human beings. Contrast [BODY] with [SOUL], which profiles a nonphysical domain of a human being; or with [CORPSE], which profiles the physical object domain but also profiles a particular region in the life domain, namely [DEAD]. Another example is [KNEEL]. Only things with knees, or something resembling knees, can kneel; hence its base domain is (higher) animals – more precisely the base domain matrix includes animals as well as time and force, since kneeling is a process (see the matrix under "communication" in Figure 1). However, it primarily profiles a particular posture, which is a spatial configuration of the object, and the domain of spatial configuration (shape) is quite deeply nested in the domain structure underlying [KNEEL].

This is still not the end of the matter of describing the domain structure underlying a concept. Recall that meaning is encyclopedic. We have focused our attention only on the most central fact about the letter T, that it is a letter of the alphabet. Langacker calls the alphabet domain the *primary domain* of the concept, since it is the domain in which the most central facts about the concept are defined. However, there are other things we know about the letter T that are also quite central. It is the twentieth letter of the alphabet, which brings in the domain of a scale (ordering; a basic domain) and measurement, which in turn presupposes numbers, which in turn presupposes the notion of a unit of an entity. The letter T also corresponds to a linguistic sound, specifically a consonant, which brings in the domain of sound sensation (another basic domain), vocal articulation (a very abstract domain), and (again) language or communication. And there is much more specific knowledge that is quite peripheral to its meaning, for example that it is the initial of my wife's last name, which presupposes a whole host of abstract domains based on other abstract domains and ultimately a wide range of basic domains.

Whether these other domains form part of the matrix of the concept of the letter T depends on whether the concept of the letter T profiles such things as the fact that it is the twentieth letter of the alphabet, the initial of my wife's last name, etc. Langacker does not precisely answer this question. In the passage quoted above (1987: 163), Langacker states that activation of a concept (presumably, its profile) "facilitates (but does not always necessitate)" the activation of more peripheral knowledge about that concept. He later says that some routines (that is, pieces of knowledge) are sufficiently central to be activated almost every time (1987: 163). This implies that the central-peripheral relation is defined in terms of necessitation vs. facilitation of activation; facilitation can perhaps be thought of as a priming effect. Other factors, such as contextual priming, presumably can convert "facilitation" of activation of peripheral knowledge to actual activation of that knowledge in particular speech events where that peripheral knowledge is relevant.

The activation of the base domain of a profiled concept, on the other hand, is presumably necessary, since the definition of a base domain is the semantic structure presupposed by the profiled concept. This implies that the whole structure given in the diagram is going to be activated. Langacker does not explicitly state this, but he does suggest that the profile-base relation is a matter of attention, in a generalized model of attention which includes multiple loci of attention, which in turn could be modelled in terms of intensity of activation (1987: 188). One could extrapolate that the less direct the involvement of the domain in the definition of the concept, the less intense its activation will be when the concept is activated.

All of the above cognitive semantic structures – encyclopedic definitions, central vs. peripheral knowledge, profile and base, basic and abstract domains – are necessary for the definition of a single meaning of a word (Langacker 1987: 164, fn. 12). There is no apparatus given above for describing multiple meanings of a word. In a later chapter (1987: Chapter 10), Langacker argues for a "schematic network" (cf. Lakoff's 1987 notion of a radial category) for describing different uses of a word which combines both classical and prototype notions. All uses of a single word are related through various types of extensions from an original meaning ("original" in the ontogenetic sense); in addition, a more schematic meaning subsuming many or all of the specific uses can arise and fit into the network. Metaphor and metonymy are two types of extensions of word meaning; they represent different uses of a particular word. We now turn to the role of domains in licensing these semantic extensions.

## 3. Domains, metaphor and metonymy

The term "metaphor" has been used for many different kinds of figurative language, depending in part on the theory of metaphor subscribed to by the analyst. I will examine the types of metaphors that are central to Lakoff and Johnson's (1980) theory of metaphor. Lakoff and Johnson's theory can be illustrated by the contrast in the following two sentences:[4]

(2) *She's in the living room.*
(3) *She's in a good mood.*

Lakoff and Johnson employ a cognitive semantic model and analyze this type of metaphor as a conceptualization of one domain in terms of the structure of another independent domain, that is, a mapping across domains. The two domains, the source domain and the target domain, do not form a domain matrix for the concepts involved. In this example, the use of *in* in (3) for the relation between a person and her emotional state does not mean that the speaker has constructed a profile for metaphorical *in* simultaneously encoding a spatial relation and an emotional relation. Only the emotional domain is profiled in (3); however, the emotional domain is conceptualized as having the same or similar structure to space by the use of the predicate *in*.

As we saw in Section 2, if one accepts Lakoff and Johnson's theory of metaphor, as I do, one must be more specific as to what domain or domains are involved in a metaphor. I argue that the two domains being compared are base domains, that is, the bases of the profiled predication. In this case, the two domains are, as indicated in the informal description in the preceding paragraph, location and emotion, the base domains of the two uses of *in* in (2) and (3). (Actually, *in* involves containment, so more than location is involved in the source domain.)

In order to get an accurate description of a metaphor, the description of the metaphor has to be formulated in such a way that the two base domains are equated. For example, Lakoff and Johnson (1980: 73) describe the following example as an instance of a metaphor they describe as AN OBJECT COMES OUT OF A SUBSTANCE:

(4) *I made a statue out of clay.*

The metaphorical expression is *out of.* Its base domain in the metaphorical usage is creation (that is the meaning of *make* selected in this sentence); the literal meaning has motion as its base domain, so the metaphor can be phrased as CREATION IS MOTION. Of course, both of these abstract domains, creation and motion, have multiple domains in their base matrices; for example, motion involves time, change and location.

Likewise, one must be careful to define the metaphor in terms of the base domain of the words in question. This is not always easy. Consider the metaphor described by Lakoff and Johnson (1980: 49) as LOVE IS A PATIENT; the following examples are theirs:

(5) *This is a* sick *relationship.*
(6) *They have a* strong, healthy *marriage.*
(7) *The marriage is* dead – *it can't be* revived.
(8) *Their marriage is* on the mend.
(9) *We're getting* back on our feet.
(10) *Their relationship is* in really good shape.
(11) *They've got a* listless *marriage.*
(12) *Their marriage is* on its last legs.
(13) *It's a* tired *affair.*

First, the metaphor is probably best described as LOVE IS A BODILY STATE. The words *sick*, *strong*, *healthy*, *listless* and *tired* all have a bodily state as the base. The phrases *back on our feet*, *in really good shape*, and *on its last legs* are themselves metaphors whose target domain is also bodily states. However, the words *dead* and *revived* are arguably profiled in the domain of life, which is one of the domains underlying the domain of living things which in turn underlies the domain of bodily states (see the domains underlying "human beings" in Figure 1).[5] They are part of another metaphor, LOVE IS LIFE, which can generate metaphorical expressions using words profiled in the domain of living things:

(14) *Their letters kept their love* alive.
(15) *Her selfishness* killed *the relationship.*
(16) *His effort to understand her* breathed new life into *their marriage.*

Of course, LOVE IS A BODILY STATE and LOVE IS LIFE are metaphors coherent with each other, since bodily states presuppose the notion of life. However, the metaphors cannot be lumped together under something like "love is a living thing", since there are many other aspects of living things that are not metaphors for love, specifically those associated with the body (bodily activities, such as spitting, sweating; or the body itself, e.g. its parts; etc.).

The role of domains in metaphor is quite central to the definition of that concept in Lakoff and Johnson's model. However, to be more precise about the phenomenon that I am examining, I will use the term *domain mapping* to describe metaphor (though since in the Lakoff-Johnson model, the two terms are virtually synonymous, I will continue to use the term "metaphor"). The role of domains in metonymy, on the other hand, is not direct, although it is more pervasive than has generally been noted, once a careful examination of the domain structure underlying a concept is undertaken.

The traditional definition of metonymy is a shift of a word-meaning from the entity it stands for to a "contiguous" entity (Ullmann 1957: 232; cf. Lakoff and Johnson 1980: 35 and Taylor 1989: 122). Entities are contiguous because they are associated in experience (Lakoff and Johnson 1980: 39–40). Lakoff and Turner argue that metonymy, unlike metaphor, "involves only one conceptual domain. A metonymic mapping occurs within a single domain, not across domains" (Lakoff and Turner 1989: 103). However, as we have seen above, a concept is profiled against an often very complex domain structure or matrix, even if there is only one abstract domain as the base. In fact, in the next sentence, Lakoff and Turner switch to describing metonymy as a mapping within a schema; the term "schema" is more amenable to describing a complex domain structure (cf. Taylor 1989: 87). And Lakoff (1987: 288) describes a metonymic mapping as occurring "within a single conceptual domain, which is structured by an ICM [idealized cognitive model]" – which Langacker equates with an abstract domain. Thus, the generalization should be rephrased as "a metonymic mapping occurs within a single domain matrix, not across domains (or domain matrices)". Of course, the domain matrix possesses a unity that is created by experience – the real point of Lakoff's position.[6]

This is indeed the critical difference between metaphor and metonymy. Metaphor is a mapping between two domains that are not part of the same matrix; if you say *She's feeling down,* there is no spatial orientation domain in the matrix of the metaphorical concept of emotion being expressed; HAPPY IS UP involves two different concepts with their own domain structures underlying them. In metonymy, on the other hand, the mapping occurs only within a domain matrix. However, it is possible for metonymy, as well as for other lexical ambiguities, to occur across domains within a domain matrix. In this way, domains do play a significant role in the interpretation of metonymy.[7] I will now illustrate some examples of this role.

Consider the following typical examples of metonymy:

(17) *Proust spent most of his time in bed.*
(18) *Proust is tough to read.*
(19) Time *magazine is pretty vapid.*
(20) Time *took over* Sunset *magazine, and it's gone downhill ever since.*

Sentence (17) and (19) are considered "literal", (18) and (20) "metonymic". However, in the encyclopedic view of semantics, the works of Proust and the company that produces *Time* magazines are part of the concepts of [PROUST] and [TIME-MAGAZINE] respectively. However, they are less central than the fact that Proust was a person and *Time* is a magazine, not least because they are quite extrinsic to the central concepts. The domain matrix of an encyclopedic characterization of [PROUST] will include the domain of creative activity. Since Proust's claim to fame is that he is a writer, and the work produced is a salient element in the domain of creative activity, the metonymic shift is quite natural (and, in fact, is quite productive). Nevertheless, the metonymic shift also involves a shift of domains within the domain matrix (schema, frame, script) for *Proust.* A similar argument applies to *Time magazine:* a secondary domain for magazines is that of the process of publication, in which the publishing company is a salient entity. The metonymy that shifts reference from the magazine to the company also shifts domains from the magazine as an object with semantic content to the domain of publication. We will call this conceptual effect *domain highlighting* (cf. Cruse 1986: 53), since the metonymy makes primary a domain that is secondary in the literal meaning.

Domain highlighting appears to be a necessary though not sufficient condition for metonymy, which also involves shift of reference, at least in the most typical occurrences thereof. Thus, the relation between domain highlighting and metonymy differs from that between domain mapping and metaphor, since domain mapping does appear to be definitional for metaphor. While domain highlighting appears to be a consequence of many if not all instances of metonymy, it also occurs in other types of lexical ambiguity that have not always been considered metonymy. Consider the following sentences:

(21) *This book is heavy.*
(22) *This book is a history of Iraq.*

The concept [BOOK] is profiled in (at least) two primary domains, the domain of physical objects and the domain of meaning or semantic content. In (21), the physical object domain of *book* is highlighted by virtue of the requirements of the predicate *heavy.* In (22), on the other hand, the semantic content domain of *book* is highlighted, again due to the requirements of the predicate *be a history of Iraq*. (There is another reading of (21) which does refer to the semantic content domain, which I will discuss below.)

It is not clear that there are in fact two different entities being referred to in (21) and (22). From a conceptual point of view, however, the concept symbolized by *this book* is different in (21) and (22). It is not an example of metonymy in the usual sense of that term because the elements profiled in each domain are highly intrinsic; no reference is made to external entities. For both of these reasons, the word *book* is not always treated as metonymic, or even ambiguous, in these sentences.

Another oft-cited example illustrates the distinctness of the domains of space and physical material in characterizing physical objects (see, for example, Cruse 1986: 65; Taylor 1989: 124):

(23) *I broke the window.*
(24) *She came in through the bathroom window.*

These two uses of *window* are usually analyzed as an ambiguity; in the encyclopedic semantic view, they highlight the physical object and shape or topological domains of the concept [WINDOW] respectively. The interpretation of [WINDOW] as an opening in the shape domain is somewhat extrinsic because it makes crucial reference to what is around it – contrast the use of *window* to describe a physical object in a hardware store showroom – though it appears to be less extrinsic to the concept [WINDOW] than the publishing company and writings in examples (18) and (20) above. The existence of examples such as *window* in (23) and (24) suggests that there is a continuum between the clear cases of metonymy and the highlighting of highly intrinsic facets of a concept as in (21) and (22). The existence of this continuum suggests that domain highlighting plays a role in lexical ambiguities other than metonymy (assuming that one does not want to extend the term "metonymy" to the book and window examples).

It may not be the case that domain highlighting within the domain matrix of a word is involved in all cases of metonymy. In some cases, the shift of prominence of domains in the matrix is quite subtle, and sensitive to the semantics of the associated words. For example, consider the following examples of synecdoche, a phenomenon usually subsumed under metonymy (Ullmann 1957: 232; Lakoff and Johnson 1980: 36; examples from Lakoff and Johnson 1980: 36–37):

(25) *We need a couple of strong bodies for our team.*
(26) *There are a lot of good heads in the university.*
(27) *We need some new faces around here.*

Since a part has the whole as its base domain, it appears that no domain selection is involved in these examples. But in fact in an encyclopedic characterization of *body, head,* and *face* the domain matrix of each part is different, since each body part is associated with different human qualities and behaviors. The selection of *bodies* in (25) is sanctioned by the need to highlight the physical strength/ability domain underlying the domain of human beings; *heads* in (26) by the need to highlight the domain of human intelligence; while *faces* in (27) is a cross-linguistically widespread synecdoche for persons as a whole, the presence or absence thereof being what is the topic of (27) (cf. Lakoff and Johnson 1980: 36–37). The synecdoche is in fact highlighting precisely the domain that is relevant to the predication. Compare (25)–(27) to (28)–(30), in which the choice of parts-for-whole is different:

(28) ??*We need a couple of strong faces for our team.*
(29) ??*There are a lot of good bodies in the university.*
(30) ??*We need some new heads around here.*

While a sentence such as (29) is interpretable, it does not mean the same thing as (26).

Another example of metonymy which involves a subtle shift in domain prominence is

(31) *I filled up the car.*

In (31), it is understood that it is the gas tank that is filled, not the main body of the car. This interpretation is possible only because the phrase [fill up VEHICLE], without the substance indicated, is conventionally interpreted as "fill up with fuel"; only by explicitly indicating the substance can it be interpreted as "the interior of the car", and only by explicitly indicating the gas tank can it be interpreted as "fill the gas tank" with some substance other than fuel:

(32) *I filled up the car with gasoline and set it on fire.* [gas tank or interior of car]
(33) *I filled up the car with sand.* [interior of car only]
(34) *I filled up the gas tank with sand.*

The two meanings of *fill up* are profiled in two different domains: the more general meaning in the domain matrix of substances and containers (shape), and the more specific meaning in the more abstract domain of fuelling, which is based on the substances/containers domain as well as a domain of fuel-requiring mechanical objects. The interpretation of *car* as "gas tank of car" involves the highlighting of the domain of fuelling in the domain matrix of [CAR] as well as a shift to the relevant part of the car; in fact, it is the highlighting of that domain by the predicate *fill up* that sanctions the shift of reference (at least when the conventional expression was first coined).

The analysis of metonymy in an encyclopedic theory of meaning, whether or not a secondary domain is highlighted in the process, casts a different light on a problem in semantic representation raised by Nunberg (1979). Nunberg presents an analysis of metonymy arguing from a non-encyclopedic view of semantics. Nunberg argues that there should be one "basic" denotation of a polysemous term, e.g. for *Proust*, *Time magazine,* and *window.* Metonymic uses are to be derived by a set of pragmatic functions that shift the meaning to the appropriate referent. Nunberg argues that the basic meaning is ultimately undecidable because any word (or at least, any noun) can be used to refer to the type of entity, a token of the type, and also the name for the entity, and a token of the name (the latter two are expressed orthographically with quotation marks, but are not phonologically distinct):

(35) *A cat is a mammal.*
(36) *His cat is called Metathesis.*
(37) *"Cat" has three letters.*
(38) *"Cat" here has a VOT of 40 ms.* [referring to a spectrograph of an occurrence of the word]

In the encyclopedic approach, there is no "basic" meaning; all metonymic meanings are present in the encyclopedic semantic representation. This is also true for the meanings which Nunberg finds ultimately undecidable. Any symbolized concept will have as part of its encyclopedic definition the phonological entity that symbolizes it, and instantiations of the concept (more precisely, concepts of instantiations of the concept type).

This last question leads us to another problem of metonymy: where to locate it in the interaction of words and phrases in semantic composition, or, to put it more generally, conceptual combination. The standard view is that metonymy represents an ambiguity (or pragmatic extension) of the noun, so that in (17)–(31) and (35)–(38), it is a question of the meaning of the noun phrase being shifted from its "basic" or "normal" meaning. Langacker (1984, 1987: 7.3.4) argues for the opposite point of view: the ambiguity is in the predicate (in traditional terms), not the noun phrase (argument). Consider the following examples:

(39) *We all heard the [trumpet].* (Langacker 1987: 271, ex. (24a))
(40) *This is a striped [apple].*

The traditional analysis is that the bracketed nouns symbolize "sound of the trumpet" and "surface of the apple" respectively, and *trumpet* and *apple* are ambiguous. Langacker argues that we should treat the noun phrases as really symbolizing the entities they appear to be symbolizing, namely the trumpet and the apple, and that the reference to the sound/surface is a characteristic of the predicate, so that *hear* can profile "hear the sound of [noisemaking object]" and *striped* can profile "striped surface of [three-dimensional opaque object]". Langacker takes this position for (39) and (40) in order to avoid any syntactic derivational or transformational relation that would "delete" the *sound of [the trumpet] and surface of [the apple].* Although Langacker does not discuss metonymy by name, (39) and (40) are closely related to prototypical instances of metonymy, and an active zone analysis for metonymy is in the spirit of the cognitive grammar view that there is a direct symbolic relation between word and meaning.

Langacker's argument in favor of this position notes the idiosyncrasy and

conventionality of the ability of particular predicates to allow "metonymic" noun phrase arguments. For example, *hear* can also take an NP that symbolizes the sound itself:

(41) *We all heard the sound of the trumpet.*

Langacker describes the "metonymized" referent as the *active zone* of the entity symbolized by the argument NP. Thus, the sound produced by the trumpet, and the surface of the apple, are the active zones of the profiled entity, but do not match the profile of the entity itself.

While Langacker's alternative analysis seems reasonable for a number of examples such as those with perception verbs, there are other examples in which the traditional analysis seems more appropriate, and this suggests that a different approach to the question should be taken. For example, predicates describing the actions of national governments virtually always allow the country itself to be the agent of the action:

(42) *Germany pushed for greater quality control in beer production.*
(43) *The United States banned tuna from countries using drift nets.*
(44) *Myanmar executed twenty Muslim activists.*

Also, many of the same predicates allow the seat of government or the head of state to function as the agent; although some significant semantic differences are found so that interchangeability is not possible in all contexts, it is possible to use all three when it is actually the government (rather than the head of state alone) that makes the decision:

(45) *France/Paris/Mitterrand will hold a referendum on the Maastricht treaty.*

It would seem odd to consider every action verb attributable to an act of government to be ambiguous between "act of [a government]", "act of the government located in and ruling [a country]", "act of the government seated in [a capital city]", and "act of the government led by [a head of state]".[8]

In other cases, the metonymic extension is an idiosyncrasy of the noun, not of the predicate:

(46) *I ate roast chicken for dinner.*
(47) **I ate roast cow for dinner.*

One cannot argue that there is an ambiguity in *eat* so that it can mean "eat the flesh of [an animal]", since (47) is unacceptable.[9] The word *chicken* must clearly

be taken to stand for "the meat thereof". Nevertheless, there is a clear metonymic relation between chicken flesh and chicken "on the hoof" (to borrow a collocation from Nunberg), which is productive with less commonly eaten animals:

(48) *I ate grilled rattlesnake for dinner.*
(49) *I ate roast tapir for dinner.*
(50) *I ate pan-fried armadillo for dinner.*

If it were not for the existence of examples such as (47), one might have argued that the metonymy resides in the predicate rather than in the noun.

To some extent, the issue of whether the metonymy can be localized in the predicate or in the noun is a red herring: the metonymy occurs by virtue of the collocation of the predicate and the noun, that is, the semantic composition of the two. The encyclopedic view of meaning supports this approach. One of Langacker's motivations for his analysis is to treat the surface object of *hear, the trumpet*, as the "real" object of the verb, without some syntactic transformation that claims that the underlying object of *hear* is the noun phrase "the sound of the trumpet".[10] But in the encyclopedic view of the meaning of *trumpet*, the sound it produces is a quite salient (albeit somewhat extrinsic) aspect of the profiled concept. Conversely, part of the encyclopedic characterization of *hear* is that objects produce sounds that people hear. Thus, one can have one's semantic cake and eat it too: (part of) the profile of *trumpet* is the object of *hear,* and (part of) the profile of what is heard is the object producing the sound.[11] The same is true of the act-of-government examples: a salient part of the profile of a country, a capital city, and a head of state in the encyclopedic definition of those concepts is the government that rules the country, is seated in the capital city, and is headed by the head of state, respectively. Of course, as I describe in more detail in the following section, it is the semantics of the predicate that highlights the relevant aspect of the encyclopedic profile of the concept symbolized by the noun; the metonymic interpretation arises only in the combination of noun and predicate.

## 4. Differences between domain mapping and domain highlighting

In the preceding section, Lakoff and Johnson's analysis of metaphor as domain mapping was adopted and it was argued that the source and target domains are the base domains of the "literal" and "figurative" concepts symbolized by the word. It was also argued that an essential part of metonymy is the highlighting of an aspect of a concept's profile in a domain somewhere in the entire domain matrix or domain structure underlying the profiled concept. Those analyses imply that a central aspect of figurative language is the manipulation of experiential domains

in understanding and communication. In the case of metonymy, the manipulation of domains plays a significant role, but metonymy cannot be reduced to domain highlighting, and domain highlighting is found in other types of lexical ambiguity for which the term "metonymy" may not be appropriate. I will henceforth use the terms "domain mapping" and "domain highlighting" to describe the semantic phenomena that are under examination in this paper. I will now explore under what circumstances one would expect to find domain mapping and domain highlighting in linguistic expressions.

Consider the following examples from Chapter 6 of Lakoff and Johnson (1980), on one type of metaphor, and the subsequent examples from Chapter 8, on metonymy; the figure of speech is italicized as in the original:

(51) He's *in* love.
(52) We're *out* of trouble now.
(53) He's *coming out of* the coma.
(54) I'm *slowly getting into* shape.
(55) He *entered* a state of euphoria.
(56) He *fell into* a depression. (Lakoff and Johnson 1980: 32)
(57) He likes to read the *Marquis de Sade.*
(58) He's in *dance.*
(59) *Acrylic* has taken over the art world.
(60) The *Times* hasn't arrived at the press conference yet.
(61) Mrs. Grundy frowns on *blue jeans.*
(62) *New windshield wipers* will satisfy him. (Lakoff and Johnson 1980: 45)

A glance at these examples and many others suggests that metaphor is associated with predicates (not just verbs, but also prepositions and adjectives), and metonymy with nouns (hence the focus of Nunberg's paper on nominal metonymy). However, this initial hypothesis is simply incorrect. Examples (63)–(66) below involve domain mapping with nouns, and examples (67)–(70) involve domain highlighting with verbs:

(63) *mouth of a person, an animal, a bottle, a cave, a river* (Cruse 1986: 72)
(64) *handle of a door, suitcase, umbrella, sword, spoon* (Cruse 1986: 74)
(65) *tree, phrase structure tree, family tree, clothes tree*
(66) *cup* [for drinking], *acorn cup, resin cup, cup* [for capstan], *cup* [golf hole], *bra cup* (Dirven 1985)
(67) *She swore foully.*
(68) *She swore loudly.*
(69) *The vase fell quickly.*
(70) *The vase fell far.*

In examples (63)–(66), the different uses of *mouth*, *handle*, *tree* and *cup* are undoubtedly profiled in different domains, as the explicit or implicit nominal or genitive modifiers suggest. There is a resemblance in shape and function in all of the examples, resemblances which appear to be of the image-schematic kind characteristic of metaphors. These are generally agreed to be nominal metaphors, or at least a figurative phenomenon closely akin to metaphor which involves domain mapping in essentially the same way.

In examples (67)–(70), a verb which has more than one primary domain associated with it has one or the other domain highlighted by virtue of the adverb associated with it. In (67), the content of the imprecation is highlighted, while in (68) it is the sound volume that is highlighted. In (69), the time and change domains in the matrix underlying motion are highlighted, while in (70) it is the location/distance domain.

Although domain mapping and domain highlighting can occur with a word of any lexical category, there is a generalization underlying the distribution of these two cognitive semantic phenomena. In (63)–(66), domain mapping is induced by the nominal/genitive dependents on the noun that is figuratively interpreted. In (67)–(70), domain highlighting is induced by the adverbial modifier to the verbal predicate. In order to formulate the distribution of domain mapping and domain highlighting, we must examine the cognitive grammar description of syntactic/semantic composition.

One of the criteria for the centrality of knowledge to a particular concept is its intrinsicness: the extent to which it refers to (or rather, does not refer to) entities external to that concept. Some concepts, however, inherently involve extrinsic entities; these are called *relational concepts*. The external entities that relational concepts "include" correspond roughly to the arguments of a predicate in formal semantics; examples include [EAT], which inherently makes reference to an eater, an item eaten, and to a lesser extent to the implement used by the eater in eating.[12] A relational concept contains only a schematic representation of the extrinsic entities associated with it, in our example the eater, the thing eaten, etc. *Things* (a technical term in cognitive grammar) are nonrelational concepts, however (Langacker 1987: 6.1.1). Relational concepts are divided into *atemporal relations* and *processes,* which correspond roughly to those relational concepts that are construed as static (i.e., construed atemporally) and those that are construed as unfolding over time (for the purposes of this paper it is not necessary to describe this distinction in detail). Things are the semantic structures symbolized by nouns, while relations are symbolized by verbs, adjectives, adverbs, and prepositions.

Syntactic/semantic composition, that is, symbolic composition in cognitive grammar, involves two aspects: what the semantic type of the resulting complex expression is, and how the component expressions are fitted together. The phrase *the fat book* and the sentence *The book is fat* symbolize two different semantic sorts: the phrase symbolizes a thing, while the sentence symbolizes a "state of affairs" (in cognitive grammar terms, in *imperfective process).* The two constructions differ (among other things) in their *profile determinant,* that is, the component element that determines the semantic type of the whole. In the phrase, *book* is the profile determinant, since it is also a thing (we are ignoring the semantic contribution of *the*). In the sentence, *book* is not the profile determinant; if we ignore the contribution of *be*, one could say that *(being) fat* is the profile determinant.[13] As can be seen by the different status of *book* and *fat* in the phrase and in the sentence, profile determinacy is a function of the construction into which words enter.

This leaves the matter of how words are combined semantically. Relationality may appear to underlie semantic composition in cognitive grammar, but this is not precisely correct. In the canonical case of a main verb and the subject and object dependent on it, as in *Mara sings,* this appears to be the case: the subject is nonrelational, and the predicate is relational; the subject referent "fills the slot" for the singer in the relational semantic structure for *sing*. But what about *Mara sings beautifully*? Here *beautiful(ly)* is a relational structure with a "slot" for a process, and *sings* "fills that slot". The fact that *sings* is inherently relational is irrelevant to the combination of *sings* and *beautifully.* Thus, in one and the same sentence, *sings* is both an entity with "slots" to be filled, and a "filler" for another entity's "slot".

In one of Langacker's most insightful analyses of the relation between syntax and semantics, he argues that it is not relationality that governs symbolic combinations, but an independent phenomenon which he calls autonomy and dependence. In most grammatical combinations, one predication can be identified as the autonomous one and the other as the dependent one using the following definition: "One structure, D, is dependent on the other, A, to the extent that A constitutes an elaboration of a salient substructure within D" (Langacker 1987: 300). Let us examine our example *Mara sings beautifully* with respect to this definition. *Mara* (that is, the semantic structure symbolized by *Mara*) does indeed elaborate a salient substructure of *sings*, namely the schematic singer in its semantic representation that makes it a relational predication (concept). Having compared *Mara* to *sings,* we must reverse this process and compare *sings* to *Mara:* does *sings* elaborate a salient substructure of *Mara*? The answer is "no", but it is not a categorical answer; after all, the semantic representation of *Mara* is encyclopedic, and part of the encyclopedic knowledge about Mara is that the speaker knows that Mara sings. But this is a very nonsalient substructure of *Mara*. Hence, we can say that *sings* is dependent and *Mara* is autonomous, relative to each other.

Now let us compare *sings* and *beautifully. Sings* elaborates a salient substructure of *beautifully,* namely the schematic process that makes it a relational predication. But *beautifully* does not elaborate a salient substructure of *sings,* even though *sings* is relational. At best, *sings* has a not very salient substructure representing the manner in which the process is executed, and *beautifully* elaborates that; but that substructure is not nearly as salient in the semantic representation for *beautifully* as the substructure of *beautifully* that is elaborated by *sings.* So on balance *beautifully* is the dependent predication and *sings* is autonomous. Note that, by this analysis, *sings* is dependent relative to *Mara*, but autonomous relative to *beautifully.* Autonomy and dependence are relative notions, and that is exactly what is needed to describe this aspect of semantic composition.

We may now characterize the conditions under which domain mapping and domain highlighting occurs: domain mapping occurs with dependent predications, and domain highlighting occurs with autonomous predications. As the preceding discussion of *sings beautifully* demonstrates, "dependent" does not necessarily correspond with "relational" (verbs, adjectives, etc.), and "autonomous" does not necessarily correspond with "nonrelational" (nouns). Thus, there is no connection between metaphor/domain mapping and relational predications, or between metonymy (more precisely, domain highlighting) and nonrelational predications. This will account for the cases in (63)–(70). But let us begin with the "typical" cases, (51)–(62).

In (51)–(56), the metaphorical expressions are dependent on the subject and object (more precisely, the object of the preposition in all but [55]); hence they are the ones subject to domain mapping. But in particular it is the autonomous expressions on which they are dependent that induce the domain mapping: *love*, *trouble*, *the coma*, *shape*, *euphoria* and *depression* are all profiled as states (physical or emotional) of a human being, and those expressions require the metaphorical interpretation of the container-based directional prepositions and verbs.
In contrast, in (57)–(62), the expressions that manifest domain highlighting are all autonomous relative to the main verbs which are dependent on them. And, conversely, the domain highlighting is induced by the dependent expressions in relation to which the italicized expressions are autonomous. For example, in (57) *read* requires that the object be understood as a text; in (60) *arrive* requires that the subject be interpreted as a person (or at least as an animal, but no animal is salient in the domain matrix of *Times*);[14] and in 62, *satisfy* requires that the subject be some completed event.[15] These examples all illustrate the principle to be discussed in Section 5: that in the grammatical combination of an autonomous and a dependent predication, the dependent predication can induce domain highlighting in the autonomous one, and the autonomous predication can induce domain mapping in the dependent one. Now let us turn to the other cases.

Examples (67)–(70) are straightforward: it is clear that the verb is autonomous relative to the adverb, and it is the adverb that induces the domain highlighting. Again, it is important to note that the word in question be autonomous relative to the word that is inducing the domain highlighting.

Examples (63)–(66) are more difficult, because an argument must be made that the nouns *mouth*, *handle*, *tree*, and *cup* are dependent on their nominal/genitive modifiers, and can be so construed even when no such modifiers are present. This latter question will be discussed in Section 5. *Mouth* and *handle* are what are called "relational nouns", since they represent parts of wholes; it is those wholes which make up the genitive modifiers. Langacker argues (1987: 185) that relational nouns such as part nouns do not profile the thing (in this case, the whole) that they are related to (what he calls a *landmark*); otherwise they would no longer be nouns/things. Instead, the landmark is a very salient substructure in the base. Of course, the structures in the base are part of the semantic structure of the concept (see Section 2 above). On the other hand, the part elaborated by the head noun is not as salient a substructure of the whole symbolized by the genitive as the whole is for the part. Thus, in the expression *the mouth of the river* (or *the river's mouth,* or *the river mouth*), *mouth* is on balance more dependent on *river,* and *river* is more autonomous relative to *mouth.* And it is *river* that induces the domain mapping for *mouth.*

The same argument can be applied to *handle* and other relational nouns; can it also be applied to *tree*, *cup*, and other nonrelational nouns that have metaphorical interpretations? In the cases illustrated, the answer is "yes". In some of the examples, e.g. *bra cup*, the word is functioning as a relational noun (part/whole). In the examples *phrase-structure tree* and *family tree*, the modifying nouns essentially name the base domain of the head noun's profile. As such, they are in a relation very much like a part-whole relation: the base domain taken as a whole is a quite salient substructure of the profiled concept, while the profiled concept is not a very salient substructure of the base domain (on average, no more so than any other concept in the domain). In *clothes tree*, *clothes* elaborates a much more salient substructure of *tree* – the tree is made expressly for the purpose of hanging clothes – than *tree* does in *clothes.* An example like *acorn cup* is a closer call: the cup is "for" the acorn and so *acorn* elaborates a salient substructure for *cup*; but the acorn is often conceived of sans cup, and so *cup* elaborates a less salient substructure of *acorn.* While there appears to be no general principle by means of which we can say that the metaphorically interpreted noun is the dependent member, partly because the semantics of noun-noun compounding seems to be so open-ended (Downing 1977), it seems to be a not unreasonable hypothesis given the examples just discussed, and should be investigated further.

## 5. The unity of domain revisited

In the last section, I argued that domain mapping can occur to a dependent predication when the autonomous predication it is dependent on induces it; and domain highlighting can occur to an autonomous predication when the predication dependent on it induces it. The reason for this is that the grammatical combination of a dependent predication and the autonomous predication(s) it is dependent on must be interpreted in a single domain (or domain matrix). Consider again a simple example of metaphor and metonymy:

(71) *She's in a good mood.* (=(3))
(72) *Proust is tough to read.* (=(18))

In (71), the relational predication *(be) in* is interpreted metaphorically in the target domain of emotion. This renders the sentence semantically coherent because the subject of *be* and the complement of *in* are in the domain of emotion. In (72), Proust is interpreted metonymically because the complex predicate *be tough to read* requires an entity in the domain of semantic content and the metonymic interpretation provides just such an entity in that domain.

In both of these cases, and in all such cases in general, there is an attempt to "match" the domain of the dependent predication and of the autonomous predications that elaborate it. Sentences such as (71) and (72) that do not match domains in the "literal" interpretations of the elements are not rejected as semantically incoherent. Instead, the listener attempts to interpret one or more elements figuratively, using metaphor or metonymy (or other cognitive processes that we have not discussed here). In other words, there is a background assumption on the part of the listener that sentences are semantically coherent. These background assumptions I call the "conceptual unities". The conceptual unity discussed in this paper is the unity of domain.

This account leaves two questions as yet unanswered: the scope of the semantic unit that requires conceptual unity, and the source of the required conceptual unity. We now take up these questions in turn.

It should be clear from our description of conceptual adjustments of domains that the scope of the unity of domain is the dependent predication and the autonomous predications it is dependent on, but no more. That means that if a word enters into grammatical relations with more than one other word – for example, *sings* compared to *Mara* and *sings* compared to *beautifully* – it is possible that it will be interpreted in different domains for each of the grammatical relations it contracts.

The first example of this is illustrated by another problem that Nunberg (1979) found with this analysis of a basic and derived meanings for nouns that allow metonymy. In some examples, the basic and a derived meaning must be simultaneously attributed to a single occurrence of the word:

(73) *Cædmon, who was the first Anglo-Saxon poet, fills only a couple of pages in this book of poetry.*
(Nunberg 1979: 167, ex. 29)

The single occurrence of the word *Cædmon* is used to refer both to the person and to his works. This problem disappears in the encyclopedic view of metonymy. Both domains are present in the domain matrix of the complex. For the word *Cædmon*, more than one part of its domain matrix can be highlighted simultaneously. However, the triggers are found in different grammatical relations: *Cædmon* with respect to the non-restrictive relative clause *who was the first Anglo-Saxon poet*, and with respect to the main clause *fills only a couple of pages in this book of poetry. Cædmon* is the autonomous predication in both cases, but relative to different dependent predications.[16]

The same is true of the following example, in which the main predicate highlights the physical object domain of the object NP, but its PP modifier highlights the semantic content domain:

(74) *I cut out this article on the environment.*

Example (20), repeated below as (75), provides an example of the same phenomenon involving anaphora, with *Sunset magazine* referring to the company and anaphoric *it* referring to the magazine's content:

(75) Time *took over* Sunset *magazine, and it's been downhill ever since.*
(=(20))

In fact, different modifiers (adjuncts) in a single phrase can highlight different domains of the head:

(76) *a thin, dog-eared monograph on hallucinogenic mushrooms of the Pacific Northwest*

In (76), the two adjectival modifiers highlight the physical object domain of *monograph* and the prepositional phrase postmodifier highlights the semantic content domain. Here also, the predication *monograph* enters into two different grammatical relations with two different predications which are dependent on it.

If a predication is dependent on more than one autonomous predication, then the whole combination must obey the conceptual unity of domain:

(77) *I won't buy that idea.*

Not only must *buy* be mapped into the domain of mental activity, but the subject *I* also has the domain of the mind highlighted (the person as a being with mental capacities, not a physical object, for instance). *Idea*, of course, has mental activity as its (primary) base domain.

We now turn to the second question, whether or not one can predict what the domain of the combination of a dependent predication and the autonomous predication(s) it is dependent on will be. It turns out that this is not decidable, because, not surprisingly, unexpressed contextual knowledge can enter into the semantic determination of the domain in which an utterance is interpreted.

Either the autonomous or dependent predication in a grammatical unit can have its domain adjusted, via domain mapping or domain highlighting. In the simplest cases, such as (71) and (72), either the autonomous or the dependent predication is interpreted "literally" – that is, as the most intrinsic entity profiled in the concept's primary domain(s) – and the other element of the sentence has its domain adjusted. As (71) and (72) demonstrate, there is no a priori directionality, requiring either the autonomous or the dependent predication to be interpreted literally. In fact, both may be interpreted figuratively, as in (1), repeated here as (78), or (79):

(78) *Denmark shot down the Maastricht treaty.* (=(1))
(79) *Sales rose to $5m last year.*

In (78), the domain of political force is highlighted in the subject NP, and there is a domain mapping in the main verb from weaponry to political action. In (79), the value (price) domain rather than the object, service, etc. domain is highlighted in the subject NP, while there is a domain mapping in the verb from vertical motion to increase in quantity, specifically monetary quantity.

One could identify the object NPs *Maastricht treaty* and *$5m* in (78) and (79) as the source of the figurative interpretations of the subject and the verb, since they "literally" refer to the political activity and monetary value domains, respectively. However, it is not always possible to attribute the figurative interpretations of the parts of a construction to some "literally" interpreted element in the clause. In some examples, only contextual properties can provide the "source" of the figurative interpretations. Consider again the following example:

(80) *This book is heavy.* (=(21))

The profile of the concept symbolized by the word *book* inhabits two domains, physical objects and meaning (semantic content). However, the predicate *heavy* can be interpreted "literally" in the physical object domain, or it can be shifted metaphorically to the meaning domain. Thus, there are interpretations of both subject and predicate in both the physical object and meaning domains, and in fact this sentence is ambiguous out of context for precisely that reason. Another example of this is the following sentence:

(81) *The newspaper went under.*

One interpretation of this sentence has both subject and predicate interpreted figuratively. Metonymy and metaphor interact to produce the interpretation. "The company producing the newspaper went bankrupt". However, there is also another interpretation, "The physical paper went under the surface of the water"; cf. *The boat went under.* Since one of the domains in the matrix of [NEWSPAPER] is that of physical objects, which undergo motion, which is the "literal" domain of [GO UNDER], this other interpretation is possible as well.

These examples demonstrate that the correct literal or figurative interpretations of the elements of sentences is not decidable from the elements of the sentence by themselves. The domain in which a predication is interpreted can be determined by context. This is possible because the autonomy-dependence relation is a relationship between semantic structures, which need not be overtly expressed in an utterance. A semantic structure symbolized by a word in a sentence can contract an autonomy-dependence relation with a semantic structure left unexpressed in the context. This is why the nominal metaphors in (63)–(66) can be interpreted metaphorically without the nominal modifiers upon which they are dependent being present in the utterance. For example, *cup* [for drinking, for a golf hole, for a capstan] is interpreted in whatever domain is prominent in the context of the speech event. In fact, an interpretation in any domain is possible, short of semantic incompatibility (and conventional limitations on the figurative interpretations of particular words and phrases). This is not surprising, considering that this is generally the case in semantic interpretation.

## 6. Conclusion

In this paper, I have argued that particular grammatical constructions, those that combine a dependent grammatical element with the autonomous elements it is dependent on, must be interpreted in a single domain (the unity of domain). This is a necessary part of the interpretation of such constructions, which include almost all of the common grammatical constructions, for example predicate-argument, head-modifier, noun-genitive, verb-adverb. In order to achieve the semantic coherence specified by the unity of domain, there must often occur an adjustment of the domains of the individual words in the construction. Domain adjustment is also a major factor, if not the major factor, in a significant portion of what are usually called "metaphors" and "metonymies". In order to focus on this aspect of the interpretation of words, I have more precisely characterized the conceptual semantic phenomena that I have described as "domain mapping" and "domain highlighting" respectively. In the case of metonymy, it is particularly appropriate to choose a different term to describe the domain adjustment involved.

The conceptual unity of domain is one of at least three conceptual unities. The second is the unity of mental space, including "physical" space and time. A mental space is a conceptual construct that is used to describe the ontological status of entities and situations – e.g. a belief, a desire, a counterfactual hypothesis, or even reality at a particular location in time or space (Fauconnier 1985). Fauconnier (1985) describes in detail the types of conceptual mappings that are required in interpreting sentences in which predicates and arguments originate in different mental spaces, namely the variety of counterpart relations. Consider for example, example (82), which builds a belief mental space M for Margaret's belief:

(82) *Margaret believes that her sister bought a car.*

In (82), assume that Margaret has a sister in "reality" (R; that is, mutually believed space). The complement of *believes* must be interpreted in Mary's belief space M, so the phrase *her sister* must designate individuals in M, which the listener normally takes to be the counterparts of Margaret and her sister in M. Likewise, *a car* must be interpreted as designating an individual in M, whether or not there is a counterpart in R. The crucial point for us here is that all of the entities in the complement are interpreted in M, and if the "normal" interpretation of a linguistic expression is to an entity in a mental space other than M, e.g. Margaret in (82), it must be interpreted as referring to a counterpart in M to be coherent.

The third is the unity of selection (cf. the minor propositional act of selection in Croft 1990), in which predicate and argument must match in individuation, quantification or number (Talmy's 1985 "plexity") and genericness (generic vs. specific, or type vs. token). These construals have been called granularity coercions (Hobbs 1985; Croft in prep.). The necessity of the unity of selection is illustrated in the following examples:

(83) *She is resembling her mother more and more every year.* [stative predicate construed as an inchoative process]

(84) *"Fresh walnut meats"* [substance construed as a set of individuated objects]

(85) *Cats have whiskers.* [bare plural construed as reference to a kind with generic predicate]

(86) *Cats were lounging on the patio.* [bare plural construed as reference to a set of cats with specific predicate]

The latter unity has been the topic of a considerable amount of work in formal semantics, but no satisfactory unified account has been presented as yet (though see Croft in prep.).

There is some reason to believe that these three conceptual unities are the most important ones in imposing semantic coherence on an utterance. Langacker (1991: 33) argues that both nominal and verbal structure involves three levels of organization: the level of a concept type, manifested in a bare noun or bare verb stem; the level of a grounded instance of the type, manifested in a full nominal with determiner and a full finite clause; and an intermediate level of an instance of the type, corresponding to the grammatical unit at which quantification occurs. The conceptual unity of domain is at the level of the type: a concept type is defined against its base domain. The unity of mental space is at the level of a grounded instance of a type: grounding involves situating the instance with respect to speaker/hearer knowledge (Langacker 1987: 126–127), which is modelled by mental spaces (1991: 97). Finally, the unity of selection is at the level of the instance, since it is at that level that individuation and quantification occur. The conceptual unities represent the reqirement that dependent verbal predications must be semantically coherent with respect to the autonomous nominal predications that they are dependent on.[17]

In comprehending an utterance, the listener assumes the unities of domain, mental space, and selection, and attempts to interpret the sentence as conforming to those unities, employing metaphor, metonymy, granularity, counterpart relations, and other *focal adjustments* (Langacker 1987: 3.3) where necessary. The listener is under a strong Gricean convention that the speaker is being semantically coherent, particularly at the lower levels of semantic composition, such as predicate-argument and head-modifier constructions. For that reason, the listener will generally try as much as possible to adjust the meanings of the parts to yield a coherent interpretation of the whole. The conceptual unities of domain, mental space, and selection are a significant part of what it means for an utterance to be coherent. This adjustment is how the interpretation of the parts is influenced by the meaning of the whole, as described in the introduction. If such focal adjustments do not yield sensible interpretations, or are conventionally prohibited due to the constructions and inflections involved, the listener may assume the sentence is incoherent. A better understanding of the specific types of coherence (the unities) will cast much more light on the "irregularities" of the process of semantic composition. Nevertheless, the process can never be made fully algorithmic. As we observed for the unity of domain, elements of an utterance interact with context, that is, conceptual structures already activated to various levels at the time of the speech event. This will be true for the other unities as well. But this fact is not surprising, and in fact should be of some comfort for those of us who believe that the expressiveness and flexibility of language is essentially open-ended.

## Notes

* An earlier version of this paper was presented at the second International Cognitive Linguistics conference in Santa Cruz, California, in 1991. I am grateful to members of that audience, particularly George Lakoff and Eve Sweetser, for their comments, and to my semantics students, especially Tim Clausner, for many discussions of the ideas contained herein; and to Dirk Geeraerts, René Dirven and an anonymous reviewer for extensive and detailed comments that greatly improved the content of this paper. None of these people bear any responsibility for the content as presented, of course.

1. Centrality is clearly closely related to prototypicality, in the sense of prototypical properties rather than prototypical instances of a category, as the reference to Rosch's analysis of prototypes suggests. However, centrality pertains to the organization of knowledge in the mind, not the categorization of individuals which both gave rise to that knowledge structure and employs that structure.
2. Grammatical morphemes are also predications, of course; however, I will not be discussing them in this paper.
3. There are actions that involve human beings but do not require mental ability, for example seeing a person. But seeing something does not require that something to be a person, only activities inherently referring to mental abilities do.

   It is also possible for other entities to write, e.g. for an animal to be taught to produce writing. This is a deviation from the idealized cognitive model (Lakoff 1987) of writing. An abstract domain is a conceptual structure, and Lakoff convincingly argues in his book (and elsewhere) that conceptual structures involve idealization. Langacker observes that an abstract schema is essentially an idealized cognitive model (1987: 150, fn. 4), which is in turn analogous to the notion of a frame. At any rate, the domain structure represents the presuppositions of the ideal case.
4. Lakoff and Johnson describe a large class of phenomena as metaphors, some of which are probably better accounted for by other cognitive processes. For example, they describe a metaphor MORE OF FORM IS MORE OF CONTENT (1980: 127), illustrated by the intensification represented in *He ran and ran and ran;* this is more likely to be an example of iconic motivation (Haiman 1983, 1985).
5. One could argue that "alive" and "dead" are bodily states also, but they are clearly of a different kind from "listless" or "healthy".
6. Rene Dirven suggests that this characterization will not distinguish between *Tea was a large meal for the Wicksteeds* (metonymy) and *Drinking Kriek-Lambiek is not just drinking, it is eating and drinking together* (metaphor). The first case is clearly metonymy, since the whole meal is profiled in a domain matrix that includes tea. However, drinking Kriek-Lambiek is profiled in a domain consisting of drinking and not eating;

   this is its source domain, and the target domain is the matrix of both drinking and eating.
7. In some cases, domain mapping occurs between two domains, one of which happens to be in the matrix of the other. This appears to be what is going on with what Goossens (1990) calls "metaphor from metonymy", illustrated below:

(i) *"Oh dear", she giggled, "I'd quite forgotten".* (Goossens 1990: 328)
(ii) *"Get out of here!" he thundered.*

In these cases the usual interpretation is that the act of speaking takes on metaphorical properties of giggling and thundering. As Goossens observes, the metaphor applies to the message (as intended by the speaker) as well as the medium. I would analyze this as a domain mapping, but the source domain (sound) is one of the domains in the matrix of the target (speaking) – hence the appearance of being "metonymy". Goossens' examples of "metonymy within metaphor", on the other hand, appear to be exactly that:

(iii) *She caught the minister's ear and persuaded him to accept her plan.* (Goossens 1990: 334)

*Ear is* a metonymy for "attention", and that metonymy is itself embedded in a metaphorical use of *catch.*

8. The last interpretation, with the head of state, often is ambiguous, but that is because the predicates describing acts of governments can also describe acts of individuals, so that *Bush lobbied against the biodiversity treaty* can mean the US government, but can also mean (and is more likely to mean) Bush the individual.
9. The unacceptability is due to the historical idiosyncrasy that English speakers appropriated Norman French words to symbolize "the meat thereof" for cows, pigs and sheep *(beef, pork, mutton).* However, this does not make the synchronic situation any less idiosyncratic.
10. This is quite clear in Langacker (1984), in which he uses the same analysis to argue against a "Tough-movement" analysis as in *Hondas are easy to fix.* In the Tough-movement examples, easiness is being attributed to some inherent property of the surface subject, e.g. the make of automobile, and that property is described as "easy to fix".
11. This is true of any sound produced by any sound-producing object, not just the intended sound of objects like trumpets whose purpose is to produce sound. The collocation of a noun symbolizing an object with *hear* will result in the highlighting of any salient sound associated with the object: *I hear the boats on the canal* can refer to any sound produced by the boats – the horn, their splashing, gliding through the water, the people talking on them, etc.
12. In this respect the notion of a relational concept is richer than that of a predicate: less centrally involved extrinsic entities are part of the concept. In fact, one can add manner and other more peripherally involved entities to the entities inherently involved in the act of eating.
13. Cognitive grammar accommodates the fact that some expressions may have no profile determinant, or even more than one profile determinant (Langacker 1987: 291–292).
14. There is another interpretation of *arrive,* as in *The Times arrived at my doorstep,* in which case the physical-object interpretation is possible. In fact, both interpretations are possible in both contexts (see examples 80–81 below), but the adjuncts favor one reading over the other.
15. The other examples involve not just domain highlighting of the autonomous predica-

tions but also domain mapping (metaphor) in the dependent predications; this will be discussed in Section 5.

16. If one reverses the two clauses, the sentence is less acceptable (thanks again to René Dirven for pointing this out to me):

    (iv) ?*Cædmon, who fills only a couple of pages in this anthology, was the first Anglo-Saxon poet.*

    This is due to the fact that although both metonymic interpretations can be accessed from a single occurrence, one meaning is more established than the other (Cruse 1986: 68–71). Nevertheless, an analysis of metonymy must still account for the fact that it is possible for the same linguistic expression to simultaneously highlight two aspects of the concept symbolized by that expression.
17. The notion of conceptual unity is very similar to the notion of "isotopie" (Greimas 1966; Rastier 1987). However, I am using "conceptual unity" to refer only to the three levels of organization of a clause or phrase, whereas isotopie is used for a much wider range of phenomena of semantic coherence.

## References

Croft, William
1990 A conceptual framework for grammatical categories (or, a taxonomy of propositional acts). *Journal of Semantics* 7: 245–279.
in prep. Aspect, countability and the unity of selection.
Cruse, D. Alan
1986 *Lexical Semantics.* Cambridge: Cambridge University Press.
Dirven, René
1985 Metaphor as a means for extending the lexicon. In *The Ubiquity of Metaphor: Metaphor in Language and Thought,* Paprotté, W. and R. Dirven, (eds.), 85–119. Amsterdam/Philadelphia: John Benjamins.
Downing, Pamela
1977 On the creation and use of English compound nouns. *Language* 53: 810–842.
Fauconnier, Gilles
1985 *Mental Spaces.* Cambridge, MA: MIT Press.
Gibbs, Raymond W. Jr.
1990 Psycholinguistic studies on the conceptual basis of idiomaticity. *Cognitive Linguistics* 1: 417–451.
Goossens, Louis
1990 Metaphtonymy: The interaction of metaphor and metonymy in expressions for linguistic action. *Cognitive Linguistics* 1: 323–340.
Greimas, Algirdas-Julien
1966 *Sémantique structurale: recherche de méthode.* Paris: Librairie Larousse.
Haiman, John
1980 Dictionaries and encyclopedias. *Lingua* 50: 329–357.

1983 Iconic and economic motivation. *Language* 59: 781–819.

1985 *Natural Syntax*. Cambridge: Cambridge University Press.

Hobbs, Jerry

1985 Granularity. *Proceedings of the Ninth International Joint Conference on Artificial Intelligence,* 432–435. Tokyo: International Joint Conference.

Lakoff, George

1987 *Women, Fire and Dangerous Things: What Categories Reveal about the Mind.* Chicago: University of Chicago Press.

1990 Invariance Hypothesis: Is abstract reason based on image-schemas? *Cognitive Linguistics* 1: 39–74.

Lakoff, George and Mark Johnson

1980 *Metaphors We Live By.* Chicago: University of Chicago Press.

Lakoff, George and Mark Turner

1989 *More than Cool Reason: A Field Guide to Poetic Metaphor.* Chicago: University of Chicago Press.

Langacker, Ronald W.

1984 Active zones. In *Proceedings of the Tenth Annual Meeting of the Berkeley Linguistics Society,* Brugman, Claudia et al. (eds.), 172–188. Berkeley: Berkeley Linguistics Society.

1987 *Foundations of Cognitive Grammar.* Vol. I: *Theoretical Prerequisites.* Stanford: Stanford University Press.

1991 *Foundations of Cognitive Grammar.* Vol. II: *Descriptive Application.* Stanford: Stanford University Press.

Lyons, John

1977 *Semantics.* 2 vols. Cambridge: Cambridge University Press.

Nunberg, Geoffrey

1979 Nonuniqueness of semantic solutions: Polysemy. *Linguistics and Philosophy* 3:143–184.

Rastier, François

1987 *Sémantique interpretative.* Paris: Presses Universitaires de France.

Rosch, Eleanor

1978 Principles of categorization. In *Cognition and Categorization,* Eleanor Rosch and Barbara Lloyd (eds.), 27–48. Hillsdale, NJ: Lawrence Erlbaum.

Searle, John

1979 Literal meaning. In *Expression and Meaning.* John Searle, 117–136. Cambridge: Cambridge University Press.

Talmy, Leonard

1985 Lexicalization patterns: Semantic structure in lexical forms. In *Language Typology and Syntactic Description*, Vol. 3: *Grammatical Categories and the Lexicon,* Timothy Shopen (ed.), 57–179. Cambridge: Cambridge University Press.

1988 Force dynamics in language and cognition. *Cognitive Science* 12: 49–100.

Taylor, John R.

1989 *Linguistic Categorization: Prototypes in Linguistic Theory.* Oxford: Oxford University Press.

Turner, Mark
1990 Aspects of the Invariance Hypothesis. *Cognitive Linguistics* 1: 247–55.
Ullmann, Stephen
1957 *The Principles of Semantics*. 2nd ed. New York: Barnes and Noble.
Wierzbicka, Anna
1987 *English Speech Act Verbs*. New York: Academic Press.
1988 *The Semantics of Grammar*. Amsterdam/Philadelphia: John Benjamins.

# Chapter 9
# Mental spaces

## Conceptual integration networks
## *Gilles Fauconnier and Mark Turner*

*Gilles Fauconnier and Mark Turner*

### 1. Introduction

Much of the excitement about recent work on language, thought, and action stems from the discovery that the same structural cognitive principles are operating in areas that were once viewed as sharply distinct and technically incommensurable. Under the old view, there were word meanings, syntactic structures, sentence meanings (typically truth-conditional), discourse and pragmatic principles, and then, at a higher level, figures of speech like metaphor and metonymy, scripts and scenarios, rhetoric, forms of inductive and deductive reasoning, argumentation, narrative structure, etc. A recurrent finding in recent work has been that key notions, principles, and instruments of analysis cut across all these divisions and in fact operate in non-linguistic situations as well. Here are some of them:

- *Frames* structure our conceptual and social life. As shown in the work of Fillmore, Langacker, Goldberg, and others, they are also, in their most generic, and schematic forms, a basis for grammatical constructions. Words are themselves viewed as constructions, and lexical meaning is an intricate web of connected frames. Furthermore, although cognitive framing is reflected and guided by language, it is not inherently linguistic. People manipulate many more frames than they have words and constructions for.
- *Analogical mapping*, traditionally studied in connection with reasoning, shows up at all levels of grammar and meaning construction, such as the interpretation of counterfactuals and hypotheticals, category formation , and of course metaphor, whether creative or conventional.
- *Reference points, focus, viewpoints, and dominions* are key notions not only at higher levels of narrative structure, but also at the seemingly micro-level of ordinary grammar, as shown convincingly by Langacker (1993); Zribi-Hertz (1989); Van Hoek (1997); Cutrer (1994), among others.
- *Connected mental spaces* account for reference and inference phenomena

This article is a reprint with revisions of an article published in 1998 in *Cognitive Science* 22(2): 133–187. 

across wide stretches of discourse, but also for sentence-internal multiple readings and tense/mood distributions. Mappings at all levels operate between such spaces, and like frames they are not specifically linguistic. (Fauconnier 1997; Dinsmore 1991; Cutrer 1994; Fauconnier and Sweetser 1996).

– *Connectors and conceptual connections* also operate at all levels, linking mental spaces and other domains for coreference, for metonymy (Nunberg 1978), and for analogy and metaphor (Turner 1991; Sweetser 1990).

There are other notions that apply uniformly at seemingly different levels, such as figure/ground organization (Talmy 1978), profiling, or pragmatic scales. Running through this research is the central cognitive scientific idea of *projection* between structures. Projection connects frames to specific situations, to related frames, and to conventional scenes. Projection connects related linguistic constructions. It connects one viewpoint to another and sets up new viewpoints partly on the basis of old. It connects counterfactual conceptions to non-counterfactual conceptions on which they are based. Projection is the backbone of analogy, categorization, and grammar.

In the present study, we show that *projection typically involves conceptual integration*. There is extensive previous research on varieties of projection, but not on conceptual integration. Empirical evidence suggests that an adequate characterization of mental projection requires a theory of conceptual integration. We propose the basis for such a theory and argue that conceptual integration – like framing or categorization – is a basic cognitive operation that operates uniformly at different levels of abstraction and under superficially divergent contextual circumstances. It also operates along a number of interacting gradients. Conceptual integration plays a significant role in many areas of cognition. It has uniform, systematic properties of structure and dynamics.

The nature of mapping between domains has enjoyed sustained attention as a central problem of cognitive science, and voluminous literatures have developed in this area, including studies by those who call their subject "analogy" or "similarity" (e. g., Hofstadter 1985, 1995a; Mitchell 1993; French 1995; Keane, Ledgeway, and Duff 1994; Holyoak and Thagard 1989, 1984; Forbus, Gentner, and Law 1994; Gentner 1983, 1989; Holland, Holyoak, Nesbett, and Thagard 1986), studies by those who call their subject "metaphor" (e.g., Lakoff and Johnson 1980; Lakoff and Turner 1989; Sweetser 1990; Turner 1987; Indurkhya 1992; Gibbs 1994) and studies that consider cross-domain mapping in general (e.g., Fauconnier 1997; Ortony 1979a, 1979b; Glucksberg and Keysar 1990; Turner 1991).

Our immediate goal is *not* to take a stand on issues and problems of cross-space mappings. Those issues are many and the debates over them will continue and will be further enriched, we hope, by taking blending into consideration.

What we *will* be suggesting is that models of cross-space mapping do not by themselves explain the relevant data. These data involve conceptual integration and multiple projections in ways that have typically gone unnoticed. Cross-space mapping is only one aspect of conceptual integration, and the existing body of research on the subject overlooks conceptual integration, which it is our intention to foreground and analyze here. As we move through the data that crucially involves both cross-space mapping and conceptual integration, we will remark that much of it is neither metaphoric nor analogical.[1]

We take it as an established and fundamental finding of cognitive science that structure mapping and metaphorical projection play a central role in the construction of reasoning and meaning. In fact, the data we analyze shows that such projections are even more pervasive than previously envisioned. Given the existence and key role of such mappings, our focus is on the construction of additional spaces with emergent structure, not directly available from the input domains.

We also rely on another fundamental finding of cognitive science, the capacity for mental simulation, as demonstrated in Johnson-Laird (1983), Kahneman (1995), Grush (1995), Schwartz and Black (1996), Barsalou (1996) among others. In our analysis, the simulation capacity assists in the on-line elaboration of blended spaces ("running the blend"). There is the added twist that simulation can operate on mental spaces which need not have potential real world reference.

Our methodology and argumentation take the following form. Since the cognitive process of conceptual integration has been largely overlooked, it is useful to give evidence for its operation in a wide variety of areas. Since conceptual integration has uniform structural and dynamic properties, it is important to reveal this uniformity behind the appearance of observational and functional diversity. We proceed analytically and empirically, by showing that central inferences, emotions, and conceptualizations, not explained in currently available frameworks, are accounted for elegantly by the conceptual integration model. The argumentation often takes the following specific form: a particular process of meaning construction has particular input representations; during the process, inferences, emotions and event-integrations emerge which cannot reside in any of the inputs; they have been constructed dynamically in a new mental space – the blended space – linked to the inputs in systematic ways. For example, *They dug their own financial grave* draws selectively from different and incompatible input frames to construct a blended space that has its own emergent structure and that provides central inferences. In this case, the blended space has become conventional.

The diversity of our data (of which only a small sample appears in the present paper) is necessary to support our claim for generality. (In showing that cell division is a basic process, it is necessary to study it for many kinds of cells. In arguing that natural selection is a general principle, it is necessary to exemplify it for widely different organisms and species.) In arguing that conceptual integration is a basic cognitive operation, we must show that it operates in many different kinds of cases.

Conceptual blending is not a compositional algorithmic process and cannot be modeled as such for even the most rudimentary cases. Blends are not predictable solely from the structure of the inputs. Rather, they are highly motivated by such structure, in harmony with independently available background and contextual structure; they comply with competing optimality constraints discussed in Section 6, and with locally relevant functional goals. In this regard, the most suitable analog for conceptual integration is not chemical composition but biological evolution. Like analogy, metaphor, translation, and other high-level processes of meaning construction, integration offers a formidable challenge for explicit computational modeling.

Special cases of conceptual blending have been discussed insightfully by Koestler (1964), Goffman (1974), Talmy (1977), Fong (1988), Moser and Hofstadter (ms.), and Kunda, Miller and Clare (1990). Fauconnier (1990) and Turner (1991) also contain analyses of such phenomena. All these authors, however, take blends to be somewhat exotic, marginal manifestations of meaning. We will show here that the process is in fact central, uniform, and pervasive.

The data and analysis we consider here suggest many psychological and neuropsychological experiments (Coulson 1997), but in the present work our emphasis is on the understanding of ecologically valid data. Research on meaning, we suggest, requires analysis of extensive ranges of data, which must be connected theoretically across fields and disciplines by general cognitive principles.

We start our report with an effective but somewhat idealized example of blending, in order to illustrate the issues and terminology. We then outline the general process of conceptual integration and the systematic dynamic properties of blends. We work through some case-studies in a variety of areas. Section 6 presents the competing optimality principles under which conceptual integration operates.

## 2. An illustration

### 2.1. The riddle of the Buddhist monk

Consider a classic puzzle of inferential problem-solving (Koestler 1964):

> A Buddhist monk begins at dawn one day walking up a mountain, reaches the top at sunset, meditates at the top for several days until one dawn when he begins to walk back to the foot of the mountain, which he reaches at sunset. Making no assumptions about his starting or stopping or about his pace during the trips, prove that there is a place on the path which he occupies at the same hour of the day on the two separate journeys.

Our demonstration of the power of blending is likely to be more effective if the reader will pause for a moment and try to solve the problem before reading further. The basic inferential step to showing that there is indeed such a place, occupied at exactly the same time going up and going down, is to imagine the Buddhist monk walking both up and down the path on the same day. Then there must be a place where he meets himself, and that place is clearly the one he would occupy at the same time of day on the two separate journeys.

The riddle is solved, but there is a cognitive puzzle here. The situation that we devised to make the solution transparent is a fantastic one. The monk cannot be making the two journeys simultaneously on the same day, and he cannot "meet himself." And yet this implausibility does not stand in the way of understanding the riddle and its solution. It is clearly disregarded. The situation imagined to solve the riddle is a blend: it combines features of the journey to the summit and of the journey back down, and uses emergent structure in that blend to make the affirmative answer apparent. Here is how this works.

### 2.2. Mental space

In our model, the input structures, generic structures, and blend structures in the network are *mental spaces.* Mental spaces are small conceptual packets constructed as we think and talk, for purposes of local understanding and action. Mental spaces are very partial assemblies containing elements, and structured by frames and cognitive models. They are interconnected, and can be modified as thought and discourse unfold. Mental spaces can be used generally to model dynamical mappings in thought and language. Fauconnier (1994), Fauconnier (1997), Fauconnier and Sweetser (1996).

Blending is an operation that takes place over conceptual integrations networks. Conceptual integration networks often involve many mental spaces. Blending can occur at many different sites in the network. A blended space can have multiple input spaces. Blending is a dynamic process that can happen repeatedly in the same network. Conceptual work can moreover be done at any time at any site in the network. For simplicity, the static diagrams we use in this article involve only a few mental spaces. The purpose of these diagrams is to help clarify the principles of blending. The diagrams themselves are not to be overinterpreted as having any place in conceptual integration theory. In these diagrams, the mental spaces are represented by circles, elements by points (or sometimes icons) in the circles, and connections between elements in different spaces by lines. The frame structure recruited to the mental space is represented either outside in a rectangle or iconically inside the circle.

## 2.3. Input spaces

There are at least two input spaces to a blend. In the case of the Buddhist Monk, each is a partial structure corresponding to one of the two journeys.

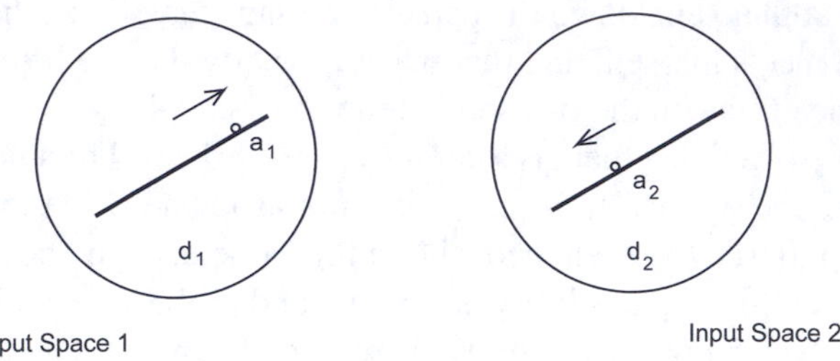


*Figure 1.*

$d_1$ is the day of the upward journey, and $d_2$ the day of the downward journey. $a_1$ is the monk going up, $a_2$ is the monk going down.

## 2.4. Cross-space mapping of counterpart connections

There is a partial cross-space mapping between the input spaces. The cross-space mapping connects counterparts in the input spaces. It connects the mountain, moving individual, day of travel, and motion in one space to the mountain, moving individual, day, and motion in the other space.

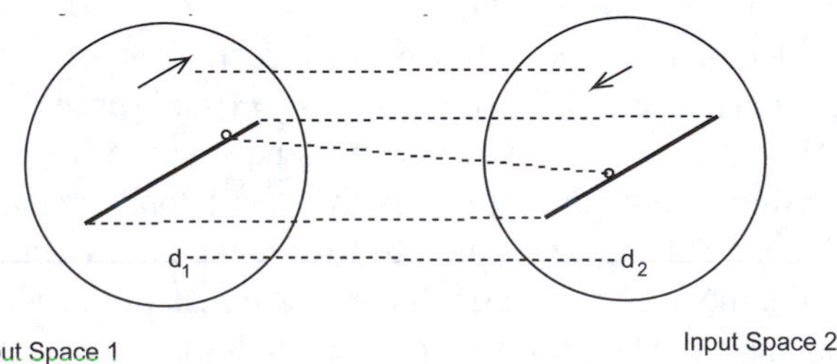


*Figure 2.*

## 2.5. Generic space

There is a *generic space*, which maps onto each of two inputs. The generic space contains what those two inputs have in common at any moment in the development of the conceptual integration network. In the case of the Buddhist Monk, the generic space has a moving individual and his position, a path linking foot and summit of the mountain, a day of travel. It does not specify the direction of motion or the actual day. (At this point in our exposition, it will not be clear why our model needs a generic space in addition to a cross-space mapping. Later, we will argue that powerful generic spaces can themselves become conventional and serve as resources to be drawn on in attempts to build new cross-space mappings in new integration networks.)

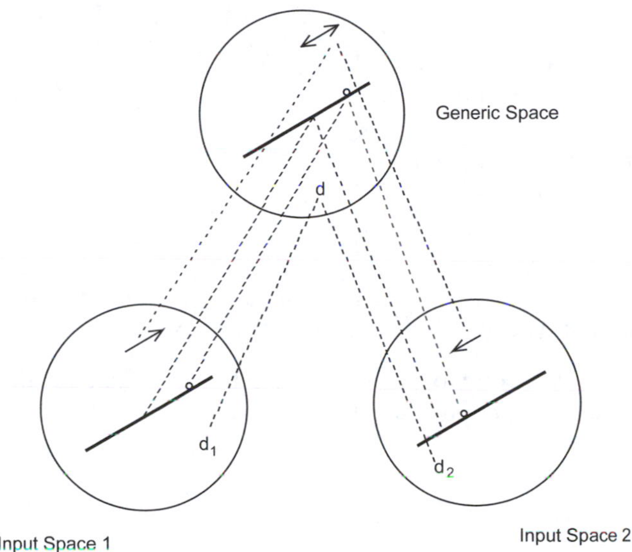


*Figure 3.*

## 2.6. Blend

The input spaces project to another space, the blend. In the blend, the two counterpart identical mountain slopes are mapped onto a single slope. The two days of travel, $d_1$ and $d_2$, are mapped onto a single day d' and therefore fused. While in the generic space and each of the input spaces there is only one moving individual, in the blend there are two moving individuals. The moving individuals in the blend and their positions have been projected from the inputs in such a way as to preserve time of day and direction of motion, and *therefore the two moving individuals cannot be fused.* Input 1 represents dynamically the entire upward journey, while Input 2 represents the entire downward journey. The projection into the blend preserves times and positions. The blend at time t of day d' contains a counterpart of a1 at the position occupied by $a_1$ at time t of $d_1$, and a counterpart of $a_2$ at the position occupied by $a_2$ at time t of day $d_2$.

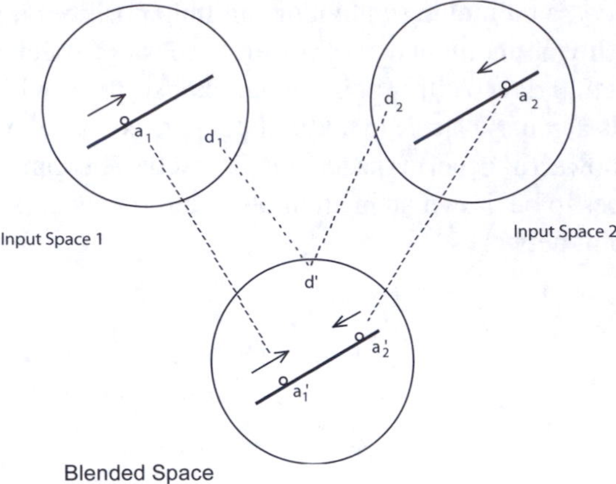


*Figure 4.*

## 2.7. Selective projection

The projection of structure to the blend is selective. For example, the calendrical time of the journey is not projected to the blend.

## 2.8. Emergent structure

The blend contains emergent structure not in the inputs. First, *composition* of elements from the inputs makes relations available in the blend that did not exist in the separate inputs. In the blend but in neither of the inputs, there are two moving individuals instead of one. They are moving in opposite directions, starting from opposite ends of the path, and their positions can be compared at any time of the trip, since they are traveling on the same day, d'.

Second, *completion* brings additional structure to the blend. This structure of two people moving on the path can itself be viewed as a salient part of a familiar background frame: two people starting a journey at the same time from opposite ends of a path. By *completion*, this familiar structure is recruited into the blend. We know, from "common sense," i.e. familiarity with this background frame, that the two people will necessarily meet at some time t' of their journey. We do not have to compute this encounter afresh; it is supplied by completion from a pre-existing familiar frame. There is no encounter in the generic space or either of the inputs, but there is an encounter in the blend, and it supplies the central inference.

Importantly, the blend remains hooked up to the Inputs, so that structural properties of the blend can be mapped back onto the Inputs. In our example, because of the familiarity of the frame obtained by completion, the inference that there is a meeting time t' with a common position p is completely automatic. The mapping back to the input spaces yields:

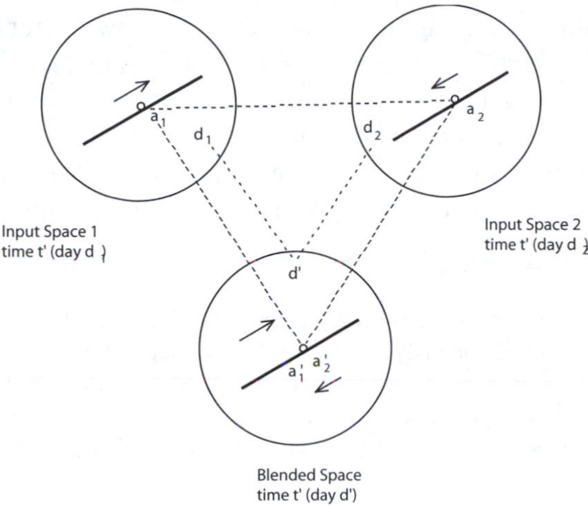


*Figure 5.*

Since the projection of individuals into the blend preserves positions on the path, we "know" through this mapping that the positions of $a_1$ and $a_2$ are the "same" at time t' on the different days, simply because they are the same, by definition, in the frame of two people meeting, instantiated in the blend by their counterparts $a_1$' and $a_2$'.

It is worth emphasizing that the pragmatic incongruity in the blend of the same person traveling in two opposite directions and meeting himself is disregarded, because the focus of the problem is the meeting point and its counterparts in the Input spaces. Blends are used cognitively in flexible ways. By contrast, in examples we discuss later, similar incongruities in the blend get highlighted and mapped back to the Inputs for inferential and emotional effect. Incongruity makes blends more visible, but blends need not be incongruous – incongruity is not one of their defining characteristics.

Notice also that in this blend, some counterparts have been fused (the days, the path on the different days, and the corresponding times on different days), others have been projected separately (the monk on the way up, the monk on the way down, the directions of motion). Projection from the Inputs is only partial – the specific dates of the journeys are not projected, nor the fact that the monk will stay at the top for a while after his upward journey. But the blend has new "emergent" structure not in the Inputs: two moving individuals whose positions can be compared and may coincide, and the richer frame of two travelers going in opposite directions on the same path and necessarily meeting each other. This emergent structure is crucial to the performance of the reasoning task.

Rather amazingly, the Buddhist monk blend shows up in real life. Hutchins (1995) studies the fascinating mental models set up by Micronesian navigators to sail across the Pacific. In such models, it is the islands that move, and virtual islands may serve as reference points. Hutchins reports a conversation between Micronesian and Western navigators who have trouble understanding each other's conceptualizations. As described in Lewis (1972), the Micronesian navigator Beiong succeeds in understanding a Western diagram of intersecting bearings in the following way:

> He eventually succeeded in achieving the mental tour de force of visualizing himself sailing simultaneously from Oroluk to Ponape and from Ponape to Oroluk and picturing the Etak bearings to Ngatik at the start of both voyages. In this way he managed to comprehend the diagram and confirmed that it showed the island's position correctly. [The Etak is the virtual island, and Ngatik is the island to be located.]

Previous insightful work by Kahneman (1995), Schwartz and Black (1996), Barsalou (1996), has emphasized the role of imaginative mental simulation and depiction in making inferences about physical scenarios. In the riddle of the Buddhist Monk, the physical system we are interested in consists of the sequence of the monk's departing, traveling up the hill, reaching the top, waiting, departing, traveling down the hill, and reaching the bottom. Imagining a mental depiction of this scenario does not solve the riddle, but representing it isomorphically as two input spaces to a blend and imagining a mental depiction of that blend does indeed create an event of encounter in the blend which points to a solution, not for the blend, but for the input spaces and therefore identically for the original scenario. Mental simulation, in this case, depends indispensably upon conceptual blending to provide the effective scenario to begin with.

## 3. The network model of conceptual integration

In this section, we present the central features of our network model, keyed to the illustration we have just given. In Section 5, we present advanced aspects of the model.

The network model is concerned with on-line, dynamical cognitive work people do to construct meaning for local purposes of thought and action. It focuses specifically on conceptual projection as an instrument of on-line work. Its central process is conceptual blending.

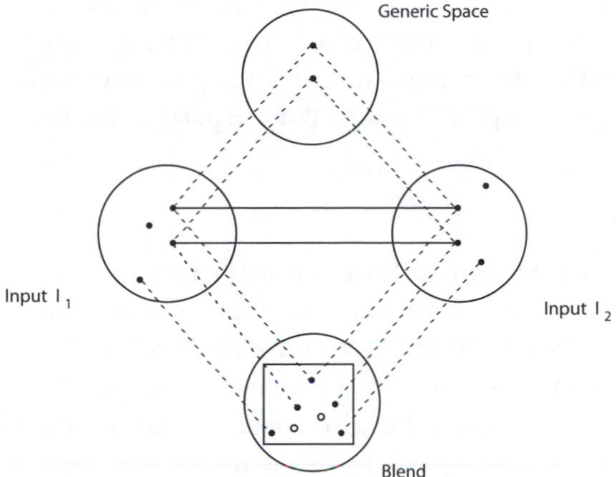


*Figure 6.*

### 3.1. Mental spaces

The circles in Figure 6 represent mental spaces. We show the crucial four mental spaces for the monk example: the two inputs, the generic, and the blend. There are also background frames recruited to build these mental spaces, such as the background frame of two people approaching each other on a path. We emphasize that this is a minimal network. Networks in other cases of conceptual integration may have yet more input spaces and even multiple blended spaces.

### 3.2. Cross-space mapping of counterpart connections

In conceptual integration, there are partial counterpart connections between input spaces. The solid lines in Figure 6 represent counterpart connections. Such counterpart connections are of many kinds: connections between frames and roles in frames; connections of identity or transformation or representation; metaphoric connections, etc. In the monk example, the monks, paths, journeys, days, and so on are counterparts.

### 3.3. Generic space

As conceptual projection unfolds, whatever structure is recognized at any moment in the conceptual work as belonging to both of the input spaces constitutes a generic space. At any moment in the construction, the generic space maps onto each of the inputs. It defines the current cross-space mapping between them. A given element in the generic space maps onto paired counterparts in the two input spaces.

### 3.4. Blending

In blending, structure from at least two input mental spaces is projected to a third space, the "blend." In the monk example, the two input spaces have two journeys completely separated in time; the blend has two simultaneous journeys. Generic spaces and blended spaces are related: blends contain generic structure captured in the generic space, but also contain more specific structure, and can contain structure that is impossible for the inputs, such as two monks who are the same monk.

### 3.5. Selective projection

The projection from the inputs to the blend is typically partial. In Figure 6, not all elements from the inputs are projected to the blend.

There are three operations involved in constructing the blend: *composition, completion, and elaboration.*

### 3.6. Composition

Blending composes elements from the input spaces, providing relations that do not exist in the separate inputs. In the monk riddle, composition yields two travelers making two journeys. Fusion is one kind of composition. Counterparts may be brought into the blend as separate elements or as a fused element. Figure 6 represents one case in which counterparts are fused in the blend and one case in which counterparts are brought into the blend as distinct entities. In the monk example, the two days in the inputs are fused into one day in the blend, but the two monks from the inputs are brought into the blend as distinct entities.

### 3.7. Completion

Blends recruit a great range of background conceptual structure and knowledge without our recognizing it consciously. In this way, composed structure is *completed* with other structure. The fundamental subtype of recruitment is pattern completion. A minimal composition in the blend can be extensively completed by a larger conventional pattern. In the monk example, the structure achieved through composition is completed by the scenario of two people journeying toward each other on a path, which yields an *encounter.*

### 3.8. Elaboration

Elaboration develops the blend through imaginative mental simulation according to principles and logic in the blend. Some of these principles will have been brought to the blend by completion. Continued dynamic completion can recruit new principles and logic during elaboration. But new principles and logic may also arise through elaboration itself. We can "run the blend" indefinitely: for example, the monks might meet each other and have a philosophical discussion about the concept of identity. Blended spaces can become extremely elaborated.

### 3.9. Emergent structure

Composition, completion, and elaboration lead to emergent structure in the blend; the blend contains structure that is not copied from the inputs. In Figure 6, the square inside the blend represents emergent structure.

## 4. Applications

### 4.1. The debate with Kant

The monk example presents a salient and intuitively apparent blend, precisely because of its pragmatic anomaly. But our claim is that blends abound in all kinds of cases that go largely unnoticed. Some are created as we talk, others are conventional, and others are even more firmly entrenched in the grammatical structure. We discuss in Fauconnier and Turner 1996 the situation in which a contemporary philosopher says, while leading a seminar,

> I claim that reason is a self-developing capacity. Kant disagrees with me on this point. He says it's innate, but I answer that that's begging the question, to which he counters, in *Critique of Pure Reason,* that only innate ideas have power. But I say to that, what about neuronal group selection? He gives no answer.

In one input mental space, we have the modern philosopher, making claims. In a separate but related input mental space, we have Kant, thinking and writing. In neither input space is there a debate. The blended space has both the modern philosopher (from the first input space) and Kant (from the second input space).

In the blend, the additional frame of *debate* has been recruited, to frame Kant and the modern philosopher as engaged in simultaneous debate, mutually aware, using a single language to treat a recognized topic.

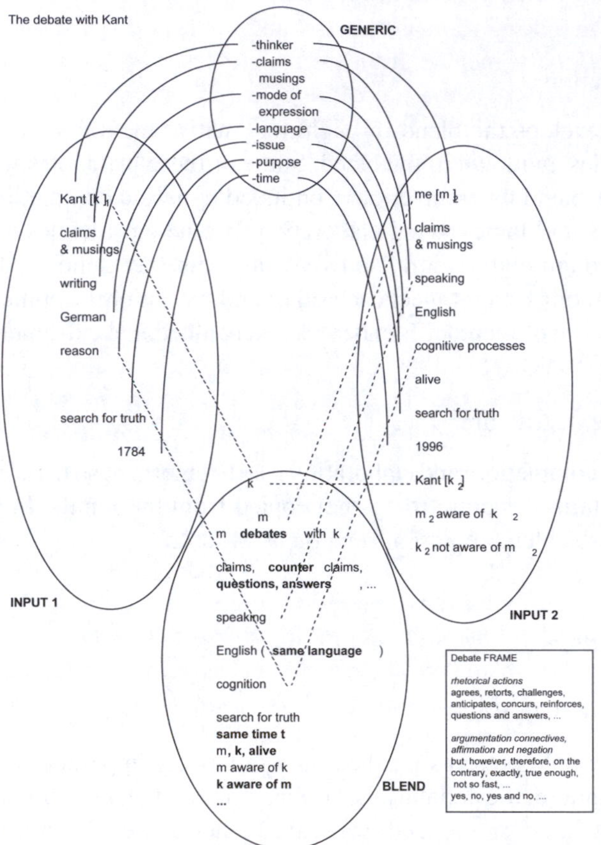


*Figure 7.*

The debate frame comes up easily in the blend, through pattern completion, since so much of its structure is already in place in the composition of the two inputs. Once the blend is established, we can operate cognitively within that space, which allows us to manipulate the various events as an integrated unit. The debate frame brings with it conventional expressions, available for our use. We know the connection of the blend to the input spaces, and the way in which structure or inferences developed in the blend translate back to the input spaces.

A "realist" interpretation of the passage would be quite fantastic. The philosophy professor and Kant would have to be brought together in time, would have to speak the same language, and so on. No one is fooled into thinking that this is the intended interpretation. In fact, using a debate blend of this type is so conventional that it will go unnoticed.

And yet, it has all the constitutive properties of blending. There is a *Cross-space mapping* linking Kant and his writings to the philosophy professor and his lecture. Counterparts include: Kant and the professor, their respective languages, topics, claims, times of activity, goals (e.g. search for truth), modes of expression (writing vs. speaking). There is *Partial projection to the blend*: Kant, the professor, some of their ideas, and the search for truth are projected to the blend. Kant's time, language, mode of expression, the fact that he's dead, and the fact that he was never aware of the future existence of our professor are not projected. There is *Emergent Structure* through *Composition*: we have two people talking in the same place at the same time. There is *Emergent Structure* through *Completion*: two people talking in the same place at the same time evoke the *cultural frame* of a conversation, a debate (if they are philosophers), an argument. This frame, the debate frame, structures the blend and is reflected by the syntax and vocabulary of the professor (*disagrees*, *answer*, *counters*, *what about*, ...).

This example allows us to observe that blends provide *Integration of Events*: Kant's ideas and the professor's claims are integrated into a unified event, the debate. Looking back now to the monk example, we see that the blend in that case integrated into a single scenario various events of uncertain relation spread out over time. Blends provide a space in which ranges of structure can be manipulated uniformly. The other spaces do not disappear once the blend has been formed. On the contrary, the blend is valuable only because it is connected conceptually to the inputs. The monk blend tells us something about the inputs. The debate with Kant tells us something about the inputs.

### 4.2. Complex numbers

Conceptual projection enables us to extend categories to cover new provisional members. The blended space that develops during such a projection merges the original category with its new extension. When categories are extended permanently, it is the structure of this blend that defines the new category structure, thus carving out a novel conceptual domain. The history of science, and of mathematics and physics in particular, is rich in such conceptual shifts. (See Fauconnier and Turner 1994; Lakoff and Núñez 2000; Lansing, p.c.) It is customary to speak of models either replacing or extending previous models, but the pervasiveness and importance of merging may have been underestimated.

Consider as an example the stage of mathematical conceptual development at which complex numbers became endowed with angles (arguments) and magnitudes. Square roots of negative numbers had shown up in formulas of sixteenth-century mathematicians and operations on these numbers had been correctly formulated. But the very mathematicians who formulated such operations, Cardan and especially Bombelli, were also of the opinion that they were "useless," "sophistic," and "impossible" or "imaginary." Such was also the opinion of Descartes a century later. Leibniz said no harm came of using them, and Euler thought them impossible but nevertheless useful. The square roots of negative numbers had the strange property of lending themselves to formal manipulations without fitting into a mathematical conceptual system. A genuine concept of complex number took time to develop, and the development proceeded in several steps along the lines explained above for analogical connections and blending.

The first step exploited the preexisting analogical mapping from numbers to one-dimensional space. Wallis is credited with having observed – in his *Algebra* (1685) – that if negative numbers could be mapped onto a directed line, complex numbers could be mapped onto points in a two-dimensional plane, and he provided geometrical constructions for the counterparts of the real or complex roots of $ax^2 + bx + c = 0$ (Kline 1980). In effect, Wallis provided a model for the mysterious numbers, thereby showing their consistency, and giving some substance to their formal manipulation. This is of course a standard case of extending analogical connections; geometric space is a source domain partially mapped onto the target domain of numbers. The mapping from a single axis is extended to mapping from the whole plane; some geometric constructions are mapped onto operations on numbers. Notice that neither the original mapping nor its extension requires more than two domains. We do not need a generic space, since there is no assumption in work like Wallis's that numbers and points in a plane share properties at some higher level of abstraction. The necessary structure is already present in the conceptual domain of two-dimensional space because it already contains the notion of distance which is expressed directly by means of numbers. (Of course, this source domain has a conceptual history of its own. We argue elsewhere that in fact it is itself the product of a non-trivial conceptual blend.) Nor does it involve a blend; numbers and points remain totally distinct categories at all levels. Although the mapping proposed by Wallis showed the formal consistency of a system including complex numbers, it did not provide a new extended concept of number. As Morris Kline reports, Wallis's work was ignored: it did not make mathematicians receptive to the use of such numbers. In itself, this is an interesting point. It shows that mapping a coherent space onto a conceptually incoherent space is not enough to give the incoherent space new conceptual structure. It also follows that coherent abstract structure is not enough, even in mathematics, to produce satisfactory conceptual structure: In Wallis's representation, the metric geometry provided abstract schemas for a unified interpretation of real and imaginary numbers, but this was insufficient cognitively for mathematicians to revise their domain of numbers accordingly.

In the analysis developed here, the novel conceptual structure in the mathematical case of numbers is first established within a blended space. In the blend, but not in the original inputs, it is possible for an element to be simultaneously a number and a geometric point, with cartesian coordinates (a,b) and polar coordinates (r,θ). In the blend, we find interesting general formal properties of such numbers, such as

$$(a, b) + (a', b') = (a+a', b+b')$$
$$(r, \theta) \times (r', \theta') = (rr', \theta + \theta')$$

Every number in this extended sense has a real part, an imaginary one, an argument, and a magnitude. By virtue of the link of the blend to the geometric input space, the numbers can be manipulated geometrically; by virtue of the link of the blend to the input space of real numbers, the new numbers in the blend are immediately conceptualized as an extension of the old numbers (which they include by way of the mapping). As in Wallis's scheme, the mapping from points on a line to numbers has been extended to a mapping from points in a plane to numbers. This mapping is partial from one input to the other – only one line of the plane is mapped onto the numbers of the target domain – but it is total from the geometric input to the blend: all the points of the plane have counterpart complex numbers. And this in turn allows the blend to incorporate the full geometric structure of the geometric input space.

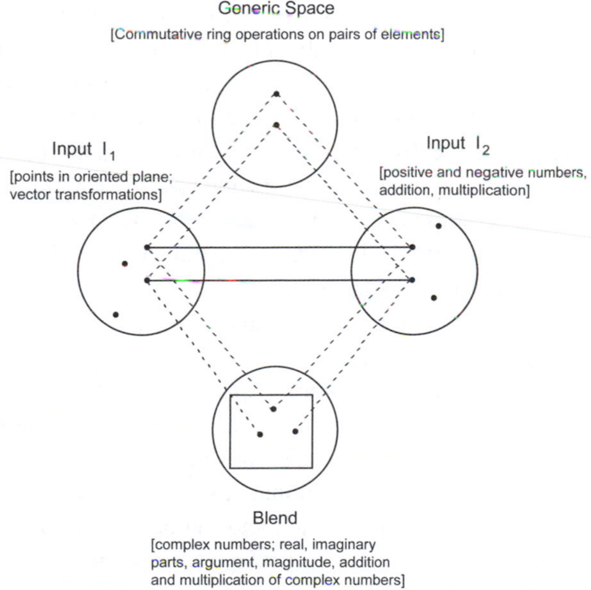


*Figure 8.*

Interestingly, when a rich blended space of this sort is built, an abstract generic space will come along with it. Having the three spaces containing respectively points (input 1), numbers (input 2), complex point/numbers (blend) entails a fourth space with abstract elements having the properties "common" to points and numbers. The relevant abstract notions in this case are those of "operations" on pairs of elements. For numbers, the specific operations (in the target domain) are addition and multiplication. For points in the plane, the operations can be viewed as vector transformations – vector addition, and vector composition by adding angles and multiplying magnitudes. In the blended space of complex numbers, vector addition and number addition are the same operation, because they invariably yield the same result; similarly, vector transformation and number multiplication are conceptually one single operation. But such an operation can be instantiated algorithmically in different ways depending on which geometric and algebraic properties of the blend are exploited.[2]

In the generic space, specific geometric or number properties are absent. All that is left is the more abstract notion of two operations on pairs of elements, such that each operation is associative, commutative, and has an identity element; each element has under each operation an inverse element; and one of the two operations is distributive with respect to the other. Something with this structure is called by mathematicians a "commutative ring."

The emergence of the concept of complex numbers with arguments and magnitudes displays all the constitutive properties of blending. There is an initial *cross-space mapping* of numbers to geometric space, a *generic* space, a *projection* of both inputs to the blend, with numbers fused with geometric points, *emergent structure* by *completion* (arguments and magnitudes), and by *elaboration* (multiplication and addition reconstrued as operations on vectors).

The blend takes on a realist interpretation within mathematics. It constitutes a new and richer way to understand numbers and space. However, it also retains its connections to the earlier conceptions provided by the Input spaces. Conceptual change of this sort is not just replacement. It is the creation of more elaborate and richly connected networks of spaces.

Under our account, then, the evolution and extension of the concept of number includes a four-space stage at which the concept of complex number is logically and coherently constructed in a blended space, on the basis of a generic space structured as a commutative ring. (That generic space is not consciously conceptualized as an abstract domain when the full-blown concept of complex number gets formed. It becomes a conceptual domain in its own right when mathematicians later study it and name it.) The abstract and mathematical example of complex numbers supports the functioning of projection in conceptual integration networks, with their blended and generic spaces,[3] and confirms that we are dealing with an aspect of thought that is not purely linguistic or verbal. It highlights the deep difference between naming and conceptualizing; adding expressions like $\sqrt{-1}$ to the domain of numbers, and calling them numbers, is not enough to make them numbers conceptually, even when they fit a consistent model. This is true of category extension in general.

### 4.3. Digging your own grave

Coulson (1997) examines remarkable elaborations of the metaphor *to dig one's own grave*. Consider the familiar idiomatic version of the metaphor. *You are digging your own grave* is a conventional expression typically used as a warning or judgment, typically implying that (i) you are doing bad things that will cause you to have a very bad experience, and (ii) you are unaware of this causal relation. A conservative parent who keeps his money in his mattress may express disapproval of an adult child's investing in the stock market by saying, *you are digging your own grave*.

At first glance, what we have here is a straightforward projection from the concrete domain of graves, corpses, and burial to abstract domains of getting into trouble, unwittingly doing the wrong things, and ultimate failure. Failing is being dead and buried; bad moves that precede and cause failure are like events (grave-digging) that precede burial. It is foolish to facilitate one's own burial or one's own failure. And it is foolish not to be aware of one's own actions, especially when they are actions leading to one's very extinction.

But a closer look reveals extraordinary mismatches between the purported source and target of this metaphor. The *causal structure* is inverted. Foolish actions cause failure, but grave-digging does not cause death. It is typically someone's dying that prompts others to dig a grave. And if the grave is atypically prepared in advance, to secure a plot, to keep workers busy, or because the person is expected to die, there is still not the slightest causal connection from the digging to the dying. In the exceptional scenario in which a prisoner is threatened into digging his own grave, it is not the digging that causes the death, and the prisoner will be killed anyway if he refuses. The *intentional structure* does not carry over. Sextons do not dig graves in their sleep, unaware of what they are doing. In contrast, figurative digging of one's own grave is conceived as unintentional misconstrual of action. The *frame structure* of agents, patients, and sequence of events is not preserved. Our background knowledge is that the "patient" dies, and then the "agent" digs the grave and buries the "patient." But in the metaphor, the actors are fused and the ordering of events is reversed. The "patient" does the digging, and if the grave is deep enough, has no other option than to die and occupy it. Even in the unusual real life case in which one might dig one's own grave in advance, there would be no necessary temporal connection between finishing the digging and perishing. The *internal event structure* does not match. In the target, it is certainly true that the more trouble you are in, the more you risk failure. Amount of trouble is mapped onto depth of grave. But again, in the source there is no correlation between the depth of a person's grave and their chances of dying.

Now recall the rationale often proposed for metaphor: Readily available background or experiential structure and inferences of the source are recruited to understand the target. By that standard, and in view of the considerable mismatch, *digging one's own grave* should be a doomed metaphor. In fact, it's a very successful one.

This paradox dissolves when we consider, in addition to the two input spaces, the blended space. In metaphoric cases, such as this one, the two inputs are the "source Input" and the "target Input." The blend in *digging one's own grave* inherits the concrete structure of graves, digging, and burial, from the source Input. But it inherits causal, intentional, and internal event structure from the target Input. They are not simply juxtaposed. Rather, *emergent* structure specific to the blend is created. In the blend, all the curious properties noted above actually hold. The existence of a satisfactory grave causes death, and is a necessary precondition for it. It follows straightforwardly that the deeper the grave, the closer it is to completion, and the greater the chance for the grave's intended occupant to die. It follows that in the blend (as opposed to the Input source), digging one's grave is a grave mistake, since it makes dying more probable. In the blend, it becomes *possible* to be unaware of one's very concrete actions. This is projected from the target Input, where it is indeed fully possible, and frequent, to be unaware of the significance of one's actions. But in the blend, it remains *highly foolish* to be unaware of such concrete actions; this is projected from the source Input. And it will project back to the target Input to produce suitable inferences (i.e. highlight foolishness and misperception of individual's behavior).

We wish to emphasize that in the construction of the blend, a single shift in causal structure, *the existence of a grave* causes *death*, instead of *death* causes *the existence of a grave*, is enough to produce *emergent* structure, specific to the blend: undesirability of digging one's grave, exceptional foolishness in not being aware of it, correlation of depth of grave with probability of death. The causal inversion is guided by the target, but the *emergent* structure is deducible within the blend from the new causal structure and familiar common-sense background knowledge. This point is essential, because the *emergent* structure, although "fantastic" from a literal interpretation point of view, is supremely efficient for the purpose of transferring the intended inferences back to the target Input, and thereby making real-world inferences. This emergent structure is not in the Inputs – it is part of the cognitive construction in the blend. But, also, it is not *stated* explicitly as part of the blend. It just follows, fairly automatically, from the unstated understanding that the causal structure has been projected from the target, not from the source.

The integration of events in the blend is indexed to events in both of the input spaces. We know how to translate structure in the blend back to structure in the inputs. The blend is an integrated platform for organizing and developing those other spaces. Consider a slightly fuller expression, *with each investment you make, you are digging your grave a little deeper.* In the target Input, there are no graves, but there are investments; in the source Input, the graves are not financial, but one does dig; in the blend, investments are simultaneously instruments of digging, and what one digs is one's *financial grave.* A single action is simultaneously investing and digging; a single condition is simultaneously having finished the digging and having lost one's money. Digging your own grave does not kill you, but digging your own financial grave does cause your death/bankruptcy.

Such blends can of course be elaborate, as in Seana Coulson's example from an editorial in the *UCSD Guardian*: *The U.S. is in a position to exhume itself from the shallow grave that we've dug for ourselves.* In this blend, the digger is identical to the body buried, which can exhume itself. This is impossible for the source Input, but possible for the target Input, where a nation can be in bad conditions but try to get out of them. In the blend, the ease of exhuming is related to the depth of the grave. This logic is available from both source and target Inputs: the shallower the grave, the easier the exhumation; the less bad the conditions, the easier it is to improve them. As in *you are digging your own grave*, the actor is responsible but unaware, his actions were unwise, he is culpable for not recognizing that his actions were unwise, and the consequences of those actions are undesirable.

Pattern completion is at work in developing this blend. In recent U.S. history, there have been many disparate events, only some caused by actors, only some caused by American actors, and almost none caused by any single actor. Nonetheless, the blend asks us to integrate those many disparate target events, by blending them with a template, available to the blend from the source Input, of a single integrated action by a single actor, namely, digging as done by a digger. To do so, we must construct in the target a single entity, "the United States," that is causal for those many disparate events, which are in turn causal for current conditions in the United States. In the blend, the United States is a person, whom we want to convince to begin the process of self-exhumation.

### 4.4. Analogical counterfactuals

Consider an analogical counterfactual of the type studied by Fauconnier (1990, in press): *In France, Watergate would not have harmed Nixon.* Uncontroversially, understanding this counterfactual includes building a generic space that fits both *American politics* and *French politics.* It includes a leader who is elected, who is a member of a political party, and who is constrained by laws. This skeletal generic space fits the space of *American politics* and *French politics* so well and intricately that it is natural for someone to project a great deal more skeletal information from *American politics* into the generic space on the assumption that it will of course apply to *French politics*.

The rhetorical motive for saying, *In France, Watergate wouldn't have done Nixon any harm* is exactly to stop someone from projecting certain kinds of information to the generic space on the assumption that it applies to *French politics*. The speaker lays down a limit to this projection by constructing a specific, counterfactual, and pragmatically anomalous blend.

Into this blend, the speaker has projected information associated with President Nixon and the Watergate break-in. Nixon and Watergate and so on are brought into the blend with only skeletal properties, such as being a president who breaks laws in order to place members of a political party at a disadvantage. It may be that such information in fact in no way belongs to *French politics*, that something like Watergate has in fact never happened in *French politics*. No matter, it can be imported to the blend from the "Nixon in America" input. Additionally, from the "France" input, we can project to the blend French cultural perspectives on such an event.

This counterfactual blended space operates according to its own logic. In this counterfactual blend, an illegal act directed with the knowledge of the elected leader against the opposing political party leader will not cause the public outrage associated with Watergate. For this central inference to take place, we must have both the nature of the event from the "Nixon in America" input and the general cultural attitudes from the "France" input. The blend is not a side-show or curiosity or merely an entertaining excrescence of the projection. It is the engine of the central inferences.

The constitutive properties of blending are apparent: cross-space mapping of the Input U.S. and France spaces; generic politics space; selective projection – Nixon and Watergate on the one hand, the frame of French politics on the other; emergent structure:

- composition provides a Watergate-like event in France;
- elaboration includes the explicit predication that the president is not harmed.
- Finally, there is projection back to the Inputs: France has features that the U. S. does not have.

Clearly, in the case of such an analogical counterfactual, the construction of meaning cannot be mistaken as an attempt to impose structure from the one input onto the other. In fact, this particular analogical counterfactual is trying to do exactly the opposite. It is trying to make clear in just what areas information projected from one input cannot be imposed on the other. Moreover, its purpose is to illuminate not only the nature of the "France" Input, but also the nature of the "America" Input. The inferences are thus not one-way. They can go from the counterfactual space to both of the Inputs.

Nor are the analogical connections exclusively positive. It is disanalogy rather than analogy that is the central assertion of the statement. We recognize that a scenario can be shared by *American politics* and *French politics* but that in certain key respects these spaces have negative counterparts rather than positive counterparts. The utterance sets up a blend exactly for the purpose of illuminating these counterparts and their negative relation to each other. The projection in the case of *In France, Watergate would not have harmed Nixon*, is thus not direct, not one-way, and not exclusively positive. This example lets us add to our model of conceptual projection the feature that even when, as in analogy, one input is in some way "understood" by projection from the other, *the projection is in general not direct, not one-way, and not exclusively positive.*

Of course, one may object to the assertion about France. One can respond, "You are wrong, look at all the harm the Greenpeace incident did to Mitterand." This can be interpreted as asking us to change the blend so that the illegal act is now general enough to include not only acts directed at an opposing political party but even acts directed against any opposing group (Greenpeace). It asserts that the space does indeed include cultural perspectives that, contrary to the previous assertion, do apply to both *American politics* and *French politics*. This, in turn, has the effect of expanding the generic space. This is a fundamental and general point that will arise repeatedly in our analyses: the array of spaces is built up dynamically and inventively in order to achieve a conceptual projection. Our network model dictates no fixed sequence in this construction of meaning. It additionally accords notable place to energetic and imaginative effort and revision. It should also be emphasized that while the English sentence *In France, Watergate ...* instructs us to perform a blend, it considerably underspecifies what blend to perform. There are countless other interpretations of this sentence corresponding to different blending choices (e.g., it could be about the love of the French for Nixon, or the consequences for Nixon of living in France rather than running for a second term, and so on). Rather remarkably, we are capable of constructing the "right" blend in context, in spite of the sparse grammatical clues.

We might ask, in what space does it hold that Watergate does not harm Nixon? Not in the "Nixon in America" Input, or the "France" Input, or in the Generic space. But if we shift to the blend, then the claim holds. It appears that a central part of conceptual projection is knowing how to construct a blend and how to shift to that blend in order to do real conceptual work, with the consequence that the vestiges of that real conceptual work are often projected to the one or both of the Inputs. But the structures of the blended space that would be impossible in the other spaces are left behind in such projection. That they are left behind does not mean that they are not indispensable to the central conceptual work.

Counterfactuals are not exotic curiosities of language. They are central to reasoning in everyday life (Kahneman 1995), and to scientific reasoning (Goodman 1947). Tetlock and Belkin (1996) show that argumentation in political science relies indispensably and extensively on counterfactual thought. Turner (1996a) shows that political scientists and others have not taken into account the complex blending that underlies the construction of counterfactuals, and the great range of conceptual structure and knowledge that it recruits without our noticing it (Turner and Fauconnier, in press). The biases smoothly integrated into the blend may serve the rhetorician, but not the social scientist.

### 4.5. Category extension and change

We frequently organize new material by extending a conventional category to it. Usually, these on-line category extensions are provisional, for local purposes, often purposes of expression and naming. Consider the attested case in which a handout for an academic talk has one column with elements listed 1 through 7, and another column with elements listed A through F. During the question period, people begin referring unselfconsciously to "Number E." The inputs to this blend are (i) the counting numbers and (ii) the alphabet, ordered in its customary linear fashion. The generic space has only a well-ordered ordinal sequence. It defines the counterparts in the two Inputs. The blend has the well-ordered ordinal sequence, but also has, linked to it and thus to each other, two paired sets of counting numbers, one of which is the "real" counting numbers and the other of which is the alphabet. But the blend does not have, for example, arithmetic properties from the input space with counting numbers, or spelling from the space with the alphabet.

In other cases, the blend may lead to permanent category change. Consider the phrase "same-sex marriage". In Turner and Fauconnier (1995), we show in detail how expressions with this syntactic form can be systematically used to trigger blends. For *same-sex marriage*, the Inputs are the traditional scenario of marriage on the one hand, and an alternative domestic scenario involving two people of the same sex on the other. The cross-space mapping may link prototypical elements like partners, common dwellings, commitment, love, etc. Selective projection then recruits additional structure from each Input, e.g. social recognition, wedding ceremonies, mode of taxation, and so on from the first Input of "traditional marriage," and same sex, no biologically common children, culturally defined roles of the partners, and so on from the second Input. Emergent properties will characterize this new social structure reflected by the blend.

At that stage of the construction, *same-sex marriage* will not be a subcategory of *marriage* for those who view *marriage* as having criterial attributes (e.g. heterosexual union for the sake of children) that *same-sex marriage* does not have. But now there can be pressure for these criterial attributes to change. The pressure comes from the activated generic space which made the blend possible. If that generic space (people living in a household, division of labor, mutual protection, financial planning done as a unit, or whatever) is understood to provide the essential criteria for the notion *marriage*, then *same-sex marriage* becomes a banal subcategory of the more general notion. Analogy and blending drive categorization. Clearly, different people using the same words in the same language may nevertheless entertain different categorization schemes. The same expression "same-sex marriage" may correspond to an analogical and conflictual blend for one person, and to a straightforward subcategory for another. Interestingly, the clashing conceptions of two such persons will still share a large amount of meaning.

### 4.6. Regatta

Let us consider another case in which it is clear that the motivation for constructing the blend is to tell us something about an important input. A modern catamaran *Great American II*, sailing from San Francisco to Boston in 1993, is being compared to a clipper, *Northern Light*, that made the same run back in 1853. A few days before the catamaran reached Boston, observers were able to say:
At this point, *Great American II* is 4.5 days ahead of *Northern Light*.

This expression frames the two boats as sailing on the same course during the same time period in 1993. It blends the event of 1853 and the event of 1993 into a single event. All the conditions for blending obtain. There is a *cross-space mapping* which links the two trajectories, the two boats, the two time periods, positions on the course, etc. *Projection to the blend* from the Inputs is partial: the 1853 date is dropped, as are the 1853 weather conditions, the purpose of the trip, and so on. But the blend has rich *emergent structure*: like the traveling monks, the boats are now in a position to be compared, so that one can be "ahead" of the other. This structure itself, two boats moving in the same direction on the same course and having departed from San Francisco on the same day, fits into an obvious and familiar *cultural frame*, that of a *race*. This yields additional emergent structure by *completion*. The race frame in the blended space may be invoked more explicitly, as in:

> At this point, *Great American II* is barely maintaining a 4.5 day lead over *Northern Light*.

"Maintaining a lead" is an intentional part of a race. Although in reality the catamaran is sailing alone, and the clipper's run took place 140 years before, the situation is described in terms of the blended space, in which, so to speak, the two boats left San Francisco on the same day in 1993, and are engaged in a race to Boston. As in the monk example, no one is fooled by the blend: the clipper has not magically reappeared. The blend remains solidly linked to the Inputs. Inferences from the Blend can be projected back to the inputs: in particular, the speeds and positions of the two boats on their respective runs many years apart can be projected back to the inputs. Another noteworthy property of the *race* frame in the blend is its emotional content. Sailors in a race are driven by emotions linked to winning, leading, losing, gaining, and so forth. This emotional value can be projected to Input 2. The solitary run of *Great American II* is conceived, thanks to the blend, as a race against the nineteenth century clipper, and can be lived with corresponding emotions.

The attested report that prompted our interest in the "boat race" was actually a magazine article in *Latitude 38*, which contained the following:

> As we went to press, Rich Wilson and Bill Biewenga were barely maintaining a 4.5 day lead over the ghost of the clipper Northern Light, ...

The blend, here, has become reified. An explicit referent, the ghost, is set up for the opponent of *Great American II* in the blended space. The mapping is more extensive, although still implicit. "*Ghost*" allows the projection from Input 1 that the clipper no longer (i.e. in 1993) exists. But the starting times are still fused, and it is understood that the "ghost" is retracing the exact run of the record-holding clipper.

Again, nobody is fooled into confusing the blend with reality. There is no inference that the sailors actually saw a ghost ship or even imagined one. The construction and operation of the blend is creative, but also conventional in the sense that readers know immediately and without conscious effort how to interpret it.

Because blending is neither deterministic nor compositional, there is more than one way to construct an acceptable blend, and this is confirmed by our boat race example. The preferred reading seems to be that *4.5 days* is the difference between the time N it took *Great American II* to reach its current position (point A), and the time N+4.5 it took *Northern Light* back in 1853 to reach point A. Under that interpretation, the boats' positions in the initial spaces (*1853*, *1993*), and in the blend, are their positions (point A for GA, and point B for NL) after N days, which is the time on the clock in the *1993* space at the time of writing. In this reading, the 4.5 days are a time in the *1853* space – the time it took NL to get from B to A. Another conceivable reading has this reversed, taking the time on the clock in the *1853* space and the 4.5 days in the current *1993* space. Under that interpretation, *Northern Light* got to point B' after N days, *Great American II* got to point A after N days, and it took *Great American II* 4.5 days to get from B' to A.

Other readings may be available. Suppose *Great American* II is following a different course from its illustrious predecessor's, so that positions on the two journeys cannot be directly compared. But suppose also that experts can estimate, given current positions, how long it "should" take *Great American II* to reach Boston. Then, the example sentence could be interpreted as saying that, given its current position, *Great American II* should end up making the run to Boston in 76 days, 8 hours minus 4.5 days, i.e. in 71 days, 20 hours. This time, in the blended space of *1853* and the experts' hypothetical *1993* space, *Great American II* reaches Boston 4.5 days ahead of Northern Light.

All these readings involve blended spaces. The blended space is different in each case, and its structure accounts for the corresponding difference of truth values in the interpretations. This is a nice point: far from being fuzzy and fantastic, the blends allow a totally precise quantified evaluation of the truth conditions they impose on the actual world.

### 4.7. The desktop

Now take a superficially very different example, offered by Dan Gruen, which involves the performance of a specific activity. Human-computer interfaces are often structured by the concept of a desktop, on which objects rest and can be manipulated and used to perform actions. The appearance of the computer screen carries icons corresponding to objects on a desktop. They can be opened and closed, put away, and so on. When working with the icons, we think of them and act upon them in some ways as we would on actual desktop material, and in some ways as when dealing with general computer commands. Clearly, the entire activity is coherent and integrated, once learned. It is not hampered by its obvious literal falsities: there is no actual desk, no folders, no putting of objects into folders, no shuffling of objects from one folder to another, no putting of objects into the trash, and so on.

The created blend has considerable emergent structure. For instance, dragging icons with the mouse belongs to neither moving objects on a desktop nor giving standard symbolic commands, or *a fortiori* using the machine language. The user is not manipulating this computer interface by means of an elaborate conscious analogy, but as an integrated form with its own coherent structure and properties. From an "objective" point of view, this activity is totally novel – it shares no physical characteristics with moving real folders, and it is novel even for the traditional user of a computer who has issued commands exclusively from a keyboard rather than from a mouse. Yet the whole point of the desktop interface is that the integrated activity is immediately accessible and congenial. The reason, of course, is that a felicitous blend has been achieved which naturally inherits, in partial fashion, the right conceptual structure from both inputs, and then cultivates it into a fuller activity under pressure and constraints from reality and background knowledge.

The desktop example also nicely illustrates the non-arbitrary nature of blending: not just any discordant combination can be projected to the blend. Some discordant structure is irrelevant because it has no bad consequences – e.g., the trash can and the folders both sit on the desktop – but other discordant structure is objectionable – dragging the icon for a floppy disk to the trash as a command to eject the disk from the drive is notoriously disturbing to users. The inference from the domain of working at a desk that everything going into the trash is lost, and from the domain of computer use that everything deleted is irrecoverable, interfere with the intended inference that the trash can is a one-way chute between two worlds – the desktop interface and your actual desk.

Another point illustrated by the example is that input spaces are themselves often blends, often with an elaborate conceptual history. The domain of computer use has as input spaces, among possible others, the domain of computer operation and the domain of interpersonal command and performance. It is common to conceive of the deletion of files as an operation of complete destruction performed by the system at the command of the user. In fact, in the domain of actual computer operation, the files are not erased by that command, and can often be recovered. The user's sense of "deletion" is already a blend of computer operation and human activity. More generally, it is the fact that, by means of blending, keyboard manipulation is already conceived as simultaneously typing and high-level action and interaction that provides the appropriate partial structure to later blends like desktops with icons. The existence of a good blend can make possible the development of a better blend.

## 5. Advanced aspects of the network model

The previous sections have outlined the general characteristics of the cognitive operation of blending as reflected in superficially very diverse cases. Blending as a cognitive operation is elegant and uniform, but offers a great variety of different instantiations. A general program of research arises from inquiring into the general features of blending, the variety of purposes it serves, and the different ways in which it can be formally applied. In this section, we consider further general features of blending and constraints on the process. In subsequent sections, we consider more detailed taxonomies of blends according to structure, function, status with respect to reality, and internal logic. In all of these sections, we present research questions for the theory of blending and offer in some cases provisional or partial answers.

### 5.1. Spaces, domains, and knowledge

A mental space is built up in part by recruiting structure from (possibly many) conceptual domains and from local context. We can build different and incompatible spaces by recruiting from the same conceptual domain. Consider a personification of death as an evil magician versus a benevolent magician: the evil magician makes objects disappear forever, while the benevolent magician transforms objects into other objects. The evil magician is a personification for a standard notion of death; the benevolent magician is a personification for a notion of death as involving reincarnation. In each case, one input space is built up by recruiting from the conceptual domain for *magician* and the other is built up by recruiting from the conceptual domain for *death*. But the two cases recruit different structure. The generic spaces have different event structure (deletion versus transformation). The blended spaces have different structure (evil versus benevolent magician). The feature of *evil* versus *benevolent* arises as an inference from blending – in the source conceptual domain of magic, there is nothing evil about making an object vanish and nothing benevolent about turning it into something else; but in the blend, the object is *us*, and our attitudes about out own vanishing or transformation provide the evaluations.

Consider also *Italian is the daughter of Latin*" versus *Latin is the daughter of Italian* [because students of Italian become interested in studying Latin]. Each has input spaces built up from conceptual domains of progeneration and languages, but quite different structure is recruited from the conceptual domains into the input spaces. *Italian is the daughter of Latin: her ostentatious beauty is really a rebellion against her mother's austerity* recruits yet different structure from these conceptual domains to the input spaces. All three of these examples have the identical underlying conceptual domains, but quite different input spaces, generic spaces, and blends.

In our network model of conceptual projection, meaning is not constructed in any single space, but resides in the entire array and its connections. The "meaning" is not contained in the blended space. We know each space in the array – no matter how elaborate the network – and can work and modify all of them and their connections. During blending, conceptual work may be required at any site in the conceptual array. Spaces, domains, and frames can proliferate and be modified. Blending can be applied successively during that proliferation. Achieving useful counterpart structure and useful integration may require activating different input mental spaces, changing the recruitment of structure to them, establishing different generic connections between them, projecting different structure from the inputs to the blend, recruiting different frames to the blend, projecting different structure from the blend back to the inputs, multiplying the blends, and so on.

### 5.2. Integration of events

A fundamental motivating factor of blending is the integration of several events into a single unit. For example, although the boat race blend depends upon extensive connection of counterparts across different spaces, it also has integration of events: the sailing from one space is integrated with the sailing from the other space into a single event of racing, and this is the central point of the blend. In the desktop case, an action performed by the user of the computer is a single event that conceptually integrates the computer command and the manipulation of office items. It thus integrates both event components and conceptual counterparts. Even metaphoric mappings that ostensibly look most as if they depend entirely on the construction of metaphoric counterparts can have integration of events as a principal motivation and product. *He digested the book* of course has metaphoric counterparts, such as food and book, but it also projects an integration of events. In the source, digesting already constitutes an integration of a number of different events. But its counterpart in the target is, independent of the metaphor, a series of discrete events – taking up the book, reading it, parsing its individual sentences, finishing it, thinking about it, understanding it as a whole, and so on. The integrity in the source is projected to the blend so that this array of events in the target acquires a conceptual integration of its events into a unit. On one hand, the metaphor blends conceptual counterparts in the two spaces – eating and reading. On the other hand, the metaphor helps us to integrate some distinct event sequences in the space of reading. The blend exploits the integrity of events already present in the space of eating, and exports that integrity of events to the target space of reading. In the "digesting" metaphor, we export the integrity in the blend to induce an integrity of events in the target (picking up book, reading lines, finishing book, thinking about it, etc.). In the boat race, we export the integrity of events in the blend to induce an integrity of events in 1993 (preparing the boat, raising money, waving goodbye to well-wishers at the dock, trimming the sails, keeping the log, arriving at Boston, parting afterward, etc. etc. etc.) In both cases, there is a great range of events in one space (reading, 1993) that comes to acquire the integrity of an event structure in the blend (digesting, race). In some cases, like "digesting the book," the integration of events is already provided in one of the inputs and is recruited by the blend to provide integration for the other input. In other cases, like the boat race, the integration emerges in the blend.

In grammar, certain abstract scenarios are represented by corresponding grammatical constructions. A given construction goes with a given schematic scenario. To describe events using that construction is to prompt the hearer to integrate those events into that schematic scenario. *John kicked the ball over the fence* describes events of kicking and motion of the ball in a direction. It uses a construction that represents the schematic scenario in which an action causes an object to move in a direction. When we use the same construction to describe an act of praying and an event of boys coming home in *We prayed the boys home*,'[4] we are prompting hearers to integrate the events into the pattern of caused motion.

### 5.3. Recruiting and integrating internal connections from the inputs into the blend

Inputs will have internal connections that are motivated conceptually and experientially. For example, if the topic is a newspaper company, that company is linked to the newspaper (its product), the building (its location), its publicly-traded shares, and so on. As Nunberg (1978) has discussed, these connections motivate expressions like *The newspaper is on Main Street*, *The newspaper went out of business*, *The newspaper was sold for fifty million dollars*, and so on.

Blends make use of these connections in several creative ways. Consider the following example of a cartoon representing a powerful newspaper company about to succeed in a hostile takeover of a weaker automobile company that will be eliminated by selling off its assets. The cartoon shows a giant printing press smashing a car. This is a metaphorical blend like those we have seen in Section 4: input one has the stronger and weaker objects; input two has the contest between companies. The cross-space mapping is the basic metaphor that maps stronger objects destroying weaker objects to winning and losing. The strong heavy object is mapped onto the powerful newspaper company; the weaker object is mapped onto the weaker automobile company. But in the blend, we find the printing press as the strong heavy object and the car as the weak object. This is an efficient exploitation of internal connections: the printing press is a salient instrument of producing newspapers, and cars are the salient products of automobile companies. In the input, the printing press is not an instrument of destruction, but it has a force-dynamic function associated with crushing which can be associated with a car-smashing machine of the sort used in recycling automobiles. In the blend, the printing press is fused with both the company and the car-smashing machine. What is going on here? The blend must achieve three goals. First, given that the cartoon is a visual representation, the blend must be concrete and specific. Second, it must fit the frame of stronger and weaker object. Third, these objects in the blend must be properly connected to the companies in input two. The companies in input two, being abstract, cannot in themselves provide the corresponding concrete elements in the blend. The weaker and stronger objects in input one are concrete but not specific, and so cannot in themselves provide the corresponding specific elements in the blend. But we can exploit internal connections in the inputs to make the elements in the blend adequate. The printing press and the car are concrete, specific objects associated with the companies that can also be fit into the frame of the stronger object destroying the weaker object. They fit this frame in part because the printing press intrinsically has force-dynamic structure capable of destruction and in part because we are familiar with car-smashing machines. In the blend, two elements are simultaneously (i) two concrete, specific objects; (ii) a stronger object destroying a weaker object; and (iii) two companies.

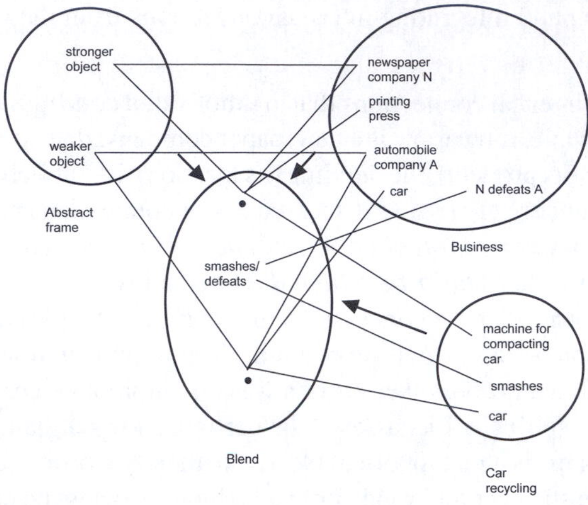


*Figure 9.*

Clearly, such a blend is creative. Not just any connections will do. There has to be a search for elements that simultaneously satisfy a number of constraints. Below, we will discuss some candidate constraints for recruiting internal connections to blends.

## 5.4. Opportunism and path-dependency

Although the laws of biology motivate all biological change, it is not possible to predict the evolution of a species, since its evolution will depend at each step on local accidents. The genetic structure that evolution has to work with at any moment depends upon the history of those accidents. The path of accidents shows opportunistic exploitation of existing structures of the organism or features of the environment. We can speak because an existing mammalian supralaryngeal airway, previously adapted for breathing and eating, could be opportunistically adapted for speech, at the cost, as Darwin observed, of making us liable to choke to death on our food.

Similarly, blending shows us that reason looks for accidents to exploit opportunistically. It is accidental that fusing the monk's paths and days but not the monks results in a blend that is easily completed by our standard frame of *two people approaching each other along a path*, but this serendipitous accident, once found, provides the solution to the problem. The printing-press blend is effective only because we know about printing presses and about car-recycling machines that happen to share a force-dynamic structure with printing presses. Had historical accident given us a world without these car-recycling machines (e.g., the world in 1950) and with a different prototypical method of printing (e.g., spraying ink), an entirely different blend would be required in order to achieve specificity, concreteness, conformity to the frame of stronger and weaker object, and proper connection to the companies in input two. Constructing that blend would require opportunism in the seeking of accidents to exploit.

Opportunism is sometimes displayed as a mark of wit: Consider *Banging a Tin Cup With a Silver Spoon*. This headline announced a news story about Orange County, whose financial managers lost much of the county's assets betting heavily on interest trends. Although the county remained extremely rich, it declared bankruptcy and asked creditors for debt forgiveness. The reporter described the county as a *wealthy deadbeat*. In one blend, Orange County is personified as a beggar with a tin cup. In another, it is personified as a wealthy individual with a silver spoon. Both of these blends are conventional. In a hyper-blend of these two blends, the county is personified as a wealthy beggar. It is accidental that a person can hold both a tin cup and a silver spoon and bang the cup with the spoon in the manner of a beggar drawing attention to his begging. The headline asks for applause for its ingenuity in finding these accidental connections. This turns out to be a general property of blends: they are judged to be better according as they exploit more accidental connections.

## 5.5. Entrenchment

Like other forms of thought and action, blends can be either entrenched or novel. *Digging your own grave* is a complex blend entrenched conceptually and linguistically. The Buddhist monk blend is novel and is used for only that one riddle. We often recruit entrenched projections to help us do on-line conceptual projection. On-line projections and entrenched projections are not different in kind; entrenched projections are on-line projections that have become entrenched. Our seemingly fixed projections are highly entrenched projections of an imaginative sort. Because the mechanisms of projection are shared in the two cases, entrenched structures are subject to transformation under work by on-line projection.

## 5.6. Fusion

### *5.6.1. Fusion of counterparts*

Blending can fuse counterparts in input spaces. In the monk example, the days are fused and the positions are fused; in the debate with Kant, fusion operates over issues, languages used, and modes of expression for debate.

But the fusion is not always simple. In the debate blend, the time of the debate is a fusion – there is only one time in the blend, not two times. But it is neither the time of the inputs nor some combination of them. It is a special transcendent time – it would be odd to say, "Two years ago, Kant disagreed with me, when I thought reason was a self-developing capacity."

### *5.6.2. Non-fusion of counterparts*

Blending need not fuse counterparts in input spaces. In the monk example, the two monks are not fused. In regatta, the two boats are not fused. In the debate with Kant, Kant and the modern philosopher are not fused.

### *5.6.3. Combination of non-counterparts*

Blends can combine non-counterpart elements that come from different inputs. Consider The Grim Reaper, which is a blend with several input spaces, including a space of harvest and a space of particular human death. A reaper in input 1 is the counterpart of Death in input 2, not of the skeleton, but since Death as a cause is metonymically associated with *skeleton* as an effect, the blend can combine the reaper (from one input) with the skeleton (from the other), even though they are not counterparts. Similarly, elements in a single input space that are metonymically related can be combined in the blend. Priests, monks, mourners, and members of lay brotherhoods that are associated with dying, funerals, burial, and afterlife are metonymically associated with Death. They are not counterparts of Death, but in the blend, an attire we associate with them – robe and cowl – can be the attire of The Grim Reaper. The cowl, pulled over the head of The Grim Reaper, at once evokes both connotations of death and the impression of Death as mysterious, unknown, and set apart from human society.

The possibility of combining non-counterparts on the basis of metonymic connections – like the connection between Death and a skeleton – gives blending a great power: the blend can combine elements that contribute to the desired effect *even though those elements are not counterparts.* The combined elements "go together" in evoking the same effect even if they do not "go together" according to the counterpart connections between the input spaces. In general, there are several vital conceptual relations that connect elements in mental spaces – Change, Identity, Time, Space, Cause-effect, Part-whole, Representation, Role-Value,

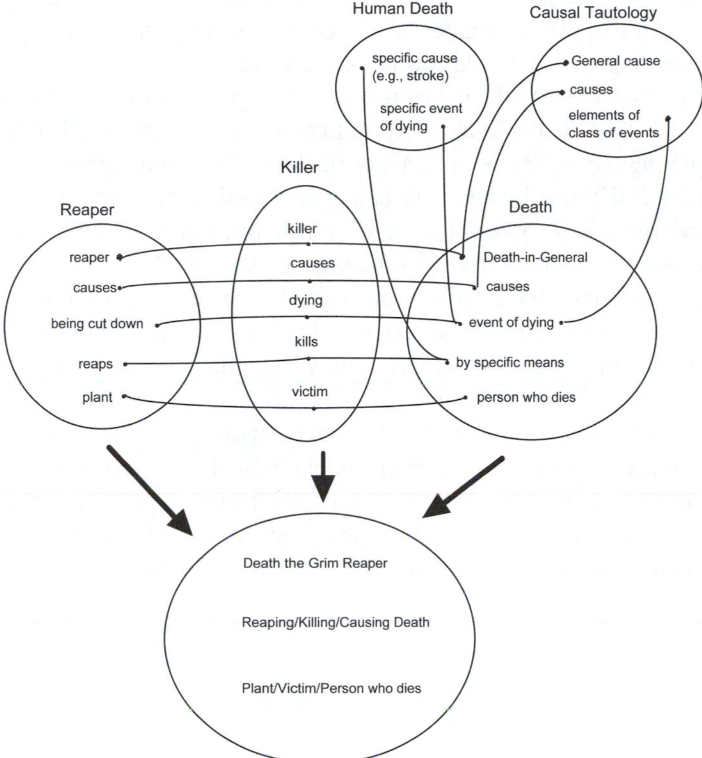


*Figure 10.*

Analogy, Disanalogy, Property, Similarity, Category, Intentionality, Uniqueness – and under blending these vital conceptual relations can be compressed to create more powerful and efficient structure in the blend. Compression in the blend of non-counterparts is routine. In *He was red-hot with anger; I could see smoke coming out his ears*, *heat* in one input has the metaphoric counterpart *anger* in the other input, but *anger* has a metonymic connection to physiological reactions, including redness of skin and increased body heat. *Heat* in the blend combines *heat* from the source input, *anger* from the target input, and *body heat* from the target input, even though the two "heats" in the inputs are not counterparts in the metaphor. (See the study by Lakoff and Kövecses, described in Lakoff, 1987.) The Birth Stork blend, which is based on the counterparts provided by the conventional metaphor BIRTH IS ARRIVAL, ingeniously provides a stork-with-diaper-sling that has as its counterpart in one input the vehicle of ARRIVAL and in the other input general causal processes of birth; the diaper belongs to neither of these counterparts, but because the baby, which is the product of birth, is metonymically associated with diapers, the diaper can be combined with the general process of birth and used concretely as part of the blend-vehicle.

The Birth Stork network makes use of some pre-existing blends. When an element in one state is later in a different state, we can compress this into a space in which the element undergoes a "change of state." When an element in one location is later in a different location, we can compress this into a space in which the element undergoes a "change of location." In general, when two spaces are related by both counterfactuality and temporal distance, we have the chance to compress those spaces and their vital relations into a single "change" blend. These two networks, "change of state" and "change of location" have, as metaphor theorists have noted, served as inputs to a further blend in which the change of state is blended with the change of location, as in *the water is coming to a boil.*

There is a third network related to these two: in one space, there is an element, but in a temporally prior space, there is no element. These two spaces also have outer-space vital relations of counterfactuality and time, and, following the general pattern, they are compressed into a single blend in which the element is always there, but undergoes a change of state from non-existence to existence.

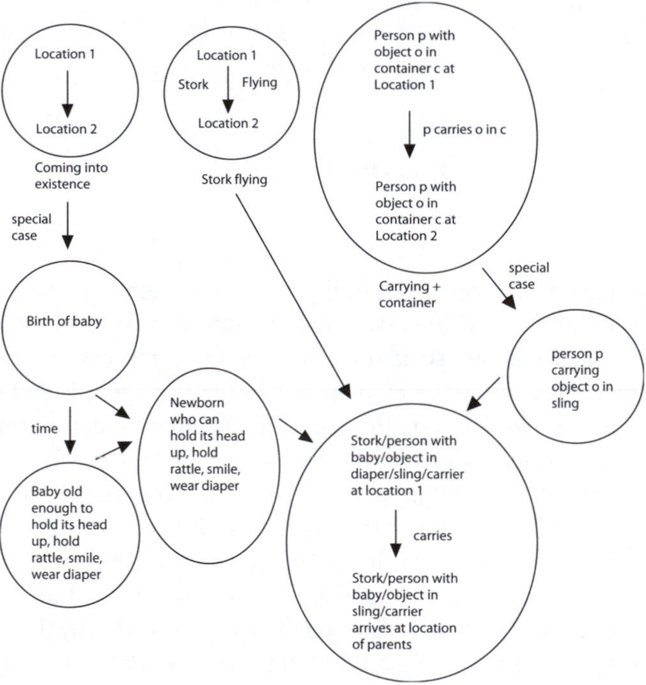


*Figure 11.*

This third blend of nothing-then-something is blended with the standard change of state/location blend into a very standard blend of "coming into existence." In this way, we understand the passage from nothing to something as motion from one location to another. This "coming into existence" blend is naturally used to frame birth as the coming into existence of the baby: "Has the baby arrived yet?" "It's on its way." "It should be here any day now."

Figure 11 takes as one of its inputs this already complicated blend of "coming into existence."

### 5.7. Biases

Composition, completion, and elaboration all recruit selectively from our most favored patterns of knowing and thinking. This makes blending a powerful cognitive instrument, but it also makes it highly subject to bias. Composition, completion, and elaboration operate for the most part automatically and below the horizon of conscious observation. This makes the detection of biases difficult. Seepage into the blend can come from defaults, prototypes, category information, conventional scenarios, and any other routine knowledge.

## 6. Overarching goals and governing principles

There is one overarching goal driving all of the principles of conceptual integration:

- Achieve human scale.

The constitutive and governing principles have the effect of creating blended spaces at human scale. The most obvious human scale situations have direct perception and action in familiar frames that are easily apprehended by human beings: an object falls, someone lifts an object, two people converse, one person goes somewhere. They typically have very few participants, direct intentionality, and immediate bodily effect and are immediately apprehended as coherent.

Once blending achieves a human-scale blend, the blend also counts as human-scale, and so can participate in producing other human-scale blends, in a bootstrapping pattern that characterizes much of cultural evolution.

To achieve a human-scale blend will often require imaginative transformations of elements and structure in integration network as they are projected to the blend. There are several sub-goals that are worth noting. They are:

- Compress what is diffuse.
- Obtain global insight.
- Strengthen vital relations.
- Come up with a story.
- Go from many to one.

Not all phenomena that meet the constitutive principles of conceptual integration are equally good blends. Some blends are better than others. There are governing principles that a blend can meet more or less well. These principles compete. In this technical sense, they are "optimality" principles. Here we discuss some of the governing principles we have been able to substantiate and some of these more specific blend structures.

Intensifying vital relations

*Compress what is diffuse by scaling a single vital conceptual relation or transforming vital conceptual relations into others. This is intensification of vital relations.*

Maximizing vital relations

*Create human scale structure in the blend by maximizing vital relations.*

Integration

*The blend must constitute a tightly integrated scene that can be manipulated as a unit. More generally, every space in the blend structure should have integration.*

Topology

*For any input space and any element in that space projected into the blend, it is optimal for the relations of the element in the blend to match the relations of its counterpart.*

Web

*Manipulating the blend as a unit must maintain the web of appropriate connections to the input spaces easily and without additional surveillance or computation.*

Unpacking

*The blend alone must enable the understander to unpack the blend to reconstruct the inputs, the cross-space mapping, the generic space, and the network of connections between all these spaces.*

Relevance

*All things being equal, if an element appears in the blend, there will be*

> *pressure to find significance for this element. Significance will include relevant links to other spaces and relevant functions in running the blend.*

## 6.1. Satisfaction of the governing principles in some basic kinds of conceptual integration network

### *6.1.1. Mirror networks*

To see a standard strategy of satisfying these governing principles, consider again three examples: the Buddhist monk, the Debate, and Regatta. Of course, they all have cross-space mapping, selective projection to the blend, and a generic space that applies to both inputs. In addition, in each of these cases, all of the spaces share a rich frame and much of its content: in the Buddhist monk, all the spaces have *man walking along a mountain path*; in the Debate, all the spaces have *philosopher musing on a philosophical problem*; in Regatta, all the spaces have *boat sailing along an ocean course.*

A *mirror network* is a conceptual integration network in which all spaces, inputs, generic, and blend, share topology given by an organizing frame. An organizing frame for a mental space is a frame that specifies the nature of the relevant activity, events, and participants. An abstract frame like *competition* is not an organizing frame, because it does not specify a cognitively representable type of activity and event structure.

Regatta, Debate with Kant, and the Buddhist monk are all mirror networks. Typically, in a mirror network, the common frame F inheres in the more elaborate frame FB in the blend. In the boat race example, the shared organizing frame *boat sailing along an ocean course* inheres in the more elaborate frame in the blend of *sailboats racing along an ocean course.* In the debate with Kant, the shared organizing frame *philosopher musing on a problem* inheres in the more elaborate frame in the blend of *philosophers debating about a problem.* In the Buddhist monk, the shared organizing frame *man walking along a mountain path* inheres in the more elaborate frame in the blend of *two men meeting on a mountain path.*

An organizing frame provides a topology for the space it organizes – that is, it provides a set of organizing relations among the elements in the space. When two spaces share the same organizing frame, they share the corresponding topology and so can easily be put into correspondence. Establishing a cross-space mapping between inputs is straightforward when they share the same organizing frame.

While spaces in a mirror network share topology at the level of an organizing frame (we call this frame topology or TF), they may differ at a more specific level (specific topology or TS). For example, in the boat race network, there are two elements that fit the role *boat* in the organizing frame and so have identical TF topology. More specific relations, however, define finer topologies that often differ. For example, in the boat race network, one of the elements fits the more specific frame *nineteenth-century clipper on a freight run* and the other fits the more specific frame *late-twentieth-century exotic catamaran on a speed run*. The two more specific frames are different, and so the topologies are different at the TS level. More precisely, we reserve the term "specific" or TS for finer topology that specifies values of roles that are in the organizing frame. These values may themselves be roles of a more finely specified frame. In our example, *boat* is a role of the organizing frame, *clipper* gives that role a more specific value and is itself a role of a more specific frame *clipper on a freight run*. Features of these more specific values – like monohull versus catamaran – can be projected to the blend.

There will also be incidental topology, TI, in both input spaces. We use the term TI for finer topology that does not have to be included or specified, given the organizing frame. In our example, it may be fully part of the actual ocean voyages that dolphins escort the boats and that they pass by a certain uncharted island, but these are not assigned a role in the organizing frame. In general, features of incidental topology can also be projected to the blend.

The selection of an organizing frame for a space is not a once-and-for-all decision. The organizing frame can be modified and elaborated as the integration network is constructed. Topology at the TF, TS, or TI level may come to be promoted or demoted as needed. For example, *obstacles* may be a role in the frame *boat making an ocean voyage*, and if the clipper has difficulty traveling near the uncharted island because of technical problems of navigation that had not been solved in 1853 while the catamaran has difficulty traveling near dolphins because it is forbidden under international law from sailing through a school of dolphins, then *uncharted island* for the clipper and *dolphins* for the catamaran get promoted to the TS level as fitting the role *obstacle*, while *uncharted island* for the catamaran and *dolphins* for the clipper remain at the TI level.

Organizing frame is shared by all spaces:

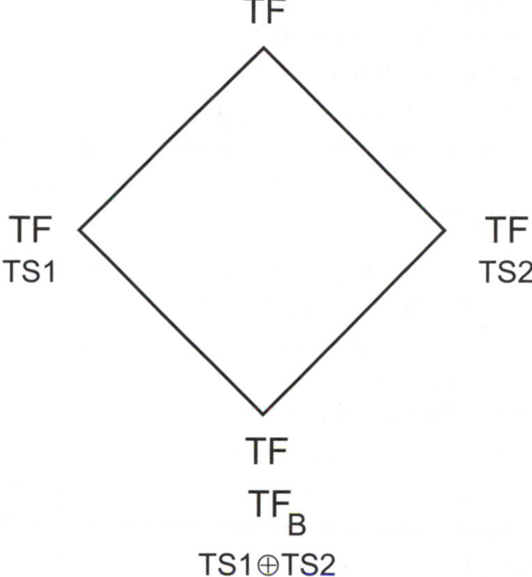


*Figure 12.* Mirror network

### *6.1.2. Shared topology network*

In a conceptual integration network over two inputs, the topology of the generic space is always shared by all four spaces – the blend, the two inputs, and the generic space. We will call a structure in which all spaces share the topology of a generic space a *shared topology network*. Four-space blends are *shared topology networks*, but multiple blends need not be, as we shall see below.

A mirror network is a shared topology network whose shared topology is moreover an organizing frame. Other shared topology networks do not share organizing frame but do share topology. For example, simple metaphors such as the portrayal of two business competitors as boxing opponents do not have a shared organizing frame: the source input in the example has *boxing* as its organizing frame, while the target input has *business competition* as its organizing frame. But the source and target inputs do share a higher-level structure of *competition* which gives them a shared topology and makes the cross-space mapping and the generic space possible.

The case of complex numbers is another example, where one input has the organizing frame of two-dimensional geometry and the other has the very different organizing frame of real/imaginary numbers. The development of the cross-space mapping and the recognition of the topology shared by the inputs required a long and arduous period of conceptual work by mathematicians, and it was only at the end of the historical process that the generic space defined by this cross-space mapping came to be recognized and named: a commutative ring.

We can now define a *mirror network* briefly and more systematically as a *shared topology network* whose generic space, cross-space mapping, and shared topology are all given by virtue of a shared organizing frame for all spaces.

### 6.1.3. Single-scope networks

A shared topology network is *single-scope* if the inputs have different organizing frames and one of them is projected to organize the blend. Its defining property is that the organizing frame of the blend is an extension of the organizing frame of one of the inputs but not the other: $TF_B > TF_1$.

The case of the two boxing business competitors is a single-scope network, whose generic space has an abstract relation of adversarial competition between two agents. The blend inherits the frame of Input 1, *boxing*. The cross-space mapping is metaphoric, with Input 1 as the source and Input 2 as the target.

In a simple metaphoric blend like this, projection from inputs to blend is highly asymmetric: one of the inputs but not the other supplies the organizing frame and therefore frame-topology. This is why it seems appropriate to call that input the *source input*. The projection of the source frame to the blend carries with it linguistic constructions (e.g., vocabulary) used to evoke the source frame. Of course, there are projections from the target input to the blend that also provide linguistic constructions for the blend, but they refer to elements below the TF level, at the TS or TI level. For example, if the two business competitors are named Murdoch and Iacocca, we may say that *Murdoch knocked Iacocca out*: *knocked out* belongs to the TF level of the source while *Murdoch* and *Iacocca* belong to the TS level of the target.

Any particular simple metaphoric single-scope network may have inhering within it a higher-order conventional metaphoric mapping, called by Lakoff and Johnson (1980) a *basic metaphor*. Such a basic metaphor is highly productive and inheres in indefinitely many particular constructions of meaning but is itself abstract. For example, the blend structure for the boxing business competitors is an active, on-line, specific conceptual structure that has inhering within it the abstract, basic metaphor of competition as physical combat. A basic metaphor itself never constitutes an active, complete, on-line construction of meaning. It always requires additional conceptual specification and projection to supply a particular construction of meaning.

### 6.1.4. Double-scope networks

A shared topology network is *double-scope* if the inputs are organized by different frames but some topology is projected from both frames to the blend to build the frame of the blend. Gruen's example of the computer desktop interface is a double-scope network. The two principal inputs have different organizing frames, the frame $F_1$ of office work with folders, files, trashcans on one hand, and the frame $F_2$ of traditional computer commands on the other. (There is also the lesser input of *choosing from a list.*) In the blend, some of the elements have F1 topology from one input while others have F2 topology from the other input.

The metaphor *digging your own grave* is also a double-scope network with frame structure projected from both inputs. Death and graves come from the source input of the "dying" scenario, but causality and intentionality are projected from the target input of discretionary action and mistakes that lead to failure, in the following way. In the target input, making mistakes is unintentional and brings one closer to failure. The blend receives this causal and intentional structure by selective projection from the target input: in the blend, digging is unintentional and brings one closer to death. But in the source input, both the causal order and the intentionality have the reverse structure: in this source, it is someone's dying that causes the grave to be dug and the digging is moreover intentional. The temporal order of events in the blend (digging before dying, making mistakes before failing) is also taken from the target input, not the source input.

Complex numbers are another case of a double-scope network. The inputs are respectively two dimensional space and real/imaginary numbers. Frame structure is projected from each of the inputs, e.g., angles, rotations, and coordinates from two-dimensional space, and multiplication, addition, and square roots, from the space of numbers.

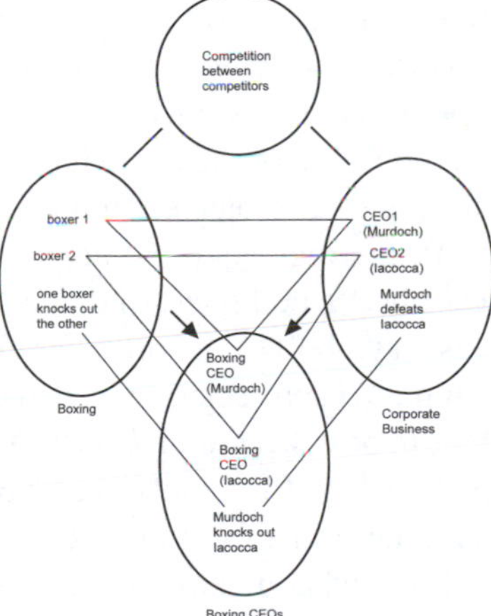


*Figure 13.* Double-scope network

We also see a double-scope network in *same-sex marriage*: input 1 has marriage but not same-sex partners; input 2 has same-sex partners but not marriage. The blend takes marriage from the TF level of input 1 and same-sex from the TF level of input 2.

In all these cases, as in most networks, the blended space develops emergent structure of its own, and ends up with a richer specific frame $F_B$. For example, in the case of complex numbers, multiplication in the blend includes addition of angles. This operation is unavailable in either of the inputs. The input of two-dimensional space doesn't have multiplication; the input of numbers doesn't have angles.

There is a gradient between single-scope and double-scope networks. Consider as an example the case in which one person, observing that the Vatican seems to be flat-footed in the metaphorical boxing match over abortion, says, "I suppose it's hard to bob and weave when you have a mitre on your head." The Pope's competition with an adversary is portrayed as a boxing match, where the Pope is impeded as a boxer by the mitre he is obliged as Pope to wear on ritual occasions, and we interpret this as meaning (with respect to the input space with the Pope) that his obligation as Pope to remain dignified impedes him in his competition. In the input space with the Pope, there is a relationship at the level of the organizing frame between the Pope and dignified behavior and also between the Pope and his mitre. The cross-space mapping between inputs does not give counterparts in Input 1 for the *required dignity* or *required headgear* elements in Input 2. The Pope's obligation and his headgear in Input 2 both project to the headgear of the boxing Pope in the blend.

In the organizing frame of the input of boxing, the boxers have no headgear that is an impediment. In the blend, the organizing frame is slightly different: it contains the role *heavy headgear that makes fighting difficult*. This organizing frame is an extension of the frame of boxing, not of the frame of Pope and Roman Catholicism. Specifically, the frame of the blend has all the roles of *boxing*. But, the headgear – namely, the mitre – is projected from input 2. In that input 2 frame, there is a crucial relation R: the dignity of the Pope makes it harder for him to compete because he must always be honest and decorous. In input 2, the role *mitre* is directly linked (as a symbol) to the role *dignity and obligation* of *Pope*. The crucial relation R in input 2 is projected to R' in the blend: the mitre/dignity makes it harder for the Pope to box. *Mitre* and *dignity* in input 2 are both projected to the same element in the blend, and, crucially, they have no counterpart in input 1. The blend gets an organizing frame from input 1 but also the frame-level relation R from input 2, and this is what makes it double-scope.

In the blend, we find all the elements of the frame of boxing plus the heavy and unwieldy mitre on the boxer's head. It turns out that having a heavy object on the head is an impediment to fighting, and so we have a very natural and automatic pattern completion of the blend, leading to a new frame *boxing as impeded by heavy headgear*. This frame is an extension of the organizing frame of input 1, not of input 2, but it is nonetheless double-scope. Recall that in *digging your own grave*, the cross-space mapping connected incompatible counterpart relations, such as direction of causality, and that to project causal direction to the blend, it was necessary therefore to choose one rather than the other of these counterpart relations. In the Pope example, because relation R in input 2 has no counterpart relation in input 1 (and *a fortiori* no incompatible counterpart relation), it can be projected to the blend (appropriately extended by completion), and no choice needs to be made between incompatible counterpart relations.

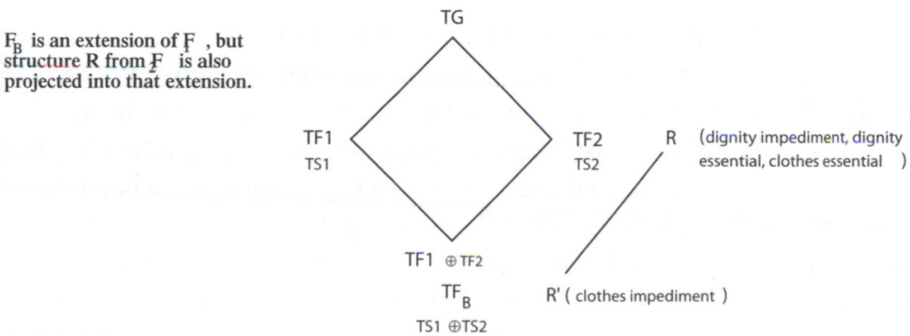


*Figure 14.* Asymmetric double-scope network

All conceptual projection appears to be particularly sensitive to certain kinds of abstract structure: causal relations, image-schematic relations, modalities, basic ontological categories, and event-shape. There are cases in shared topology networks where a relation is unspecified in the generic space but specified in incompatible ways in the inputs. For example, in the frame network of the Buddhist monk, all four spaces share the frame *man walking along a (directed) mountain path*, but Input 1 has a direction for that motion (up), and Input 2 has a different direction for that motion (down). The specific direction of the motion is part of the event-shape of the motion, and moreover it is projected from each input into the blend. This does not create a clash in the blend, because the counterpart monks in the inputs are not fused when projected to the blend, so we have in the blend one monk ascending and the other descending. The two specific directions do not correspond in the inputs and are not connected in the cross-space mapping.

### *6.1.5. Simplex networks*

A basic kind of conceptual integration network we have not explored in this article is a simplex network. Briefly, a simplex network has an abstract frame as one input and as the other input a specific situation that has no organizing frame at all for the purpose of the integration, and so no potential for competition with the organizing frame of the first input. For example, *Sally is the daughter of Paul* has the kinship frame *daughter-ego* as one input and as the other input a specific situation containing nothing but Sally and Paul. In the blend, Sally is framed as *daughter* and Paul is framed as *ego.* There is crucial emergent structure in this blend: the blend has a role *daughter of Paul* that is unavailable from either input. Moreover, the *ego* role in the kinship input is specified in the blend to be a father rather than a mother.

### 6.2. Vital relations

Before we complete the taxonomy of blend structures by topology, we must discuss a further governing constraint, concerning the compression of vital relations. Recruiting special connections in one of the inputs can be used to bring in additional structure that assists in satisfying the governing principles. Where an element in the blend has a topology that does not match the topology of a counterpart in one input, special connections internal to that input can be recruited to increase topological connections and help satisfy other governing principles.

For example, in the Birth Stork blend, the diaper has a topology of being used as a sling (and more generally as part of the vehicle), which does not match the topology of the diaper in the Newborn input. But bringing the diaper into the blend helps satisfy Web, since it establishes more connections to the Birth space; and Unpacking, since it includes an element of the Birth space along with elements from the space of Transport; and Relevance, since an alternative way of carrying the baby – in a paper sack, or net, for example – would not have the Relevance of close association with the baby in the Birth space.

The analysis is similar for the cowl worn by the Grim Reaper. In the blend, the cowl has a topology – attire of the agent – that is not matched by the cowl in the input space. But exploiting the special and distant connection in the Death space of the relationship between dying and the priest and the attire of the priest, and thereby bringing the cowl into the blend, helps satisfy Web, Unpacking, and Relevance.

The skeleton as the form of the Grim Reaper is slightly more complicated, because in this case the skeleton in the Death input has some useful topology – on its own, it is frightening or at least impressive as a salient result of the death of a human being. Exploiting the special connection in the Death input of the relationship between dying and the final result of a skeleton, in order to bring the skeleton into the blend, helps satisfy Topology as well.

We have seen a continuum of blend structures – from simplex networks to mirror networks to single-scope and double-scope networks. Along this continuum, the topological connections in the basic cross-space mapping between input spaces typically grow weaker, but other connections are employed for the purpose of maximizing Topology, Integration, and Web. By contrast, as this continuum is ascended, it grows easier to satisfy Unpacking since the blend increasingly incorporates special connections from one input without counterparts in the basic cross-space mapping. Generally, along this continuum, as the basic cross-space topology is weakened, Unpacking is strengthened.

Intensification of vital relations

> *When an element is projected from an input to the blend and a second element from that input is projected because of its vital relation to the first, intensify the vital relation in the blend.*

We saw above that blending can compress non-counterpart elements from a single input, such as Death, the cowl of the priest, and the skeleton of the person who has died. The metonymic distance is large between abstract death as the general cause of all deaths and the cowl worn by a certain kind of participant in a ritual associated with particular deaths. But in the blend, the metonymic connection is direct: the cowl is the attire of Death. Similarly, the skeleton after decomposition of the body is a distant product of death. But in the blend the skeleton is actually a body part of Death. The fact that metonymy is preserved in such cases can be viewed as a consequence of Topology. The Intensification of Vital Relations constraint additionally specifies that the metonymies get tighter under projection: distant cause-effect is compressed into part-whole.

Satisfying the Intensification of Vital Relations constraint is not a matter of blindly projecting vital relations. The internal integration of the blend provides opportunities for some acceptable vital relations but not for others. Since Death is an active person in the blend, and active persons are known to have skeletons (although they are not normally visible), the part-whole relation between the skeleton and the body becomes available as the counterpart of the distant cause-effect relation in the input. Intensifying Vital Relations under projection typically optimizes integration in the blend, since it helps build a tighter and more easily manipulated unit.

Now we return to the taxonomy of blend structures by topology.

### *6.2.1. Single-scope network with compression of vital relation*

Suppose the example of the boxing business competitors is elaborated slightly – the competitors are now a newspaper magnate and an automobile magnate, and they are identifiable in part because one has a rolled-up newspaper in his back pocket and the other has a car key on a key ring hanging out of his back pocket, each with an appropriate label. The organizing frame of the blend is still projected from the Boxing input, so the network is single-scope. But there is a frame relation in Input 2 that, in accord with the intensification of vital relations constraint, is projected to the TI level of the blend. The frame-relation in Input 2 is that the newspaper is the commercial product of the magnate's activities. The newspaper in the blend is connected to a newspaper in Input 2. The newspaper in Input 2 has no counterpart in Input 1 and its relevant topology in Input 2 – product of the magnate's activities – is not the topology in the blend – copy of newspaper read by the boxer-magnate. The blend has an element – newspaper – projected from an input but the topology of that element in the blend is inherited from neither input. The metonymy between the magnate and the newspaper as commercial product in the blend is tightened under projection, so that it becomes part of the magnate's appearance. The analysis is similar for the car key.

### *6.2.2. Double-scope network with intensification of vital relation*

Recall the visual cartoon in which the printing press smashes the car. We pointed out that the printing press and car have topology in the blend (the press crushes and the car is crushed) that their counterparts in Input 2 do not have (the press is an instrument of making newspapers and the car is a salient product of the automobile company). Additionally, the printing press and car in Input 2 have no counterparts in Input 1. Interestingly, the elements that did not project their input-topology (printing press and car) end up being the only objects in the blend. This contrasts with the cartoon where the newspaper-in-the-back-pocket is only an optional element in the frame organizing the blend. The cartoon of the printing press smashing the car is remarkable because it is a case where Integration and Topology are maximized by recruiting vital relations in Input 2. Because the topologies of strong and weak object on the one hand and competing companies on the other will match only at a very abstract level, we find that in addition to the companies, objects closely connected to them are projected to the blend in a way that closely matches and elaborates the Input 1 topology of strong and weak objects.

This blend structure is double-scope because the topology of strong and weak object comes from Input 1 but the topology of intentionality (the printing press intends to crush the car and the car hates it) comes from Input 2, where it is attached not to the printing press and the automobile but rather to the respective companies. The projection to the printing press and the car in the blend is symmetric: their topology in the blend matches frame topology in both inputs.

This example emphasizes that conceptual projection is a dynamic process that cannot be adequately represented by a static drawing. Once the conceptual projection is achieved, it may look as if the printing press has always corresponded to the stronger object and the car to the weaker. But in the cross-space mapping, the printing press and the car play no role; they have no counterparts in Input 1. Rather, the cross-space counterparts are stronger object and newspaper company, weaker object and automobile company. Under projection of the metonymies from Input 2, the printing press *in the blend* becomes the counterpart of the stronger object in Input 1, and the car *in the blend* becomes the counterpart of the weaker object in Input 1.

This example also shows that identity is metonymy of zero distance. The metonymic relation in Input 2 between company and commercial product is transformed into identity in the blend, where the printing press is identically both a printing press and the newspaper company to which it is metonymically related as an instrument (in one of the inputs).

#### *6.2.3. Double-scope network with intensification of vital relations and additional frame recruitment*

Suppose the cartoon now contains the newspaper magnate operating the printing press to smash the car, which is being driven by the car magnate. Here the blend structure becomes elaborate through the recruitment to the blend of an additional adversaries-with-instruments frame in which adversaries fight with opposing instruments, and in which the winning adversary has the superior instrument. Now the printing press and car in Input 2 have counterparts in the adversaries-with-instruments frame: in input 2, the printing press is a symbol of a capacity for productivity that is an instrument of corporate competition, and the car is a product that is an instrument of corporate competition; these instruments in Input 2 are the counterparts of the instruments in the adversaries-with-instruments frame. Now, the topology of opposing instruments in the blend matches the topology of opposing instruments in the adversaries-with-instruments frame. This frame has the useful property of aligning superiority of instrument with superiority of adversary. In this case, we see that exploiting special internal connections in Input 2 makes it possible to recruit a frame that makes Topology much stronger in the blend structure.

### 6.3. Governing principles and single-scope networks

In the single-scope network exemplified by the business competitors portrayed metaphorically as boxers, Integration in the blend is automatically satisfied because the blend inherits an organizing frame from the source, boxing. Topology is satisfied between blend and source for the same reason. But Topology is also satisfied between blend and target because the conventional metaphor of competition as physical combat has aligned the relevant topologies of the source and target input spaces. Thus, when an element in the blend inherits topology from an element in either input that is involved in the cross-space metaphoric mapping, the topology it inherits is automatically, by virtue of the metaphor, compatible with the topology of that input element's counterpart in the other input. Web is similarly satisfied by this shared topology. Unpacking is provided just as it was for a mirror network – although the blend is integrated at the TF level, it is disintegrated at the TS level. Suppose, for example, that the competitors are represented in a cartoon as boxing in business suits. This lack of integration between business suits and boxing prompts us to unpack to two different spaces, one of boxing and one of business. In the same way, if we know that *Murdoch* and *Iacocca* refer to businessmen and not boxers, then their use in the sentence *Murdoch knocked out Iacocca* directs us to the TS level of the input of businessmen, and this helps satisfy Unpacking.

### 6.4. Governing principles and double-scope networks

In a double-scope network, Topology, Integration, and Web are not satisfied in such an automatic and routine fashion: it is necessary to use a frame that has been developed specifically for the blend and that has central emergent structure. (This may be why double-scope networks – such as the desktop, complex numbers, and digging your own grave – are often typically thought of as more creative, at least until they become entrenched.) In double-scope networks, then, we expect to see increasing competition between governing principles and increasingly many opportunities for failure to satisfy them.

The computer desktop provides an illustration of many of these competitions and opportunities for failure. First let us consider an aspect of the desktop blend in which Topology clashes with Integration, and Integration of the blend wins. The purpose of the blend is to provide an integrated conceptual space that can serve as the basis for integrated action. The basic integrative principle of the computer desktop is that everything is on the two-dimensional computer screen. But in the input space of real office work, the trashcan is not on the desktop. By Topology, the location of the trashcan as not on the desktop would be projected to the computer interface blend; but doing so would destroy the internal integration of the blend, which is why, on the computer screen desktop, the trashcan is on the desktop. Integration of the blend in this case can only be achieved by relaxing the topology constraint as we develop a new frame for the blend.

There are at least two reasons why we are content to relax topology in this way. First, the topology that is being dropped from the desktop input is incidental to the cross-space mapping – the three-dimensionality of the office and the position of trashcans under desks has no counterpart in the cross-space mapping to the input of computer operation. Second, as we have mentioned, the purpose of constructing this blend is to develop a conceptual basis for extended action, and not to draw conclusions about the input space of offices. In a contrasting case, like the Buddhist monk, the purpose is to draw conclusions about topology of input spaces – specifically coincidence of locations and times. In such a case, relaxing Topology is likely to allow inferences in the blend that would project wrongly or not at all back to the input, and so defeat the purpose of the blend. In that case, Topology is not relaxed.

It is also possible for the frame elaborated for a blend to fail to satisfy the governing constraints. The most noticeable such failure for the computer desktop is the use of the trashcan both as the container of what is to be deleted and as the instrument of ejecting floppy disks. This failure involves failures of Integration, Topology, and Web.

The trashcan-for-both-deletion-and-ejection violates Integration for the frame elaborated for the blend in three ways. First, in the frame elaborated for the blend, the dual roles of the trashcan are contradictory, since one ejects the floppy disk to keep it rather than discard it. Second, in the frame elaborated for the blend, all other operations of dragging one icon to another have as their result that the first is *contained* in the second, but that is not so in the uniquely exceptional case of dragging the floppy to the trashcan. Third, for all other manipulations of icons on the desktop, the result is a *computation*, but in this case it is a physical *interaction* at the level of hardware.

The trashcan-for-both-deletion-and-ejection violates Topology. In the input of office spaces, putting an object in a folder or in the trashcan results in containment. This topology is projected to the blend. The trashcan in the desktop is like any icon that represents a metaphoric container: if we drag a file to a folder icon or to the trashcan icon, the file is then deposited there, and this is the topology of the input of office spaces. However, putting the floppy disk icon into the trashcan icon so as to eject it is an exceptional and contrary case that violates the projection of topology from the input of offices. It also violates topology by not preserving the relation Input 2 (the space of real offices) that items transferred to the trashcan are unwanted and destined to become non-retrievable.

The trashcan-for-both-deletion-and-ejection also violates Web. The very opportunity of ejecting floppy disks from the computer desktop creates non-optimal web connections, since sometimes the floppy disk is "inside" the world of computer operations and sometimes it is "inside" the world of the real office.

We now turn to questions of optimality in word-processing programs on the desktop. The command sequence Select-Copy-Paste on word-processing applications violates both Topology and Web. It violates Topology as follows. In the Input where text is actually copied by scribes or Xerox machines, copying (after selection) is a one-step operation. There is no pasting and no clipboard. Properties specific to the Integration in the blend make it convenient to decompose this operation into two steps, but they do not map topologically onto corresponding operations in the Input of "real copying."

The labels "Copy" and "Paste" chosen for these two operations in the blend also violate Web: the Copy operation in the blend (which actually produces no visible change in the text) does not correspond to the Copy operation in the Input (which does produce visible change); the Paste operation, which does produce change, is closer to "copying" in the Input, but the label "Paste" suggests a counterpart (pasting), which is not even part of the copying process. Not surprisingly, these flaws in the overall blend lead to mistakes by novice users. They click Copy instead of Paste, or try sequences like: Select – Select Insertion Point – Copy. This fails miserably because the first selection (not marked for copying) is lost when the second selection occurs, and anyway Copy at that point is the wrong command. Mistakes like this are interesting however, because they represent the user's effort to maintain optimal Topology and Web connections. If double selection were possible on the blended interface (as it is, in terms of attention, in the Input), Copy and Paste could easily be reintegrated into a single process operating on both selections, and the attempted sequence would be viable. In fact, the Microsoft Word® application being used to type the present text has a keyboard command (with no counterpart in the menus) which comes closer to this conception.

The "Cut and Paste" method of moving text is a less severe violation, because the projected operations from the "office" Input are plausible and properly web-connected. But it does add conceptual complexity to what is more easily conceived of as simple unitary "moving." Recent versions of Word® have added to the interface the possibility of selecting and dragging text directly to the appropriate location. The portion of text does not actually "move" (only the arrow does) until the mouse is unclicked.

Despite all these failures to satisfy optimality principles, nonetheless the desktop blend draws rich and effective structure from familiar frames, and users are able to use it in a rudimentary fashion very quickly and to learn the elaborated frame, warts and all. The non-optimality creates difficulty for novices, who are reluctant to put the floppy disk in the trashcan since by topology it should then be lost, but this difficulty is forgotten by advanced users, who learn a less optimal but more elaborate blend.

The fact that in double-scope networks the organizing frame of the blend is not available by extension from the organizing frame of either input increases chances of non-optimality and of competition between the governing principles, but it also offers opportunity for creativity in attempting to satisfy the governing principles. Pressure to satisfy governing principles in highly complex double-scope networks has historically given rise to some of the most fundamental and creative scientific discoveries. The development of the concept of complex numbers in mathematics, discussed in chapter four, is a case in point. The complex number blend turns out to be a double-scope shared topology network. Some key elements in each input have no counterparts in the basic cross-space mapping. The operation of multiplication for numbers has no counterpart in the geometry input, and the angles of vectors in the geometry input have no counterparts in the number input. The blend, however, inherits both the multiplication operation from the frame of the "number" input and the vector angle from the frame of the "geometric" input. This is already enough to make it a double-scope shared topology network, since multiplication in the blend has TF2 topology while angle in the blend has TF1 topology. But furthermore, in the blend, multiplication includes addition of angles as one of its constitutive components. This is discovered by running the blend; it turns out to be a highly unexpected essential property of the new concept of number which has emerged. So in this instance, the pressures to satisfy optimality in this double-scope shared topology network led to important mathematical discovery. Jeff Lansing has pointed out to us other marvelous examples of important scientific blends leading to discovery (by Fourier, Maxwell, and Faraday), which suggests that this is a general process. We emphasize that this type of creativity is possible by virtue of the competition of governing principles and the power of blending to accommodate them.

Unpacking is actually relatively easy to satisfy in the double-scope case since key elements in the blend cannot all be projected back to the same organizing frame of one of the inputs. For example, in *digging your own grave*, the grave-digger is responsible for the death, and this structure cannot be provided by the single organizing frame of digging graves, making it clear that the blend must be unpacked to the organizing frames of different inputs.

### 6.5. Competition among pressures motivated by optimality

At the top level of our model, there are general constitutive principles characteristics of all blend structures, like cross-space mappings. At a lower level, there are governing principles like Integration. But these governing principles themselves compete, as we have seen and as we will discuss further, and that competition results in a variety of yet lower-level governing pressures for constructing the blend. In this section, we discuss the candidate governing pressures for which we have found evidence.

Non-disintegration

> *Neutralize projections and topological relations that would disintegrate the blend.*

For example, as we saw above in the section called "Governing principles and double-scope networks," since the integrative principle of the computer desktop blend is that everything is on the computer desktop, Topology must be relaxed in projecting the trashcan to the blend so as to filter out the three-dimensionality of the real office space. In the regatta example, weather in 1853 (even if known) is not projected because it would clash with the projected 1993 weather. In the Debate with Kant, the language, German, from Input 1, is not projected; Integration in the debate frame requires a single language.

Non-displacement

*Do not disconnect valuable web connections to inputs.*

The computer desktop has web connections to the space of computer operations, in which all shifts of focus require only a simple click. For example, if a user is running five different applications on the desktop and wants to see only one of them, he can click "Hide Others" (conversely, "Show others"); to see a given document partially occluded by another, he need only click anywhere on the desired document. But in the space of offices, to hide everything on your desk except the one thing you wish to focus on would require complex physical operations. If these operations were all projected to the blend, it would sever its useful web connections to the input of computer operation. Function guides competition here. The web connection to "change of focus" in the computer operations input is important because the desktop interface is designed to run a computer. If its function were to simulate the working environment of an office worker, then the complexity of the physical operations would be maintained at the expense of computing efficiency.

Non-displacement combines with Integration to force novel integrations in the blend. For instance, in the case of the metaphor *digging one's own grave*, the blend's causal, temporal, and intentional structure (*digger is unaware of his actions, a deep enough grave causes death*) are projected from the target space of mistakes and failure. This web connection is crucial to the reasoning, but would be destroyed if the commonplace structure of the source (death followed by conscious grave-digging by somebody else) were projected. In the Nixon-in-France example, we project to the blend Nixon, but not his U.S. citizenship, which would prevent him from being president of France, thus cutting off a crucial web link from the blend to the second input.

Non-interference

*Avoid projections from input spaces to the blend that defeat each other in the blend.*

For example, in the space of office work, we often write "discard" across the top of an outdated version to be discarded. In the computer desktop, the icon for a file has only one place for a label. If we projected to the computer desktop the operation of labeling the document "discard" by making a click-command that put that label on the icon, we would lose the title of the file. So the "title" label and the "discard" label from the space of office work defeat each other if both are projected to the blend.

In a counterfactual blend like *If Napoleon had been the son of Alexander, he would have won the battle of Waterloo*, we do not attempt to project Napoleon's actual father. There is no inference that if Napoleon had been the son of Alexander, Charles Bonaparte would have been Alexander, although formally this leads to an integrated scene. (If the goal is to point out that Napoleon lacked some military qualities that perhaps Alexander possessed, it is odd to say *If Charles Bonaparte had been Alexander, Napoleon would have won the battle of Waterloo.* But if we really mean that some deficiency was actually transmitted by Charles, through genes or education, then the counterfactual sounds ok. The blend in that case contains an efficient father appropriately connected to Charles and Alexander.) The traits of fathers Alexander and Charles would defeat each other in the blend.

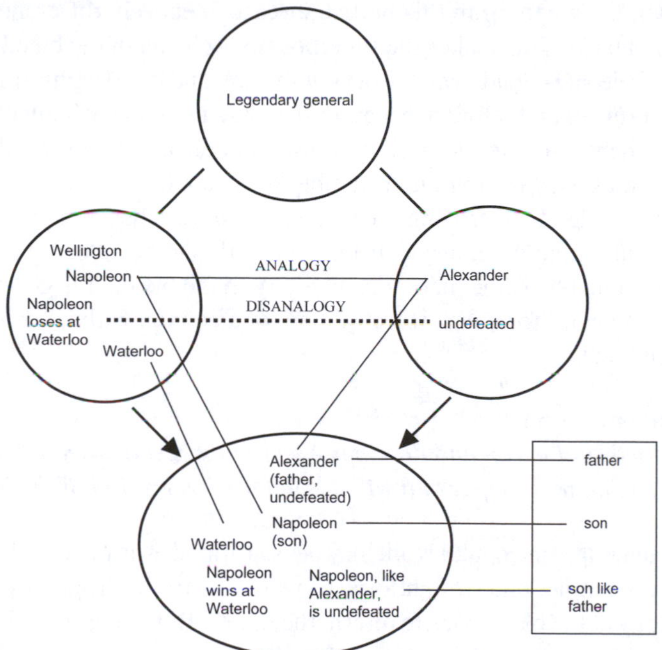


*Figure 15.*

In the metaphor of Death as the Grim Reaper, Death, which inherits from the cadaver its skeleton, could additionally inherit its shredded, decayed clothing. The cowl would thus be shredded, but this interferes with the projection of the cowl as a piece of clothing of a live priest at the funeral. Technically, the projections from the blend to the input, of the skeleton, the sickle, etc., are one-to-one, but the projection of the shredded cowl would be one-to-many (the priest's head-dress/ the dead man's hat). Similarly, in a "bad" desktop blend, the projection (from the blend to the space of real offices) of the label on the desktop file would be one-to-many: the title of a document, or the instruction to discard it.

Non-ambiguity

*Do not create ambiguity in the blend that interferes with the computation.*

The method of ejecting floppy disks "through" the trash on the computer desktop violates several constraints, as we have seen above. It also violates non-ambiguity. Superposition of icon a over icon b "means" copying/inserting the contents of a "into" b. So a plausible interpretation of the disk icon's being moved over the trashcan icon is that the contents of the disk are transferred to the trashcan. But in fact, the meaning in this particular case is entirely different ("eject disk from computer"). This makes the superposition schema in the blend ambiguous. Similarly, a debate-blend, which works with Kant and philosophy, might fail with a deity or prophet and religion, because we would not know whether to count victory in the debate as superior religious insight or as heresy. We would not have a straightforward way of running the ambiguous blend.

A cartoon blend advertising the magazine *Success* has a man blended into a rocket shooting into outer space. People judge this to be a "bad metaphor." One reason, presumably, is the inherent ambiguity in the blend: it is good for a rocket to fly, but not good for a man to be shot out of a cannon with no control over his actions and fate.

Backward projection

*As the blend is run and develops emergent structure, avoid backward projection to an input that will disrupt the integration of the input itself.*

During blending, conceptual work may be performed at any site in the conceptual array. For example, one straightforward way to optimize Topology is to project the topology of the blend back to reform the inputs. But doing so will conflict with the original Integration of the inputs. Usually, this is undesirable, which gives rise to pressure to avoid backward projection.

For example, under pressure from Integration, the desktop blend places the trashcan on the desktop, but projecting this relation backward to the input of the actual desks would disrupt their efficient use. In the grave-digging metaphor, we do not want to start thinking, through backward projection to the source input, that digging graves actually causes death. We do not interpret the printing press cartoon as additionally suggesting that smashing cars with a printing press is a good idea.

Many blends, however, have the purpose of modifying the structure of an input. Coulson (1995) considers such blends.

### 6.6. The Topology Constraint and the Invariance Hypothesis

One goal of the network model is to account for inferencing during conceptual projection. For example, we have shown in our pedagogical riddle of the Buddhist monk that if the blend and its inputs have the same co-occurrence of locations and times (under Topology) and this mirroring survives as we run the blend (under Web), then the inference of an *encounter* in the blend entails inferences for the inputs which effectively solve the riddle.

An earlier attempt to account for inferencing during conceptual projection in the special case of metaphor goes under the name of "the invariance principle" – launched by analysis in Turner (1987: 143–148), stated briefly in Lakoff and Turner (1989: 82), and analyzed in Lakoff (1989), Turner (1991: 172–182), Lakoff (1993), and Turner (1996b). The invariance principle proposes that in metaphor, we attempt to project image-schematic structure (with inferences) from source to target while avoiding the creation of an image-schematic clash in the target. Importing new image-schematic structure to the target by projection does not violate the invariance principle if the original target is appropriately indeterminate. Asserting by means of the metaphor that the target's image-schematic structure is to be overridden does not violate the constraint, since the changed target contains no clash.

Our network model of conceptual projection extends and modifies the invariance principle. We emphasize the importance of image-schematic topology in all conceptual projection, not only metaphoric projection. In the network model, there are productive matches of image-schematic structure between inputs, generic space, and blend. First, consider the generic space and the inputs. The structure of the finished generic space, taken as applying to both inputs, frequently contains extensive image-schematic structure, as in the riddle of the Buddhist monk, where the two input spaces do not stand in metaphoric relation (we do not understand the descending monk by metaphoric projection from the ascending monk or conversely).

Second, consider the blend and the inputs. There is always important matching of image-schematic topology between blend and inputs under Topology: the Buddhist monk blend requires an extensive topological match between parts of the blend and each of the inputs.

But the Topology constraint is not a generalization of the invariance principle to non-metaphoric cases. The Topology constraint does not require that we project image-schematic structure from one input to the other or from the blend to the inputs. It does require that we project image-schematic structure from the inputs to the blend. In the Buddhist monk riddle, we do not import image-schematic structure from one input to the other, because *the detailed relevant image-schematic structure already exists in each input independently of the other input*. Furthermore, although we "understand" the Buddhist monk input spaces by drawing on the image-schematic structure of the "encounter" in the blend, we do not project that image-schematic structure from the blend to the inputs; quite the contrary. The blend has the image-schema for "encounter"; the inputs do not have it; we do not project that image-schema to the inputs; instead, we infer from this image-schema in the blend a different and complicated relation of image-schemas between the inputs: namely, there exists in each input a time-location pair, and these two pairs in the two inputs have the identical times and the identical locations.

Topological structure in the blend may be elaborated that is important for the construction of meaning but that is not projected identically back to the inputs. This is clearest in the case of science fiction or fantasy blends meant for entertainment, where we are not solving over the inputs, and where Topology and Web may be thoroughly relaxed, but it is also true for cases where inferences are drawn for the inputs: the existence of the race in the *Great American II* blend is crucial for the construction of meaning and inference, but the race structure in the blend does not displace the structure of the inputs in which each boat is making a solitary run. Each space in the conceptual projection has a different structure, and each space is useful.

Now let us consider examples that are felt to be clearly metaphoric. What is the relationship for clearly metaphoric cases between the topology constraint – which we claim applies to all integration networks – and the invariance principle – which was advanced exclusively for the metaphoric cases? The network model, far from eliminating the need for a theory of metaphor and a consideration of the mapping of image-schemas, requires such a theory, in the following way. Consider the status of the generic space and the origin of its content. Typically, the generic space contains image-schematic topology, which is taken to apply to two inputs. Often, much or even all of that content is supplied processually by activating a conventional metaphoric mapping between the domains underlying the two inputs. Indeed, in many cases, some of them quite important, it may be that the image-schematic structure belongs to the target only because metaphoric projection installed it in the target. In sum, a counterpart mapping is needed to launch on-line blending, and that counterpart structure is often supplied by activating a conventional metaphor, and the counterpart structure may have been created by the basic metaphor projection rather than merely picked out as a template for the projection.

Now consider the case where the metaphoric meaning that arises in an integration network is not supplied by activating a conventional conceptual metaphor. In these cases, the invariance principle survives with modification into our model. Under the topology and web constraints, the projection of image-schematic structure from the source space plays an important role in blending. Under the topology constraint and the non-disintegration pressure for the inputs, image-schematic clashes are avoided in the target space. Moreover, if there is a clash of topology between source and target, then since it is the target we care about, we typically prefer the topology in the target: structure in the blend needed to deliver inferences for the target will accord with the important image-schematic structure in the target as opposed to the source. We see a clear example of this in digging your own grave, where the causal, intentional, frame, and internal event structure of the blend suit the topology of the target space but not at all that of the source space, although some structure – the foolishness of failing to recognize concrete actions – comes from the source into the blend. In general, the topology of the blend needed for delivering inferences for the target cannot do so if it conflicts with the protected topology of the target. A clash of this nature is to be avoided. This principle is equivalent in spirit and effect to the invariance principle's proposal that an image-schematic clash is not to be created in the target.

But the network model and its Topology principle differ from the two-domain model of metaphor and its invariance principle. Under the invariance principle, all the inferential structure had to be supplied by either the target and its protected image-schematic structure or by the source image-schematic structure projected to the target. We have demonstrated that the blend often has *emergent structure* available from neither input but important for inferencing. In *digging your own grave*, there is important causal structure and event structure: the person addressed is digging a grave and the existence of a satisfactory grave causes death. This structure is image-schematic, but it is not given by either input. The causal structure of the blend is the inverse of the causal structure of the source, and in the target it is not given, prior to the blend, that the person addressed is performing bad acts, that performing them completes in a cumulative manner a certain gradual action, or that completing that action causes disaster. This image-schematic structure, with its inferences, is developed in the blend so as to permit the projection of certain inferences to the target that the target can accept.

Similarly, the desktop has emergent structure provided by neither input, such as dragging a file icon from the hard disk icon to the floppy disk icon to *duplicate* the file onto the floppy disk rather than *move* it off the hard disk and onto the floppy disk. The image-schematic topology of the blend in this instance violates the topology of the source of actual desktops and moving things on them, and it is not given by the target space of symbolic computer commands, although it can be projected there.

There is another important difference. The two-domain model of metaphor with its invariance principle is not a theory of the development of metaphoric mappings. In our view, the development of a conventional metaphoric mapping involves conceptual integration. In cases where useful inferences or structure have emerged in the blend and become thoroughly conventional, the blend itself becomes the conventional conceptual structure of the "target" domain. Additionally, blending is always available to someone who activates a conventional metaphor, and many of the conventional metaphors studied so far, like ANGER IS HEAT or The Grim Reaper, are actually conventional blends.

## 7. Additional dimensions of conceptual integration

### 7.1. Activation

In Fauconnier and Turner (1994), we provided a taxonomy of blends by kind of conceptual activation. The parameters in this taxonomy are: the number and type of spaces involved; the degree to which any particular space in the array is active as a working space in which new on-line conceptual construction must be done; the degree of blending and of abstraction; whether the vocabulary transfer is on-line or permanent; the number of conceptual domains involved in building up the inputs and the blend; whether or not the conceptual domain involved is consciously focused upon; and the extent to which the blended space gives birth to a new conceptual domain. The existence of a blended space does not entail that it serve as the basis for an imaginary conceptual domain, like the ghost ships of the boatrace example or the sinners of Dante's hell. Most blends, while serving important local cognitive functions, have no corresponding conceptual domains.

### 7.2. Functions of blends and topic spaces

The function of the desktop blend is to provide an integrated activity that the computer user can inhabit; naturally, the integration principle dominates. But in the monk example, the function of the blend is to solve for a puzzle in the inputs; naturally, the web principle dominates. The many examples analyzed in previous work on blending supply a survey of functions of blends. They include: reasoning on inputs (the monk example); adding meaning and emotion to inputs (enthusiasm in the boat race example); creating rhetorical presence (Oakley 1995) for some aspect of the inputs (*If gnatcatchers were dolphins, we would not be permitting them to become extinct*); jokes (analyzed by Seana Coulson); conceptual change (*artificial life*); cultural change (*same-sex marriage*); provisional category extension (*he's a real fish*); enhancing one of the inputs (the debate with Kant enhances the modern philosophy teacher's authority, status, etc.); supplying new action (desktop); providing integrated conceptual structure over an unintegrated array (as in giving the structure of caused motion to unintegrated events in *John sped the toy car around the Christmas tree*); and integrating the performance of actions (learning to ski). It is important to remember that functions cannot be predicted from structural features.

For functional reasons, the input spaces are rhetorically unequal. For example, in the boat race, it is 1993 that the reporter cares about and talks about. It is 1993 that he is interested in understanding and reporting fully. We label 1993 the *topic space* of the projection. It is possible for there to be more than one topic space (in the monk example, both spaces are equally topic spaces). It is also possible for the topic space to shift: if we are descendants of the captain of *Northern Light*, it may be 1853 that we care about understanding. Coulson (1995) shows that a source input space in a metaphoric projection can be the topic space.

## 8. Summary and further results

Conceptual integration – "blending" – is a basic cognitive operation. Conceptual integration networks involve input spaces, generic spaces, and blended spaces. There is a cross-space mapping of counterpart connections between input spaces and selective projection of structure from the inputs to the blend. Blends develop through composition, completion, and elaboration. Blends provide the possibility of backward projection to the inputs of inferential and other structure. Conceptual integration networks arise under competing governing principles of Topology, Integration, Web, Unpacking, Relevance, Intensification of Vital Relations, and Maximizing Vital Relations. Some basic patterns of satisfying these constraints are simplex networks, mirror networks, single-scope networks, and double-scope networks.

There are many other results of this research that can only be referred to here, without further explanation. We provide an analysis of grammatical constructions used to evoke conceptual integration, and of the way those grammatical constructions can be composed to evoke compositions of conceptual integrations. We analyze the mechanisms of frame integration, including composition of frame integrations. Unsurprisingly, we find that the construction of meaning is not truth-conditionally compositional: construction of meaning is not just a matter of specifying contextual elements and composing truth conditions. However, it turns out that there *is* compositionality at the level of the general schemes for conceptual integration networks and at the level of the syntactic forms that prompt for those schemes. We show that one purpose of grammatical constructions is to prompt for conceptual integrations of certain types. We also show that there is a process of *formal* blending at the level of grammar that is parallel to the process of *conceptual* blending, and that the two processes interact in intricate ways. In particular, conceptual blending can guide formal blending to produce new grammatical constructions suited to evoke just those conceptual blends. In these ways, blending is a central process of grammar. We analyze the role of conceptual integration in conceiving of space, form, and motion. We explore typical uses of conceptual integration in literature and the visual arts. We argue that conceptual integration interacts with cognitive activities like category assignment, analogy, metaphor, framing, metonymy, grammatical constructions, and so on. Moreover, the model of conceptual intergation suggests that these are not sharply distinguished kinds of cognitive activity. Distinctions among the products of conceptual integration are real, but arise from a number of interacting graded dimensions of difference. A number of locations in the grid of all these dimensions stand out as prototypes or cognitive reference points, and these locations have been given the name "categorization," "framing," "metaphor," and so on. These reference points are convenient, but there are not sharp divisions in the very nature of the types of phenomena that fall under these labels. The underlying cognitive operations are general, while the differences stem from the nature of the appropriate domains and mappings and the many interacting dimensions along which they vary.

Further research on blending is presented at http://blending.stanford.edu.

## 9. Conclusion

This paper has presented evidence for a general cognitive operation, conceptual integration, which builds up networks of connected spaces – inputs, generic, and blended spaces. The construction of such networks depends quite generally on establishing cross-space mappings of the sort commonly studied in theories of metaphor and analogy. But metaphor and analogy phenomena are only a small subset of the range of conceptual integration phenomena. Conceptual integration networks are equally prominent in counterfactuals, category extension, event integration, grammatical constructions, conceptual change (as in scientific evolution), and literary and rhetorical invention. The salient feature of such networks is the construction of a blended space, which develops specific emergent structure and dynamics while remaining linked to the overall network. Projection in a network can occur in different ways and in different directions, as we analyze in the taxonomy of Section 6. Theories of metaphor and analogy have typically focused on the case where projection is one-way (from a "source" to a "target") and they have overlooked the construction of blended spaces. Accordingly, the overall picture is even richer than previously envisioned, and any explicit computational modeling of the entire process will presumably face obstacles in addition to the already formidable ones encountered for analogy. At the same time, however, the conceptual integration view yields a far more unified general conception of meaning construction at all levels, and this should prove to be a major simplification.

It is remarkable that blending – a general-purpose, fundamental, indispensable cognitive operation, routinely employed in a variety of domains, commonly interactive with other cognitive operations that have received extensive analysis – should have received so little systematic attention in the study of cognition and language. The routine and largely unconscious nature of blending may have helped it escape scrutiny. The many well-known spectacular blends – sirens, mermaids, chimerae, space aliens, cybernetic organisms, Bambi – may have made blending seem merely exotic. Blending is a central, orderly, powerful, systematic, and commonplace cognitive operation. We have proposed a theoretical model of its constitutive and governing principles.

## Notes

1. There is widespread agreement in research on analogy and metaphor that cross-space mappings operate and transfer inferences by extracting or creating common schematic structure. The modeling of such processes has typically focused on the stage at which two domains are already appropriately structured and alignment takes place. Most researchers acknowledge, however, that this is only a part (perhaps even a small part) of the entire process, given the richness of domains and the corresponding multitude of ways to structure them (or "re-represent" them). These issues are discussed in many places (e.g. Burns 1995; Hofstadter 1985, 1995a,b; Holyoak and Thagard 1994; Forbus et al. 1997; Hummel and Holyoak 1996). The work we present in this article does not bear directly on this issue (but see note 3). It takes as given the undeniable, but admittedly still poorly understood cognitive capacity for schema induction and cross-domain mapping.

   What we find with respect to cross-space mappings is:

   - they operate in many phenomena other than metaphor and analogy;
   - they operate extensively in the construction of simple everyday sentence meaning;
   - they operate not just between a source and a target, but more generally between the various spaces of a conceptual integration network, including generic and blended spaces.

   Our analyses of conceptual integration do, inevitably, have some consequences for the research on cross-space mapping. For example, we find evidence against all three of the claims in Dedre Gentner's classic paper on structure mapping (Gentner 1983). (i) We find that, as a general principle, analogy is not compositional; the meaning of an analogy does not derive from the meaning of its parts. For example, "This surgeon is a butcher" has as part of its central meaning "incompetence," which is not available from either the input for the surgeon or the input for the butcher, but which is emergent in the blend. Personifying Death as a magician who is evil because he makes people disappear depends upon the emergence of *evil* in the blend: absent the blend, Death is not intentional and hence not evil, and a magician who performs disappearing tricks is not evil either. (ii) We find, as a general principle, that mapping does depend upon specific content of the domains and not just on structural properties: the attribution of incompetence to the surgeon-butcher depends upon attitudes toward what happens to human bodies. (iii) We find, as a general principle, that there are not clean distinctions in kind between various products of conceptual projection and conceptual integration, but rather several interacting gradients of distinction. On the other hand, we concur in general with Holyoak and Thagard (1989) and Holland, Holyoak, Nisbett, and Thagard (1986) that pragmatic goals and purposes influence mapping, and with Keane, Ledgeway, and Duff (1994) that cognitive constraints (including, e.g., constraints on working memory, influence from background knowledge, influence of prior activity) influence mapping.

2. For example, if $(r,\theta) = a + bi$ and
$(r',\theta') = a' + b'i$ , then
$(r,\theta) \times (r', \theta') = (rr', \theta+\theta') =$
1. $(a+bi) \times (a'+b'i) = aa'-bb' + (a'b+ab')i$
3. Douglas Hofstadter (p.c.) reports his discovery of how to "make" new geometries by blending. Taking projective geometry as a generic, and Euclidean as a source, he obtained a dual target for the latter, and a new "contrajective" geometry as a blend of the Euclidean and the Euclidual. Adrian Robert (in press) has shown that informal proofs in mathematics involve massive on-line blending of schematic structures, performed unconsciously by authors and readers of proofs.
4. "So far, the people of this small textile town in northwestern Carolina have been unable to pray Mrs. Smith's two little boys home again." (NY Times). This is an example of the Caused Motion construction studied in particular by Goldberg (1994), who explicitly addresses the issue of fusing grammatical constructions, within the framework of Construction Grammar (Fillmore and Kay nd ms). We see this fusion as the reflex of conceptual blending. Fauconnier and Turner (1996) and Mandelblit (1997) offer detailed accounts of the Causative Construction in French and Hebrew respectively, using the blending approach. We also see Langacker's general approach to grammar as very congenial to the one described here. In Langacker's Cognitive Grammar, schemas are put in correspondence and integrated in succession to form functional assemblies. Interestingly, emergent structure also develops at this elementary level of sentence formation.

## References

Barsalou, Lawrence
1996 Perceptual symbol systems. Manuscript, University of Chicago.
Burns, Bruce
1995 *Fluid Concepts and Creative Analogy:* A Review. *AI Magazine* 16(3): 81–83.

Coulson, Seana
1995 Analogic and metaphoric mapping in blended spaces. *Center for Research in Language Newsletter* 9(1): 2–12.
1997 Semantic leaps: Frame-shifting and conceptual blending. Ph. D. dissertation, University of California, San Diego.
Cutrer, Michelle
1994 Time and tense in narratives and everyday language. Ph.D. dissertation, University of California, San Diego.
Dinsmore, John
1991 *Partitioned Representations.* Dordrecht: Kluwer.
Fauconnier, Gilles
1994 *Mental Spaces.* New York: Cambridge University Press.
1997 *Mappings in Thought and Language.* Cambridge: Cambridge University Press.
1990 Domains and Connections. *Cognitive Linguistics* 1(1): 151–174.
Fauconnier, Gilles and Eve Sweetser
1996 *Spaces, Worlds, and Grammar.* Chicago: University of Chicago Press.
Fauconnier, Gilles and Mark Turner
1994 Conceptual projection and middle spaces. UCSD: Department of Cognitive Science Technical Report 9401. Available from http://cogsci.ucsd.edu.
1996 Blending as a central process of grammar. In *Conceptual Structure, Discourse, and Language*, Adele Goldberg (ed.), Stanford: Center for the Study of Language and Information. Distributed by Cambridge University Press.
2002 *The Way We Think.* New York: Basic Books.
Fillmore, Charles J. and Paul Kay
Undated ms. On Grammatical Constructions. University of California at Berkeley.
Fong, Heatherbell
1988 The stony idiom of the brain: A study in the syntax and semantics of metaphors. Ph.D. dissertation. University of California, San Diego.
Forbus, Kenneth D., Dedre Gentner, and Keith Law
1994 MAC/FAC: A model of similarity-based retrieval. *Cognitive Science* 19: 141–205.
Forbus, Kenneth D., Dedre Gentner, Arthur Markman, and Ronald Ferguson
1997 Analogy just looks like high level perception: Why a domain-general approach to analogical mapping is right. Manuscript, Northwestern University.
Freeman, Margaret
1997 Grounded spaces: Deictic -self anaphors in the poetry of Emily Dickinson. *Language and Literature* 6(1): 7–28.
French, Robert M.
1995 *The Subtlety of Sameness.* Cambridge, MA: The MIT Press.
Gentner, Dedre
1983 Structure-mapping: A theoretical framework for analogy. *Cognitive Science* 7: 155–170.
1989 The mechanisms of analogical reasoning. In *Similarity and Analogical Reasoning*, S. Vosniadou and A. Ortony (eds.), 199–241. Cambridge: Cambridge University Press.

Gibbs, Raymond W., Jr.
1994 *The Poetics of Mind: Figurative Thought, Language, and Understanding.* Cambridge: Cambridge University Press.

Glucksberg, Sam and Boas Keysar
1990 Understanding metaphorical comparisons: Beyond similarity. *Psychological Review* 97: 3–18.

Goffman, Ervin
1974 *Frame Analysis.* New York: Harper and Row.

Goldberg, Adele
1994 *Constructions.* Chicago: University of Chicago Press.

Goodman, Nelson
1947 The problem of counterfactual conditionals. *Journal of Philosophy* 44: 113–128.

Grush, Rick
1995 Cognition and emulation. Ph.D. dissertation, University of California, San Diego.

Hofstadter, Douglas
1985 Analogies and roles in human and machine thinking. In *Metamagical Themas,* D. Hofstadter, chapter 24. New York: Bantam Books.
1995a *Fluid Concepts and Creative Analogies.* New York: Basic Books.
1995b A Review of *Mental Leaps: Analogy in Creative Thought.* AI Magazine, 16(3): 75–80.

Holland, John H., Keith J. Holyoak, Richard E. Nisbett, and Paul Thagard
1986 *Induction: Processes of Inference, Learning, and Discovery.* Cambridge, MA: Bradford Books/MIT Press.

Holyoak, Keith J. and Paul Thagard
1989 Analogical mapping by constraint satisfaction. *Cognitive Science* 13: 295–355.
1994 *Mental Leaps: Analogy in Creative Thought.* Cambridge, MA: MIT Press.

Hummel, John and Keith Holyoak
1996 LISA: A computational model of analogical inference and schema induction. In *Proceedings of the Eighteenth Annual Conference of the Cognitive Science Society,* Garrison Cottrell (ed.), 352–357. Lawrence Erlbaum: Mahwah, NJ.

Hutchins, Edwin
1995 *Cognition in the Wild.* Cambridge: MIT Press.

Indurkhya, Bipin
1992 *Metaphor and Cognition: An Interactionist Approach.* Dordrecht: Kluwer.

Johnson-Laird, Philip N.
1983 *Mental Models.* Cambridge, MA: Harvard University Press.

Kahneman, Daniel
1995 Varieties of counterfactual thinking. In *What Might Have Been: The Social Psychology of Counterfactual Thinking,* Neal J. Roese and James M. Olson (eds.). Lawrence Erlbaum: Hillsdale, N.J.

Keane, Mark T., Time Ledgeway, and Stuart Duff
1994 Constraints on analogical mapping: A comparison of three models. *Cognitive Science* 18: 387–438.

Kline, Morris
1980 *Mathematics: The Loss of Certainty.* Oxford: Oxford University Press.

Koestler, Arthur
1964 *The Act of Creation.* NY: Macmillan.

Kunda, Ziva, Dale T. Miller, and Teresa Clare
1990 Combining social concepts: the role of causal reasoning. *Cognitive Science* 14: 551–577.

Lakoff, George
1987 *Women, Fire, and Dangerous Things.* Chicago: University of Chicago Press.
1989 The invariance hypothesis: Do metaphors preserve cognitive topology? Paper delivered at the Duisburg Cognitive Linguistics Conference. Available from the Linguistic Agency at the University of Duisburg.
1993 The contemporary theory of metaphor. In *Metaphor and Thought*, Andrew Ortony (ed.), 202–251. 2nd ed. Cambridge: Cambridge University Press.

Lakoff, George and Mark Johnson
1980 *Metaphors we Live By.* Chicago: University of Chicago Press.

Lakoff, George and Rafael E. Núñez
2000 *Where Mathematics Comes From.* New York: Basic Books.

Lakoff, George and Mark Turner
1989 *More than Cool Reason: A Field Guide to Poetic Metaphor.* Chicago: Chicago University Press.

Langacker, Ronald W.
1987 *Foundations of Cognitive Grammar*, vol. I: *Theoretical Prerequisites.* Stanford: Stanford University Press
1991 *Foundations of Cognitive Grammar*, vol. II: *Descriptive Application.* Stanford: Stanford University Press.
1993 Reference-point constructions. *Cognitive Linguistics* 4(1): 1–38.

Lewis, David
1972 *We, the Navigators. The Ancient Art of Landfinding in the Pacific.* Honolulu: The University Press of Hawaii.

Mandelblit, Nili
1997 Grammatical blending: Creative and schematic aspects in sentence processing and translation. Ph.D. dissertation, University of California, San Diego.

Mandelblit, Nili and Oron Zachar
in press The notion of unit and its development in Cognitive Science. *Cognitive Science.*

Mitchell, Melanie
1993 *Analogy-Making as Perception.* Cambridge: MIT Press.

Moser, David and Douglas Hofstadter
undated ms. Errors: A royal road to the mind. Center for Research on Concepts and Cognition. Indiana University.

Nunberg, Geoffrey
1978 *The Pragmatics of Reference.* Bloomington, IN: Indiana University Linguistics Club.

Oakley, Todd
1995 Presence: the conceptual basis of rhetorical effect. Ph. D. dissertation, University of Maryland.

Ortony, Andrew
1979a Beyond literal similarity. *Psychological Review* 86: 161–180.
1979b The role of similarity in similes and metaphors. In *Metaphor and Thought*, A. Ortony (ed.), 186–201. Cambridge: Cambridge University Press.

Robert, Adrian
in press Blending in the interpretation of mathematical proofs. In *Conceptual Structure, Discourse, and Language*, II Jean-Pierre Koenig et al. (eds.), Stanford: Center for the Study of Language and Information. Distributed by Cambridge University Press.

Schwartz, Daniel L. and John B. Black
1996 Shuttling between depictive models and abstract rules: Induction and fallback. *Cognitive Science* 20: 457–497.

Sweetser, Eve
1990 *From Etymology to Pragmatics: The Mind-as-Body Metaphor in Semantic Structure and Semantic Change*. Cambridge: Cambridge University Press.
1997 Mental spaces and cognitive linguistics: A cognitively realistic approach to compositionality. Fifth International Cognitive Linguistics Conference.

Talmy, Leonard
1977 Rubber-sheet Cognition in Language. *Proceedings of the 13th Regional Meeting of the Chicago Linguistic Society* 13: 612–628.
1978 Figure and ground in complex sentences. In *Universals of Human Language*. Volume 4: *Syntax,* Joseph H. Greenberg (ed.), 625–649. Stanford: Stanford University Press.

Tetlock, Philip and Aaron Belkin
1996 Counterfactual thought experiments in world politics: Logical, methodological, and psychological perspectives. In *Counterfactual Thought Experiments in World Politics: Logical, Methodological, and Psychological Perspectives*, Philip E. Tetlock and Aaron Belkin (eds.), 3–38. Princeton: Princeton University Press.

Turner, Mark
1987 *Death is the Mother of Beauty: Mind, Metaphor, Criticism.* Chicago: Chicago University Press.
1991 *Reading Minds: The Study of English in the Age of Cognitive Science.* Princeton: Princeton University Press.
1996a Conceptual blending and counterfactual argument in the social and behavioral sciences In *Counterfactual Thought Experiments in World Politics*, Philip Tetlock and Aaron Belkin (eds.), 291–295. Princeton: Princeton University Press.
1996b *The Literary Mind: The Origins of Language and Thought.* New York: Oxford University Press.

Turner, Mark and Gilles Fauconnier
1995 Conceptual integration and formal expression. *Journal of Metaphor and Symbolic Activity* 10(3): 183–04.

in press Conceptual Integration in Counterfactuals. In *Conceptual Structure, Discourse, and Language*, II, J.-P. Koenig (ed.). Stanford: Center for the Study of Language and Information. Distributed by Cambridge University Press.

Van Hoek, Karen
1997 *Anaphora and Conceptual Structure.* Chicago: University of Chicago Press.

Veale, Tony
1996 Pastiche: A metaphor-centred computational model of conceptual blending, with special reference to cinematic borrowing. Manuscript.

Zbikowski, Lawrence
1997 Conceptual blending and song. Manuscript, University of Chicago.

Zribi-Hertz, Anne
1989 Anaphor binding and narrative point of view: English reflexive pronouns in sentence and discourse. *Language* 65: 695–727.

# Chapter 10
# Frame semantics

## Frame semantics
*Charles J. Fillmore*

### 1. Introduction

With the term 'frame semantics' I have in mind a research program in empirical semantics and a descriptive framework for presenting the results of such research. Frame semantics offers a particular way of looking at word meanings, as well as a way of characterizing principles for creating new words and phrases, for adding new meanings to words, and for assembling the meanings of elements in a text into the total meaning of the text. By the term 'frame' I have in mind any system of concepts related in such a way that to understand any one of them you have to understand the whole structure in which it fits; when one of the things in such a structure is introduced into a text, or into a conversation, all of the others are automatically made available. I intend the word 'frame' as used here to be a general cover term for the set of concepts variously known, in the literature on natural language understanding, as 'schema', 'script', 'scenario', 'ideational scaffolding', 'cognitive model', or 'folk theory'.[1]

Frame semantics comes out of traditions of empirical semantics rather than formal semantics. It is most akin to ethnographic semantics, the work of the anthropologist who moves into an alien culture and asks such questions as, 'What categories of experience are encoded by the members of this speech community through the linguistic choices that they make when they talk?' A frame semantics outlook is not (or is not necessarily) incompatible with work and results in formal semantics; but it differs importantly from formal semantics in emphasizing the continuities, rather than the discontinuities, between language and experience. The ideas I will be presenting in this paper represent not so much a genuine theory of empirical semantics as a set of warnings about the kinds of problems such a theory will have to deal with. If we wish, we can think of the remarks I make as 'pre-formal' rather than 'non-formalist'; I claim to be listing, and as well as I can to be describing, phenomena which must be well understood and carefully described before serious formal theorizing about them can become possible.

In the view I am presenting, words represent categorizations of experience, and

Originally published in 1982 in *Linguistics in the Morning Calm*, Linguistic Society of Korea (ed.), 111–137. Seoul: Hanshin Publishing Company. Reprinted with permission.

each of these categories is underlain by a motivating situation occurring against a background of knowledge and experience. With respect to word meanings, frame semantic research can be thought of as the effort to understand what reason a speech community might have found for creating the category represented by the word, and to explain the word's meaning by presenting and clarifying that reason.

An analogy that I find helpful in distinguishing the operation and the goals of frame semantics from those of standard views of compositional semantics is between a grammar and a set of tools – tools like hammers and knives, but also like clocks and shoes and pencils. To know about tools is to know what they look like and what they are made of – the phonology and morphology, so to speak – but it is also to know what people use them for, why people are interested in doing the things that they use them for, and maybe even what kinds of people use them. In this analogy, it is possible to think of a linguistic text, not as a record of 'small meanings' which give the interpreter the job of assembling these into a 'big meaning' (the meaning of the containing text), but rather as a record of the tools that somebody used in carrying out a particular activity. The job of interpreting a text, then, is analogous to the job of figuring out what activity the people had to be engaged in who used these tools in this order.

## 2. A private history of the concept 'frame'

I trace my own interest in semantic frames through my career-long interest in lexical structure and lexical semantics. As a graduate student (at the University of Michigan in the late fifties) I spent a lot of time exploring the co-occurrence privileges of words, and I tried to develop distribution classes of English words using strings of words or strings of word classes as the 'frames' within which I could discover appropriate classes of mutually substitutable elements. This way of working, standard for a long time in phonological and morphological investigations, had been developed with particular rigor for purposes of syntactic description by Charles Fries (Fries 1952) and played an important role in the development of 'tagmemic formulas' in the work of Kenneth Pike (Pike 1967), the scholars who most directly influenced my thinking during this period. Substitutability within the same 'slot' in such a 'frame' was subject to certain (poorly articulated) conditions of meaning-preservation or structure-preservation, or sometimes merely meaningfulness-preservation. In this conception, the 'frame' (with its single open 'slot') was considered capable of leading to the discovery of important functioning word classes or grammatical categories. As an example of the workings of such a procedure, we can take the frame consisting of two complete clauses and a gap between them, as in *John is Mary's husband – he doesn't live with her.* The substitution in this frame of *but* and *yet* suggests that these two words have (by this diagnostic at least) very similar functions; insertion of *moreover* or *however* suggest the existence of conjunctions functioning semantically similarly to *but* and *yet* but requiring sentence boundaries. The conjunctions AND and OR can meaningfully be inserted into the frame, but in each case (and in each case with different effect) the logical or rhetorical 'point' of the whole utterance differs importantly from that brought about by *but* or *yet*. In each of these cases, what one came to know about these words was the kind of structures with which they could occur and what function they had within those structures.

In the early sixties, together with William S.-Y. Wang and eventually D. Terence Langendoen and a number of other colleagues, I was associated with the Project on Linguistic Analysis at the Ohio State University. My work on that project was largely devoted to the classification of English verbs, but now not only according to the surface-syntactic frames which were hospitable to them, but also according to their grammatical 'behavior', thought of in terms of the sensitivity of structures containing them to particular grammatical 'transformations.' This project was whole-heartedly transformationalist, basing its operations at first on the earliest work on English transformational grammar by Chomsky (1957) and Lees (1961), and in its later stages on advances within the theory suggested by the work of Peter Rosenbaum (Rosenbaum 1967) and the book which established the standard working paradigm for transformationalist studies of English, Chomsky (1965). What animated this work was the belief that discoveries in the 'behavior' of particular classes of words led to discoveries in the structure of the grammar of English. This was so because it was believed that the distributional properties of individual words discovered by this research could only be accommodated if the grammar of the language operated under particular working principles. My own work from this period included a small monograph on indirect object verbs (Fillmore 1961) and a paper which pointed to the eventual recognition of the transformational cycle as an operating principle in a formal grammar of English (Fillmore 1963).

The project's work on verbs was at first completely syntactic, in the sense that what was sought was, for each verb, a full account (expressed in terms of subcategorization features) of the deep structure syntactic frames which were hospitable to it, and a full account (expressed in terms of rule features) of the various paths or 'transformational histories' by which sentences containing them could be transformed into surface sentences. The kind of work I have in mind was carried on with much greater thoroughness by Fred Householder and his colleagues at Indiana University (Householder et al 1964), and with extreme care and sophistication by Maurice Gross and his team in Paris on the verbs and adjectives of French (Gross 1975).

In the late sixties I began to believe that certain kinds of groupings of verbs and classifications of clause types could be stated more meaningfully if the structures with which verbs were initially associated were described in terms of the semantic roles of their associated arguments. I had become aware of certain American and European work on dependency grammar and valence theory, and it seemed clear to me that what was really important about a verb was its 'semantic valence' (as one might call it), a description of the semantic role of its arguments. Valence theory and dependency grammar did not assign the same classificatory role to the 'predicate' (or 'VP') that one found in transformationalist work (see, e.g., Tesnière 1959); the kind of semantic classifications that I needed could be made more complete and sensible, I believed, if, instead of relying on theoretically separate kinds of distributional statements such as 'strict subcategorization features' and 'selectional features,' one could take into account the semantic roles of all arguments of a predication, that of the 'subject' being simply one of them. Questioning, ultimately, the relevance of the assumed basic immediate-constituency cut between subject and predicate, I proposed that verbs could be seen as basically having two kinds of features relevant to their distribution in sentences: the first a deep-structure valence description expressed in terms of what I called 'case frames', the second a description in terms of rule features. What I called 'case frames' amounted to descriptions of predicating words that communicated such information as the following: 'Such-and-such a verb occurs in expressions containing three nominals, one designating an actor who performs the act designated by the verb, one designating an object on which the actor's act has a state-changing influence, and one designating an object through the manipulation of which the actor brings about the mentioned state change.' In symbols this statement could be represented as [— A P I], the letters standing for 'Agent', 'Patient' and 'Instrument'. Actually, the kind of description I sought distinguished 'case frames' as the structures in actual individual sentences in which the verbs could appear from 'case frame features' as representations of the class of 'case frames' into which particular verbs could be inserted. In the description of 'case frame features' it was possible to notice which of the 'cases' were obligatory, which were optional, what selectional dependencies obtained among them, and so on (see Fillmore 1968).

We were developing a kind of mixed syntactic-semantic valence description of verbs, and we noticed that the separate valence patterns seemed to characterize semantic types of verbs, such as verbs of perception, causation, movement, etc. Within these syntactic valence types, however, it seemed that some semantic generalizations were lost. There seemed to be important differences between *give it to john* and *send it to chicago* that could not be illuminated merely by showing what syntactic rules separate *give* from *send*, just as there seemed to be semantic commonalities between *rob* and *steal*, *buy* and *sell*, *enjoy* and *amuse*, etc., which were lost in the syntactic class separation of these verbs.

My ultimate goal in this work in 'case grammar' (as the framework came to be called) was the development of a 'valence dictionary' which was to differ importantly from the kinds of valence dictionaries appearing in Europe (e.g., Helbig and Schenkel 1973) by having its semantic valence taken as basic and by having as much as possible of its syntactic valence accounted for by general rules. (Thus, it was not thought to be necessary to explain, in individual lexical entries, which of the arguments in a [V A P I] predication of the type described above was to be the subject and which was to be the object, since such matters were automatically predicted by the grammar with reference to a set of general principles concerning the mapping from configurations of semantic cases into configurations of grammatical relations.)

Although the concept of 'frame' in various fields within cognitive psychology appears to have origins quite independent of linguistics, its use in case grammar was continuous, in my own thinking, with the use to which I have put it in 'frame semantics'. In particular, I thought of each case frame as characterizing a small abstract 'scene' or 'situation', so that to understand the semantic structure of the verb it was necessary to understand the properties of such schematized scenes.

The scene schemata definable by the system of semantic cases (a system of semantic role notions which I held to be maximally general and defining a minimal and possibly universal repertory) was sufficient, I believed, for understanding those aspects of the semantic structure of a verb which were linked to the verb's basic syntactic properties and to an understanding of the ways in which different languages differently shaped their minimal clauses, but they were clearly not adequate for describing with any completeness the semantic structure of the clauses containing individual verbs.

This theory of semantic roles fell short of providing the detail needed for semantic description; it came more and more to seem that another independent level of role structure was needed for the semantic description of verbs in particular limited domains. One possible way of devising a fuller account of lexical semantics is to associate some mechanism for deriving sets of truth conditions for a clause from semantic information individually attached to given predicates; but it seemed to me more profitable to believe that there are larger cognitive structures capable of providing a new layer of semantic role notions in terms of which whole domains of vocabulary could be semantically characterized.

My first attempt to describe one such cognitive structure was in a paper on 'Verbs of judging' (Fillmore 1971) – verbs like *blame*, *accuse*, *criticize* – for which I needed to be able to imagine a kind of 'scene schematization' that was essentially different from the sort associated with 'case frames'. In devising a framework for describing the elements in this class of verbs, I found it useful to distinguish a person who formed or expressed some sort of judgment on the worth or behavior of some situation or individual (and I called such a person the Judge); a person concerning whose behavior or character it was relevant for the

Judge to make a judgment (I called this person the Defendant); and some situation concerning which it seemed relevant for the Judge to be making a Judgment (and this I called simply the Situation). In terms of this framework, then, I chose to describe *accuse* as a verb usable for asserting that the Judge, presupposing the badness of the Situation, claimed that the Defendant was responsible for the Situation; I described *criticize* as usable for asserting that the Judge, presupposing the Defendant's responsibility for the Situation, presented arguments for believing that the Situation was in some way blameworthy. The details of my description have been 'criticized' (see esp. McCawley 1975), but the point remains that we have here not just a group of individual words, but a 'domain' of vocabulary whose elements somehow presuppose a schematization of human judgment and behavior involving notions of worth, responsibility, judgment, etc., such that one would want to say that nobody can really understand the meanings of the words in that domain who does not understand the social institutions or the structures of experience which they presuppose.

A second domain in which I attempted to characterize a cognitive 'scene' with the same function was that of the 'commercial event' (see Fillmore 1977b). In particular, I tried to show that a large and important set of English verbs could be seen as semantically related to each other by virtue of the different ways in which they 'indexed' or 'evoked' the same general 'scene'. The elements of this schematic scene included a person interested in exchanging money for goods (the Buyer), a person interested in exchanging goods for money (the Seller), the goods which the Buyer did or could acquire (the Goods), and the money acquired (or sought) by the seller (the Money). Using the terms of this framework, it was then possible to say that the verb *buy* focuses on the actions of the Buyer with respect to the Goods, backgrounding the Seller and the Money; that the verb *sell* focuses on the actions of the Seller with respect to the Goods, backgrounding the Buyer and the Money; that the verb *pay* focuses on the actions of the Buyer with respect to both the Money and the Seller, backgrounding the Goods, and so on, with such verbs as *spend, cost, charge*, and a number of others somewhat more peripheral to these. Again, the point of the description was to argue that nobody could be said to know the meanings of these verbs who did not know the details of the kind of scene which provided the background and motivation for the categories which these words represent. Using the word 'frame' for the structured way in which the scene is presented or remembered, we can say that the frame structures the word-meanings, and that the word 'evokes' the frame.

The structures I have mentioned so far can be thought of as motivating the categories speakers wish to bring into play when describing situations that might be independent of the actual speech situation, the conversational context. A second and equally important kind of framing is the framing of the actual communication situation. When we understand a piece of language, we bring to the task both our ability to assign schematizations of the phases or components of the 'world' that the text somehow characterizes, and our ability to schematize the situation in which this piece of language is being produced. We have both 'cognitive frames' and 'interactional frames', the latter having to do with how we conceptualize what is going on between the speaker and the hearer, or between the author and the reader. By the early seventies I had become influenced by work on speech acts, performativity, and pragmatics in general, and had begun contributing to this field in the form of a number of writings on presuppositions and deixis (see, e.g., Fillmore 1975). Knowledge of deictic categories requires an understanding of the ways in which tenses, person marking morphemes, demonstrative categories, etc., schematize the communicating situation; knowledge of illocutionary points, principles of conversational cooperation, and routinized speech events, contribute to the full understanding of most conversational exchanges. Further, knowing that a text is, say, an obituary, a proposal of marriage, a business contract, or a folktale, provides knowledge about how to interpret particular passages in it, how to expect the text to develop, and how to know when it is finished. It is frequently the case that such expectations combine with the actual material of the text to lead to the text's correct interpretation. And once again this is accomplished by having in mind an abstract structure of expectations which brings with it roles, purposes, natural or conventionalized sequences of event types, and all the rest of the apparatus that we wish to associate with the notion of 'frame'.

In the mid-seventies I came into contact with the work of Eleanor Rosch (Rosch 1973) and that of Brent Berlin and Paul Kay (Berlin and Kay 1969) and began to see the importance of the notion of 'prototype' in understanding the nature of human categorization. Through the work of Karl Zimmer (Zimmer 1971) and Pamela Downing (Downing 1977) on the relevance of categorizing contexts to principles of word-formation and, in work that reflects fruitful collaboration with Paul Kay and George Lakoff, I began to propose descriptions of word meanings that made use of the prototype notion. One generalization that seemed valid was that very often the frame or background against which the meaning of a word is defined and understood is a fairly large slice of the surrounding culture, and this background understanding is best understood as a 'prototype' rather than as a genuine body of assumptions about what the world is like. It is frequently useful, when trying to state truth conditions for the appropriateness of predicating the word of something, to construct a simple definition of the word, allowing the complexity of fit between uses of the word and real world situations to be attributed to the details of the prototype background frame rather than to the details of the word's meaning. Thus we could define an *orphan* as a child whose parents are no longer living, and then understand the category as motivated against a background of a particular kind: in this assumed background world, children depend on their parents for care and guidance and parents accept the responsibility of providing this care and guidance without question; a person without parents has a special status, for society, only up to a particular age, because during this period a society needs to provide some special way of providing care and instruction. The category *orphan* does not have 'built into it' any specification of the age after which it is no longer relevant to speak of somebody as an orphan, because that understanding is a part of the background prototype; a boy in his twenties is generally regarded as being able to take care of himself and to have passed the age where the main guidance is expected to come from his family. It is that background information which determines the fact that the word *orphan* would not be appropriately used of such a boy, rather than information that is to be separately built into a description of the word's meaning. In the prototype situation, an orphan is seen as somebody deserving of pity and concern; hence the point of the joke about the young man on trial for the murder of his parents who asked the court for mercy on the grounds that he was an orphan: the prototype scene against which society has a reason to categorize some children as orphans does not take into account the case in which a child orphans himself.

As a second example of a category that has to be fitted onto a background of institutions and practices we can consider the word *breakfast*. To understand this word is to understand the practice in our culture of having three meals a day, at more or less conventionally established times of the day, and for one of these meals to be the one which is eaten early in the day, after a period of sleep, and for it to consist of a somewhat unique menu (the details of which can vary from community to community). What is interesting about the word *breakfast* is that each of the three conditions most typically associated with it can be independently absent still allowing native speakers to use the word. The fact that someone can work through the night without sleep, and then at sun-up have a meal of eggs, toast, coffee and orange juice, and call that meal breakfast, shows clearly that the 'post-sleep' character of the category is not criterial; the fact that someone can sleep through the morning, wake up at three o'clock in the afternoon, and sit down to a meal of eggs, toast, coffee and orange juice, and call that meal *breakfast*, shows that the 'early morning' character of the category is also not criterial; and lastly, the fact that a person can sleep through the night, wake up in the morning, have cabbage soup and chocolate pie 'for breakfast', shows that the 'breakfast menu' character of the concept is also not criterial. (This in spite of the fact that an American restaurant that advertises its willingness to serve breakfast at any time is referring precisely to the stereotyped breakfast ingredients.) What we want to say, when we observe usage phenomena like that, is not that we have so far failed to capture the true core of the word's meaning, but rather that the word gives us a category which can be used in many different contexts, this range of contexts determined by the multiple aspects of its prototypic use – the use it has when the conditions of the background situation more or less exactly match the defining prototype.

The descriptive framework which is in the process of evolving out of all of the above considerations is one in which words and other linguistic forms and categories are seen as indexing semantic or cognitive categories which are themselves recognized as participating in larger conceptual structures of some sort, all of this made intelligible by knowing something about the kinds of settings or contexts in which a community found a need to make such categories available to its participants, the background of experiences and practices within which such contexts could arise, the categories, the contexts, and the backgrounds themselves all understood in terms of prototypes.

## 3. Further illustrations and some terminological proposals

A 'frame', as the notion plays a role in the description of linguistic meanings, is a system of categories structured in accordance with some motivating context. Some words exist in order to provide access to knowledge of such frames to the participants in the communication process, and simultaneously serve to perform a categorization which takes such framing for granted.

The motivating context is some body of understandings, some pattern of practices, or some history of social institutions, against which we find intelligible the creation of a particular category in the history of the language community. The word *week-end* conveys what it conveys both because of the calendric seven-day cycle and because of a particular practice of devoting a relatively larger continuous block of days within such a cycle to public work and two continuous days to one's private life. If we had only one 'day of rest' there would be no need for the word *week-end*; one could simply use the name of that day. If we had three days of work and four days of rest, then too it seems unlikely that the name for the period devoted to one's private life would have been given that name. (If the work week is gradually shortened, the word *week-end* might stay; but it is unlikely that the category could have developed naturally if from the start the number of days devoted to work were shorter than the number of the remaining days. An acquaintance of mine who works only on Wednesdays, pleased at being able to enjoy 'a long week-end', recognizes that the word is here being used facetiously.)

The word *vegetarian* means what it means, when used of people in our culture, because the category of 'someone who eats only vegetables' is a relevant and interesting category only against the background of a community many or most of whose members regularly eat meat. Notice that the word designates, not just someone who eats plant food, but someone who eats only plant food.

Furthermore, it is used most appropriately for situations in which the individual so designated avoids meat deliberately and for a purpose. The purpose might be one of beliefs about nutrition, or it may be one of concerns for animal life; but the word is not used (in a sentence like *John is a vegetarian.*) to describe people whose diet does not include meat because they are unable to find any, or because they cannot afford to buy it.

Occasionally one comes upon a term whose motivating context is very specific. One such is the compound *flip strength*, used, I am told, in the pornographic literature business. Some publishers of pornographic novels instruct their authors to include a certain quota of high interest words on every page, so that a potential customer, in a bookstore, while 'flipping' the pages of the book, will, no matter where he opens the book, find evidence that the book is filled with wonderful and exciting goings-on. A book which has a high ratio of nasty words per page has high flip strength; a book which has these words more widely distributed has low flip strength. As I understand the word, an editor of such a publication venture might reject a manuscript, requesting that it be returned only after its flip strength has been raised.

With this last example, it is extremely clear that the background context is absolutely essential to understanding the category. It is not that the conditions for using the word cannot be stated without this background understanding (relative flip strength of novels could easily be determined by a computer), but that the word's meaning cannot be truly understood by someone who is unaware of those human concerns and problems which provide the reason for the category's existence.

We can say that, in the process of using a language, a speaker 'applies' a frame to a situation, and shows that he intends this frame to be applied by using words recognized as grounded in such a frame. What is going on here seems to correspond, within the ordinary vocabulary of a language, to lexical material in scientific discourse that is describable as 'theory laden': the word *phlogiston* is 'theory-laden'; the reason it is no longer used in serious discourse is that nobody accepts the theory within which it is a concept. That is, nobody schematizes the physical world in a way that would give a reason to speak of part of it as *phlogiston*.

To illustrate the point with items from everyday language, we can consider the words *land* and *ground* (which I have described elsewhere but cannot forego mentioning here). The difference between these two words appears to be best expressed by saying that *land* designates the dry surface of the earth as it is distinct from the *sea*, whereas *ground* designates the dry surface of the earth as it is distinct from the *air* above it. The words *land* and *ground*, then, differ not so much in what it is that they can be used to identify, but in how they situate that thing in a larger frame. It is by our recognition of this frame contrast that we are able to understand that a bird that 'spends its life on the land' is being described negatively as a bird that does not spend any time in water; a bird that 'spends its life on the ground' is being described negatively as a bird that does not fly.

Though the details are a bit tricky, the two English words *shore* and *coast* (not differently translatable in many languages) seem to differ from each other in that while the *shore* is the boundary between land and water from the water's point of view, the *coast* is the boundary between land and water from the land's point of view. A trip that took four hours 'from shore to shore' is a trip across a body of water; a trip that took four hours 'from coast to coast' is a trip across a land mass. "We will soon reach the coast" is a natural way to say something about a journey on land; "we will soon reach the shore" is a natural way to say something about a sea journey. Our perception of these nuances derives from our recognition of the different ways in which the two words schematize the world.

The Japanese adjective *nurui* is another example of a framing word. Although not all Japanese-speaking informants support this judgment, enough do to make the example worth giving. In the usage that supports my point, *nurui*, used to describe the temperature of a liquid means 'at room temperature', but it is said mainly of liquids that are ideally hot. *Kono ocha ga nurui* (this tea is lukewarm) is an acceptable sentence in the idiolects that support my point, but *kono biiru ga nurui* (this beer is lukewarm) is not. It will be noticed that the English word *lukewarm* does not 'frame' its object in the same way. A cold liquid and a hot liquid can both become lukewarm when left standing long enough; but only the liquid that was supposed to be hot can be described as 'nurui'.

A large number of framing words appear only in highly specialized contexts, such as the term *flip strength* discussed earlier. The legal term *decedent* gives us another example of such context specialization. According to my legal informants (and my available law dictionaries) the word *decedent* is used to identify a dead person in the context of a discussion of the inheritance of that person's property. (The word *deceased*, as in the phrase 'the deceased', is also limited to legal or journalistic contexts, but it is not limited to any particular subdomain within the law.) Another example is *mufti*. Mufti, in the sense it once had in the military service, refers to ordinary clothing when worn by somebody who regularly wears a military uniform. If we see two men wearing identical suits, we can, referring to their clothing, say that one of them is 'in mufti' if that one is a military officer. The property of being 'in mufti' is obviously a property that has relevance only in the context of a military community.

Given all these examples of clear cases of terms linked to highly specific cognitive frames, we can see that the process of understanding a text involves retrieving or perceiving the frames evoked by the text's lexical content and assembling this kind of schematic knowledge (in some way which cannot be easily formalized) into some sort of 'envisionment' of the 'world' of the text. If I tell you (to be somewhat ridiculous) that the decedent while on land and in mufti last weekend ate a typical breakfast and read a novel high in flip strength, you know that I am talking about a now-dead naval officer who during the period including last Saturday and Sunday read a pornographic novel; and you know a few other things about the man, about how he spent his time, and about the setting in which this report of his activities is given. The sentence did not give you this information directly; you had to 'compute' some of it by constructing, in your imagination, a complex context within which each of the lexically signaled framings was motivated. We see in this way that there is a very tight connection between lexical semantics and text semantics, or, to speak more carefully, between lexical semantics and the process of text comprehension. The framing words in a text reveal the multiple ways in which the speaker or author schematizes the situation and induce the hearer to construct that envisionment of the text world which would motivate or explain the categorization acts expressed by the lexical choices observed in the text.

The interpreter's envisionment of the text world assigns that world both a perspective and a history. A report of somebody buying something evokes the frame of the commercial event, but sees that event, for the moment at least, from the point of view of one of its participants. Describing somebody as being *on land* locates the scene in the history of a sea voyage, by noticing that it is relevant to describe the location in this way only if this period is seen as an interruption of a period of sea travel. Saying that somebody is *at bat* locates an event as one part of a particular baseball game. Describing coffee, in Japanese, as *nurui* recognizes that it was once hot and has been allowed to 'cool'. One knows that the coffee is currently at room temperature, but also that it did not get that way by starting out as iced coffee.

Sometimes the perspective which a word assigns is not a perspective on the current scene – something that might be visible in a pictorial representation of the scene – but is that of a much larger framework. Thus, the description of someone as a *heretic* presupposes an established religion, or a religious community which has a well-defined notion of doctrinal correctness. In a community lacking such beliefs or practices, the word has no purpose. Sometimes a word situates an event in a history wider than the history of the ongoing narrative. In speaking of locations within North America, the expressions *out west* and *back east* are frequently used. The terms have the form they do because for a large portion of American families the settlement history of the country traced its way from the east coast to the west coast. European immigrants first landed on the east coast; some of them, or some of their descendants, gradually migrated westward. The eastern part of the country, where these immigrants or their ancestors once were, was *back east*; the western part of the country, not yet reached, was *out west*. The expressions are used today by people whose families did not share in this general westward movement themselves, but the terms recall the historical basis of their creation.

Earlier I spoke of the notion of deep cases as offering an account of the semantic aspects of single-clause predications which figured in the basic grammatical structure of clauses. A broader view of the semantics of grammar, one which owes a great deal to the work of Leonard Talmy (see Talmy 1980) and Ronald Langacker (Langacker 1987), sees lexical framing providing the 'content' upon which grammatical structure performs a 'configuring' function. Thinking in this way, we can see that any grammatical category or pattern imposes its own 'frame' on the material it structures. For example, the English pluperfect can be described as having as its role, in structuring the 'history' of the text world, that of characterizing the situation at a particular time (the narrative time) as being partly explained by the occurrence of an event or situation that occurred or existed earlier on. The progressive aspect, in its turn, schematizes a situation as one which is continuing or iterating across a span of time. Thus, a sentence in a narrative of the form *She had been running*, a form which combines the progressive and the pluperfect forms, can have the function of explaining why, at the narrative time point, "she" was panting, or sweating, or tired. Thus we see that the cognitive frames which inform and shape our understanding of language can differ greatly in respect to their generality or specificity: a lexical verb like *run* can give us a specific kind of physical activity image, while the pluperfect and the progressive combine, each in a general and abstract way, to shape the image of running in a way that fits the current situation and to situate the event of running both temporally and in 'relevance' into the ongoing history of the text world.

It is necessary to distinguish two importantly different ways in which the cognitive frames we call on to help us interpret linguistic texts get introduced into the interpretation process. On the one hand, we have cases in which the lexical and grammatical material observable in the text 'evokes' the relevant frames in the mind of the interpreter by virtue of the fact that these lexical forms or these grammatical structures or categories exist as indices of these frames; on the other hand, we have cases in which the interpreter assigns coherence to a text by 'invoking' a particular interpretive frame. An extremely important difference between frames that are evoked by material in the text and frames that are invoked by the interpreter is that in the latter case an 'outsider' has no reason to suspect, beyond a general sense of irrelevance or pointlessness in the text, that anything is missing. To repeat an example that I have used elsewhere, a Japanese personal letter in the traditional style is supposed to begin with a comment on the current season. Somebody who knows this tradition is able to sense the relevance of an opening sentence in a letter which speaks of the garden floor covered with leaves. The kind of understanding which allows such an interpretation comes from outside of the text itself.

Invoked frames can come from general knowledge, knowledge that exists independently of the text at hand, or from the ongoing text itself.

## 4. Frame-semantic formulations of empirical semantic observations

In this section I examine a number of observations about lexical meaning or text interpretation which permit formulations in terms of notions from frame semantics. In the following section I examine a number of traditional topics in standard semantic theorizing and raise questions about the importance they would be given in an account of linguistic meaning of the sort we have been exploring.

### 4.1 Polysemy arising from alternative framings of the same lexical item

For many instances of polysemy it is possible to say that a given lexical item properly fits either of two different cognitive frames. One possibility is that a word has a general use in the everyday language but has been given a separate use in technical language. For example, we might wish to say that the English word *angle* is understood in connection with a perceptual frame as a figure made by two lines joined at a point in a way suggested by a bent stick. Presented in terms of a competing procedural frame, an angle is thought of in terms of the rotation of a line about a point, the angle itself visually represented as the line before and after its rotation. In the procedural frame the notion of a 180 degree angle is intelligible, as is the notion of a 360 degree angle. Within the perceptual frame such notions do not fit. (The example is from Arnheim 1969: 182f.)

### 4.2. Alternate framings of a single situation

From a frame semantics point of view, it is frequently possible to show that the same 'facts' can be presented within different framings, framings which make them out as different 'facts'. Somebody who shows an unwillingness to give out money in a particular situation might be described by one person as *stingy* (in which case the behavior is contrasted with being *generous*), and by another as *thrifty* (in which case a contrast is made with being *wasteful*). The speaker who applies the *stingy*: *generous* contrast to a way of behaving assumes that it is to be evaluated with respect to the behaver's treatment of fellow humans; whereas the speaker who evaluates the behavior by applying to it a *thifty: wasteful* contrast assumes that what is most important is a measure of the skill or wisdom displayed in the use of money or other resources.

### 4.3. 'Contrast within frames' versus 'contrast across frames'

The fact that a single situation can be 'framed' in contrasting ways makes possible two ways of presenting a negation or an opposition. Using the contrasts introduced in the last paragraph, if I say of somebody, *He's not stingy – he's really generous*, I have accepted the scale by which you choose to measure him, and I inform you that in my opinion your application of this scale was in error. If on the other hand I say *He's not stingy – he's thrifty*, what I am doing is proposing that the behavior in question is not to be evaluated along the *stingy: generous* dimension but along the *thifty: wasteful* dimension. In the first case I have argued for a particular standard in the application of an accepted scale; in the second case my utterance argues for the irrelevance of one scale and the appropriateness of another.

### 4.4. Word sense creation by frame borrowing

When a speaker wishes to talk about something for which an appropriate cognitive frame has not been established, or for which he wishes to introduce a novel schematization, he can sometimes accomplish this by transferring the linguistic material associated with a frame which makes the distinctions he's interested in onto the new situation, relying on the interpreter to see the appropriateness of the transfer. Certain new senses of words can be best understood as having originated in this way; we might expect that such was the case in the importation of the term *bachelor* into the terminology appropriate to fur seal society, to use the example made common in lexical semantics discussion from the reminder, in Katz and Fodor (1963), of the use of the word *bachelor* to designate 'a male fur seal without a mate during the mating season'. Lakoff and Johnson (1980) have made us aware of the value of metaphor in conceptualization and communication, making the persuasive case that in a great many domains of experience metaphors provide us with the only way of communicating about those experiences.

### 4.5. Reframing a lexical set

Various kinds of semantic change can be illuminated by considering the phenomena in frame semantic terms. One important type of change consists in reconstituting the motivating circumstances while preserving the lexical item and its basic fit with the associated scene. People observing certain usages of English with an eye to feminist concerns have noticed tendencies on the part of many speakers to have certain asymmetries in the sets of conditions for using the words in the proportion *boy: man :: girl: woman*. In particular, in the usage pattern that I have in mind, males appeared to be classified as *men* at an earlier age than that at which females are classified as *woman*. A number of people, sensing that this usage pattern revealed attitudes toward females (or a history of attitudes toward females reflected in current conventional usage possibly in independence of the user's own attitudes) which ought to be corrected. A number of speakers have succeeded in modifying their usage in a way which established the age boundary between the *boy* to *man* transition at the same place as that between the *girl* to *woman* transition. The semantic change in this case is a real one, which needs to be explained. But it would not be satisfying to see the explanation solely in changes of the meaning of the words *girl* and *woman*; the full explanation must assign the change to the underlying schematization on the part of the language user. The realities (of people of both sexes getting older) have not changed, nor have the available choices of linguistic material; what has changed (in some speakers) is the underlying schematization, the circumstances motivating the category contrasts.

### 4.6. Relexicalizing unchanged frames

A second kind of semantic change, which oddly can be illustrated with the same words, is one in which the links between words and their frames are changed, but the underlying schematization remains unchanged. The effort to respond to society's new sensitivity to the connections between language and attitudes is perhaps easiest to manage in the short run if it does not require something as deeply cognitive as a reschematization of the domain. A superficial rule-of-thumb for bringing about the appearance of a raised consciousness in the realm of language and sexism is a mechanical principle like "Where I am inclined to say *girl* I should instead say *woman* ". A person who adopts this rule may find that in most cases it performs very well; but one sometimes finds oneself trapped – as in the experience of an acquaintance of mine – when talking about very young females; my friend found himself, several times, using the word *woman* when talking about an eight-year-old girl. The fact that this friend would never accidentally use the word *man* when talking about an eight-year-old boy shows that the change in question is not of the reschematization type discussed in the previous paragraph. An equally clear example of the same phenomenon (as I have discussed elsewhere – Fillmore 1972) is in the use of the word *suspect* where the speaker or writer might have been inclined to use such a word as *burglar, murderer, arsonist*, or more generally, *culprit*. Conscious of the legal doctrine that a person is to be considered innocent until proven guilty, and conscious too of the danger of committing libel, journalists and police officers have learned to identify persons accused of crimes but not (yet) legally held to be guilty of them as *suspects*. A change in usage which would clearly reflect the adoption of the legal doctrine mentioned above about guilt and innocence as the underlying cognitive frame would not result in some of the frequent mistakes people make in the use of the word *suspect*. The word *suspect* is supposed to be used of a person who is suspected of committing the crime in question; for it to be used appropriately, there has to be some specific person of whom it can be said that that person is suspected by someone of committing the crime. The current journalistic use of *suspect* even when nobody has been accused of the crime shows that the change is of the superficial kind, following the application of a rule of thumb that says, "Wherever I am inclined to say *culprit* (etc.), I should instead say *suspect*." I have in mind such usages as can be found in reports like "Police investigating the murder have found no clues as to the identity of the suspect."

### 4.7. Miscommunication by frame conflict

The law provides many contexts in which specific new framings need to be constructed for familiar words. The notion *innocent* mentioned above is an example. In both everyday language and legal language there is a contradictory opposition between *innocent* and *guilty*. In everyday language, the difference depends on whether the individual in question did or did not commit the crime in question. In legal language, by contrast, the difference depends on whether the individual in question has or has not been declared guilty by the court as a result of legal action within the criminal justice system. This disparity of schematization is responsible for frequent misunderstandings in the use of these words. An example of such misunderstandings (which I have discussed in Fillmore 1978) was in a conversation between a prospective juror and lawyers in a voir dire hearing in a municipal court in Berkeley. The attorney for the defense asked the prospective juror "Do you accept the American legal doctrine that a man is innocent until proven guilty?" The citizen answered that a person should be treated as innocent until proven guilty, but that it would be strange to say that he was actually innocent. The attorney asked again, saying, "I'm talking about the doctrine that a man *is* innocent until proven guilty. Do you or do you not accept that doctrine?" The citizen answered that if the man *is* innocent, then there is no need for a trial. (This rude answer excused the man from jury duty.) This little bit of miscommunicating could easily have been avoided. The citizen was not really being asked whether or not he accepted a particular legal doctrine, but whether or not he was willing to adopt for the purpose of discussion in the trial which was about to start the framing of the words *innocent* and *guilty* provided by the criminal justice institutions in place of the everyday use of these same words.

### 4.8. Reformulations in technical language

Legal contexts give us further ways of seeing changes between general and special-purpose framings of words. In many cases this is because the everyday sense of a word does not cover all cases in which it should be appropriate to use the word. In the prototype case of events fitting the word *murder*, one person (A), intending to kill a second person (B), acts in such a way as to cause that person to die. This prototype does not cover a case in which A, intending to kill B, aims his gun at B, and kills C (who is standing next to B) instead. Some of the properties of *murder* relate A and B; others relate A to C. The question somebody needs to answer, of course, is whether, for the purposes of the law, it is proper to say that A murdered C. The law does this, not by modifying the definition of *murder* so that it will cover this 'wrong-target' case, but by adding to the system of legal semantics a statutory interpretation principle called 'Transfer of Intent' according to which A's intent to kill B is fictitiously transferred to C so that the definition of *murder* can fully fit what A did to C. With respect to judgments of reprehensibility and legal provisions for punishment, A's killing of C should be treated in the same way as A's successful killing of B would have been. The Transfer of Intent principle makes it possible for the non-prototypic case to fall under the same definition.

Other such reinterpretations in the law are equally founded on intentions associated with the prototypical case. The concept of *forcible entry* involves one person gaining entry to another person's property by overcoming the resistance of persons trying to prevent that person's entry. The usual definition of *forcible entry*, however, includes not only the situation in which the intruder physically overpowers the other, but also the situation in which, as it is usually put, "resistance would be unavailing". If you, being twice my size and strength, insist on being admitted to my apartment, and I meekly let you enter (on the reasonable grounds that if we had a fight, I would lose), then too you can be charged with *forcible entry*. A third example is *oral agreement*. Basically an *oral agreement* is a contract or agreement which two parties entered into orally, that is, without putting the agreement in a written form and without signing our names to it. The importance of the notion *oral agreement* in the law is that the conditions of its authenticity and its bindingness distinguish it from agreements that are fully written out and signed. The critical difference, for the given legal purposes, is the presence or absence of the signatures of the principals. The important part of the contrast, then, is that between being signed and not being signed. Accordingly, provisions made in the law for *oral agreements* also apply to written agreements which happen not to be signed. The prototype background in which the notion *oral agreement* is motivated, is one in which agreements are either made by word of mouth or by means of documents which are written and signed. In situations which depart from the prototype the law has needed to determine which aspect of the prototype contrast is legally the most salient (the presence or absence of the signatures supporting a written document) and let that be the criterion which specifies the contrast.

### 4.9. Frames for evaluation

One important area in which semantic interpretation depends crucially on lexical framing is that of attributions of value. Evaluative adjectives can contain in their meanings reference to the dimensions, scales, or standards according to which something is evaluated, as with adjectives like *fragrant, tasty, efficient, intelligent*, etc. In many cases, however, an adjective is abstractly evaluative (as with the English words *good* and *bad*) and interpretations of their attributive use depend on knowledge of the ideational frames to which they are indexed. The fact that speakers of English are able to interpret such phrases as *a good pencil, good coffee, a good mother, a good pilot*, etc., shows that they are able to call into their consciousness for this purpose the fact that a pencil is used for writing and can be evaluated for how easy or efficient it is to write with it, or how clearly its traces appear on the paper, the fact that coffee is a drink and can be evaluated for its taste, its contribution to the drinker's alertness, etc., that mothers and pilots do what they professionally and conventionally do and can be evaluated for how easily, how effectively, and how efficiently they do it. The point was made earlier that cognitive frames called on to assist in text interpretation may derive from general background knowledge or may be brought into play by the textual context. This is particularly true in the case of the interpretation of evaluative adjectives, since some nouns have frames associated with them whose evaluative dimensions are provided in advance, while others designate things that could be evaluated only if the context provided some basis for the evaluation. When we come across the phrase *a good stick* we expect to find in the context some explanation of a situation within which one stick could function better than another (for propping a window open, for repelling a raccoon, for skewering marshmallows, etc.). A general concept of 'framing' involves contextualizing or situating events in the broadest sense possible; within linguistic semantics proper the concern is with patterns of framing that are already established and which are specifically associated with given lexical items or grammatical categories.

### 4.10. Script evocation

I said earlier about cognitive frames that to speak of one of its elements is to speak of the others at the same time. More carefully put, to speak of one part of a frame is to bring to consciousness, or to raise into question, its other components. This effect is particularly striking in connection with the kinds of frames known as 'scripts', frames whose elements are sequenced types of events. Text understanding that makes use of scriptal knowledge (on which see Schank and Abelson 1977) involves the activation of whole-scale scripting of events on the presentation of an event that can be seen to part of such a script. Thus, in a textlet like "He pushed against the door. The room was empty." we make the two sentences cohere by assuming that the goal somebody might have in pushing against a door is to get that door open, and that if one succeeded in getting the door open by such an act, one could then be in a position to notice whether the room was empty. Reading between the lines, we expand the text to mean: "He pushed against the door. *the door opened. he looked inside. he saw that* The room was empty."

### 4.11. Frames for texts

Discussion of text structure on the part of Robert Longacre and others shows that languages or cultures can differ with respect to the ways in which texts with particular communicative goals can have particular conventionalized forms. Recipes in English make consistent use of imperatives. In Hungarian recipes, first person plural descriptions are the norm. And Longacre has described (in conversation) a language lacking in procedural discourse uses narrative form for such purposes. Here it would be difficult to believe that languages differ from each other in the presence of material usable for particular kinds of discourse, it seems rather to be the case that traditions of language use within the culture develop in different ways in texts with different communicative goals.

## 5. Frame-semantic formulations of issues in technical semantics

In this section I examine a small number of topics that one traditionally finds in standard treatises on technical semantics: proportionality, paradigms, taxonomies, syncategorematicity, the supposed contrast between 'dictionary' and 'encyclopedia', the goal of descriptive simplicity and redundancy elimination, and, lastly, the troubled notion of 'lexical presupposition'.

### 5.1. Proportionality

One of the most frequently used heuristic devices for discovering and demonstrating the existence of semantic features in the vocabulary of a language is that of setting up a proportionality involving four words and asking for intuitive agreement about the identity of pairwise differences among them. Believing that man is to woman as boy is to girl, we set up the ratio *man*: *woman* :: *boy*: *girl*. Others frequently used are *come: go :: bring: take, look: see :: glance: glimpse, inhale: exhale :: sniff: snort,* and *man: woman :: bachelor: spinster.* The approach which sees the basic semantic relations as holding among words taken in isolation fails to help us become aware of the possibly quite separate ways in which individual members of these proportions are fitted onto, or frame, their reality. I have already pointed out that in many people's speech the differentiating criterion for *boy* vs. *man* might be importantly different from that for *girl* vs. *woman; bring* is separate enough in its semantics from *come* for it to have acquired quite separate patterns of dialect variation; and the motivation for the categories *bachelor* and *spinster* appear to be considerably different, in spite of one's inclination, as a systematizer, to put the two words together. One might wish to propose that the abstract structural patterns underlying these word groups are simple and straightforward, in the ways suggested by the proportions, even though certain facts about the world make the domain look less orderly. I think such a proposal is not helpful, because it is not one which asks the analyst to look for the background and motivating situations which separately give reasons for the existence of the individual categories, one by one.

## 5.2. Paradigms

A prime example of semantic structure among lexical items is the 'paradigm'; and the best example of a lexical-semantic paradigm is the kind of display of livestock terms represented by Table 1.

*Table 1.*

| cattle | sheep | horse | swine |
|---|---|---|---|
| cow | ewe | mare | sow |
| bull | ram | stallion | boar |
| steer | wether | gelding | barrow |

Here the proposal that we have a closed system of terms tied together by such features as General, Female, Male, and Neuter, cross-cut by features identifying species (Bovine, Ovine, Equine, Porcine), seems very attractive. Unfortunately the display disguises many facts about both these words and the domain which they appear to cover. *cattle* and *swine* are plurals; *sheep* and *horse* are not. The words *wether* and *barrow* are known only to specialists. In the case of *cattle, cow* and *bull* appear to have the status of 'basic level objects' (in the sense of Rosch 1973), whereas the general terms have that function in the case of *sheep* and *horse*. In the case of *swine*, a word not in the table, namely *pig*, is the best candidate for 'basic level object' status.

In short, the regularities apparent in the paradigm (and this set of terms – together with terms for young, newborn, etc. – make up what is generally accepted as the best example of a semantic paradigm) are misleading. To which we ought to add the Neuter category of the words in the bottom row is not just a 'neutral' category operating in the same line of business as the categories Female and Male. The category is differently motivated in the different species, which is another way of saying that one has different reasons for castrating a bull and a horse, one might do it at different (relative) ages, etc,

### 5.3. Taxonomies

The next most common kind of lexical semantic formal structure is the 'semantic taxonomy', a semantic network founded on the relation 'is a kind of'. Scientific taxonomies have obvious uses in scientific discourse, and research that has led to the uncovering of folk taxonomies has been among the most important empirical semantic research yet done. But there are two aspects of taxonomic structures that argue against regarding them as representing merely a formal system of relationships founded on a single clear semantic relation. The first is that at different levels in a taxonomy the community might have had different reasons for introducing the categories; the second is that the usual tree-form display of the elements of a taxonomy does not show how it is that particular elements in the taxonomy are 'cognitively privileged categories' in important ways. Both of these points can be illustrated with a 'path' in a taxonomy of zoological terms in English, namely

*animal*
*vertebrate*
*mammal*
*dog*
*retriever*

Of this set of words, *dog* and *animal* seem to be the cognitively privileged categories, privileged in the sense that they are the words that would most ordinarily be used when in everyday natural talk one is describing one's experiences. *vertebrate* and *mammal* are terms whose employment fits a particular kind of interactional or contextual schema (that of scientific discourse),while *retriever* as a category occurs most naturally as an answer to a question about what kind of a dog one has. Suppose that you, hearing a splash in my back yard, were to ask me what that noise was, and suppose the fact is that my pet retriever fell in the family swimming pool. As a way of explaining the source of the noise, it would be natural for me to say "An animal fell in the pool" or "A dog fell in the pool", but it would be very unnatural for me to say "A vertebrate fell in the pool" or "A mammal fell in the pool", and unnatural in a different way for me to say "A retriever fell in the pool". The latter three terms seem to appear more natural in utterances used in acts of classifying, but seem unnatural when used in acts of referring. This functional difference is not revealed within the logic of a standard taxonomic tree.

### 5.4. Syncategorematic terms

It has frequently been discussed (e.g., Austin 1964, Lecture VII) that a word like *imitation* does not semantically modify a word it grammatically modifies in the standard 'set intersection' way. Rather, it combines with the meaning of its partner to form a fairly complex concept. Something correctly described as *imitation coffee* looks like coffee and tastes like coffee, and it looks and tastes like coffee not by accident, but because somebody manufactured it so that it would have these properties; but, whatever it is, it is not made of coffee beans. Understanding the category, in fact, requires understanding the role of coffee in our lives and (perhaps) the reasons someone might have for making a coffee substitute.

By contrast a word like *real* appears to contribute nothing at all to the noun to which it is attached as a modifier. To describe something as *real coffee* is to do nothing more than to assert that something is coffee, against the background of (the possibility of) somebody's suspicion that it is imitation coffee. As with *imitation*, a part of a full understanding of an expression with *real* is knowing the reasons one might have for providing substitutes for the thing in question. The notion *real coffee* makes sense to us because we know that in some settings coffee is scarce, and we know that some people find coffee damaging to their health or held offensive by their religion. We can understand a category like *real gold* or *real diamond* because we can imagine a reason why somebody might choose to produce fake gold or fake diamonds, and we can imagine why someone might have doubts about the authenticity of particular samples. By contrast, a notion like *real pants* is unintelligible, because it is impossible to imagine something looking like pants and functioning like pants which do not, by virtue of those properties alone, count as being genuine pants.

### 5.5. Redundancy elimination

A common goal in structural semantics is the elimination or minimization of redundant information in the semantic description of lexical items. Frequently a semantic theorist will declare that the goal of a 'semantic dictionary' is that of saying just enough about each word in the language to guarantee that it is semantically in contrast with each other word in the language (Bendix 1966). It is a goal which presupposes the analyst's ability to have an overview of the entire lexical repertory of the language. Such a goal is completely antithetical to the goals of frame semantics, since frame semantics aims at discovering what categorizing functions the word serves in the contexts in which its use is motivated. This kind of knowledge is in principle attainable independently of knowledge about other words in the language, except for those relatively few cases in which the 'mosaic' image is appropriate, the image by which the meaning given to any one word is dependent on the meanings of its neighboring words (as in Trier 1931).

### 5.6. Dictionary vs. encyclopedia

The various structuralist approaches that find a goal of redundancy elimination relevant, also find it intelligible to draw a clear distinction between 'dictionaries' and 'encyclopedias'. In particular, certain scholars insist on a distinction between purely semantic information about words and encyclopedic information about the designata of words. Somebody holding this view might expect to be able to justify certain characteristics of carpenters (or the concept *carpenter*) as belonging to the semantic category of the noun, other distinct characteristics of carpenters as simply being true of the individuals who satisfy the criteria associated with the category. A frame-semantic approach would rather say that communities of men contain individuals who by trade make things out of wood, using particular kinds of tools, etc., etc., and would note that these people are called *carpenters.* The possibility of separating some features of a full description of what carpenters do as related to the concept and others as related to the people does not seem important. There is a distinction to be made between knowledge about words and knowledge about things, but it is not to be made in a way that serves the interests of the semanticists I have just been describing. True 'encyclopedic' information about carpenters as people might say something about wages, union affiliations, job related diseases, etc.; such information is not a matter of dispute.

### 5.7. Simplicity of description

While in respect to redundancy elimination it has appeared that standard approaches value simplicity and frame-semantic approaches do not, there is another sense in which simplicity of description is enhanced by the frame semantics approach. A recent lively discussion between Paul Kay and Linda Coleman on the one hand (Coleman and Kay 1981) and Eve Sweetser on the other hand (Sweetser 1981) concerns the possibility of a prototype background of assumptions (or, as Sweetser calls it, a 'folk theory') as providing the grounding for a simplified definition of the noun *lie*. On the Kay/ Coleman account, a *lie* is something which is (1) false in fact, (2) believed by the speaker to be false, and (3) said in order to deceive.

Sweetser's suggestion is that if we can characterize a folk theory of human communication involving cooperation, expressing what one believes, etc., then it is possible to describe a *lie* as simply a 'false statement', those other understandings we have about the concept falling out through an understanding of why one would bother to produce a false statement.

### 5.8. Presupposition

Claims about 'presuppositional' information being associated with individual lexical items have not received a good press. I find that within frame semantics, the concept of lexical presupposition does not seem unjustified. Consider the case of a verb like English *chase*, a verb for which a lexical presuppositionist might be inclined to say that when it is used of two beings moving in the same course, the movement of the one in front is presupposed, independently of whether the movement of the individual designated by the subject of the verb is asserted, denied, questioned, or supposed. In a setting in which one person is running, especially where it is understood that that person is fleeing, it is relevant to consider whether some other person is or is not going to try to prevent that first person from getting away. (My illustration is with people, but that's not an important condition.) The verb *chase* exists as a category by recognition of such relevance. If I ask, "Did anybody chase him?", or if I say "We didn't chase him", our reason for understanding that 'he' was running (fleeing) is that we know the kind of situation against which the category *chase* has a reason for being. It is in that sense, it seems to me, that one can talk about lexical presuppostions.

## 6. Concluding remarks

In this paper I have argued for a view of the description of meaning-bearing elements in a language according to which words (etc.) come into being only for a reason, that reason being anchored in human experiences and human institutions. In this view, the only way in which people can truly be said to understand the use to which these meaning-bearing elements are being put in actual utterances is to understand those experiences and institutions and to know why such experiences and institutions gave people reasons to create the categories expressed by the words. The semanticist's job is to tease out the precise nature of the relationship between the word and the category, and the precise nature of the relationships between the category and the background. I believe that some of the examples I have offered have shown the advantages of looking at language in this way.

## Note

1. For a recent attempt to differentiate these terms, see Beaugrande 1981: 303.

## References

Arnheim, Rudolf
1969 *Visual Thinking*. Berkeley: University of California Press.
Austin, John L.
1964 *Sense and Sensibilia*. (Reconstructed from manuscript notes by Geoffrey J. Warnock.) Oxford University Press.
Beaugrande, Robert de
1981 Design criteria for process models of reading. *Reading Research Quarterly* 16(2): 261–315.
Bendix, Edward H.
1966 *Componential Analysis of General Vocabulary: The Semantic Structure of a Set of Verbs in English, Hindi and Japanese*. Bloomington: Indiana University Press.
Berlin, Brent and Paul Kay
1969 *Basic Color Terms*. Berkeley: University of California Press.
Chomsky, Noam A.
1957 *Syntactic Structures*. The Hague: Mouton
1965 *Aspects of the Theory of Syntax*. Cambridge, MA: M.I.T. Press
Coleman, Linda and Paul Kay
1981 Prototype semantics. *Language* 57: 26–44.
Downing, Pamela
1977 On the creation and use of English compound nouns. *Language* 53: 810–842.
Fillmore, Charles J.
1961 *Indirect Object Constructions in English and the Ordering of Transformations*. The Hague: Mouton.
1963 The position of embedding transformations in a grammar. *Word* 19: 208–301.
1968 The case for case. In *Universals in Linguistic Theory*, Emmon Bach and Richard Harms (eds.), 1–90. New York: Holt, Rinehart & Winston.
1971 Verbs of judging: An exercise in semantic description. In *Studies in Linguistic Semantics*, Charles J. Fillmore and D. Terrence Langendoen (eds.), 272–289. New York: Holt, Rinehart and Winston.
1972 On generativity. In *The Goals of Linguistic Theory*, Stanley Peters (ed.), 1–19. Englewood Cliffs: Prentice Hall.
1975 *Santa Cruz Lectures on Deixis*. Bloomington: Indiana University Linguistics Club.
1977a The case for case reopened. In *Syntax and Semantics 8: Grammatical Relations*, Peter Cole and Jerry Sadock, (eds.), 59–82. New York: Academic Press.

1977b Topics in lexical semantics. In *Current Issues in Linguistic Theory*, Roger W. Cole (ed.), 76–138. Bloomington: Indiana University Press.

1978 On the organization of semantic information in the lexicon. In *Papers from the Parasession on the Lexicon*, 1–11. Chicago: The Chicago Linguistic Society.

Fries, Charles C.

1952 *The Structure of English*. New York: Harcourt, Brace & World.

Gross, Maurice

1975 *Méthodes en syntaxe*. Paris: Hermann.

Helbig, Gerhard and Wolfgang Schenkel

1973 *Wörterbuch zur Valenz und Distribution deutscher Verben*. Leipzig: VEB Verlag Enzyklopädie.

Householder, Fred W., et al.

1964 *Linguistic Analysis of English*, Final Report on NSF Grant No. GS-108.

Katz, Jerrold J. and Jerry A. Fodor

1963 The structure of a semantic theory. *Language* 39: 170–210.

Lakoff, George and Mark Johnson

1980 *Metaphors We Live By*. Chicago: University of Chicago Press.

Langacker, Ronald W.

1987 Foundations of Cognitive Grammar. vol. 1: *Theoretical Prerequisites*. Stanford: Stanford University Press.

Lees, Robert B.

1960 *The Grammar of English Nominalizations*. The Hague: Mouton

McCawley, James D.

1975 Verbs of bitching. In *Contemporary Research in Philosophical Logic and Linguistic Semantics*, David Hockney et al. (eds.), 313–332. Dordrecht: Reidel.

Pike, Kenneth L.

1967 *Language in Relation to a Unified Theory of the Structure of Human Behavior*. The Hague: Mouton.

Rosch, Eleanor H.

1973 On the internal structure of perceptual and semantic categories. In *Cognitive Development and the Acquisition of Language*, Timothy E. Moore (ed.), 111–144. New York: Academic Press.

Rosenbaum, Peter S.

1967 *The Grammar of English Predicate Complement Constructions*. Cambridge, MA: MIT Press

Schank, Roger C. and Robert P. Abelson

1977 *Scripts, Plans, Goals and Understanding: An Inquiry into Human Knowledge Structures*. Hillsdale, N.J.: Lawrence Erlbaum.

Sweetser, Eve E.

1981 The definition of *lie:* An examination of the folk theories underlying a semantic prototype. Unpublished ms.

Talmy, Leonard

1980 Grammar and cognition. Unpublished ms. University of California at San Diego, Cognitive Science Program.

Tesnière, Lucien
1959 *Elements de syntaxe structurale*. Paris: Klingksieck.

Trier, Jost
1931 *Der deutsche Wortschatz im Sinnbezirk des Verstandes*. Heidelberg.

Wilson, Deirdre
1975 *Presuppositions and Non-Truth-Conditional Semantics*. London: Academic Press.

Zimmer, Karl E.
1971 Some general observations about nominal compounds. In *Working Papers on Language Universals* 5: 1–24. Stanford: Stanford University Press. (Reprinted in 1981 in *Wortbildung*, Leonard Lipka and Hartmut Günther (eds.), 233–257. Darmstadt: Wissenschaftliche Buchgesellschaft Darmstadt.)

# Chapter 11
# Construction Grammar

## The inherent semantics of argument structure: The case of the English ditransitive construction[1]
*Adele E. Goldberg*

### 1. Introduction

In their *Language* article, "The learnability and acquisition of the dative alternation", J. Gropen, S. Pinker, M. Hollander, R. Goldberg, and R. Wilson (1989) provide a compelling account of how it is that the ditransitive syntax can be used productively with new and novel verb forms, and yet resist full productivity over any generally defined domain. They suggest lexico-semantic rules which operate on narrowly defined verb classes producing verbs with slightly altered semantics, whose arguments are mapped onto the ditransitive syntax by general linking rules. The identification of narrowly defined verb classes is done on the basis of specific morphophonological and semantic criteria. In this paper, I summarize their arguments, and, while accepting the idea that narrowly circumscribed domains of local productivity need to be identified, I will argue that there is a more revealing characterization of the phenomenon than that offered. Specifically, I will argue that the semantic constraints involved are more felicitously associated directly with the construction as a whole than with the lexicosemantic structure of the verbs.

In the second half of the paper, I will analyze the specific semantics involved, arguing that several important generalizations have been overlooked. In this section I will also identify several systematic metaphors associated with the construction, showing that expressions such as "Mary gave Joe a kiss", and "Mary's behavior gave John an idea" are instances of a large and productive class of expressions which are based on systematic metaphors.

### 2. A discussion of J. Gropen, S. Pinker, M. Honander, R. Goldberg, and R. Wilson (1989)

It has been a long standing puzzle that the ditransitive syntax may be used somewhat but not completely productively. That it can be used somewhat produc-

Originally published in 1992 in *Cognitive Linguistics* 3(1): 37–74.

tively is clear from evidence that the syntactic pattern can be extended to new and hypothetical verb forms; for example, the new lexical item *fax* can be used ditransitively as in:

(1) *Joe faxed Bob the report.*

Also, hypothetical lexical items are readily adapted to the ditransitive syntax. For example, if we define a new verb, *shin* to mean "to kick with the shin" it is quite natural for us to allow this new verb to be used ditransitively, as in:

(2) *Joe shinned his teammate the ball.* (Marantz 1984: 177)

At the same time, the pattern is not completely productive within any generally defined class of verbs. Apparently closely related words show distinct differences as to whether they allow ditransitive syntax:

(3) a. *Joe gave the earthquake relief fund $5.*
b. **Joe donated the earthquake relief fund $5.*
(4) a. *Joe told Mary a story.*
b. **Joe whispered Mary a story.*
(5) a. *Joe baked Mary a cake.*
b. **Joe iced Mary a cake.*

Brown and Hanlon (1970) have shown that children are neither corrected nor mis-comprehended more often when they speak ungrammatically, so that they have no recourse to "negative evidence" that could allow them to either unlearn or avoid learning the above type of ungrammatical sentences. An apparent paradox arises then, since if speakers have a productive mechanism that allows them to extend the use of the ditransitive syntax to new and novel verbs, it is not clear what prevents speakers from overgeneralizing to produce the above ill formed examples.

Gropen et al. propose a solution to this paradox. A broad range rule is proposed to capture the necessary conditions for ditransitive syntax. The broad range rule states in effect that a prospective possessor must be involved, i.e., that the first object must be understood to be a prospective possessor.[2] This general rule does not provide sufficient conditions, however, there being many verbs which can be understood to involve a prospective possessor which do not allow ditransitive syntax (cf. *donate*, *contribute*, *pull*, *shout*, *choose*, *credit*, *say*).

Sufficient conditions are determined by a set of narrow range rules which classify verbs into narrowly defined semantic classes. The specific classes that Gropen et al. propose are the following:

1. Verbs that inherently signify acts of giving, e.g., *give*, *pass*, *hand*, *sell*, *trade*, *lend*, *serve*, and *feed*.
2. Verbs of instantaneous causation of ballistic motion, e.g., *throw*, *toss*, *flip*, *slap*, *kick*, *poke*, *fling*, *shoot*, *blast*.
3. Verbs of sending, e.g., *send*, *mail*, *ship*.
4. Verbs of continuous causation of accompanied motion in a deictically-specified direction: *bring*, *take*.
5. Verbs of future having (involving commitments that a person will have something at some later point), e.g., *offer*, *promise*, *bequeath*, *leave*, *refer*, *forward*, *allocate*, *guarantee*, *allot*, *assign*, *advance*, *award*, *reserve*, *grant*.
6. Verbs of communicated message e.g., *tell*, *show*, *ask*, *teach*, *pose*, *write*, *spin*, *read*, *quote*, *cite*.
7. Verbs of instrument of communication, e.g., *radio*, *e-mail*, *telegraph*, *wire*, *telephone*, *netmail*, *fax*.
8. Verbs of creation, e.g., *bake*, *make*, *build*, *cook*, *sew*, *knit*, *toss* (when a salad results), *fix* (when a meal results), *pour* (when a drink results).
9. Verbs of obtaining, e.g., *get*, *buy*, *find*, *steal*, *order*, *win*, *earn*, *grab*.

Before continuing with Gropen et al.'s argument, we might make several small comments on this particular set of subclasses. First, the fifth subclass, "Verbs of future having," actually can be seen to conflate three distinct subclasses. Some of the verbs are used in expressions which imply that the subject actually acts to cause the first object to receive the second object at some later point in time (e.g., *bequeath*, *leave*, *forward*, *allocate*, *assign*), some of the verbs are used in expressions which imply the subject acts to cause the first object to receive the second object at some later point in time only if the *satisfaction conditions* (Searle 1983) associated with the act denoted by the predicate hold, (e.g., *promise*, *guarantee*, *owe*), and finally some are used in expressions which imply that the subject only *enables* the first object to receive the second object (e.g., *permit*, *allow*). Each of these classes will be discussed in more detail below.

The sixth class, verbs of communicated message, should be understood to include verbs whose inherent semantics involves a communicative act, in order to distinguish this class from similar verbs such as *say*, *assert*, *claim*, and *doubt* which might be described as verbs of propositional attitude. Understood in this way, several of the verbs listed by Gropen et al. seem to be misclassified; for example, *pose*, *spin* and *cite do* not obviously fall into the class of "verbs of communicated message", and accordingly, are not (at least in my dialect) readily dativizable:

(6) ?**Bill posed him a problem.*
(7) ?**Bill spun her a fairy tale.*

(8) ?**Bill cited him a passage.*

Both this class and the seventh class, verbs of instrument of communication, should be classified as metaphorical classes since they are based on a systematic metaphor which involves understanding meaning as being packaged in linguistic form and sent between interlocutors. This metaphor, often referred to as the Conduit metaphor (Reddy 1979), is described in more detail in the section below on metaphorical extensions.

Finally, at least one additional subclass should be added to the list of subclasses. This involves verbs of refusal (e.g., *refuse, deny*), e.g., *Bill refused Joe a raise*; *The committee denied him tenure*. Expressions involving these verbs imply that the subject refuses to cause the first object to receive the second object.[3]

In any case, we need only accept the spirit of Gropen et al.'s analysis, that narrowly defined semantic subclasses need to be identified, in order to accept Gropen et al.'s conclusion that this type of narrow circumscription allows us to capture the fact that other subclasses of verbs which refer to the same kind of general events, but do not fall into any of the above particular classes, fail to dativize. Their examples of such non-dativizing classes are as follows:

1. Verbs of fulfilling (X gives something to Y that Y deserves, needs, or is worthy of): **I presented him the award*; **I credited him the discovery*; **Bill entrusted/trusted him the sacred chalice*; **I supplied them a bag of groceries*. [I would also include in this class non-dativizing *concede, furnish*, and *donate*.]
2. Verbs of continuous causation of accompanied motion in some manner: **I pulled John the box. *I carried/pushed/schleped/lifted/lowered/hauled John the box.*
3. Verbs of manner of speaking: **John shouted/screamed/murmured/whispered/yodeled Bill the news.*
4. Verbs of propositions and propositional attitudes: **I said/asserted/questioned/claimed/doubted her something.*
5. Verbs of choosing: **I chose/picked/selected/favored/indicated her a dress.*

Gropen et al. also provide experimental evidence to show that speakers are sensitive to certain morphophonological constraints. In particular, verbs with particular morphemes such as *per-*, *con-*, *-mit*, *-sume* and polysyllabic verbs with non-initial stress are disallowed. These constraints largely coincide with distinctions between Latinate and native vocabulary, and between specialized and more basic vocabulary; however, we clearly would not want to ascribe recourse to etymological information to children, and the experiments in support of these particular constraints controlled for semantic information. Therefore, the constraints are stated in terms of morphophonology. These constraints are used to explain the following:

(9) *Chris bought/*purchased/*obtained/*collected him some food.*
(10) *Jan told/*explained/*reported/*announced Chris a story.*

However the constraints do not apply to every narrowly defined classes of verbs. Verbs of future having, in particular, are not subject to this constraint:

(11) *Chris assigned/allotted/guaranteed/bequeathed him the tickets.*

The class of instrument-of-communication verbs and the class of creation verbs also include verbs which are exceptions to the morphophonological constraint:

(12) *Chris e-mailed/radioed/arpanetted him a message.*
(13) *Chris xeroxed/thermofaxed/nroff'd him a copy.*

Gropen et al. suggest that each of the verbs in examples 12–13 is classified independently of the morphological criteria as a special kind of complex stem having a noun or name as its root. They cite evidence that tacit knowledge that a word's stem is from another category allows it to be treated specially with respect to morphological processes (Pinker and Prince 1988). To account for these cases, we can state the generalization that a verb from any class which is understood to have a noun or name as its root, is not constrained by the morphophonological constraint.

The narrowly defined subclasses of verbs together with the morphophonological constraint provide a high degree of predictive power. A new or nonsense verb which falls into one of the recognized narrow classes of verbs and which, if applicable, obeys the morphophonological constraint, is automatically licensed to be used ditransitively (however see note 3). Verbs in conflict with these constraints are ruled out. This circumscribing of narrow domains in which the ditransitive is locally productive goes a long way toward accounting for the apparent paradox which Gropen et al. set out to resolve: that the ditransitive syntax can be extended to new and novel verbs, but at the same time is not available to all verbs of any broadly defined class (I refer the reader to Pinker 1989 for a detailed investigation of partial productivity).

## 3. Lexical idiosyncrasy

There remains room for a degree of lexical idiosyncrasy. One expected source of idiosyncrasy stems from the fact that the determination of which narrowly-defined class a given verb belongs in is not always entirely clear-cut. For example, I have suggested that *bequeath* falls into the dativizing class of verbs of future having, along with *leave*, *forward*, *allocate*, etc. However, it seems it might be possible to instead classify *bequeath* in the non-dativizing class of verbs of fulfilling (X gives something to Y that Y deserves, needs, or is worthy of), along with *present*, *credit*, *entrust*, *donate*, etc. Because of these two classification possibilities, we would expect *bequeath* in fact to dativize in some dialects, and not to dativize in others. In general, in the case of verbs that may fall into one of two classes, one which can appear ditransitively and one which cannot, we would expect to find some dialectal variation in whether the verbs can be used ditransitively.

Another source of lexical idiosyncrasy is evidenced by the fact that speakers I have checked with occasionally report different degrees of grammaticality even among verbs which are uncontroversially within the same narrow range class. For example, *throw* and *blast* both fall within the class of verbs of instantaneous causation of ballistic motion and yet:

(14) a. *She threw him a cannonball.*

is decidedly better for most speakers than,

(14) b. *She blasted him a cannonball.*

Similarly,

(15) a. *Sally designed him a house.*

is judged to be more grammatical than,

(15) b. *Sally created him a house.*

although both *design* and *create* should fall in the same class of verbs of creation.

This lexical idiosyncrasy can in part be accounted for by a phenomenon which Gropen et al. identify in the same 1989 article. They show that people "tend to be conservative" in their use of lexical items. Specifically they show experimentally that people tend to use lexical items in the same constructions in which they heard those items used, but that they can, if properly primed, extend the uses to new patterns (cf. also Bybee 1985). This phenomenon provides evidence that people store in memory the specific syntactic patterns that a word is heard used with (see also Bybee 1985, Langacker 1987 for particular usage-based models of grammar). This being the case, a certain degree of lexical idiosyncrasy is to be expected.

The existence of some degree of lexical idiosyncrasy, however, should not be taken to undermine the existence of narrowly defined semantic subclasses of verbs that occur in the ditransitive construction. Although the exact formulation of the classes has differed, the existence of such subclasses has been noticed by Green (1974), Oehrle (1976), and Wierzbicka (1986). And, as has just been discussed (and is spelled out in more detail in Pinker 1989), the existence of such classes begins to explain the phenomenon of partial productivity.

## 4. The theoretical framework

In their acquisition experiment, Gropen et al. show that the semantic restriction that a prospective possessor must be involved is operable as soon as the ditransitive syntax is produced, there being no period of unconstrained overgeneralization. For example, none of the following possible types of overextensions were ever uttered by any of the children:

(16) **Amy took Chicago the road. (Amy took the road to Chicago.)*
(17) **Betty threw the tree the box. (Betty threw the box to the tree.)*
(18) **Alex put his head a gun. (Alex put a gun to his head.)*
(19) **Babs took fun a trip. (Babs took a trip for fun.)*

This calls into question the idea that the dative rule is fundamentally a syntactic operation; there is no clear reason why a syntactic operation would be constrained by an arbitrary semantic condition as soon as the syntactic operation is learned. Moreover, since an unconstrained rule would be easier to learn and represent (Fodor ms.) and would provide more expressive power (Pinker 1989), it is not clear why the semantic constraints on this putative syntactic rule are not ignored by new generations of speakers.

For these reasons, Gropen et al. propose that the prepositional/ditransitive alternation results from a semantic rule rather than being the product of a syntactic transformation. Specifically, they suggest that productive use of the ditransitive syntax is the result of a lexicosemantic rule which takes as input a verb with the semantics, *X causes Y to go to Z* and produces the semantic structure *X causes Z to have Y*. The double object syntax, they argue, is then predictable from near universal linking rules mapping the arguments of a verb with the meaning *X causes Z to have Y* into the ditransitive form. In this way, they argue that the dative rule produces a "conceptual gestalt shift", that it is, in effect, a semantic operation on lexical structure.

There are several problems with the rule based account Gropen et al. put forward. It creates a basic asymmetry between the ditransitive and prepositional constructions, since on their account, the argument structure that is mapped into the ditransitive syntax is derived from the argument structure that would be mapped onto a prepositional paraphrase. However, there appears to be little empirical evidence to warrant postulating such an asymmetry. Gropen et al.'s own evidence shows that both constructions are learned at roughly the same time, neither predictably preceding the other in children's speech; therefore an argument based on the chronology of acquisition is immediately undermined. Moreover, as is well known, there are ditransitive expressions which have no prepositional counterpart, for example:

(20) a. *Her mother allowed Jane a candy bar.*
 b. **Her mother allowed a candy bar to Jane.*
(21) a. *The music gave him a headache.*
 b. **The music gave a headache to him.*
(22) a. *Jane refused Fred a kiss.*
 b. **Jane refused a kiss to Fred.*

The asymmetrical relationship implicit in the idea of a rule that takes a "cause to go" semantic structure and changes it into a "cause to have" semantic structure appears to be an historical remnant from transformational accounts which postulated that ditransitive forms were transformationally derived from paraphrases with *to* or *for.* An alternative account will be suggested below which avoids the necessity of postulating rules or transformations on either syntactic or semantic structure.

Another problem with the rule based account is that many of the verb classes do not involve verbs which basically mean: "X causes Y to go to Z". Specifically, verbs of creation (*bake*, *make*), verbs denoting acts whose associated satisfaction conditions imply future having (*promise*, *offer*), verbs of permission (*permit*, *allow*), and verbs of refusal (*deny*, *refuse*) do not involve verbs that mean "cause to go". In order to account for these cases, several distinct rules would need to be postulated.

Further, many verbs clearly do not come to mean "cause to have". For example, the verbs *bake*, *draw* in:

(23) *Joe baked Sally a cake.*
(24) *Joe drew Sally a picture.*

do not under any plausible interpretation mean "cause to have". In general, it is not clear that the meanings of the verbs are changed at all. For example, there is no reason to think that two senses of *send* are involved in the following examples:

(25) a. *I sent a package to him.*
 b. *I sent him a package.*

The sending involved is exactly the same.

There is an alternative account which avoids these difficulties while at the same time capturing the idea that the ditransitive syntax crucially reflects a specific semantics. The alternative is to attribute the semantics directly to the construction instead of to the specific verbs involved. This type of solution has been suggested by Fillmore (1987). Via the literal superimposition of a series of slides, Fillmore suggested that the meaning of an expression is arrived at by the superimposition of the meanings of open class words with the meanings of the grammatical elements. Adopting Fillmore's insight, we can view the construction as imposing a certain semantic construal on the scene described. That is, the semantics of "X causes Y to have Z", or what I will describe as "X causes Z to receive Y", can be attributed directly to the skeletal syntax, [Subj [Verb Obj Obj2]].[4] What are described as narrow range lexicosemantic rules by Gropen et al. can be reinterpreted as narrowly defined classes of verbs which are conventionally associated with the construction. The verb *throw* on this account does not come to mean "cause to receive" when used ditransitively; instead *throw* simply means "throw". The implication of caused reception is contributed, not by the verb, but by the construction.

On this account no asymmetry between the ditransitive and prepositional paraphrase is assumed. In fact, once we recognize that both syntactic structures are paired with identifiable semantics, the alternation itself can be seen to be a result of semantic overlap between the two constructions. It is a fact about the world that causing something to move somewhere is systematically related to causing someone to receive something. We no longer need to state a rule in the grammar linking these two constructions.

This account also allows us to avoid a proliferation of verb senses; we need only postulate one verb *send* which has the same sense in both:

(26) a. *I sent a package to him.*
b. *I sent him a package.*

The sending scene referred to in both sentences is compatible with a description in terms of *I caused a package to go to him* or *I caused him to receive a package*, with little if any noticeable change in meaning so either construction is licensed.

Pinker argues that a major motivation for positing lexical rules is that they tell us which verb stems we can use with the construction (Pinker 1989). However, it is not necessary to postulate rules that alter the inherent semantics of the verbs – we can say that the particular verb classes are conventionally associated with the construction. The overall interpretation, then, is an effect of the principles of integration, not rules operating on lexical semantics.

There are additional reasons to prefer this account. Below we will see that there are specific semantic constraints on the subject and direct object as well as on the verb. The subject must intend the transfer and the direct object must be understood to be a willing recipient. It will turn out that these constraints, just like the morphophonological constraint that Gropen et al. propose, can be overridden in certain delimitable subclasses of expressions, but they nonetheless need to be stated as constraints on the use of ditransitive syntax. The fact that these constraints refer to the subject and the first object undermines attempts to link the semantic constraints solely to the verb's semantics. In the same way, the systematic metaphors that are discussed in the next section are not describable without direct reference to the entities which are encoded as arguments in the ditransitive syntax. For example, a metaphor to be discussed below, Directed Actions are Transferred Objects crucially refers to the entity which is coded as the second argument, i.e., the action. It is only the semantics of the second argument which differentiates:

(27) *John gave Mary an apple.*
(28) *John gave Mary a wink.*

It is also clear that there are several verbs in the narrowly defined class of creation verbs which do not inherently signify creation; however these verbs can be associated with a scene of creation when used in conjunction with particular direct objects. For example, Gropen et al. include *fix*, and *pour* in their list of verbs of creation because of such expressions as:

(29) *Fix dinner.*
(30) *Pour a drink.*

These expressions refer to scenes of creation, but the creation involved is not part of the *verbs'* semantics. *Pour* and *fix* retain their normal meanings in these expressions. It is the verb together with the direct object which describes a scene of creation and therefore licenses the ditransitive syntax.

Another benefit to attributing the semantics directly to the construction is that it is more parsimonious. The rule-based account must postulate not only separate verb senses, but also a special form-meaning correspondence in the form of a linking rule. That is, despite the fact that Gropen et al. imply that the construction results simply from applying near universal linking rules to the "X causes Z to have Y" argument structure, in point of fact, one of the necessary linking rules needs to be postulated specifically for this construction. The linking rule mapping the possessed entity to the second object position is unique to this construction. Moreover, another stipulation is required to capture the fact that the proposed verb senses only occur in this construction. That is, *throw* for example, does not mean "cause to have" except when used ditransitively. This fact cannot follow simply from the proposed linking rules since other verbs which lexically code "cause to have", such as *give*, can be used derivatively and with other valences with the same meaning. On our account, only a single form-meaning correspondence need be postulated, that the skeletal construction, [Subj [Verb Obj Obj2]] is paired with a particular semantics. No new verb senses are required, and so no stipulation of where these verb senses can occur is necessary.

Finally, by associating the semantics directly with the construction, there is a natural way to capture the intuition that the *give*-class of verbs is more central to the construction than the other classes. What needs to be noted is that the semantics associated with these lexical items is redundant with the semantics of the construction. The other classes of lexical items are only compatible with the construction in the sense that they are able to accommodate the transfer interpretation, but do not lexically code transfer.[5]

The idea that the meanings of lexical items can accommodate to the meanings of the constructions has been discussed at some length by, among others, Talmy (1977), Fillmore (ms.) and Carter (1988). What is at issue in the case of the ditransitive is whether the transfer interpretation of ditransitive expressions must be posited in the meaning of each of the verbs involved or whether we can attribute the transfer interpretation to the meaning of the construction. For the reasons just outlined, it makes sense to associate the transfer interpretation directly with the construction.

In the theory of Construction Grammar, as articulated by Fillmore, Kay, and O'Connor (1988), Fillmore (1988), Kay (1988), and Lakoff (1987), the units of language are taken to be form-meaning correspondences that are not strictly predictable from knowledge of the rest of the grammar; these correspondences are called *constructions*. Words and morphemes are taken to be instances of constructions, as are larger phrasal form-meaning correspondences. Since the existence of the ditransitive structure in English is not predictable from knowledge of the rest of English grammar, and since it is advantageous to view the structure as being associated with a particular semantic interpretation for the reasons just outlined, a constructional analysis of the English ditransitive is warranted, i.e., the ditransitive argument structure can be seen to be a *construction* in the Construction Grammar sense of the term, a pairing of both form and meaning. By referring to a construction, instead of to a "case frame", "valence", or "subcategorization frame", I intend to underscore the point that the construction, with a specific meaning to be detailed below, exists independently of the individual verbs that may occur with it.

## 5. The semantics

We are now in a position to turn our attention to the description of the construction's semantics. This section owes a great debt to Cattell (1984), Green (1974), and Oehrle (1976), for their detailed analyses of hundreds of ditransitive expressions. In what follows, several aspects of the semantics are discussed: the construction is shown not to be associated with a single fixed meaning, but instead is associated with a category of related meanings; specific constraints on the subject and direct object are argued for; and several systematic metaphors are identified and discussed, revealing the general, systematic, productive nature of forms that are often assumed to be idiosyncratic. Before these issues are addressed, however, I will briefly defend my choice of the term "recipient" as opposed to "possessor" to describe the semantics associated with the first object position.

## 6. On the notion recipient

I have been referring to the semantic role of the first object position as "recipient" instead of as "possessor". This is done for several reasons. Many of the metaphors involving transfer (to be described below) do not map the implication that the recipient possesses the transferred entity after reception. For example,

(31) *Joe gave Mary an insult.*

does not imply that Mary "possesses" an insult, but only that Mary "received" an insult. Similarly,

(32) *Jan gave Chris a punch.*

does not imply that Chris "possesses" a punch, but only that he "received" a punch. If we describe the role as that of a "recipient" instead of "possessor" these facts pose no problem. The fact that a possessive relationship is usually implied follows automatically from the fact that what is received is normally subsequently possessed.

Moreover, noticing that a recipient is involved in ditransitive expressions may be a first step toward motivating the double object syntax of the construction. Those interested in the semantics of the direct object since Jakobson have noted that *recipients* of force and effect make for good direct objects (Jakobson 1984 [1938]; Langacker 1987; Rice 1987). (Of course this is not to say that all direct objects are recipients; clearly the objects of cognition verbs such as *believe, see,* and *know* would present difficulties for such a claim.)

Finally, the construction has been shown to be associated with a scene of transfer (I have been using "scene" in the sense of Fillmore [1975] to mean any coherent individuatable perception, memory experience, action or object). Describing the first object as a "recipient" more adequately captures the dynamic character of this semantics. It is for these reasons that I consider "recipient" to be a more appropriate description for the semantics of the first object than "possessor".

## 7. Polysemous interpretation

It is widely recognized that many ditransitive expressions do not strictly imply that the second object is successfully transferred to the first object. For example, "Chris baked Jan a cake" does not strictly imply that Jan actually receives the cake. It may happen that Chris is mugged by cake-thieves on the way over to Jan's. In fact many of the narrowly defined verb classes described by Gropen et al. can be seen to give rise to slightly different interpretations.

Expressions involving verbs of creation (e.g., *bake*, *make*, *build*, *cook*) and verbs of obtaining (e.g., *get*, *grab*, *win*, *earn*) do not strictly imply that the subject causes the first object to receive the second object. As was noted above, "Chris baked Jan a cake" does not strictly imply that Jan receives the cake. Transfer is rather a *ceteris paribus* implication. What is implied by this example is that Chris baked a cake with the intention of giving the cake to Jan.

Expressions involving verbs which imply that the subject undertakes an obligation (e.g., *promise*, *guarantee*, *owe*) also do not strictly imply transfer. For example, *Bill promised his son a car* does not imply that Bill actually gives his son a car, or even that Bill intends to give his son a car. Rather, transfer is implied by the "satisfaction conditions" associated with the act denoted by each predicate (Searle 1983). A satisfied promise for example does imply that the promisee receives whatever is promised.

Expressions involving verbs of future having (e.g., *bequeath*, *leave*, *refer*, *forward*, *allocate*, *allot*, *assign*) imply that the subject acts to cause the first object to receive the second object at some future point in time. This class differs from the last two classes in that no intention or obligation of future action on the part of the subject is implied; i.e., the subject's role in the transfer is accomplished by the action referred to by the predicate.

Expressions involving verbs of permission (e.g., *permit*, *allow*) imply that the subject *enables* the transfer to occur by not preventing it, not that the subject actually *causes* the transfer to occur. For example, *Joe allowed Billy a popsicle* implies only that Joe enabled, or did not prevent Billy from having a popsicle, not that Joe necessarily caused Billy to have a popsicle.

Expressions involving verbs of refusal (e.g., *refuse*, *deny*) express the negation of transfer, for example:

(33) *Joe refused Bob a raise in salary.*
(34) *His mother denied Billy a birthday cake.*

Here transfer is relevant in that the possibility for successful transfer has arisen, the subject is understood to refuse to act as the cause of the reception.

Because of these differences, the semantics involved can best be represented as a category of related meanings. In this sense the ditransitive can be viewed as a case of *constructional polysemy*: the same form is paired with different but related senses. The slightly different senses associated with the construction would have to be accounted for by a rule-based account as well. Narrow range rules would have to be modified to account for differences in implication; this could certainly be done. However, polysemy has been shown to be a natural and recurring phenomenon in natural language in many studies (for example, Brugman 1988; Haiman 1978; Lakoff 1987; Lindner 1981; Sweetser 1990). Moreover, accounting for these differences in terms of constructional polysemy allows us to capture the relationships between the different senses in a natural way, instead of postulating an unstructured collection of rules. In particular, a polysemous analysis allows us to recognize the special status of the central sense of the construction.

The central sense can be argued to be the sense involving successful transfer of an object to a recipient, i.e., the subject agentively causes the second object to be transferred to the first object. There are several reasons to postulate this class as the central sense. It involves concrete, as opposed to metaphorical or abstract (here, potential) transfer, and concrete meanings have been shown to be more basic diachronically (Traugott 1988; Sweetser 1990) and synchronically (Lakoff and Johnson 1980). Further this is the class most metaphorical extensions (described below) are based on. For example,

(35) a. *Mary taught Bill French.*

implies that Bill actually learned some French, i.e., that metaphorical transfer was successful. This is in contrast to:

(35) b. *Mary taught French to Bill.*

in which no such implication is necessary. Similarly,

(36) a. *Mary showed her mother the photograph.*

implies that her mother actually saw the photograph, whereas for many speakers, no such implication is necessary in,

(36) b. *Mary showed the photograph to her mother (but her nearsighted mother couldn't see it).*

These facts can be accounted for once we recognize actual successful transfer as the central sense of the construction; we need only state that metaphorical extensions have as their source domain, the central sense. Finally, successful transfer is argued to be the central sense because the other classes can be represented most economically as extensions from this sense.

The different senses are of course not unrelated to the differences in the meanings of the verbs which enter into the construction. That is, it is clear that the lexical items which occur in a particular expression play a role in deciding which sense of the ditransitive will be implied. For example, it is not an accident that the verb *refuse* combines with the ditransitive construction to imply that the subject refuses to cause the first object to receive the second object. For this reason it is possible to understand the different senses just described as resulting from principles of integration between the central sense of the construction and the particular verb classes that enter into it. On this view, the construction is directly associated only with the central sense of actual transfer, the differences in interpretation resulting from principles of integration existing between the central sense and the different classes of verbs involved.

At the same time, the various senses, or alternatively, the principles of integration, are not predictable and must be conventionally associated with the construction. For example, it is not predictable from knowing the rest of English, that verbs of creation will be allowable in the ditransitive construction in the first place; moreover, it is not predictable that ditransitive expressions involving verbs of creation will imply intended transfer instead of actual transfer or general benefaction. Because of this, the various different possible senses are listed; it should be borne in mind that it is possible to view them as principles of integration operating between the central sense of the construction and the classes of verbs which enter into it.

The suggestion here of allowing for a fairly specific central sense of the construction and also postulating separate related senses or principles of integration which make reference to specific verb classes, can be contrasted with the possibility of postulating a single abstract sense for the construction and allowing the verbs' semantics to fill out the meaning. Since the latter approach is attractive in being more simple, let me take time to demonstrate why an abstractionist account fails to adequately account for the data.

Several researchers (e.g., Wierzbicka 1986; Paul Kay. p.c.; Frederike Van der Leek, p.c.) have suggested that there is a uniform meaning associated with the ditransitive, and that is simply that there is some kind of special effect on the first object. It is claimed that the nature of this effect is inferred pragmatically. Several problems are apparent with this suggestion.

First, there is no non-circular reason to think that first object is any more affected in the following (a) cases than in the corresponding (b) cases:

(37) a. Chris baked Pat a cake.
 b. *Chris baked a cake for Pat.*
(38) a. *Chris promised Pat a car.*
 b. *Chris promised a car to Pat.*
(39) a. *Chris kicked Pat the ball.*
 b. *Chris kicked the ball to Pat.*

In fact, there is no obvious definition for "affected" which implies that the Pat is necessarily affected in:

(40) *Chris baked Pat a cake.*

Pat may never receive the cake, and in fact may never even know about the cake.

Also undermining the claim that the first object is necessarily affected in the ditransitive construction is the fact that this argument is often only marginally passivizable, and passive is generally accepted to be positively correlated with affected subjects:

(41) **Lou was bought a gift.*
(42) **Lou was boiled an egg.*
(43) **Pat was flung a sweater.*
(44) **She was nudged a beer.*
(45) **She was baked a cake.*

Finally, it is not possible to construe the first object as affected in just any pragmatically-inferable way. For example, even if we know that there are an agent, a patient, and a goal involved (this we may know by the semantic roles on, e.g., Kay's account), it is possible to pragmatically infer that the way the goal is affected is by the agent throwing the patient at the goal. However, the following cannot be interpreted in this way:

(46) *Pat threw Chris the ball.*
(47) *Pat hit Chris the ball.*

That is, these examples cannot be interpreted to mean that Pat threw the ball at Chris. They can only mean that Pat threw or hit the ball so that Chris would receive the ball. This fact is unexplained by the abstractionist account.

Another abstractionist analysis that is sometimes offered is that the first object semantic role be described as a *prospective possessor*, thus allowing the semantics to be abstract enough to cover all of the possible interpretations of actual, intended, future, or refused transfer (e.g., Goldsmith 1980). However, this suggestion, and in fact more generally, any abstractionist account, is subject to several criticisms.

One general problem is that an abstractionist account cannot capture the intuition that transfer in general, and *give* in particular are more basic to the construction. *Give*, in fact, is the most prototypical ditransitive verb because its lexical semantics is identical with the construction's semantics. I take this to be a strong enough intuition to be worth worrying about. In fact, I performed an informal experiment to gauge the strength of the intuition that *give* codes the most basic sense of the construction. I asked ten non-linguists what the nonsense word *topamased* meant in the following sentence:

(48) *She topamased him something.*

A full six out of ten subjects responded that *topamased* meant "give". This fact cannot be attributed simply to effects of general word frequency because there are several other words that are allowable in this construction and are more frequent than *give*. Thus, according to Carroll et al.'s *Word Frequency Book* (1971), that used a 5,000,000 word corpus, *give* occurred 3366 times, while *tell* occurred 3715 times; *take* 4089 times; *get* 5700 times; and *make* 8333 times. Only *tell* of these other words was given as a response, and it was only given by one speaker. None of the other words were given as responses. One might raise the objection that while *give* is not the most frequently occurring word overall, it is nonetheless the most frequently word in this construction. However, the point of the experiment was exactly to test whether speakers were aware of the close relationship between *give* and this particular construction; the results seem to indicate that they are.

A related problem stems from the fact that not all ditransitive expressions are equally acceptable. That is, there are certain benefactive ditransitives, to be described below in terms of a systematic metaphor, which are acceptable to varying degrees, with some speakers allowing them more freely than others. Examples of this type include:

(49) *Hit me a home run.*
(50) *Crush me a mountain.*
(51) *Rob me a bank.*

These expressions are severely restricted in use (Oehrle 1976). For example, they are noticeably more felicitous as commands:

(52) a. *Hit me a home run.*
b. ?*Alice hit me a home run.*

Also, they are more acceptable when the recipient is referred to by a pronoun:

(53) ?*Hit Sally a home run.*

On our account, we can understand these cases to be a limited extension from the basic sense; we do not need to put them on a par with other ditransitive examples, and yet we can still treat them as related to the rest of the ditransitives. However, on an abstractionist account, we have to choose whether to include them as ditransitives or exclude them from the analysis. If we include them, we have no way to account for their marginal status and special constraints. If we exclude them, we fail to capture the obvious similarity they bear to other ditransitives, both in their syntax and in their semantics.

Another problem is that it is not predictable that verbs of creation will combine with the ditransitive to imply intended transfer instead of actual or future transfer. For example,

(54) *Chris baked Mary a cake.*

can only mean that Chris intends to give Mary the cake. It cannot mean that Chris necessarily gave or will give the cake to Mary.

Finally, an abstractionist account does not readily allow us to account for the fact, mentioned previously, that the metaphorical extensions are based on an actual transfer, not potential or intended transfer. That is, if we only postulate an abstract constraint on the first object position, we have no natural way of accounting for the fact that the metaphorical extensions imply that the first object is an actual recipient, and not a prospective recipient or goal. However, on our account that constructional polysemy is involved, we can say that the metaphorical extensions have as their source domain, the central sense of actual transfer.

These problems arise for any abstractionist account; therefore, such an account can be seen to be unsatisfactory. Instead, a polysemous semantics is warranted. The related senses are diagrammed in Figure 1.

## 8. Motivating the links

The links between the senses can be shown to be natural by showing that analogous links are found elsewhere in language. In this way, it is possible to demonstrate that no *ad hoc* machinery is necessary to account for the polysemous relations. For example, to see that the link between senses A and B, i.e., a link between actual and intended transfer, is natural, notice that a parallel link between actualization and intention can be found in two interpretations of the English present progressive tense. These two interpretations are exemplified in the following:

(55) a. *Not right now, I'm working.*
b. *Tomorrow, I'm working all day.*

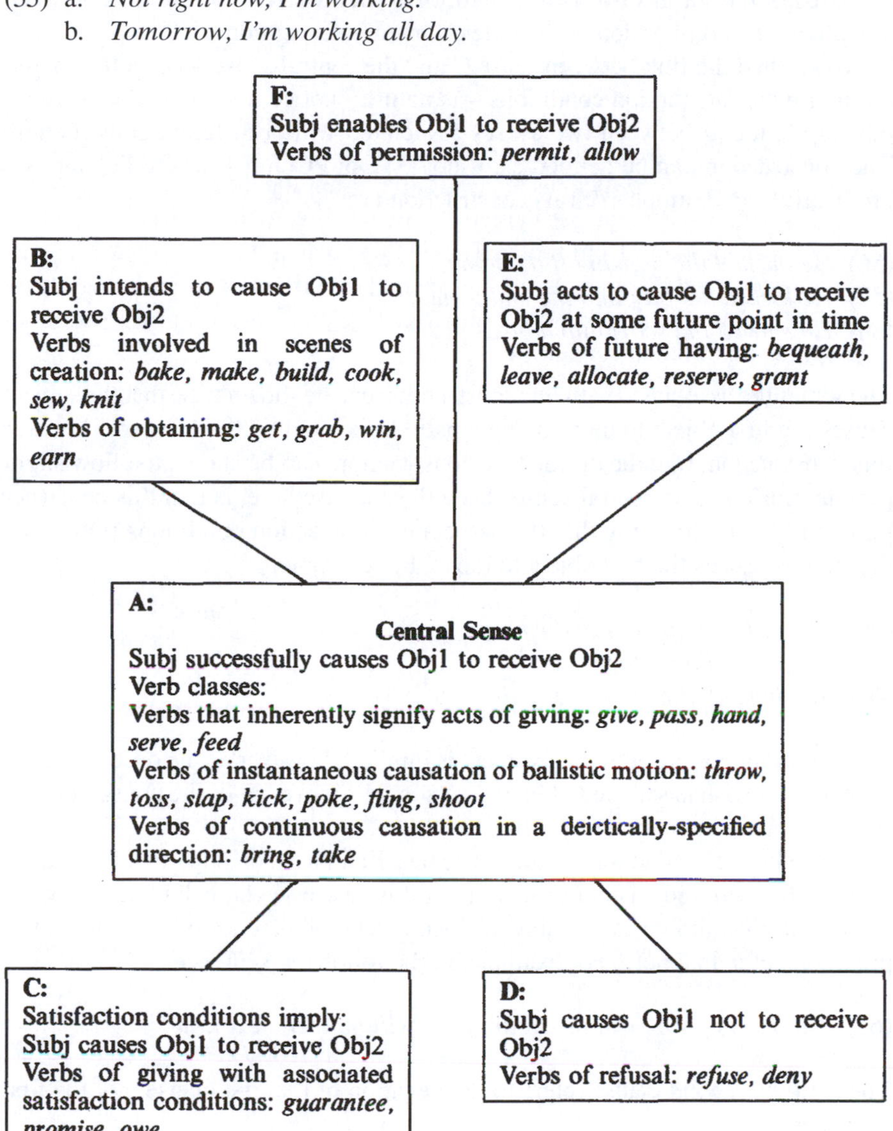

F:
Subj enables Obj1 to receive Obj2
Verbs of permission: permit, allow
B:
Subj intends to cause Obj1 to receive Obj2
Verbs involved in scenes of creation: bake, make, build, cook, sew, knit
Verbs of obtaining: get, grab, win, earn
E:
Subj acts to cause Obj1 to receive Obj2 at some future point in time
Verbs of future having: bequeath, leave, allocate, reserve, grant
A:
Central Sense
Subj successfully causes Obj1 to receive Obj2
Verb classes:
Verbs that inherently signify acts of giving: give, pass, hand, serve, feed
Verbs of instantaneous causation of ballistic motion: throw, toss, slap, kick, poke, fling, shoot
Verbs of continuous causation in a deictically-specified direction: bring, take
C:
Satisfaction conditions imply:
Subj causes Obj1 to receive Obj2
Verbs of giving with associated satisfaction conditions: guarantee, promise, owe
D:
Subj causes Obj1 not to receive Obj2
Verbs of refusal: refuse, deny


*Figure 1.* Polysemous senses of the ditransitive construction

In the first example, the working is actualized, while in the second example, the working is intended and will, as a *ceteris paribus* implication, be actualized. If the parallel between the two interpretations of the present progressive and the two uses of the ditransitive is accepted, then the existence of the link between actualization and intention in the latter is made unexceptional.

To see that the link between sense C and the central sense – i.e., a link based on pragmatic satisfaction conditions – is natural, notice that an analogous relationship is found between two senses associated with a different construction. The construction can be defined as: [Subj [V Obj PComp]], where PComp is a predicative PP. Examples of this construction are:

(56) *He pushed the napkin off the table.*
(57) *He kicked the ball into the end-zone.*
(58) *He shoved the scarf into a box.*

The semantics associated with this construction can be shown to be that the subject causes the first object to move along a path designated by the PComp. However this construction, like the ditransitive construction, can be shown to allow slight permutations on this central sense. The relevant case here, is that this construction can be used to imply that the associated satisfaction conditions imply that the subject causes the first object to move. For example:

(59) *She ordered him out of the house.*
(60) *She asked him into the room.*
(61) *She invited him out to her cabin.*

In these examples, no actual movement is implied; however, if the order, request, invitation or wish is satisfied, then the person will move out of the house, into the room, or out to her cabin, respectively.

Sense D is related to the central sense by a link based on negation. It has been more difficult to find an analogous link for this case elsewhere, but the following is a possible candidate. A possibly analogous relation is required for some interpretations of *it* anaphora. For example, in the following sentence,

(62) *The 76'ers didn't win this year, but it will happen next time.*

The *it* in the second clause refers to the negation of the first clause, not the first clause itself.

Sense E, that the subject is understood to act to cause the first object to receive the second object at some future point in time, involves expressions which imply that the subject performs some crucial act in a causal chain which, if uninterrupted, will naturally result in the first object receiving the second object. This relationship can be found in the pragmatic principle that allows us to answer the question,

A: How did you get here?
with the response,
B: I hopped on a bus.

The act of hopping on a bus is understood to be the crucial act in a causal chain which, if uninterrupted, naturally results in actualized transportation.

Finally, the link between the central sense and sense F is based on the relationship between causation and enablement. It should not be surprising that the ditransitive construction can accommodate cases of enablement since it is often the case that causers and entities which enable function the same syntactically. For example, so-called causative verbs in English allow subjects which actually only enable as well as subjects which are truly causative. Some examples are: "Forgetting to set my alarm made me oversleep". "Leaving the butter out all day is what melted it".[6]

## 9. Volitionality of the subject

There are certain semantic constraints on the ditransitive syntax which, although occasionally recognized (e.g., Green 1974), have not been incorporated into most theories of argument structure. The reason these constraints are often overlooked is that there appear to be exceptional cases. However, the exceptional cases form a delimitable class that can be seen to involve a general systematic metaphor (of the type described in Lakoff and Johnson 1980). It will be shown that the constraints do in fact hold in the source domain of the metaphor.

To identify the first constraint, notice that each of the verbs described so far independently selects for a volitional subject. This generalization can be captured by assigning a constraint on the subject's volitionality directly to the construction.

The volitionality must extend so that not only is the action described by the verb performed agentively, but also so that the transfer is intended. For example, in:

(63) *Joe painted Sally a picture.*

Joe must be understood to intend to give the picture to Sally. It cannot be the case that Joe painted the picture for someone else and later happened to give it to Sally. Similarly, in:

(64) *Bob told Joe a story.*

It cannot be the case that Bob told the story to someone else, and Joe just happened to overhear.[7] This constraint accounts for the illformedness of the following examples:

(65) **Joe threw the outfielder the ball he had intended the firstbaseman to catch.*
(66) **Hal brought his mother a cake since he didn't eat it on the way home.*
(67) **Joe took Sam a package by leaving it in his trunk where Sam later found it.*

This is not to say that the first or second object of the ditransitive cannot be given a transparent interpretation. The description used to pick out the objects may be understood to be the speaker's description, not the subject's. For example, it is acceptable to say:

(68) *Oedipus gave his mother a kiss.*

despite the fact that Oedipus did not realize he was kissing his mother. Likewise, it is acceptable to say:

(69) *Joe gave Mary a sweater with a hole in it.*

even if Joe did not intend to give Mary a defective sweater. Also, it is not necessarily contradictory to use "accidentally" in ditransitive expressions, for example: *Joe accidentally loaned Bob a lot of money* [by mistaking Bob for Bill, his twin; without realizing that Bob would skip bail with it; instead of giving the money as a gift as he had intended].

While I do not attempt to untangle the relevant issues here, I appeal to the fact that the same possibilities of interpretation occur with other expressions which are generally agreed to require volitional subjects. For example, *murder* is a verb which is universally recognized as selecting for a volitional subject. Still, it is possible to say without contradiction,

(70) *Joe accidentally murdered Mary* [although he had meant to murder Sue/ although he had only meant to knock her unconscious].

What I am suggesting, then, is whatever notion of volitionality is adopted to deal with verbs such as *murder*, should be also used to capture the semantic requirement of the subject position of the ditransitive construction.

The existence of this constraint has been obscured by examples such as:

(71) *The medicine brought him relief.*
(72) *The rain bought us some time.*
(73) *She got me a ticket by distracting me while I was driving.*

(74) *She gave me the flu.*
(75) The music lent the party a festive air.
(76) *The missed ball handed him the victory on a silver platter.*

In these examples the subject is not volitional. Even when the subject is an animate being, as in examples (73) and (74), no volitionality is required. However these examples form a delimitable class of expressions, as each is an instance of a particular conventional systematic metaphor, Causal Events are Transfers.[8] This metaphor involves understanding causing an effect in an entity as transferring the effect, construed as an object, to that entity. Evidence for the existence of this metaphor, independent of the ditransitive construction, comes from the following expressions:

The Catch-22 situation *presented* him with a dilemma.
The unforeseen circumstances *laid* a new opportunity *at our feet.*
The document *supplied* us with some entertainment.
The report *furnished* them with the information they needed.

Further evidence, both for the existence of the metaphor, and for it motivating the ditransitive examples (67)–(72), comes from the polysemy of each of the predicates involved in those examples. The predicates *bring*, *buy*, *get*, *give*, *lend* and *hand* are used to imply causation, but each of their central senses involve transfer by an agent to a recipient. The link between these senses is accounted for by appeal to the metaphor. *Bring*, *buy*, *get*, *give*, *lend* and *hand* here involve the metaphorical transfer of effect; i.e., each of the examples (71)–(76) implies that the subject is the cause of the first object being affected in some way by "receiving" the second object.

This class can be represented as follows:

Name of Metaphor: Causal Events are Transfers

Source Domain: Subject causes Obj to receive Obj2
Target Domain: Subject is the cause of Obj being affected by Obj2
Subj: cause
Obj: affected party
Obj2: effect

Recognizing the metaphor allows us to divorce ourselves from the often made, but erroneous claim that examples such as

(77) *Sally gave Bill a headache.*
(78) *Mary's behavior gave John an idea.*

are idiosyncratic. In fact, they are actually instances of a general, productive and principled class of expressions based on the Causal Events are Transfers metaphor.

Returning to the statement of the constraint that the subject must intend the transfer, we can now see the necessity of recognizing this metaphor. By identifying the metaphor, we are able to understand the exceptional cases to be licensed by it; we can recognize that the volitionality constraint is satisfied in the source domain of the metaphor. At the same time, this metaphor differs from the other metaphors to be described below in not mapping volitionality to the target domain; however, the fact that volitionality is not mapped in this metaphor, follows from the fact that the target domain is concerned with abstract causes. Abstract causes cannot necessarily be volitional because they are not necessarily human. Each of the other metaphors described below, on the other hand, involve human actors in the target domain as well as in the source domain, and in each of the target domains, the volitionality constraint is respected.

## 10. Semantic constraints on the first object

It has long been realized[9] that the first object must be an animate being to account for the following:

(79) *He sent who/*where a letter?*[10]

This constraint, however, just like the constraint that the subject must intend the transfer, is somewhat obscured by expressions licensed by the Causal Events are Transfers metaphor described above. For example:

(80) *The paint job gave the car a higher sale price.*
(81) *The tabasco sauce gave the baked beans some flavor.*
(82) *The music lent the party a festive air.*

In none of these examples is the first object an animate being; however, in the source domain of the metaphor, the affected party is understood to be a recipient, i.e., an animate being. That is, the constraint is satisfied in the source, but not the target domain of the metaphor.

An additional semantic constraint is that the first object be understood to be a beneficiary or a willing recipient.[11] This constraint is needed to account for the following example:

(83) **Sally burned Joe some rice.*

Example 83 is unacceptable even if malicious intentions are attributed to Sally; however, it *is* acceptable in the context that Joe is thought to like burnt rice. Furthermore, one cannot felicitously say:

(84) **Bill told Mary a story, but she wasn't listening.*
(85) **Bill threw the coma victim a blanket.*

In these examples, the first object is not understood to be a willing recipient, and accordingly, these examples are unacceptable.

This constraint may be responsible for the slight difference in meaning between the following two examples provided by Robert Wilensky (p.c.):

(86) a. *She fed lasagna to the guests.*
b. *She fed the guests lasagna.*

Most speakers find the first example to be somewhat less polite than the first. Since "feed" is normally used with reference to the food intake of babies or animals, the impoliteness of the first example is not surprising; what requires explanation is the fact that the second example is interpreted to be more polite. The constraint that the first object must be construed as a willing recipient can account for this since the ditransitive version has the effect of imposing the interpretation that the guests are willing agents, thereby according them more respect.

That the recipient is expected to be willing should not be confused with the idea that the recipient is expected to benefit from the transfer. Thus, while,

(87) *Jack poured Jane an arsenic-laced martini.*

does not imply that Jane will benefit from imbibing the martini, it does presuppose that she is expected to willingly drink the martini.

In some cases, however, the issue of the recipient's willingness or unwillingness is irrelevant to whether transfer is successful. These involve expressions in which actual successful transfer is implied:

(88) *Bill gave the driver a speeding ticket.*
(89) *Bill gave Chris a headache.*
(90) *Chris gave Bill a kick.*[12]

Nonetheless, all cases in which the first object is required to *accept* the transferred object in order for transfer to be successful imply that the first object is assumed to be a willing recipient.

## 11. Other metaphors

In the discussion about the constraint that the subject must intend the transfer, we described a systematic metaphor, Causal Events are Transfers, which licenses exceptions to the constraint. This is just one of several metaphors which license the use of the ditransitive construction. The metaphors can be understood to be further extensions from the central sense of literal transfer. The source domain of each of these metaphors is the central sense of actual successful transfer.

The Conduit Metaphor, described and named by Michael Reddy (1979) involves communication *traveling across* from the stimulus to the listener. The listener understands the communication upon "reception". Evidence for the metaphor includes:

He *got the ideas across to* Jo.
His thoughts *came across from* his speech.
Jo received the information from Sam.
Jo got the information from Bill.

This metaphor licenses the following examples:

(91) *She told Jo a fairy tale.*
(92) *She wired Joe a message.*
(93) *She quoted Joe a passage.*
(94) *She gave Joe her thoughts on the subject.*

This class can be represented as follows:

Name of Metaphor: CONDUIT

Source Domain: Subject causes Obj to receive Obj2
Target Domain: Subj communicates Obj2 to Obj
Subj: speaker
Obj: listener
Obj2: information

A related metaphor involves understanding perceptions as entities which move toward the perceiver. The perception is understood to be perceived upon "reception". Evidence for the metaphor includes the following:

The view *knocked me over.*
I *caught* a glimpse of him.
I missed that sight.

I had a view of the orchestra.
He *let me have* a look.

This metaphor licenses the following examples:

(95) *He showed Bob the view.*
(96) *He gave Bob a glimpse.*

Source Domain: Subject causes Obj to receive Obj2
Target Domain: Subj acts to cause Obj to see Obj2
Subj: actor
Obj: perceiver
Obj2: perception

Another metaphor involves understanding actions that are intentionally directed at another person as being entities which are transferred to that person. Evidence for the metaphor includes:

He *blocked* the kick.
He *c*aught the kiss she threw to him.
All he got from her was a goodbye wave.
Joe took a punch from Bill.
She couldn't get a smile out of him.
She threw a parting glance in his direction.
She ta*rgeted him* with a big smile.
Bob *received* a slap/kick/kiss/smile from Jo.

This metaphor licenses the following expressions:

(97) *She blew him a kiss.*
(98) *She shot him a keep-quiet look.*
(99) *She gave him a wink.*
(100) *Jo gave Bob a punch.*
(101) *She threw him a parting glance.*

This class can be represented as follows:

Name of Metaphor: Actions which are directed at a Person are Entities which are Transferred to the Person.

Source Domain: Subject causes Obj to receive Obj2
Target Domain: Subj performs an action (Obj2) which is directed at Obj

Subj: actor
Obj: recipient
Obj2: action

Another metaphor extends the use of the ditransitive to the speech act domain. This metaphor is used in reference to the situation where a person agrees to accept certain facts and assumptions. The metaphor involves understanding these facts and assumptions as objects which are given to the person who is making the argument to be used in the building of the argument. (The idea of *building an argument* assumes another metaphor, Arguments are Constructed Objects). If the facts or assumptions do not need to be agreed to because they are in some sense self-evident, then they may be called "givens" where no explicit "giver" is necessary. We can title this metaphor, Facts and Assumptions that are Agreed to are Objects which are Given. Evidence for the metaphor includes the following expressions,

I'll *let you have that much.*
I don't want to give up that assumption.
Accept that as a given.
If you take that assumption away, you don't have a great argument.
If you don't *have* that assumption, you're not *left with much.*
Even *granted* that, your argument is still full of holes.

This metaphor licenses the following:

(102) *I'll give you that assumption.*
(103) *I'll grant you that much of your argument.*

Name of Metaphor: FACTS AND ASSUMPTIONS THAT ARE AGREED TO ARE OBJECTS WHICH ARE GIVEN.

Source Domain: Subject causes Obj to receive Obj2
Target Domain: Subject agrees to accept Obj2 for the sake of Obj's argument
Subj: actor
Obj: builder of an argument
Obj2: fact or assumption

The final metaphor to be discussed here licenses ditransitive expressions which are often assumed not to involve a possessor at all. The following examples come from Green 1974:

(104) *Crush me a mountain.*
(105) *Cry me a river.*
(106) *Slay me a dragon.*
(107) *They're going to kill Reagan a commie.*

These expressions can be seen to involve metaphorical transfer once the following metaphor is recognized. The metaphor involves understanding actions which are performed for the benefit of a person as objects which are transferred to the person. The metaphor is exemplified in the following expressions:

He *owes* you many favors.
By slaving away quietly for him, she has given more than he deserves.
The senator claimed never to have received any favors.
He always *gets* what he wants out of people.
He graciously *offered* a ride to the airport.

The mapping of this metaphor is different from the others in that the source domain of this metaphor is not "Subj causes Obj to receive Obj2" as it was in each of the other metaphors. In particular, the second object is not the received object in the mapping; rather it is the action performed that is the received object. This metaphor, then represents an extended use of the ditransitive. And, as we might expect, there is wide dialectal variation in the degree of acceptability of these expressions. In fact, these cases are subject to their own special constraints. As noted previously, they are more acceptable as commands:

(108) a. *Cry me a river.*
b. ?*Sally cried me a river.*

And they are more acceptable with pronouns in first object position:

(109) ?*Cry Joe a river.*

These cases can be seen to be a limited extension from the central sense of the construction. This class can be represented as follows:

Name of Metaphor: ACTS THAT ARE PERFORMED FOR THE BENEFIT OF A PERSON ARE OBJECTS WHICH ARE GIVEN TO THAT PERSON.

Source Domain: Subject causes Obj to receive an Object
(not necessarily designated by Obj2)
Target Domain: Subject Performs an Action for the Benefit of Obj
Subj: actor
Obj: person whom action is performed for the benefit of
Obj2: Obj acted on by Subj

## 12. Exceptions

There remain a few ditransitive expressions that are exceptional.

Some uses of *ask* can be fit into the pattern described above if they are interpreted as instances of the Conduit metaphor. For example,

(110) *She asked Sam a question.*

can be understood to mean she caused Sam to "receive" a question. However, other uses of *ask* are clearly exceptional, for example,

(111) *She asked Sam his name/his birthday/his marital status.*

This type of example clearly does not imply that Sam potentially receives his name, his birthday or his marital status. Grimshaw (1979) discusses these "concealed questions" at some length. She argues that noun phrases such as those above, that are semantically questions, can appear as arguments of any verb which subcategorizes for an NP in that position and which selects for a question complement. Thus example (111) is motivated by factors which are independent of the ditransitive construction, resulting in a case of "target-structure conspiracy" in the sense of Green (1973).

*Forgive* and especially *envy* as used in:

(112) *He forgave her her sins.*
(113) *He envied the prince his fortune.*

are also exceptional. The subjects in these cases are not causal and no reception is involved. However, these predicates have illuminating semantic histories. *Forgive* and *envy* historically had senses that were closely related to *give*. *Forgive* used to mean "to give or grant" (OED: 452). *Envy* used to mean "to give grudgingly" or "to refuse to give a thing to" (OED: 232). This of course is not evidence that *forgive* or *envy* are part of the synchronic semantic pattern outlined above. But the historical facts do suggest that these predicates were at least at one time associated with this sort of pattern. These facts also of course suggest that the construction can occasionally be frozen without continuing reference to the original semantics.

However, it seems reasonable that syntactic change should tend toward patterns that are more transparent to the speaker. If the construction with the semantics I have outlined is psychologically real, then it would be natural for odd cases of ditransitives involving *forgive* and *envy* to drop out of use. And in fact I myself find archaic sounding sentences involving *forgive* and *envy* much more acceptable than modern sounding sentences. For example:

(114) a. *She forgave him his sins.*
b. ?**She forgave him his goof.*
(115) a. *She envied him his vast fortune.*
b. ?**She envied him his extensive stock portfolio.*

Nonetheless, *envy* and *forgive* are synchronically exceptional, and must be learned individually.[13]

## 13. Prepositional paraphrases

An analysis of the ditransitive construction would not be complete without some reference to the existence of prepositional paraphrases. That is, many ditransitive expressions can be paraphrased using either *to* or *for:*

(116) a. *John gave Mary an apple.*
b. *John gave an apple to Mary.*
(117) a. *John baked Mary a cake.*
b. *John baked a cake for Mary.*

The question that arises, on the account presented here, is not why some verbs are allowed to undergo a lexical or syntactic rule that alters the semantic structure or the subcategorization frame of the verb, as it is typically taken to be. Rather, the question becomes: how are the semantics of the independent constructions related such that the classes of verbs associated with one overlap with the classes of verbs associated with another?

From the rephrasing of this traditional question, it becomes clear that a full answer requires an independent semantic analysis of the constructions associated with the prepositional paraphrases. Although such an analysis is being undertaken as part of a larger project in which several argument structure constructions and their interrelations are analyzed (Goldberg 1992), a full analysis is not yet at hand. However, some initial reflections may be in order.

There is a metaphor in English that involves understanding possession as being located next to, transferring an entity to a recipient as causing the entity to move to that recipient, and transferring ownership away from a possessor as taking that entity away from the possessor. Evidence for the existence of such a metaphor includes:

They *took* his house *away* from him.
He *lost* his house.
Suddenly several thousand dollars *came into* his possession.

This metaphor is motivated by the fact that giving typically involves movement from a possessor to a recipient; however it is clear that such motion is not literally implied by the transference of ownership. For example, in,

(118) *She gave her house to the Moonies.*

no actual transfer of the house is necessarily implied.

The relevance of the metaphor for the issue at hand relates to the fact that prepositional paraphrases involving *to* can be seen to be a subset of a more general construction which can be termed the Caused Motion construction: [Subj [V Obj PCOMP]], where PCOMP is a predicative PP (this construction was mentioned briefly above). This construction can be seen to involve a family of related senses, much like we have seen for the ditransitive, but the central sense of this construction can be argued to involve the caused motion of the Obj referent along the path designated by PCOMP. As in the case of the ditransitive construction, metaphorical extensions of this basic sense are allowed. The metaphor just discussed, then, can be seen to provide a metaphorical extension of the basic sense of caused motion to the domain of possession. This is why we find a fair degree of overlap between classes of verbs associated with the ditransitive, and with the caused-motion construction.

At the same time, it is clear that not all expressions can be alternately expressed using either of the ditransitive or the caused-motion constructions. To some extent, these differences stem from the differences in the semantics associated with the particular constructions. For example, expressions involving verbs of refusal (e.g., *refuse*, *deny*) cannot occur with prepositional paraphrases because they are not readily understood in terms of caused motion.

(119) **She refused a raise to Joe.*
(120) **His mother denied a cake to Billy.*

Conversely, there are cases of caused motion that do not involve a recipient:

(121) He kicked the ball to the endzone.

As we would expect, since we have argued that the ditransitive construction necessarily involves a recipient, such expressions cannot be expressed in the ditransitive construction:

(122) **He kicked the endzone the ball.*

On the other hand, there are cases which could conceivably be associated with both constructions, and yet are not. For example, although verbs of continuous causation, such as *push*, *carry*, *pull*, etc., can be associated with the caused-motion construction, they cannot be used in the ditransitive construction. What needs to be borne in mind to understand these cases, is that these constructions do not generalize as broadly as possible; instead, as was discussed at length in the first part of this paper, particular narrowly defined classes of verbs and particular metaphors are conventionally associated with the constructions.

## 14. Conclusion

I have argued that the semantics associated with the ditransitive syntactic pattern is more felicitously associated directly with the construction as a whole than with the lexicosemantic structure of the verbs. This allows us to view the alternation between the ditransitive and prepositional paraphrases as arising from a semantic overlap between the two constructions. It is a fact about the world that the semantics associated with the two patterns are related; we no longer require a rule in the grammar mapping one pattern onto the other. In this way we need not posit an unwarranted asymmetrical relationship between the two argument structures. Moreover, by directly associating the semantics with the argument structure, we avoid the necessity of positing *ad hoc* new verb senses that appear only with this argument structure.

The semantics involved has been shown to be highly specific. In the central sense, the argument structure is associated with a scene of transfer between a volitional agent and a willing recipient. Permutations on this basic sense can be identified with narrowly defined subclasses of verbs. Following Gropen et al., the subclasses are defined by specific morphophonological and semantic criteria; in addition, systematic metaphors have been shown to license extensions from the basic sense of literal transfer.

A larger project is currently underway in which several argument structure constructions are analyzed (Goldberg 1992). It is argued that the ditransitive is by no means unique in being associated with a particular polysemous semantics and allowing metaphorical extensions (see also Haiman 1978; Emanatian 1990; Lakoff 1987; Sweetser 1990). In this work, several questions raised by a constructional approach to argument structure are addressed, including the nature of verb representation and the interrelations between various constructions.

# Notes

1. I would like to thank Claudia Brugman, Jane Espenson, Michele Emanatian, Paul Kay, Jean-Pierre Koenig, Laura Michaelis, Steven Pinker, Eve Sweetser, Robert

Wilensky and especially Charles Fillmore and George Lakoff for their extremely helpful criticisms and suggestions. All errors are solely my own.

2. It is important to note that, for purposes of exposition, I use grammatical relation terms to refer both to the linguistic entity and the referent of the linguistic entity. Thus for example, in saying "the first object must be a recipient", I intend that there is a constraint on the first object position such that its referent must be understood as a recipient.
3. This class and the class of verbs of permission (*permit, allow*) actually have a slightly different status in the theory proposed by Gropen et al. and Pinker (1989), because the verbs in this class do not alternate with prepositional paraphrases. They are also unique in not forming productive subclasses:
   a. Sally permitted/allowed/*let/*enabled Bob a kiss.
   b. Sally refused/denied/*prevented/*disallowed/*forbid him a kiss.

   One way to account for the non-productivity of these classes is to stipulate that a necessary condition on a subclass being productive is that the subclass have more than two members (Pinker 1989).
4. Here and below, I assume that the second NP is a type of grammatical object distinct from the direct object. In doing so, I am following the analysis explicitly argued for in Dryer (1986), and the analysis implicit in labeling the second object Obj0, as is done in LFG (e.g., Bresnan and Moshi 1990). Evidence that the second NP is a type of object comes from the fact that it lacks a preposition, that it is passivizable in British English, and that it is notionally a direct object. Evidence that it is distinct from a direct object comes from the fact that it obligatorily follows the first object when both are present, and that it is not passivizable in American English.
5. The *give*-class of verbs may be viewed in fact as motivating the existence of the construction. That is, language users may note a correlation between the syntactic form and the semantic interpretation associated with expressions involving these lexical items. Speakers are then able to abstract away from the particular lexical items, allowing the construction to achieve independent status. Once this occurs, the construction can be used to impose its meaning on other novel lexical items. (I thank Charles Fillmore for suggesting the idea that lexical subcategorization frames may motivate constructions.)
6. It has been suggested to me (Dirk Geeraerts, p.c.) that some of these links may be interpretable as *metonymic* extensions from the central sense.
7. Subjects which metonymically stand for volitional beings are also acceptable:
   a. The bank loaned him the money.
   b. His company promised him a raise.
   c. The orchestra played us the symphony.
8. I would like to thank Dirk Geeraerts and Alan Schwartz for indicating that this metaphor could be stated in terms of transfer.
9. See for example, Green 1974: 103.
10. This particular succinct example comes from an anonymous reviewer of an earlier draft.
11. Many theories capture this constraint by postulating a beneficiary role for the first object position of expressions which are paraphrasable with a benefactive *for* phrase.

12. These final two examples happen to be based on metaphors. What is relevant here is that successful (metaphorical) transfer is implied, i.e., (89) implies that Chris has a headache, and (90) implies that Bill received a kick.
13. These facts suggest that a diachronic study of the ditransitive construction may yield valuable insights. They also raise the question of the exact extent to which the pattern described here is psychologically real and not a diachronic generalization. Addressing these issues would require diachronic and experimental studies, which, although I hope to take up at some point in the future, go beyond the scope of the present work.

## References

Bresnan, Joan and Lioba Moshi
1990 Object asymmetries in comparative Bantu syntax. *Linguistic Inquiry* 21 (2): 147–186.
Brugman, Claudia
1988 *The Story of* Over*: Polysemy, Semantics, and the Structure of the Lexicon.* New York: Garland.
Brown, Roger and Canaille Hanlon
1970 Derivational complexity and order of acquisition in child speech. In *Cognition and the Development of Language*, John R. Hayes (ed.), 155–207. New York: Wiley.
Bybee, Joan
1985 *Morphology: A Study of the Relation between Meaning and Form.* Amsterdam/Philadelphia: Benjamins.
Carroll, John, Peter Davies, and Barry Richman
1971 *Word Frequency Book.* New York: Houghton Mimin Company.
Carter, Richard
1988 Compositionality and polysemy. In *On Linking: Papers by Richard Carter*, Levin Beth and Carol Tenny (eds.), 167–204. (MIT's Lexicon Project Working Papers 25.) Cambridge: Center for Cognitive Science, MIT.
Cattell, Ray
1984 *Composite Predicates in English. Syntax and Semantics*, Vol. 17. Sydney: Academic Press.
Dryer, Matthew
1986 Primary objects, secondary objects, and antidative. *Language* 62(4): 808–845.
Emanatian, Michele
1990 Chagga consecutive construction. In *Current Approaches to African Linguistics*, vol. 7, J. Hutchison and V. Manfredi (eds.), 193–207. Dordrecht: Foris.
Fillmore, Charles J.
1975 An alternative to checklist-theories of meaning. In *Proceedings of the First Conference of the Berkeley Linguistic Society* 1: 123–131.
1987 Stanford summer linguistics institute lectures.

The mechanisms of Construction Grammar. *Proceedings of the Fourteenth Annual Meeting of the Berkeley Linguistic Society* 14: 35–55.

Fillmore, Charles J., Paul Kay, and Catherine O'Connor
1988 Regularity and idiomaticity in grammatical constructions: The case of *let alone*. *Language* 64: 501–538.

Fodor, Jerry A.
Undated ms. The procedural solution to the projection problem.

Goldberg, Adele
1992 Argument structure constructions. Ph.D. dissertation, University of California, Berkeley.
1989 A unified account of the semantics of the ditransitive construction. *Proceedings of the Fifteenth Annual Meeting of the Berkeley Linguistic Society* 15.

Goldsmith, John
1980 Meaning and mechanism in language. In *Harvard Studies in Syntax and Semantics* 3, Susumu Kuno (ed.), 423–448. Cambridge, MA: Harvard University Press.

Green, Georgia
1973 A syntactic syncretism in English and French. In *Issues in Linguistics,* Kachru Braj, Robert Lees, Yakov Malkiel, Angelina Piertrangeli, and Sol Saporta (eds.). Urbana: University of Illinois Press.
1974 *Semantics and Syntactic Regularity.* Bloomington: Indiana University Press.

Grimshaw, Jane
1979 Complement selection and the lexicon. *Linguistic Inquiry* 10(2): 279–326.

Gropen, Jess, Steven Pinker, Michelle Hollander, Richard Goldberg, and Ronald Wilson
1989 Learnability and acquisition of the dative alternation in English. *Language* 65: 203–257.

Haiman, John
1978 A study in polysemy. *Studies m Language* 2(1): 1–34.

Jakobson, Roman
1984 *Russsian and Slavic Grammar: Studies* 1931–1981, Linda R. Waugh and Morris Halle (eds.). Berlin: Mouton de Gruyter,. (Originally published in 1938.)

Kay, Paul
1988 *Even.* Berkeley Cognitive Science Report 50.

Lakoff, George
1987 *Women, Fire. and Dangerous Things: What Categories Reveal About the Mind.* Chicago: University of Chicago Press.

Lakoff, George and Mark Johnson
1980 *Metaphors We Live By.* Chicago: University of Chicago Press.

Langacker, Ronald
1987 *Foundations of Cognitive Grammar* Vol. I. Stanford: Stanford University Press.
1987 Grammatical ramifications of the setting/participant distinction. *Proceedings of the Thirteenth Annual Meeting of the Berkeley Linguistic Society* 13: 383–394.

Lindner, Susan
1981 A lexico-semantic analysis of verb-particle constructions with *UP* and *OUT*. Ph.D. dissertation. University of California, San Diego

Marantz, Alec P.
1984 *On the Nature of Grammatical Relations.* Cambridge, Mass: MIT Press.

Oehrle, Richard T.
1976 The grammatical status of the English dative alternation. Ph.D. dissertation, Cambridge, MA, MIT.

Pinker, Steven
1989 *Learnability and Cognition: the Acquisition of Argument Structure.* Cambridge, MA: MIT Press.

Pinker, Steven and Alan Prince
1988 On language and connectionism: Analysis of a parallel distributed processing model of language acquisition. *Cognition* 28,73–193.

Reddy, Michael
1979 The Conduit Metaphor. In *Metaphor and Thought*, A. Ortony (ed.), 284–324. Cambridge: Cambridge University Press.

Rice, Sally
1987 Participant and non-participants: Toward a cognitive model of transitivity. UCSD dissertation.

Searle, John R.
1983 *Intentionality: An Essay in the Philosophy of Mind.* Cambridge: Cambridge University Press.

Sweetser, Eve
1990 *From Etymology to Pragmatics.* Cambridge University Press.

Traugott, Elizabeth C.
1988 Pragmatic strengthening and grammaticalization. *Proceedings of the Fourteenth Annual Meeting of the Berkeley Linguistic Society* 14: 406–416.

Weiner, Edmund S.C. and John A. Simpson
1971 *The Compact Edition of the Oxford English Dictionary.* Oxford: Oxford University Press.

Wierzbicka, Anna
1986 The semantics of "internal dative" in English. *Quaderni di Semantica* 7(1): 140–142.

# Chapter 12
# Usage-based linguistics

## First steps toward a usage-based theory of language acquisition*

*Michael Tomasello*

In usage-based models of language – for example, those of Langacker (1987, 1988, 2000), Bybee (1985, 1995), and Croft (2000) – all things flow from the actual usage events in which people communicate linguistically with one another. The linguistic skills that a person possesses at any given moment in time – in the form of a "structured inventory of symbolic units" – result from her accumulated experience with language across the totality of usage events in her life. This accumulated linguistic experience undergoes processes of entrenchment, due to repeated uses of particular expressions across usage events, and abstraction, due to type variation in constituents of particular expressions across usage events. Given this focus on usage events and the processes of language learning that occur within these events, a crucial item on the research agenda of usage-based models of language is, or should be, the study of how human beings build up the most basic aspects of their linguistic competence during childhood.

From the point of view of research in child language acquisition, perhaps the most attractive feature of usage-based models is their openness on the question of what are the linguistic units with which people operate. For example, usage-based theories explicitly recognize that human beings learn and use many relatively fixed, item-based linguistic expressions such as *How-ya-doin?*, *Could you please ...*, *I'm simply amazed*, and *You keep out of this* – which, even when they are potentially decomposable into elements, are stored and produced as single units (see Bybee and Scheibman 1999 for psycholinguistic evidence focused on *I dunno*). On the other hand, people also operate with some highly abstract linguistic constructions such as, in English, the ditransitive construction, the resultative construction, and the caused motion construction – based on commonalities in the forms and functions of a whole host of different specific expressions (Goldberg 1995). Finally, people also control many "mixed" constructions that revolve around concrete and particular linguistic items but are partly abstract as well, for example, the "What's X doing Y" construction, as in *What's that fly doing my soup?* (Kay and Fillmore 1999) – which has its own distinctive linguistic form

Originally published in 2000 in *Cognitive Linguistics* 11(1/2): 61–82.

and communicative function (see Michaelis and Lambrecht 1996 and Fillmore et al. 1988 for other mixed constructions).

The important methodological point is that the psycholinguistic units with which people operate are identified through observation of their language use. Since it is obvious to all empirically oriented students of language acquisition that children operate with different psycholinguistic units than adults (Tomasello 2000), this theoretical freedom to identify these units on the basis of actual language use, rather than adult-based linguistic theory, is truly liberating. My procedure in this article, therefore, will be to examine children's early use of language in an effort to identify what are the psycholinguistic units – in terms of both complexity and abstractness – with which the process of language acquisition begins. I will also seek to identify some of the developmental processes by means of which children's use of language becomes more adult-like over time.

## 1. The emergence of language

Following the general strictures of cognitive linguistics, to identify the fundamental units of language use we must begin with basic processes of human cognition and communication. Following the general lead of many functionally oriented theorists, my candidate for the most fundamental psycholinguistic unit is the utterance (see especially Croft 2000). An utterance is a linguistic act in which one person expresses towards another, within a single intonation contour, a relatively coherent communicative intention in a communicative context.

### 1.1. Understanding communicative intentions

For current purposes, a communicative intention may be defined as one person expressing an intention that another person share attention with her to some third entity (Tomasello 1998a). This is not a trivial cognitive achievement, and indeed the expression and comprehension of communicative intentions is a species-unique characteristic of *Homo sapiens* (Tomasello 1999). It is thus interesting to note that there are currently no observations indicating that nonhuman primates use any vocalization to direct the attention of groupmates to any external entity such as a predator or food. (Vervet monkeys make different alarm calls for different predators, but a close inspection of the way they use these calls leads to the conclusion that "monkeys cannot communicate with the intent to modify the mental states of others because... they do not recognize that such mental states exist", Cheney and Seyfarth 1990: 310). Nor are there any observations indicating that nonhuman primates use any facial or manual gesture to direct the attention of groupmates to an external entity; they do not point, hold up objects to show them to others, or even offer objects to others (chimpanzees raised by humans sometimes learn to point or use "symbols", but only for imperative, not declarative, purposes – which suggests that they may be attempting to direct the behavior, not the attention, of others; Tomasello and Camaioni 1997). The simple fact is that nonhuman primates do not as a matter of course in their natural environment "express an intention that another share attention with them to some third entity" – perhaps because they do not understand that others have attention (Tomasello and Call 1997).

Prelinguistic human infants are able to discriminate sounds and associate particular experiences with them (Haith and Benson 1997), but they do not comprehend and produce linguistic symbols until about their first birthdays. They do not do this quite simply because they do not yet understand communicative intentions. From about their first birthdays, however, infants begin to understand that when other persons are making funny noises at them they are trying to manipulate their attention with respect to some external entity. This understanding is one manifestation of a momentous shift in the way human infants understand other persons – which occurs at around nine to twelve months of age, as indicated by the near simultaneous emergence of a wide array of joint attentional skills involving outside objects. This includes such things as following into the gaze direction and pointing gestures of others, imitating the actions of others on objects, and manipulating the attention of others by pointing or holding up objects to "show" them to others declaratively. The first language emerges on the heels of these non-linguistic triadic behaviors (involving you, me, and it) and is highly correlated with them – in the sense that children with earlier emerging skills of nonlinguistic joint attention begin to acquire linguistic skills at an earlier age as well (Carpenter, Nagell, and Tomasello 1998). Similarly, children with autism have problems with joint attention and language in a correlated fashion, that is, those who have the poorest nonlinguistic joint attentional skills are those who have the poorest language skills (Sigman and Capps 1997). When children begin to understand the actions of others as intentional in general, they also begin to understand the communicative actions of others as intentional in the sense that they are aimed at directing attention.

Even given the ability to understand communicative intentions in general, it is still far from straightforward to determine a specific communicative intention in a specific usage event. Wittgenstein (1953) in particular analyzed the many problems involved (e.g., he pointed out the fundamental indeterminacy of ostensive definitions; see also Quine 1960) and concluded that communicative intentions can only be comprehended if they are experienced within the context of some already familiar "form of life" that serves as their functional grounding. In language acquisition, these are what Bruner (1983) called joint attentional "formats" – mutually understood social interactions between child and adult that constitute the shared presuppositions and joint attentional framework of the usage event (see also Tomasello, in press). It is easy to see that over ontogenetic time the forms of life that structure early language acquisition turn into the wider knowledge bases that a number of cognitive-functional linguists have pointed to as crucial in the proper characterization of linguistic meaning. The frames, scripts, and other larger entities within which specific linguistic forms gain their communicative significance – as specified, for example, in Fillmore's (1988) frame semantics and Langacker's (1987) base-profile distinction – have their ontogenetic roots in the nonlinguistically learned and experienced joint attentional formats of child language acquisition. Within these larger intersubjectively shared wholes, children come to understand utterances as attempts to manipulate or "window" the attention of other persons with respect to particular aspects of these interaction-encompassing background frames (Talmy 1996).

And so, if we take the understanding of communicative intentions as primary in the child's initiation into linguistic communication, our fundamental unit of analysis must be the most complete and coherent communicative act, the utterance – which is most reliably identified by its simultaneous functional and prosodic coherence. Children come to understand utterances as they come to understand the intentional actions, including communicative actions, of others. They do this within the context of intersubjectively shared forms of life – joint attentional formats – which constitute the medium within which skills of linguistic communication function and grow. Thus, in the current view, utterances are the primary units of linguistic communication since they are used to express complete and coherent communicative intentions, and other smaller units of language are communicatively significant only by virtue of the role they play in utterances.

### 1.2. Holophrases and early word combinations

Children naturally want to understand all of what an adult is trying to communicate to them in an utterance, and so when they attempt to communicate with other people they attempt to produce (i.e., to reproduce) the entire utterance – even though they often succeed in (re)producing only one linguistic element out of the adult's whole utterance. This kind of expression has often been called a "holophrase" since it is a single linguistic symbol functioning as a whole utterance, for example, *That!* meaning "I want that" or *Ball?* meaning "Where's the ball?" (Barrett 1982). The child's attempt is thus not to reproduce one component of the goal-directed communicative act but rather the entire goal-directed act, even though she may only succeed in producing one element. This element is often the one designating the "new" aspect of the situation (Greenfield and Smith 1986), and so it is possible to think of holophrases as kind of primitive predications, with joint attentional formats serving as a kind of topical ground (although young children are clearly not adult-like in explicitly establishing shared topics with an interlocutor and then predicating something about the topic that is new for *her*, the interlocutor).

Holophrases come in many forms; they do not just correspond to single adult words. Thus, most children also have in their early language some so-called frozen phrases that are learned as holophrases but will at some point be broken down into their constituent elements, for example, *Lemme-see*, *Gimme-that*, *I-wanna-do-it*, *My-turn*, and many others (Lieven et al. 1992). This is of course especially true of children learning languages less isolating than English (e.g., Inuktitut; Allen 1996). And so what the holophrastic child needs to do to become a syntactically competent language user is to be able to move in both directions – from part to whole and from whole to part. She must be able either to "break down" or to "fill out" her holophrases so that she can express her communicative intentions in the more linguistically articulated way of adult speakers. Learning how to do this depends on the child's ability to comprehend not only the adult utterance as a whole, but also the functional role being played by the different linguistic elements in that whole. This is the beginnings of grammar.[1]

One could imagine that children learn holophrases, or perhaps even words disembodied from any particular speech act function, and then combine these in situations in which they both are relevant – with both words having roughly equivalent status. For example, a child has learned to name a ball and a table and then spies a ball on a table and says, "Ball table". There may be some initial linguistic productions that are like this for some children, including both "successive single-word utterances" (Bloom 1973) and some word combinations. But in fact most of children's early multiword speech shows a functional asymmetry between constituents, that is, there is one word or phrase that seems to structure the utterance in the sense that it determines the speech act function of the utterance as a whole (often with help from an intonational contour), with the other linguistic item(s) simply filling in variable slot(s). This kind of organization is responsible for what has been called the "pivot look" of early child language, which is characteristic of most children learning most of the languages of the world (Braine 1976; Brown 1973). Early multi-word productions are thus things like: *Where's the X?*, *I wanna X*, *More X*, *It's a X*, *I'm X-ing it*, *Put X here*, *Mommy's X-ing it*, *Let's X it*, *Throw X*, *X gone*, *I X-ed it*, *Sit on the X*, *Open X*, *X here*, *There's a X*, *X broken*, and so on and so forth.

These early word combinations serve the same kinds of functions as early holophrases (indeed many begin their life in one way or another as a holophrase); they simply have a bit more grammatical structure in the sense that they have constant linguistic material that (i) has some internal complexity in some cases (in adult eyes and perhaps the child's as well), and (ii) they have at least one open slot in which many different lexical items and phrases may be placed. Because of this wholistic, utterance-level organization along with open slots, we may call these utterance schemas (see Wray and Perkins 2000 for a similar proposal).

## 2. The emergence of grammar

Because young children are learning a particular natural language, their early utterances will for the most part be describable with the traditional, adult-based structural categories of that language. But from a psycho-linguistic point of view, it is not at all clear that children are actually operating with adult-like categories. Thus, when the child says something like "Wanna play horsie", it is possible that she understands infinitival clauses in general; it is possible that she understands something like *Wanna + activity wanted;* and it is possible that this is an undifferentiated holophrase. The only way to begin to resolve the issue is to look at this particular child's usage of the word *want* or *wanna*, her use of the word *horsie* and related terms, and her use of other apparent complement clause constructions with other words. In syntactic analyses based on generative grammar and its offshoots this is never done – the child's utterance is simply treated as if it were an adult utterance – and in more functionally based analyses it is often not done with enough critical rigor (e.g., with attention to issues of data sampling).

The issue at stake here is the nature of children's underlying linguistic representations. Do they consist primarily of concrete, item-based utterance schemas and other constructions, or do they consist of more abstract linguistic "rules" (plus a lexicon to fill out the rules with semantic content)? Methodologically, the key issue is children's productivity or creativity with language. To the extent that they are operating with concrete words, phrases, and utterance schemas, children's productivity will be tied to this specific linguistic material (e.g., filling in slots in item-based utterance schemas). To the extent that they are working with highly abstract syntactic rules they should be much more productive, while still being canonical, with all structures of their language. Choosing between these alternatives is, or should be, an empirical matter based on distributional analyses (and experiments) of the language use of particular children during particular developmental periods – just as the structures of particular languages are, or should be, determined through distributional analyses (and experiments) of their speakers' actual language use (Croft 2000; Dryer 1997).

### 2.1. Verb islands and other item-based constructions

Early work in developmental psycholinguistics, such as that of Braine (1976) and Bowerman (1976), found many highly concrete, highly local, item-based patterns in corpora of many different children learning many different languages.

The conclusion was thus that child language was not fully adult-like. But these researchers seemingly could not believe their own eyes and so maintained that whereas children learned some item-based formulae early on (some children more than others), most children also possessed a number of more abstract linguistic representations from early on as well. Other researchers at this time spent some effort trying to discover whether there were other kinds of abstract schemas underlying children's early utterances, such as nonlinguistic sensory-motor cognition (e.g., Brown 1973).

Recent research suggests, however, that most of young children's early language is not based on abstractions of any kind, linguistic or otherwise – with the exception that they control from early on some item-based structures with highly constrained "slots".[2] For example, in a detailed diary study Tomasello (1992) found that most of his English-speaking daughter's early multi-word speech revolved around specific verbs and other predicative terms. That is to say, at any given developmental period each verb was used in its own unique set of utterance-level schemas, and across developmental time each verb began to be used in new utterance-level schemas (and with different TAM morphology) on its own developmental timetable irrespective of what other verbs were doing during that same time period. There was thus no evidence that once the child mastered the use of, for example, a locative construction with one verb that she could then automatically use that same locative construction with other semantically appropriate verbs. Generalizing this pattern, Tomasello (1992) hypothesized that children's early grammars could be characterized as an inventory of verb-island constructions (utterance schemas revolving around verbs), which then defined the first syntactic categories as lexically based things such as "hitter", "thing hit", and "thing hit with" (as opposed to subject/agent, object/patient, and instrument; see also Tomasello and Brooks 1999). Lieven, Pine, and Baldwin (1997; see also Pine et al. 1998) found some very similar results in a sample of 12 English-speaking children, namely, they found that 92 percent of their children's earliest multi-word utterances emanated from one of their first 25 lexically-based patterns, which were different for each child (see also Pine and Lieven 1997).

A number of systematic studies of children learning languages other than English have also found basically item-based organization. For example, in a study of young Italian-speaking children Pizzuto and Caselli (1992, 1994) found that of the six possible person-number forms for each verb in the present tense, about half of all verbs were used in one form only, and an additional 40 percent were used with two or three forms. Of the ten percent of verbs that appeared in four or more forms, approximately half were highly frequent, highly irregular forms that could only have been learned by rote – not by application of an abstract rule. In a similar study of one child learning to speak Brazilian Portugese, Rubino and Pine (1998) found adult-like subject-verb agreement patterns only for the parts of the verb paradigm that appeared with high frequency in adult language (e.g., first-person singular), not for low frequency parts of the paradigm (e.g., third-person plural). The clear implication of these findings is that Romance-speaking children do not master the whole verb paradigm for all their verbs at once, but rather they only master some endings with some verbs – and often different ones with different verbs. (For additional findings of this same type, see Serrat 1997 for Catalan; Behrens 1998 for Dutch; Allen 1996 for Inuktitut; Gathercole et al. 1999 for Spanish; Stoll 1998 for Russian; and Berman and Armon-Lotem 1995 for Hebrew.) It should also be noted that syntactic overgeneralization errors such as *Don't fall me down* – which might be seen as evidence of more general and categorical syntactic knowledge – are almost never produced before about two-and-a-half to three years of age (see Pinker 1989).

Finally, experiments using novel verbs have also found that young children's early productivity with syntactic constructions is highly limited. For example, Tomasello and Brooks (1998) exposed two- to three-year-old children to a novel verb used to refer to a highly transitive and novel action in which an agent was doing something to a patient. In the key condition the novel verb was used in an intransitive sentence frame such as *The sock is tamming* (to refer to a situation in which, for example, a bear was doing something that caused a sock to "tam" – similar to the verb *roll* or *spin*). Then, with novel characters performing the target action, the adult asked children the question: *What is the doggie doing?* (when the dog was causing some new character to tam). Agent questions of this type encourage a transitive reply such as *He's tamming the car* – which would be creative since the child has heard this verb only in an intransitive sentence frame. The outcome was that very few children produced a transitive utterance with the novel verb, and in another study they were quite poor at two tests of comprehension as well (Akhtar and Tomasello 1997). As a control, children also heard another novel verb introduced in a transitive sentence frame, and in this case virtually all of them produced a transitive utterance – demonstrating that they can use novel verbs in the transitive construction when they have heard them used in that way. Moreover, four- to five-year-old children are quite good at using novel verbs in transitive utterances creatively, demonstrating that once they have indeed acquired more abstract linguistic skills children are perfectly competent in these tasks (Pinker et al. 1987; Maratsos et al. 1987; see Tomasello 2000 for a review). Finally, Akhtar (1999) found that if 2.5- to 3.5-year-old children heard such things as *The bird the bus meeked*, when given new toys they quite often repeated the pattern and said such things as *The bear the cow meeked* – only consistently correcting to canonical English word order at 4.5 years of age. This behavior is consistent with the view that when two-to-three-year-olds are learning about *meeking* they are just learning about *meeking*; they do not assimilate this newly learned verb to some more abstract, verb-general linguistic category or construction that would license a canonical English transitive utterance.

The general conclusion is clear. In the early stages, children mostly use language the way they have heard adults using it. This leads to an inventory of item-based utterance schemas, with perhaps some slots in them built up through observed type variation in that utterance position. The reason that children do not operate with more abstract linguistic categories and schemas is quite simply because they have not yet had sufficient linguistic experience in particular usage events to construct these adult-like linguistic abstractions.

### 2.2. Imitative learning, entrenchment, and abstraction

If children are acquiring mainly item-based constructions early in development – and children acquiring different languages acquire different item-based constructions – an important part of the process must be some form of imitative learning. Imitation has been almost banished from the study of child language because it is most often defined as the child repeating verbatim what an adult has just said without understanding its meaning, and indeed this process very likely does not play a central role in language acquisition. But, there are forms of social learning called cultural learning in which the learner understands the purpose or function of the behavior she is reproducing (Tomasello et al. 1993). Thus, Meltzoff (1995) found that 18-month-old infants attempted to reproduce the intentional action they saw an adult attempting to perform, even when that action was not carried through to completion, Carpenter, Akhtar, and Tomasello (1998) found that 16-month-old infants attempted to reproduce an adult's intentional, goal-directed actions, but not her accidental actions. In the case of language, if they are to use a piece of language in an adult-like way, children must understand and reproduce both its surface linguistic form and its underlying communicative function – in the sense of using it in connection with the same communicative intention (Tomasello 1998a, 1999).

Cultural learning of this type works simultaneously on multiple hierarchical levels, and indeed it must work in this way if the child is to become creative with conventional, culturally based skills. As a nonlinguistic example, a child may see an adult use a stapler and understand that his goal is to staple together two pieces of paper. In some cases, the child may understand also that the goal/function of placing the papers inside the stapler's jaws is to align them with the stapling mechanism inside the stapler, and that the goal/function of pressing down on the stapler is to eject the staple through the two papers – with both of these sub-actions being in the service of the overall goal/function of attaching the two sheets of paper. To the extent that the child does not understand the sub-functions, she will be lost when she encounters some new stapler, for example, one whose stapling mechanism works differently (e.g., does not require pressing down). Only to the extent that the child understands the relevant subfunctions, will she be able to adapt to this new situation creatively (e.g., adjusting her behavior to effect the same outcome with the new stapling mechanism). The comparable linguistic example is that the child hears an adult say "I stapled your papers" and comprehends not only the utterance and its overall communicative intention, but also, for example, the word *stapled* and its communicative subfunction in the utterance (the contribution it is making to the utterance as a whole), along with the phrase *your papers* and its communicative subfunction in the utterance – with *your* serving a sub-function within that phrase. Again, only if the child performs some "functionally based distributional analysis" of this type will she be able in the future to use these linguistic elements creatively in novel utterances.

Reconceptualized in this way to include intention reading, my claim is that cultural (imitative) learning is more important in language development, especially in the early stages, than has traditionally been recognized. This is clear in the data reviewed in the foregoing, which revealed that before their third birthdays children use individual verbs and syntactic constructions in just the way they have heard and understood them being used – with only very limited abilities to go beyond what they have heard. Interestingly, there are two phenomena of child language acquisition that are often taken to be evidence against imitative learning, but which are actually evidence for it – if we look at exactly what children do and do not hear. First, many young children say things like "Her open it", an accusative subject which they supposedly have not heard from adults. But children hear things like "Let her open it" or "Help her open it" all the time, and so it is possible that when they say these things they are simply reproducing the end part of the utterances they have heard. Very telling is the fact that children almost never make the complementary error "Mary hit I" or "Jim kissed she" – the reason being that they never hear anything like this anywhere. A similar account can be given for some of the findings going under the general rubric of optional infinitives (Rice 1998). Children hear a very large number of nonfinite verbs right after nominative nouns, especially in questions such as "Should he open it?" and "Does she eat grapes?" The child might then later say, in partially imitative fashion: "He open it" and "She eat grapes".

It is also important that children seem to have special difficulties in going beyond what they have heard when they have heard it multiple times, that is, it is entrenched. Thus, Brooks, Tomasello, Lewis, and Dodson (1999) modeled the use of a number of fixed-transitivity English verbs for children from 3;5 to 8;0 years – verbs such as *disappear* that are exclusively intransitive and verbs such as *hit* that are exclusively transitive. There were four pairs of verbs, one member of each pair typically learned early by children and used often by adults (and so presumably more entrenched) and one member of each pair typically learned later by children and used less frequently by adults (less entrenched). The four pairs were: *come-arrive*, *take-remove*, *hit-strike*, *disappear-vanish* (the first member of each pair being more entrenched). The finding was that, in the face of adult questions attempting to induce them to overgeneralize, children of all ages were less likely to over-generalize the strongly entrenched verbs than the weakly entrenched verbs; that is, they were more likely to produce *I arrived it* than *I comed it*. This finding suggests not only that children say what they hear, but that the more they hear it the more it seems to them that this is the only way it can be said.

The imitative learning and entrenchment of particular linguistic forms cannot be the whole story of language acquisition, however, since children do at some point go beyond what they hear from adults and create novel yet canonical utterances. As noted above, they do this first by creating "slots" in otherwise item-based schemas (Tomasello et al. 1997). It is not known precisely how they create these slots, but one possibility is that they observe in adult speech variation in that utterance position and so induce the slot on the basis of "type frequency". In general, in usage-based models the token frequency of an expression in the language learner's experience tends to entrench an expression – enabling the user to access and fluently use the expression as a whole (Langacker 1988; Krug 1998; Bybee and Scheibman 1999) – whereas the type frequency of an expression (i.e., the number of different forms in which the language learner experiences the expression or some element of the expression) determines the creative possibilities, or productivity, of the construction (Bybee 1985, 1995). Together, these two types of frequency – along with the corresponding child learning processes – may explain the ways in which young children acquire the use of specific linguistic expressions in specific communicative contexts and then generalize these expressions to new contexts based on various kinds of type variations they hear – including everything from type variation in a single slot to type variation in all of the constituents of a construction. The extent of type variation needed for different kinds of productivity is not known at this time, and indeed after a certain point in development it may be that type variation in the slots of constructions becomes less important as these slots come to be more precisely defined functionally.

Another possibility – not mutually exclusive but rather complementary to the foregoing – is that abstract constructions are created by a relational mapping across different verb-island constructions (Gentner and Markman 1997). For example, in English the several verb-island constructions that children have with the verbs *give*, *tell*, *show*, *send*, and so forth, all share a "transfer" meaning and they all appear in a structure: NP+V+NP+NP (identified by the appropriate morphology on NPs and VPs). The specific hypothesis is thus that children make constructional analogies based on similarities of both form and function: two utterances or constructions are analogous if a "good" structure mapping is found both on the level of linguistic form and on the level of communicative function. Precisely how this might be done is not known at this time, but there are some proposals that a key element in the process might be some kind of "critical mass" of exemplars, to give children sufficient raw material from which to construct their abstractions (Marchman and Bates 1994).

In either case, the main point is that young children begin by imitatively learning specific pieces of language in order to express their communicative intentions, for example, in holophrases and other fixed expressions. As they attempt to comprehend and reproduce the utterances produced by mature speakers – along with the internal constituents of those utterances – they come to discern certain patterns of language use (including patterns of token and type frequency), and these patterns lead them to construct a number of different kinds of (at first very local) linguistic categories and schemas. As with all kinds of categories and schemas in cognitive development, the conceptual "glue" that holds them together is function; children categorize together things that do the same thing (Mandler 1997). In this case, children understand as instances of the same kind of linguistic units those that serve "the same" or "similar" communicative functions in utterances.

### 2.3. Usage-based syntactic operations

Given that children are acquiring linguistic constructions of various shapes and sizes and degrees of abstraction throughout early development (i.e., building their linguistic inventories), we may now ask about their ability to put these constructions together creatively in order to adapt to the exigencies of particular usage events. Tomasello, Lieven, Behrens, and Forwergk (to appear) addressed this issue in a naturalistic study of one two-year-old child learning English. The novelty was that this child's language was recorded using extremely dense taping intervals. Specifically, the child was recorded in linguistic interaction with her mother for one hour per day, five days per week, for six weeks – making the taped data roughly five to ten times denser than most existing databases of child language, and accounting for approximately eight to ten percent of all of the child's utterances during this six-week period. In order to investigate this child's syntactic creativity, all of her 500+ utterances produced during the last one-hour taping session at the end of the six-week period were designated as target utterances. Then, for each target utterance, there was a search for "similar" utterances produced by the child (not the mother) in the previous six weeks of taping. Was it an utterance she had said before exactly? Was it an utterance based on some highly frequent schema from before but with a new linguistic item in the slot? Was it an utterance pieced together from previously mastered language in some more creative way? Or did the target utterance have no previous precedents in the child's productive language at all?

The main goal was thus to determine for each utterance recorded on the final day of the study what kinds of syntactic operations were necessary for its production, that is to say, in what ways did the child have to modify things she had previously said (her "stored linguistic experience") to produce the thing she was now saying. We may call these operations "usage-based syntactic operations" since they explicitly take into account that the child does not put together each of her utterances from scratch, morpheme by morpheme, but rather, she puts together her utterances from a motley assortment of different kinds of pre-existing psycholinguistic units. And so, following the usage-based models of Bybee (1995), Langacker (2000), and Croft (2000), the question was how this child was able to "cut and paste" together her previously mastered linguistic constructions in order to create a novel utterance in a specific usage event. What was found by this procedure was:

– Of the 455 intelligible utterances produced, 78 percent were utterances that this child had said before during the previous six weeks of sampling – in exactly this same form as whole utterances. Many of these were utterance routines like *Thank-you*, *There-you-go*, etc., but many were simply frequently used multi-word utterances such as *Where's Daddy?*
– Another 18 percent of the target utterances were things the child had said before but with one minor change, that is, they consisted of an established utterance schema plus other linguistic material "filled in" or "added on". For example, the child had said many scores of times previously *Where's X*, but on the target tape she said *Where's the butter?*, which was new (*butter* having been said on five occasions previously in other linguistic contexts). As another example, the child said *I got one here*, which was new. But she had said *I got one* seven times previously, and she had added *here* onto the end of utterances many scores of times previously.
– Only four percent of this child's target utterances were different from things she had said before in more than one way. These mostly involved the combination of "filling in" and "adding on" to an established utterance schema. For example, the child said creatively *I want tissue lounge*, which seemingly derived from the utterance schema *I want object* (which she had said over 50 times previously), with a slotting in of the word *tissue* (which she had said nine times previously in other contexts), and adding on of the word *lounge* (which she had said three times previously in other contexts).
– There were exactly three utterances (less than one-half of one per cent) that could not be accounted for in a relatively straightforward application of this procedure, and two of these were heavily scaffolded by the immediate discourse context (i.e., the child took some other utterance not from her stored linguistic experience but rather from her mother's immediately preceding speech).

It is thus clear that in the vast majority of cases, this child's creative utterances were based directly on things she had said before many times previously. Moreover, in the vast majority of cases, one of the pieces of language on which the child's creative utterance was based was what we called an utterance schema. Utterance schemas were things the child had said before as full utterances with some variation in one (or, infrequently, more than one) slot – such things as *Where's the X?*, *I wanna X*, *More X*, *It's a X*, *I'm X-ing it*, *Put X here*, *Mommy's X-ing it*, *Let's X it*, and so forth. Importantly, these utterance schemas were things that the child had said before, on average, an estimated 150 times during the previous six weeks, and the other language used in these creative utterances (e.g., to fill the slot) had been said before, on average in one or another context, an estimated 70 times during the previous six weeks (these estimations are aimed at reflecting the child's total experience as projected from our ten-percent sample). Further evidence for the psychological reality of these utterance schemas derives from the fact that there were virtually no insertions of linguistic material into previously invariant sequential strings within the schemas (e.g., the child never put adverbs or other modifiers into the middle of an established utterance schema) or substitutions of linguistic material into places that did not already have established slots. It is also important that there was almost perfect functional consistency across different uses of these utterance schemas; the child filled the slot with the same kind of linguistic item or phrase (e.g., an object word or a locative phrase) across the six-week period of study.

The usage-based approach is also quite revealing in the case of more complex constructions. For example, Diessel and Tomasello (in press) looked at seven children's earliest utterances with sentential complements and found that virtually all of them were composed of a simple sentence schema that the child had already mastered combined with one of a delimited set of matrix verbs (see also Bloom 1992). These matrix verbs were of two types. First were epistemic verbs such as *think* and *know*. In almost all cases children used *I think* to indicate their own uncertainty about something, and they basically never used the verb *think* in anything but this first-person, present tense form; that is, there were virtually no examples of *He thinks....*, *She thinks...*, etc., virtually no examples of *I don't think...*, *I can't think...*, etc., and virtually no examples of *I thought...*, *I didn't think...*, etc. And there were almost no uses with a complementizer (virtually no examples of *I think that...*). It thus appears that for many young children *I think* is a relatively fixed phrase meaning something like *Maybe*. The child then pieces together this fixed phrase with a full sentence as a sort of evidential marker, but not as a "sentence embedding" as it is typically portrayed in more formal analyses. The second kind of matrix verbs are attention-getting verbs like *Look* and *See* in conjunction with full finite clauses. In this case, children use these "matrix" verbs almost exclusively in imperative form (again almost no negations, no nonpresent tenses, no complementizers), once more suggesting an item-based approach not involving syntactic embedding. Thus, when examined closely, children's earliest complex sentences look much less like adult sentential complements (which are used most often in written discourse) and much more like various kinds of "pastiches" of various kinds of established item-based constructions.

The findings of both of these studies are best explained by a usage-based model in which children's early linguistic competence is organized as an inventory of item-based constructions, many of which are best characterized as utterance schemas since they structure whole utterances. Fluency with a construction is a function of its token frequency in the child's experience (entrenchment); creativity with a construction emanates from the child's experience of type variation in one or more of its constituents (abstraction). In this way, children build up in their linguistic inventories a very diverse set of constructions – concrete, abstract, and mixed – to call upon as needed in particular usage events. Putting together a creative utterance then involves usage-based syntactic operations in which the child in some way integrates already mastered constructions and elements of various shapes, sizes, and degrees of abstraction in some way that is functionally appropriate for the usage event at hand.

## 3. Conclusion

The study of language acquisition has always tagged along behind models from linguistics – because to study how children acquire something we should first know what that something is. The new usage-based models of cognitive and functional linguistics offer some exciting new perspectives for developmentalists because they are concerned with the actual psychological processes by means of which individuals comprehend and produce utterances. But cognitive and functional linguists have something to learn from developmental psycholinguists as well. If we are interested in people's "stored linguistic experience", and how they use that experience in acts of linguistic communication, it would seem relevant to investigate systematically the processes by which linguistic experience is built up and used in human ontogeny.

The general picture that emerges from my application of the usage-based view to problems of child language acquisition is this: When young children have something they want to say, they sometimes have a set expression readily available and so they simply retrieve that expression from their stored linguistic experience. When they have no set expression readily available, they retrieve linguistic schemas and items that they have previously mastered (either in their own production or in their comprehension of other speakers) and then "cut and paste" them together as necessary for the communicative situation at hand – what I have called "usage-based syntactic operations". Perhaps the first choice in this creative process is an utterance schema which can be used to structure the communicative act as a whole, with other items being filled in or added on to this foundation. It is important that in doing their cutting and pasting, children coordinate not just the linguistic forms involved but also the conventional communicative functions of these forms – as otherwise they would be speaking creative nonsense. It is also important that the linguistic structures being cut and pasted in these acts of linguistic communication are a variegated lot, including everything from single words to abstract categories to partially abstract utterance or phrasal schemas.

Irrespective of the accuracy of the current proposals, there can be no doubt that it is time for cognitive functional linguistics and the study of child language acquisition to come together (Tomasello 1998b). The view I am espousing here is that the most promising theoretical frameworks in which this might be done are the new usage-based models in which (i) the units of language with which people operate are not presupposed or prejudged, (ii) there is an explicit concern with processes of communication in usage events, and (iii) the primary research questions are how human linguistic competence has evolved historically and how today it develops ontogenetically.

## Notes

* Thanks to Holger Diessel and Elena Lieven for comments on a previous version of the manuscript.

1. One could argue that holophrases are already in a sense grammatical since in many instances the child seems to control an intonational contour and to combine it productively with some phonologically expressed linguistic symbol. But it is in fact unknown the degree to which young children productively combine intonation and phonology, and indeed it is just as likely that in the beginning children use each linguistic symbol in the same way as adults (although in some cases the adult, and so the child, uses it in more than one way, e.g., both *Ball!* and *Ball?*).
2. It could be argued that repeated tokens of *I'm sorry* represent an abstraction of a single utterance type, with the same reasoning also applying to the constant segment of formulae such as *Wanna* __. However, I am focusing, as is common, on possible abstractions across utterance types, not tokens.

## References

Akhtar, Nameera
1999 Acquiring basic word order: Evidence for data-driven learning of syntactic structure. *Journal of Child Language* 26: 339–356.

Akhtar, Nameera and Michael Tomasello
1999 Young children's productivity with word order and verb morphology. *Developmental Psychology* 33: 952–965.
Allen, Shanley
*1996* *Aspects of Argument Structure Acquisition in Inuktitut*. Amsterdam/Philadelphia: John Benjamins.
Barrett, Martin
1982 The holophrastic hypothesis: Conceptual and empirical issues. *Cognition* 11: 47–76.
Behrens, Heike
1998 Where does the information go? Paper presented at MPI workshop on argument structure, Nijmegen.
Berman, Ruth and S. Annon-Lotem
1995 How grammatical are early verbs? Paper presented at the *Colloque International de Besancon sur l'Acquisition de la Syntaxe*. November, Besancon, France.
Bloom, Lois
1973 *One Word at a Time*. The Hague: Mouton.
1992 *Language Development from Two to Three*. Cambridge: Cambridge University Press.
Bowerman, Melissa
1976 Semantic factors in the acquisition of rules for word use and sentence construction. In *Normal and Deficient Child Language*, D. Morehead and A. Morehead (eds.), Baltimore: University Park Press.
Braine, Martyn
1976 Children's first word combinations. Monographs of the Society for Research in Child Development 41(1).
Brooks, Patricia, Michael Tomasello, Lawrence Lewis, and Kelly Dodson
1999 Children's overgeneralization of fixed transitivity verbs: The entrenchment hypothesis. *Child Development* 70: 1325–1337. Brown, Roger
*A First Language: The Early Stages.* Cambridge, MA: Harvard University Press.
Bruner, Jerome
1983 *Child's Talk*. New York: Norton.
Bybee, Joan
1985 *Morphology*. Amsterdam/Philadelphia: John Benjamins.
Regular morphology and the lexicon. *Language and Cognitive Processes* 10: 425–455.
Bybee, Joan and Joanne Scheibmann
1985 The effect of usage on degrees of constituency: The reduction of *don't* in English. *Linguistics* 37: 575–596.
Carpenter, Malinda, Nameera Akhtar, and Michael Tomasello
1998 14- through 18-month-old infants differentially imitate intentional and accidental actions. *Infant Behavior and Development* 21: 315–330.
Carpenter, Malinda, Katherine Nagell, and Michael Tomasello
1998 Social cognition, joint attention, and communicative competence from 9 to 15 months of age. Monographs of the Society for Research in Child Development 255.

Cheney, Dorothy and Robert Seyfarth
1990 *How Monkeys See the World.* University of Chicago Press.
Croft, William
2000 *Explaining Language Change: An Evolutionary Approach.* London: Longman.
Diessel, Holger and Michael Tomasello
in press Why complement clauses do not have a *that*-complementizer in early child language. *Proceedings of Berkeley Linguistic Society.*
Dryer, Mathew
1997 Are grammatical relations universal? In *Essays on Language Function and Language Type*, Joan Bybee, John Haiman and Sandra Thompson (eds.), 115–143. Amsterdam: John Benjamins.
Fillmore, Charles
1988 Toward a frame-based lexicon. In *Frames, Fields, and Contrast*, A. Lehrer and E. Kittay (eds.), 75–102. Hillsdale, NJ: Erlbaum. Fillmore, Charles, Paul Kaye, and Mary O'Connor
1988 Regularity and idiomaticity in grammatical constructions: The case of *let alone*. *Language* 64: 501–538.
Gathercole, Virginia, Eugenia Sebastian, and Pilar Soto
1999 The early acquisition of Spanish verbal morphology: Across-the-board or piecemeal knowledge? *International Journal of Bilingualism* 3: 133–182.
Gentner, Dedre, and Arthur Markman
1997 Structure mapping in analogy and similarity. *American Psychologist* 52: 45–56.
Goldberg, Adele
1995 *Constructions: A Construction Grammar Approach to Argument Structure.* University of Chicago Press.
Greenfield, Patricia and Joshua Smith
1986 *Structure of Communication m Early Language Development.* New York: Academic Press.
Haith, Marshall and Janet Benson
1997 Infant cognition. In *Handbook of Child Psychology*, vol. 2, D. Kuhn, D. and R. Siegler (eds.) New York: Wiley.
Kay, Paul and Charles Fillmore
1999 Grammatical constructions and linguistic generalizations. *Language* 75: 1–33.
Krug, Manfred
1998 String frequency: A cognitive motivating factor in coalescence, language processing, and language change. *Journal of English Linguistics* 26: 286–320.
Langacker, Ronald W.
1987 *Foundations of Cognitive Grammar*, vol. 1. Stanford University Press.
1988 A usage-based model. In *Topics in Cognitive Linguistics*, B. Rudzka-Ostyn (ed.), 127–161. Amsterdam: John Benjamins.
2000 A dynamic usage-based model. In *Usage-Based Models of Language*, M. Barlow and S. Kemmer (eds.). Stanford: SLI Publications.

Lieven, Elena, Julian Pine, and Helen Dresner Barnes
1992 Individual differences in early vocabulary development. *Journal of Child Language* 19: 287–310.

Lieven, Elena, Julian Pine, and Gillian Baldwin
1997 Lexically-based learning and early grammatical development. *Journal of Child Language* 24: 187–220.

Mandler, Jean
1997 Representation. In *Cognition, Perception, and Language*, vol. 2: *Handbook of Child Psychology*, D. Kuhn, D. and R. Siegler (eds.). New York: Wiley.

Maratsos, Michael, Ronald Gudeman, Patricia Gerard-Ngo, and Ganie DeHart
1987 A study in novel word learning: The productivity of the causative. In *Mechanisms of Language Acquisition,* B. Mac Whinney (ed.). Hillsdale, NJ: Erlbaum.

Marchman, Virginia and Elizabeth Bates
1994 Continuity in lexical and morphological development: A test of the critical mass hypothesis. *Journal of Child Language* 21: 339–366.

Meltzoff, Andrew
1995 Understanding the intentions of others: Re-enactment of intended acts by 18-month-old children. *Developmental Psychology* 31: 838–850.

Michaelis, Laura and Knud Lambrecht
1996 Toward a construction-based theory of language function: The case of nominal extraposition. *Language* 72: 215–247.

Pine, Julian, and Elena Lieven
1997 Slot and frame patterns in the development of the determiner category. *Applied Psycholinguistics* 18: 123–138.

Pine, Julian, Elena Lieven, and Carolyn Rowland
1998 Comparing different models of the development of the English verb category. *Linguistics* 36: 4–40.

Pinker, Steven
1989 *Learnability and Cognition: The Acquisition of Verb-Argument Structure.* Cambridge MA: Harvard University Press.

Pinker, Steven, David Lebeaux, and Laura Frost
1987 Productivity and constraints in the acquisition of the passive. *Cognition* 26:195–267.

Pizutto, Elena and Christina Caselli
1992 The acquisition of Italian morphology. *Journal of Child Language* 19: 491–557.
1994 The acquisition of Italian verb morphology in a cross-linguistic perspective. In *Other Children, Other Languages*, Y. Levy (ed.). Hillsdale, NJ: Erlbaum.

Quine, Willard
1960 *Word and Object.* Cambridge, MA: MIT Press.

Rice, Mabel (ed.)
1998 *Toward a Genetics of Language.* Mahwah, NJ: Erlbaum.

Rubino, Rafael and Julian Pine
1998 Subject-verb agreement in Brazilian Portugese: What low error rates hide. *Journal of Child Language* 25: 35–60.

Serrat, Elissabet
1997 Acquisition of verb category in Catalan. Unpublished dissertation.
Sigman, Marian and Lisa Capps
1997 *Children with Autism: A Developmental Perspective.* Cambridge: Harvard University Press.
Stoll, Sabine
1998 The acquisition of Russian aspect. *First Language* 18: 351–378.
Talmy, Leonard
1996 The windowing of attention in language. In *Grammatical Constructions: Their Form and Meaning*, M. Shibatani and S. Thompson (eds.). Oxford: Oxford University Press.
Tomasello, Michael
1992 *First Verbs: A Case Study of Early Grammatical Development.* Cambridge University Press.
1998a Reference: Intending that others jointly attend. *Pragmatics and Cognition* 6: 219–234.
1998b The return of constructions. *Journal of Child Language* 75: 431–447.
1999 *The Cultural Origins of Human Cognition.* Cambridge, MA: Harvard University Press.
2000 Do young children have adult syntactic competence? *Cognition* 74: 209–253.
in press Perceiving intentions and learning words in the second year of life. In *Language Acquisition and Conceptual Development*, Melissa Bowerman and Steven Levinson (eds.). Cambridge University Press.
Tomasello, Michael, Nameera Akhtar, Kelly Dodson, and Laura Rekau
1997 Differential productivity in young children's use of nouns and verbs. *Journal of Child Language* 24: 373–387.
Tomasello, Michael and Patricia Brooks
1998 Young children's earliest transitive and intransitive constructions. *Cognitive Linguistics* 9: 379–395.
1999 Early syntactic development: A Construction Grammar approach. In *The Development of Language*, M. Barrett (ed.). Psychology Press.
Tomasello, Michael and Josep Call
1997 *Primate Cognition.* Oxford University Press.
Tomasello, Michael and Luigia Camaioni
1997 A comparison of the gestural communication of apes and human infants. *Human Development* 40: 7–24.
Tomasello, Michael, Ann Kruger, and Hiliary Ratner
1993 Cultural learning. *Behavioral and Brain Sciences* 16: 495–552.
Tomasello, Michael, Elena Lieven, Heike Behrens, and Heike Forwergk
to appear Early syntactic creativity: A usage based approach. Submitted for publication.
Wittgenstein, Ludwig
1953 *Philosophical Investigations.* New York: MacMillan.
Wray, Alison and Michael Perkins
2000 The functions of formulaic language: An integrated model. *Language and Communication* 20: 1–28.

# Epilogue
# Trajectories for further reading

*Dirk Geeraerts*

Starting with each of the twelve chapters in the present collection, we will now lay out some paths for further reading: what are the options if you want to know more about the basic concepts that were introduced in this reader? And, more importantly still, what other domains of enquiry are popular within Cognitive Linguistics, beyond the dozen or so basic ideas? The suggestions can obviously not be exhaustive, compared to the 7000 titles at present included in the digital *Bibliography of Cognitive Linguistics*, but they should help the reader to find his or her way in the considerable literature that is available in the domain of Cognitive Linguistics. In this sense, the present list is not just about further reading, but also about how to chart the territory of Cognitive Linguistics beyond the core areas. Remember also that more general pointers for further reading were already mentioned in the introductory chapter to this volume: Kristiansen, Achard, Dirven, and Ruiz de Mendoza (2006) as a companion volume to the present one, Geeraerts and Cuyckens (forthcoming) as a comprehensive reference work, and Violi (2001), Taylor (2003a), Ungerer and Schmid (1996), Dirven and Verspoor (2004), Croft and Cruse (2004), and Evans and Green (2006) as introductory textbooks.

### Chapter 1. Cognitive Grammar

The central ideas of Ron Langacker may be found in his two-volume *Foundations of Cognitive Grammar* (1987, 1991). Important collections of papers that expand upon the foundational work are Langacker (1990, 1999). An excellent book-length introduction to the grammatical framework developed by Langacker is provided by Taylor (2002). Solid examples of work directly inspired by Langacker's approach to grammar include Achard (1998), Casad (1992), Chen (2003), Dabrowska (1997), García-Miguel (1999), Heyvaert (2003), Janda (1993), Kemmer (1993), Maldonado (2002), Matsumoto (1996), Newman (1996), Rice (1987), Smith (1994), Taylor (1996), Van Hoek (1997), Verhagen (2005). These references are obviously indicative only: once you get started with publicatons like these, you will easily come across other relevant work. In addition to the actual theoretical and descriptive work, it may be interesting to get a more personal view of Cognitive

Grammar: Langacker (2004) is an interview with Ricardo Maldonado, and Newman (2004), in a festschrift for Langacker edited by Lewandowska-Tomasczcyk and Kwiatkowska (2004), looks back at the birth period of Cognitive Grammar in Langacker's lectures of 1977.

## Chapter 2. Grammatical construal

The culmination of Len Talmy's work so far is his two-volume *Toward a Cognitive Semantics* (2000a, 2000b), which consists largely of revised versions of seminal papers published earlier. Unlike Langacker, Talmy has not had many students, but that hasn't prevented his work from being highly influential. Two characteristic topics are force dynamics and lexicalization patterns. The first involves the linguistic representation of force-based interactions and causal relations. Talmy's distinction between four basic types of interaction has been fruitfully applied to areas like modals (Sweetser 1990), grammatical typology (Croft 1991), spatial terms (Cienki 1998), causal verbs (Kemmer and Verhagen1994; Soares da Silva 2003), and a variety of other lexical items (Vandeloise 1996).

Talmy's notion of lexicalization patterns introduces the distinction between 'verb-framed' and 'sattelite-framed' languages, depending on the way in which information about the path or the manner of motion is coded in the language. This distinction has inspired a lot of typological research, including studies of a psycholinguistic nature, as in the work of Slobin (1996, 2000 among others); further extensions include gesture research (McNeill 2000) and metaphor studies (Özçaliskan 2005).

While Ron Langacker's Cognitive Grammar and Len Talmy's Cognitive Semantics are the most articulated frameworks for the description of grammatical meaning that have been developed in the context of Cognitive Linguistics, systematic comparisons of the two approaches are difficult to find. A good starting-point is Croft and Wood (2000).

## Chapter 3. Radial network

The preposition *over* plays a role in Cognitive Semantics that is somewhat comparable to that of *bachelor* in Katzian semantics: from Brugman (1981, 1988) over Vandeloise (1990), Cuyckens (1991), Deane (1992), Geeraerts (1992), and Dewell (1994), to Tyler and Evans (2003), it has been a rallying-point for competing forms of semantic analysis. The focus on *over* is typical for a broader interest in spatial language: see Zelinsky-Wibbelt (1993), Pütz and Dirven (1996), Cuyckens and Radden (2002) for significant collective volumes, and Herskovits

(1986), Vandeloise (1991, 2001), Svorou (1994), Levinson (2003) as a sample of relevant monographs.

More generally, network models of semantic description are a standard element of the analytic toolkit of Cognitive Linguistics, regardless of whether they take a radial or an alternative form. Dividing the examples of such network descriptions over the different network forms introduced in Chapter 3, Chapter 4, and Chapter 5 would be somewhat artificial. Rather, samples from different linguistic domains that use network and prototype models may be the best way to establish the fruitfulness of the descriptive technique. Lexical examples abound, which is no surprise, given that the descriptive models were initially developed in the field of lexical semantics; to name just a few examples, see Rudzka-Ostyn (1988, 1989, 1995) for specifically systematic applications of the descriptive models. Examples of network or prototype-based studies in morphology include Tuggy (1992), Janda (1993), Taylor (1996); in phonology: Van Langendonck (1999), Bybee (2001), Kristiansen (2003); and in syntax: Rice (1987), Tuggy (1996), Iwata (1998), Chen (2003). But to repeat, these are only samples; numerous other instances could be found easily.

So far, there have been few attempts to formalize network analyses in other ways than through the graphical representations that are popular in Cognitive Linguistics. The relationship with connectionist models in Artifical Intelligence has however inspired some work: see Regier (1996), Zlatev (1999), and Bybee and McLelland (2005) for examples.

## Chapter 4. Prototype theory

An overview of prototype-theoretical developments within Cognitive Linguistics is provided by Mangasser-Wahl (2000); references to the foundational works of Rosch are found in Chapter 4. Volumes with specific attention for prototypicality include Tsohatzidis (1989) and Geeraerts (2006). While the descriptive applications of prototype theory are covered by the references in the previous section, there are some theoretically relevant issues to be mentioned here. First, the flexibility inherent in a prototype-theoretical conception of semantic structure leads to questions about semantic change and to a confrontation with diachronic semantics: see Geeraerts (1997) for a diachronic interpretation of prototype theory, and more broadly Blank (1997), Blank and Koch (1999), Traugott and Dasher (2005). Second, although prototype theory originated in psycholinguistic categorization research, the link with psychology faded while prototypicality was developed within linguistics. Counteracting that tendency, see Cuyckens, Sandra, and Rice (1997) for critical questions about the psychological reality of prototype analyses in linguistics. Finally, the empirical study of prototypicality presented in Geeraerts, Grondelaers, and Bakema (1994) introduces a shift from a semasiological towards an onomasiological perspective, i.e. a perspective in which the choice between alternative categories rather than the semantic flexibility within one category becomes the central focus of attention. Such a shift signals a transition from the question 'Why is it that x can be designated by A?' to the question 'What determines the choice for A rather than B as a designation for x?' If Cognitive Linguistics is primarily concerned with categorization, the second question would seem to be closer to actual processes of categorization than the first. For the elaboration of the onomasiological research perspective, see Grondelaers and Geeraerts (2003).

### Chapter 5. Schematic network

Given the links between the concept of schematic network and some of the other chapters, most of the directly relevant pointers will be found elsewhere in this overview of further reading: among the suggestions included in the previous two paragraphs, and among those in the final two paragraphs. At this point, reading tips are restricted to the problem of polysemy (as opposed to monosemy or generality), which plays an important role in the background of Chapter 5. The problem is an important one in Cognitive Linguistics: the structure of polysemy (either with a focus on the overall structure of the polysemous network, or with a focus on the metaphorical, metonymical links within the network) is of central interest to Cognitive Linguistics – but what about the elements in the network? Should descriptions maximalize polysemy, or should they be parsimonious? The question has been debated many times in Cognitive Linguistics, and there is no canonical position. Noteworthy contributions to the debate include Sweetser (1986, 1987), Geeraerts (1993a), Cruse (1995), Schmid (2000), Janssen (2003), Taylor (1992, 2003b), Zlatev (2003b), Allwood (2003). For volumes focusing on the theoretical nature of polysemy, see Lewandowska-Tomaszczyk (1998), Peeters (2000), Cuyckens and Zawada (2001), Ravin and Leacock (2002), Nerlich, Todd, Herman, and Clarke (2003), Cuyckens, Dirven, and Taylor (2003).

### Chapter 6. Conceptual metaphor

Besides the basic reading provided by Lakoff and Johnson (1980) and Lakoff (1987), see Kövecses (2002) for a comprehensive introduction to metaphor theory within Cognitive Linguistics. Edited volumes of specific interest include Paprotté and Dirven (1985), Ortony (1993), Gibbs and Steen (1999), Barcelona (2000), Baicchi, Broccias, and Sans (2005). Popular areas of application for metaphor theory (the domain is vast, to be sure) are the study of emotion concepts (Kövecses 1986, 2000; Athanasiadou and Tabakowska 1998), literary and stylistic studies (Turner 1987; Lakoff and Turner 1989; Tabakowska 1993; Turner 1996; Freeman 1995; Fischer and Nänny 2001; Semino and Culpeper 2002), religious discourse (Boeve and Feyaerts 1999; Feyaerts 2003), gesture (McNeill 2000), and ideology and cultural models (Dirven, Frank, and Ilie 2001; Dirven, Hawkins, and Sandikcioglu 2001; Lakoff 2002; Dirven Frank, and Pütz 2003; Chilton 2004). Reddy (1979) is a ground-breaking metalinguistic metaphor analysis, i.e. an analysis of the imagery we use to talk about language and concepts. For an interview with George Lakoff, see Pires de Oliveira (2001).

From a theoretical point of view, three specific issues deserve to be mentioned. First, the experiential perspective of Cognitive Linguistics leads to a specific interest of metaphor researchers in the embodiment of metaphors, i.e. the way in which they may be based in prelinguistic (bodily, sensor-motor) experience: among many others, see Gibbs (2005) and Grady (1997). The latter introduces the notion of 'primary metaphor' for fundamental metaphorical patterns like *good is up*: from very early on in an individual's experience, these concepts correlate, and it may be only later that the two domains as such are cognitively separated by the individual. The embodied nature of language has important philosophical ramifications, involving questions about objectivity and the cartesian mind/body dualism: see Johnson (1987), Lakoff and Johnson (1999), Damasio (1994), Geeraerts (1993b). A more literal, materialist version of embodiment is the Neural Theory of Metaphor developed by Lakoff (2003), which looks at the neurophysiological correlates of metaphor.

Second, while the focus on embodied cognition tends to have universalist leanings (the body would seem to be a universal of human experience), the metaphorical understanding of a given target domain also exhibits cultural and historical variation. This is reflected by quantities of comparative and culture-specific research: see Kövecses (2005) for an overview, and compare Wierzbicka (1991), Dirven (1994), Palmer (1996), Yu (1998) for examples of research into cultural specificity and language. The recognition of cultural diversity also leads a number of scholars to stress the social nature of language as foundational: researchers like Sinha & Jensen de López (2000), Zlatev (2003a), Harder (2003), Bernárdez (2005) emphasize that the experientialist nature of Cognitive Linguistics does not only refer to material factors (taking embodiment in a physical and physiological sense) but that the cultural environment and the socially interactive nature of language should be recognized as primary elements of a cognitive approach.

Third, from Traugott (1985) to Haser (2005), critical questions have been voiced with regard to the validation of the metaphorical hypothesis: how do you establish that a metaphorical pattern is not just present in the surface form of the language, but actually influences the way people think? At this point, experimental research becomes of prime importance: see the brief remarks at the end of the next section.

## Chapter 7. Image schema

The first elaborate treatment of the notion of image schema is to be found in Johnson (1987); the current state of affairs is adequately represented in a collective volume edited by Hampe (2005). Image schemas have been fruitfully and intensively applied in the semantic analysis of linguistic forms with a primary spatial meaning, like many prepositions and verbal particles. For a sample of such work, see Radden (1985), Rudzka-Ostyn (1985), Casad (2004), Ekberg (1997), Hampe (2002). Other types of meaning have been analyzed as well from an image schematic point of view: see Soares da Silva (2003) on causatives, Peña Cervel on emotion terms (2003), and Cienki (2005) on the analysis of gestures. (The latter application, by the way, links up with a lively field of inquiry in which Cognitive Linguistics is applied to the analysis of gesture and sign languages: see McNeill 1995, 2000; Wilcox 2001; Taub 2001; Liddell 2003; Wilcox 2004.) But image schemas have not only been applied, they have also been critically questioned. Theoretically interesting contributions include Brugman (1990), Krzeszowski (1993), Kennedy and Vervaeke (1993), Johnson (1993), Cienki (1997), Clausner and Croft (1999).

Gibbs's work is laid down in a number of volumes: Gibbs (1994, 1999, 2005). His work is not just important because of its thematic focus on figurative language and thought, but also because he is one of the pioneers of using an experimental method in Cognitive Linguistics. Together with the use of corpus data and neurophysiological evidence, experimental research is one of the cornerstones of an empirically validated Cognitive Linguistics. However, it is not yet the case that experimentation (or empirical research in the broad sense) is dominant within Cognitive Linguistics: see Gonzalez-Marquez, Mittelberg, Coulson, and Spivey (forthcoming) for an introduction to different empirical methods in Cognitive Linguistics. Convincing examples of experimental methods in Cognitive Linguistics may be found in work such as Sandra and Rice (1995), Frisson, Sandra, Brisard, and Cuyckens (1996), Sanders and Noordman (2000), Boroditsky (2001), Bowerman and Choi (2003), Verspoor and Lowie (2003), Coulson (2004), Giora (2003), Matlock, Ramscar, and Boroditsky (2004).

## Chapter 8. Metonymy

The literature on metonymy within Cognitive Linguistics may to a large extent be found in a number of collective volumes: Panther and Radden (1999), Barcelona (2000), Dirven and Pörings (2002), and Panther and Thornburg (2003). Theoretically speaking, the discussions largely involve the demarcation of the notion of metonymy. The domain hypothesis as put forward by Croft has an immediate appeal because of the simple way in which it allows for a distinction between metaphor and metonymy: metaphor as a conceptual relationship between different domains, metonymy as a conceptual relationship between a single domain, or at least, a domain matrix. However, the difficulties encountered in establishing an operation definition of 'domain' have led a number of people to the exploration of theoretical alternatives. Basically, there are three different trends. First, Ruiz de Mendoza and Otal Campo (2002) represent a trend towards refinements of the domain approach, by distinguishing between domain expansions and domain reductions. Second, there is a trend that stresses the role of metonymy as a conceptual operation through which one concept (the source) provides access to another concept (the target): see Radden and Kövecses (1999), Panther (2005). The semiotic notion of indexicality plays a definitional role in this approach. Third, there are attempts to refine the traditional conception of metonymy in terms of contiguity: Koch (2001), Peirsman and Geeraerts (2006).

The latter article also exemplifies another important area of metonymy research within Cognitive Linguistics, viz. the attempt to classify different types of metonymy. In Peirsman and Geeraerts (2006), this takes the form of identifying metonymical patterns of the part/whole type, and determining the relations between those types. With regard to the latter, Feyaerts (1999) explores the existence of metonymical hierarchies, in which more schematic and more specific metonymical patterns co-exist. In other cases, the classificatory attempt takes the form of distinguishing between different phenomena that would traditionally be classified as identical: see Paradis (2004) for a distinction between 'facets' and metonymy.

## Chapter 9. Mental spaces

The mental spaces (or 'blending' or 'conceptual integration') framework is elaborated in a number of monographs and collective volumes: Fauconnier (1994, 1998), Fauconnier and Sweetser (1996), Coulson (2001), Fauconnier and Turner (2002). The fruitfulness of the approach may be measured by the various problems and fields to which it is applied: compositionality (Sweetser 1999), humor (Coulson 1996), literary analysis (Turner 1996, Freeman 2000), narrative structure (Oakley 1998). Particularly interesting from the point of view of theory formation in

Cognitive Linguistics is the combination of a conceptual integration approach with other typical subjects of analysis within Cognitive Linguistics: see Coulson and Oakley (2003) on blending and metonymy, and Broccias (2003) on blending and schemas.

## Chapter 10. Frame semantics

The development of frame semantics beyond its initial formulation may be traced in Fillmore (1985, 1987, 1992), and Fillmore and Atkins (1992, 1994, 2000). References to the older articles will be found in Chapter 10; a number of these are reprinted in Fillmore (2003). On a very practical and descriptive level, the frame idea is currently being implemented in the FrameNet project (http://framenet.icsi.berkeley.edu/) which takes the form of a corpus-based on line dictionary for English. For the importance for descriptive lexicography of frame semantics, see Atkins (1994) and Fontenelle (2003). Although the concept of frame is generally accepted as part of the descriptive repertoire of Cognitive Linguistics, and in spite of early descriptive interest as in Dirven, Goossens, Putseys, and Vorlat (1982), the theoretical status of the concept has perhaps been less investigated than could be expected: see Lehrer and Kittay (1992) and Lutzeier (1992) for comparisons between different approaches to lexical structure (semantic fields, frames, prototypes, and lexical relations); further, see Coulson (2001) for the importance of frames for mental space theory, and compare Glynn (2004), who delineates the general question about the relationship between Construction Grammar, semantic field theory, and frame semantics.

## Chapter 11. Construction Grammar

Like almost all other branches of Cognitive Linguistics, Construction Grammar is not a single, neatly delineated model of grammatical description; it is rather a bundle of closely related but at the same time competitive approaches. Major strands within Construction Grammar are represented by Goldberg (1995, 2006), Kay (1997), Croft (1999), Fillmore (2002), Michaelis and Ruppenhofer (2002), Boas (2003), and Bergen and Chang (2005). Important edited volumes covering the full spectrum of Construction Grammar are Goldberg (1996), Shibatani and Thompson (1996), Foolen and Van der Leek (2000), Fried and Östman (2004), Östman and Fried (2005), Fried and Boas (2005).

The differences of emphasis between the different forms of Construction Grammar may be summarized as follows. Kay and Michaelis work most directly along the lines set out by Fillmore; see the seminal paper Fillmore, Kay, and O'Connor

(1988). This approach pays a lot of attention to the formal aspects of constructions, linking up with Head-Driven Phrase Structure Grammar as a formal model for the description of grammar. The Goldberg line of investigation draws on Langacker and Lakoff style network analyses, with an emphasis on the description of constructional networks, while at the same time insisting on psychological realism and experimental backing up of the analyses. This concern is shared by the Embodied Construction Grammar propagated by Bergen and Chang, who try to add neurophysiological evidence to the empirical basis of Construction Grammar. Radical Construction Grammar as developed by Croft has a typological orientation. It is 'radical' in the sense that it assumes that constructions are not derived from their constituent parts, but that the component entities (like word classes) are rather derived from the constructions they appear in.

From a certain point of view, Ron Langacker's Cognitive Grammar may also be considered a type of construction grammar: Langacker himself offers an insightful comparison of the main types of Construction Grammar in Langacker (2005).

A fruitful methodological enrichment of Construction Grammar is offered by the so-called 'collostructional' method of Gries and Stefanowitsch (Stefanowitsch and Gries 2003; Gries and Stefanowitsch 2006). Using a collocational analysis of corpus data, it allows for a characterization of constructions in terms of the items that typically occur in the constructions. Further, Construction Grammar links up with various other domains of research within Cognitive Linguistics. The link with acquisitional research may be followed in connection with Chapter 12. Historical research on the development of constructions is being incorporated into grammaticalization research: see Traugott (2003), Ziegler (2004).

Grammaticalization, broadly defined, is the process through which an entity or a construction becomes a conventional part of a grammar. More narrowly, it involves the process through which open class lexical items develop into closed class items (like prepositions) or morphemes. Grammaticalization is a thoroughly researched area within Cognitive Linguistics in its own right: for a basic bibliography, see Heine, Claudi, and Hünnemeyer (1991), Traugott and Heine (1991), Hopper and Traugott (1993), Lehmann (1995), Heine (1997), Brinton and Traugott (2005).

## Chapter 12. Usage-based linguistics

The major reference for Tomasello's work is his 2003 book. For other work coming out of his research team, see Diessel (2004). Tomasello's article in the present collection could be the starting-point for readings in two different directions: on the one hand, that of applied research within Cognitive Linguistics, on the other, that of the ramifications of the usage-based approach. In these suggestion for further reading, we will focus on the latter, but a few brief indications about the former line may be useful. Apart from Tomasello, other sources for research into language acquisition and language development in the context of Cognitive Linguistics include Bowerman and Levinson (2001). A broader view of the language acquisition debate, including a systematic appraisal of the Chomskyan 'language instinct' approach, may be found in Sampson (2005). Applied linguistics in a broad sense, specifically also including language teaching, is represented by volumes like Pütz, Niemeier and Dirven (2001a, 2001b), Achard and Niemeier (2004).

The notion 'usage-based' was introduced by Langacker (1988, 2000) and in a sense popularized by the volume edited by Barlow and Kemmer (2000). Next to the acquisitional aspects, there are two features of the usage-based approach that need to be explored: the descriptive, and the methodological aspect.

Methodologically speaking, the inevitable basis for usage-based models of grammar is usage data, and the natural form that non-elicited usage data take is that of a corpus. Now, corpus data were indeed used from early on in the history of Cognitive Linguistics. The methodology of early European studies in Cognitive Linguistics in particular has tended to be more corpus-based than the early American studies: see e.g. Dirven, Goossens, Putseys and Vorlat (1982), Rudzka-Ostyn (1988), Geeraerts, Grondelaers, and Bakema (1994). At the same time, it is not the case that the methodology of Cognitive Linguistics, in accordance with its self-declared usage-based status, is as yet predominantly that of corpus linguistics. Specifically, there would seem to be room for more quantification and statistics in the analysis of the corpus data: see Tummers, Heylen, and Geeraerts (2005) for a state of the art.

Descriptively speaking, an overview of some of the most quantitatively inspired work provides a good picture of the areas in which the idea of a usage-based grammar has so far been applied most intensively: in language change research (Bybee 2001, 2003; Krug 2000); in sociolinguistic language variation research (Speelman, Grondelaers and Geeraerts 2003); in quantitative analyses of grammatical variation (Grondelaers, Speelman and Geeraerts 2002; Gries 2003; Rohdenburg and Mondorf 2003); and in functional discourse analysis (Sanders and Gernsbacher 2004). Qunatitative studies of the latter type link up with a broader field of discourse and pragmatic studies within Cognitive Linguistics: see Nuyts (1992), Liebert, Redeker and Waugh (1997), Koenig (1998), Van Hoek, Kibrik and Noordman (1999), Fischer (2000), Zelinsky-Wibbelt (2000), Marmaridou (2002) for representative volumes and monographs.

The type of grammatical model that is gradually emerging (but that is far from stabilized) from quantitative usage-based studies like the ones mentioned is a multivariate one in which the occurrence of grammatical phenomena is simultaneously determined by forces of different kinds: conceptual, discursive, variational. The latter factor in particular may need to be worked in more systematically than has so far been the case; see Geeraerts (2005) and Kristiansen and Dirven (2006) for the emerging notion of Cognitive Sociolinguistics.

## References


Achard, Michel
1998 *Representation of Cognitive Structures: Syntax and Semantics of French Sentential Complements*. Berlin/New York: Mouton de Gruyter.

Achard, Michel and Susanne Niemeier (eds.)
2004 *Cognitive Linguistics, Second Language Acquisition, and Foreign Language Teaching*. Berlin/New York: Mouton de Gruyter.

Allwood, Jens
2003 Meaning potentials and context: Some consequences for the analysis of variation in meaning. In *Cognitive Linguistic Approaches to Lexical Semantics*, Hubert Cuyckens, René Dirven, and John Taylor (eds.), 29–66. Berlin/New York: Mouton de Gruyter.

Athanasiadou, Angeliki and Elzbieta Tabakowska (eds.)
1998 *Speaking of Emotions: Conceptualisation and Expression*. Berlin/New York: Mouton de Gruyter.

Atkins, Beryl T.S.
1994 Analyzing the verbs of seeing: A frame semantics approach to lexicography. *Proceedings of the Twentieth Annual Meeting of the Berkeley Linguistics Society* 42–56. Berkeley: Berkeley Linguistics Society.

Baicchi, Annalisa, Cristiano Broccias, and Andrea Sans (eds.)
2005 *Modelling Thought and Constructing Meaning. Cognitive Models in Interaction*. Milan: FrancoAngeli.

Barcelona, Antonio (ed.)
2000 *Metaphor and Metonymy at the Crossroads: A Cognitive Perspective*. Berlin/New York: Mouton de Gruyter.

Barlow, Michael and Susanne Kemmer (eds.)
2000 *Usage-based Models of Language*. Stanford: CSLI Publications.

Bergen, Benjamin K. and Nancy Chang
2005 Embodied construction grammar in simulation-based language understanding. In *Construction Grammars: Cognitive Grounding and Theoretical Extensions*, Jan-Ola Östman and Mirjam Fried (eds.), 147–190. Amsterdam/Philadelphia: John Benjamins.

Bernárdez, Enrique
2005 Social cognition: variation, language, and culture in a cognitive linguistic typology. In *Cognitive Linguistics. Internal Dynamics and Interdisicplinary Interaction*, Francisco J. Ruiz de Mendoza and Sandra Peña Cervel (eds.), 191–222. Berlin/New York: Mouton de Gruyter.

Blank, Andreas
1997 *Prinzipien des lexikalischen Bedeutungswandels am Beispiel der romanischen Sprachen*. Tübingen: Max Niemeyer.

Blank, Andreas and Peter Koch (eds.)
1999 *Historical Semantics and Cognition*. Berlin/New York: Mouton de Gruyter.

Boas, Hans C.
2003 *A Constructional Approach to Resultatives*. Stanford: CSLI Publications.

Boeve, Lieven and Kurt Feyaerts (eds.)
1999 *Metaphor and Godtalk*. Bern: Peter Lang.

Boroditsky, Lera
2001 Does language shape thought? Mandarin and English speakers' conceptions of time. *Cognitive Psychology* 43: 1–22.

Bowerman, Melissa and Stephen C. Levinson (eds.)
2001 *Language Acquisition and Conceptual Development*. Cambridge: Cambridge University Press.

Bowerman, Melissa and Soonja Choi
2003 Space under construction: Language-specific spatial categorization in first language acquisition. In *Language and Mind: Advances in the Study of Language and Cognition*, Dedre Gentner and Susan Goldin-Meadow (eds.), 387–427. Cambridge, Mass.: The MIT Press.

Brinton, Laurel and Elizabeth C. Traugott
2005 *Lexicalization and Language Change*. Cambridge: Cambridge University Press.

Broccias, Cristiano
2003 *The English Change Network: Forcing Changes into Schemas*. Berlin/New York: Mouton de Gruyter.

Brugman, Claudia
1981 The story of *over*. MA thesis, University of California at Berkeley.
1988 *The Story of* Over*: Polysemy, Semantics, and the Structure of the Lexicon*. New York: Garland.
1990 What is the Invariance Hypothesis? *Cognitive Linguistics* 1: 257–266.

Bybee, Joan
2001 *Phonology and Language Use*. Cambridge: Cambridge University Press.
2003 Cognitive processes in grammaticalization. In *The New Psychology of Language*, Volume II, Michael Tomasello (ed.), 145–167. Mahwah, N.J.: Erlbaum.

Bybee, Joan and James L. McLelland
2005 Alternatives to the combinatorial paradigm of linguistic theory based on domain general principles of human cognition. *The Linguistic Review* 22: 381–410.

Casad, Eugene H.
1992 Cognition, history, and Cora *yee*. *Cognitive Linguistics* 3: 151–186.
2004 Imagery through the ages. In *Imagery in Language. Festschrift in Honour of Professor Ronald W. Langacker*, Barbara Lewandowska-Tomaszczyk and Alina Kwiatkowska (eds.), 115–158. Frankfurt: Peter Lang.

Chen, Ron
2003 *English Inversion: A Ground-before-Figure Construction*. Berlin/New York: Mouton de Gruyter.

Chilton, Paul
2004 *Analysing Political Discourse: Theory and Practice*. London/New York: Routledge.

Cienki, Alan
1997 Some properties and groupings of image schemas. In *Lexical and Syntactical Constructions and the Construction of Meaning*. Marjolijn Verspoor, Kee Dong Lee, and Eve Sweetser (eds.), 3–16. Amsterdam/Philadelphia: John Benjamins.
1998 STRAIGHT: An image-schema and its metaphorical extensions. *Cognitive Linguistics* 9: 107–149.
2005 Image schemas and metaphoric gestures. In *From Perception to Meaning. Image Schemas in Cognitive Linguistics*, Beate Hampe (ed.), 421–441. Berlin/New York: Mouton de Gruyter.

Clausner, Timothy C. and William Croft
1999 Domains and image schemas. *Cognitive Linguistics* 10: 1–31.

Coulson, Seana
1996 Menendez Brothers virus: Blended spaces and internet humor. In *Conceptual Structure, Discourse, and Language*, Adele E. Goldberg (ed.), 67–81. Stanford: CSLI Publications.
2001 *Semantic Leaps: Frame-shifting and Conceptual Blending in Meaning Construction*. Cambridge: Cambridge University Press.
2004 Electrophysiology and pragmatic language comprehension. In *Experimental Pragmatics*, Ira Noveck and Dan Sperber (eds.), 187–206. San Diego: Palgrave Macmillan.

Coulson, Seana and Todd Oakley
2003 Metonymy and conceptual blending. In *Metonymy and Pragmatic Inferencing*, Klaus-Uwe Panther and Linda Thornburg (eds.), 51–79. Amsterdam/Philadelphia: John Benjamins.

Croft, William and D. Alan Cruse
2004 *Cognitive Linguistics*. Cambridge: Cambridge University Press.

Croft, William
1991 *Syntactic Categories and Grammatical Relations*. Chicago: The University of Chicago Press.
1999 *Radical Construction Grammar: Syntactic Theory in Typological Perspective*. Oxford: Oxford University Press.

Croft, William and Esther J. Wood
2000 Construal operations in linguistics and artificial intelligence. In *Meaning and Cognition,* Liliana Albertazzi (ed.*),* 51–78. Amsterdam/Philadelphia: John Benjamins.

Cruse, D. Alan
1995 Between polysemy and monosemy. In *New Trends in Semantics and Lexicography*. Henryk Kardela and Gunnar Persson (eds.), 25–34. Umeå: Swedish Science Press.

Cuyckens, Hubert
1991 *The Semantics of Spatial Prepositions in Dutch*. PhD thesis, Universitaire Instelling Antwerpen.

Cuyckens, Hubert and Britta Zawada (eds.)
2001 *Polysemy in Cognitive Linguistics*. Amsterdam/Philadelphia: John Benjamins.

Cuyckens, Hubert and Günter Radden (eds.)
2002 *Perspectives on Prepositions.* Tübingen: Max Niemeyer.

Cuyckens, Hubert, Dominiek Sandra, and Sally Rice
1997 Towards an empirical lexical semantics. In *Human Contact through Language and Linguistics*, Birgit Smieja and Meike Tasch (eds.), 35–54. Frankfurt: Peter Lang.

Cuyckens, Hubert, René Dirven, and John Taylor (eds.)
2003 *Cognitive Approaches to Lexical Semantics.* Berlin/New York: Mouton de Gruyter.

Dabrowska, Ewa
1997 *Cognitive Semantics and the Polish Dative.* Berlin/New York: Mouton de Gruyter.

Damasio, Antonio R.
1994 *Decartes' Error: Emotion, Reason, and the Human Brain.* New York: Grosset/Putnam.

Deane, Paul D.
1992 Polysemy as the consequence of internal conceptual complexity: The case of *over. Proceedings of the Eastern States Conference on Linguistics (ESCOL)* 9: 32–43.

Dewell, Robert B.
1994 *Over* again: On the role of image-schemas in semantic analysis. *Cognitive Linguistics* 5: 351–380.

Diessel, Holger
2004 *The Acquisition of Complex Sentences.* Cambridge: Cambridge University Press.

Dirven, René and Marjolijn Verspoor
2004 *Cognitive Exploration of Language and Linguistics.* Second Revised Edition. Amsterdam/Philadelphia: John Benjamins.

Dirven, René
1994 *Metaphor and Nation: Metaphors Afrikaners Live by.* Frankfurt: Peter Lang.

Dirven, René and Ralf Pörings (eds.)
2002 *Metaphor and Metonymy in Comparison and Contrast.* Berlin/New York: Mouton de Gruyter.

Dirven, René, Bruce Hawkins, and Esra Sandikcioglu (eds.)
2001 *Language and Ideology. Volume I: Theoretical Cognitive Approaches.* Amsterdam/Philadelphia: John Benjamins.

Dirven, René, Roslyn Frank, and Cornelia Ilie (eds.)
2001 *Language and Ideology. Volume II: Descriptive Cognitive Approaches.* Amsterdam/Philadelphia: John Benjamins.

Dirven, René, Roslyn Frank, and Martin Pütz (eds.)
2003 *Cognitive Models in Language and Thought: Ideology, Metaphors, and Meanings.* Berlin/New York: Mouton de Gruyter.

Dirven, René, Louis Goossens, Yvan Putseys, and Emma Vorlat
1982 *The Scene of Linguistic Action and its Perspectivization by* Speak, Talk, Say, *and* Tell. Amsterdam/Philadelphia: John Benjamins.

Ekberg, Lena
1997 Image schemas and lexical polysemy: The case of Swedish *runt* (around). *Trondheim Working Papers in Linguistics* 25: 23–42.

Evans, Vyvian and Melanie Green
2006 *Cognitive Linguistics. An Introduction*. Edinburgh: Edinburgh University Press.

Fauconnier, Gilles
1994 *Mental Spaces: Aspects of Meaning Construction in Natural Language*. Cambridge: Cambridge University Press.
1998 *Mental Spaces, Language Modalities, and Conceptual Integration*. Mahwah, N.J.: Lawrence Erlbaum.

Fauconnier, Gilles and Eve E. Sweetser (eds.)
1996 *Spaces, Worlds, and Grammar.* Chicago: The University of Chicago Press.

Fauconnier, Gilles and Mark Turner
2002 *The Way We Think: Conceptual Blending and the Mind's Hidden Complexities*. New York: Basic Books.

Feyaerts, Kurt
1999 Metonymic hierarchies: The conceptualization of stupidity in German idiomatic expressions. In *Metonymy in Language and Thought*, Klaus-Uwe Panther and Günter Radden (eds.) 309–332. Amsterdam/Philadelphia: John Benjamins.

Feyaerts, Kurt (ed.)
2003 *The Bible through Metaphor and Translation: A Cognitive Semantic Perspective*. Bern: Peter Lang.

Fillmore, Charles J.
1985 Frames and the semantics of understanding. *Quaderni di Semantica* 6: 222–254.
1987 A private history of the concept 'frame'. In *Concepts of Case*, René Dirven and Günter Radden (eds.), 28–36. Tübingen: Gunter Narr.
1992 'Corpus linguistics' vs. 'computer-aided armchair linguistics'. In *Directions in Corpus Linguistics*, Jan Svartvik (ed.), 35–66. Berlin/New York: Mouton de Gruyter.
2002 Mini-grammars of some time-when expressions in English. In *Complex Sentences in Grammar and Discourse*, Joan Bybee and Michael Noonan (eds.), 31–59. Amsterdam/Philadelphia: John Benjamins.
2003 *Form and Meaning in Language. Volume 1. Papers on Semantic Roles*. Stanford: CSLI Publications.

Fillmore, Charles J. and Beryl T.S. Atkins
1992 Toward a frame-based lexicon: The semantics of *risk* and its neighbours. In *Frames, Fields, and Contrasts: New Essays in Semantic and Lexical Organization*, Adrienne Lehrer and Eve F. Kittay (eds.), 75–102. Hillsdale, N.J.: Erlbaum.
1994 Starting where dictionaries stop: The challenge of corpus lexicography. In *Computational Approaches to the Lexicon*, Beryl T.S. Atkins and Antonio Zampolli (eds.), 349–393. Oxford: Oxford University Press.

2000 Describing polysemy: the case of *crawl*. In *Polysemy: Theoretical and Computational Approaches*, Yael Ravin and Claudia Leacock (eds.), 91–110. Oxford: Oxord University Press.

Fillmore, Charles, Paul Kay, and Catherine O'Connor
1988 Regularity and idiomaticity in grammatical constructions: the case of *let alone*. *Language* 64: 501–38.

Fischer, Kerstin
2000 *From Cognitive Semantics to Lexical Pragmatics: The Functional Polysemy of Discourse Particles*. Berlin/New York: Mouton de Gruyter.

Fischer, Olga and Max Nänny (eds.)
2001 *Iconicity in Language and Literature. Volume 2: The Motivated Sign*. Amsterdam/Philadelphia: John Benjamins.

Fontenelle, Thierry (ed.)
2003 FrameNet and Frame Semantics. Thematic issue of the *International Journal of Lexicography* 16: 233–361.

Foolen, Ad and Frederike Van der Leek (eds.)
2000 *Constructions in Cognitive Linguistics*. Amsterdam/Philadelphia: John Benjamins.

Freeman, Margaret H.
1995 Metaphor making meaning: Dickinson's conceptual universe. *Journal of Pragmatics* 24: 643–666.
2000 Poetry and the scope of metaphor: Toward a cognitive theory of literature. In *Metaphor and Metonymy at the Crossroads: A Cognitive Perspective*, Antonio Barcelona (ed.), 253–281. Berlin/New York: Mouton de Gruyter.

Fried, Mirjam and Hans Boas (eds.)
2005 *Grammatical Constructions. Back to the Roots*. Amsterdam/Philadelphia: John Benjamins.

Fried, Mirjam and Jan-Ola Östman (eds.)
2004 *Construction Grammar in a Cross-Language Perspective*. Amsterdam/Philadelphia: John Benjamins.

Frisson, Steven, Dominiek Sandra, Frank Brisard and Hubert Cuyckens
1996 From one meaning to the next: The effects of polysemous relationships in lexical learning. In *The Construal of Space in Language, and Thought*, Martin Pütz and René Dirven (eds.), 613–647. Berlin/New York: Mouton de Gruyter.

García-Miguel, José M.
1999 Grammatical relations in Spanish triactant clauses. In *Issues in Cognitive Linguistics*. Leon de Stadler and Christoph Eyrich (eds.), 447–469. Berlin/New York: Mouton de Gruyter.

Geeraerts, Dirk
1992 The semantic structure of Dutch *over*. *Leuvense Bijdragen* 81: 205–230.
1993a Vagueness's puzzles, polysemy's vagaries. *Cognitive Linguistics* 4: 223–272.
1993b Cognitive semantics and the history of philosophical epistemology. In *Conceptualizations and Mental Processing in Language*, Richard A. Geiger and Brygida RudzkaOstyn (eds.), 53–79. Berlin/New York: Mouton de Gruyter.

1997 *Diachronic Prototype Semantics. A Contribution to Historical Lexicology.* Oxford: Oxford University Press.

2005 Lectal data and empirical variation in Cognitive Linguistics. In *Cognitive Linguistics. Internal Dynamics and Interdisciplinary Interactions*, Francesco J. Ruiz de Mendoza and Sandra Peña Cervel (eds.), 163–189. Berlin/New York: Mouton de Gruyter.

2006 *Words and Other Wonders. Papers on Lexical and Semantic Topics.* Berlin/New York: Mouton de Gruyter.

Geeraerts, Dirk and Hubert Cuyckens (eds.)

forthc. *Handbook of Cognitive Linguistics*. New York: Oxford University Press.

Geeraerts, Dirk, Stefan Grondelaers, and Peter Bakema

1994 *The Structure of Lexical Variation. Meaning, Naming, and Context.* Berlin/New York: Mouton de Gruyter.

Gibbs, Raymond W.

1994 *The Poetics of Mind: Figurative Thought, Language, and Understanding.* Cambridge: Cambridge University Press.

1999 *Intentions in the Experience of Meaning*. Cambridge: Cambridge University Press.

2005 *Embodiment and Cognitive Science*. Cambridge: Cambridge University Press.

Gibbs, Raymond W. and Gerard J. Steen (eds.)

1999 *Metaphor in Cognitive Linguistics*. Amsterdam/Philadelphia: John Benjamins.

Giora, Rachel

2003 *On our Mind: Salience, Context, and Figurative Language*. New York: Oxford University Press.

Glynn, Dylan

2004 Constructions at the crossroads: The place of construction grammar between field and frame. *Annual Review of Cognitive Linguistics* 2: 197–233.

Goldberg, Adele E.

1995 *Constructions: A Construction Grammar Approach to Argument Structure.* Chicago, University of Chicago Press.

2006 *Constructions at Work. The Nature of Generalization in Language*. Oxford: Oxford Univresity Press.

Goldberg, Adele E. (ed.)

1996 *Conceptual Structure, Discourse, and Language*. Stanford: CSLI Publications.

Gonzalez-Marquez, Monica, Irene Mittelberg, Seana Coulson, and Michael J. Spivey (eds.)

forthc. *Methods in Cognitive Linguistics*. Amsterdam/Philadelphia: John Benjamins.

Grady, Joseph

1997 THEORIES ARE BUILDINGS revisited. *Cognitive Linguistics* 8: 267–290.

Gries, Stefan Th.

2003 *Multifactorial Analysis in Corpus Linguistics: A Study of Particle Placement.* London: Continuum Press.

Gries, Stefan Th. and Anatol Stefanowitsch (eds.)
2006 *Corpora in Cognitive Linguistics. Corpus-based Approaches to Syntax and Lexis.* Berlin/New York: Mouton de Gruyter.

Grondelaers, Stefan, Dirk Speelman, and Dirk Geeraerts
2002 Regressing on *er.* Statistical analysis of texts and language variation. In *6th International Conference on the Statistical Analysis of Textual Data*, Anne Morin and Pascal Sébillot (eds.), 335–346. Rennes: Institut National de Recherche en Informatique et en Automatique.

Grondelaers, Stefan and Dirk Geeraerts
2003 Towards a pragmatic model of cognitive onomasiology. In *Cognitive Approaches to Lexical Semantics*, Hubert Cuyckens, René Dirven, and John Taylor (eds.), 67–92. Berlin/New York: Mouton de Gruyter.

Hampe, Beate
2002 *Superlative Verbs: A Corpus-based Study of Semantic Redundancy in English Verb-Particle Constructions.* Tübingen: Gunter Narr.

Hampe, Beate (ed.)
2005 *From Perception to Meaning. Image Schemas in Cognitive Linguistics.* Berlin/New York: Mouton de Gruyter.

Harder, Peter
2003 The status of linguistic facts. Rethinking the relation between cognition, social institution, and utterance from a functional point of view. *Mind and Language* 18: 52–76

Haser, Verena
2005 *Metaphor, Metonymy, and Experientialist Philosophy: Challenging Cognitive Semantics.* Berlin/New York: Mouton de Gruyter.

Heine, Bernd
1997 *Cognitive Foundations of Grammar.* Oxford: Oxford University Press.

Heine, Bernd, Ulrike Claudi, and Friederike Hünnemeyer
1991 *Grammaticalization: A Conceptual Framework.* Chicago: The University of Chicago Press.

Herskovits, Annette H.
1986 *Language and Spatial Cognition: An Interdisciplinary Study of Prepositions in English.* Cambridge: Cambridge University Press.

Heyvaert, Liesbeth
2003 *A Cognitive-Functional Approach to Nominalization in English.* Berlin/New York: Mouton de Gruyter.

Hopper, Paul J. and Elizabeth C. Traugott
1993 *Grammaticalization.* Cambridge: Cambridge University Press.

Iwata, Seizi
1998 *A Network Approach to Verbal Semantics.* Tokyo, Kaitakusha.

Janda, L. A.
1993 *A Geography of Case Semantics: The Czech Dative and the Russian Instrumental.* Berlin/New York: Mouton de Gruyter.

Janssen, Theo
2003 Monosemy versus polysemy. In *Cognitive Approaches to Lexical Semantics*, Hubert Cuyckens, René Dirven, and John Taylor (eds.), 93–122. Berlin/New York: Mouton de Gruyter.

Johnson, Mark
1987 *The Body in the Mind : The Bodily Basis of Meaning, Imagination, and Reason*. Chicago: The University of Chicago Press.
1993 Conceptual metaphor and embodied structures of meaning: A reply to Kennedy and Vervaeke. *Philosophical Psychology* 6: 413–422.

Kay, Paul
1997 *Words and the Grammar of Context*. Stanford: CSLI Publications.

Kemmer, Suzanne E.
1993 *The Middle Voice*. Amsterdam/Philadelphia: John Benjamins.

Kemmer, Suzanne and Arie Verhagen
1994 The grammar of causatives and the conceptual structure of events. *Cognitive Linguistics* 5: 115–156.

Kennedy, John M. and John Vervaeke
1993 Metaphor and knowledge attained via the body. *Philosophical Psychology* 6: 407–412.

Koch, Peter
2001 Metonymy: Unity in diversity. *Journal of Historical Pragmatics* 2: 201–244.

Koenig, Jean-Pierre (ed.)
1998 *Discourse and Cognition: Bridging the Gap*. Stanford: CSLI Publications.

Kövecses, Zoltan
1986 *Metaphors of Anger, Pride and Love: A Lexical Approach to the Structure of Concepts*. Amsterdam/Philadelphia: John Benjamins.
2000 *Metaphor and Emotion. Language, Culture, and Body in Human Feeling*. Cambridge: Cambridge University Press; Paris: Editions de la Maison des Sciences de l'Homme.
2002 *Metaphor: A Practical Introduction*. Oxford: Oxford University Press.
2005 *Metaphor in Culture: Universality and Variation*. Cambridge: Cambridge University Press.

Kristiansen, Gitte
2003 How to do things with allophones: Linguistic stereotypes as cognitive reference points in social cognition. In *Cognitive Models in Language and Thought: Ideologies, Metaphors, and Meanings*, René Dirven, Roslyn Frank, and Martin Pütz (eds.), 69–120. Berlin/New York: Mouton de Gruyter.

Kristiansen, Gitte and René Dirven (eds.)
2006 *Cognitive Sociolinguistics*. Berlin/New York: Mouton de Gruyter.

Kristiansen, Gitte, Michel Achard, René Dirven, and Francisco J. Ruiz de Mendoza (eds.)
2006 *Cognitive Linguistics: Current Applications and Future Perspectives*. Berlin/New York: Mouton de Gruyter.

Krug, Manfred
2000 *Emerging English Modals: A Corpus-Based Study of Grammaticalization*. Berlin/New York: Mouton de Gruyter.

Krzeszowski, Tomasz P.
1993 The axiological parameter in preconceptual image schemata. In *Conceptualizations and Mental Processing in Language,* Richard A. Geiger and Brygida Rudzka-Ostyn (eds.), 307–329. Berlin/New York: Mouton de Gruyter.

Lakoff, George
1987 *Women, Fire, and Dangerous Things: What Categories Reveal about the Mind*. Chicago: The University of Chicago Press.
2002 *Moral Politics: How Liberals and Conservatives Think*. 2nd edition. Chicago: The University of Chicago Press.
2003 The brain's concepts. The role of the sensory-motor system in reason and language. *Working papers of the NTL Group at the International Computer Science Institute (ICSI)*. Berkeley: University of California, Berkeley.

Lakoff, George and Mark Johnson
1980 *Metaphors We Live by*. Chicago: The University of Chicago Press.
1999 *Philosophy in the Flesh: The Embodied Mind and its Challenges to Western Thought*. Chicago: The University of Chicago Press.

Lakoff, George and Mark Turner
1989 *More than Cool Reason: A Field Guide to Poetic Metaphor*. Chicago: The University of Chicago Press.

Langacker, Ronald W.
1987 *Foundations of Cognitive Grammar. Volume 1: Theoretical Prerequisites*. Stanford: Stanford University Press.
1988 A usage-based model. In *Topics in Cognitive Linguistics*, Brygida Rudzka-Ostyn (ed.), 127–161. Amsterdam/Philadelphia: John Benjamins.
1990 *Concept, Image, and Symbol: The Cognitive Basis of Grammar*. Berlin/New York: Mouton de Gruyter.
1991 *Foundations of Cognitive Grammar. Volume 2: Descriptive Application*. Stanford: Stanford University Press.
1999 *Grammar and Conceptualization*. Berlin/New York: Mouton de Gruyter.
2000 A dynamic usage-based model. In *Usage-based Models of Language*, Michael Barlow and Susanne Kemmer (eds.), 1–63. Stanford: CSLI Publications.
2004 A visit to Cognitive Grammar: Interviewed by Ricardo Maldonado. *Annual Review of Cognitive Linguistics* 2: 305–319.
2005 Construction grammars: Cognitive, radical, and less so. In *Cognitive Linguistics: Internal Dynamics, and Interdisciplinary Interaction*, Francisco J. Ruiz de Mendoza and Sandra Peña Cervel (eds.), 101–159. Berlin/New York: Mouton de Gruyter.

Lehmann, Christian
1995 *Thoughts on Grammaticalization*. Munich: Lincom Europa.

Lehrer, Adrienne and Eva F. Kittay (eds.)
1992 *Frames, Fields and Contrasts: New Essays in Semantic and Lexical Organization*. Hillsdale, N.J.: Lawrence Erlbaum.

Levinson, Stephen C.
2003 *Space in Language and Cognition: Explorations in Cognitive Diversity*. Cambridge: Cambridge University Press.

Lewandowska-Tomaszczyk, Barbara (ed.)
1998 *Lexical Semantics, Cognition and Philosophy*. Lódz, Poland: Lódz University Press.

Lewandowska-Tomaszczyk, Barbara and Alina Kwiatkowska (eds.)
2004 *Imagery in Language. Festschrift in Honour of Professor Ronald W. Langacker*. Frankfurt: Peter Lang.

Liddell, Scott K.
2003 *Grammar, Gesture, and Meaning in American Sign Language*. Cambridge: Cambridge University Press.
Liebert, Wolf-Andreas, Gisela Redeker, and Linda Waugh (eds.)
1997 *Discourse and Perspective in Cognitive Linguistics*. Amsterdam/Philadelphia: John Benjamins.
Lipka, Leonhard
2002 *English Lexicology. Lexical Structure, Word Semantics, and Word-Formation*. Tübingen: Gunter Narr.
Maldonado, Ricardo
2002 Objective and subjective datives. *Cognitive Linguistics* 13: 1–65.
Mangasser-Wahl, Martina
2000 *Von der Prototypentheorie zur empirischen Semantik*. Frankfurt: Peter Lang.
Marmaridou, Sophia S. A.
2002 *Pragmatic Meaning and Cognition*. Amsterdam/Philadelphia: John Benjamins.
Matlock, Teenie, Michael Ramscar, and Lera Boroditsky
2004 The experiential basis of motion language. In *Linguagem, cultura e cognição: Estudos de linguística cognitiva,* Augusto Soares da Silva, Amadeu Torres, and Miguel Gonçalves (eds.), 43–57. Coimbra: Almedina.
Matsumoto, Yo
1996 Subjective motion and English and Japanese verbs. *Cognitive Linguistics* 7: 183–226.
McNeill, David
1995 *Hand and Mind: What Gestures Reveal About Thought*. Chicago: The University of Chicago Press.
McNeill, David (ed.)
2000 *Language and Gesture*. Cambridge: Cambridge University Press.
Michaelis, Laura A. and Josef Ruppenhofer
2002 *Beyond Alternations: A Constructional Model of the German Applicative Pattern*. Stanford: CLSI Publications.
Nerlich, Brigitte, Zazie Todd, Vimala Herman, and David D. Clarke (eds.)
2003 *Polysemy: Flexible Patterns of Meaning in Mind and Language*. Berlin/New York: Mouton de Gruyter.
Newman, John
1996 *Give: A Cognitive Linguistic Study*. Berlin/New York: Mouton de Gruyter.
2004 The quiet revolution: Ron Langacker's Fall Quarter 1977 lectures. In *Imagery in Language. Festschrift in Honour of Professor Ronald W. Langacker*, Barbara Lewandowska-Tomaszczyk and Alina Kwiatkowska (eds.), 43–60. Frankfurt: Peter Lang.
Nuyts, Jan
1992 *Aspects of a Cognitive-pragmatic Theory of Language. On Cognition, Functionalism, and Grammar.* Amsterdam/Philadelphia: John Benjamins.
Oakley, Todd V.
1998 Conceptual blending, narrative discourse, and rhetoric. *Cognitive Linguistics* 9: 321–360.

Ortony, Andrew (ed.)
1993 *Metaphor and Thought*. 2nd edition. Cambridge: Cambridge University Press.
Östman, Jan-Ola and Mirjam Fried (eds.)
2005 *Construction Grammars: Cognitive Grounding and Theoretical Extensions*. Amsterdam/Philadelphia: John Benjamins.
Özçaliskan, Seyda
2005 Metaphor meets typology: Ways of moving metaphorically in English and Turkish. *Cognitive Linguistics* 16: 207–246.
Palmer, Gary B.
1996 *Toward a Theory of Cultural Linguistics*. Austin: University of Texas Press.
Panther, Klaus-Uwe
2005 The role of conceptual metonymy in meaning construction. In *Cognitive Linguistics: Internal Dynamics and Interdisciplinary Interaction,* Francisco J. Ruiz de Mendoza and Sandra Peña Cervel (eds.), 353–386. Berlin/New York: Mouton de Gruyter.
Panther, Klaus-Uwe and Günter Radden (eds.)
1999 *Metonymy in Language and Thought*. Amsterdam/Philadelphia: John Benjamins.
Panther, Klaus-Uwe and Linda Thornburg (ed.)
2003 *Metonymy and Pragmatic Inferencing*. Amsterdam/Philadelphia: John Benjamins.
Paprotté, Wolf and René Dirven (eds.)
1985 *The Ubiquity of Metaphor. Metaphor in Language and Thought*. Amsterdam/Philadelphia: John Benjamins.
Paradis, Carita
2004 Where does metonymy stop? Senses, facets, and active zones. *Metaphor, and Symbol* 19: 245–264.
Peeters, Bert (ed.)
2000 *The Lexicon-Encyclopedia Interface*. Oxford: Elsevier Science.
Peirsman, Yves and Dirk Geeraerts
2006 Metonymy as a prototypical category. *Cognitive Linguistics*, forthcoming.
Peña Cervel, Sandra
2003 *Topology and Cognition: What Image Schemas Reveal about the Metaphorical Language of Emotions*. München: Lincom.
Pires de Olivera, Roberta
2001 Language and ideology: An interview with George Lakoff. In *Language and Ideology. Volume I: Theoretical Cognitive Approaches*, René Dirven, Bruce Hawkins, and Esra Sandikcioglu (eds.), 23–47. Amsterdam/Philadelphia: John Benjamins.
Pütz, Martin and René Dirven (eds.)
1996 *The Construal of Space in Language and Thought*. Berlin/New York: Mouton de Gruyter.
Pütz, Martin, Susanne Niemeier, and René Dirven (eds.)
2001a *Applied Cognitive Linguistics I: Theory and Language Acquisition*. Berlin/New York: Mouton de Gruyter.

2001b *Applied Cognitive Linguistics II: Language Pedagogy*. Berlin/New York: Mouton de Gruyter.

Radden, Günter

1985 Spatial metaphors underlying prepositions of causality. In *The Ubiquity of Metaphor. Metaphor in Language and Thought*, Wolf Paprotté and René Dirven (eds.), 177–207. Amsterdam/Philadelphia: John Benjamins.

Radden, Günter and Zoltan Kövecses

1999 Towards a theory of metonymy. In *Metonymy in Language and Thought*, Klaus-Uwe Panther and Günter Radden (eds.), 15–59. Amsterdam/Philadelphia: John Benjamins.

Ravin, Yael and Claudia Leacock (eds.)

2002 *Polysemy: Theoretical and Computational Approaches*. Oxford: Oxford University Press.

Reddy, Michael J.

1979 The conduit metaphor – A case of frame conflict in our language about language. In *Metaphor and Thought*, Andrew Ortony (ed.), 284–324. Cambridge: Cambridge University Press.

Regier, Terry

1996 *The Human Semantic Potential: Spatial Language and Constrained Connectionism*. Cambridge, Mass., The MIT Press.

Rice, Sally

1987 Towards a transitive prototype. *Proceedings of the Thirteenth Annual Meeting of the Berkeley Linguistics Society* 422–434. Berkeley: Berkeley Linguistics Society.

Rohdenburg, Günter and Britta Mondorf (eds.)

2003 *Determinants of Grammatical Variation in English*. Berlin/New York: Mouton de Gruyter.

Rudzka-Ostyn, Brygida

1985 Metaphoric processes in word formation. The case of prefixed verbs. In *The Ubiquity of Metaphor: Metaphor in Language and Thought*, Wolf Paprotté and René Dirven (eds.), 209–242. Amsterdam/Philadelphia: John Benjamins.

1988 Semantic extensions into the domain of verbal communication. In *Topics in Cognitive Linguistics*, Brygida Rudzka-Ostyn (ed.), 507–554. Amsterdam/Philadelphia: John Benjamins.

1989 Prototypes, schemas, and cross-category correspondences: The case of *ask*. *Linguistics* 27: 613–661.

1995 Metaphor, schema, invariance: The case of verbs of answering. In *By Word of Mouth: Metaphor, Metonymy, and Linguistic Action in a Cognitive Perspective*, Louis Goossens, Paul Pauwels, Brygida Rudzka-Ostyn, Anne-Marie Simon-Vandenbergen, and Johan Vanparys (eds.), 205–243. Amsterdam/Philadelphia: John Benjamins.

Ruiz de Mendoza, Francisco J. and José Luis Otal Campo

2002 *Metonymy, Grammar, and Communication*. Albolote: Editorial Comares.

Sampson, Geoffrey R.

2005 *The 'Language Instinct' Debate*. Revised edition. London: Continuum.

Sanders, Ted J. M. and Leo G. M. Noordman
2000 The role of coherence relations and their linguistic markers in text processing. *Discourse Processes* 29: 37–60.
Sanders, Ted J. M. and Morton Ann Gernsbacher
2004 Accessibility in text and discourse processing. *Discourse Processes* 37: 79–89.
Sandra, Dominiek and Sally Rice
1995 Network analyses of prepositional meanings: Mirroring whose mind – the linguist's or language user's? *Cognitive Linguistics* 6: 89–130.
Schmid, Hans-Jörg
2000 *English Abstract Nouns as Conceptual Shells*. Berlin/New York: Mouton de Gruyter.
Semino, Elena and Jonathan Culpeper (eds.)
2002 *Cognitive Stylistics: Language and Cognition in Text Analysis*. Amsterdam/Philadelphia: John Benjamins.
Shibatani, Masayoshi and Sandra A. Thompson (eds.)
1996 *Grammatical Constructions: Their Form and Meaning*. Oxford: Oxford University Press.
Sinha, Chris and Kristina Jensen de López
2000 Language, culture, and the embodiment of spatial cognition. *Cognitive Linguistics* 11: 17–41.
Slobin, Dan I.
1996 Two ways to travel: Verbs of motion in English and Spanish. In *Grammatical Constructions: Their Form and Meaning*, Masayoshi Shibatani and Sandra A. Thompson (eds.), 195–219. New York: Oxford University Press.
2000 Verbalized events: A dynamic approach to linguistic relativity and determinism. In *Evidence for Linguistic Relativity*, Susanne Niemeier and René Dirven (eds.), 107–138. Amsterdam/Philadelphia: John Benjamins.
Smith, Michael B.
1994 Agreement and iconicity in Russian impersonal constructions. *Cognitive Linguistics* 5: 5–56.
Soares da Silva, Augusto
2003 Image schemas and category coherence: The case of the Portuguese verb *deixar*. In *Cognitive Approaches to Lexical Semantics*, Hubert Cuyckens, René Dirven, and John Taylor (eds.), 281–322. Berlin/New York: Mouton de Gruyter.
Speelman, Dirk, Stefan Grondelaers, and Dirk Geeraerts
2003 Profile-based linguistic uniformity as a generic method for comparing language varieties. *Computers and the Humanities* 37: 317–337.
Stefanowitsch, Anatol and Stefan Th. Gries
2003 Collostructions: Investigating the interaction between words and constructions. *International Journal of Corpus Linguistics* 8: 209–243.
Svorou, Soteria
1994 *The Grammar of Space*. Amsterdam/Philadelphia: John Benjamins.
Sweetser, Eve E.
1986 Polysemy vs. abstraction: Mutually exclusive or complementary? *Proceedings*

*of the Twelfth Annual Meeting of the Berkeley Linguistics Society*. 528–538. Berkeley: Berkeley Linguistics Society.

1987 The definition of *lie*. An examination of the folk models underlying a semantic prototype. In *Cultural Models in Language and Thought*, Dorothy Holland and Naomi Quinn (eds.), 43–66. Cambridge: Cambridge University Press.

1990 *From Etymology to Pragmatics. Metaphorical and Cultural Aspects of Semantic Structure*. Cambridge: Cambridge University Press.

1999 Compositionality and blending: Semantic composition in a cognitively realistic framework. In *Cognitive Linguistics: Foundations, Scope, and Methodology*, Theo Janssen and Gisela Redeker (eds.), 129–162. Berlin/New York: Mouton de Gruyter.

Tabakowska, Elzbieta

1993 *Cognitive Linguistics and Poetics of Translation*. Tübingen: Gunter Narr.

Talmy, Leonard

2000a *Toward a Cognitive Semantics, Vol. I: Concept Structuring Systems*. Cambridge, Mass., The MIT Press.

2000b *Toward a Cognitive Semantics, Vol. II: Typology and Process in Concept Structuring*. Cambridge, Mass., The MIT Press.

Taub, Sarah

2001 *Language from the Body: Iconicity and Metaphor in American Sign Language*. Cambridge: Cambridge University Press.

Taylor, John R.

1992 How many meanings does a word have? *Stellenbosch Papers in Linguistics* 25: 133–168.

1996 *Possessives in English: An Exploration in Cognitive Grammar*. Oxford: Clarendon Press.

2002 *Cognitive Grammar*. Oxford: Oxford University Press.

2003a *Linguistic Categorization*. 3rd edition. Oxford: Oxford University Press.

2003b Polysemy's paradoxes. *Language Sciences* 25: 637–655.

Tomasello, Michael

2003 *Constructing a Language: A Usage-Based Theory of Language Acquisition*. Cambridge, Mass.: Harvard University Press.

Traugott, Elizabeth C.

1985 Conventional and dead metaphors revisited. In *The Ubiquity of Metaphor. Metaphor in Language and Thought*, Wolf Paprotté and René Dirven (eds.), 17–56. Amsterdam/Philadelphia: John Benjamins.

2003 Constructions in grammaticalization. In *Handbook of Historical Linguistics*, Brian D. Joseph and Richard D. Janda (eds.), 624–627. Oxford: Blackwell.

Traugott, Elizabeth C. and Richard B. Dasher

2005 *Regularity in Semantic Change*. Cambridge: Cambridge University Press.

Traugott, Elizabeth C. and Bernd Heine (eds.)

1991 *Approaches to Grammaticalization*. Amsterdam: John Benjamins.

Tsohatzidis, Savas L. (ed.)

1989 *Meanings and Prototypes: Studies in Linguistic Categorization*. London: Routledge.

Tuggy, David

1992 The affix-stem distinction: A cognitive grammar analysis of data from Orizaba Náhuatl. *Cognitive Linguistics* 3: 337–637.

1996 The thing is is that people talk that way. The question is why? In *Cognitive Linguistics in the Redwoods. The Expansion of a New Paradigm in Linguistics*, Eugene H. Casad (ed.), 713–752. Berlin/New York: Mouton de Gruyter.

Tummers, José, Kris Heylen, and Dirk Geeraerts

2005 Usage-based approaches in Cognitive Linguistics: A technical state of the art. *Corpus Linguistics and Linguistic Theory* 1: 225–261.

Turner, Mark

1987 *Death is the Mother of Beauty. Mind, Metaphor, Criticism*. Chicago: The University of Chicago Press.

1996 *The Literary Mind: The Origins of Thought and Language*. Oxford: Oxford University Press.

Tyler, Andrea and Vyvian Evans

2003 Reconsidering prepositional polysemy networks: The case of *over*. In *Polysemy: Flexible Patterns of Meaning in Mind*, Brigitte Nerlich, Zazie Todd, Vimala Herman, and David D. Clarke (eds.), 96–160. Berlin/New York: Mouton de Gruyter.

Ungerer, Friedrich and Hans-Jörg Schmid

1996 *An Introduction to Cognitive Linguistics*. London/New York: Longman.

Van Hoek, Karen

1997 *Anaphor and Conceptual Structure*. Chicago: The University of Chicago Press.

Van Hoek, Karen, Andrej A. Kibrik, and Leo Noordman (eds.)

1999 *Discourse Studies in Cognitive Linguistics*. Amsterdam/Philadelphia: John Benjamins.

Van Langendonck, Willy

1999 Markedness and prototypical speaker attributes. In *Issues in Cognitive Linguistics,* Leon de Stadler and Christoph Eyrich (eds.), 567–576. Berlin/New York: Mouton de Gruyter.

Vandeloise, Claude

1990 Representation, prototypes, and centrality. In *Meanings and Prototypes. Studies in Linguistic Categorization*, Savas L. Tsohatzidis (eds.), 403–437. London, New York: Routledge.

1991 *Spatial Prepositions: A Case Study from French*. Chicago: The University of Chicago Press.

1996 'Touching': A minimal transmission of energy. *Cognitive Linguistics in the Redwoods. The Expansion of a New Paradigm in Linguistics*, Eugene H. Casad (ed.), 541–566. Berlin/New York: Mouton de Gruyter.

2001 *Aristote et le Lexique de l'Espace: Rencontres entre la Physique Grèque et la Linguistique Cognitive*. Stanford : CSLI Publications.

Verhagen, Arie

2005 *Constructions of Intersubjectivity: Discourse, Syntax, and Cognition*. Oxford: Oxford University Press.

Verspoor, Marjolijn, and Wander Lowie
2003 Making sense of polysemous words. *Language Learning* 53 2003: 547–86.

Violi, Patrizia
2001 *Meaning and Experience*. Bloomington: Indiana University Press.

Wierzbicka, Anna
1991 *Cross-cultural Pragmatics: The Semantics of Social Interaction*. Berlin/New York: Mouton de Gruyter.

Wilcox, Phyllis P.
2001 *Metaphor in American Sign Language*. Washington: Gallaudet University Press.

Wilcox, Sherman
2004 Cognitive iconicity: Conceptual spaces, meaning, and gesture in signed language. *Cognitive Linguistics* 15: 119–147.

Yu, Ning
1998 *The Contemporary Theory of Metaphor: A Perspective from Chinese*. Amsterdam/Philadelphia: John Benjamins.

Zelinsky-Wibbelt, Cornelia (ed.)
1993 *The Semantics of Prepositions: From Mental Processing to Natural Language Processing*. Berlin/New York: Mouton de Gruyter.

Zelinsky-Wibbelt, Cornelia
2000 *Discourse and the Continuity of Reference: Representing Mental Categorization* . Berlin/New York: Mouton de Gruyter.

Ziegler, Debra
2004 Reanalysis in the history of *do*: A view from construction grammar. *Cognitive Linguistics* 15: 529–574.

Zlatev, Jordan
1999 Situated embodied semantics and connectionist modeling. In *Cognitive Semantics: Meaning and Cognition*, Jens Allwood and Peter Gårdenfors (eds.), 173–194. Amsterdam/Philadelphia: John Benjamins.

2003a Beyond cognitive determination. Interactionism in the acquisition of spatial semantics. In *Ecology of Language Acquisition*, Jonathan Leather and Jet van Dam (eds.), 83–107. Amsterdam: Kluwer Academic Publishers.

2003b Polysemy or generality? Mu. In *Cognitive Approaches to Lexical Semantics*, Hubert Cuyckens, René Dirven, and John Taylor (eds.), 447–494. Berlin/New York: Mouton de Gruyter.